THERE'S ONLY ONE F IN FULHAM

30 YEARS (AND MORE!) OF FULHAM FC AND TOOFIF

DAVID LLOYD

To Mum and Dad. The Best.

This book would not have been possible without the love and support of my gorgeous wife, Heather, and our four children, Matt, Ellen, Carys and Morgan.

The levels of support and goodwill for this project have been extraordinary, and very humbling. Simply saying thank you doesn't seem enough somehow; but thank you. The difficult bit is to ensure that everyone's included here. Thanks to Bob, Lois and Steve Leven for proofreading the vast bulk of the text. Thanks to Alan Smith and the Fulham Supporters Trust – specifically Tom Greatrex and Mike Gregg for picking up the baton and supporting the venture. Special mention to the FST's Gerry Pimm for taking on the extra mantle of agony uncle. Earlier in the "journey", Michael Heatley stepped in to help guide the project when it looked to be going nowhere. However, the fella who's ensured we got to finishing line with an end product that's fit for purpose is the wondrous Mike Jones, a design wizard and someone who's always prepared to go the extra mile (and then some!). Master lensman Ken Coton generously supplied a batch of (superior!) photos whenever my cupboard was bare. Thanks, too, to Julian Newton in this regard. Ray Lewington, as you'd expect, has come up trumps with the foreword – thanks, Ray. You wouldn't be reading this now had it not been for the excellence and advice of Gareth Roberts, Tracey Firth and the brilliant staff at Bishops Printers. And the finished product has been considerably enhanced thanks to the input of Melvin Tenner, Bill Plummer, Bill Muddyman, Paul Johnson, David Daly, Roger Scoon, Dave Gardner, Jean Tigana and all the fabulous people I've had the privilege of interviewing. Thanks, too, to Sammy James and all at Fulhamish for promoting the book via their online store. Thanks to Rachael Oakley at Byline Publishing for all the help and support – and for purchasing the first copy! Seems I'm also contractually obliged to pay homage to Les Strong (at least that's what his, er, "agent" told me). THANK YOU. And Come On You Whites!

Published in 2018
by DL Books,
11 Johnson's Close,
Carshalton, Surrey SM5 2LU

© David Lloyd 2018

David Lloyd has asserted his right to be identified as the author of this work, in accordance with the Copyright, Designs and Patents Act, 1988.

A CIP catalogue record for this book is available from the British Library.

ISBN 978-1-9165017-0-6

Designed by Mike Jones.

Printed and bound by Bishops Printers Ltd.
Walton Road, Farlington, Portsmouth PO6 1TR

PICTURE CREDITS
Photography © David Lloyd 2018

Except: Page 7 © Crystal Palace FC; Pages 20 to 22 © Gordon McLeod; Pages 38, 41 & 57 (bottom); Page 62 © Julian Newton; Pages 106 & 107 (top) © Ken Coton; Pages 114 (top & bottom) & 115 (bottom) © Bill Plummer; Pages 138 & 141 © Ken Coton; Page 182 © Julian Newton; Page 188 © John O'Farrell and Tim Goffe; Pages 220 (right), 221 (top), 226, 229 © Ken Coton; Page 234 © Bill and Andy Muddyman; Page 238 © Melvin Tenner; Pages 261, 280 (top), 281 & 286 (top) © Ken Coton; Page 297 © Ken Adam; Pages 298, 309 © Ken Coton; Page 317 © Getty; Page 353 © Matt Lloyd; Page 360 © Morgan Lloyd.

Every effort has been made to trace copyright holders and to obtain their permission for the use of copyright material. The publisher apologises for any errors or omissions in the above list and would be grateful if notified of any corrections that should be incorporated in future reprints or editions of this book.

Contents

Introduction

Family comes first, and this selection of fanzine-related anecdotes, reminiscences, insights and interviews is dedicated above all to my nearest and dearest.

My wonderful wife Heather has had to endure TOOFIF-speak for the entirety of our marriage. Even my proposal to the lovely lady took place at a Fulham gathering! Our four children, Matt, Ellen, Carys and Morgan, are our pride and joy. Love you all loads!

Fulham FC is renowned as a family club, and long may that continue. This humble tome is therefore also dedicated to Fulham supporters everywhere – but specifically the hardy band that stuck with the Club during the tough times. You know who you are; it's just a shame that the latter-day overlords don't. Without your tireless efforts it's almost certain that there'd be no club today to lord over

On that note, I sincerely hope this little lot doesn't come over as some sort of egotistical exercise. It's essentially a compilation of what's transpired in and around the production of the fanzine, hopefully presented in an informative, entertaining and authentic fashion. That said, I'm proud of having got stuck in to all sorts of Fulham-related matters over the years. Fact is, though, I could name scores, maybe hundreds, of supporters who have risen in magnificent fashion to the various testing challenges presented by following our favourite football club over the last 30 years, either with expertise or advice or simply pitching in to do things such as mending stand seats and painting terrace stanchions. And there'll be many others whose names I don't know and whose involvement hasn't come onto my radar. So there's absolutely no "Big I Am" involved in any of this – I'm just one of many who have done their bit and chipped in along the way.

Top right: Blackmail Corner! That's me with younger brother Gareth posing with Fulham striker Steve Earle on the Putney End terracing back in the day. What a tie! But at least it's black and white!

Far right: In Cassis, South of France, with Jean Tigana, a supreme host.

Below: The Lloyd clan. Back row: Dad, Matt and Morgan. Front: Heather, Ellen and Carys. My pride and joy.

This book has been penned from the viewpoint of an ordinary punter. But one who's always known that there's an extraordinary tale to tell. With all the material at my disposal – having luckily been on hand for so many announcements and unveilings, and having been embroiled in so much of the campaigning efforts by supporters – this David-on-the-Spot was raring to go. Throw in the three decades of attending football matches and accompanying TOOFIFs and it was clear that this was a unique opportunity – one that only yours truly could cock up!

Personally, I far prefer the quiet life. If pressed into service then I'll do so diligently and to the best of my abilities, but ideally from somewhere in the background. When principals are involved, though, I can be pretty stubborn. And when FFC's future was threatened in the late 1980s, the Supporters' Club committee, of which I was part, leapt into action. By that time, TOOFIF had been launched. So it all got rather hectic. Still, it'd only be for a year or two, right…?

"You'll note that nowhere in any of this have I claimed to be a representative of anyone, or anyone's spokesman. That's 'cos I'm not. I'm just the fanzine editor." *TOOFIF 64*

The "Results" panel...

The text has been arranged chronologically, wherever possible, and linked to the issue(s) of the fanzine out at that time. These mini-chapters are interspersed with a selection of stand-alone articles.

The side panel's four coloured boxes represent the four footballing divisions. The box representing the tier in which Fulham were competing at the time contains the team's results during the lifetime of the issue(s) in question, together with FFC's best and worst league positions during that period. The book's fore-edge showcases the Club's amazing rollercoaster journey. It's an astonishing stat, but the only berth that Fulham haven't filled during the past 30 years is rock bottom, 92nd. Not for the want of trying, some might say!

TOP TIER

SECOND TIER

THIRD TIER

FOURTH TIER

Foreword by Ray Lewington

Thirty years, eh? So much has happened in that time! When we were on a bit of a downer, the contents of TOOFIF could be tough going – no one likes to read how badly they're doing. But the fanzine's always been produced with a real passion and with the best intentions of helping Fulham FC.

Whereas those employed at the Club have to deal with the practical side of things, the supporters, the lifeblood of any club, focus on the emotional aspect. And there's nothing wrong with that. All that emotion and passion is what sets English football apart from the rest.

When you've just lost a game of football, and you're feeling low because of any number of things, criticism can hurt. But give it a couple of hours and you soon come down to earth. Often you'll think, "If I'd have been watching that, I'd have said much the same." Or worse! When things are going well, and the supporters are that much more positive, it makes for a great atmosphere and a genuine bond develops. It's an emotional game all said and done, and I've always been prepared to give an opinion or three as a player and then as a coach. So, as long as no line is crossed, fanzines are fine with me.

I'll never forget David coming to visit me in hospital some years ago when I was at a low ebb. It's the mark of the guy and something I'll remember far more than any perceived criticism contained in the pages of TOOFIF.

Reflecting on the last 30 years at Fulham, "ups and down" barely covers it. Those with long memories will recall that I joined Fulham in 1980 as a player, just after the Club had been relegated to Division Three. We clawed our way back under Malcolm Macdonald and very nearly made it back-to-back promotions before that wonderful side was ripped apart because of backstage politics.

I had a season with Sheffield United then Ray Harford got in touch. He'd just resigned as Fulham boss and said there was a job going – as Player-Manager. He also said, as a mate, not to touch it! I was naïve and had stars in my eyes, but I was in. That period was tough, to put it mildly, and I got badly bruised. However, that whole experience proved invaluable. And my bond with Fulham and the fans became that much stronger.

I returned to Craven Cottage when Chris Coleman was in charge. By then, the whole place had been transformed – no more training at Banstead for a start! Mohamed Al Fayed had overseen Fulham's march to the Premier League and had ensured that the Club's infrastructure matched his ambitions. A few years later, in came Roy Hodgson. What a fantastic period that was, from the Great Escape of 2008 to the amazing Europa League adventures of 2010.

I've got so much time for the Fulham supporters who stuck with the team when times were bad – even those who gave me real grief! When a Club's down on its luck for whatever reason, and gates are down to four or five thousand, those loyal fans who turned up every week and supported the Club just by being there deserve a medal in my book. And I couldn't help but reflect on those times when we got to Hamburg. Good luck to all those people who have come along on the back of the Club's successful years, I'm not knocking them, but those who fought for the Club's survival and who continued to pay to watch every week when their likely "reward" was yet another defeat, well they thoroughly deserved their moment in Hamburg. And at Wembley last May come to that! Emotions were high at both Finals (and yes, I was at Wembley, with my wife Ann) and I was so chuffed for all the fans, but especially for those whose loyalty had been tested to the limit.

Make no mistake, Fulham is a lovely football club. And I've got a special attachment to the Club and the people. Craven Cottage is a unique ground. You'd be surprised at how many players of other clubs love coming to the place. When I was with the national side, conversations would often turn to playing at such a fantastic Thames-side setting, and these are guys who've played at the best stadiums in the world.

Going back to my earliest days at Fulham, I was told that the bulldozers would soon be moving in. That would have been a travesty. It was all a bit make do and mend in those days. And defeats to teams such as Hayes (home; 0-2) and Chester (away; 7-0) was a world apart from taking on and beating the superstars of Shakhtar and Juventus.

See, I told you "ups and downs" barely covers it!

Left: Ray Lewington, a fantastic servant to FFC from the moment he signed as a player in 1980.

Above right: These days Ray is Assistant Manager at Crystal Palace, working alongside Roy Hodgson – a partnership made in Fulham!

Tom Greatrex

The last 30 years have seen some incredible ups and downs on the pitch for Fulham – from the nadir of 1996, sitting 91st and losing to the only team below us in the League, to a European tournament final and a narrow extra-time defeat. That period has also coincided almost completely with the various twists, turns and sometimes fortunate events in the as-yet-not-quite-finally-resolved battle to secure Fulham's long-term future at Craven Cottage.

From when, in the mid-1980s, then Chairman and owner Ernie Clay had managed to persuade the Church Commissioners to sell him the freehold of Craven Cottage, the questions over the future of the ground have always been there in the background. Whether explicitly, openly and without pretence or covertly, secretly and with elaborate justification, every chairman and owner since has had plans to redevelop the ground, and all but the current Chairman have suggested that moving Fulham away from our historic home was an inevitability. That none have succeeded in doing so on a permanent basis – although it got very close on more than one occasion – is part of the remarkable story of our remarkable Club, its fans and the support and affection from a wider community.

From its first edition, that remarkable story has been told through the pages of TOOFIF – and particularly, vitally, during the period before the high-media profile that came with Mohamed Al Fayed's ownership. In a world not yet introduced to social media and the Internet, TOOFIF was often the only source of what was really going on as well as detailing the misgivings, suspicions and doubts of fans. While the Fulham Park Rangers proposal was a naked attempt to profit from the value of the Cottage site with no pretence of any residual responsibility for the football clubs involved, subsequent ideas have been more subtly proposed. The last-minute about-turn and withdrawal of support for the Council's compulsory purchase of Craven Cottage in return for a much-needed financial injection from the property company who retained ownership of the ground was a turning point for some. While the merits or otherwise of that move were long debated in

TOOFIF and elsewhere, it was a supreme irony that a downturn in the London property market did for the developers and gave us a welcome reprieve. An early entry in the list of final games at the Cottage came and went.

Over the years there have been various schemes for redeveloping a ground that had been unchanged since the 1970s Riverside Stand was constructed. Before Al Fayed's takeover, a 15,000-capacity ground with flats around the perimeter – probably something similar to what Leyton Orient's Brisbane Road has become – would have kept us home but limited our ability to grow. The Al Fayed grand plan of a 30,000-capacity ground would have sacrificed the Cottage but maintained the listed, and thanks to fans, restored Stevenage Road façade. Both took years to get through planning approval and various legal challenges on behalf of a minority of local residents who often gave the impression they would rather that if the Club could not be driven out of business, then relocating it elsewhere would suit them just as well. Both involved compromise and a realism among supporters who could see the bigger picture of keeping Fulham in Fulham as a battle worth joining and winning, albeit imperfectly. Both schemes ended up on the scrapheap.

In all of the twists and turns, that Fulham's eventual move away from Craven Cottage came at the behest of a calculated deceit is one of the most disappointing and dispiriting episodes in our recent off-pitch history. The home fixture against Leicester City, managed by Micky Adams, at the end of our first Premier League season was celebrated as the next last game at the Cottage before a temporary move to Loftus Road while the 30,000 stadium was to be built. However, I had discovered a few days before that the new stadium was not going ahead. I attended that game almost in a daze, quietly fuming at what I knew (but couldn't say) was going to happen next. While the eventual final, final game was a low-key early round of the InterToto Cup, the managed release of the let-down came soon afterwards: the new scheme couldn't be built, and the Club was looking at a new site near White City. They tried to portray this as being linked to our historic home because it happened to be in the same London borough; the Club had employed some "very expensive consultants" to show we could fill a 40,000-plus stadium; and, finally, a divide-and-rule argument that was to subsequently be comprehensively demolished by events – that Fulham fans would have to choose between Craven Cottage and playing at the top level.

Below: Tom Greatrex spearheaded the Back to the Cottage campaign. Tom is Chairman of the Fulham Supporters' Trust these days – and also somehow finds the time to be Chairman of Supporters Direct, too.

And unlike any attempt before, for the first time since 1896 Fulham were not playing football at Craven Cottage, with ownership of the site quietly transferred to a separate entity.

Compared to the amateurishness, or perhaps arrogance, of late 1980s property developers that supporters could (and did) unite against, the operation employed by those advising Al Fayed to promote a future away from Craven Cottage was professional, sophisticated and well-resourced. It was also supported by a large number of fans whose gratitude to the owner for his largesse, which had been responsible for a step change in our on-field fortunes, meant they could contemplate a future away from Craven Cottage.

For fans who took a different view – while they could understand why others were unconvinced – it was a grim, depressing and unpleasant experience to be challenging the Club's view. Supporters are fanatics. Both these terms are indicative of wanting to be on the same side as "your" Club – an institution you identify with, love and cherish. It's not something you want to be fighting.

Creative protests, media-friendly stunts and statements of support from former players and managers were collected to keep attention high, and to try to explain to fans what we thought was going on, and put pertinent questions to the Club. The profile of our owner helped in that respect, but also led to some calculated remarks in response, questioning how far we could be considered supporters, a determined attempt to undermine our efforts and question our motivation through a guerrilla war of press statements. We certainly found out which former players and managers backed up their previous statements about Craven Cottage when there was a difference of view with the Club, and who didn't. Suffice it to say, the respect and affection with which I held Bobby Robson is head and shoulders above that of a much more recent former manager who had gone on to manage England, as a result.

Just as in the first TOOFIF decade, looking at back issues from 2002 to 2004 now is a reminder of how, even in the age of messageboards and a 24-hour sports news channel with schedules to fill, the authoritative fanzine was a crucial conduit for both the detail, and tone, of the emerging Back to the Cottage campaign.

The important work happened behind the scenes – we were very fortunate to assemble a group of like-minded fans with expertise in law, finance, construction, planning, politics and with good connections – to find out what was happening. One day the full story will doubtless be told, but a combination of mysterious litigation, competition for development sites, property inflation, time and good fortune meant that the plans we developed for how you could return to Craven Cottage and satisfy ground regulations for relatively small amounts of money were, eventually, effectively adopted by the Club.

It was described as a temporary return as an alternative to a third year at Loftus Road while a new site continued to be sought, but secure in the knowledge it would both be exceptionally difficult to get the Club out of the Cottage a second time and to find another site, that soon changed. The trend for identikit new grounds, out of town, difficult to get to, having no character and little atmosphere declined, and having a ground of age and character became part of the attraction that has since been heavily marketed.

Two plans for replacement Riverside stands have since been given permission, with the most recent due to begin construction in less than a year. Once a new stand is built, then there will be no justification again for planning to move the Club away from Craven Cottage. In public statements, the current Chairman has repeatedly made that intention to stay at our historic home clear. As we get more familiar with his approach, and as trust and relationships build, there is nothing to suggest that this time anything other than the future at the Cottage will be secured for the long term. Yet, as the last 30 years chronicled by TOOFIF have demonstrated, there have been good intentions, promises, plans and proposals before. None, other than the one suggested by fans to get us back home for the lowest financial outlay, have come to fruition.

The lesson from all of this is the value of the consistency, knowledge, commitment and passion of supporters in challenging, questioning and scrutinising what goes on in the name of the Club we all love. TOOFIF has been an integral part of that over three decades, and while from time to time that has meant being unpopular, almost ostracised and barely tolerated, the bigger picture of the unique and lasting connection between Club and ground has been almost continuously maintained, even when it has seemed futile.

That Fulham are at Craven Cottage, and look set to remain for the long term, is in part testament to the efforts of a series of supporters' organisations engaged in various different, but related, campaigns over 30 years. The most important – and lasting – consequence of those has been to help the Club understand and appreciate, through different ownerships, in periods of harmony and dissent alike, that not only is there something special, unique and of emotional value about our historic home, but also that Craven Cottage is an integral part of Fulham Football Club and always will be. Without TOOFIF that simply would not have been possible.

Tom Greatrex, EST Chairman, summer 2018

Above: Fulham supporters rallied behind the Back to the Cottage campaign. This photo was taken in Stevenage Road, near the main gates of the Club, after a march from Stamford Bridge to underline our desire to return to our historic home.

"That Fulham are at Craven Cottage, and look set to remain for the long term, is in part testament to the efforts of a series of supporters' organisations engaged in various different, but related, campaigns over 30 years."

Rise of a Cottage Industry

So what right have I got to produce a Fulham fanzine? Funnily enough, give or take the odd expletive, those were the words somewhat forcibly directed at yours truly outside the Recreation Ground, Aldershot, back in March 1988 when Issue 1 made its bow. The Fulham supporter in question (who, bless him, still gets his regular TOOFIF fix to this day) didn't hold back, with either his aggressive demeanour or his beer-tainted breath. But it was a valid question. The answer? No more right than any other Fulham fan, I guess. In fact, in early 1988 I had no idea what a fanzine was, let alone how to produce one. But I loved all things football and was a fervent supporter of Fulham FC, and that had to count for something.

Raised in Wimbledon, well before the rise and fall of Wimbledon FC, I lived with my Welsh-born folks, Bryn and Eirwen, sister Gwyneth and brother Gareth (spot the Welshness?), two doors along from ardent, long-time FFC season-ticket holders Reg and Joan Stockham. When Joan was unable to attend a reserve game at Craven Cottage, Reg took me along instead; I was nine years old. And that was it; well and truly hooked. I can't remember the fixture, but I'm pretty sure Johnny Haynes and Les Barrett were strutting their stuff for the second string. Playtime football sessions at Dundonald Primary School were thereafter the stage for my Haynes and Barrett impressions (yeah, yeah, more akin to Les Haynes and Johnny Barrett…). Anyway, these were enough to persuade Dundonald's Class Six teacher and games master Mr Cumes – who decades later I discovered had a first name, Stan, and that he'd worked behind the scenes at Craven Cottage on matchdays – to include me in the school football team, even though until a mid-teens growth spurt I was more akin to Cliff Carr in stature.

Almost immediately the FFC matchday routine was set; 93 bus to Putney Bridge, into the ground early – Putney End in those days – at 1pm, watch the First Division fare from behind the goal, then meet the Stockhams afterwards for a lift home in their green Mini. Fulham didn't win too many games back then, and season after season developed into battles to avoid the trapdoor down to Division Two. But it was utterly brilliant, and the riverside setting, complete with flags of the First Division clubs fluttering on Thames-side flagpoles, was breathtakingly magnificent. Being one of the 47,290 that crammed into Craven Cottage on 27 March 1967 to watch Fulham hold Manchester United – Best, Law, Charlton et al – to a 2-2 draw was heady stuff indeed. And, at four-foot-nothing, a bit scary, if truth be told. It was all a far cry from another 2-2 draw, and with another "United", at the Cottage, almost 30 years later. This encounter, in which we shared the spoils with Hartlepool United on 10 February 1996, was watched by a mere 3,700 supporters in a dilapidated stadium strewn with weeds, and with some sections deemed unsafe and therefore closed to the public. More pertinently, that result left us in our worst-ever position, one off the foot of the entire Football League and staring into the abyss of oblivion. By then, of course, TOOFIF was well and truly established.

In the mid-'60s I was at Rutlish School, Merton Park, in the same intake as future FFC midfielder Terry Bullivant – who once made a big thing of me having come to school in odd socks, and whose best mate Pete Sponder once decided my school blazer deserved a literal look, and so set fire to it during French. While I was wearing it. *C'est la vie*! Also at the school was Barry Medwin, son of former Fulham coach and ex-Wales international Terry Medwin. (Other subsequent Rutlish football graduates include Steve Finnan, Chris Perry and Jason Cundy.)

Bored while confined to bed with the real-deal flu aged 15 or so, I cobbled together a wordsearch and some Fulham quizzes, as you do! A few years down the line they resurfaced during a clear-out, so I sent them to the-then Fulham programme editor – and more recently a Club Director before his untimely death in 2014 – Dennis Turner, who invited me to become a regular contributor. Aside from producing quizzes, I ghosted Cliff Carr's captain's column for a season (I was a lot taller than our diminutive skipper by then!), cobbled together the Juniors' and Reserves' match reports and then graduated to assembling the troublesome visitors' pages – irksome and time-consuming because of the reliance on topical material being sent by post from the clubs in question. In those

Opposite page: This motley crew, led by Dennis Turner (front, middle) were responsible for putting together the Fulham programme in 1983-84. Four years later the bloke in the white trainers co-founded TOOFIF.

Below: Fulham goalkeeper Tony Macedo keeps his eyes fixed on the ball as Manchester United's Denis Law, in typically acrobatic fashion, goes for the spectacular in front of a packed Putney End. Meanwhile, tucked away in the crowd, and barely able to see over the hoardings, is a future TOOFIF editor.

long-lost pre-internet days, such inside info invariably arrived late, or sometimes not at all. Worth saying too that, unlike several others on the team, I was among the few who contributed to every home programme at the time; that's not said for point-scoring purposes but to highlight the folly of a daft (and, frankly, insulting) decision made by the Club once Jimmy Hill came in as Chairman. Anyway, with no mod cons like email on tap, the final task was to deliver the copy by hand at first light to Ward & Woolverton printers in Mitcham – which involved becoming yet another frustrated motorist inching along the A238 from Merton Park to Colliers Wood, then, after dumping an info-packed envelope with Ward (or was it Woolverton?), heading back to Wimbledon and finding somewhere to park the car before jumping on a train. There was a full day's work in Central London still to contend with.

After kicking off my working life in the personnel field, I made an overdue Steed Malbranque-like sidestep into journalism, becoming a reporter on *LT News*, staff newspaper of London Transport. The poor people of Hammersmith and Fulham also had to endure my mangled prose in the local papers; my Fulham match reports appeared in the *Fulham Chronicle* and the *Hammersmith & Fulham Gazette*, as well as the short-lived *Wimbledon Recorder*. All of which meant that it came as something of a shock to learn that after five-plus years as a volunteer I'd been dropped from FFC's programme team. And unceremoniously so.

The gang of contributors came from far and wide, so the only time we met en masse was during the summer months at Craven Cottage. Once the customary "team photo" was out of the way, the following season's duties were divvied out. On checking by phone with the editor (and future TOOFIF regular) Chris Mason when that summer's meeting was likely to happen, he sheepishly replied, "It took place last week – er, haven't you heard from Jimmy Hill?" "Er, no."

When JH returned to FFC as Chairman in 1987, one of his concerns was the number of free passes doled out to Fulham fans. Programme contributors received passes as a reward for their considerable efforts. So too FFC Lottery Ticket sellers. Come to that, those who worked for Fulham Directors, let's say at Deans Blinds in Wimbledon for example, would also be looked after. In typical Jimmy Hill style, he'd simply taken a red pen to the list of programme contributors and struck through some of them, willy-nilly. No questions; no research. It was a low blow in my opinion; as well as a highly unbusiness-like and stupid one as it turned out. You see my family were also Lottery Ticket sellers, and my mum worked for Deans Blinds at the time (and incidentally became a good mate of former groundsman Albert Purdy, a foreboding, legendary figure at the Cottage back in the day; by this time he was a foreboding, legendary cleaner at Deans Blinds). So if it was a free ticket I was after, then I was covered from several angles. Thing is, in those days I was playing at a decent level of senior football on Saturdays, so – and it's almost sacrilegious to admit this – I was only coming to Fulham for the final half-hour when I had 2pm kick-offs or when the fixtures didn't clash.

Therefore, not only had I been sacked from the programme team without the courtesy of a phone call or letter from the Club, but they could have continued using my services, be they good, bad or indifferent, for years to come at no cost to the Club whatsoever. Free ticket or no free ticket. I'm also pretty sure that at the time I was the only contributor, apart from the editor, with a day-job in the field of journalism. So I had more relevant experience than most of those who'd been retained, too. It still rankles all these years later – not the decision itself, you understand, that's the Club's prerogative however much I may bleat, but the not being told. In any case, despite this self-righteous stance, it's perfectly feasible that my submissions were deemed a pile of error-strewn claptrap; but if so, no one told me that either. Either way, bless you, Jimmy Hill.

Within months of the above decision, and with the Fulham Park Rangers pantomime still a talking point, up popped the name of David Preston along with the suggestion that he and I should start a fanzine. Whatever that was. And whoever he was, come to that. After a few false starts

Aldershot 0 Fulham 1	
26.03.88	10th
Northampton Town 3 Fulham 2	
02.04.88	11th
Fulham 3 Rotherham United 1	
04.04.88	9th
Grimsby Town 0 Fulham 2	
09.04.88	8th

1st
2nd
3rd
4th
5th
6th
7th
8th
9th
10th
11th
12th
13th
14th
15th
16th
17th
18th
19th
20th
21st
22nd
23rd
24th

(when it became evident that "David Preston" and "exceptional writing ability" were a snug fit, but that "DP" and "reliability" were somewhat less so!) we gradually put together some ideas and duly informed the club of our intentions: to produce a regular punchy magazine that, while always supportive of the Club, would offer an alternative view to the often bland, enforced PR-speak typically peddled by football clubs up and down the country. The general idea was to offer some hard-hitting articles along with plenty of laughs. We weren't looking much beyond frank terrace opinions and concerns intermingled with features such as silly names, crazy haircuts and tales of convoluted away trips. The Club's response was as surprising as it was indicative of the way FFC operated back then.

In essence, the Club weren't keen, but by the same token couldn't prevent us going ahead with the venture. Wouldn't it be more appropriate, however, for us to use our undoubted skills for the benefit of the Club, they suggested? Hmm, like writing for the programme, for example?

In an ironic twist, the Club Director whose signature appeared at the foot of the letter, David Gardner, went on to become one of TOOFIF's most loyal supporters!

So we forged ahead with issue no.1. The Recreation Ground, Aldershot, was the unlikely setting for our first effort, a lightweight edition in retrospect, but one that was the culmination of a massive head-scratching exercise that produced no end of splinters. David P's brother Martin kindly allowed us to use a computer (what the hell was a computer?) in his publishing house and appointed one of his designers to produce an eye-catching masthead. The fella in question came up with a bog-standard two-deck effort in basic Helvetica font, which must have taken him all of 15 seconds, and then tried to make the most of our naïveté by charging us for the privilege! He was given a sharp verbal blast from Martin Preston for his damned cheek – and, in one of those beautiful twists, the subject also came up years later across a desk when I interviewed him for a job! No, he didn't get the advertised post.

The first editorial emphasised our honourable intentions, but it's true to say that we'd have measured the mag's longevity in days rather than decades. David Preston, with his ferocious appetite for all things social, went his merry way after Issue 5, whereas yours truly, with evidently no wish for any sort of social life, stubbornly clung on for what turned out to be an incredible ride, spanning 30 years and counting!

Things weren't particularly great at FFC as we claimed a valuable away victory at Aldershot in the spring of '88. But very few could have foreseen what was around the corner – and no one could have predicted the longer-term scenario. Indeed,

Fanzines (and Along Came TOOFIF)

The fanzine's name truly came about in the dead of night. Co-editor David Preston and I had bandied one or two potential titles around, but nothing quite hit the mark. One suggestion, Fulham Fallout (name of UK punk band The Lurkers' 1978 debut album), eventually became the title of our letters pages. The eureka moment came after I'd had my sleep disturbed by a noisy neighbour. Drowsy and dishevelled, I shuffled towards the loo… then, approaching the door, WALLOP! No, I hadn't banged my head; instead, from nowhere: "There's Only One F In Fulham". Neat. Although bang from Anfield, in fact. Well sort of. It was a hark-back to an occasional terrace chant that had been given an airing by Fulham's travelling contingent during our 10-0 Littlewoods Cup massacre at Liverpool in September 1986. Sorted. A great title (one of the best, we've been told over the years), if maybe a tad long. However, when you consider that Gillingham's (excellent) fans' mag was called *Brian Moore's Head Looks Uncannily Like the London Planetarium*, ours was positively catchy by comparison!

When Fulham's inaugural fanzine hit the streets it was at the vanguard of the extraordinary football fanzine explosion. A few, such as *The City Gent* (Bradford City), *The Oatcake* (Stoke City), *Terrace Talk* (York City) and *Leyton Orientear* (any wild guesses?), had started the trend, but by the time Issue 2 of TOOFIF went on sale there were dozens of examples up and down the leagues. Before long they could be counted in their hundreds.

As was the case at many other clubs, Fulham fans were treated to more than one 'zine in due course. Alongside TOOFIF came *Where's Ara?* in late 1993 and, five years after that, *Where Were You…?*. There was also *Cottage Pie*, referred to as a fanzine by some but actually the Supporters' Club magazine, produced for a while by, er, yours truly. Far from seeing the newcomers as a threat, I embraced their arrival, freely offering advice and assistance. Both of the other Fulham 'zines were very different to TOOFIF anyway, and in a sense it was the more the merrier. I couldn't stop them coming out, so why not go along with the flow? In the event, neither lasted that long – a shame as they made a far better fist of their debut issues than we did. But if nothing else, TOOFIF had staying power!

CALLING all Fulham Fans !

A number of supporters are getting together to produce their own fanzine to reflect the thoughts and views of the club's fans — and they are appealing to all other Fulham supporters to help out.

The organisers want to hear from anyone who might like to contribute articles or have

Fulham FC fanzine needs you!

any ideas on how to distribute and print the magazine.

It is hoped that the first issue will be on sale within the next two to three weeks, so get in touch now.

The only credentials required are enthusiasm, a love of Fulham Football Club and a sense of humour.

Anyone who would like to become involved in the project should contact Dave Lloyd (31 The Quadrant, Wimbledon SW20 8SW) or Dave Preston (37 Ember Lane, Esher, Surrey).

matters were to get a whole lot worse, almost terminally so. And then, in the most unlikely of developments, Fulham Football Club made an extraordinary recovery from the brink of extinction to reach the heady heights of the top flight once again while also, wonder of wonders, enjoying an epic journey to reach the final of a major European competition. Truly a roller-coaster ride of jaw-dropping proportions – and TOOFIF was there to cover the lot, capturing the full gamut of emotions along the way… ⚽

There's Only One F In Anfield

Third Division Fulham's League Cup exploits in 1986-87 came to an end following a narrow 3-2 defeat to all-conquering Liverpool – the Reds having powered to the League and FA Cup double just a few months before. Hmm, doesn't sound so bad when it's put like that, does it? It's almost heroic.

What that opening paragraph slightly overlooks is that the enjoyable five-goal skirmish under the lights at Craven Cottage was the tie's second leg; the first game between the sides in that season's second round finished in record-busting style at Anfield. Liverpool won 10-0.

"You could say that things didn't exactly go to plan!" said Fulham's Brian Cottington wryly many years later. "It was a wonderful draw for us – and it was very exciting to go to Anfield. As a club we weren't mixing with those sorts of teams at the time, and certainly not with the calibre of players Liverpool had in their ranks. So it was as exciting as it was daunting."

It must have been a daunting occasion for midfielder Kevin Hoddy, who made his Fulham debut at Anfield. "We had quite a young, reshuffled team," confirmed Cottington. "That included Kevin – but it was hardly a dream debut! The amazing thing is that we had the first chance of the game. Dean Coney was sent on his way thanks to a great through ball by one of our midfielders; "Dixie" chipped the ball over Bruce Grobbelaar only to see it hit the bar and bounce down and away to safety. A turning point? Probably not! Liverpool turned on the style and it was backs to the wall for us from then to the final whistle.

"I was at right-back that night," recalled Cottington, "and up against my Irish countryman Ronnie Whelan. He turned me inside out. Fact is, it was men against boys on the night. The result hurt us all, and yet it was somehow a privilege to see at close quarters just how good these superstars really were. They would have given anyone a proper hiding that night; they were amazing. It was a great game to watch from where I was, anyway!"

A fair proportion of the 13,498 crowd were Fulham supporters, and they were determined to enjoy their day out and even embraced the result.

From Issue 1:

Hello, good morning/afternoon/ evening and welcome.

Hello and welcome to a brand new fanzine all about the best club in the world (well, SW6 anyway). We are no doubt preaching to the converted in saying that there is something special about following Fulham, albeit an incredibly frustrating experience from time to time. It was with this in mind – and not necessarily for the benefit of those of us who may not be orthographers (spelling experts!) – that the fanzine's title was chosen. The feeling for Fulham really does run deep, and most football supporters in general can tell a tale or two about the Club.

But that is not to say that everything in the Cottage garden is rosy – far from it. Indeed, leaving aside the off-the-field problems, the team have spent three months on the crest of a slump. There are, of course, plenty of suggestions from the terraces. Some are extremely valid. Others lack a degree or two of savvy. And some are physically impossible! However, all these "miracle cures" are argued with great passion, which is where *There's Only One F In Fulham* comes in.

We aim to stimulate interest in the Club and provide a forum for such views. But if this is to succeed we need your contributions. This is your chance to put pen to paper on any subject relating to Fulham (or football in general) and seeing it and your name in print.

We are standing next to our desk-top publishing machine (okay, potato & printing set plus front-room table) awaiting the torrent of replies…

"Our fans were absolutely superb," said Cottington. "They could see we were trying but were simply being outclassed, big time. They never stopped singing – even chanting 'We want eight…we want nine!' after they'd scored their seventh and eighth goals. They also sang 'There's Only One F in Fulham' with great gusto."

In years to come, that particular line would become a feature of Fulham FC matchdays once the TOOFIF salesforce became established!

Outclassed and outgunned, the tie was nevertheless only at the halfway mark. So how do you prepare for the return leg in such circumstances? Chris Mason, editor of Fulham's matchday programme, took the whimsical route: with a picture of Maradona praying ("We felt that a player at prayer might be a suitable front cover image as far as tonight's game is concerned."). ⚽

Above: Brian Cottington recalls our fans being "absolutely superb" during the 10-0 hammering at Liverpool.

Below: Fulham FC 19??–?? with Chairman David Bulstrode in the middle of the front row. Player-Manager Ray Lewington (to the right of Bulstrode) evidently had a lot of faith in his outfield players, hence the lack of goalkeepers!

Early Doors

Having sent the Club a copy of Issue 1 we received the following from Jimmy Hill:

"I admire your enthusiasm in producing such a magazine, but quite selfishly wonder whether the time and trouble might not be spent on cold-blooded mercenary ways of keeping Fulham FC alive.

"In being honest, there are aspects of the magazine that I read which I would not enjoy if I happened to be one or two of the players that were mentioned and on that basis I do not approve, but it is a free country and you must do what you feel you must do. However, I do not think it would be an advantage for you to be in the Riversiders' Bar after home matches for reasons which, with some thought, must be fairly obvious."

We responded in TOOFIF's Summer Newsletter No 1 *(above right)* as follows:

"The Chairman's missive [indicates that] there are some people who are not too keen on our humble publication. We realise that we're not going to appeal to everyone, but we feel that the tone of the letter is unnecessarily patronising and written with little appreciation of our intentions – not to mention the veiled threat of violence from hard-done-by players.

Quizballs From Issue 2

1. How many times did Roger Brown kick the ball out of the ground during his career? a) 3; b) 8; or c) 476

2. Who is the odd one out? a) Benito Mussolini; b) Genghis Khan; c) Jimmy Hill

3. List the following in decreasing order of popularity: a) Ernie Clay; c) David Bulstrode; c) John Beck

4. Geoff Banton – animal, vegetable or mineral?

5. When was the last time that anything was rung up on the till in any of the Club bars?

"We are not about vindictive campaigns against players or insulting criticisms. Apparently, one of the 'upset' players is Gary Elkins. Any references to him have been pretty mild in our opinion. The fact remains that, up to now, his abilities or otherwise have been the main focus of our postbag." ⚽

Leave it out, son!

Many of us mere mortals can only stand and listen in wonderment at some of the highly intellectual instructions proffered by many of the game's superstars up and down the country. In this issue, top personality-coach Buck Jarkett helps us cast some light on this verbal minefield [the name of Fulham's first-team coach at the time was Jack Burkett; what a coincidence!]…

One of the things that really annoys me is all them experts slagging off English football and the way that it's played. What a load of old cobblers! Me and the gaffer work all bleedin' week on all kinds of things so that the lads can get a result and I think it's high time I let you in on the closely guarded secrets of how to coach a football team.

FULHAM FOOTBALL CLUB (1987) LIMITED

CRAVEN COTTAGE STEVENAGE ROAD LONDON SW6 6HH
TELEPHONE 01-736 6561

Mr. D. Preston,
Ember Lane,
Esher

26th April 1988

Dear David,

Thank you very much for sending a copy to me of "There's only one 'F' in Fulham".

I admire your enthusiasm in producing such a magazine, but quite selfishly wonder whether the time and trouble might not be spent on cold-blooded mercenary ways of keeping Fulham Football Club alive.

In being honest, there are aspects of the magazine that I read which I would not enjoy if I happened to be one or two of the players that were mentioned and on that basis I do not approve, but it is a free country and you must do what you feel you must do. However, I do not think it would be an advantage for you to be in the Riversiders' Bar after home matches for reasons which with some thought must be fairly obvious.

All good wishes.

Yours sincerely,

Y. Haines

p.p. Jimmy Hill
Chairman

(signed in Mr. Hill's absence)

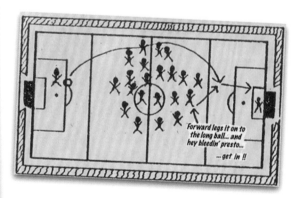

Forward legs it on to the long ball... and hey bleedin' presto...

...get in !!

Left: From the off FFC Chairman Jimmy Hill disapproved of TOOFIF. At the time this was something of a knee-jerk reaction, but in due course it was perfectly understandable given the amount of flak and personal comments that came his way.

Above: A typical Buck Jarkett tactics board, chock-full of technical wizardy and footballing insight.

From the Boardroom, Issue 2

We can appreciate people's apprehension towards the sudden appearance of a magazine such as ours. While it is true that some of the articles may contain one or two barbed comments, we are not out to criticise Fulham FC (nor its employees) for criticism's sake. Indeed we hope to foster the feeling for the Club (and all that it entails) and just maybe entice one or two newcomers to see what all the fuss is about. But then neither must it be a bland mag either.

Producing a fanzine covering Fulham FC does present a problem or two, which come as a result of the Club's apparent openness. Other fanzines have sprung up as a result of their club's "behind-closed-doors" policy, offering only a hint or two to the true supporters of what is really going on. That is very different at Fulham where matters are discussed much more openly – take for instance the recent forum at Craven Cottage and the airing of the Kenny

Achampong issue in the last issue of *Cottage Pie*.

So our fanzine is not necessarily a crusade. Where we can score heavily, however, is reflecting more accurately the views of the man or woman on the terraces. We have received very many comments from Fulham supporters regarding Issue 1 – all of which (to date!) have been complimentary and, of course, we thank you for taking the trouble to pass on your views.

1. Make sure you can shove a "y" on the end of every player's name, so Linekery, Butchy, Browny, Scotty and so forth. Of course, this doesn't work with Dowie, Langley or Storey; my advice is not to sign such players. It just gets too complicated.

2. Ensure that all your players own a suit. Players and the like get all sorts of stick for being yobs, so dressing up smart'll shut up all the arty-farty clean-up-the-game campaigners. Or interfering twats as I like to call them.

3. Give them intensive coaching on all the highly technical phrases involved in the game (in a ruddy loud voice, naturally!):

"Back door"
"Give it, give it (son)"
"Down the line"
"110 per cent"
"Great knock son"
"To feet, to feet"
"Lay it, lay it"
"More effort guys"
"Get back and face"
"Long ball, long ball"
"Man on, man on"
"Step it up"
"Give and go"

These are just a few, but without them your team would have no chance of doing well. Remember that if you keep repeating any given phrase you've got a much better chance of winning the game. To help you understand, here's a good example of chat between professional footballers that I picked up on a recent visit to Fulham:

Get there Big Jim… win it, win it… give, give… back door Scotty… turn… turn… down the line… knock it, give it… go on Kenny, son… pass it, pass it… hit the box… pass it you pratt, pass it… far post, far post… little dink, little dink, Pongo… pass it, pass it… lay it back, lay it, lay it… hit the naffing thing…HIT IT!... oh f**k it!!

This is what it's all about, and quite frankly I'm mystified as to why Fulham, with so many good callers in the team, are stuck where they are in the Third Division. ⚽

"DON'T share a beach with the Fulham lads this summer," advised Radio 2's commentator after this game at Chesterfield where Gordon Davies, Jeff Hopkins and assistant manager Jack Burkett were all shown the red card.

Those in attendance at Saltergate had a different story to tell — one in which none of the supposed villains of the piece were the main protagonists. As far as Fulham were concerned referee Parker, suitably dressed in black, had that dubious distinction.

This was a fairly nondescript showing by Fulham who had already resigned themselves to yet another season of third division football. Chesterfield, on the other hand,

CHESTERFIELD 1 FULHAM 0

needed at least a point to be sure of avoiding the play-offs. Chesterfield had the added insurance, although they probably did not know it, that Fulham have failed to win their final away game of the season since 1961.

Jamie Hewitt missed a golden opportunity for the home side in the fourth minute when he put a penalty kick wide of Jim Stannard's right post, but Chesterfield settled their early nerves when Dave Waller's 22nd goal of the season six minutes later put them ahead.

As half-time approached Fulham's Gordon Davies had a couple of plausible penalty appeals turned down, but it was after the break that the Welshman really got in the thick of things.

After Peter Scott had been booked for a foul, Davies and Chesterfield's Darren Wood followed suit with an off-the-ball clash. Davies put the ball in the net in the 67th minute, but after initially allowing the goal referee

Parker noticed an offside flag and the goal was ruled out.

Worse was to follow for the visitors inside four crazy minutes.

Paddy McGeeney fell to the ground after a challenge by Davies which resulted in his second bookable offence and subsequent dismissal.

Then as the visitors were attempting to bring on substitute Steven Greaves for his senior debut, Jeff Hopkins' few impolite words of advice to a linesman resulted in him following Davies down the tunnel. Not to be outdone, Burkett rushed onto the field to add his voice to the argument and he too received his marching orders.

Just to round things off Mr Parker booked Jeff Eckhardt and Jim Stannard in the final minutes to give Fulham a 6-1 victory in the misdemeanours count, but no points from the last game of the season.

Fulham 1 Chester City 0	
15.04.88	7th
Fulham 3 Southend United 1	
23.04.88	7th
Preston NE 2 Fulham 1	
30.04.88	8th
Fulham 0 Bury 1	
02.05.88	9th
Chesterfield 1 Fulham 0	
07.05.88	9th

1st
2nd
3rd
4th
5th
6th
7th
8th
9th
10th
11th
12th
13th
14th
15th
16th
17th
18th
19th
20th
21st
22nd
23rd
24th

Above and right: Fulham's routine season closer at Chesterfield turned out to be anything but. Our lot had nothing to play for while the Spireites were fighting relegation. Referee Parker took centre stage, however, and astonishingly showed three red cards — to Gordon Davies, Jeff Hopkins and coach Jack Burkett — and exasperated the whole travelling contingent.

On the Campaign Trail

As the 1988-89 season kicked off, so TOOFIF went into campaigning mode...

Those of you who attended the special meeting at the Cottage in July will be aware that our "lovely landlords" have finally come up with their plans for the redevelopment/total destruction of Craven Cottage.

Without getting into the realms of "rear elevations" and "front sections", it appears they want to demolish three-quarters of the ground, leaving only the protected Stevenage Road Stand and the Cottage intact. The Eric Miller Stand will be replaced by a couple of thousand flats and a couple of rows of terracing (eight, actually) while the Hammersmith and Putney Ends will be drastically reduced so as to accommodate a couple of hundred more flats – leaving the ground capacity at a level more suited to the Dan Air Counties League than the Third Division of the Football League.

Apart from the eradication of all the seating in the Miller Stand, the restaurant, bars and Riverside Suite would also be reduced to rubble. This would not only lessen the facilities available to supporters (and the consequent loss of precious income to the Club) but also, in the guise of the Riverside Suite, rid the community of a valuable and much-used facility.

Of course, to you and me these plans are complete flights of fancy and totally outside the guidelines laid down by the Council in their planning brief. However, one never knows and it is down to every single Fulham supporter to ensure that these ridiculous notions are booted once and for all into touch.

At the time of writing, Hammersmith & Fulham Council are considering the applications as well as the many hundreds of letters protesting at the scheme. With any luck the application will be turned down, though that will probably lead to an appeal to the Department of Environment. If such a scenario should occur, a Public Inquiry would be set up to assess the rights and wrongs of the whole affair. There is also the possibility that the Council would slap a Compulsory Order on the ground, which would also be discussed at the enquiry. This would all happen early next year, so particularly in view of the Council beginning to get the jitters about the next local elections, now is the time to start bombarding them with your protests. HELP KEEP FFC ALIVE. ⚽

On the telly

An unplanned-for knock-on effect of producing a fanzine, at least back in 1988, was taking on media work, which included going on the telly. Given that I've always had a face for radio and a voice for mime, it's not something I particularly relish doing. When other Fulham supporters, such as Allan Gould, Melvin Tenner, Tom Greatrex, the late Dennis Turner, David Hamilton or, more recently, Richard Osman are seen or heard spreading the FFC word, they always seem to come across with much more gravitas than yours truly.

I was a nervous wreck the first time I went on the radio to discuss Fulham's plight. It was a live chat during a half-time break at the Cottage with LBC's on-site match reporter Phil Mison, himself a long-time Fulham fan. Allan Gould and I were designated Fulham Supporters' Club representatives, and we were to be quizzed about the latest chapter in the Club's interminable ground saga. It was important to get the Supporters' Club message over clearly and concisely. In the event I was Mark Fotheringham to Allan's Mark Schwarzer as I bumbled my way through the interview in the Fulham press box; okay, no own goals perhaps, but Allan came across as a far more authoritative voice.

A change in employment helped a little; production of *LT News*, the London Transport staff journal produced in various guises since

Opposite page: Jim Hicks, cover star of Issue 3, takes drastic action to avoid being interviewed for the mag. In fact, the ever-genial Jim had been a guest at a football dinner and needed to "escape" the motley Broomfield FC crew to catch his train home.

Below: A rabbit-caught-in-the-headlights moment captured by a TV camera. Melvin Tenner (bottom pic) was a key figure during the Club's troubled years, fronting not only the Supporters' Club Committee but also, in due course, the Fulham 2000 fundraising project.

DAVID LLOYD
Fulham Supporters Club

FULHAM 2000
TO COMMEMORATE THE SIGNIFICANT CONTRIBUTION TO THE RESTORATION OF CRAVEN COTTAGE AND THE FACADE OF THE STEVENAGE ROAD STAND FROM FULHAM 2000, A SUPPORTERS' ORGANISATION FORMED IN DIFFICULT TIMES TO HELP FULHAM FOOTBALL CLUB REMAIN AT ITS HISTORIC HOME.
APRIL 1999

1914, was shunted to an out-of-house agency and, with my reporting job axed, I was flukily retained by the company as a Press Officer. Inside a couple of years, I'd somehow risen to second in command – Press and Public Affairs Manager, no less – and gained invaluable experience along the way (especially as LT and its successive Chairmen were regularly in the firing line!), even if I far preferred being on the other side of the news fence.

However, this experience proved particularly useful when, as a consequence of Fulham's downward spiral in the early 1990s, the Club's staffing numbers reached an all-time low. With my phone number having been circulated via FSC press releases, and by that point being contacted on TOOFIF matters too, I found myself undertaking much of the Club's basic Press and PR work – unseen. It was no big deal, really, simply a case of providing factual background information for the most part, and of course reminding those asking the questions that I was giving them guidance as an outside operative. Now and then this led to being interviewed by the media; however, unlike the instances I'd witnessed at first hand at London Transport, this was generally non-controversial, non-political stuff with no potential "out-to-get-you" time-bomb tucked away in the list of questions. In essence I was merely a point of contact, and any such interviews were generally space-fillers for the media outlets, but there was still a need to behave responsibly. It may have been an easy-fill for them, but, from the Fulham supporters' perspective, it was imperative that our Club's predicament was broadcast.

More and more interviews followed and, with Fulham desperately needing coverage

of their ever-worsening plight, it all became a necessary evil, even if by then I'd grown in confidence and was fully au fait with the Fulham issues of the day. A bizarre episode unfolded on the back of a Club announcement about the ground. BBC Newsroom South-East were to broadcast a live early evening link from Craven Cottage featuring a Club Director, and I was invited to add my two-penn'orth as Supporters' Club Press Secretary. Only trouble was, when I trundled along to the Cottage just after 6pm, not only had the Director subsequently declined to take part but the presenter was embroiled in a traffic snarl-up in Hammersmith.

"It's all down to you," said the candid cameraman with a steely smile as he set up his equipment on the Hammersmith End terracing. "In which ear do you normally have the earpiece, guv?" "Well I can narrow it down to one of two," I replied pretty unhelpfully, adding that I hadn't done this sort of live-to-camera stuff before. The cameraman's eyes seemed to glaze over a little and his smile was a lot less steely; a lot less smiley in fact.

Within seconds we were "on". And with still no sign of the reporter, it was left to an under-rehearsed "anchor" in the studio to pose some diluted questions, which allowed me more scope to put across the supporters' angle on things, especially with nobody else around to interrupt! "Blimey, you carried that off well," blurted the cameraman as I handed back the mic and earpiece afterwards. Had he looked at me 45 seconds after that generous remark, he'd have noticed that I was sitting down on the famous old terracing shaking like a bloody jelly. ⚽

Cardiff City 1 Fulham 2	
27.08.88	7th
Fulham 1 Southend United 0	
03.09.88	2nd
Mansfield Town 3 Fulham 1	
10.09.88	7th
Fulham 1 Bury 0	
17.09.88	3rd
Bolton Wanderers 3 Fulham 2	
20.09.88	6th
Huddersfield Town 2 Fulham 0	
01.10.88	11th
Fulham 2 Wolves 2	
05.10.88	12th
Bristol City 1 Fulham 5	
08.10.88	6th
League Cup	
Fulham 1 Brentford 1	
30.08.88	Round 1 1st leg
Brentford 1 Fulham 0	
06.09.88	Round 1 2nd leg

1st
2nd
3rd
4th
5th
6th
7th
8th
9th
10th
11th
12th
13th
14th
15th
16th
17th
18th
19th
20th
21th
22th
23th
24th

Merger Madness: a Recap

Just as things started to get a bit hairy again on the ground front, TOOFIF co-editor Dave Preston reminded the mag's readers in Issue 5 of the background to the merger mania and the events of February/March 1987...

At a time when things (yet again) aren't going too well on the pitch, we can always seek some solace by looking back to the events of nearly two years ago that threatened the very existence of our beloved Fulham. As an indirect result of the mass supporters' campaign that followed, came the emergence of TOOFIF. Co-editor David Preston reflects on those traumatic times…

I gleaned the dreaded news from that most illustrious of sports journos, Michael Wale, while innocently tuning in to the BBC's *London Plus* one Monday evening. There they were, QPR Chairman Jim Gregory standing side-by-side with David Bulstrode to announce the formation of this exciting new club!

After an initial period of disbelief I reached for the phone to impart the news to my mates – Fulham and Rangers fans alike. In the course of one conversation I vowed to do something about it. So what, you might think? In all of my previous 24 years I had studiously avoided doing something about anything whatsoever; but for some ridiculous reason this was different.

A few more phone-calls led to a chat with our then Supporters' Club Chairman Mr Guard who informed me that there was some kind of meeting down at The Crabtree the following day. I arrived, with a QPR mate, to be greeted by a film crew and a "slate" behind the bar – maybe this merger business wasn't quite so bad after all!

After copious quantities of lager and a fair bit of conversation we were, at least, all united in our total opposition and that saving Fulham FC was our first priority. Even so, we still weren't sure about how we were going to achieve this – but all that was to change in the next 48 hours.

The Football Supporters' Association were trying to initiate a united front against all the merger talk, with Wimbledon and Palace also under threat. A meeting was organised to get all the interested parties to formulate a plan of action, although in QPR's case this was more difficult as their Official Supporters' Club had come out in support of the proposed Fulham Park Rangers. The meeting took place in a dingy pub at Vauxhall – liberal supplies of alcohol were once again on hand, and this time cameras from BBC TV News were present. After an hour or so a group of bedraggled QPR fans marched in declaring their undying hatred for all things Marler.

The first decision taken was to organise some kind of protest for the following Saturday – sit-ins. For once, the League computer had got it right with ourselves, QPR and the Dons all playing at home. Rangers fans were to register their protest as the teams ran out, Fulham at half-time and Wimbledon at the end of their match. It was agreed that every effort should be made not to delay our respective matches for too long lest we get branded as louts and hooligans.

Dominic Guard and Brendon Gleeson then mentioned that Hammersmith & Fulham Council had promised the Town Hall for some form of public meeting and it was agreed to book this for the following Monday evening.

Naturally, none of us had the money to buy the Club but there was some encouragement from Jimmy Hill following his televised confrontation with Bulstrode. To this end, I contacted the esteemed TV pundit and informed him of our plans. He expressed a great deal of caution about

THE WRITE APPROACH

Did you know that when closing a letter to a Prince the phrase 'I remain, Sir, your most humble and obedient servant' should be used if protocol is to be observed? That much came to light when the Supporters' Club wrote to the Prince of Wales asking for his support on the ground development issue.

Certainly the Supporters' Club's letter-writing machine has been working overtime of late. Indeed, initial reaction when asked by the editor to pen this piece was something akin to 'Not another ruddy article!' But then, we thought, there's only a few days before the inquiry kicks off in earnest and writer's cramp (and red hot typewriters) will then give way to concerted concentration as the listening process begins. In any case, you SHOULD know what we've been up to.

Some 45 supporters helped to distribute 10,000 leaflets in the Craven Cottage locality recently. These leaflets merely stated the facts as known to date. As rumours and counter rumours were abounding, the Supporters' Club felt that local residents should at least be given an opportunity of reading the facts. (One other document doing the rounds refers to the inquiry being held at Fulham Town Hall and not Hammersmith. It says the inquiry begins on Monday and not Tuesday. It also states that local residents will have their 'poll tax' bumped up if the council win the CPO, which is just not true).

A further 20,000 Supporters' Club leaflets (and paid for by us) were printed for distribution to other London clubs. We received an excellent response from Chelsea supporters who helped us to dish out about 8,000 before last Saturday's match with Charlton—who themselves know a thing or two about ground problems.

The feedback was very enlightening. Many had seen the pieces in the previous day's Evening Standard and Fulham Chronicle (courtesy of, you've guessed, the Supporters' Club) and were actually on the look-out for the leaflets. Others said they had already written to the inspector in charge of the inquiry. The great majority made favourable, sympathetic noises and wished us well. Even some of the passing police commented that they hoped we won the battle. One even admitted to having sent his views to the inspector.

Meantime the letters are flooding in, Roy Hattersley MP writes: "The future of Craven Cottage is of great concern to me and I hope you will keep in touch with developments" (or lack of them, we hope, Mr Hattersley!).

Tom Pendry MP, Chairman of the House of Commons All-Party Football Committee, wrote: "the committee is very concerned about the suggested redevelopment of the soccer grounds at Fulham and Chelsea by Cabra Estates and accordingly I plan to arrange a meeting of our committee to address the issue sometime in mid-January—before the vital CPO meeting. The last thing we want to see is the demise of Fulham FC and will do whatever is in our power to prevent this."

Gordon Taylor, Chief Executive of the Professional Footballers' Association says: "I have already written in support of Fulham FC remaining at Craven Cottage and will continue to give my support in the future." In his letter to the inspectorate, Mr Taylor writes: "Having been personally involved I am very much aware of the great depth of feeling there is over Craven Cottage and, of course, Fulham FC, and vividly recall the fact that the Fulham & Hammersmith Town Hall was packed to the boards at the time of the takeover of Fulham FC by Marler Estates.

"Such intensity of feeling showed the effect that a

football club can have on its community and whilst at the present moment the football club's fortunes are not at their zenith . . . there is every opportunity that once again the club can return to its Division One days."

The depth of feeling referred to by Mr Taylor is certainly evident in replies from other supporter's clubs. Typical is Aldershot's letter to Chris Patten in which they state: "It would be a travesty if the future of one of football's most traditional clubs was to be put in jeopardy yet again by property developers.

"Indeed we, at Aldershot, only have to go back to April 25th this year when only the enthusiasm and vocal support of the many Fulham followers at our ground saw a 0-1 deficit turn into a 2-1 victory in the final minutes as they strove determined in their quest for promotion—and thus relegating ourselves in the process. What an injustice it would be if these loyal supporters of West London were to be deprived of their football stadium and, very possibly, their football team."

Councillor Gordon Prentice has stated that such letters are vital to their case. Well, the Supporters' Club feel they have done more than their bit to stimulate people's conscience. Encouragingly letters ARE flooding in to the inspector. Less encouraging is that, by and large, it is the same faces who are doing the work and giving up countless hours of their free time. One or two others have beaten their own particular drum then disappeared from view. Shame on them.

DAVID LLOYD

Allan Gould giving out leaflets prior to last Saturday's Chelsea v Charlton game. (Fulham supporters were helped enormously by Chelsea fans. 8,000 leaflets were distributed before the match in all).

At long last an issue of Cottage Pie has hit the streets. Packed with all the latest news it contains an 'exclusive' interview with Stuart Dalrymple, a report on a Supporters' Club trip to France plus a round-up of the season's Player-of-the-Month awards. Supporters' Club members can pick up their copy from the Hammersmith end kiosk or bar at today's match.

the proposed pitch invasions and felt it might lead to trouble. But we, at least, had faith in the Fulham faithful.

Saturday 28 February 1987 arrived not only with a great deal of excitement but also a fair amount of trepidation. I arrived early and took up position – along with my constant companion of the last few days, a pint of Holstein, in the saloon bar at The Crabtree. It was more like a cup-tie atmosphere as people began to assemble. Of course we couldn't publicly announce our intention to invade the pitch, but we could at least issue leaflets asking for "some sort of PEACEFUL protest" while also advertising Monday's meeting.

Clichéd it may be, but I did have to wipe a tear from my eye when I saw the Walsall fans' banner pleading "Don't Kill Fulham". The game kicked-off and, not surprisingly in view of the traumatic circumstances, the Fulham players appeared to have had the stuffing knocked out of them as they quickly went two-down.

However, this all seemed to be hardly of any consequence when news filtered through that they still hadn't kicked-off at Loftus Road due to the fans' protests. We'd informed the police of our intentions and they had agreed not to intervene as long as we didn't damage the goalposts. We all know what happened then and I can honestly say that it was one of the most moving experiences of my life. Admittedly, it did take a while to get everyone off the pitch, but it was a credit to the police, stewards, players and fans that this was done with the minimum of fuss.

The players responded by almost getting the script right – scoring twice to rescue a much-needed point. Afterwards it was incredible to meet the number of other fans from West Ham, Arsenal, QPR (eh?) and, in particular, Chelsea who had come along to the Cottage to show their support. I handed many of them petitions to send off and I was amazed to receive signatures from more than 500 Chelsea fans.

Sunday came with many headlines of the previous day's events, although there was a particularly obnoxious and patronising article in the *Express* that was effectively trying to sign our death warrant.

That afternoon there was the unusual sight of the Football League Management Committee actually doing something positive by refusing to sanction the proposed merger. The bandwagon was well

and truly beginning to roll and the public meeting at Hammersmith didn't let us down. In a totally unique atmosphere, fans of all the clubs concerned stood side-by-side as speaker after speaker denounced the traitorous plans of Bulstrode and co. Supermac was there alongside Hill, Roy Hattersley, Gordon Taylor, Brendon Batson and various members of supporters' action groups. Also present was David Dein, who within a year was welcoming Mr Bulstrode on to the Management Committee. The major points to come out of the highly charged and emotional evening were: a) Hill's announcement that he was gathering together a consortium to buy the Club; and b) the coining of the phrase "Bulldozer" Bulstrode from the FSA's Rogan Taylor.

Matters were now out of our hands. And we sat back and awaited the outcome of negotiations between the consortium and Marler, with "our boys" finally doing the business (something for which every fan should be eternally grateful). But already a lot had been achieved: Rangers' fans had quickly formed the Loyal Supporters' Association (to be totally independent of the football club); one of the bedraggled fans from the Vauxhall pub was already formulating plans for *A Kick Up The Rs*; the forming of FLAG (the Football in London Action Group) to protect and guard against any future merger mania; but most importantly, a friendship and bond between football fans from different clubs had been formed.

Many fans have claimed they were left in the dark by the Supporters' Club during the crisis, but when you consider that all this happened within a week it's remarkable that anything was done at all. And one final point: Jimmy Hill may well feel disappointed at the lack of money emanating from the Supporters' Club, and also feel that we should keep our views to ourselves, but one thing is for sure – that meeting at Hammersmith, which created such feeling and much greater awareness of the situation, was not organised or instigated by Jimmy Hill, but by THE FANS! ⚽

Fulham 5 Aldershot 1		
15.10.88	4th	
Swansea City 2 Fulham 0		
22.10.88	9th	
Fulham 3 Northampton Town 2		
25.10.88	7th	
Notts Co 0 Fulham 1		
29.10.88	4th	
Fulham 1 Blackpool 1		
05.11.88	8th	
Fulham 2 Reading 1		
08.11.88	5th	
Sheffield United 1 Fulham 0		
12.11.88	7th	
Port Vale 3 Fulham 0		
26.11.88	8th	
Fulham 0 Bristol Rov 2	9th	
03.12.88	8th	
Fulham 2 Preston NE 1		
17.12.88	8th	
Gillingham 0 Fulham 1		
26.12.88	7th	
Chesterfield 4 Fulham 1		
31.12.88	10th	
Fulham 3 Brentford 3		
02.01.89	9th	
Fulham 4 Chester City 1		
07.01.89	6th	
Southend United 0 Fulham 0		
13.01.89	5th	
Fulham 1 Mansfield Town 1		
21.01.89	7th	
Bury 3 Fulham 1		
28.01.89	8th	
Fulham 1 Huddersfield Town 2		
04.02.89	10th	
Wolves 5 Fulham 2		
11.02.89	10th	
Fulham 3 Bristol City 1		
18.02.89	9th	
Northampton Town 2 Fulham 1		
28.02.89	10th	
FA Cup		
Fulham 0 Colchester United 1		
19.11.88	Round 1	
Sherpa Vans Trophy		
Fulham 0 Brentford 2		
22.11.88	Group match	
Gillingham 2 Fulham 1		
10.12.88	Group match	

1st
2nd
3rd
4th
5th
6th
7th
8th
9th
10th
11th
12th
13th
14th
15th
16th
17th
18th
19th
20th
21st
22nd
23rd
24th

Training Day

Ordinarily, a local newspaper reporter fracturing his ankle wouldn't affect the TOOFIF regime. On this occasion, though, it was a decidedly lucky break for the mag's co-editors as we got to train with the Fulham first-teamers.

In February 1989, the *South London Guardian* had fixed up a "local hack can't hack it" training feature for the paper. However, the journo in question's injury meant that they needed a substitute; or a pair of subs as it turned out. *The Guardian* contacted manager Ray Lewington who gave us the thumbs-up to be the local paper's stand-ins.

Come the day it was nerves aplenty as we got changed at the less-than-salubrious Fire Brigade Ground, Banstead. We were decidedly sheepish as we mingled with our heroes outside the changing rooms and greeted our photographer, Gordon McLeod, who'd be snapping the action for the feature.

Dave Preston promptly announced he was a goalkeeper, so was paired with Fulham custodian and fellow fitness expert Jim Stannard. I joined the main group for a series of general warm-up stretches and running exercises. DP noted that Big Jim was continuing with his stretches and, eager to avoid anything that involved strenuous activity or even moving from a given spot, did as many stretches as he could. While sitting down, naturally. The rest of us ran. And ran. Then ran some more. Meantime, coach Jack Burkett and keepers Stannard and Lol Batty put Preston through his paces, throwing balls at him from all angles for what must have been 10 or 12 seconds. Exhausting stuff, eh Dave?

The trio of goalkeeping "specialists" did at least find the time to exchange some footballing thoughts: "Are you those bastards from 'One F In Fulham'?" was countered with "Is it true that opposing forwards nail your feet to the goal-line?" Hardly mutual respect, but it was a start.

After further punishing shuttle runs, the rest of the players were – eventually – allowed a football. But any thoughts of it being something of a breeze from that point were given a mighty boot when Doug Rougvie did precisely that to Gordon Davies, dispatching him back to the changing rooms for prompt treatment. And within minutes I received my very own shuddering welcome to Fulham, encountering Gary Elkins in a 50:50 tackle that was as fair as it was meaty.

It was a thunderous collision; Elkins (and his muscular thighs!) flew in at full force as if his life depended on it, then simply got up and carried on as if nothing out of the ordinary had happened. The ball somehow survived, squirting out in an unexpected direction, but it was still in one piece. I did my utmost to follow suit, desperately trying to remain cool despite having been well and truly battered – it was like one of those cartoon collisions with a massive "KAPOW" filling the frame and a constellation of stars flashing every which way. I staggered to my feet, determined not to look too much of a wimp.

The players' reaction to me getting up (almost) right away seemed to suggest I'd come through some sort of initiation test. Even so, it left me regretting, just at that achy, groggy moment, that I'd gone anywhere near a flipping fanzine: that challenge was meant to hurt! And it ticked that particular box all right. A thought occurred as

Opposite page right: No wonder the ball squirted off at right angles, my attention had been drawn by Robert Wilson thundering in with studs showing. That one stung, Willo! Meanwhile, Dave Preston was lying down on the job (*bottom pic*) while "training" with fellow goalkeepers Jim Stannard and Lol Batty.

Below: It's a little known fact that walking football was invented by Fulham FC as long ago as 1989! Here, Gordon Davies, Clive Walker and Andy Sayer try to out-amble TOOFIF's outfield representative.

Below right: TOOOFIF makes its bow in the Club's programme for sponsoring Gary Elkins' boots.

1 TOOFIF   2 Sue & Mel Zulker
3 5 6 Eltham Glass
4 Betty Humphries   7 Antony Prior

I got back to my feet: I wonder if Gary Elkins launched into that ferocious tackle in "football boots: sponsored by TOOFIF"? Ah, the irony.

Thankfully, the feeling returned to my legs, and we were split into two teams and played a more structured match. This was more like it, and before long the nerves went the way of the collywobbles. A few decent touches and it dawned that I could cope with it all – in fact, it was going a whole lot better than I dared hope. Don't get cocky, just go along with the flow; stay focused. I moved towards the ball to play

a routine return pass, just as Robert Wilson decided to make his own mark on proceedings.

The photographer's motordrive went into overdrive as Willo thundered in, studs up, with forearm raised to protect his face. The challenge was fierce and, unbeknown to me at the time (it was extremely muddy), inscribed a nasty six-inch gash down my shin. I only discovered the extent of the injury on showering nearly two hours later, but it sure stung like hell at the time. Being ignorant of the damage most certainly helped, as I carried on and, evidently, gained a level of respect from the players.

It also sharpened the focus. I was reasonably fit then (it was a *long* time ago!) and, somehow, not coming across as too much of an idiot. The sad aspect, and this is an indication of how far from grace the Club had fallen by 1989 (although we still managed to sneak into the Division Three Play-offs that season), was that few of the guys still slogging through the Banstead mire – my heroes – were anything above decent Sunday League standard: my lowly level. Of those who completed the session, the players who stood out as being a clear cut above the rest were Elkins, Wilson, Justin Skinner, Jeff Eckhardt and, best of the bunch by a distance, Clive Walker.

That concerted session lasted well over a couple of hours. Now, with the main thrust of training

Fulham 1 Swansea City 0	
04.03.89 9th	1st
Blackpool 0 Fulham 1	2nd
11.03.89 9th	3rd
	4th
Fulham 2 Notts County 1	5th
14.03.89 7th	6th
Fulham 2 Cardiff City 0	7th
18.03.89 6th	8th
Brentford 0 Fulham 1	**9th**
24.03.89 4th	10th
	11th
Fulham 1 Gillingham 2 h	12th
27.03.89 7t	13th
Preston NE 1 Fulham 4	14th
01.04.89 5th	15th
Chester City 7 Fulham 0	16th
05.04.89 6th	17th
	18th
Fulham 2 Chesterfield 1	19th
08.04.89 5th	20th
Fulham 1 Bolton Wanderers 1	21th
15.04.89 5th	22th
	23th
Wigan Athletic 1 Fulham 1	24th
22.04.89 5th	
Aldershot 1 Fulham 2	
25.04.89 4th	
Fulham 2 Sheffield United 2	
29.04.89 5th	
Reading 0 Fulham 1	
01.05.89 4th	
Bristol Rovers 0 Fulham 0	
06.05.89 4th	
Fulham 1 Port Vale 2	
13.05.89 4th	

Quizballs From Issue 7

1. Can you spot the odd one out?
   - a) Richard Dimbleby
   - b) Lord Beaverbrook
   - c) Ken Myers

2. How many people has Jimmy Hill taken notice of in the past year?
   - a) None
   - b) Less than none
   - c) Pointless question

3. If you had a lot of money, what would you spend it on?
   - a) The homeless
   - b) Nurses' pay rises
   - c) A midfield player from Luton

4. Can you match these drinks to the appropriate players?
   - a) 7-Up
   - b) Babycham
   - c) Anything vaguely alcoholic

5. How many times have you heard "The referee's a w****r" chanted at Fulham this season?
   - a) Once
   - b) Twice
   - c) At least once in all 23 home games

over, those still up for more headed to the top pitch for a seven-a-side game. Count me in; a bit leg-weary and quite achy but, given such a unique opportunity, definitely up for it. Before long, and boosted by a hefty dose of adrenaline, I put everything into a straightforward tackle on Clive Walker as he raced directly at me. A juicy routine tackle; my ball for sure. Mistake. "Walks" simply went up a gear, tipped the ball into space and hurdled the challenge. Easy; sheer class, ability and fitness.

Well, I say hurdled. He *almost* cleared my leg as I dived in, but in clipping it he went flying skywards before landing heavily and awkwardly. The Fire Brigade Ground, and indeed the whole of Banstead, was treated to every swearword known to man plus a few more besides as Walks made it abundantly clear he was not best pleased. All I could do was apologise; time and again. And he was still cursing and muttering half an hour or so later when we stunted up the picture wanted by the paper – hack knackered and held up by a couple of players: Walker and Andy Sayer. With Ray Lewington alongside having a proper giggle at my expense. Oh well, job done and, in

fact, hardly knackered at all. It was a genuine thrill and, battered legs or not, a day to treasure. Dave Preston, who by then had long since taken a shower and devoured a couple of all-day breakfasts, enjoyed himself immensely too.

Two days later I picked up the *Evening News* at London's Victoria Station and read the Stop Press column with a mixture of shock and embarrassment. "Fulham winger Clive Walker is a doubt for tomorrow's home game due to an injury picked up in training." Okay, so the subhead of "TOOFIF co-editor crocks Fulham's potential matchwinner" might have been in my head and not the paper, but it made for an uncomfortable train journey home. In those days Walker was one of the few who could change the course of a game in our favour, so imagine my delight and massive relief when he passed his late fitness test and scored the opening goal in our 3-1 home win over Bristol City. Clive Walker's a top bloke and to this day whenever he strolls past the TOOFIF sales pitch en route to his matchday press duties at Fulham he reminds me of one or more of those swearwords, complete with a wink and a broad smile! ⚽

Above (left): "Ivor" was so unnerved at being closely marked that he cried off early, under the premise that he'd been battered by Doug Rougvie!

Above (right): Ray Lewington, Clive Walker and Andy Sayer smile for the camera while the othher fella holds on as if his life depended on it. "Walks", all the while, was still muttering away much to Lewy's amusement.

Right: Words *and* pic by yours truly.

Nervous Fulham hang on

Glenn Thomas and Trevor Morgan battle it out. Words and pictures by DAVID LLOYD

FULHAM 1 BOLTON 1

WITH six games now remaining, Fulham are still clinging on to fifth place but only just, following this nervy draw against Bolton.

The Wanderers, for all their Sherpa Van Trophy aspirations, appeared to be one of the Londoners easier opponents in a generally tough run-in to the end of the season.

However, the visitors had other ideas and at the final whistle it was Fulham who were thankful to earn a point from the game.

Ray Lewington's men started well with plenty of passes to feet and looked to be in a different class during the opening exchanges.

The Bolton defence was made to look decidedly statuesque on several occasions with Clive Walker continually showing fellow veteran Phil Neal a clean pair of heels on the left flank.

From one such break, Walker crossed into the area where both Gordon Davies and Peter Scott had shots charged down before the ball was scrambled away.

Seemingly inspired by former Fulham maestro Johnny Haynes who was watching from the stands, skipper Doug Rougvie played an exquisite cross-field ball into the path of Michael Cole who in turn set up Peter Scott for a powerful drive which was well held by keeper Felgate.

Bolton countered strongly and only two fine Jim Stannard saves – one from Steve Thompson's 25-yard free kick and the other from Robbie Savage's close-range header – kept Fulham on level terms.

But just two minutes after the interval Fulham struck when Justin Skinner, having just seen Felgate tip his header away for a corner, got on to the end of Rougvie's flick-on from the resulting kick to head the ball home. It was nearly two minutes later when Felgate's attempted clearance hit Davies but Walker blasted wide with the goal at his mercy.

However, Bolton's strong-running and set-piece moves continued to be a threat and it was no real surprise when they equalised with 20 minutes to go. Dean Crombie missed the initial opening but Trevor Morgan made no mistake in converting Chandler's right-wing corner.

Fulham were unable to bounce back and only a couple of desperate blocks from Ronnie Mauge stopped Bolton from grabbing a last minute winner.

Left: With typical whimsy, Paul Johnson draws attention to our unexpected midweek at Chester — we were thumped 7-0!

Below: Those lovely folk at *The Standard* make their views on Fulham's predicament perfectly clear in an editorial. Good job it's not one of their beloved north London clubs that's under the cosh.

Some much-needed proof that football can still be a funny old game was assured recently at Craven Cottage when a fan intercepted Ray Lewington as he strode across the pitch on his way to collect the Barclays Third Division Manager of the Month award and handed him a can of 7-Up as a reminder of Fulham's 7-0 pasting at Chester, a result that came too late to prevent Lewington from winning the award. **Time Out**

Football in Fulham

FULHAM Football Club was always something of a joke, but an endearing, family joke. Now the club is a shadow of what it was: gates this season are as low as 4,000. The owners want to develop the ground, but Hammersmith Council has voted to purchase the site compulsorily, at a potential cost of £20m in compensation. The Council should save its ratepayers' money and let the ground be built on.

There's no I in Team

A few weeks after the training episode, I took a call in the office at London Transport. The voice claimed to be Fulham manager Ray Lewington — yeah, right! — and he wanted to know if I could take some time off work in the next few days. It certainly sounded like Ray Lewington, but come on, why would it be the man himself — was he hacked off about the District Line trains at Putney Bridge, maybe?

I humoured the caller a bit more. Yes, the major office deadlines had passed for that week, so I'd be able to take a day off if necessary. But what exactly was this about?

Turns out it was an invitation to play for Fulham Reserves against Watford's second string in a couple of days' time. "Don't worry," said the voice becoming more credible as Ray Lew every second, "it'll only be a scratch side, but we have to fulfill the Football Combination fixture or we'll get hit with a fine. Do you fancy it?" Now that certainly sounded credible; cash-strapped Fulham wouldn't want to lob out any money if they didn't have to. What was incredible, though, was being invited to play for Fulham Reserves, scratch side or not.

Ray insisted that, because of the financial implications, the fixture had to take place: "We've got to play, we can't afford not to, it's as simple as that." He went through a list of Fulham players available for the game but said that the squad would be augmented by, among others, the husband of Club Secretary Janice Baldwin, plus yours truly. If I could get the time off, that is.

Suddenly I was free that day. Whatever day it was. Did I fancy it? What sort of question was that? Of course I fancied it. Ready, willing and (relatively speaking) able. Bloody hell, this was exciting.

That evening was spent checking (about 20 times as I recall) that my boots were in good shape and packed away safely in my kit bag. All for a game still a couple of days away. Back into work the following day, elated and anticipation levels ever rising... but no running up escalators on the way in — mustn't pull any muscles. Not much in the diary for today, just a few articles to write and calls to make. The plan: take it fairly easy and prepare and look forward to facing Watford tomorrow. For Fulham. Ain't life grand?

The phone rang. Ray Lew again. My new boss, albeit temporarily. Checking that all's well and that I'm in good shape, perhaps. Or maybe letting me in on our formation and tactics. Well no, actually. "Watford have cried off. They can't raise a team," said Lew. "They'll be fined for doing that." Fined? Is that it? The footballing authorities should have thrown the flipping book at them! What a terrible let-down. So my big moment never materialised.

But for 24 hours, at least, I was a Fulham player — and immensely proud of it, too.

Absent Friends

Jeff Eckhardt and Steven Greaves: stand up and be counted. Oh yes, and Gordon Davies, and also Ronnie Mauge.

Many tickets for the Supporters' Club Player-of-the-Year dinner and dance were sold on the premise that there would be at least one star guest (ie a player) on each table. Ivor had dropped the organiser a line in advance to say that he was unable to attend, but in the event only messrs Eckhardt and Greaves were there for the meal, although Mr Mauge turned up after the pubs had closed in order to get a lesson in how to dance the twist from the organiser. Ray Lewington, naturally, was also present, but what of the others?

In particular, one thinks of Peter Scott and John Marshall who, having sat out the early part of the season as they waited in vain for a stampede of chequebook-armed managers to come in and sign them, have a testimonial season coming up at FFC. Are those same supporters who were let down so badly (after shelling out £15 per ticket) now expected to fork out more cash for their testimonial fund?

Where was Club captain Doug Rougvie – someone who had done much in a relatively short spell to help push us towards a Play-off berth and who seemingly had an encouragingly good rapport with the supporters? (Of course, we subsequently learned that the blaggard had done a highland fling and was that very night probably helping his homesick wife choose a colour scheme for their new Scottish abode. It won't be black and white, that's for sure!).

Granted, it was only 48 hours after the disappointment of the "Rovers Return" leg. And granted, the occasion didn't figure all that highly in most of the well-paid professionals' no-doubt action-packed diaries. In the circumstances the players could not be faulted for thinking twice

Top right: Club captain Doug Rougvie opted for a highland fling rather than attend the Supporters' Club dinner and dance

Opposite page: Gary Barnett and the FA Cup – can YOU spot the similarity?

Milton's Lost Paradise

The matchday programme recently carried a rather candid interview with Steve Milton. The newcomer from Whyteleafe was quoted as saying that "the attitude of the Fulham players stinks – there is no will-power to win."

What smacks about the young upstart's comments, of course, is that they are spot-on. Most of the players have preferred to pass the buck rather than the ball, which has itself been propelled to all parts of the ground via passing pigeons, stand roofs, clouds and, in Gary Elkins' case, that favourite associate of his in the Enclosure.

Some players have decided to take the easy route through matches – hiding, in essence, and only resurfacing on the odd occasions when the going's got a bit easier. That much was made apparent when Ray Lewington took the field at Bath. Despite a long spell out of first-team action, Lewy did not take long to get stuck in and take responsibility when the ball came his way. Ray's style might not always be cultured but he sure as hell had a bloody go and he ran his wotsits off while doing his utmost to chivvy those around him to do likewise.

However, as Steve himself admits, he's come to the club at a bad time.

"It's unfortunate that I've come to Fulham whilst they're going through a bad patch. But all we need is one win and I'm sure we can snap out of it. At the moment the attitude of the Fulham players stinks. There is no will power to win. Everyone has their own battles during a game and if I win my battles I've had a good game. But at the moment I'm really disappointed with our attitude especially as it isn't kept within the confines of the dressing room it's brought onto the pitch. If we go 1–0 down the heads drop. It's sickening really".

Some of his squad do not appear to possess those basic qualities; indeed, "putting in a shift" and "standing up to be counted" seem to be alien phrases to a fair few.

Naturally, the seasoned professionals (sic) at the Club were not all that impressed with Milton's comments and a "short loan period with the Sky Blues" ensued (sent to Coventry – geddit?). After the 4-0 win over hapless Wigan, one senior player (who is in his testimonial year, and whose name rhymes with "hot") is supposed to have broken the silence by asking if the degree of effort was okay that day. To be fair, the player in question (whose name sounds as if he comes from north of the border) is one of those who, if not in the superstar bracket, at least does seem to care whether we win or lose. He's also prepared to let his feelings show, as Gavin Nebbeling found out!

Milton's display against Cardiff, excellent though it was, was what you should expect from a centre-forward, yet it was exhilarating compared to the rest of the team that day – a fact reflected in the Supporters' Club votes for man-of-the-match. He polled 66 of the 68 votes cast (with Clive Walker claiming the other two).

Confidence may be a difficult factor to acquire but well-paid pros ought, at the very least, to be big enough to take responsibility on the field of play. Or are the Fulham squad members simply not good enough?

about attending. However, after thinking twice, they should all have come up with the same answer – support the supporters. And ATTEND!

In accepting the wholly deserved top award, Jeff Eckhardt remarked that he could not have performed so well that season without the rest of his colleagues, and that he had intended to thank them during his speech. To great applause, he said simply and pointedly: "Thanks, Steve."

To his great credit, Ray Lewington was visibly embarrassed and annoyed at the poor turn out of players. After accepting several awards on behalf of absent friends, including the Young Player of the Year Award on behalf of Justin Skinner (who, on the night, managed to top his "invisible man" impression of 48 hours earlier), Lewy said he had expected "a decent turn out" and they would all "get a clip". ⚽

Gary Barnett's Ears

A twilight-hours accident with a bottle of Tipp-Ex was the trigger to being chased behind the Riverside Stand by a first-team favourite. In the early days of TOOFIF the magazine pages were laid out and paginated on boards the night before the mag was required at the printers. These were the days before the fanzine operation had access to a computer at home. Instead, material was printed out on whatever computer was available – at work or via a friend – and then literally cut and pasted into place on the boards.

On this occasion all was going pretty much to plan, if slowly. It was well into the night and by then it was a case of overriding the tiredness and maintaining concentration levels. As the final snippets were pasted into place, and the bed beckoned, disaster! A nudged cabinet, a dislodged bottle of Tipp-Ex, which naturally nosedived onto one of the pages, meant that one particular article got the big white splodge treatment.

With no means of printing out a clean version of the article and a deadline looming, a quick and easy Plan B was required. But I was knackered and inspiration was in desperately short supply. That is, until a picture of the FA Cup spawned the germ of an idea… and by the morning, with help from the printer, the gap was filled with an FA Cup look-a-like feature. Trouble was, come the following Saturday when Issue 8 made its

bow, Gary Barnett was none too pleased about the suggestion that his prominent ears resembled the handles on the famous trophy. Or the fact that some of his team-mates ribbed him about it before and even during the game.

Oblivious to this, I headed as usual for the Supporters Bar post-match, which, in those days, was at the Bishops Park end of the Riverside Stand. The riverside walkway was sparsely populated, so when Barnett ambled round the corner heading for the players' bar in the centre of the stand he spotted yours truly about 30 yards away with tell-tale bag of TOOFIFs in hand.

"Oi, I want a word with you," yelled our busy midfielder, suddenly very animated and evidently not in the best of moods. With that, he broke into a run. Defaulting to full cowardly mode, I hared off into the aisle under the stand fully expecting to be nabbed. Thankfully Gary's all-action efforts in the white shirt had drained his batteries and, even with the bag of TOOFIFs slung around my neck, I was able to outrun him and make my escape. No doubt he'd get me the following week. But he never did! He was probably, even then, plotting to oversee non-league Barry Town's sortie into the First Round proper of the UEFA Cup… ⚽

Quizballs From Issue 8

1. Name the odd one out:
   a) Zico
   b) Maradona
   c) Hicks

2. Can you spot the odd one out?
   a) Daley Thompson
   b) Carl Lewis
   c) Des Bremner

3. Which of the following claimed that goal at Crewe?
   a) Jim Stannard
   b) Andy Sayer
   c) Gordon Davies

4 Who was the last Fulham player not to receive a booking?
   a) Joe Bacuzzi
   b) Len Oliver
   c) Robert Dalrymple

5. What was the last FREE event staged at the Cottage?
   a) VE-Day celebrations
   b) Promotion from the Southern League
   c) The Crucifiction?

6. On what occasion can you hear the PA system at Fulham
   a) When Jimmy Hill speaks
   b) When Jimmy Hill speaks
   c) When Jimmy Hill speaks

Fulham 1 Tranmere Rovers 2	
19.08.89	16th
Bolton Wanderers 0 Fulham 0	
26.08.89	15th
Fulham 1 Mansfield Town 0	
02.09.89	12th
Crewe Alexandra 2 Fulham 3	
09.09.89	8th
Fulham 2 Swansea City 0	
16.09.89	7th
Walsall 0 Fulham 0	
23.09.89	7th
Fulham 0 Huddersfield Town 0	
26.09.89	7th
Chester City 0 Fulham 2	
30.09.89	4th
Bristol Rovers 2 Fulham 0	
07.10.89	7th
Fulham 1 Rotherham United 1	
14.10.89	9th
Reading 3 Fulham 2	
17.10.89	11th
Fulham 2 Bury 2	
21.10.89	11th
Brentford 2 Fulham 0	
28.10.89	12th
Fulham 1 Northampton Town 1	
31.10.89	13th
Leyton Orient 1 Fulham 1	
04.11.90	13th
Fulham 2 Cardiff City 5	
11.11.89	13th
Fulham 4 Wigan Athletic 0	
25.11.89	12th
Notts County 2 Fulham 0	
02.12.89	12th
Blackpool 0 Fulham 1	
16.12.89	11th
Fulham 0 Bristol City 1	
26.12.89	11th
Fulham 2 Shrewsbury Town 1	
30.12.89	11th
Birmingham City 1 Fulham 1	
01.01.90	12th
Preston NE 1 Fulham 0	
06.01.90	12th
Fulham 2 Bolton Wanderers 2	
13.01.90	12th
Tranmere Rovers 2 Fulham 1	
19.01.90	12th
Fulham 1 Crewe Alexandra 1	
27.01.90	13th
Swansea City 4 Fulham 2	
10.02.90	17th
Mansfield Town 2 Fulham 0	
13.02.90	18th
Fulham 5 Notts County 2	
17.02.90	14th
Wigan Athletic 2 Fulham 1	
24.02.90	18th
League Cup	
Fulham 0 Oxford United 1	
23.08.89	Round 1 1st leg
Oxford United 3 Fulham 5	
30.08.89	Round 1 2nd leg
Sunderland 1 Fulham 1	
19.09.89	Round 2
Fulham 0 Sunderland 3	
03.10.89	Round 2 replay
FA Cup	
Bath City 2 Fulham 1	
19.11.89	Round 1
Fulham 2 Bath City 1	
22.11.89	Round 1 replay
Bristol City 2 Fulham 1	
09.12.89	Round 2
Leyland Daf Cup	
Peterborough United 1 Fulham 0	
08.11.89	Gp match
Fulham 0 Notts County 1	
28.11.89	Gp match

1st
2nd
3rd
4th
5th
6th
7th
8th
9th
10th
11th
12th
13th
14th
15th
16th
17th
18th
19th
20th
21st
22nd
23rd
24th

The FA Cup

Gary Barnett

Hot Property!

In the Spring of 1990 Fulham fans were pinning their hopes on the local council winning the CPO Inquiry and thereby ensuring the much-coveted Craven Cottage site remained a football stadium rather than being bulldozed and transformed into luxury flats. On the eve of that inquiry, though, the Fulham FC Board made a deal with the ground's owners to vacate the site in due course ("by May 1993 or before") in return for staged payments of up to £13m (the first £2m of which was "paid on the date of the agreement") and to withdraw their support for the CPO. This perceived U-turn outraged the supporters and resulted in further rearguard actions by fans. Amid the frenzy and general hullabaloo, the fanzine became well and truly established.

Down to the ground

The role of Fulham Supporters' Club Press Secretary would normally be as demanding as the post of Social Secretary for a Party-goers Association. In the early 1990s, Fulham FC were languishing in the lower divisions and the Club was hardly headline news material, so, apart from trying to publicise the odd fundraising disco at local level, the Press Secretary gig was a low-key, fairly cushy number. But boy did that all change, and virtually overnight.

We all knew things were far from rosy. On the pitch all the signs pointed to a continuation of the sorry downward spiral, while off it the legacy of Ernie Clay's disastrous sell-out to property developers was coming to a head. At least the proposed Fulham Park Rangers merger was a thing of the past.

By now the local Council was doing its bit, supporting a Compulsory Purchase Order (CPO) that would keep Fulham FC at Craven Cottage and out of the hands of property developers. To recap: in 1989, Vicenza Developments Ltd, a susbsidiary of Cabra who owned Craven Cottage, applied to

Hammersmith & Fulham Borough Council for planning permission to develop Craven Cottage for residential purposes. The Council then applied for an alternative development and issued a CPO for the site. The upshot was a Public Inquiry ordered by the Secretary of State set to begin on Tuesday 30 January 1990. Supporters' Club activity cranked up that week with the distribution of leaflets to residents close to Craven Cottage urging them to support the CPO and the Club's modest plans for the ground. We went into the weekend concentrating on our fixture with Crewe and being ready to attend the Inquiry on the Tuesday.

But that weekend the balloon went up. Depending on your interpretation of events, the Directors of Fulham FC had either sold out or preserved the Club's future. In short, for a staged payment of up to £13m, £2m of which was paid up front, they had agreed to allow the developers to build on the ground in due course and, when the time came, not to oppose the development. The agreement also included an agreement not to support the CPO. This just left the fundamental issue of where Fulham FC might play once they vacated the Cottage.

Suddenly our favourite football club, overlooked by the media for years, had become hot news. By mid-morning on Monday, Thames TV were keen to broadcast the views of Fulham supporters. They'd be filming at Craven Cottage at about 11am. Thankfully my boss was a big sports fan and okayed my request to take an early lunch. It turned into an extended one – I didn't get back to my desk until Wednesday morning!

After joining forces with fellow Supporters' Club committee members Allan Gould and Andy Dance at the Cottage gates, we blurted our views to the TV cameras. The general drift was that Fulham FC and its supporters been sold down the river. Having done our bits to camera we were all set to drift off ourselves but spotted local Councillor Gordon Prentice striding purposefully, and at some pace, towards the Cottage. He was fuming. Had he been sketched in cartoon form he'd have had clouds of steam billowing from his ears and an ever-reddening scowly face. He was so het-up that he didn't take any notice of our cheery greetings from across the road.

So, rather than continue towards The Crabtree, we doubled back to see whose head was about to be removed from their shoulders. Barely able to keep up, we were bemused to see the enraged Councillor come to an abrupt halt just inside the Craven Cottage gates. And there he stayed, edging from foot to foot, as we approached. We said our hellos a second time. This time they registered.

> "That weekend the balloon went up. Depending on your interpretation of events, the Directors of Fulham FC had either sold out or preserved the Club's future."

Opposite page right: Hammersmith & Fulham Council's "Keeping Faith" leaflet distributed in the run-up to the CPO Inquiry.

Below: Alland Gould (left) and David Lloyd secure a home-made banner to the Hammersmith End fencing: "HOME IS CRAVEN COTTAGE".

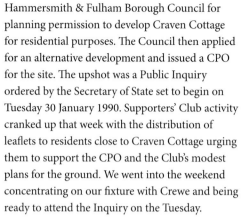

Keeping Faith.

❝ Last Sunday Fulham Football Club 87 entered into a legally binding agreement with Cabra Estates which involves leaving the Cottage and withdrawing support for the Council's Compulsory Purchase Order (CPO).

We deeply regret the Board's decision. We have worked together in partnership since 1987 with the express intention of keeping football at the Cottage. The Board's decision was taken 48 hours before the start of the Public Inquiry without the Council's prior knowledge or agreement.

Despite this let down, our basic position has not been changed. We shall be pressing ahead with the CPO because we believe the original reasons for going for it are still valid.

We firmly believe:
- The Cottage should not be built over. It is valuable open space in a crowded inner city borough.
- Craven Cottage is the only one of the 91 league grounds in England and Wales with a listed stand and other structures. It is unique. It is part of our heritage.
- Craven Cottage is the historic home of Fulham Football Club. It is part of our local identity.
- The Council's established policy is to retain football at the three grounds in the borough — Stamford Bridge, Loftus Road and Craven Cottage.

The Council's case is still strong although many will feel that our position has inevitably been undermined by the sudden and unexpected withdrawal at the 11th hour of the Club's support for the CPO.

Since 1987 all our efforts have been directed at keeping football at Craven Cottage. That is the real issue.

The issue is not about:
- negotiating the best terms to leave the Cottage;
- whether or not anyone stands to gain financially from the decision;
- the motives of the directors.

The Board admits that the threat of the CPO gave the directors extra bargaining power. We agree. But Cabra would never have promised so much money unless they believed they were in grave danger of losing the CPO Inquiry.

Despite last weekend's setback, the council is keeping faith with the supporters. Fulham without the Cottage is unthinkable.

Our message is 'support the council, support the CPO. Keep football at the Cottage.' ❞

— Comment from Cllr. Gordon Prentice

Hammersmith & Fulham
Serving our Community

The Agreement says:
- Cabra will pay the club £2 million now.
- The club will be granted a lease of Craven Cottage for 3 years.
- Cabra can terminate the lease in May 1991 or May 1992 if they have been given planning permission and are ready to start a development.
- Cabra pay the club £3.5 million when the club leave the ground.
- Cabra will, if the club wish, try to arrange for the club to share a ground for a further 3 years.
- If the club don't want to ground-share, they will be paid £500,000 more instead.
- The club would be paid another £5 million if Cabra ever obtain planning permission to redevelop the Cottage.
- If the ground were sold for over £50 million the club would receive anything above £50 million up to a maximum of £2 million more.
- The club assured Cabra that they would not support the present or any future CPO.

Leader of the Council Cllr. Mike Goodman says

❝ 'I am delighted with the way the inquiry is proceeding which clearly demonstrates the council's continued commitment to football.

There's a long way to go, but with the supporters and people of Fulham behind us, the council remains committed to our local ground, its historic ground and Britain's national sport. We shall keep the faith. ❞

Your Council helping to keep football at Craven Cottage

Gordon's face was a peculiar mix of anger and uncertainty. "Hello lads," he said breathlessly, before releasing some of his venom: "I've raced down here bloody furious at the Fulham Board; I've been used and lied to. Now, having got to within yards of the Cottage, I realise that it's probably best not to go any further. I'm so upset, I'll probably do something that I'll later regret." With that, he said his goodbyes and, deflated, trudged back along Stevenage Road.

Now that we were pretty much at the foot of the Cottage stairs, Allan suggested we should head up to see if we could scrounge a cup of tea. So we popped into the cramped reception area and, after making our cheeky request through the small hatch, were indeed given a cuppa each. Before we could start supping, though, the connecting door opened and an outstretched arm appeared. In horror-movie fashion, the fingers on the arm beckoned us in. We didn't know it, but that eerie gesture heralded an astonishing ten-hour marathon session.

The three of us shuffled through to discover that the arm belonged to Andy Muddyman. He led us to a room where Andy's dad, Bill, and Jimmy Hill were waiting, together with FFC General Manager Stuart Dalrymple. This was around noon. We were still there for the evening news – and there we were on the Football Club's telly telling our hosts what we thought of their actions. We were still there, having been treated to a fish and chips supper, for the 10 o'clock edition. Oh, and that's us on the TV again; flippin' repeats!

In the meantime we'd had the basics of the deal and the Club's stance explained to us in bizarre fashion. Bill, or it might have been Jimmy, picked up a book and, in turn, put it on our heads. The book represented Fulham FC – and when it was taken off our head, that indicated we didn't have possession of the Club any more. It was outlined to us that, given Cabra's ownership of the ground, taking a large sum of money from them for something "we" didn't own was a fantastic deal. The money would help to tide us over, then to set up somewhere else in due course and ensure the Club's survival. A new three-year lease of the football ground had been arranged, too – taking us up to 31 May 1993. We were told that, with this deal on the table, Fulham simply couldn't gamble on the CPO. So, with that in mind, they'd shaken hands on the deal with Cabra.

The three of us were asked, pointedly and individually, what we would have done in the circumstances. Allan had no doubts; he never once wavered. "Go with the CPO," he said emphatically as soon as the book was removed from his head, adding that we'd be unlikely to find any suitable new ground nearby. Andy, wearing his accountant's hat, acknowledged the plus points of the deal and, somewhat reluctantly, agreed with the Club's stance now that the situation had been explained in much more detail.

When it was my turn, while not as adamant as Allan, I acknowledged the Club's dilemma but still reckoned that the best route for the Club would have been via the Council's CPO, which would now surely be abandoned, given FFC's withdrawal of support.

Funny really that, all these years later, one of the lasting impressions of an intense and unlikely few hours in the famous old Cottage with senior Club officials desperately trying to convince us that their actions were honourable and justified are of Jimmy Hill noisily chomping on his fish and chips with his mouth open. And of us repeatedly doing our bit on the club's telly, telling our hosts precisely what we thought of their cloak and dagger tactics. Actually, the CPO inquiry did go ahead a couple of days later – with the Supporters' Club now playing a much more prominent role. The Football Club, meanwhile, although contractually obliged to withdraw their support, were privately delighted that the inquiry was going ahead as scheduled. ❖

Match	Date	Position
Fulham 3 Preston NE 1	03.03.90	16th
Fulham 1 Chester City 0	06.03.90	13th
Huddersfield Town 0 Fulham 1	10.03.90	11th
Fulham 1 Bristol Rovers 2	17.03.90	12th
Rotherham United 2 Fulham 1	20.03.90	14th
Fulham 1 Reading 2	24.03.90	16th
Bury 0 Fulham 0	31.03.90	16th
Fulham 0 Walsall 0	04.04.90	16th
Northampton Town 2 Fulham 2	07.04.90	17th
Fulham 1 Brentford 0	10.04.90	14th

1st
2nd
3rd
4th
5th
6th
7th
8th
9th
10th
11th
12th
13th
14th
15th
16th
17th
18th
19th
20th
21st
22nd
23rd
24th

The News – According to Issue 10

So much has happened in the past few weeks it really is difficult to know where to begin. One thing is certain – TOOFIF has an exclusive on its hands. No Club official and, it follows, no Club publication, is permitted by THAT deal to refer to the goings-on at the CPO inquiry. As an independent journal we can. Developments have taken such diverse twists and turns, and so many supporters are still in the dark on so many points, that we have decided to attempt to tell the full story – or at least the full story as we know it. TOOFIF's David Lloyd was on hand as the events unfurled…

Below: The fight goes on, suggests one sour-mouthed supporter in the local press

'We will fight to the end'

WHERE do we go from here? That's the justifiable reaction of Fulham fans following the board's shock decision to accept Cabra's eleventh-hour offer.

The immediate answer is Fulham Town Hall – for that is where Hammersmith and Fulham Council is laudibly going ahead with its Compulsory Purchase Order to buy the site for football.

As far as the supporters' club is concerned, our campaign remains unaltered – to keep football at Craven Cottage.

Main villain of the piece is undoubtedly former chairman Ernie Clay who sold out to the property developers in the first place. The board's dramatic cloak-and-dagger deal, the lack of consultation, all leave a very sour taste in the mouth.

Certainly, as a pure business transaction, the deal can be deemed a good one. From having no ground, no time and no money they have secured a two to three season extension plus the much vaunted £13 million – strings and all.

The major flaw concerns the fans' emotions – all fans, not just Fulham's. The overwhelming feeling that Craven Cottage IS Fulham and they would have preferred the full compulsory purchase order (CPO).

The Labour council admits the odds of winning the CPO have been damaged. But they insist that should it be successful they would offer a ground lease, on their terms of course, to Fulham FC.

If the CPO fails and Cabra's planning proposals are sanctioned the question remains – where DO we go from here?

It is staggering that the club, which as it stands has only a guaranteed two-year extension to their lease, admit to not having any alternative site in mind. And, although they have banked £2 million (part

Jimmy Hill has denied Fulham FC sold out to developers in the Craven Cottage deal. But it's left DAVID LLOYD, of Fulham Supporters' Club, with a sour taste in his mouth.

of which has gone to clear debts and part set aside for the transfer market) and will get a further £3.5 to £4 million when they vacate Craven Cottage what will that get them?

Currently, Fulham's fans would get up at dawn if a surprise friendly was arranged in the Orkneys, but few would bother to make that trip on a regular basis. Or would they?

And so to the new 'democratic' club Jimmy Hill has talked about. He said: "It was agreed voting powers should be opened up to those who supported the club's rescue."

Fine comments and certainly a move in the right direction. Those figures have now been released and as expected those who put their hands in their pockets in 1987 are rewarded now.

Eleven individuals or groups are listed from the Muddeymans down to supporters' groups. The directors' total per centage of the votes is 81.8. Those supporters who shipped in back in 1987 take 11.6 per cent and the three supporters' groups - Supporters' Club, Riversiders and Vice-Presidents each get 2.2 per cent.

We could not have expected more and at least this does give us some say. We also admit it would not be our place to get too involved in, say, heavy transfer deals. But we insist we should be consulted on more general issues, like selling up to property developers!

THE PROLOGUE

Fulham FC, as witnesses for Hammersmith & Fulham Council in the forthcoming CPO Inquiry, were apparently playing a passive role in the lead up to the hearing so, inspired by Councillor Gordon Prentice's view that "letters to Chris Patten MP (Secretary of State for the Environment) and the CPO Inspector are absolutely vital", the Supporters' Club – or rather Allan Gould, who was the main instigator – started the campaign in earnest. Almost at once all the committee members rallied to the cause.

Letters were written to every Football League supporters club, all known British fanzines (more than 300!), the FA, the Football League, the PFA, the House of Commons all-party football committee, all local MPs and even the Prince of Wales. The various parties were urged to spread the news and send their views, and hopefully support, to Chris Patten and the Inspector.

Meetings of the Football Supporters' Association and National Federation of Football Supporters were addressed. The message was simple: "Help us keep Fulham FC at Craven Cottage."

Fulham supporters then delivered 10,000 leaflets in the Craven Cottage locality, to inform residents of the goings-on and to quash some of the false rumours that were circulating. A further 20,000 leaflets were distributed to other football supporters in London. Worth noting, too, that we received excellent support from Chelsea fans who helped us to hand out 8,000 leaflets prior to their home match with Charlton Athletic.

Press packs were circulated to more than 50 concerns and, as the inquiry approached, so media interest intensified. Phone-ins took place, on Capital Gold and LBC. Gordon Prentice and Jimmy Hill trounced Emile Al-Uzaize on the Capital broadcast, so much so that a referee would have stopped the contest. Hill later admitted: "Gordon presented our case superbly and in football terms it was three points in the bag." However, the local Tory Councillor concluded with the prophetic words: "I still expect Jimmy Hill to make a deal with Cabra Estates before the opening of the inquiry."

Even the national press was taking note by now and an excellent preview piece appeared in the *Daily Telegraph*. And Jimmy Hill himself said in that Saturday's match programme (v Crewe, just three days before the inquiry): "So far so good. There is a lot of work to be done, but perhaps the CPO will prove above all else is that there are enough people around with the will and dedication to do it."

The campaign was rapidly gathering momentum and our press packs were evidently rising to the top of various journalists' in-trays. Allan Gould and yours truly were invited to present the current position on LBC radio. Allan also did so, brilliantly, on Greater London Radio and Radio Two.

We trooped away from the Crewe match disappointed (again) with the team's showing but wholly braced for the inquiry, which started on the Tuesday. At least we'd done our bit; now we could put our feet up…

'ERE WE GO, 'ERE WE GO

It is said that most people can recall where they were when Kennedy was shot. Fulham supporters of a certain age will always remember how they heard of the shock disclosure of the "deal". The jungle drums went haywire that Sunday, and far from putting our feet up it transpired that the real battle was just commencing.

The Supporters' Club sprang into action and five members met with Gordon Prentice at Hammersmith Town Hall that evening. Another press release was speedily prepared. To give you a flavour, it began: "Once again the supporters of Fulham FC have been sold down the river by their Board of Directors, for the third time in as many years." It continued: "If 'Judas' Hill is so sure that this move is for everybody's good then why hasn't he consulted anybody, fans or Council, in making this decision? What exactly does Judas Hill think he's going to get for his paltry 13 pieces of silver? That won't buy enough land in London, let alone build a new stadium. Why has he chosen to lead us into the wilderness?"

The papers were full of it on Monday. Mid-morning, and at the request of Thames TV, Allan Gould, Supporters' Club secretary Andy Dance and myself hared down to the Cottage to face the cameras and deliver our "Sold down the River" speeches. We then headed into the Cottage hoping to scrounge a cup of tea.

What followed over the next ten hours was as surprising as it was dramatic. Within two minutes of entering the Cottage we were invited to have "talks" with Jimmy Hill, plus Bill and Andy Muddyman. FFC General Manager Stuart Dalrymple was also in attendance. From the off, the conversation was frank and forceful. Cynics would suggest that: a) Of course the Club wanted to appease the supporters; and b) Obviously they would be trying to pull the wool over our eyes. When have the supporters counted for much in any case?

That might have been the case had we been seen for ten minutes or so. But that is less likely over what became a marathon session. Discussions were forthright and the first hour-and-a-half in particular included some hostile questioning and comments. When told that most Fulham fans thought of him as a "Judas" and a "money-grabbing bastard" the Chairman suddenly offered to resign. The look of shock on Bill Muddyman's face was genuine – if there was a script to this particular exchange then JH was certainly not sticking to it. From that juncture, or at least after

calming down slightly, the Chairman continued without his "BBC" or "Uncle Jim" approach, and a certain amount of mutual trust was achieved. It was at this point that it dawned on us that the CPO could still go ahead, and that as the first instalment of the deal – a small matter of two million pounds – was due imminently, all was not yet lost.

Having entered the room in total opposition to Hill and the Board, we were now prepared to concede that they had – in their opinion – acted in the best interests of Fulham FC. We, in turn, pointed out that we would be persevering with our own campaign to keep Fulham/football at Craven Cottage (which pleased them) and that as such we could not be seen to be agreeing to anything that would affect that goal.

Bill Muddyman pointed out that Hill had taken, and would no doubt continue to take, most of the flak whereas the deal was a Board decision (well, the Board minus David Gardner) and not Hill's. We accepted this, but were adamant that with Cabra offering such a sum – strings'n'all – they were obviously aware of the mounting public opinion in the Council's (and Fulham's) favour. As such, we insisted, they should have persevered with the CPO.

Above: The Supporters' Club leaflet delivered to homes near Craven Cottage prior to the CPO Inquiry.

The Club have, in a number of articles since, stressed that they had nothing to sell – Clay sold the ground in 1986 – and they were in effect being paid for their silence. In fact, as well as withdrawing their support for the CPO, Fulham FC were required by the deal to pen a letter to the Inspector in support of Cabra's planning application.

What was clear was that neither Fulham FC nor Cabra Estates were prepared to risk even a 10 per cent chance of losing the CPO. (Hill and co claimed that the Council's case had weakened in the previous few days – a point refuted by the Council.)

It was also clear that the whole issue was becoming more involved by the minute. We accepted that as supporters we were still merely pawns in the game, but here was a case of the pawns more than holding their own. Some of questions we were asking at that point were:

a) Was the deal, with all its detail and complexities, *really* thrashed out on that Saturday night/Sunday morning?

b) At what point during the negotiations (if ever) were the Board members aware that success via the CPO could mean they kept two or even six million pounds and still hang on to the Cottage?

c) If this was the case, who was the clever cookie in Fulham's team?

d) Would the CPO inquiry still go ahead? (The closing lines in Fulham's agreement with Cabra stated: "In the light of the above, Fulham FC have withdrawn their support for the CPO and do not now expect the Hammersmith & Fulham Council to continue with it.")

e) What were we, as "mere" supporters, doing getting involved with such heavy business matters and hard-nosed businessmen?

f) And were we about to become somebody's fall guys?

We cared not if we were to become fall guys as long as Craven Cottage remained our home, but we were at least aware of this possibility. We were also fast becoming aware that this was no ordinary situation. It was getting hugely complex – we were beginning to question everyone involved, and even their motives. And every new announcement seemed to present a whole host of fresh scenarios.

Our lengthy meeting at the Cottage was followed by an extraordinary general meeting of the Supporters' Club on the eve of the CPO. Hill and the Muddymans agreed to speak at the meeting and let us use the Boardroom. Questions were again fierce. They were answered fairly with the only taboo subject being the CPO itself – the deal with Cabra precluded any comment on the subject. Many still disagreed with the deal, but most now understood the reasons for it being signed.

Once Hill and Muddyman departed, next into the Boardroom was Gordon Prentice, still disenchanted and angry with the FFC Board, but totally committed to the CPO. He did, however, now require our support more than ever as he and the Council had, at a stroke, lost their star witness. The committee voted unanimously to whole-heartedly support the CPO. ⚽

More from Issue 10

With shades of 1987, a pitch demonstration was planned for the next home game – against, would you believe, Walsall, whose fans had supported us admirably last time out. The Gods, however, thought this was too cosy an arrangement and following three days of torrential rain the Craven Cottage surface resembled a series of swimming pools (just the thing for a complex of luxury flats?).

An intriguing scenario ensued before the inevitable postponement. Local Mayor and fervent Fulham fan Ian Gray had, via the *Daily Mirror*, threatened to strangle Jimmy Hill, while Mike Goodman, leader of the Council, promised to get himself arrested at the game for publicity purposes. Allan Gould, for the Supporters' Club, made the smart move of threatening to withdraw support for the CPO if any member of the Council misbehaved in any way. Council assurance was promptly issued promising no embarrassing scenes. It was a great shame that rain ultimately stopped play since many, many supporters were still in the dark about what had elapsed, and why.

Following the Walsall washout, the pitch demo was rescheduled for the next home game, versus Notts County. Between 1,500 and 2,000 supporters made their way onto the pitch at half-time. A diplomatic 1-1 score at the break ensured hearty exchanges between the two sets of supporters. The Inspector Stephen Marks was present to hear speeches from Allan Gould and

Opposite page right: "Defiant fans" – the *Fulham Chronicle* offer their take on the Notts County pitch demo.

The CPO Inquiry

After the furious activity of the previous 48 hours the opening session of the CPO inquiry could have been a dull affair. Not a bit of it. Tension gripped the public gallery as, below us, the two sides argued as to whether, with the Football Club's withdrawal of support, there was just reason to proceed. Cabra's QC was Anthony Scrivener, who later in life – in 2005 – defended former Iraqi President Saddam Hussein against mass murder charges. However, to our great relief, Stephen Marks, the Inspector of the inquiry, upheld the Council's claim that they were striving to maintain association football – and not necessarily Fulham FC – and the open space incorporated in the site. This was a major victory. All these years later, it's difficult to convey just how important such victories were. More recently, Fulham FC have enjoyed lording it as one of the top-flight elite, but in 1990 our down-at-heel Club was struggling merely to survive (and things would get worse before they got better). In late January/early February of that year there was something on the go every single day.

Terrace Talk (from the local *Gazette*)

This particular fanzine co-editor's diary has been as tightly packed as a well-hung footballer's jockstrap recently. It's got so bad that I have had to check the extensive list of appointments before being able to squeeze in a read of my favourite newspaper – *The Gazette* of course. Fulham FC has more than a little to do with the busy spell and the severe curtailment in social life. "So, what can he have been up to?" I hear the one remotely interested reader ask. Well, I'll tell you...

Sat 6 Jan Watched "the lads" go down by a single goal on Preston's plastic pitch. An above-average performance by Fulham, and had the forwards taken their chances we would have spent the coach journey home reflecting on a comfortable victory. As it was, we were treated to an, ahem, "artistic film" very loosely based on tennis.

Sun 7 Jan Played, and scored, for Broomfield FC (Leatherhead & District League Div. 2). After boring all and sundry with increasingly embellished descriptions of the majestic effort (a 485-yard diving header) I went home to turn my attentions to designing a leaflet for distribution to homes in the Craven Cottage locality.

Mon 8 Jan Spent much of the day addressing envelopes to all known British fanzines (300+!) and, when writer's cramp eased a little, the envelopes were stuffed with documents outlining the ground development saga at Fulham and asking for the respective fanzine teams' support. Then dropped leaflet artwork at the printers.

Tue 9 Jan Evening: Board of Management meeting at Fulham with Jimmy Hill, the Directors, Councillor Gordon Prentice plus other invited parties. Went "wearing" my Supporters' Club committee hat. Discussed... the ground saga. CPO given the thumbs-up.

Wed 10 Jan Decided that my girlfriend deserved a night out. Took her to the Fulham Supporters' Club committee meeting. Main topic... the ground saga.

Thu 11 Jan Evening: Addressed Football Supporters' Association re, yup, you've guessed, the ground saga. Plans were proposed to bring the whole issue to national prominence.

Fri 12 Jan Collected Fulham leaflets from printers.

Sat 13 Jan Delivered Fulham leaflets to Craven Cottage... stuck posters up in ground... met and liaised with the press... attended extraordinary meeting of the Supporters' Club (no prizes for guessing the main topic)... oh yes, watched the game, an exciting 2-2 draw with Bolton. Successfully read Clive Walker's lips after the wingman was comprehensively felled in the box by Winstanley late in the game but no penalty was given. Personally, I didn't think it was a "jolly fine decision, my old China" or that "fair play, ref – giving a penalty would have ruined that nice Mr Winstanley's weekend."

Sun 14 Jan Now player-manager of Broomfield. Masterminded a 3-1 victory by pointing out what a football looked like and the purpose of the white wooden things at either end of the pitch. Did not score. Designed Supporters' Club advert for the new Fulham newspaper, *The Cottager*.

Mon 15 Jan Interviewed Ray Lewington for local press. Sad to hear that Hugh Burns had returned to Dunfermline after his loan period. The manager was necessarily diplomatic about that penalty incident but commented that, having seen the match video twice, his view had not changed a jot since 4.36 on Saturday afternoon.

Tue 16 Jan Another night out for my girlfriend. With 40-or-so others we delivered aforementioned leaflets to houses in the Cottage locality. Fulham general manager bought us all a drink afterwards – half a shandy with 40 straws.

Wed 17 Jan Busy time in day job! No time for football stuff. Withdrawal symptoms set in. Early night.

Thu 18 Jan Man from *The Gazette* rings. "Don't forget your Terrace Talk article, will you?" Aaarrgghh. Prepared most of that then went on to complete *Cottage Pie*, the Supporters' Club magazine.

Fri 19 Jan Took annual leave to coincide with my girlfriend's day off. How sweet. Took her to Prenton Park for the evening match with Tranmere. Walker's strike put us ahead but two late Morrissey goals, the second of which was well offside (honest!), made for a long, late journey home.

Sat 20 Jan Went to Stamford Bridge to distribute "Save Fulham FC" leaflets along with several Chelsea fans who agreed to help. Received an excellent response from all concerned, and a local news photographer was there to snap the action.

We shall not be moved!

MORE than 1,500 supporters poured on to the Craven Cottage pitch at half-time of Saturday's match to voice support for the council's CPO on the ground.

In a spectacle charged with emotion many were unable to hold back tears. Followers of visiting Notts County gave their fellow fans a rousing ovation.

Supporters club spokesman Alan Gould and Councillor Gordon Prentice addressed the crowd. They condemned the board's decision to leave the Cottage and spoke with confidence about the chances of Fulham staying at their 96-year-old home.

The CPO inquiry should end today or tomorrow and a decision is expected in May.

Standing firm...defiant Fulham fans during the pitch protest.

Jimmy Hill talks the tightrope

Martin Thorpe on a light-footed display over Craven Cottage

PERHAPS Jimmy Hill would have been more at home with an Autocue or with Desmond Lynam not QCs asking him questions, but he managed to achieve what he set out to do at yesterday's public inquiry into the future of Craven Cottage — give evidence but say nothing.

For weeks now the inquiry has been a largely grey affair with planners and expert witnesses guiding the inspector on whether the local council should be allowed to compulsorily purchase the ground to save the soccer. But on the inquiry's last day a TV star was in the witness box and, as if by herd instinct, TV was there too.

Up in the public gallery of fusty Fulham town hall — all oak doors and paintings of forgotten aldermen — the fans sat distrustful of Hill but hoping for a crumb of hope over the Cottage. On the gallery's gold-painted, curlicued railings someone had even tied a "Fulham FC" scarf as if it were the fence at the Hammersmith End.

When the star player got into the box — so to speak — it was ostensibly to give evidence but really to walk a tightrope. To help their case, the council wanted him to say that, if the inquiry was won, Fulham would stay at the Cottage.

Hill did not want to say they would not — so keeping the club's options open — but was mindful of a clause in the recent deal between the Fulham board and the ground's owners, Cabra Estates. This says the board must not be seen to support the compulsory purchase on pain of jeopardising the £13 million that would ultimately come Fulham's way if the inquiry reject the compulsory purchase and Cabra build houses on the site.

It is the sort of dilemma in which TV soccer pundits often find themselves — balancing the urge to give their honest view of an offside decision against a FA disrepute charge for criticising the ref.

To help convey to Cabra the impression that Hill was not voluntarily associating with "the opposition", his solicitors requested he be sworn in — not a common practice at public inquiries as the inspector quickly demonstrated by admitting that "on the question of the swearing" he had no knowledge of how to do it. But eventually the Fulham chairman's tightrope act began.

"Were you delighted at signing the Cabra deal?" asked the Cabra QC. No, "just very pleased, because it protected the club against the downside of losing the compulsory purchase".

"Would you prefer to have the choice to stay at the Cottage rather than leave," asked the council's QC. "The more options the better," replied Hill.

But had not his intention been, until recently, to secure the club's future at Craven Cottage? "To secure the future of the club in general," he said. "I don't think you can distinguish one from the other." Hang on, was this a slip of Hill's guard? Everyone waited for an action replay, but he was soon back on the fence. If the compulsory purchase was won, would Fulham stay at the Cottage? "Whatever happens with the inquiry, the board's duty is to make the wisest decision for the club."

The inspector will decide this autumn. Who was it said referees have a difficult job?

was then questioned, first by Cabra's counsel, Mr Scrivener. Among the questions were:

Q. You have the goodwill of Fulham FC at heart?
A. Solely.

Q. Were you delighted about the Cabra deal?
A. I was very pleased. (Hill said that under the new arrangements following the Cabra deal, all Club funds would be donated to a football charity in the event of Fulham ever being wound up. No money whatsoever would be paid to Directors, shareholders or anyone else.)

All Scrivener's questioning was linked to Hill's article "The Reasons Why" that had appeared in the matchday programme for the visit of Notts County.

Hill was asked to confirm that the Board had sent a letter to the inquiry in support of Cabra's development application. He confirmed this had been done as one of the conditions of the recent agreement, but refused to confirm that leaving Craven Cottage was the preferred option for Fulham FC.

Hill's hesitation before answering many of the Cabra counsel's questions was clearly understood by those present to mean that he and the Board did not in any way rule out a future for Fulham at Craven Cottage. However, he was very careful not to risk breaching the terms of agreement with Cabra. It was then the turn of the Council's counsel, Mr Spence. Hill's answer to one question was: "You cannot distinguish the future of Fulham Football Club from the future of Craven Cottage."

Q. Would you like to have the choice of whether to accept a further £4m to leave the Cottage or to negotiate a further lease from the Council in the event that the CPO was successful?
A. The more options that are before the Board, the better. Yes! (Hill added that he was "full of hope" about the future if Fulham FC stayed at Craven Cottage.)

He was then asked: "With £2m are you even more hopeful?" Hill replied: "Yes!"

Hill confirmed that the views he'd expressed in programmes for the Bury match and others prior to the Cabra agreement remained unaltered (his view in these was that staying at Craven Cottage was vital to the future of Fulham FC).

If given the options between Fulham playing on at the Cottage or moving to a new ground elsewhere "the Board would carefully weigh up the options, taking supporters' views into account, and reach a decision in the best interests of Fulham FC."

On ground-sharing, Hill was only in favour where the ground was ideally purpose-built for

Above: Martin Thorpe covers Jimmy Hill's subpoenaed appearance at the CPO Inquiry for *The Guardian*.

Gordon Prentice and see the crowd demonstrate with banners and a show of hands that they still wished to remain at Craven Cottage. The crowd then dispersed peacefully after delaying the restart by 10 minutes. The event seemed to inspire the team; Fulham went on to record a thrilling 5-2 victory (why don't they always give it a go in such fashion?); even the Inspector was visibly engrossed.

There was a further twist to events as the CPO Inquiry entered the last week when Jimmy Hill was invited, then subpoenaed, to attend the proceedings. Hill, despite extensive experience of global live TV appearances, looked extremely nervous and fraught. This live showing was not on his terms, and a slip of the tongue could have proved disastrous. 😳

Notes prepared by Richard Jones of the FSC

Mr Magruder (Hill's solicitor) explained that the Chairman's refusal to attend prior to being summoned was not intended as a discourtesy to the Inspector; he was merely complying with the terms of the Cabra agreement of 28 January, which prevented the Club or its officials from speaking in favour of the Council's CPO. He also requested that Mr Hill be sworn in, and after some discussion an affirmation to tell the truth was given.

The Inspector imposed certain limitations on areas on which Jimmy Hill could be questioned or could make any comment. Hill made a short opening statement in which he thanked the other Directors of Fulham FC for their unprecedented generosity and efforts on behalf of the Club. He

sharing, and where Fulham FC was at least 50 per cent owner.

The Inquiry closed with a site visit by the Inspector. Whether he has become a Fulham supporter following his visit for the rousing Notts County encounter remains unclear. Hopefully, something has influenced him in favour of the Council's CPO application and that Chris Patten MP will receive the appropriate advice in two months or so. In the meantime, of course, anything can happen. ⚽

The Gould Life

Supporters' Club spokesman at the inquiry was Allan Gould. His evidence included rebuttals to several points raised by Arsenal Vice-Chairman David Dein, who spoke on behalf of Cabra.

I am 31 and attended my first match at Craven Cottage as a five-year-old. My father, a Fulham supporter for more than 50 years, took me to that match and still goes to the Cottage for every home game. Today I'm representing the Fulham Supporters' Club. The FSC reformed in 1987 along with Fulham FC (1987) Ltd. I have been a committee member for the past two years and currently hold the post of Social Secretary; I've been nominated as spokesman on the CPO.

Along with my fellow members, I am fed up with people rubbishing our football club. People who neither know nor care about it. People like David Dein, the Vice-Chairman of Arsenal and alleged "avid football fan". He says during his evidence: "During my several visits to the Club's ground I had become aware of how dilapidated the whole place had become." I wonder if the Inspector shared this opinion on his recent visits?

Mr Dein went on: "I remember attending a formal visit to the ground for one whole day with members of the FA, the DoE and the police

in my capacity as a member of the Football League management committee." This must have been in or before 1988 as he hasn't been on that committee since that date.

Mr Dein continued: "The dilapidated condition of the premises was largely due no doubt to their lack of financial resources." The Club was reluctant to spend money on major ground repairs partly due to lack of resources but also due to the short-term nature of their lease.

Dein went on: "It may be helpful if I explain the dilemma of the Club. The attendances are very low, so low that the income from all sources cannot hope to cover the running costs." As Fulham are forbidden from defending themselves, I will quote Jimmy Hill from an interview on Capital Gold Radio on Tuesday, 23 January. Our Chairman said: "The last three years have naturally been tough. In the first year we lost £300,000. In the second we lost £120,000 which means that things are going in the right direction. During that time we have paid off half-a-million pounds to buy the players' contracts from the previous owners of the Club. Our graph shows, because we have a much more efficient commercial side running now, that given reasonably fair wind, next year we should be breaking even." [Allan then catalogued some of those commercial activities, including a three-year sponsorship deal worth £100,000 with Teleconnect; ClubCall, raising around £60,000 per annum; Cottage Chance, which brings in £30-40,000 per annum; programme sales, worth around £24,000 a season; commercial sales of Club merchandise; leasing a betting office to Ladbrokes] All this doesn't suggest to me that "the Club cannot hope to cover their running costs."

[Allan then rubbished Dein's supposed knowledge of FFC, picking him up on several howlers in his evidence before continuing...] Dein states that "Two million pounds will not go very far in salvaging Fulham from the financial quagmire it is in – much of it will pay off the most pressing debts and the rest will not go far in today's transfer market." Well, that's fine by most Fulham supporters who, I believe, would be happy watching their team playing in a lower division but at an improved Craven Cottage in Stevenage Road, SW6. So much for Mr Dein! ⚽

"I am fed up with people rubbishing our football club. People who neither know nor care about it. People like David Dein, the Vice-Chairman of Arsenal and alleged 'avid football fan'."

Left: Allan Gould, Fulham Supporters' Club spokesman at the CPO Inquiry and all-round good egg.

Chance of a Lifetime

I f you don't shoot, you'll never score; if you don't buy a raffle ticket, you won't win a prize. Well it ain't always so. Having supported no end of Fulham fundraising schemes over the years, including Cottage Chance, I didn't enter this particular season (if I recall, it was £10 a month to take part). First prize each month was £1,000 with ever-decreasing amounts for the lesser places.

Down in sixth spot, or thereabouts, was the Chateau Weekend. The winners, and their partners, were whisked off en masse to FFC Vice-Chairman Bill Muddyman's chateau in the south of France for a weekend of Fulham chatter while gorging on wonderful food and wine. In the glorious sunshine. Sounds perfect!

So imagine my surprise when one of the winners, Michael Gregg – a colleague on the Fulham Supporters' Club committee – said he wasn't fussed about going and offered me his place. "For all of the hard work you've put in on behalf of the Club," insisted Michael. It was a wonderful, generous gesture, and one that prompted a life-changing moment.

Five or six couples were picked up at the airport by Bill Muddyman's people carrier and ferried to the chateau. One of the couples were Brentford fans believe it or not, but then, unlike me, they'd at least paid their Cottage Chance dues. On arrival we walked up a slight incline to be met at the apex by the main host, Bill Muddyman, who'd been joined by Club Chairman Jimmy Hill and Chief Executive Brian Naysmith. This led to the one sour note of the whole weekend. Each guest was warmly greeted with handshakes and a glass of wine, even the Brentford fans. Everyone, that is except me; in fact, Jimmy Hill pointedly ignored not only yours truly but, disgracefully in my eyes, my much better half, Heather. Not a great start.

In the event we all went on to have a superb couple of days. Bill was incredibly generous; nothing was too much trouble. And virtually nothing was off-limits, so we all made full use of the swimming pool and tennis courts. I say "virtually" – the only thing not on the agenda was any meaningful talk about Fulham's future, a massive hot potato at the time. Massive hot potatoes and anything else we cared to scoff were in plentiful supply, as was the wine from Bill's vineyard. Wine doesn't usually agree with me, but this was lovely stuff. And it was a shame not to join in! Lapping up the plentiful French sunshine was thirsty work, after all.

The chateau was picturesque and spacious. Heather and I had been given a delightful bedroom that had a spiral staircase leading up to another room affording a great view of the vineyard and surrounding countryside. It might have been the wine, but as we retired that night I'm sure there was a little green lizard gazing serenely from one of the staircase steps, daring us to go anywhere near it. I did the only thing I could think of at the time – I got down on one knee and proposed to Heather. Bill's Château de Berne wine may have influenced the timing perhaps, but it was a great move on my part.

The news of our engagement spread the following morning and everything was mellow. At least until all parties were invited to play tennis. Down at the tennis court I was told I'd be partnering Jimmy Hill against Brian Naysmith and AN Other – with everyone else watching from the adjacent grassy banks. Deep joy. I hadn't played since schooldays, and hadn't been much good then, just a fairly fit baseline scrapper. Still, Jimmy was an accomplished player, so it would all be down to him.

During the knock-up I realised I'd been given a defective racket, as the ball kept going clean through the strings, particularly whenever I attempted a swished backhand. The embarrassment! "Okay, let's get going," suggested Jimmy, somewhat nonplussed with his non-playing partner. "Try a few practice serves, then we'll play a set." I was a good bit taller since school, and, glory be, it seemed I had something

Opposite page top: Jimmy Hill prepares to receive at the far end of the court, while, at the other end, some prima donna is more interested in the camera, leaving Brian Naysmith to fend for himself during the practice session before the main event.

Below right: Something seems to have caught Jimmy Hill's attention – maybe it's the Château de Berne leaflet!

Quizballs From Issue 11

1. Which of these disappearances constitutes the greatest mystery?
   a) Lord Lucan
   b) Glen Miller
   c) Fulham's midfield

2. Can you spot the odd one out?
   a) Margot Fonteyn
   b) Rudolf Nureyev
   c) Justin Skinner

3. Who or what is currently the most popular?
   a) The Poll Tax
   b) Chelsea
   c) The Chairman of FFC

4. "Fulham have a talented youth team" – take a stab at justifying that extraordinary statement in not more than one word.

5. "We Don't Talk Anymore" was a popular hit for the evergreen Cliff Richard. To which of the following would this song be most applicable?
   a) Kenny Dalglish
   b) Marcel Marceau
   c) Jim Stannard and the Fulham defence

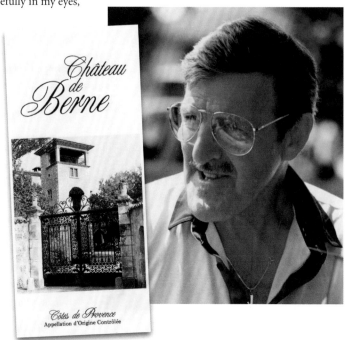

Château
de
Berne

Côtes de Provence
Appellation d'Origine Contrôlée

of a serve now. Not only did I manage to hit the ball, but I did so quite hard. And over the net, too. Okay, let's give this a go.

It wasn't quite the hush before a Wimbledon final, but there was an air of anticipation as I let rip towards the hapless Fulham fan at the other end of the court. It wasn't quite an ace, perhaps, but a fierce unreturnable winner; fifteen-love – and a smattering of applause from the spectators. Applause! Maybe we should quit now that we were ahead. Heather gave me a smile and a nod of encouragement. Hey, things were looking a little less intimidating.

Naysmith was now ready to receive. He was a useful player. Right, mate, let's see if you can handle my new-found rocket serve. Another hush. We settled, ready for the second point of the match. I lobbed the tennis ball into the air, described an almighty thrashed arc with the racket and made a fearsomely brilliant contact. The ball positively fizzed in the general direction of the receiver.

"Wow, you really caught that one well," exclaimed Jimmy Hill a nano-second later. And let's be fair, he should know. Because my howitzer of a serve had just thundered into the back of his neck, where a big angry red weal was already emerging. It was, of course, incredibly funny on a number of levels. But in a typically British way most of those present were doing their utmost to stifle their guffaws. We were guests after all. Then again Jimmy was undoubtedly hurt. And not a little shocked. "Bet you wish you'd shaken our hands when we arrived now, JH!" I thought. Or rather I didn't. That's merely a bit of artistic licence way after the event.

After a short break we continued the contest. Jimmy Hill won the set (I was there alongside him, but he did all the important stuff) and we subsequently headed off for more food and wine. With Jimmy parading a nasty bruise for the rest of our time at the chateau, it was hard to dodge the issue. The general consensus was that it had been a chance in a million – and that the make-up folk at the BBC would have their work cut out to disguise the glowing red blotch prior to JH's next appearance on the box.

Thanks, Michael, for so generously passing up the chance to go on the chateau weekend. In doing so you were indirectly responsible for setting off a chain of events that included JH's on-court mishap. Of much more significance though, it hastened wedded bliss and four wonderful children! ⚽

1st	
2nd	
3rd	
4th	
5th	
6th	
7th	
8th	
9th	
10th	
11th	
12th	
13th	
14th	
15th	
16th	
17th	
18th	
19th	
20th	
21th	
22th	
23th	
24th	

Fulham 1 Birmingham City 2
14.04.90   14th

Bristol City 5 Fulham 1
16.04.90   16th

Fulham 0 Blackpool 0
21.04.90   17th

Shrewsbury Town 2 Fulham 0
24.04.90   19th

Cardiff City 3 Fulham 3
28.04.90   20th

Fulham 1 Leyton Orient 2
05.05.90   20th

Moral Victory

Having heard of Arsenal Vice-Chairman David Dein's involvement with the CPO and his support for Cabra, Fulham fan Andrew Victory was quick off the mark with a letter to Highbury. That missive, addressed to the Gunners' Chaiman, is reproduced here, along with the brief reply from Mr Dein.

Dear Sir or Madam: As a lifelong supporter of Fulham Football Club, I was sickened to discover that one of your Directors had given "evidence" concerning the proposed demolition of Craven Cottage. I assumed a Director of such a prominent football club would be supporting the battle to save Craven Cottage. I was disgusted to discover he was, in fact, assisting the property developers!

It baffles me that Mr Dein should be in favour of another club losing its home of 96 years to developers who are entirely motivated by profit. It is an open secret that the Fulham Directors reluctantly agreed to accept a sum of money to "go quietly". They were faced with eviction at the end of May had they refused. Everybody connected to Fulham Football Club desperately wants to remain at Craven Cottage, and it is appalling that we have been stabbed in the back by Mr Dein.

In my opinion, the name of Arsenal Football Club has been soiled. Perhaps Mr Dein (who I assume cares for Arsenal) would like to imagine the feelings of Arsenal fans if a Fulham Director assisted in the demolition of Highbury!

In reply, David Dein wrote:

By the tone of your letter you clearly are not aware that I was instrumental in saving Fulham Football Club from extinction in 1987. Furthermore my evidence was totally supportive of the Board of Fulham and if my recommendations are adopted I am sure Fulham will have a far brighter future than perhaps you could envisage.

Lewington Out, Dicks In!

FULHAM FOOTBALL CLUB

TELECONNECT   TELECONNECT

Above: Alan Dicks (front row, fourth from left) poses with his squad.

THERE'S ONLY ONE F IN FULHAM
An alternative look at Fulham F.C.

INSIDE: An occasional gem amid the usual old rubbish!!

ISSUE 12 SEPTEMBER 1990 £1

THERE'S ONLY ONE F IN FULHAM
An alternative look at Fulham F.C.

SIMPLY THE BEST!

ISSUE 13 NOVEMBER 1990 £1

Right: What might have been.

Opposite page: Further ramblings in the local *Gazette*.

E very football club has its share of ups and downs, but you need to be a fairly long-in-the-tooth Fulham fan to remember our last lots of "ups". Indeed the nadir was reached last season when we finished fifth from bottom of Division Three, only escaping the dreaded drop by virtue of Cardiff's timely defeat at Bury.

In the meantime, the "Lewington Out" brigade have had their wishes granted, at least in part. Last season's manager has been moved sideways – he's now First Team Coach – to accommodate new supremo Alan Dicks. Yep, the self same Alan Dicks who guided Bristol City up to Division One in the 1970s. City went on a downward trend at the turn of the decade, since which time Dicks has been out of British football.

The thought occurs, if the new boss fares badly will we hear the less-than-massed ranks chanting "Dicks Out, Dicks Out"? Doesn't bear thinking about, does it?

On the subject of the CPO, expect the decision to go against Cabra's building proposals but also against the Council's CPO application. Much would then depend upon any recommendation to keep the Cottage site as an "open space". ⚽

What a To-do, Ron

One of the few players to stand out as a real trier in what was a trying season was Ronnie Mauge. His efforts earned him the Supporters' Club young player of the season award. Yet he'll be kicking off

the new season with Bury. Out of nowhere Ronnie got in touch with *Cottage Pie*, the Supporters' Club mag edited by Richard Jones; those comments were subsequently also aired in TOOFIF.

"The way Fulham treated me the last couple of months was diabolical. I love Fulham. I love the supporters. But the way the Club treated me – nah! So in that sense I'm glad to join Bury. They wanted me out at Fulham. They dropped me for the last four games of the season. They put Jeff Eckhardt, who's a centre-back, in midfield, they put Ray in midfield without giving me any explanations. And I just though, nah…

"I didn't really want to leave Fulham. I don't want the fans to believe I wanted to go or that I deserted them because the fans have been really good to me. To tell the truth I was forced out. I don't think it was anything to do with Ray. What I believe is that Alan Dicks wanted me out. Why? I haven't got a clue.

"The thing that gets me is that I feel bad for the supporters who don't know what really goes on. Because there was a lot of shit going on at Fulham. It came to a point when no one even knew who the manager was. No one even knew who was picking the team. There were rumours that Alan Dicks was picking the team. Now this is the story the players have been hearing, right? The reason Alan Dicks became manager is because Jimmy Hill wanted a say in how to pick the team and Ray Lewington wasn't having any.

"But some of the players are still loyal to Lew and it's all just, well, ridiculous. The last couple of months it was Alan Dicks picking the team, I'm telling you. Lew went into the background. It was a shambles and the players were confused. I got disheartened. Like, what's going on? I dunno.

"But I want to get it through to the true Fulham supporters that, honest to God, it wasn't down to me to leave Fulham. If it was down to Ray Lewington then I'd still be at Fulham today. I love the supporters and everything that they've done for me, and I'm grateful. But I was forced out." ⚽

Classical look for Cottage

IS THIS the classic shape of things to come at Craven Cottage, home of Fulham Football Club? It is, if an inquiry held earlier this year grants permission to Cabra Estates for this £20 million Quinlan Terry-designed scheme for 240 flats and a basilica-shaped community centre.

At the inquiry Hammersmith and Fulham Council opposed the demolition of Craven Cottage but Fulham FC backed the developer.

If agreed, then Cabra will pay up to £13 million for the Cottage and will pay for Fulham to share another ground for three years.

Gunning for Dein

Arsenal fanzine *The Gooner* responded to their Vice-Chairman backing Cabra Estates' proposals at the CPO inquiry. Ian Trevett wrote...

The public tribunal to decide the fate of the Council's CPO and effectively deciding the future of Fulham FC lined up as follows: Football was represented by the Fulham Supporters' Club and Hammersmith & Fulham Council;

Jimmy Hill was nowhere to be seen and eventually had to be ordered to attend; and Cabra was represented by David Dein.

Basically, Dein's evidence was a vitriolic attack on Fulham FC, its ground and its supporters. Dein's attacks range from the petty to the vicious and I believe he has brought shame on our club. What was Dein's motive? I find it hard to comprehend why a

First Division vice-chairman should find it necessary to sabotage the dreams of Third Division supporters.

I hope Fulham supporters succeed in their fight to stay at Craven Cottage. And I would like to congratulate Ian Gray and Gordon Prentice at Hammersmith & Fulham Council for supporting football. If only the national government had the same love of the game.

Yvonne Gets the Boot

The sacking of a Football Club Secretary should not be an issue that concerns the ordinary supporter. Yet the dismissal of Yvonne Haines and the handling of the whole affair has rankled many and has united all the supporters' groups. It was a move guaranteed to drive a wedge between the supporters and the Board at precisely the same time that members of the Board are calling for a more unified approach and more trust. To learn, in the same week, that a convicted fraudster has been taken on to run our lottery just adds to the feeling of unrest. Chief Executive Brian Naysmith carried out the evil deed, seemingly on a whim, and the Board have backed his action in the wake of receiving letters and petitions from supporters. Yvonne Haines' dismissal is Fulham's loss.

Yvonne's dismissal led to longstanding Fulham fan Chris Mason writing to Jimmy Hill:
I write to confirm my resignation from the team of programme contributors. You may remember that I returned my ground pass to you at half-time last Saturday week. I have been a Fulham supporter since 1951 and a programme contributor for seven years. I was editor of the programme at the time of the formation of "Fulham 1987 Ltd."

And, along with many others, I looked forward to a new and interesting chapter in the history of our Club.

Sadly, however, it seems that the changes have been for the worse. Fulham has never been a great club in terms of achievements on the field but it did have an atmosphere all of its own. This atmosphere has now been soured.

The rumour and speculation concerning the future of the Club and, more particularly, the recent behind-the-scenes changes which culminated in the disgraceful dismissal of Yvonne Haines have, in my view, tarnished the image of Fulham forever. ⚽

CPO Decision

So, the D of E has finally extracted its digit and announced, as TOOFIF forecast, a three-way draw. The Council's CPO was rejected, as were the building schemes put forward by the Council and Cabra. John Duggan has been trumpeting that he need only re-apply to get his planning through, but will the just-thwarted Council agree that easily? I suspect not. Fulham, whose lease is now virtually guaranteed to last until May 1993, now have some breathing space. We are still at Craven Cottage, and who knows what can happen in the next two-and-a-half years? ⚽

TERRACE TALK
by David Lloyd, Editor of 'There's Only One F in Fulham'

NOW is as good a time as any to see precisely what the current Fulham team is made of. Convincing victories in the last two home matches may just have given them the necessary injection of confidence – much needed after such an appalling start to the season – to make a move up the table.

The next two matches copuld well be billed as crunch games. They are both away – at Huddersfield this Saturday and at Wigan the week after. Fulham, of course, have yet to record an away league win this season. Their last such victory came, in fact, nigh on a year ago – at Huddersfield!

Despite the improved showings of late, Fulham remain deep in relegation trouble. Should they fail to pick up any points from the next six on offer, then it is safe to assume the scrap will continue between now and May. On the other hand if, say, three or more points are gained, then with two

home matches to follow (against fellow strugglers Preston and Shrewsbury), a steady climb into the top half of the table could become a reality.

Why the new-found optimism? Well, the win or two and the manner of them has helped. As has the knowledge that even at our worst – and there were some truly dreadful performances early on – we have not been taken to the cleaners. Other teams near the foot of the table have taken drubbings every three or four weeks, but not Fulham.

Our two worst defeats have been at Bournemouth – and time hasn't healed those awful memories – and Grimsby, both by 3-0. These statistics also say something about the overall standard of the division. Yet still we have foundered.

Most of the close defeats have been followed by "We woz unlucky" claims from the players.

And on most occasions such a case could be made. Trouble is, it's no good citing bad luck as the trap-door opens in May. You have to make your own luck.

Although sufficient openings were created for a hatful of goals against Crewe on Saturday, our winner needed a touch of good fortune. Crewe had not long equalised after being under the cosh for the first 45 minutes. The uneasy feeling crept in that we would buckle and have to settle for a point – or worse.

Simon Morgan thought differently. A great tackle halted a Crewe attack near the halfway line. A second challenge ensured that he kept possession, then Lady Luck intervened. The pass forward ran on kindly into Gordon Davies' path and he slotted the ball home. Ivor, as ever, took the plaudits. But there was also a huge smile of satisfaction on Morgan's face.

It's all too easy to highlight

cock-ups – like the botched substitution a few weeks ago when the wrong number was raised from the dug-out – but it's much more pleasant to record a job well done.

The lack of a robust 20 goal a season forward – promised to the team and fans since August – has not helped. A series of stop-gaps, including the pitiful Leroy Rosenoir (if only his knees were as healthy as his heart) made little impression.

Much will depend on the midfielders, particularly Justin Skinner and Jeff Eckhardt, continuing where they left off against Crewe in their support of the forwards. Both want to get away – Eckhardt had a transfer request turned down. It would be ironic that in doing the business to attract other clubs they help Fulham's cause. And not many players choose to leave winning sides when an integral part of the first choice eleven, do they?

1st
2nd
3rd
4th
5th
6th
7th
8th
9th
10th
11th
12th
13th
14th
15th
16th
17th
18th
19th
20th
21st
22nd
23rd
24th

Skulduggery at the Cottage

Fulham FC hasn't always been the cosy, friendly place for which it's famous. In fact, there was a good deal of suspicion around in the 1990s. Indeed, back then a favourite word of the moment on the terraces was "skulduggery".

It was very odd, for example, to see a convicted fraudster, Tom Enefer, put in charge of the Club's commercial affairs. True, he'd paid his dues, but this was a highly delicate time in Fulham's history and one element desperately required around the place was trust. That appointment did nothing to advance such an ideal. In due course, our doubts had more than a little substance – this is from TOOFIF 27, August '93: Factually, Enefer was a convicted fraudster who, having done his time, was taken on by [Brian] Naysmith as commercial guru, yet when he departed it was discovered that some £70,000 was unaccounted for in Fulham's "books" (please note "unaccounted for", not "stolen"!) and that the records for the scratch-off tickets were in an equally bad state. Why do you think he left?

When popular Club Secretary Yvonne Haines was sacked, seemingly on a whim, many of those who worked closely with the Club were disgusted at the decision. Yvonne, twin sister of FFC ticket office supremo Sandra Coles (who retired after nearly 40 years' service to FFC in May 2013), subsequently resurfaced as "popular club secretary" at Millwall, a position she held for 20 years before her retirement in 2012. However, back in October 1990 Yvonne's dismissal set off a curious chain of events.

Those involved with producing the matchday programme were threatening to down tools in protest and, out of the blue, I received an invitation to attend a meeting at the Cottage. Or rather to attend a meeting that, I was told most pointedly, *wasn't* taking place at the Cottage. Nudge, nudge, get the picture? Ken Simpson, who in later years would be responsible for taking presentation photos on matchdays, was another

who'd *not* been invited by Chief Executive Brian Naysmith. As soon as the meeting kicked off we were reminded very solemnly that the whole matter was not only delicate but also highly confidential, and that those in attendance had to swear to secrecy. Most of us were perfectly ready to swear.

It very soon dawned on the motley crew present that we were in effect perceived as a potential shadow programme squad; should the current incumbents carry out their threat, the Club was hell-bent on making a seamless transition and carrying on regardless – a pragmatic move, but one that was handled very poorly.

Right at the outset, Naysmith offered me the editorship. Hmm, that would have been interesting (although totally implausible) – how could I edit both the Club's official matchday programme and the independent fanzine! Being serious for half a second, had I accepted the offer then TOOFIF would naturally have had to be shelved (at the very least). Naysmith's gesture was well meant, I suppose, if done in a creepy sort of way. It was flattering too. Fact was I had no spare time to take up the offer of overseeing such a demanding production on a voluntary basis anyway. Produce around 25 home programmes a season? No chance. However, the overriding factor was that

Top right: Yvonne Haines, FFC Club Secretary in 1993, with her twin sister Sandra Coles – Fulham folk through and through.

Below: *The Guardian* was tipped off about Brian Naysmith's unsettling actions – which prompted a furious salvo from the Club in this direction. Trouble was, they were well wide of the mark!.

Bottom clipping: Fulham FC's appointment of an ex-fraudster is highlighted in the local press.

JIMMY HILL has returned from his villa in France to find Fulham in ferment over the actions of Brian Naysmith, the chief executive he appointed during the summer.

While the chairman was on holiday Naysmith sacked Yvonne Haines, the club's secretary for the past 20 years and a respected stalwart of the club through many bad times.

He had already upset the volunteer team who produce the programme at Fulham by trying to withdraw their only remuneration, their season tickets. And, unforgivably, he sounded out a replacement editorial team with a brief to make the programme "more Sun than Guardian".

Sort him out, Jimmy.

Fulham FC give ex-fraudster senior job

FULHAM Football Club is taking financial advice from a convicted fraudster who was sentenced to three years for his part in a scheme to milk an Olympic lottery.

Tom Enefer, 58, started his new job as commercial consultant on October 8. He is respons-

ible for developing the club's business affairs including the £30,000-a-year lottery.

In 1982 Enefer took part in a plot to defraud the British Olympic Lottery with his own company Enefer Consultants who were taken on by the BOA as organisers and

promoters. After police investigations, Enefer was convicted at Maidstone Crown Court in May 1985 of fraud.

He was sentenced to three years in jail but served 12 months with remission for good behaviour.

Earlier this year Brian

Naismith, Fulham's recently appointed chief executive, offered him the job.

Enefer told the Gazette yesterday: "I've got absolutely nothing to hide. I've paid the price for what I did and I can assure you Fulham FC will not be paying anything.

"I pleaded guilty, went to prison and served my time. It's all in the past and I'm as clean as a whistle. Brian recommended me to the board and Jimmy Hill the chairman and Bill Muddyman the vice-chairman were put fully in the picture before they interviewed me and con-

firmed my appointment.

Hill said he and Muddyman were quite happy with Naismith's decision to hire Enefer.

"We told Brian it was his decision," he said yesterday.

● Fulham FC secretary Yvonne Haines in shock dismissal – page 59

Mr Enefer yesterday

Haines gets boot in shock decision

Long-serving secretary is left stunned by notice

FULHAM Football Club's recent run of encouraging results, culminating in Tuesday's 2-0 win over Bury, has been accompanied by another off the pitch saga following the shock sacking of club secretary Yvonne Haines.

Haines, a popular and essential member of the Craven Cottage administration for the last 20 years, was summoned to Chief Executive Brian Naismith's office last week and was verbally given three months notice.

At the time of going to press neither Haines nor Naismith were prepared to elaborate on the reasons behind the dismissal.

But Haines told the Gazette: "It came completely out of the blue. It was Mr Naismith's decision and not the board's.

"I've done nothing to warrant dismissal and have a clear conscience. Everyone at the club, including Alan Dicks, has been wonderful to me."

Reaction from those close to the club was swift and emphatic. A petition with the names of over 450 supporters was handed to directors before they attended a board meeting on Wednesday to discuss the affair. And it was strongly rumoured that

playing staff, including coach Ray Lewington and striker Gordon Davies, were up in arms at Naismith's action.

Haines, accompanied by the club chaplain the Reverend Gary Piper at the meeting, said afterwards the ball was now in the directors' court but she would fight the decision unless an adequate reason was given. The association representing Football League employees, FLESA, will also take up the case.

Naismith, who joined the club at the beginning of August, declined to comment on the affair this week, saying it was "sub judice." However, he hit out at an article in a national newspaper which criticised his attempts to change the editorial team responsible for the club programme.

The editor for the last ten years, Dennis Turner, was told, via a third party, that Naismith wanted to change the style of the programme. David Lloyd, present editor of

"There's Only One F in Fulham" was approached to take on the editor's job but turned it down.

The programme's contributors receive nothing from the club except free tickets for home games. According to Turner the club rake in up to £40,000 a year from programme proceeds even before advertising is taken into account.

But Naismith had decided that the season ticket facility should be terminated as part of a drive to cut back on complimentary tickets. Speaking yesterday morning, Naismith said his proposal to scrap the free tickets had been rejected by Chairman Jimmy Hill and other members of the board. And he denied claims that his decision to terminate Haines' contract had caused a split between himself and members of the board.

"I am totally confident that I have got the full support of the board. It's up to the board what sort of statement it issues. Obviously I didn't enjoy breaking the news to Haines. I wouldn't like to remove someone who has been in a job for a week yet alone a number of years."

Olaf Dixon, secretary of FLESA, said yesterday that the association would be prepared to go to an industrial tribunal if the club failed to produce either adequate reasons for the dismissal or substantial remuneration for Haines.

I, too, was every bit as disappointed by Yvonne's dismissal, so with an immediate and polite "Thank you, but no thank you" I explained my reasons to Naysmith and those present and left them to it.

So it was a big surprise when, the following Saturday, a brief review of the meeting-that-wasn't appeared in *The Guardian*'s sports diary column. It didn't go down at all well in the corridors of power at Fulham. Naysmith, I'm told, assumed that I was to blame and he wanted retribution. In a below-the-belt fit of pique, he published a particularly spiteful piece blaming me for everything from the Club's lowly league position to poverty and world hunger. It was a malicious and vindictive move based on a totally false premise. It wasn't me who'd spilled the beans. In fact, I've never done that sort of thing (despite being privy to several pieces of juicy Club gossip over the years) – it's not my style; nor did it make any sense to make an improper mess on my own doorstep.

In the days that followed it became pretty darned obvious who had briefed *The Guardian*. Indeed, it was a simple process of deduction to make 2 + 2 into 4 – but that simple equation was evidently beyond the supposed brains at Fulham! Intriguingly, the actual perpetrator

Above: The "shock decision" to dismiss Yvonne Haines is announced in the local press.

Below: Hold the front page! The Club call for a ceasefire via the front cover of the matchday magazine

Fulham 0 Southend United 3	23.02.91	20th
Fulham 1 Reading 1	02.03.91	20th
Bolton Wanderers 3 Fulham 0	09.03.91	20th
Birmingham 2 Fulham 0	12.03.91	21st
Fulham 1 Bournemouth 1	16.03.91	20th
Fulham 1 Stoke City 1	19.03.91	22nd
Rotherham United 3 Fulham 1	23.03.91	23rd
Bradford City 0 Fulham 0	30.03.91	22nd
Fulham 1 Mansfield Town 0	01.04.91	20th
Chester City 1 Fulham 0	06.04.91	22nd
Fulham 4 Shrewsbury Town 0	09.04.91	20th
Fulham 0 Grimsby Town 0	13.04.91	20th
Brentford 1 Fulham 2	16.04.91	20th
Fulham 1 Swansea City 1	20.04.91	20th
Fulham 0 Brentford 1	23.04.91	20th
Bury 1 Fulham 1	27.04.91	21st
Exeter City 1 Fulham 0	04.05.91	21st
Fulham 1 Leyton Orient 1	11.05.91	21st

1st
2nd
3rd
4th
5th
6th
7th
8th
9th
10th
11th
12th
13th
14th
15th
16th
17th
18th
19th
20th
21th
22th
23th
24th

didn't get the vilification treatment. Quite the opposite, in fact – in later years he was later invited onto the Board! Needless to say, I never received any sort of apology from Naysmith or anyone else at FFC. ⚽

Nasty Tricks

I'm sorry to report that some FFC staff have resorted to what can only be called "smear campaign" tactics and that I'm among those targeted. Intriguingly, the slurs have not been connected in any way to the production of the fanzine – the contents of which could understandably raise an eyebrow or two in the Cottage and the FFC Boardroom. No, we're talking about sheer invention and supposition.

Various people connected with the Club had told me "Your name's mud with the admin staff" and when this was still so a few weeks down the line I arranged a meeting with Chief Executive Brian Naysmith. Our chat was perfectly reasonable and when we discussed the specifics he seemed to believe me. So, I was subsequently shocked – and annoyed – to be shown a copy of a letter that accused me of being a "Club-wrecker" with regard to the matters we'd discussed. The letter also branded Supporters' Club committee member Allan Gould "a liar" with regard to a completely separate issue. The pair of us were described as "crude and malicious rumour-mongers" and referred to as "supposed Fulham supporters". The letter was signed by Brian Naysmith. ⚽

Below: Hammersmith End regular Emma Hawkey, who later made a more-than-decent job of editing FFC's programme, discusses fanzines and TOOFIF in the Club's matchday publication.

IN MY VIEW

EMMA HAWKEY

Is the difference between fanzines and official programmes really so great? At Fulham, we like to think the official matchday magazine is both entertaining and informative, a forum for supporters' views as well as those of the club. But Emma Hawkey, Hammersmith End regular, welcomes the arrival of the fanzine as a healthy antidote to some of the literature currently on the soccer scene.

As fans disperse all over London at 5 O'clock on a Saturday afternoon they are recognisable as much for the match programme shoved into their back pockets as they are by their back pockets as they are by their scarves and football shirts. In pubs a short trip from the grounds there is brief post match hush as programmes are perused and new League positions hastily checked. But it is only recently that anyone has really cashed in on an interest in football literature that has been around for a long time. Collector's items now, yesterdays programmes have been lovingly hoarded for decades, sometimes the only full written history of a club.

Growing out of teen publications like *Shoot!* and *Match*, football pundits can now graduate to 90 Minutes, the 'serious' soccer monthly which sells and sells. But it is *When Saturday Comes* – a kind of *Private Eye* to *90 Minutes'* Spectator – that is the bestselling example of a new trend. The biggest and most controversial expansion in the soccer library is the fanzine section. While official programme editors must continue to toe the line, chairmen, managers and players brace themselves as fanzines multiply. And as they multiply so does the controversy which surrounds them.

Always accused of disloyalty, a threatened libel suit against Brighton's "Gull's Eye" has forced fanzine editors to reassess and formalise their publications; the Fulham fanzine "There's Only One F In Fulham" wryly claims to offer "an (almost) no holds barred forum for views on our beloved F.F.C." Police harrassment of fanzine sellers outside grounds and a general disapproval coming from football bigwigs, forced 9 M.P.s to table an early day motion before the commons last year, stating that "This house believes that the growth of football fanzines is a healthy development which reflects the desire of more soccer fans to have a say in the running of the football clubs". In my view this is right. TOOFIF, which comes 2nd in another fanzine's national top ten, for the most part, is exactly what it says it is: A forum for the views of people who are not often asked for their opinions, football fans. And more than that, it is a forum for views on a football club which really is "beloved" by those fans. Mansfield's "Follow The Yellow Brick Road" is typical when it exhorts its readers to "bring your voices back to Field Mill and start backing your team once more".

In fact, fanzines are all about these voices, that were previously only heard on the terraces. A mixture of satire, reminiscence, news, views and sometimes anger, is certainly entertaining but the best fanzine editorial also helps to open previously closed books and provide fans with important information.

Much of the content of recent editions of TOOFIF inevitably concern the future of The Cottage as the home of Fulham Football Club. Each stage of the proceedings has been carefully minuted in the fanzine, in a style that most definitely intends to inform rather than to persuade. In My view, a close examination of this kind of open and "healthy" approach to the running of football club should help to dispel a definite media relish of the sport's bad reputation. "I.D. Card Victory For Thugs", blasted Today Newspaper after last years Taylor Report, while T.V. critic Sheridan Morely merely suggests a ban on soccer matches for a "cooling off period" of ten years. "Football is sick" exclaimed David Miller in The Times. In fanzines, perhaps, English football is finding its cure.

Gardner's Question Time

David Gardner was recently dismissed from Fulham's Board of Directors. His dismissal, "in the best interests of the Club", is the latest in a line of such moves that smack of bad handling and poor timing. After being made aware that David was prepared to speak to TOOFIF, contact was made...

Was your removal from the Board a surprise?

Yes, I certainly had no warning beforehand. The Chairman and Vice-Chairman had both been away for some time prior to the Board meeting concerned, so as yet I am unclear as to what information they acted upon – and whether it was rumour, which supporters are constantly being told to ignore, or fact.

What were the reasons given, and can you appeal?

All I've been told is that it is in the best interests of the Club. Up at Rotherham the Chairman intimated that I'd supposedly revealed details of players' wages to one of the squad. I was told that there were things that Directors should and should not do. Interestingly the player in question has refuted this allegation and has suggested that Directors were using him as a scapegoat to remove me from the Board. In the meantime I am checking out the appeals procedure.

Do you feel you're the latest Fulham stalwart to be eased out?

Yes, quite possibly.

As a long-time Fulham supporter, are you worried about that trend?

Very much so. The crowd figures are decreasing with each match without such measures being taken.

Why do you feel you have been eased out?

I don't really know. Maybe because I've been honest in my opinions – although I've consistently endeavoured to support the Board's policies, whether or not I agreed with them personally.

Are you bitter?

A little, I must admit – more about the handling of the situation rather than the decision itself. It's a cliché I know, but the Club is the be-all; Boards come and go.

What are your feelings towards Fulham now?

Nothing's changed. I have supported them since 1955 but it all feels pretty strange at present. It is now nearly two weeks since the decision was announced at the Board meeting, but nothing has been said to me as yet.

Where do you go from here?

As mentioned earlier I am taking advice on business procedure, but even should there be some legal loophole I can't see myself returning to a set-up where I'm clearly not wanted. Obviously I shall remain a Fulham supporter, but I could maybe spend a little more time with Kingstonian – my local club and where I was a junior back in '58-59. I must stress that I shall not be turning my back on Fulham, and certainly not because of what has happened.

Where do Fulham go from here?

Hopefully upwards! As to the ground saga, I can't see any way we can stay at the Cottage now, unless a way is found to get the freehold back from Cabra Estates – which seems remote.

You may have disagreed with some of the Board's decisions (despite showing a united front outside of the Boardroom). Did you consider yourself a "lone voice" at times?

Yes, particularly on expenditure matters where I have felt we have been overspending and living way beyond our means. On other matters I'd better not comment at present. I wonder why I wasn't given a hint as to what was to occur at that Board meeting – which I had given prior warning I could not attend. I also wonder why the Chairman told the players en route to the Board meeting. In a democracy – one of the Chairman's favourite words – that is not supposed to happen.

Was the appointment of Alan Dicks made with the knowledge of all the Board?

No, the appointment was made solely by the Chairman – this is the most autocratic organisation that I know of.

So do you consider that the Cabra money has been well spent?

Judging by results, no. The team all too

often hasn't seemed to know what they are supposed to be doing. And yet on paper we have our strongest squad for some time. However, we have seen a lack of total commitment from some quarters, and when things have gone wrong, or not as originally planned or expected, heads have dropped too quickly.

Could there have been a more stubborn approach taken by the Board on the ground issue?

What must be re-iterated is that the freehold of Craven Cottage was lost as a result of a previous Chairman's actions, and that when the current Board took over we were only tenants on our "own" ground. The deal signed with Cabra – had it been implemented in full – was simply incredible. To have got £13m in effect for nothing would have been astounding. However, as things have worked out, questions must be raised. If the deal is so good for Fulham, why is it so difficult for Fulham to get what is contractually theirs? The way the whole business is dragging on leaves an unsavoury taste because the future remains so uncertain. At the end of the day it is the Club that matters.

Do you think the slide can be arrested?

Well it would be financially catastrophic if we went down to the Fourth – and it'll be bad enough anyway. But yes, I am sure that with a bit of sensible pruning the current squad should be able to beat anyone in the current Third Division. And certainly if one or two of the reserves and juniors come through then maybe we'll be celebrating this time next year. I certainly hope so, but as to where – well who knows!

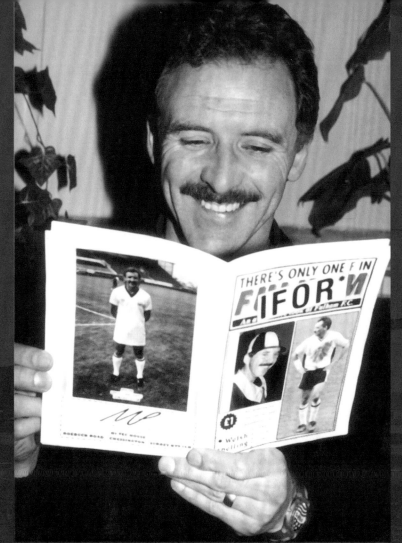

Gordon Davies

First player to get a TOOFIF testimonial issue was Ivor. With the benefit of hindsight (and having racked up considerably more, ahem, experience since then), that booklet was a pretty lame affair. Even so, it eventually added a princely £450 to the popular Welshman's testimonial fund. What the top-flight players of today could do with such a cash injection, eh? But it was one of those occasions where it seemed only right to do something, whatever the end product. As I was still playing football at weekends myself in those days I missed chunks of his first spell at the Club; sacrilege! So, why did we put Ivor on a pedestal?

Gordon Davies remains the Club's all-time leading goalscorer and is a bone fide Fulham legend. His final tally of 178 goals (159 in the League and 19 in cup competitions) were amassed during two spells at Craven Cottage. A late starter in the professional game, Ivor joined Fulham in 1978 from Merthyr Tydfil for just £4,000. He scored the winner on his debut at Blackpool and, by rattling in the goals, soon caught the eye of the Welsh management, winning 18 caps overall.

Having notched 114 goals in 247 games over six seasons, Ivor decided to try his luck in the top flight with Chelsea in November 1984 (only Ivor could do this and still remain in our good books!). He played mainly in the reserves (although he did manage a first-team hat-trick in a 4-3 win at Goodison Park) before moving to Manchester City a year later.

Ivor was transferred back to the Cottage in October 1986 and set about overhauling the goalscoring records of both Bedford Jezzard (154) and Johnny Haynes (158). Ivor always seemed to play with a smile on his face and it was that, along with a regular supply of goals, which made him such a firm favourite with the Fulham faithful with whom he enjoyed such a wonderful rapport. He scored several memorable goals, including one in front of the Cottage from near the corner flag against Chesterfield; his personal favourite performance, though, was netting three goals in a 4-3 victory at Birmingham in 1979 – "a close call between that and the terrific 4-1 win at Newcastle in October 1982", he recalls.

One great "goal" that was wrongly chalked off for offside could well have changed the course of Fulham history – his wonderful strike

Top: The ever-smiling "Ivor" takes a peek at an early version of his special TOOFIF testimonial issue.

Above right: Another grin for the team photocall, and ((*bottom*) Gordon and wife Sue as Tweedeldum and Tweedledee at a Supporters' Club disco.

against Leicester City in the spring of 1983 was incorrectly disallowed and it was the Foxes, not Fulham, who ultimately went up to the top flight that season. By contrast, Ernie Clay saw to it that our excellent squad was broken up, and an almost terminal downward spiral was set in motion. It's fair to say that during Ivor's latter seasons at Craven Cottage the set-up was more than a tad inferior to the Malcolm Macdonald years.

Ivor bowed out of Fulham following a testimonial match against Wales at the Cottage in May 1991. He was a little cheesed off at the suggestion of Chairman Jimmy Hill that his "legs had gone". On moving to Wrexham, Ivor was able to demonstrate that there was still plenty of life in the old pins by helping the Welsh side cause a major upset in defeating Arsenal 2-1 in the FA Cup, and he was able to gesture that his legs were indeed fine and dandy to the *Match of the Day* presenter... Jimmy Hill!

After Wrexham, Ivor had a brief dalliance with football management, taking charge of Norwegian club Tornado FK in 1992 (as player/manager) before heading back to the UK to join

Vauxhall Conference side Northwich Victoria, where, after netting 12 goals in 36 games, he finally hung up his boots in 1993, aged 37. No doubt inspired by his stint at the Bridge, Gordon went on to form his own pest control company and in recent years has combined this with a return to Fulham for matchday corporate hospitality duties. Rumour has it that he still tries to claim any contentious goals! ⚽

Above: Gordon (No 7) reacts sharply to fire a shot at goal.

Below: "Ivor" poses for the TOOFIF camera with fellow Wales International Jeff Hopkins.

Bottom: Glenn Hoddle in a Fulham shirt. He's pictured shortly before putting in a classy display against Wales in Gordon's testimonial match.

Left: The match report is from the local *Gazette*, whose editor evidently didn't know how to spell Johnny Haynes!

DAVID LLOYD on Gordon Davies' farewell at Craven Cottage
Ivor signs off with tears

YOU would never have caught Johnny Haines doing it. Nor George Cohen. Or even the more contemporary recipients of testimonials at Craven Cottage.

Yet after his match against Wales, the final sighting of Gordon Davies by the chanting throng below was that of a grinning dewy-eyed Welshman on the Cottage balcony – clad only in his underpants!

The crowd had listened politely as he told them that despite several requests for his shirt he was giving it to a supporter who had overcome brain surgery. Cheers rang out as the presentation was made. More cheers rang out as he subsequently took off his shorts and lobbed them down into the crowd.

Somehow it was typical 'Ivor'. The fans loved him – and not only for becoming the club's record goalscorer. He and wife Sue were well and truly bitten by the Fulham bug, and his concern for the club's future remains sincere – despite being given a free transfer.

He told the Gazette this week: " I still feel I have the ability, attitude and desire to continue in League football – and I am certainly not ready to be put out to grass just yet. It's such a shame that my future has to be away from Craven Cottage – my heart will always be at Fulham and with the wonderful supporters who have not had all that much to get excited about just lately."

He added: "I have been very fortunate to play alongside some very good players, Ray Houghton, Tony Gale and Paul Parker to name just three. Biggest disappointments of course were to narrowly miss out on promotion to Division One in the early 80s and failing in the Division Three play offs to Bristol Rovers more recently.

Having recently undergone an ankle operation – "a small one

but necessary all the same" – Ivor was only expected to ceremonially kick off his own 'big match' against a full strength Welsh side. Instead he came on for the last ten minutes to give us all a final glimpse of our hero in a Fulham shirt.

Despite his sporadic appearances last term he was for the seventh time the club's leading scorer for the season.

His latest return may only have been seven but one of those was very special, and well scripted. It might only have been from 18 inches but Ivor's strike last October against Swansea, not far from his own backyard, was his 155th League goal thereby passing Bedford Jezzard's record.

This made him Fulham's all-time record goalscorer, since he had already by-passed Johnny Haynes' tally of 157 in all competitions, at Wolves in 1989. In total he finished with 178 goals from 416 starts – not bad for a player whose first telling contribution in a Fulham shirt was to give away a penalty, at Blackpool back in 1978.

So an era ended with the match against Wales, for whom Gordon Davies played 18 times. The occasion drew 3,853 spectators, better than 14 gates at the Cottage last season. Wales cantered to a 4-1 success with goals from Dean Saunders, Ian Rush, a Jeff Eckhardt own goal and David Phillips.

The best player on the park was Glenn Hoddle, who, testimonial or not , put on a show of passing not seen at Fulham since the days of Johnny Haines.

And in a scene reminiscent of when Haines was chaired off the Wembley pitch after the 9-3 victory over Scotland in 1961, it was Gordon Davies who was hoisted onto the shoulders of hunders of Fulham fans within minutes of the final whistle. He is a hard and, almost certainly, impossible act to follow.

Top: 'Ivor' soars high and above Fulham fans salute their hero at the end of the Welsh game

Phil Lament

After Phil Stant's £50,000 move north to Mansfield he spoke to TOOFIF.

"I was deeply sorry to leave, especially since it seemed I had a good rapport with the supporters. I have received a stack of "good luck" and "best wishes" cards – it's such a shame I had to leave in such a rush. At least through these columns I can say goodbye, and also a very big "thank you" for getting behind me in such a short period of time."

Phil went on the transfer list at the end of last season because of a disagreement over where he should live. The Chairman said that his intended Northamptonshire base was too far from the Cottage and training ground, despite others already living a similar distance away. But that issue had all been settled.

"Yes I was on the list," added Phil, "and it's true that I was very annoyed at being messed about. However, I was raring to go for the new season and had come off the list. The timing of the move was, what can I say, quite amazing. I'd bought a place in Woking on the Monday and yet by the Wednesday I'd been sold. It's not exactly the way I would have chosen – all this house-moving is a real hassle. But it seems it was a case of the Club's bank putting a gun to Fulham's head. Somebody had to be sold. And that someone was me. My fee paid everyone's wages in August. Things really were that bad, apparently." ⚽

Dicks Out!

Alan Dicks could not overcome the fact that he'd been out of the British game for the best part of a decade and was sadly out of touch. Clive Walker described his training techniques as "ten years out of date". And in answer to a question from a young Fulham supporter who asked Dicks about his favourite players, Dicks referred to the Harris brothers at Chelsea (Ron Harris left Chelsea in 1980; elder sibling Allan departed in 1967). The young lad was understandably mystified.

Of course, the supporters have been blamed for his dismissal. Our chanting had affected the players so something had to be done, is how Jimmy Hill summed it up in his press release. Sorry, Jim, didn't realise that the succession of shambolic showings of the past few years was down to us.

As for TOOFIF, its overriding objective has been to further the cause of our favourite Football Club – currently in such dire straits – while (hopefully) having a little fun along the way. The fun factor's not in great supply right now. It is perfectly clear from the correspondence to the mag that the fans' feeling for their Club is deep-rooted and genuine. Having an improved football club to support and cherish is paramount. As editor of TOOFIF I'd put myself in that category. The point is, we all care

Top right: Phil Stant prepares to hold off Kevin Bond, with both players looking at a passing plane or awaiting for a lofted clearance to drop their way.

There's only one **F**in
FULHAM
An alternative look at Fulham F.C.

Fighting for survival?

Issue 16 | AUG/SEPT '91 | £1

Bury the Hatchet?

Here's part of a letter sent to FFC Chairman Jimmy Hill by supporter Martin Benjamin:

As you yourself have pointed out, communication seems to lie at the heart of the problem. You are unhappy at the way in which "rumours" are spread by people whom you judge to be malicious. Well how about this for an initiative? Bury the hatchet with "There's Only One F In Fulham".

I know this will be difficult for you to swallow! I know you believe TOOFIF to be malicious, but as an average, run-of-the-mill supporter, I must point out that TOOFIF has provided me with far more accurate information about the Club than any official publication has done. The quality of ClubCall is frankly poor and in any case it is unreasonable to expect the average fan to pay the exorbitant rates of an 0898 number every day to listen to promotional information that a normal business would provide free of charge. I know you think that TOOFIF prints unfounded gossip, but surely if this is so, the best way to influence TOOFIF is to co-operate with David Lloyd, so that he can make his editorial decisions with the full picture at his command. I think you ought to realise that whether you like it or not TOOFIF is popular with and respected by all the Fulham supporters I know; yet this does not mean that we are all in the same way against the Directors. It seems to me that a better relationship with TOOFIF could only improve the mutual respect between the Board and the rest of the supporters – what is there to lose by trying?

There's only one Fin **FULHAM**
An alternative look at Fulham F.C.

There's only one Fin **FULHAM**
An alternative look at Fulham F.C.

Dicks out!! ...Cox in??

TOOFIF ASKS ROGER MELLY IF HE'D LIKE THE JOB

Exclusive short list inside

JANUARY 1992   £1

Above left: Glenn Thomas leaps high at the front post but it's Mark Newson who makes contact and scores at Bradford.

Left: The pair congratulate each other while Peter Scott looks on impassively!

Below: It wasn't all doom and gloom under Alan Dicks. Here, Simon Morgan and Martin Pike line up with the gaffer after the Club had won the "Best Carnival Float" award at the Fulham carnival.

– even if we might demonstrate that in ways not appreciated by some people.

So what have we seen at Fulham during TOOFIF's existence? The list below forms a catalogue of disaster. We've witnessed:
• an appalling downturn in the quality of the team (which hopefully reached a nadir last season);
• the sacking of the long-standing and popular Club Secretary;
• the resignation of the programme team;
• the 11th-hour deal with Cabra Estates;
• the Council continuing with their CPO bid for the ground without the Club's backing;
• the demotion of the team manager (who heard of the decision on ClubCall);
• the appointment of a team manager who'd been out of the British game for nearly a decade;
• some illogical dealings in the transfer market;
• the sacking of a Club Director;
• the appointment of a convicted fraudster to operate commercial affairs;
• last-ditch scrambles in successive seasons to escape the demoralising drop into the Fourth Division;
• performances that must rank amongst the worst ever (some of last season's "efforts" were surely *the* worst ever);
• having to endure performances that

were devoid of tactics, spirit and effort;
• the £2m windfall from Cabra Estates frittered away. New players were unable to halt the decline and only augmented the squad and the wage bill;
• the discovery of a number of cheques stuffed into a drawer in the Cottage offices that should have been paid into Cottage Chance;
• the release (a merciful one?) of fans' favourite Gordon Davies;
• a second deal with Cabra Estates linked to a move to Stamford Bridge;
• a home defeat by a non-League club in the FA Cup first round;
• Gary Elkins becoming an instant success in the top flight once he left Fulham;

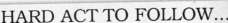

HARD ACT TO FOLLOW...

Don Mackay may have made a sound start to his managerial stint at Fulham, but what has he actually won? Here, Alan Dicks parades his 'haul' of silverware - the shield for the best float at the Fulham Carnival - with the help of two burly minders. Can you follow *that*, Don?

Chester City 2 Fulham 0	17.08.91	22nd
Fulham 0 Birmingham City 1	24.08.91	22nd
Torquay United 0 Fulham 1	31.08.91	18th
Fulham 0 West Brom 0	03.08.91	18th
Fulham 3 Swansea City 0	07.09.91	10th
Stoke City 2 Fulham 0	14.09.91	11th
Bury 3 Fulham 1	17.09.91	16th
Fulham 2 Leyton Orient 1	21.09.91	12th
Bournemouth 0 Fulham 0	27.09.91	9th
Fulham 0 Brentford 1	05.10.91	15th
Bradford City 3 Fulham 4	12.10.91	13th
Bolton Wanderers 0 Fulham 3	19.10.91	8th
Fulham 1 Preston NE 0	26.10.91	7th
Fulham 0 Hull City 0	02.11.91	6th
Huddersfield Town 3 Fulham 1	06.11.91	9th
Hartlepool United 2 Fulham 0	09.11.91	12th
Fulham 1 Stockport County 2	23.11.91	13th
Darlington 3 Fulham 1	30.11.91	15th
Birmingham City 3 Fulham 1	21.12.91	16th
Fulham 2 Torquay United 1	26.12.91	16th
Fulham 2 Chester City 2	28.12.91	17th
West Brom 2 Fulham 3	01.01.92	15th
Peterborough United 4 Fulham 1	11.01.92	15th
Fulham 0 Shrewsbury Town 0	18.01.92	16th
Exeter City 1 Fulham 1	25.01.92	16th
Fulham 1 Wigan Athletic 1	28.01.92	16th
Fulham 1 Bolton Wanderers 1	01.02.92	16th
Preston NE 1 Fulham 2	08.02.92	15th
Fulham 4 Darlington 0	11.02.92	12th
Reading 0 Fulham 2	15.02.92	12th
Fulham 0 Peterborough United 1	22.02.92	12th
Wigan Athletic 0 Fulham 2	28.02.92	10th
Shrewsbury 0 Fulham 0	03.03.92	10th

League Cup
Charlton Athletic 4 Fulham 2	21.08.91	Round 1 1st leg
Fulham 1 Charlton Athletic 1	27.08.91	Round 1 2nd leg

FA Cup
Fulham 0 Hayes 2	15.11.91	Round 1

Autoglass Trophy
Maidstone United 2 Fulham 6	23.10.91	Gp match
Fulham 2 Gillingham 0	20.11.91	Gp match
Fulham 2 Gillingham 0	14.01.92	Round 1
Fulham 0 Wrexham 2	25.02.92	Quarter-final

1st
2nd
3rd
4th
5th
6th
7th
8th
9th
10th
11th
12th
13th
14th
15th
16th
17th
18th
19th
20th
21st
22th
23rd
24th

WHISTLE BLOWER

Tony Moss

The year of the fanzine

TEN YEARS after the birth of the first football magazine written and produced by fans themselves, 1991 saw an explosion of new offerings.

There are now nearly 400 titles — Wimbledon alone having five (one per fan, perhaps) — with the wit and wisdom spread ever thinner. What started out as a vital voice for true supporters has become serious business, with clubs producing their own pseudo fanzines and groups like Class War jumping on the bandwagon with Our Day Will Come, with the rallying cry of "Balls to the Super League".

1991 also saw the first Fanzine of the Year Awards ceremony, with the winners leaving their trophy forgetfully behind in the bar at Birmingham New Street station. To avoid such calamity, we shall be sending our fanzine awards by special Red Star delivery. Consult Ian Woosnam for arrival details.

FANZINE of the Year: There's Only One F in Fulham. Unerringly accurate insights into the craven goings-on inside and outside the Cottage, especially its essential football dictionary: Targetman — striker who doesn't score. Enthusiastic — runs about a lot. Inspirational — shouts a lot. Consistent — boring. Chunky — fat. Cultured — slow. Bustling — uses his elbows. Long-serving — nobody wants him. Former international — over 35, if he's a day. Much-travelled — awkward bastard.

• and now the belated sacking of Alan Dicks, with the related press notice apparently putting the blame on us fans for daring to voice our disapproval.

Little wonder then that we are at such a low ebb and that the fun has all but disappeared from following Fulham. Little wonder, too, that the increased displeasure is permanently just below the surface and is frequently directed at players at the first hint of a bad bounce, even if the sentiments are aimed at higher up the management structure. It is not surprising, then, that the players in turn have become so edgy at home. What a vicious circle; the manager had to go. Hopefully the team's playing fortunes will take an upward swing with a sound managerial appointment. ⚽

Ivor wrecks 'em!

FA Cup third round day is always a big date on the footballing calendar. Except, that is, when you've been knocked out by non-League Hayes at home in round one! However, even with Fulham having a Saturday off, the question Fancy going to see Wrexham play at the weekend?" isn't one that's guaranteed to set the pulses racing. Mind you, up front for the Welsh side at the time was a certain Gordon Davies, who'd left Craven Cottage in May 1991, so the suggestion suddenly had that much more appeal.

The questioner, stalwart Fulham supporter and good mate Allan Gould, then slapped down several trump cards. "They're playing Arsenal in the Cup. We'll take our other halves and make a real weekend of it." Sounds good. "Oh, and we'll be staying at Ivor and Sue's gaff." Even better – a few days away, and as guests of Fulham's record goalscorer and his wife!

Apparently, Allan and his other half Frances had access to a holiday cottage in Yorkshire and had joked with Gordon that his Cheshire home, midway (well, sort of) between London and Yorkshire, was conveniently situated for a coffee stop. Gordon suggested that he and Frances stop by one weekend, maybe take in a game, and why not bring a pal. Unable to find one, Allan asked me to join him, along with my better half, Heather.

Wrexham v Arsenal in the FA Cup. Bottom versus top. A potential goal-fest, with Ivor and his Wrexham colleagues in line for plenty of practice at taking kick-offs! Let's hope Ivor can take a joke, as he'll be in line for plenty of post-match mickey-taking following the expected thrashing!

On arriving in Cheshire we just had time to meet and greet – and hand over a good luck card signed by a host of Fulham supporters – before setting off for the Racecourse Ground. No worries, we could catch up properly a half-hour or so after the final whistle. The four of us took our places in the Mold Road Stand. As you'd expect, the ground was buzzing. Before the kick-off, Wrexham's no.7 gave us a cheeky wave before the match settled into the expected routine – one-way traffic.

The previous season Arsenal were League Champions while Wrexham finished bottom of Division Four. The visitors tore into their hosts but couldn't find the net. In fact, it was two minutes before the break when a great run by Paul Merson set up Alan Smith for the opening goal. Here we go, we thought. And yet the anticipated deluge never followed. Instead, Wrexham just about weathered the onslaught, breaking to create chances of their own now and again.

And that was the pattern, Arsenal in charge with Wrexham threatening occasionally, until the final ten minutes. At that point, David O'Leary clambered all over Ivor just outside the Arsenal box and the linesman flagged furiously for the infringement. O'Leary, just as furiously, disagreed – which made what happened next all the funnier. Mickey Thomas placed the ball carefully

Davies: I've still got the legs

GORDON Davies explained how he tried to embarrass the BBC's Match of the Day pundit Jimmy Hill, the Fulham chairman, after helping to humiliate Arsenal in Wrexham's magnificent FA Cup win.

The 36-year-old former Fulham striker looked up to the stands and pointed at his legs, saying afterwards: "I've got four good friends of mine who are Fulham fans staying with me.

"About three months before the end of last season it was brought to my notice that Jimmy Hill wanted me out because my legs had gone and I couldn't do the business any more.

"It was just a little reference to Mr Hill to show him that I've still got a pair of legs and I can still do the business."

Davies is now rethinking his next career move after Saturday's win. He was due to go out to Norway on January 20 — eight days before the fourth round — to become player-manager of third division champions Tornado.

Above left: Gordon Davies (at the front) and his Wrexham team-mates celebrate their 2-1 victory over Arsenal. In the cutting (above), "Ivor" insists his legs hadn't "gone" – although they're nowhere to be seen in the photo! He even refers to four Fulham fans staying with him. "Good friends"? Whoever could he mean?

then thundered a left-foot special into the top-left corner beyond David Seaman for one of the most memorable of FA Cup goals.

Within two minutes Ivor squared the ball to Steve Watkin and he squirted the ball into the net from about five yards for 2-1 and Wrexham held out for one of the great all-time FA Cup upsets. In the Mold Road Stand, four folk from The Smoke were going barmy. Any hopes of meeting Ivor within half an hour of the finish were promptly dashed as he and several team-mates were caught up in a flurry of post-match interviews.

Full credit must be paid to Arsenal as they made their departure. Although clearly disappointed, they showed real class in signing a stack of autographs for the numerous supporters, mainly beaming Welshmen, when

they could just as easily have slunk on to the waiting coach.

When our genial host did finally appear, knackered but sporting his trademark cheery smile, we headed back to base where we were treated to a truly superb spread courtesy of Sue. As *Match of the Day* neared so Gordon took his place, cross-legged on the floor, in front of the telly to enjoy a re-run of the afternoon's events.

As soon as Jimmy Hill appeared, we were treated to Gordon in mimic mode, doing a better Jimmy Hill than the fellow on the box – and it was evident that our record goalscorer wasn't best pleased at having been released by the Fulham Chairman, who'd suggested in so doing that the Welshman's legs had gone. Cue many comments from Ivor whenever he came into shot on the telly, delivered in Jimmy Hill tones, of the "looks like my legs are okay there" variety! Surreal.

In his various post-match interviews Ivor was gracious enough to comment on the good-luck card from Fulham supporters, saying it had given the whole Wrexham team a lift beforehand. He also mentioned the quartet of Fulham fans in the stand who'd come along to lend their support.

Regarding that card, Ivor told TOOFIF a few days later: "Mickey Thomas, Joey Jones and myself were busy trying to lift the youngsters' morale at the time – trying to get their minds off the enormity of the game. Then the card came in signed by a number of the Thames Bank Travellers. Some of the polite messages were great fun to read, as were those you couldn't repeat! As well as giving me a personal lift, it also gave the lads a bit of a laugh and helped to break the tension. It was certainly a nice surprise before such an important fixture." ⚽

THE FULHAM FOOTBALL CLUB

SUPPORTERS' CLUB CALENDAR 1992

Bland Awareness

How I agree with Steven Tyrell's comments about the state of the programme (TOOFIF19). It's as bland as your average football commentator and as interesting as a party political broadcast. In the Reading proggy we had another three-quarter-page photo of the latest starlet to sign – fine, if only the rest of the issue were as in-depth. And what about that penalty competition bit on the inside back cover? Look at the print size – is it that big for the sake of short-sighted fans or because it was the only way the editor could fill the space? The latter I feel.

Also, don't the photo captions make interesting reading? "Mark Kelly gets in his cross" and "Sean Farrell heads for goal" – bet they spent hours thinking of them! The letters column is about as illuminating as a box of used matches. I know of many supporters who have penned letters to the Club but have not received a reply either personally or through the letters column. These letters must have disappeared into the same black void as all that money we received from Cabra.

No, give me TOOFIF any day. It might only come out every so often, but it's well worth waiting for and at least gives the impression that the production team cares about our great little Club – even if I don't always agree with all the sentiments expressed. The letters column in TOOFIF proves that there are Fulham supporters out there putting pen to paper. Well done to them, and to TOOFIF for making it such an interesting read. ⚽

David Berryman

Top right and opposite page: Spot the diehards! Fulham fans en route to Orient from Putney Pier demonstrate their attachment to Craven Cottage.

Opposite page top: Paul Johnson contemplates a nightmare scenario.

Below: Some blithering idiot gets a chance to witter on in the local *Gazette*.

Looking ahead at the Cottage, with Only One F In Fulham

Fanzine editor *David Lloyd* takes at look at the past month at the Cottage – and reminds fans that although everything looks rosy, the battle is not over yet

THE RECENT news about Craven Cottage has been welcomed throughout the sporting world but especially, of course, down in this corner of SW6.

When the euphoria has died down, however, it is worth remembering that we have merely had another stay of execution and that apart from overcoming a major hurdle nothing has actually been achieved as yet. That may seem to be a 'downbeat' message on the back of such 'up beat' news and accompanying headlines but that is the reality.

To regain the freehold almost £8 million has to be found, and quickly. Although we've been given a 10 year lease on the ground the rent, which is minimal for the first three years, it escalates to around £500,000 a year for the ensuing seven. So it's clear we have to secure the ground soon. At least we have the resolve to succeed and are being well piloted by the Fulham 2000 crew.

The immediate message to all those who have stalled over becoming members of Fulham 2000 is to stall no longer, get your £10 contribution in as soon as possible (these should be sent to 'Fulham 2000,' Freepost, W14 OBR). To use a footballing analogy, it's

no good a winger cleverly sidestepping a tackle from the full back if his ensuing unchallenged cross then sails aimlessly into the crowd. We must maintain our determination and concentration to ensure that our 'last ball' is delivered with accuracy and precision.

Meanwhile noises of the threatening variety are being made by the Manager and Chairman: "Crowds of 3,500 aren't enough. . . Unpopular decisions will have to be made in the summer. . . We've got to balance the books," etc, etc. On the face of it that's fair enough. Football clubs should be run in a business like way – it's crazy that clubs, particularly those in modest positions such as Fulham, have allowed their finances to run so out of control. Costs have spiralled ever upwards while attendances have dwindled, and little has been seemingly achieved in generating extra income.

It's clear that in future players' contracts should be structured so that they get paid in direct relation to the league position and the number of spectators attracted. The players at Don Mackay's disposal this season should have managed to achieve a play-off place, injuries or no injuries, and such an arrangement might well have been the impetus they required. That or a rockets up their backsides!

Similarly we are forever being told by the Club that more should be coming through the turnstiles (ie it's our fault!). But what is the club doing about it? Where apart from the wonderful in the Gazette (creep), are the mentions in the press that would give the impression of Fulham being a vibrant club? In particular why such poor relations with the Standard? What is

the club doing to attract those less than stoic souls away from their TV screens?

The announcement of the new lease should have been jumped upon by the club and even more so with the almost simultaneous news that they'd secured a shirt sponsor. More people could surely have been enticed in for the Bradford game if a higher profile approach had been taken. As it was, it was like just another game – no special attractions, no concessions to say, local schoolchildren on the day, not even any balloons. Another chance missed.

Meantime, the on pitch entertainment value has been generally very poor. As suggested earlier in this piece the players are good enough – certainly in this below average second division – but a magic ingredient, a spark has been sadly missing. We've had excuses of the pitch being below par and the supposed bobbles have affected our confidence and our natural passing game. If only we'd failed playing a natural passing game.

Now we're being told that sacrifices will have to be made, that senior players (on higher wages) are to be released, that the Reserve team is to be dropped, and that next years first team could be made up of predominantly YTS lads. If such measures are deemed necessary then it's fine by me. It'll be quite a novelty to have the club running on a sound financial footing – but don't blame those of us who've been paying out good money week in week out. We'll still be there next season, but what about doing something positive to entice the many former Fulham fans back to the Cottage, or day I say it, some new ones?

48

FULHAM ALL AT SEA? SUPPORTERS GO CRUISING DOWN THE RIVER TO SCUPPER MOVE TO 'BRIDGE'

FULHAM supporters staged a floating demonstration yesterday against the club's controversial decision to leave Craven Cottage, its home for 96 years, at the end of this season and turn the historic Thames-side ground over to the property developers. A pleasure-boat taking 120 members of the Fulham Supporters' Club from Putney to Greenwich, on the way to the match at Leyton Orient, was bedecked with banners opposing the move to Stamford Bridge

Fulham 0 Exeter City 0	
07.03.92 10th	1st
Fulham 1 Huddersfield Town 0	2nd
10.03.92 10th	3rd
Hull City 0 Fulham 0	4th
14.03.92 11th	5th
Fulham 1 Hartlepool United 0	6th
20.03.92 10th	7th
Stockport County 2 Fulham 0	8th
27.03.92 10th	9th
Fulham 1 Stoke City 1	10th
31.03.92 11th	11th
Swansea City 2 Fulham 2	12th
04.04.92 11th	13th
	14th
Fulham 1 Reading 0	15th
07.04.92 10th	16th
Fulham 4 Bury 2	17th
11.04.92 10th	18th
Leyton Orient 0 Fulham 1	19th
18.04.92 10th	20th
Fulham 2 Bournemouth 0	21st
20.04.92 7th	22nd
Brentford 4 Fulham 0	23rd
26.04.92 9th	24th
Fulham 2 Bradford City 1	
02.05.92 9th	

Bridge of Sighs

All the vibes are that we'll be kicking off next season at Stamford Bridge. Even as these notes are being penned, officials of Cabra and Chelsea are meeting to try to get some common ground (geddit? But then it's no laughing matter, is it?). Yesterday morning, before our match with Bury, there was a Board of management meeting at Craven Cottage. Top of the agenda was "the move to Stamford Bridge".

Another item, incredibly, was "the celebrations for the move". *Celebrations!* Some supporters may well make the short journey up the road, but I don't think that anyone will feel like celebrating. How can they be so out of touch with the mood of the supporters? You'll note that Club officials are all talking as if there's no other option apart from starting next season at Chelsea. Every opportunity is taken in the programme to mention the fact. In Reading's programme for the match before their visit to the Cottage, they urged their fans to go to Fulham as it would be the last time Reading would play there. I wonder who's been spreading the word? And yet the Council remain resolute that there will be no groundsharing. Even Cabra boss John Duggan was quoted yesterday as saying there will be no ground sharing. So what the hell is happening. I expect we'll be the last ones to know! ⚽

Air of Confidence

Whisper it very quietly, but Fulham fans are going into the new season with an almost unheard of air of confidence – about matters on and off the field!

On the playing front there is no reason to suspect that with a continuation of last season's form we shouldn't be "there or thereabouts". There is no doubting, as Don Mackay insists in a chat with TOOFIF, that the team will be giving 100 per cent in every match. Which, of course, is how it should be. As to the off-the-field affairs, well the great news is that we are still at Craven Cottage and have a season in which to strike a deal with Cabra, who are ailing so badly that they would struggle to buy a house-brick these days let alone fund a luxury housing development. Shame!

The summer months have seen a furious rearguard action by, in particular, the Supporters' Club. They gave evidence at the Public Inquiry into the ground's future and were so thorough that the Council's QC drew on their evidence for his final speech. No chance has been missed, either, to lobby interested parties about the Club's situation.

Meantime the Club, too, have been active. They have taken the matter to the High Court where they attempted to get the clause of silence lifted, saying that, in fact, they wanted to stay at the Cottage. Cabra appealed, and won. So the latest murmurings were that Fulham were considering taking the issue to the House of Lords. In a sense, however, they have made their point: by their very appeal they have indicated their intent. Although now bound once again by the clause of silence this would not prevent Fulham officials from explaining their change of heart were they to be subpoenaed by the Council.

So as we start the new season (with or without the completion of electrical work), where do we stand? Deal number two with Cabra, which involved the Club negotiating, and to be seen negotiating, with Chelsea with a view to sharing the Bridge has elapsed and we are now back to the former arrangements. This entails having a further season at the Cottage – a season for the supporters, if necessary, to come to the Club's aid financially. As for the £10,000-a-day penalty payment, well that is still clocking up but this is, as it stands, only paper money. Although now totalling in excess of £8m that would have to be fought for through the courts. Nevertheless it offers a very handy bargaining position.

Cabra's share price has nosedived to just 3p and their position is, to say the least, precarious. John Duggan was "asked to step down" from the chairmanship during the summer and the new set-up promises a "change of direction". If they were to go belly-up, bids for the freehold would be made under cover, so on the one hand we could attain the Cottage for a paltry figure, but on the other this could allow someone else to step in.

Cabra's application to "transform" Craven Cottage has been consistently turned down by the Council; any future development plans could only be of a limited nature. Therefore it is unlikely another property company would come in at present, more so given that the constraints demand that football, or at least a field sport, would have to be accommodated on the site. The only way forward seems to be for Fulham and Cabra to come to an arrangement; the question remains whether Fulham, i.e. Bill Muddyman, can raise sufficient funds.

Whether by accident or design, the Board now have the slight edge. They have spent hundreds of thousands of pounds in ensuring that we have at least one more season at the Cottage, and as long as we continue to get the right vibes we should put our money where our mouths are. The Supporters' Club for instance is known to be proposing a fundraising scheme aimed specifically at saving – and retaining – the ground. This would be handled separately from any existing scheme, and by wholly trustworthy personnel. More news on this is bound to follow as the season opens.

The simplest way, of course, to bring in some money is to cajole a friend or lapsed supporter to come along to a game. With a little bit of luck Don Mackay could well ensure that they don't need too much persuading. Here's to being 20 points clear and having a 999-year lease by Christmas! ⚽

Ground Control

Melvin Tenner, Chairman of Fulham Supporters' Club, issued the following statement at a Public Inquiry at Fulham Town Hall in June 1992.
Craven Cottage, Fulham's home since 1896, fell into the hands of SB Properties, a subsidiary of Marler Estates, in 1986. The actions of Fulham's Chairman in the previous three years led many to question his motives, and when in 1985 the

Opposite page right: Fulham Supporters' Club Chairman Melvin Tenner gets to issue a statement at the 1992 Public Inquiry.

Below: Simon Morgan and Don Mackay make it onto the cover of *Cottage Pie*.

COTTAGE PIE

AUGUST 1992

THE FULHAM SUPPORTERS CLUB OFFICIAL MAGAZINE

Church Commissioners sold him the freehold of the ground without covenants stipulating football use, property men scented money. In the months between the ground's purchase and its resale, reputable developers offered between £3-4million for the site. Marler's successful bid was a rather surprising £9m. The new owner's principals feigned interest in the Club until permission for partial development of the ground lapsed in February 1987. (Cabra Estates settled out of court a subsequent legal action brought by Kilroe Enterprises, a company which lent money to Fulham in 1985 in return for the Club's support of its scheme.) Following the untimely death of its Chairman (Sir Eric Miller), Marler sold its then very valuable real estate to Cabra, whose objective was clear from the beginning: to make a property profit from something hitherto as sacred as a famous football ground.

Cabra's shares, placed at 110p for the Marler deal, stood at 6¾p at the opening of this appeal. The unwillingness of the company's two banks, Midland and the Royal Bank of Scotland, to provide security for payments due to Fulham FC (1987) under the terms of a 1990 agreement between the parties has resulted in the accrual of penalties exceeding £5m, rising at the rate of £10,000 a day (under a second agreement signed last summer this debt was frozen until June 1, 1992, since when Cabra's burden has begun to increase by identical increments).

Buildings at Craven Cottage listed for their historical and architectural importance were deemed by the last Inquiry's Inspector to have been properly listed and appropriately placed in Grade 2, a finding that led Cabra to propose their wholesale removal, and re-erection at an alternative site. In these circumstances, and in the present economical climate, we wish to reaffirm that, since 1987, the ardent wish of the Directors, supporters and friends of Fulham Football Club has been to secure our future at Craven Cottage. It is our view that the most appropriate and viable development at the ground would be one that ensured the continuing presence of football.

The importance of Craven Cottage to the heritage and traditions of British football, as well as its ambiance and location, make it a unique sporting venue. The Stevenage Road Stand and the Cottage itself are prime examples of the work of the Scottish engineer Archibald Leitch, who dictated the shape and form of dozens of football grounds between 1900 and 1939. The stand's gable is one of only three surviving, while the Stevenage Road façade is one of the finest pieces of Leitch's work extant south of the border. Craven Cottage itself is a famous and much-loved landmark of English football.

In the event that Fulham FC is compelled to leave its home, Fulham supporters would

wish that the site remains a sporting venue, as designated by the Hammersmith & Fulham Council in its Unitary Development plan. We can see no reason why the local community should suffer the loss of a recreational facility, and the imposition of luxury flats for which there is no demand in the borough simply to help a beleaguered company out of financial difficulties of its own making.

Craven Cottage has considerable scope for repair and refurbishment, and it should be recorded that both Fulham FC and its supporters are ready to invest time and money on the ground if and when there is some security of tenure. Plans to bring additional investment and sponsorship into the Club are advanced and would accelerate on rejection of Cabra's appeal. Lotteries initiated in 1990 are steadily reducing the Club's annual deficit, and season ticket sales are at their highest for many years following an inspiring second half of last season.

In a recent survey, 79 per cent of respondents said they would invest in Fulham at Craven Cottage. The use of the ground by local organisations and companies continues to grow, bringing much-needed income and fostering goodwill and support.

In his Inquiry Report, Stephen Marks stated: "…if, as has happened before at Fulham, assistance can be found from benefactors, and if the numerous fundraising activities continue to contribute to the funds, it would not be wrong to say with certainty that the Club would not be able to support itself at Craven Cottage." We go further: those who work for, support and truly cherish Fulham are determined to ensure that this happens. Those of Cabra's shareholders not in receivership would obviously like to see the site free of football encumbrance, but Craven Cottage is as important to Fulham's meaning as the players who have created memories there throughout this century, and will not be surrendered lightly. ⚽

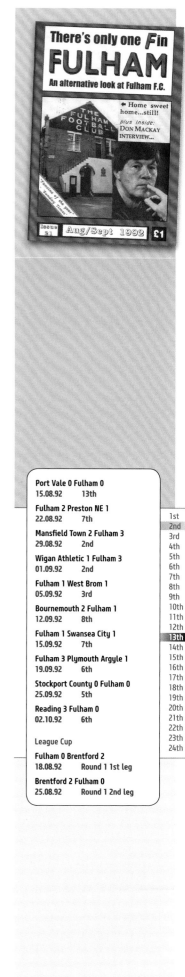

Port Vale 0 Fulham 0		
15.08.92	13th	
Fulham 2 Preston NE 1		
22.08.92	7th	
Mansfield Town 2 Fulham 3		
29.08.92	2nd	
Wigan Athletic 1 Fulham 3		
01.09.92	2nd	
Fulham 1 West Brom 1		
05.09.92	3rd	
Bournemouth 2 Fulham 1		
12.09.92	8th	
Fulham 1 Swansea City 1		
15.09.92	7th	
Fulham 3 Plymouth Argyle 1		
19.09.92	6th	
Stockport County 0 Fulham 0		
25.09.92	5th	
Reading 3 Fulham 0		
02.10.92	6th	
League Cup		
Fulham 0 Brentford 2		
18.08.92	Round 1 1st leg	
Brentford 2 Fulham 0		
25.08.92	Round 1 2nd leg	

1st
2nd
3rd
4th
5th
6th
7th
8th
9th
10th
11th
12th
13th
14th
15th
16th
17th
18th
19th
20th
21th
22th
23th
24th

Hotfoot to Brighton

Hard to believe in these days of frittered £11m transfer dealings that we were once scraping for every penny. Two hardy individuals, Gary Billing and Alex Ferguson (no, not that one) decided to do their bit to swell the Club's coffers. Fulham's away game at the Goldstone Ground, Brighton, in November 1992 was the targeted fixture: this doughty duo would make their way to the game on foot, overnight and all the way from Craven Cottage.

On the Friday evening a group of us waved Alex and Gary off. It's a mark of the fellow that Club captain Simon Morgan made a point of coming along. He also promised to be there to greet them the following day; if they got there in time. If they got there at all! This was a tough challenge given that the gruesome twosome were hardly Olympic athlete material. They were, though, TOOFIF stalwarts. Gary's booming tones could be heard the length and breadth of Stevenage Road on matchdays during the mag's first decade, and he helped take TOOFIF sales to an all-time high. Alex, aka The Traveller,

Right: Doughty duo Alex Ferguson and Gary Billing are met aat the Goldstone Ground, Brighton, by Don Mackay, having walked overnight from Craven Cottage to raise desperately needed funds for the Club.

Opposite page right: Gary and Alex line up with Julian Hails, Glenn Thomas and Gavin Nebbeling

Below: As autumn turns to winter, here's one scribe's take on how things were going at FFC.

Below right: A review in *Shoot!* – "one of the best fanzine names" but the interview with Don Mackay is "creepy".

Opposite page, bottom: Cabra's fortunes continue to nosedive. Shame.

was proud to contribute his own highly individual accounts of sundry footballing awaydays until his untimely death in 2006. With a wealth of material available, TOOFIF was proud to maintain that arrangement long after his sad demise.

As Gary, aka Cap'n Beaky, and Alex set off to cover their first half-mile up to Fulham Palace Road, the TOOFIF Editor demonstrated his whole-hearted backing for the dynamic duo by offering a cheery wave then heading home for a cup of cocoa and bed. A support vehicle would, however, accompany them through the night. And it was as well that it did.

Fanzine editor David Lloyd on the season so far

Crazy Fulham

The season is almost a quarter of the way through, so we asked *David Lloyd*, editor of the Fulham fanzine There's Only One F In Fulham, to take a look at how the Whites are doing. Here's his report.

YOU DON'T have to be crazy to be a Fulham supporter, but it sure helps!

The team's latest antic was to go three down to a poor Hull side – goals that fell in the "soft" category at that – before rallying to earn a draw with a late leveller.

Yes, we're a funny lot – you should try flogging fanzines to a crowd that has just seen its team go two down at home inside the first four minutes.

"One F in Fulham? There's more than one F out there on the Park!," was the reply. "You should rename it 'Five past three and we're two-nil down, mate'. There's more life in my grandad's Y-fronts than in Fulham's back four!" And so it went on.

When goal number three went in after three Hull players had seemingly been offside the linesman's parentage was severely questioned. Yet Simon Morgan's corker into the roof of the net bought a buzz to the place.

Strange, isn't it – mathematically 0-2 is as bad as 1-3, but the fact we had scored gave the crowd real hope.

Gary Brazil poached another to reduce the arrears further and Fulham being Fulham they completed the comeback with a deflected goal near the end. Udo Onwere may not have heard the rumblings of "Udo Unawary" prior to his strike but he milked the applause as the ball arched over keper Fettis.

Cofmments from the Fulham crowd are legendary. These have been of the wise-cracking variety in the main, but certain players have been the subject of special attention.

Frank Large, a centre forwad with more clubs than Tommy Docherty, managed goals galore for all of them except Fulham and received his fair share of ribald ridicule. So did Peter O'Sullivan, whose work down the flanks wasn't always appreciated by those in the enclosure.

Gary Elkins had a 'special bond' with those same fans, maybe since all his clarances seemed to end up there! He has managed to bounce back at least, in the Premier League no less with Wimbledon.

Wayne Kerrins was not so fortunate. He suffered so badly that in the latter stages of an unremarkable spell with the club he was unable to play at home, such was the abuse.

Strangely one of the latter-day targets has been Gary Brazil, arguably the most gifted player on the books.

Having beenone of those ever presents and one to escape the sorrows of being substituted it may have taken his absence through injury earlier this season for fans to realise what they were missing. Certainly he did himself no harm in scoring two goals on his return against Plymouth and when the crowd started chanting his name he alleged to have saidL "Blimey, this can't be Fulham!"

There is little doubt the off-the-field turmoil has affected players and fans. As the club slipped nearer and nearer the Fourth Division and a fatal move away from the cosy Cottage, it is little wonder the dwindling band of supporters became more and more disenchanted.

This disenchantment obviously spilled onto the pitch. Thankfully the arrival of Don Mackay and his man management skills has stopped the rot on the playing front and the abuse, much of it understandable if not wholly deserved, is being overtaken again by wit.

"Johnny Marshall, don't you know about space? You should, there's enough on your head!"

"If Big Jim had taken any longer to get up, Greenpeace would have moved in to refloat him."

Yep, we're a funny lot at the Cottage!

● Action as Fulham battle it out against Hull City

FANZINE CHOICE

There's only one F in Fulham

There's only one Fin **FULHAM**
An alternative look at Fulham F.C.

← Home sweet home...still!

plus inside: DON MACKAY INTERVIEW...

Issue 11   Aug/Sept 1992   £1

One of the best fanzine names going, the actual content is pretty good, too. This edition addresses some serious issues, particularly the continuing battle for Craven Cottage, without becoming too depressing. The interview with Fulham boss Don Mackay was a bit creepy, though.

When TOOFIF caught up with the intrepid pair the following morning, with the Goldstone Ground still three or four miles away, Gary and Alex were really struggling. Gone was the jaunty air and jovial smiles of the night before, replaced by a sombre mood and anguished grimaces. Their stamina wasn't really a problem; their resolve certainly wasn't – but their feet were a bloody mess.

Every step was painful, with burst blisters upon burst blisters, and their distress was all too evident. But on they plodded, and somehow they bravely limped into Old Shoreham Road, Hove, where – true to his word – Simon Morgan was one of the welcoming committee of players and supporters. The quips were soon flying: "Don't think you'll pass a fitness test today, guys!" "Hope you don't have to walk back again tonight!" "They

look half-dead, but they're still fitter than Jim Stannard!" "'Half-dead' you say – you must be talking about Mark Cooper?!"

Gary and Alex were so done-in and in so much discomfort that they could barely muster a retort of any kind; highly unusual behaviour for those two vociferous rapscallions! Once they headed into the bowels of the Goldstone Ground for a clean-up, it became apparent just how bad a state their feet were in: horrible, and definitely not for the squeamish! But there was a lorry-load of bandages and antiseptic in the place to ensure that, after extensive treatment, they could be escorted onto the pitch to meet Olympic gold medallist Sally Gunnell and our former winger Clive Walker, who was clad in Brighton's fetching "Tesco" kit. The boys done good!

Oh yes, and we came out on top in the match, winning 2-0. In fact, we walked it! ⚽

Fulham 3 Hull City 3	
10.10.92	11th
Burnley 5 Fulham 2	
17.10.92	12th
Fulham 1 Chester City 0	
24.10.92	10th
Exeter City 1 Fulham 2	
31.10.92	10th
Fulham 0 Stoke City 0	
03.11.92	10th
Bradford City 3 Fulham 2	
07.11.92	11th
Fulham 1 Bolton Wanderers 4	
21.11.92	13th
Brighton & HA 0 Fulham 2	
28.11.92	10th
Fulham 0 Mansfield Town 0	
05.12.92	9th
Fulham 0 Rotherham United 1	
12.12.92	12th
Blackpool 1 Fulham 1	
20.12.92	12th
Leyton Orient 0 Fulham 0	
26.12.92	12th
Fulham 1 Hartlepool United 3	
28.12.92	12th
Swansea City 2 Fulham 2	
09.01.93	12th
FA Cup	
Northampton Town 3 Fulham 1	
14.11.92	Round 1
Autoglass Trophy	
Gillingham 3 Fulham 3	
08.12.92	Gp match
Fulham 2 Leyton Orient 2	
15.12.92	Gp match
Port Vale 4 Fulham 3	
12.01.93	Round 2

1st
2nd
3rd
4th
5th
6th
7th
8th
9th
10th
11th
12th
13th
14th
15th
16th
17th
18th
19th
20th
21st
22nd
23rd
24th

Cabra calls in the liquidators

CABRA Estates, the property company that owns the grounds of both Chelsea and Fulham football clubs, yesterday called in provisional liquidators.

The decision came two days after its bankers, Royal Bank of Scotland and Midland Bank, called in their loans to the group. Cabra's shares were suspended at 2p on Tuesday. Liquidators, rather than the more usual receivers, were appointed because there was no charge over the assets.

The liquidation does not affect Cabra's subsidiaries, including those that own the football stadi-

By Heather Connon
City Correspondent

ums. Frank Blin of Coopers & Lybrand, one of the joint liquidators, assured Chelsea fans that the move should not affect the club's future at Stamford Bridge.

"Prior to our appointment, discussions for the sale of the Stamford Bridge ground were under way and I understand that these were at a fairly advanced stage," he said. "I also understand that both the directors of Chelsea and Cabra are of the view that, if the

negotiations could be completed satisfactorily, this would enable Chelsea to remain at Stamford Bridge if they wished."

Chelsea is believed to be negotiating the purchase of a long lease with the Royal Bank, which has secured its loan on the ground.

The position of Fulham, which was expecting a £5m payment in compensation for leaving its Craven Cottage ground when the lease expires at the end of the season, is less clear. Mr Blin said that "all the various options" available, "including discussions with Fulham" will be considered.

Coffee From Brazil

If there's been one player who's received an unmerited amount of flak on the terraces and in TOOFIF, it's Gary Brazil – in my opinion, of course! The game, and a fanzine's content, is all about opinions. The vitriol that was aimed at Brazil, though, would suggest he's among the worst players to ever play for the Club, which is so far from the truth as to be laughable.

No one's suggesting Brazil didn't have his faults – he was hardly the best at one-on-ones with opposing keepers for example; neither was he the type to fling himself at a header if there was a big centre-half anywhere in the vicinity, which was often the case in the frequently brutal world of lower-league football. But for a lot of people Gary Brazil, who was responsible for many of the best moments featured in our goals of the season videos, simply couldn't do anything right.

A cultured footballer who, at our level at the time (Division Two/third tier), would have been best employed behind the target man or front two, the wiry Brazil often found himself played out wide, or even as the main target man. Hardly ideal. For all that he did wrong, perceived or otherwise, he did an awful lot right – but still the flak kept on flying. And he didn't like it one bit. I plucked up the courage to ask him if he'd like to do an interview for TOOFIF in which he could explain his side of things and attempt to build some bridges. I was delighted when he agreed to do so.

Armed with tape machine and notebook I was welcomed into chez Brazil and, with no desperate rush to get on with the interview, enjoyed an in-depth off-the-record chat. After an understandably awkward first few minutes we got on extremely well. Gary's wife kindly offered to make us both a coffee before we got down to record anything; then she'd leave us alone. Seemed like a great idea; things were indeed going well.

Coffee and biscuits were duly served and, as it was a warm day, Gary pulled the sliding window open a tad to let in a pleasant breeze from the back garden. But what should have been idyllic promptly became catastrophic. With the window ajar in strolled the family cat, not that anyone knew it at the time. From nowhere, the sharp-clawed moggy leapt up, blind-side, from behind the cream-coloured sofa, landing ever-so-briefly on the apex of the furniture before continuing its superfast feline descent onto my lap, latching on with its claws. Even Gary Brazil jumped. Not nearly as much as me, though, and certainly not as much as my cup of coffee, the contents of which went everywhere. In the realms of how to make friends and influence people it doesn't rank right

up there. In how to disfigure a sofa, though, it was massive bonus points all round.

To be fair, Gary ultimately thought the whole episode was hilarious. I can't honestly say that his wife shared that view. No idea what the bloody cat thought; it had bolted out into the garden as startled as we were. Despite the shambles, we went ahead with the interview, which appeared in TOOFIF 24 – and, yes, Gary Brazil continued to get loads of flak from the terraces.

Shortly before I left the Brazil household, Gary took a call from John Marshall. A group of players were heading to Wimbledon Dog Track there and then, and I was cordially invited to join them. It would have been a hoot, except that I had already arranged to go out with my wife that night. Oh, and if I'm honest my coffee-splattered trousers and shirt combo probably didn't meet the dress code.

How does the current set-up compare with those at your previous clubs?
Sheffield United and Newcastle are very big clubs. Preston are a little like Fulham in that they're a once-proud club striving to get back into the big time. Fulham is getting much more of a warmer atmosphere and a family feeling to it. That wasn't the case when I first came to the Club – this group of players definitely want the Club to do well, with a good degree of passion – and the fans, too, are now pulling with us.

One of your colleagues has described you as a model professional. Do you feel he has a point, or did Julian Hails know you were about to be interviewed and simply wanted you to repay the compliment in print?
No, I paid Julian a few quid! It's interesting what Julian says. I think the senior players at the Club have a duty to help the younger lads. I took notice of Julian when he was still at college. I likened him to myself in terms of size, his wispy nature and willingness to take people on. However, you can give advice to as many people as you like, but it's

> *"Gary's wife kindly offered to make us both a coffee before we got down to record anything; then she'd leave us alone. Seemed like a great idea; things were indeed going well."*

Top right: Gary Brazil is all set to cut in on goal at Scarborough's McCain Stadium.

Opposite page bottom: This column in the local *Gazette* from January 1993 includes the first mention of Fulham 2000 "The Craven Cottage Crusade".

Below: Gary Brazil almost smiles for the TOOFIF camera.

only those who'll listen to their seniors and then make up their own minds who will get on. Julian's a clever lad and it's often forgotten that it's less than a year since he made the first team. If he's picked up anything from me, then I'm honoured.

You've had a good rapport with fans elsewhere, but you've suffered a mauling from some of our fans, and indeed in TOOFIF. How do you cope?
Cope? Hmm… you have to have broad shoulders – even someone of my size has to have broad shoulders! You have to have the type of character where you're not going to give in. It's easy to start feeling sorry for yourself when it seems 80 per cent of the crowd are after your neck. You've just got to have the strength of character to say "Right, I'm going to show you!" – that's certainly the attitude I adopted as there's absolutely no way that, after good spells at Preston and Newcastle, I was going to buckle. And yet it got the stage at Deepdale last year that when my name was read out over the Tannoy the Preston fans applauded and cheered politely while Fulham fans booed me. I had to check my shirt to see who I was playing for!

You had a stormer in that game, and scored…
When the ball went in some of the Fulham fans were a bit quiet – maybe if someone else had scored they might have cheered louder on the day. I don't know why things got that bad – although I'd be the first to admit that when I first came to the Club I wasn't playing as well as perhaps I've managed in the last 12 months or so. It certainly wasn't for the lack of trying; neither was it because I don't give a damn, as that's not the way I am. Each time I go onto the pitch I want to do really well. Maybe it was because I was being moved around a lot on the pitch and not settling into one position – but that would only be making excuses. I knew I wasn't playing up to the standard expected of me, and expected by me. But that said, I don't think I

deserved the type of criticism that was directed at me. It all seemed to get out of hand.

Some of the comments in TOOFIF weren't all that supportive either…
No, they didn't exactly do my cause any good – especially as I know so many fans read the magazine and that some of those might just not have made up their minds but were simply jumping on the bandwagon a bit. It can be nasty. I'd be lying if I said it doesn't matter, because it does. It hurts when you're getting stick, but if you're the sort of person who then decides to hide in a corner and who doesn't want the ball for fear of making an error then you're going to go under. Luckily I'm not made like that – I want the ball as often as possible – and if I make mistakes, well, perhaps they show up because I don't hide.

Have such comments spurred you on or did you give a mental two-fingers to your tormentors?
There was a point when I had to completely cut the fans off, all of them, just so I could go about my job and try to do so to the best of my ability. When things started to turn and the team and I were doing well and yet I was still receiving stick, I must admit I thought; "Well sod you lot!" I knew I was doing pretty well and, to be fair, most of the supporters recognised that too – but there was still an element of the crowd that did not want to know. I'd be walking into Craven Cottage at 1.45 on a Saturday afternoon a week after, say, scoring a hat-trick at Maidstone and yes I was getting booed and being told to "Get lost Brazil", or a lot worse, and I just thought: "What's going on?"

Is that happening now?
No, not really. The vast majority are really good now. I don't mind honest criticism, but there are still the idiots – every club has them – who relish in criticising your every move.

Fulham 2 Stockport County 1 16.01.93 11th	1st
Plymouth Argyle 1 Fulham 1 23.01.93 11th	2nd 3rd
Preston NE 1 Fulham 2 30.01.93 10th	4th 5th
Fulham 1 Port Vale 2 06.02.93 10th	6th 7th
West Brom 4 Fulham 0 13.02.93 11th	8th 9th
Fulham 1 Wigan Athletic 1 20.02.93 11th	10th 11th
Hull City 1 Fulham 1 27.02.93 12th	12th 13th
Fulham 1 Bournemouth 1 02.03.93 12th	14th 15th
Fulham 0 Reading 0 06.03.93 12th	16th 17th
Huddersfield Town 1 Fulham 0 10.03.93 14th	18th 19th 20th
Rotherham United 1 Fulham 1 06.04.93 14th	21st 22nd 23rd
Fulham 1 Leyton Orient 0 10.04.93 13th	24th
Hartlepool United 0 Fulham 3 12.04.93 13th	

An update on Craven Cottage – by fanzine editor David Lloyd

DAVID LLOYD, the man behind There's Only One F In Fulham fanzine, gives Whites supporters an insight into what is really going on at their club.

"WHAT'S it like playing at Stamford Bridge, then?" is a question travelling Fulham fans are often asked.

You can't really blame the questioners since information on Fulham's plight is hardly making headline news in southern-based editions of the national press, let alone those north of Watford. Even the majority of the faithful fans who watch virtually every Fulham match have struggled to keep up with developments, or indeed non-developments.

What is known for certain, however, is that Fulham's lease runs out in May and once again a black cloud is looming over the future of Craven Cottage.

With the demise of Cabra Estates, negotiations are being handled by the Royal Bank of Scotland and it is understood that at least one firm bid for the freehold has been made by the Fulham board. But at around a quarter of the bank's valuation of £10m, it was rejected.

What had been expected by now was the result of Cabra's appeal against the refusal of planning permission for Craven Cottage. This is obviously a key announcement since it will

give a clearer indication of the site's worth. Yet there is no way of knowing when the announcement will be made, despite the fact that the inspector's report was delivered to the Department of Environment back in October! The delay would appear to be political.

Fulham fans have gone as far as seeking an early day motion in Parliament, pointing out to the Secretary of State that Cabra has gone into liquidation and under no circumstance should planning permission be granted. That motion received considerable support from MPs and surprisingly gained more support on the day than other national and international issues that were making headline news.

But one thing is becoming very clear: the Royal Bank's very close ties with the Government itself makes it a highly sensitive issue.

While all this is difficult to get across to the layman in an interesting form – and it has dragged on interminably – Fulham themselves have not helped matters.

True, they are still apparently bound by the clause of silence as part of the Cabra deal, but away from that they haven't exactly been pushing the club's profile either.

Thankfully the Gazette has managed to keep its readers in touch but the Evening Standard in particular is hardly awash with news. In the absence of good old-fashioned investigative re-

porting the club should have been pumping the media – the Standard especially – with information, gossip, trivia, anything, if only to give the appearance of a vibrant club.

But no, weeks go by and the only noticeable absentee from round-up columns on London's clubs is you-know-who. You could be forgiven for thinking that Fulham didn't exist at times.

At least the supporters have not been idle. You know, the unpaid amateurs who devote untold hours to the club's cause because they care. As well as instigating what publicity the club has received recently (the Golden Years book, the sponsored walk to Brighton, etc) they are about to launch Fulham 2000: The Craven Cottage Crusade.

After spending months preparing the way with a massive behind-the-scenes exercise, the organisers are at last stepping up a gear and in the next couple of weeks will launch a propaganda exercise detailing the club's plight, culminating in a huge fund-raising scheme.

The object, of course, is to ensure that Fulham FC remains at Craven Cottage. Further details are available from Richard Jones on 081 397 5651 (home).

To go on the ever-growing mailing list please write to Mark Pollard, 49 Parkstead Road, Putney SW15 5AN. In the meantime watch this space!

Above: Gary Brazil celebrates.

You were cheered off after giving a sound showing at Orient, despite receiving a hefty buffeting on the pitch…

Yes, it was nice to be applauded. But then everyone did well at Orient. I don't think it would have made any difference who came off; whoever it was would've been cheered that day.

What's your favourite position, Gary – behind the front two perhaps?

I enjoy playing there, yes, as it's hard for people to pick me up there. But I still think I currently serve more of a purpose as an out-and-out front man.

Guess it all depends on who's available on the day?

Precisely! But I can see myself playing behind the front two and doing well. It's nice that the manager has options and can play a few of us in various positions; just look at Jeff Eckhardt. In the absence of Mark Kelly, the manager played me as a wide left player or left-sided midfielder, which I admit I don't overly enjoy. I prefer a more attacking role.

How do you rate the current squad? We've had a dip in form of late, are we good enough for promotion?

I was asked this many times at the start of the season. I said I felt our squad was strong enough to at least make the Play-offs and make promotion, and I stick by that. Having sat out much of the season and watched the opposition, there aren't many teams that make you think, "Bloody hell, they're a good side!" We've got to get our act together; if we do we'll be up there. It's down to us – if we fail, it's down to us – there's no making excuses, we've got to find that consistency. ⚽

Grounds for Optimism

The spotlight has been turned once again onto Craven Cottage: will we still be playing at the magnificent old stadium next season? No one really knows at this stage, but my gut reaction – for what it's worth – is that we might well be. This is based on nothing more than listening to the vibes and, I suppose, trying to remain positive. One thing is certain, however: the success of the newly launched Fulham 2000 is imperative. If nothing else, it could tempt a few ex- or floating supporters out of the woodwork. But the beauty of the scheme is that anyone can become a member for £10. In due course it is hoped that a series of offers will be made to Fulham supporters related to the amount of money pledged to the fundraising effort. For the time being, we must recruit as many people as possible, and swing public opinion in our favour.

These notes are being penned the day after the launch so much more will be known in the coming weeks and months. As you all know the whole ground issue is such a complex business – each piece of "news" that emerges has more than one interpretation which makes it doubly difficult to get the message out to the fan on the terraces, particularly since the Club remain silent. That may not be the case for much longer. Indeed, at the Fulham 2000 press launch Melvin Tenner suggested that, as he understood it, there is no legal constraint against the Club speaking out and their silence is now due to the fact that they do not wish to antagonise the Royal Bank of Scotland while striving to strike a deal. It would seem that the behind-the-scenes wranglings are on a knife-edge and we can only hope that the resolution of the powers-that-be matches ours as far as staying at the Cottage is concerned.

The message is clear: Fulham supporters want to stay at the Cottage. Football fans everywhere would no doubt back that sentiment. Various arms of the Club have been receiving correspondence wishing us luck in our quest for some time now. One of the aims of Fulham 2000 is to harness this feeling. Main aim, of course, is to do everything possible to help Fulham remain at their home.

Have no doubt, eviction is currently staring us in the face. As it stands we are out on 31 May and at the launch we made a big fuss of the fact that we had just 100 days left on the site. That's 100 days after being there for nearly 100 years. It's understood that the Royal Bank of Scotland have been holding out for an unreasonably high fee – possibly as high as £12m – for the freehold, while another option could be a shortish-term lease, say ten years, during which time Fulham would have to find such a sum, but in the meantime the Club would also have to pay a whopping rent.

Don Mackay has suggested that £15m would be a prohibitive sum to pay for the ground (not unreasonably, he'd like some of that "pot" to be made available to him to spend on strengthening the team) but it's not so prohibitive as it sounds. Having regained the freehold we would then have other sources of revenue open to us, not least the supporters' contributions through Fulham 2000 and various grants, particularly those from the Football Trust.

Other sources, though, put the "real" value of the ground at less than £1m – much more realistic since it would seem very unlikely now that permission can ever be granted for a Canary Wharf or even Chelsea Harbour-type development on the site. A modest development may be allowed, but that on its own wouldn't make the scheme's backers sufficient return on their capital layout. On the other hand, a modest development including a football pitch is possible and should the Royal Bank choose to join Fulham FC in such plans then both parties would benefit.

Some fans would say that it is worth paying any price to regain the freehold. That's fine if someone out there has several million tucked under their

> *"The message is clear: Fulham supporters want to stay at the Cottage. Football fans everywhere would no doubt back that sentiment."*

mattress, but that is not a plausible option. Looking at it purely in business terms, why should we expect Bill Muddyman & Co to stump up a sum that is many times above their perceived valuation?

What we must do is exert pressure on the Royal Bank. If Fulham 2000 gains a sufficiently high profile, the Bank will soon be aware of football fans' feelings on the subject. As well as joining the scheme, supporters should continue with their letter-writing. Comments should be addressed to The Rt. Hon. Lord Younger of Prestwick, Chairman, Royal Bank of Scotland plc, 42 St. Andrews Square, Edinburgh EH2 2YE. Should you happen to bank with them you could consider withdrawing your money and switching banks. The RBS wouldn't like that, for sure!

It shouldn't go unnoticed that Johnny Haynes was up before dawn in order to travel from Edinburgh on the first flight on Saturday morning (having been at a special function the night before, for Denis Compton) to get to the Fulham 2000 launch. And yet he tirelessly fielded everything that was thrown at him by the media. His only hesitation came when asked if he'd brought his boots with him (if only!). David Hamilton, too, did his share, as did Sharon Duce – and even George

Best flew the flag, having made a surprise entrance before the end. The whole press conference was handled with superb professionalism by the Fulham 2000 crew, something that hasn't always been the case with some of Fulham's back-room staff in the recent past.

But enough of the back-slapping. Nothing has been achieved thus far. So, fill in your Fulham 2000 application form and send in your ten quid – and encourage as many of your mates to do the same. What must be clear is that we intend to stay at the Cottage, and it's a message we must shout to the heavens. With enough public opinion behind us, then anything's possible!

The Fulham 2000 organisers would like nothing better than to spend all money raised on physical improvements to Craven Cottage, but this can only come when the ground is ours once more. In the meantime, they will not hesitate to direct all resources available at persuading the Royal Bank to see sense.

Above and top left: The Fulham 2000 campaign is launched and Johnny Haynes and George Best pose for the TOOFIF camera.

Top: The Fulham 2000 head honchos (from left) Geoff Faulkner, Alan Williams, Richard Jones and Melvin Tenner are joined by an interloper who evidently hadn't received the dress code memo.

Farewell Bobby

Just as the Fulham 2000 campaign got underway so it was announced that Bobby Moore (*right*) had cancer. Then, within days, he was gone. Having received the ultimate in red cards (and what a diabolical and ill-judged decision by the person in charge) so the tributes and obituaries followed. Perhaps the most poignant remarks came from Bobby's former England team-mate and fellow World Cup winner George Cohen: "I had cancer from 1976 to '82 and it's a terrible strain on the family. I just hope he didn't suffer." The rest of George's quote was typical of other tributes: "He was a man who conducted himself in the right way. He was very dignified and it is tragic he should go this way; 51 is no age. Most will remember him for his football, but I

remember him as a person; he never had a bad word for anyone."

Most of Mooro's career was spent, of course, at West Ham. However, he still managed to clock up 150 games during a wonderful swansong for Fulham. With delicious irony, Fulham and Moore battled through 11 matches to reach the 1975 FA Cup Final to face... West Ham. One of his best games came during that run – at Everton, then top of the First Division. The Toffees surely expected an easy passage to the Sixth Round against Second Division FFC. Bobby Moore clearly revelled in being back on the big stage and was keen to show that he was still able to strut his stuff. With most of the 45,000 crowd screaming for a home win, Bobby did as much as anyone to stem the blue tide, performing in his

customary calm, unruffled and supremely confident style. On this occasion he added the occasional audacious touch too – such as coolly flipping the ball up while being pressurised in his own penalty area and then flicking it back with perfect weight to Peter Mellor. This was despite the fact that the whole of Merseyside was seemingly bearing down on him. Anyone else would have hoofed the ball into Row Z; but then Bobby Moore wasn't anyone else.

Opportunity Knocks

How ironic that the first inkling of the great news about the ground should be heard on the local radio at Huddersfield (after that shoddy performance it was just about the only thing that prevented mass suicide on the coach journey home!). When the whispers became reality the following morning, the news was indeed worth savouring. At long last we have managed to attain some sort of stability and a base from which to launch great things; hopefully! Let's face it, we've suffered a severe decline over the past decade. Standards have been allowed to slip alarmingly in all departments. Now we have a terrific opportunity, if you'll pardon the pun, to build on the news.

However, it's important to remember that, even though the recent news is as welcome as it is terrific, we haven't actually achieved anything as yet. But we now have the opportunity to buy back the freehold of Craven Cottage. Presently there is the not insubstantial sum of almost £8m to find – and within three years, not ten. In case you're not aware, although we've been given a ten-year lease, the rent, which is minimal for the first three years, then rises sharply for the ensuing seven to a figure believed to be about £500,000 per annum. So it's clear we need to secure the ground sooner rather than later. The immediate message to all those who have stalled over making their £10 contributions to Fulham 2000 is "stall no longer" – those contributions are every bit as important now as they were before the news broke.

There's no doubt that the Fulham 2000 crew's success in publicising the Club's plight, and the ensuing stampede to become a member, has helped to sway the issue. The media campaign was well organised and well received. The coverage in the press of the Club's position and the rounds of media interviews carried a lot of weight. As a result, just weeks after saying that they were not interested in a deal on the ground at any price, the Royal Bank of Scotland changed their stance.

All parties must have been impressed with the manner in which the Fulham 2000 crew brought the matter out into the open. On the one hand the movement was akin to the proverbial swan, moving majestically in an assured and dignified style belying the fact that beneath the surface it was a mad thrash – with many hours of research, preparatory work and consultation being undertaken. And all somehow organised around other responsibilities involving family and work. In many cases the day job came a very poor second and family life became almost non-existent. So, while the feeling about remaining at the Cottage remains euphoric, please don't forget the efforts of the Fulham 2000 committee in particular, their ever-suffering other halves, and also the many helpers who were willingly roped in along the way. Without their Herculean efforts the situation would probably have remained shambolic.

Those who wrote to the Bank should realise that those letters were effective. Those efforts demonstrated the strength of feeling, and the Bank themselves conceded that our fans were "eminently decent folk"

Top right: TOOFIF's *We can Dream* character captures the mood perfecclty courtesy of Paul Johnson.

Below: How Fulham FC released the news to the media that they had negotiated a ten-year lease for Craven Cottage, during which they could buy back the ground – if sufficient funds could be found.

FULHAM FOOTBALL CLUB (1987) LIMITED

CRAVEN COTTAGE STEVENAGE ROAD LONDON SW6 6HH
TELEPHONE 071-736 6561
FAX 071-731 7047

Press Release by Fulham F.C.

The Board of Fulham Football Club is delighted to announce that it has reached agreement with the Royal Bank of Scotland to continue to lease Craven Cottage for the next decade during which time it will have the opportunity to purchase outright it's famous home.

This will bring to an end the long period of uncertainty which has surrounded the Club's future for the past few years. The Directors of the Club have worked extraordinarily hard to put together this deal which in shape, is comparable with that recently struck with Chelsea F.C. The terms allow Fulham to pay a reasonably low introductory rent over the first three seasons whilst they seek the partial redevelopment which will be fundamental to their ongoing ability to fund both the ensuing rental payments and the agreed option price of just under £8m.

The Fulham Board have praised highly, the imaginative and energetic efforts of The Royal Bank in finding a seemingly impossible accomodation to the catastrophic situation which followed the demise of the ill–fated Cabra plc.

GRORTY DICK

the independent WBA Fanzine

EDITOR: Andy Beaglehole
c/o 7 Ruth Close, Tipton, Staffs, DY4 0AR

SUBSCRIPTIONS/INVOICES: CONTACT STEVE CARR
021 556 3886

Dear Fulham 2000:

It's every football supporters sweating black nightmare to lose their home ground. The altar of memories, the tradition, even the infuriating home defeats that make a club unique. Take away a base and part of the club is missing, never to be replaced. I can't fully imagine the full horror of such a prospect.

But even from a hundred+ miles away, it's so heartening to read how supporters have fought for their club. I hope that my supporters could conduct such an eloquent campaign in the same circumstances. I also hope that we will never have to.

Here's a cheque for a tenner. Seems the least we can do to show supporter solidarity. Hang on in there – we're all rooting for you !

ANDY BEAGLEHOLE
EDITOR - GRORTY DICK

Left: West Brom's *Grorty Dick* was just one of a whole host of fanzines to support the Fulham 2000 cause.

and that they were keen to come to an amicable solution. However, there were also clear signs that the Bank weren't comfortable with Fulham 2000's more aggressive stance, although they were just stating the truth of the matter. Prior to the Fulham 2000 launch the Bank were all sweetness and light, saying they wanted to be reasonable, etc, etc. Their idea of being "reasonable", however, was (in a letter in late December) to threaten to evict Fulham at the end of the season. The combination of supporters' letters and Fulham 2000's approach helped to force the issue.

And let's not forget the FFC Board when dishing out the praise. It's been a helter-skelter route so far, but the bottom line is that we are still at Craven Cottage – a position that was but a pipedream until just recently. It was a close-run thing, but we're still at our historic home and the Board members are willing to invest in Fulham's future at Craven Cottage. We should do likewise.

We've had excellent support from non-Fulham fans. All the other fanzines were targeted, and many rushed to help with their ten quids along with coverage of our plight in their publications. Sod's Law being what it is,

no sooner had our original mailshot taken place so the details of the new deal were announced. Consequently we had to burn the midnight oil once again to explain that while the news was most welcome, nothing had changed on the fundraising front – we had merely been given a stay of execution.

Overall the news is wonderfully upbeat, but the real danger is thinking that our troubles are over. We have overcome a major hurdle, but, just like a winger jinking his way past a series of tough tackles, all that skill and effort is a waste of energy if the ensuing cross sails aimlessly into the crowd. We must maintain our determination and concentration to ensure that our "final ball" is delivered with accuracy and purpose. ⚽

Fulham 1 Blackpool 0	
17.04.93	13th
Fulham 4 Burnley 0	
24.04.93	12th
Chester City 2 Fulham 3	
01.05.93	11th
Fulham 1 Exeter City 1	
08.05.93	12th

1st
2nd
3rd
4th
5th
6th
7th
8th
9th
10th
11th
12th
13th
14th
15th
16th
17th
18th
19th
20th
21st
22nd
23rd
24th

Fulham secure future

FOOTBALL: Fulham yesterday secured their future at Craven Cottage for at least the next ten years, putting an end to fears that this may be the club's last campaign at the stadium by the River Thames. Fulham will lease the ground from its owners, the Royal Bank of Scotland, with an option to buy it for £8 million during that period. The announcement follows five years of uncertainty over the site, which developers wanted to use to build houses and flats. The Fulham chairman, Jimmy Hill, said: "It is not VE Day but it is like El Alamein. It has been a big battle but we have come through it and we are now going in a new direction." The club also unveiled plans to develop an all-seater stadium with a capacity of 15,000 at Craven Cottage, and to construct 136 flats.

Fulham 2000 Latest

On the Fulham 2000 front, membership has risen to 3,400 – that's £34,000 for the coffers. Equally good news is that the "pot" has been boosted by £12,000 from sales of limited edition ceramic Craven Cottages. Committee members continued to meet every fortnight during the summer, and are still hopeful of reaching agreement with the Board about fundraising schemes. It's strange how the Board appear to be dragging their heels on this. Perhaps they're surprised at how well the Fulham 2000 gang has done with fairly limited exposure to date. A further three-pronged launch by the fans'-led initiative is imminent: a furtherance of the membership drive; a second package that'll be aimed at supporters; and a third appeal directly targeting businesses. Sure, this is still a helluva long way from the magic seven-and-a-half million quid needed but, with the months ticking away, it's a credible start. With the backing of the Board, this push could

all be orchestrated in a more concerted manner. Come on chaps, we're all in this together… ⚽

Top right: Ceramic Cottages were all the rage in Summer 1993!

Opposite page right: Andrew Pulver offers his take on our Club's parlous state and the Fulham 2000 campaign in *Time Out*.

Below: Latest news on the ground front. This clipping is from the *Daily Telegraph* in October 1993.

Clouding the Issue

There's only one "f" in frustration (and, come to think of it, only one "f" in the word that often precedes it – at least where Fulham is concerned). Can someone explain what the hell is going on? Here we are heading into November and we're doing so under a big, black cloud. We currently stand one off the bottom of the division and any hard news is almost impossible to obtain. And November is traditionally our bad month!

Oops, there goes the TOOFIF Ed into doom and gloom overdrive. Unfortunately, that's the way things appear. If we can dispense with such red herrings as who we should buy should a non-existent £100,000 be made available, the question of whether Ara (Bedrossian) should have been secured earlier and whether or not the team would've been doing better had we moved to Chelsea, then we're left with the bottom line: the Club is going backwards.

Prior to the Hull game, the team had been offering ever-worsening performances, both in terms of entertainment and points. This squad of players has the wherewithal to beat the teams that have whipped us (with the exception of Liverpool) and yet the approach has, quite visibly, been all wrong. Off the pitch, the fans have been kept in the dark about the latest on the ground situation while the Board appears to be stonewalling any suggestions and progress by the Fulham 2000 folk. Indeed, there was more information in the Hull programme, only read by about 200 travelling Fulham supporters, about our plight than in all the home programmes put together. So it's hardly surprising that the troops are getting restless.

Let's get something straight: while we all dream of supporting a club that's consistently bringing in the silverware, all we want here – at least in the present circumstances – is

The Stevenage Road stand — the scheme would have demolished all but the brick facade   *Picture: Richard Watt*

Gummer saves stand in extra-time

By John Grigsby, Local Government Correspondent

THE only football stand in England which is listed as being of special architectural or historic interest has been saved from demolition.

Mr Gummer, Environment Secretary, has dismissed two appeals over plans to redevelop Fulham Football Club in west London.

The project would have involved the demolition of all but the brick facade of the Grade II Stevenage Road grandstand, built in 1905. The celebrated Craven Cottage pavilion, which is also listed, would have been converted into flats.

The ruling focuses the spotlight on one of the pio-neering and almost forgotten heroes of the modern game of association football.

The buildings are the earli-est, and one of the most unchanged and therefore sig-nificant, works of Archibald Leith, who although not an architect or even a promi-nent engineer, was the lead-ing football stand designer of his time.

His work influenced the design of grounds across Europe.

The Stevenage Road build-ing is the earliest example of a two-tiered design and the first in which the technique of lattice beams and trusses with curved tie members was used.

The ground is also consid-ered to be unique because of Craven Cottage, a two-storey pavilion, placed diagonally next to the stand.

Hammersmith and Fulham Council said that the domes-tic scale of the cottage and the stand harmonised with its setting.

Mr Gummer agreed that the proposed development would be of "a very high stan-dard appropriate to this important riverside loca-tion". However, he also accepted the judgment of his inspector that this was not enough to allow the demoli-tion of the listed buildings.

He does not rule out the redevelopment of the site if the scheme ensured the pres-ervation of the listed buildings.

At one stage it was expected that Fulham would share a ground with Chelsea. But the club struck a deal which enables it to lease Cra-ven Cottage for 10 years with an opportunity to buy the ground for £8 million.

However, it depends heavily on the successful development of the site for mainly residential use.

Sport

Preview

Craven desires

Andrew Pulver on Fulham 2000

By any standards, it's been a rotten season so far for Fulham. They've failed to register a single home win, they're bumping along second from bottom of the Endsleigh Division 2 (propped up only by Barnet, who hardly count); and to compound the misery they're drawn away to Yeovil in the first round of the FA Cup. The tie with the legendary Somerset giant-killers means, for the first (and most likely the last) time this season, that Fulham will come under the scrutiny of BSkyB's live coverage: the cameras are presumably coming along not for the quality of the football but so that the assembled Monday night audience can dance on the Cottagers' mangled remains.

The only piece of positive news that the Fulham faithful have to cling on to is the recent announcement that the hallowed turf of Craven Cottage has, for the time being at least, been saved from the spectre of developers. The club has been offered the chance by current owners Royal Bank of Scotland to buy back the ground for some £7.5 million which must happen by June 1996, when the rent on the ten-year lease will soar to unaffordable levels.

There's many a slip, though, and this is merely the latest instalment of a saga that's been running since 1989, when now-bankrupt Cabra Estates made their first moves to take over Fulham's prime piece of river frontage. The Fulham 2000 campaign was set up in the summer of 1992 as an independent supporters' initiative to raise funds.

David Lloyd is a committed member of Fulham 2000: he also edits the successful fanzine *There's Only One F in Fulham*. But his loyalties, like others, are being strained. 'We're banging our heads against a brick wall. You'd have thought the club would have been only too happy . . . It's particularly galling when you think how much energy has been put into setting up the Fulham 2000 thing. I can't for the life of me work out why the fundraising aspect of it is being delayed by the club. There hasn't even been a bucket collection.'

For all the supporters' resentment, Chairman Jimmy Hill is sticking to his guns, pointing out that the hundreds of thousands of the fans might raise is a drop in the ocean. 'Don't get me wrong,' says Lloyd. 'I've got a lot of time for the bloke. He's come a long way because of his stubbornness, and you have to respect that. But he's got

a tendency to talk down to the supporters, and say the wrong thing at the wrong time. He's written in the programme, for example, complaining that not enough people are turning up. Fair point. But the people reading it have turned up, and they end up feeling slighted.'

Everybody at Fulham is very tight-lipped about the future, for the Bank's offer has more than a whiff of give-with-one-hand-take-away-with-the-other about it. Lloyd is indignant that fans have learned more about the club's problems through the programme notes of another club (Hull City on Oct 16) than through their own.

It's the survival of the club, as much as the ground, that's at stake.

'Let's put it this way,' Lloyd continues. 'There is a case — I'm not suggesting that it is likely, mind — for the winding-up of Fulham FC. The nightmare for us is that the men on the board are just seeing out time: in three years we'll be in Division 3, we'll be paying half a million plus in rent, the crowds'll have gone to nothing. They'll just point the finger at the supporters again, saying we should have moved to Chelsea. But there's no guarantee that if we'd have moved we'd have done any better. The worst possible thing that could happen now is that we're allowed to drift.'

However, something else positive happened just a few days ago: the return of stylish Cypriot midfielder Ara Bedrossian ('the guy we were desperate to hang on to,' comments Lloyd) after a typically muddled story of inter-club loan, wage complaints and overseas negotiation. Lloyd, however, is still grinding his teeth. 'Lots of people have a soft spot for Fulham: it's a grand site, there's a wealth of ex-star players, there's a lot of people wanting us to get back to a position of respectability. We don't want to be battling, as we are, for the title of London's worst football club. It's all so frustrating because there's so much going for the place.'

You can join Fulham 2000 by writing to Freepost, London W14 0BR. Membership is £10.

---

some stability. We yearn for a team that's performing to its full potential (please note, that doesn't necessarily meaning winning every week. That said, in this poor division if we played to our full potential that would surely translate into racking up a fair few victories.). And we're desperate for regular progress reports on how the quest to raise £7m+ is going. Many, many people from all over the country have signed up and paid the tenners to Fulham 2000. But in the meantime what do we hear from the Club? Nothing. The silence is deafening. ⚽

Heartfelt Pleas

Issue 29 is packed with examples of the fans' frustrations. With no one, apart from the Board, exactly sure of what is going on – and some suggest that they don't know either – fans can only argue their case based on what they perceive to be happening. Typical of the TOOFIF post-bag is the following:

After 30 years of following Fulham through thick and thin, I feel I can't take any more. It is so sad to see what has been allowed to happen to this Club. I now leave after matches feeling angry and frustrated. I have kicked the cat so often it has left home. I am being forced to watch my football elsewhere, probably the local park since my loyalties will always be with Fulham. But I am not prepared to keep paying to watch performances knowing we will probably lose because we are unable to score goals. Everyone knows we desperately need a striker – apart from the people that run Fulham FC it seems.

It's going to be another wasted season. The ground is in a state of disrepair, and there is no sign of the Club raising the money to save the ground, apart from Fulham 2000. I believe there is an on-going plan to run the Club down, and I am just another one voting with his feet. What else can I do?

I've come to the conclusion that the Club has no ambition or interest in promotion. I only hope that the few remaining fans can make enough noise to bring attention to our plight before is it too late.

As with most correspondence to TOOFIF, this is written from the heart. It (and similar offerings) highlights how distant the Board members are from the supporters. These supporters – of Fulham as well as those of other clubs, don't forget – make up an army who have consistently said they are willing to help. However, since the flurry of activity that signalled the launch of Fulham 2000 there has been little progress, save the all-important news of the new lease. Trouble is, we're now well into the decisive three-year spell and the multi-million pound goal is as distant as ever. Crucial time has been wasted, and just as worrying is that the terrific head of steam that had been built up has all but evaporated.

Comments such as these will, I'm sure, not find favour with the powers-that-be. No doubt we'll be labelled "so-called supporters" and be told that we must show patience. Patience! We've shown nothing but patience for years! Supporters who turn up week in, week out, home and away, should be cultivated not preached at. But then PR is something alien to this Club at present. The really frustrating thing is that despite the downward spiral of recent seasons, there are plenty of us left who really care.

Are we being left to wallow in the mire, and ultimate closure through lack of interest? Can that really be the plan? ⚽

There's only one F in **FULHAM**
An alternative look at Fulham F.C.

ARA'S BACK!

INSIDE: Peter Storey, Colin McCarthy, Ronnie Maugé, Tom Loorke, Teddy Maybank, James Lawrence, Gary Cobb, Frannie Ward, Clive Walker...

Issue 29 November 1993 £1

Match	Date	Position
Hartlepool 0 Fulham 1	14.08.93	10th
Fulham 1 Cardiff 3	21.08.93	14th
Bristol Rovers 2 Fulham 1	28.08.93	16th
Fulham 0 Wrexham 0	31.08.93	18th
Fulham 1 Bradford City 1	04.09.93	19th
Burnley 3 Fulham 1	11.09.93	21st
Barnet 0 Fulham 2	14.09.93	17th
Fulham 0 York City 1	18.09.93	20th
Huddersfield Town 1 Fulham 0	25.09.93	22nd
Fulham 2 Leyton Orient 3	02.10.93	23rd
Fulham 0 Bournemouth 2	09.10.93	23rd
Hull City 1 Fulham 1	16.10.93	23rd
Fulham 0 Stockport 1	23.10.93	23rd
Reading 1 Fulham 0	30.10.93	23rd
Exeter City 6 Fulham 4	02.11.93	23rd
Fulham 0 Brighton & HA 1	06.11.93	23rd
Rotherham United 1 Fulham 2	20.11.93	23rd
Fulham 3 Swansea City 1	27.11.93	22nd
Cardiff City 1 Fulham 0	11.12.93	23rd
Fulham 2 Hartlepool 0	17.12.93	21st
Fulham 0 Port Vale 0	27.12.93	21st
Plymouth 3 Fulham 1	28.12.93	21st
Fulham 0 Brentford 0	01.01.94	22nd
Cambridge United 3 Fulham 0	03.01.94	22nd
Blackpool 2 Fulham 3	08.01.94	22nd

League Cup

Fulham 2 Colchester United 1	17.08.93	Round 1 1st leg
Colchester United 1 Fulham 2	24.08.93	Round 1 2nd leg
Fulham 1 Liverpool 3	21.09.93	Round 2 1st leg
Liverpool 5 Fulham 0	05.10.93	Round 2 2nd leg

Autoglass Trophy

Fulham 4 Brighton & HA 1	28.09.93	Gp match
Reading 1 Fulham 0	10.11.93	Gp match
Bristol Rovers 2 Fulham 2	01.12.93	aet Round 2
FFC win on pens		
Fulham 1 Reading 0	11.01.94	Southern Area Quarter-final

1st
2nd
3rd
4th
5th
6th
7th
8th
9th
10th
11th
12th
13th
14th
15th
16th
17th
18th
19th
20th
21st
22nd
23rd
24th

Good News Corner

TOOFIF has been accused by the powers-that-be of being too negative – can you Adam and Eve it??!! The mag is compiled almost entirely from submissions, so one would tend to think that if these are in any way representative then the negative tone would have something to do with the fact that the Club isn't exactly on an even keel at present. Oops, that's a bit negative! Then again, a return of nine points from 15 games and sitting 23rd in the table isn't really the place to be, is it? Do you know that it's reached the point that Club officials have suggested TOOFIF should devote a page per issue to good news. What a novel idea, we thought. Perhaps the programme should take note, too. Anyway, here goes...

1. Ara's back.
2. We're still ahead of Barnet.
3. We scored a goal against Liverpool.
4. We scored a goal against Bradford – who, let's face it, are one of the better teams in our division this season.
5. Hartlepool aren't very good.
6. Cardiff are pretty poor.
7. Huddersfield are worse.
8. Thanks heavens for Barnet.
9. Martin Ferney signed a new contract at the start of the season.
10. We win loads of corners.
11. The Reserves aren't bottom of the Combination again.
12. The new shirts are now on sale.
13. The Club's washing powder is great – don't the shirts come up lovely and white?
14. We're through to the next round of the Autoglass.
15. Every month you can be a winner with Cottage Chance.
16. You can't make out what Ken Myers is saying at half-time.
17. Ernie Clay's in Portugal.
18. Alan Dicks is in the US.
19. Tom Enefer is anywhere but SW6.
20. The programme has had a revamp.
21. We're still at the Cottage.
22. GMB is the bestest union in the whole wide world.
23. The pitch looks lush and in excellent condition (nice one, Steve!).
24. Simon Morgan has been called up for the UK diving team.
25. The Board consists of truly wonderful human beings ever-ready and willing to listen and work with the supporters.
26. An announcement regarding a major fundraising drive by Fulham 2000 will be made in the next, um, few weeks or months.
27. There's nothing from The Traveller in this issue.
28. Barnet – we love you.

Above: Steve McGee – responsible for keeping the Craven Cottage pitch in "lush and excellent condition".

Below: Vice-Captain Jeff Eckhardt brought some levity to the table.

Programme notes

With discontent in the air, a submission to TOOFIF 29 not only stirred up a right old hornets' nest but also a pointed attack on yours truly in the match programme. The article by Alex Sims, "Pathetic Programmes", is reproduced here to highlight how daft the whole situation was. As you'll see, the issues raised by Alex were wholly resolvable and within the Club's remit (whereas matters on the field can be affected by circumstances outside their control, such as a bad bounce of the ball, an "iffy" decision or basic bad luck). The whole premise of his piece, though, was based on the fact that the programme team had (worthily) boasted that they'd be conveying the Club's image in the best possible way. Those ideals, and by implication "the Club's image", were well and truly knocked askew by a string of cock-ups. Anyway, see what you think: here's how it all panned out...

PATHETIC PROGRAMMES

My estimation of Jeff Eckhardt has suddenly shot up since he wrote "From the Vice-Captain's Table" in the Bournemouth programme. It was the first genuinely humorous article in there all season – deliberately humorous, that is. However, the "ability" of almost everyone else who contributes to the organ has kept me laughing virtually non-stop since August. I can sum it up in one word: pathetic!

I quote from page 6 of the first issue v Colchester: "[We intend] to convey the image of FFC in the best possible way." Well, you could have fooled me! I could fill the whole of this issue with examples of the cock-ups, mis-prints, mis-spellings, plain bad grammar and such like that have somehow slipped past the editor's eagle eye. Let's just concentrate on the worst examples…

1. In that same Colchester programme is a profile of Terry Angus that is almost illegible because (aside from the inevitable grammar and typing errors – "on and out attack" is a new one on me!) somebody had forgotten to mention that you use inverted commas for direct speech. Also, the introduction to Colchester United ended with an unusual sentence: "Happily the…" Happily what? I'm dying to know. Similarly "Hearsay" ended with "whilst Gavin…"

Hmm, okay let's give the team the benefit of the doubt and put it down to teething troubles.

2. The Cardiff programme was on another plane, and included a genuine classic. "On the Road" told us how to get to Colchester. Dead simple, really. Just follow the M4 to junction 18 and follow the signs to Bath. Nothing to it. What an unusual ground-share scheme!

3 Apparently Bradford City remained in the First Division from 1908 until 1992 and inexplicably seem to have played, and won, two Coca-Cola cup ties at both Crewe and Darlington on the same August night. Really?

4. The £1.50 Liverpool "special" had two real clangers. Okay, so the photos are slightly better, but if you have to repeat photos from previous programmes please don't change the name of the player in the meantime. The acrobatics from Farrell are now Brazil's – are you sure? And as for the goal at Burnley, one must assume that the editor wasn't at the game because the "cheeky 25-yard chip" is shown two inches above as a sidefoot along the ground.

5. That wonderful moment against Liverpool is captured on camera. So what photos are we to be offered? The lads celebrating wildly? Farrell lobbing Brucie? Brucie backpedalling in vain? Oh no. We get the ball crossing the line, on its own! No Brucie, no Farrell, no crowd scenes; no point!

6. And what about page 27 of the Bournemouth programme? Here we were being told how to get to Liverpool by car or train. Pity the game had been played four days earlier!

The other classic from this programme was the less-than-generous offer that "…you could watch your kids run out with the Black & Whites here at the Cottage" for a "cool" £145,000! Not forgetting VAT! What a snip! That section was signed by Commercial Manager Ken Myers. Any takers, I wonder, Ken?

Conveying the image of FFC as amateurish, imprecise, irrelevant and worthy of ridicule is not funny for me and other supporters. The ghost of former Chairman Tommy Trinder has yet to be laid and I'm sick of people treating us as a joke. Get professional – or get out! ⚽

Above: Acrobatics from Sean Farrell – or is it Gary Brazil? Alex Sims would love to know!

Below: Fulham hosted Liverpool in the League Cup, but the day's souvenir programme contained errors.

This Time Next Year…

Derek Trotter always had dreams of being a millionaire. And yet Del Boy wouldn't have done so by producing TOOFIF! All those lovely people who've trundled along to the fanzine sales pitch over the years can testify that it's darned obvious there's no money in shifting fanzines. Not enough for me to merit a visit from the fashion police anyway. In the mag's early years it ran at a substantial loss; despite having much higher sales during those campaigning times, the printing costs were considerably higher too. Even so, we honoured pledges for kit sponsorship – with Sean Gore, Gary Elkins and Gary Brazil among those being stuck with having the letters "TOOFIF" printed under their sponsorship pictures in the matchday programme. But they survived.

When Fulham drew Liverpool in the Coca-Cola Cup in 1993, a rare bonanza payday looked to be in the offing. Gates at Craven Cottage at the time were around the 3-4,000 mark. The preceding game (a 0-1 loss to York City) attracted 3,595. Liverpool's visit was bound to result in a capacity crowd approaching 14,000. And with a new issue heading to the printers, time to "up" the print-run by 1,000 copies to cater for the extra demand. A no-brainer; I'd be quids in, no problem.

Er, a big problem, in fact. It rained. Or rather, it deluged. All flipping night. A crowd of 13,599 braved the monsoon to see us go down 1-3; but hardly anyone wanted to stop to buy a fanzine. And why would they, given that the vast majority of the mags had been transformed into a mushy pulp despite being housed on a palette. Instead of the hoped-for £1,000-ish profit, the TOOFIF accounts showed a loss of that magnitude.

It was a big hit to the pocket, and all very frustrating, but that's what can happen.

Even so, there were still some sly personal digs from the Club that income from fanzine sales was being squirrelled away somehow. Really? In fact, TOOFIF continued to donate money over the years, only without making a too much of a song and dance about it.

This is probably the appropriate time to declare that on top of channelling sums to FFC via the youth team and player sponsorship, TOOFIF has backed Fulham-supported charities plus the Fulham 2000 and Back to the Cottage campaigns as well as supporting the Princess Diana Fund (1997), September 11 Fund (2001), Indian Ocean Tsunami (2004) and, in various years, Help a London Child, Comic Relief and Charing Cross Hospital. We've also sponsored an FFC safety officer's tabard.

So, while we're not claiming to be angels, we're defintely not millionaires either!

Under Attack

View from the TOP

JIMMY HILL

PHOTO: Mike Jones

LONG-TIME Fulham supporter Anne Morris rang Clubline to ask me this most interesting and original question. "I've read the Fulham fanzine, TOOFIF, for many years and mostly enjoyed it. But recently I've become concerned. It seems to be a powerful and respected publication both amongst Fulham supporters and recently, the national press. But increasingly I feel that TOOFIF have power without responsibility. What contribution do you think it makes to this Club? And what do you think about fanzines in general?"

"This is something that has occupied my mind for a long time now, with regard to fanzines generally, and Fulham's fanzine in particular. I want to make one thing clear first of all because I'm quite sure this conversation – or your question and my answer – will be dealt with in our fanzine, in a fair way, I hope.

If you've been born with a long chin as I was you really become quite used to people having fun at your expense. From the school playground onwards, people will joke and laugh about a physical characteristic, so I'm the last person in the world to get worried when people laugh at me. If you've been a professional player and missed the occasional open goal, or even worse, if you've been the Chairman or the Manager of a football club that's not winning any matches, people are bound to have fun at your expense. Those who've seen me on television tend to view me as someone who takes football very seriously – I'm always ready to argue my corner. Those who know me much better – and probably those who know me best are those who shared a dressing room when I played, like Bedford Jezzard, Tosh Chamberlain, Johnny Haynes and the others – they know that even if I don't have quite Vinny Jones's sense of fun, I do have a sense of humour, and I am prepared, when the joke is at my expense, to have a laugh at myself. The mickey-taking element of fanzines up and down the country I find most enjoyable, and I must admit I feel guilty sometimes about the laughs I'm having at other people's expense. So that's one side of it. Nobody minds the laughs and the criticism, especially about the game because you can argue about that all night. Look at the problem we're having trying to find a new England manager. People say to me: "Who's going to be the new England manager? Who would you choose?" Well, you might as well take a whopping great pin and stick it in a directory which the Managers' Association might have, and hope that you've got the right one. All the discussion, the argy-bargy – that's fine; all part of being involved in a football club. Where it goes over the top – and this is something that really has to be understood – is that the Club is desperately fighting for survival at the moment, and unlike, say, the Conservatives in the House of Commons where everything they do is contested by the Opposition on parties, football clubs aren't strong enough to have an opposition at the moment. We are not strong enough to cope with the kind of undermining that has gone on in TOOFIF, of almost every department in the Club. It goes beyond a laugh and a joke when something goes wrong. It is a constant and demeaning – and MEANT to be demeaning – process of those who run our football club. And it is damaging.

To make matters worse, TOOFIF provides very little money for the Club. We need money at the moment, more than anything else. The tasks of buying back this ground, of balancing the books and becoming a viable, fighting force in the Second Division and hopefully, in the end, further up the ladder; these are vital. However well we run our affairs, there are going to be full stops missing from the programme, there are going to be other errors because human beings were not made perfect. In all areas of the Club's activities we'll try to make those errors minimal. What football clubs need is support, forgiveness, help, aid, finance – all these things. They're prepared to put up with mickey-taking, but not just constant opposition. That is only destructive, and makes one wonder why the meaning of the word 'supporter' in the context of many fanzines has been eroded." The above words were spoken 'off the cuff' on Clubline and are reproduced here not as a declaration of war against TOOFIF but rather an invitation to peace. As we prime the pumps with the Supporters Club under the '2000' banner for the mammoth task of forging a future for the Club at Craven Cottage, it should be blindingly apparent that we all need to be pushing in the same direction. To do otherwise would be unforgivable.

Jimmy Hill
Chairman

The Chairman's Christmas Message can be heard from noon on Christmas Eve on 0891 44 00 44

"I've said it before, but to ram it home to those who may only read this bit, the tone of any particular issue of TOOFIF only reflects the post-bag of preceding weeks."

Above: Given the personal flak that Jimmy Hill received in the mag it was perhaps not surprising that he chose to respond. This appeared in the match day programme for the visit of Hartlepool in December 1993. His accusation, though, that TOOFIF provides "very little money for the Club" was wide of the mark – and an odd thing to say given that he'd frequently admitted that he'd not put in a penny himself.

Right: The same programme carried further accusations, and these were just as inaccurate. No reference was made about the fact that a number of fanzine folk, including the Ed, had independently offered their services to help the programme compilers; those services were declined.

Opposite page right: Don Mackay – Issue 29 carried criticism of the manager.

'HearSAY'

MULL THIS ONE OVER!

It's been a very long snooze, but we at the Cottage do still regard Fulham FC as something of a "sleeping giant". Unfortunately that acclaim doesn't spread as far as we might think. One Fulham supporter choked on his beer in a Norfolk pub recently when a local journalist claimed never to have heard of our mighty Black & Whites. He was soon put right, but quickly added insult to injury when he compared us to his local Anglian Combination side. "Oh," he said, "you mean like Mul Barton Utd?" It really is time that this sleeping giant woke up ...

TOOFIF TOO MUCH

For a magazine that so frequently criticises the board for failing to disclose details of the Club's financial position, the Fulham fanzine, TOOFIF, is remarkably unforthcoming about its own. The editor used to state that it was a non-profit making enterprise but somewhere along the line these words have mysteriously disappeared....

CURIOUSER AND CURIOUSER

One more thing about our friends at the fanzine. A recent article entitled "Pathetic Programmes" highlighted the printing errors which have dogged the Match day magazine so far this season. We were accused of "Conveying the image of F.F.C. as amateurish; imprecise; irrelevant and unworthy of ridicule." So it came as a bit of a shock to find that these very extracts were sent to the National newspapers; the same story appeared in The Independent two weeks ago, courtesy of TOOFIF. All very peculiar.

SORRY SURREY

On-site bookies Surrey Racing made an unexpected loss as Fulham charged to a 3-1 victory over Swansea last month. Their price? 18-1. Well done those optimists amongst you.

COTTAGE JINX

Hartlepool may be a touch jittery about playing at the Cottage today. They did win 3-1 here on 28th December 1992, but the North-easterners did not score another League goal until March 7th 1993, two and a half months later.

Here's a response to the "publicity" afforded to TOOFIF in recent matchday programmes…

After the mauling taken by TOOFIF in the Hartlepool programme in particular, here are the thoughts of the editor. Jimmy Hill's piece was well written and, on the whole, quite fair. It's interesting, however, that he says we provide "very little money for the Club." Let me assure you Mr Hill, what little profit made over the years has been passed on to Fulham. Luckily, TOOFIF's sales have been pretty constant despite dwindling crowds – if "gates" rose then the Club would get a much larger bung. But that, I'm afraid, is beyond TOOFIF's control, although quite definitely within the Club's.

TOOFIF has, from day one, sponsored players' kits. Some pledges have been rash on my part, as, with paltry profits from the mag, I've had to honour such pledges from my own pocket. Undaunted, TOOFIF has also sponsored a steward's tabard, donated sweatshirts to the Junior Black & Whites, and made donations to various fundraising activities at Fulham. It's just that we've not boasted about it. However, I do recall a boast by Jimmy Hill that he's not put a penny in himself.

What of the other criticisms:

1. I have **never** sent cuttings to national newspapers (and the paper referred to was *The Guardian* not *The Independent*, so you even got the one fact in that piece wrong!);

2. The programme states that TOOFIF "frequently criticises the Board for failing to disclose details of the Club's financial position." Maybe I'm losing my marbles, but I can't recall doing that even once!

3. The inference that the Ed – me – is making a financial killing (if only!) is also false. A change *has* occurred recently; I'm now self-employed (no secrets there) and TOOFIF now operates under that banner, but the Club will continue to receive sponsorship in exactly the same way.

For a programme that so frequently stated its stance of independence from the Football Club, its views now, spookily, seem to follow the party line. The editor used to state that "the views expressed were not necessarily those of the Football Club." Somewhere along the way those words have mysteriously disappeared.

I've said it before, but to ram it home to those who may only read this bit, the tone of any particular issue of TOOFIF only reflects the post-bag of preceding weeks. Certainly Issue 29 was critical of Mr Mackay (and to a lesser extent Mr Hill) but that's exactly the mood of the camp. The clause referred to in the previous paragraph still applies to TOOFIF – I'd far and away prefer to be editing a publication that was leading the cheers for a thriving and successful football club. But that's just not the case. I'm assured by Club personnel that things are getting better. That's great news. But there's a long way to go.

As for Mr Hill's closing remarks, I want to declare that TOOFIF is firmly behind Fulham 2000 and will be trumpeting the cause once details are known.

NB. As well as offering to help out with the programme already this season, I have been to see Mr Summers regarding the poor results shown on the press front. I have relevant, front-line experience in the Press and PR field. It's not my fault that having made the approach that you – the Club – felt able to ignore it. In my opinion, it's the Club's loss (oh, the arrogance!).

There's only one **F**in
FULHAM
An alternative look at Fulham F.C.

"HELLO AND WELCOME TO FULHAM CLUBLINE ON 0891 44 00 44…"

Special non-gloomy edition

Issue 30 ☆ **January 1994** £1

1st
2nd
3rd
4th
5th
6th
7th
8th
9th
10th
11th
12th
13th
14th
15th
16th
17th
18th
19th
20th
21st
22nd
23rd
24th

Fulham 0 Hull City 1
15.01.94   22nd

Bournemouth 1 Fulham 3
22.01.94   20th

Fulham 1 Reading 0
30.01.94   17th

Stockport County 2 Fulham 4
05.02.94   16th

Autoglass Trophy

Fulham 2 Wycombe Wanderers 2
08.02.94
aet Southern Area Semi-final
Wycombe win on pens

You see, Mr Hill and co, I *am* on your side. When mistakes are made on this side of the fence I am the first to hold up my hands. That seems not to be the case in other quarters where, apparently, things are constantly viewed through a rosy hue. (I should say, however, that the programme editor has already apologised for the inaccuracies included and has offered me the right of reply.)

Anyway, the following arrived the Saturday morning after the Hartlepool game:

Dear TOOFIF

Am I alone in being pretty stunned that a man such as Jimmy Hill, with the considerable financial clout and media contacts that he has at his disposal, has chosen to launch a full-scale attack on the integrity of a tiny publication (circulation @1,500?) run single-handedly and on a veritable shoestring? If the editor was in it for profit, surely he would have seen the error of his ways many moons ago.
Tony Berry
• Circulation is nearer 1,800, Tony, but printing alone accounts for about £1,300. Ed.

Well Programmed

As a contributor, I presumably fall into the "pathetic" category outlined by Alex Sims in his detailed criticism of the much-maligned programme recently. First off, ALL the mistakes highlighted by Mr Sims were valid criticisms, with the photo of Gary Brazil's "chip" against Burnley being one of many errors to have littered my own pieces so far this season. However, a number of points deserve a reply on behalf of the programme team.

For example, the repeat of the Supporters' Club news in the Bournemouth programme was a mistake on the part of the printers.

The debate goes on. With the Programme Team still reeling from his fanzine-based attack on this publication, ALEX SIMS is keen to put the record straight.........

Dear Editor

Having read David Roodyn's article in the Brighton programme I would like the right of reply to put into perspective his comments about me, my previous article in TOOFIF, and the contents of the fanzine.

If you could print this letter (preferably in full) perhaps it might help to lay to rest what I, personally, consider a myth: the rift between different groups of supporters at the club.

There were two ways to reply to Mr Roodyn; I guess he would be expecting another "cynical" attack. However, I prefer to write a conciliatory letter of explanation. I'm afraid he is grossly misinformed and misunderstood my motives. Indeed, your publication appears incapable of understanding the whole concept and philosophy of a fanzine - or is it that you don't want to understand it?

Mr Roodyn writes about the "cynicism and divisiveness" and my "disgruntled motives". Strong words! Was it divisive to point out that, in the opinion of many readers on the terraces, the programme was embarrassing? I'm afraid it was a fact. Was it cynical of me to write to TOOFIF instead of yourselves? Well, possibly! I'm sorry to say I thought you probably wouldn't print the letter. I hope you'll prove me wrong and print this one. As for my motives, Mr Roodyn is very wide of the mark. I thought the article was clear enough - my only motives are to care passionately about F.F.C and it's image.

Whenever I show the fanzine to non-Fulham supporters they are unanimous in their praise for the obvious love and dedication to the Club which shines through. Clearly, it's not all going to be sunshine and roses when you remember what has happened to the club in the recent past. Are you really surprised that some fans are a bit cynical? The officials at the club have to work hard to convince the fans that we are not being sold down the river again. I believe Mr Hill and the board are doing a good job. I hope my confidence is not misplaced. Furthermore, when a team is bottom but one of the old 3rd Division a fanzine is bound to reflect the supporters' frustrations. The letter from a Spurs fan made me laugh - what does he know about suffering with your club? - two or three seasons out of the top league?

Have you read other club's fanzines Mr Roodyn? Some of them are appalling in their attitude - spending all their energies attacking other clubs (ask our friend from Spurs) and spreading hate between supporters. Is that what you prefer? TOOFIF is above most of that, I hope, and you should be proud of the fact. We don't promote hate, as a rule we show love of the club, mixed with worry, bemusement and yes, some anger. In short, a reflection of the emotions on the terraces.

A genuine fanzine is mostly written by the "die-hards" - they are people who pay out substantial amounts of money to watch Fulham week in and week out. Please don't preach to me in such a patronising tone about "fellowship" between supporters 200 miles apart (as wonderful as that is). I've been watching Fulham for 28 years and I keep in touch from 1500 miles away. Because of the club. I'm flying back to England for Christmas mainly to watch our 4 games - and I'm not the only one!

Others writing in the fanzine may not go so often to watch the team but it is these people we need to attract, as Mr Hill and Mr Mackay keep reminding us. They, too, have a voice and should be heard. The fanzine gives them the chance to opinionate. I don't agree with many letters, some are very personal attacks (unlike mine, Mr Roodyn) which are made public to prove that the organisation is open and frank. I applaud the chairman's recent clarifications in the programme. This is exactly what stops those rumours and silly comments from spreading. We need more explanations please!

Finally, congratulations on a vastly improved effort for the last two programmes. I'm sorry Mr Roodyn, but you know full well I wasn't talking about "typographical errors". The quality and lay-out have never been in doubt, Mr Cain is a very good writer and Dominic Guard's article in the Brighton programme was quite superb. The photos were also much better. I'd like to think the improvement would have occurred without TOOFIF's "heavy" criticism.

We are not (very) cynical but really concerned for the club we love, as I am sure you all are. Prove us wrong, print this letter, and together let's get Fulham back where it belongs. Extending an olive branch at Christmas!

Alex Sims
Huelva, Spain

Right: Alex Sims gets his point across – several points, actually – in the matchday programme.

Left: While waiting for a corner kick to be taken, Terry Angus contemplates life without inverted commas.

Right: Fanzine of the week, but *The Sun*'s Matt Walker is far from impressed...

Below: ...However, those awfully nice folk at *The Guardian* promptly waded in to defend TOOFIF!

WHICH newspaper hounded out Graham Taylor with non-stop insults such as Turnip and Norse manure? And which newspaper last week gave the fanzine There's Only One F In Fulham three out of 10 because "it produces attack after scathing attack on manager Don Mackay and what an awful bore it becomes"?

from 'The Guardian'

FANZINE of the week

Sorry, but there is only one F in awful

● Sunsport's regular fanzine feature this week goes to Craven Cottage on the banks of the Thames. The long-suffering fans feel sold down river and make it clear in their magazine 'There is only one F in Fulham'.

By MATT WALKER

FULHAM fans have just about had enough.

The November issue of 'There is only one F in Fulham' produces attack after scathing attack on manager Don Mackay.

And what an awful bore it all becomes.

The alarm bells are ringing louder these days at Craven Cottage. The 'Mackay Out' campaign has begun in earnest in the fanzine.

Article after article slags off the Cottagers' manager and there are no holds barred as the fans really get stuck in.

THIS scores a bore – Fulham's scathing fanzine.

Apparently at the 'Meet the Manager' night Mackay complained the fanzine was too negative.

One fuming supporter replied in the letters page, writing: "Just in case you are reading this, Don, here is a positive thought: Mackay OUT!"

But it is not just Mackay in the firing line.

Infamous chairman Jimmy Hill is also bombarded. Retirement is the only solution in the minds of the fans.

These 'devoted' supporters have obviously decided the two men are to blame for the demise of the club — not the players.

But, having read one page of this fanzine, it feels as if you have read them all.

Virtually all the pieces are about the terrible Mackay and how he must be sacked to save the club from ruin.

It really is very boring and, come the back pages, you could be excused for falling asleep.

This fanzine is really not worth a quid — and I certainly will not be rushing out to buy next month's issue.

Having seen the proof of the page that should have appeared, it was all the more annoying to see that the printers had instead used a repeat of the page from the Leyton Orient edition.

Similarly, the Terry Angus interview – with its glaring omission of inverted commas – as well as other errors in the Colchester programme were ominous examples of up-and-coming cock-ups by Morgan Print. I conducted the interview in question – how do you think I felt?

The Fulham supporters quite rightly see TOOFIF as a vehicle to voice their discontent (and there's been plenty of scope lately) but view the programme as the voice of the Club, warts and all. When that publication is riddled with errors, that only compounds the image of incompetence that currently surrounds the Club as a whole. ⚽

Jonathan Sim

Evil Under *The Sun*

What a peculiar review by *The Sun*! Peculiar in that it appeared a good month after Issue 29 hit the streets and on a weekend that Fulham didn't have a game. However, the main comment to make is that, while TOOFIF welcomes comments and constructive criticism, this is surely a case of the pot calling the kettle black.

Being a fanzine editor, you soon learn to take the rough with the smooth. But the only thing *The Sun* has homed in on is that the reviewed edition mercilessly slags off Messrs Mackay and Hill. That's bloody rich coming from the organ that made an artform out of crucifying Bobby Robson and Graham Taylor – a point picked up by *The Guardian* the following weekend. The records of Robson and Taylor were infinitely superior to Mackay's, too.

A fanzine's content is almost exclusively based on what is contributed by the fans of the club in question, and the content of TOOFIF 29 was wholly representative of the postbag. What leapt from the pages was the frustration with how things are apparently being handled at Craven Cottage, both on and off the pitch.

Given the facts (and numerous rumours!), it's little wonder that fans were fed up. At the time of issue only Barnet were below us in the division, we'd failed to register a single win at home, many performances (and choice of tactics) had been appalling and the Fulham 2000 scheme – of which we'd heard very little after the initial launch – was seemingly being baulked by the Club.

Hmm, better bring this little piece to a halt now – it's in danger of becoming "an awful bore"! ⚽

View From Near the Bottom

Anne Morris? Who she? According to Jimmy Hill's Column (in the Hartlepool programme), this long-time supporter rang him on Clubline and posed a "most interesting and original question" regarding TOOFIF. Evidently she has read TOOFIF for many years and mostly enjoyed it. However, of late she has become concerned as she feels that the fanzine is a powerful and respected publication, yet has power without responsibility.

I won't concern myself too much with Jimmy Hill's reply, save only to say that it was fairly predictable if reasonably put together. And, of course, he is entitled to his view. Doubtless others may wish to comment in more detail about his outlook. Yet I would certainly wish to take issue with his suggestion that TOOFIF is in some way trying to undermine the running of the Club and that its criticisms are constant and demeaning – and "meant to be demeaning". Not only is this not true nor supported by any facts but it is yet another attack on the fans. TOOFIF regularly features a range of views and is open to any supporter to contribute letters, articles and so on.

Anne Morris, this includes you! If you have been a long-time supporter and reader of TOOFIF you will know that your views (whatever they are) are most welcome. I wonder, then, why you haven't made your views known for publication in TOOFIF? By the way, when Mr Hill was giving you his answer, did you ask him if a good example of "demeaning" was when he and that motley crew of grinning celebs and luvvies took part in that infamous and appalling "Fulham RIP" river/coffin demonstration? Perhaps you were one of those supporters who threw bricks at the boat?

Although "power without responsibility" has an impressive-sounding ring to it, it's actually a pretty empty and meaningless phrase when applied, as it was, to a magazine, or indeed to the media generally. Theatre, film, art critics, political commentators et al have this so-called power without responsibility. As, of course, do TV pundits much closer to home. I mean, who'd be a Blackburn ball-girl?

Gordon Bennett (pseudonym of a TOOFIF regular)

Give a Little Whistle

There has been much comment about the quality and nature of both TOOFIF and the programme, with both publications being put in the spotlight by a rather curious – if not bizarre – debate at a time when we should really be concentrating on what is actually happening on the pitch.

Both magazines have their supporters and detractors but, for the most part, it would seem that both are bought by supporters keen to read anything about their favourite club. Given the lack of media attention, or interest, and little or none created, it is hardly surprising that supporters swoop for TOOFIF, the programme and, latterly, *Where's Ara?*.

I have no doubt that the TOOFIF editor – and the contributors – would like or prefer to shout from the rooftops in praise of a Fulham team living up to expectations and marching triumphantly towards promotion while regularly putting the opposition to the sword. The crowds would increase significantly and so would the print run and sales, too.

Above right: Jimmy Hill, whose comments in the matchday programme prompted responses from fanzine regulars Gordon Bennett and Ron Motson.

Opposite page right: In other news, Fulham beat Port Vale 3-0. Or to be more precise, a TOOFIF team trounced Port Vale fanzine *The Memoirs of Seth Bottomley* by that scoreline on BBC Radio 5's *Over The Moon – Sick as a Parrot* quiz. The triumphant trio, The Ed, David Preston and John Gordon, are pictured with the show's question master, Rory McGrath.

TOOFIF's Day in *The Sun*

We start this issue's overview of the fanzine scene by having a look at *The Sun*. Their goals section on a Monday has started to run fanzine reviews, and I think that the people writing them are missing the point. They seem to bang on about humour as if it is the only important thing about a fanzine. Sure, any decent fanzine should have a fair sprinkling of humour but a fanzine's main job is to campaign for the fans.

One recent review had a go at the excellent One F in Fulham for being too depressing. This is a fanzine dedicated to a team second to bottom of the Second Division, fighting to keep their ground and they also have Jimmy Hill as their Chairman. So it's not surprising that things might be a little downbeat. It is a step forward that papers such as *The Sun* are giving fanzines publicity, but they should really get people writing the reviews who know what they're talking about.

From the Ipswich fanzine
Those Were The Days

However, a glance at the League table tells its own story. Harsh words, perhaps, but the actuality. So there's ample reason for supporters to be frustrated and disgruntled and to ask what's going on. It's hardly surprising that some feel a change at the top is needed and that such opinions are expressed in writing. Those who have contrary opinions can also express themselves, and do so. Hopefully the ensuing debate will be constructive rather than destructive.

The programme becomes an issue because, whether it is independent of the parent club or not, it is perceived as the voice of the Club. And when it isn't saying very much and/or when news isn't forthcoming, and when it contains horrendous mistakes, people will be inclined to hold a low opinion of it. Typographical mistakes are inevitable but careless captions, wrong identification of players in captions (Jim Stannard being mistaken for Roger Freestone is a recent example) and statistical errors can and should be avoided.

That said, I'd say that the current programme team have certainly raised the quality of it, although the concerted attacks on TOOFIF seem somewhat unnecessary, a waste of space and, in truth, constitute another attack on the supporters. The inaccurate and mendacious comments should have been avoided and are no credit to whoever was responsible for them. We all want a good programme, which becomes a written history of the Club as well as an update on the life and activity within the Club.

We also want a good fanzine but, of course, it reflects fans' perceptions of the Club, thus is an alternative look at Fulham FC from the bizarre to the hysterical, the nostalgic to the historical, (hopefully) factual to the occasionally scurrilous. No home should be without it! Intriguingly, the Club has yet to refute any stories for inaccuracies if I'm not mistaken.

Turning to that infamous "review" in *The Sun*, I believe most supporters will treat it with the contempt it deserves. Critics of TOOFIF and others have been quick to comment how TOOFIF was slagged off by the newspaper in question – indeed several club officials appeared to be somewhat gleeful.

I read lots of daily newspapers and in doing so have been aware of the praise afforded to TOOFIF in publications such as *The Times*, *Sunday Times*, *Observer*, *Guardian*, *Telegraph*, *Independent* and *Time Out*. I also "read" *The Sun*. Do you know that since that three-out-of ten review I haven't seen anything else written by "Matt Walker". In fact, when I rang *The Sun*'s sports desk, the person who answered had never heard of him. And I have had no response to my message for him to give me a buzz, either. Now, I'm not saying that TOOFIF was "set up" (couldn't happen, could it?), but it increasingly looks that way. Compare their review and mark of our fanzine with those of other much worse, badly produced, badly written and frankly inept fanzines and you'll see what I mean.

I have my own idea of what's taken place, and perhaps the source of that particular attack lies much closer to our corner of SW6. Fact is, though, all this programme versus TOOFIF stuff only acts as a smokescreen to real and much more pertinent issues. ❖

Ron Motson (pseudonym of a TOOFIF regular)

There's only one Fin
FULHAM
An alternative look at Fulham F.C.

You can always be sure of a load of TOSH with TOOFIF

Issue 31   February 1994   £1

Fulham 1 Blackpool 0	
12.02.94	15th
Fulham 0 Bristol Rovers 1	
19.02.94	16th
Wrexham 2 Fulham 0	
22.02.94	17th
Fulham 3 Burnley 2	
05.03.94	17th

1st
2nd
3rd
4th
5th
6th
7th
8th
9th
10th
11th
12th
13th
14th
15th
16th
17th
18th
19th
20th
21st
22nd
23rd
24th

Alan Dicks and Don Mackay

In TOOFIF's 25th year Fulham were lording it in the Premier League and the extraordinarily gifted Dimitar Berbatov was leading our line. It's fair to say that you wouldn't put fellow frontman George Georgiou in the "extraordinarily gifted" bracket – in his short spell at the Cottage, the hirsute striker was more noted for throwing litter from his car window (in shock when a cat supposedly ran in front of his motor) than putting the ball in the back of the net. But while the players weren't generally top-drawer material, our downward spiral in the early 1990s was down to mismanagement as much as anything else.

All these years later, it's very hard to put into words just how abject Fulham's on-pitch showings became as we headed for the bottom division; some "performances" simply defied description. The mood off the field was hardly rosy given all the problems about the ground, but a decent level of concerted effort on the pitch would have injected a sense of hope. Alan Dicks, manager from July 1990 to December '91, proved to be hopelessly out of his depth in the Fulham hotseat (prompting one of the most memorable of TOOFIF covers!). And, after an initial flurry of optimism, his successor, Don Mackay (January '92 to March '94), was unable to check our slide either.

Without a doubt, we should have been pushing for promotion, especially as we'd had the Cabra millions to spend – an absolute fortune in those lower-division days – but that unexpected bonus was, scandalously, simply frittered away. Dicks took overall control from Ray Lewington in 1990. Having spent four years in charge on a shoestring budget (come to think of it, shoestrings were considered a luxury), Lewy was demoted to assistant manager when Dicks moved in. Successful in the 1970s at Bristol City, and before that assistant manager to Jimmy Hill at Coventry, Dicks had been out of the British game for

a decade when Hill, by now FFC Chairman, installed him as Fulham manager.

The move was a disaster. He was a lovely bloke, but so out of touch. His single season at Fulham was summed up by one utterly shambolic result: Fulham 0 Hayes 2. We were that poor at the time, our FA Cup dismissal hardly registered as a shock result. Just as you can tell when a group of players are well drilled and pulling in the same direction (think of our team ethic under Micky Adams, Roy Hodgson or, more recently, Slaviša Jokanović), it's also easy to spot when things are going awry. Under Alan Dicks things were going very badly askew.

From TOOFIF 15, April 1991: It was extremely worrying at the manager's forum the other week that the only person apparently unconcerned about Fulham's lowly position was Alan Dicks. He was either very brave or particularly thick-skinned to attend in the first place, but once installed in the hotseat he seemed intent on blinding us with science – trouble was, he failed to convince even those who had previously been prepared to give him the benefit of the doubt. Questions were answered in one of two ways: a) "That's your opinion."

Above right: Genial Alan Dicks, a lovely bloke but hopelessly out of touch.

Below: George Georgiou, who apparently panicked at the sight of a cat. Good job he never faced Wolves!

Opposite page right: A host of ex-players and celebs are paraded at the Cottage to mark the full launch of Fulham 2000.

Cat caused it

FULHAM football player George Georgiou has been fined £100 for tossing litter from the sunroof of his Ford Escort saloon.

Georgiou, who admitted the offence, blamed his actions on a cat crossing his path.

He told Wimbledon Magistrates Court: "As I recall a cat ran out in front of me and my instincts made me throw the litter out of the window to avoid hitting the cat."

Georgiou was fined £100 and ordered to pay £82 costs.

GEORGE GEORGIOU

or b) "That's nothing to do with me." He failed to recognise the genuine feeling for the Club from supporters who, with every reason to rant and rave, persistently probed with articulate questions that were both reasoned and reasonable. The two players either side of him, Phil Stant and Martin Ferney – who, incidentally received 100 per cent support from the audience – were clearly embarrassed. Well, we've been embarrassed almost all season!

Supporters' groups had frequent meetings with Jimmy Hill and co in those days, and it's fair to say that the perpetual dismal showings were mentioned more than once! The Chairman's reaction was incredibly condescending, along the lines of: supporters had to show patience (arrgh, "patience"; just how many times was that word rammed down our throats!? The truth is, we showed remarkable forbearance), there were no major problems boys and girls; it would all come good.

Naturally, we hardly expected the Chairman to simply respond with "Okay chaps, whatever you say…" or "You lovely, loyal supporters may have a point…" Or indeed to lay into his manager in our presence. However, we hoped for some sort of reaction, evident by an improvement in team harmony and performance. If that wasn't possible, then the Board should act on the fans' droll yet apposite "Dicks Out" mantra. But we were merely supporters; what did we know?

A fair bit as it turned out. Years later, in his Testimonial brochure, Simon Morgan outlined: "'Dicks Out' was a smashing man. Whatever we may have thought about his managerial capabilities, we were all impressed by his charm, friendliness and politeness. Unfortunately, these count for little in the cruel world of a football dressing room. Give the players an inch and they will take a mile and they found it easy to ride roughshod over his attempts at discipline.

"His ideas and methods were hopelessly outdated and a gulf emerged between him and Ray Lew. The final straw came the day after the Hayes shambles. 'Dicks Out' ordered us to watch a video of the whole debacle. As we sat in his office, he came in, fast-forwarded the video to the first goal, briefly talked us through it and then

left, saying he had to go shopping with his wife. Jimmy Hill sacked him on the train home from Darlington after another heavy defeat."

So in came Don Mackay. He talked a good game and made a good impression on the supporters and the players. In his first season we finished ninth; and if memory serves me right, that was enough for him to be chaired around the pitch by fans after the last home game. Affable and punchy in Meet-the-Manager sessions, Mackay also gained brownie points for grabbing a paintbrush when supporters and a clutch of players got together during pre-season in an attempt to tart up the tired old stadium. But we soon became a tired old team and Mackay outstayed his welcome.

Cue the same pattern of conversation with the Chairman as above. This was no "toys out of the pram" moment after losing a couple of games. This was serious. So serious that by the time Mackay was eventually sacked in March 1994, we were bound for the basement division. It's quite likely that penniless Fulham felt they didn't have the means to pay him off before this; if so, it proved to be a grave error of judgement.

Simon Morgan said: "Mackay managed to convey the impression in the press that he was a strict disciplinarian, but the reality was that the players did pretty much as they pleased. The sad thing was that we had a team capable of winning promotion, but it lacked the will, discipline and organisation. If he could have stamped his authority on the Club, things could have been so very different. In my opinion, Mackay became little more than a puppet for Jimmy Hill, and he lost the players' respect one afternoon when we all went to the Chairman's house for tea. As the players and JH sat around the table discussing where we were going wrong, Mackay acted as the waiter. The lads, of course, made the most of it: 'Pass the sauce, Don,' or 'Any more steak, Don?' As we sat around drinking and smoking cigars, he was doing the washing up. No respect, no hope."

At least this tale demonstrates that the Chairman was concerned about our predicament, but Mackay undisputedly remained in charge for far too long. Oh well, fourth-tier football here we come. So much for showing patience, eh Jim? ⚽

York City 2 Fulham 0
12.03.94   19th

Fulham 3 Barnet 0
15.03.94   17th

Fulham 1 Huddersfield Town 1
19.03.94   18th

Leyton Orient 2 Fulham 2
26.03.94   18th

Fulham 0 Cambridge United 2
29.03.94   19th

Port Vale 2 Fulham 2
02.04.94   20th

Fulham 1 Plymouth Argyle 1
04.04.94   20th

Brentford 1 Fulham 2
09.04.94   20th

Bradford City 0 Fulham 0
13.04.94   20th

Fulham 0 Exeter City 2
16.04.94   20th

Brighton & HA 2 Fulham 0
23.04.94   21st

Fulham 1 Rotherham United 0
30.04.94   20th

Swansea City 2 Fulham 1
07.05.94   21st

1st
2nd
3rd
4th
5th
6th
7th
8th
9th
10th
11th
12th
13th
14th
15th
16th
17th
18th
19th
20th
21st
22nd
23rd
24th

Slithering Downwards

Just when you thought it couldn't get any worse, Fulham manage to get relegated to the basement division. Yup, Division bloody Four (in all but name). We had no divine right to remain in Division Two and we'd flirted with the drop before, yet it's still hard to take in. Last year's division was pretty awful, but we still ended up being one of the four worst teams. Those teams that made strides towards the upper reaches did so by somehow stringing a few results together and then riding on the ensuing boost of confidence. There was precious little style or panache.

We should not have gone down. It's so easy to pass comments after the event. But us poor souls who've suffered week in, week out (and shelled out hard-earned cash for the "privilege") had realised things were well off-kilter many moons ago. And we had constructively and politely made the powers-that-be at FFC aware of our concerns.

The loyal hardcore supporters have continued to stump up to Cottage Chance, Fulham 2000 and chipped in with sponsorship and other donations – and for what? Indecision! It's great news that the financial side of the Club's affairs is in better shape than for many years – even if we remain a Jim Stannard punt from regaining the freehold – but scant attention, it seems, was being paid to the team.

Some performances were abysmal and made me almost ashamed to be a Fulham fan. Had we gone down to the Third with all guns blazing; had we been a poor side that had at least shown passion and fight on the majority of occasions then it would have been easier to take. But we didn't – we slithered ever-downwards with barely a whimper.

Who wants to write this way about one's favourite team? I know I don't. And who wants to be an editor of a magazine that has spent much of its existence spouting doom and gloom? I bloody well don't.

I don't think that we're asking for anything that's too outrageous: simply a group of players that give their absolute all and play to some sort of team framework. We're not the footballing experts here – at least we're not those employed in a professional capacity – but as regular spectators who support the team come what may our opinions are valid.

Not everyone was overjoyed about the appointment of Ian Branfoot, and I remain as wary as the average Fulham fan. But there are clear signs that we may be about to turn the corner. There has already been a marked improvement in fitness levels and, with the new signings looking useful (if on the, er, old side) there's some real competition for places. Okay, this is based only on the pre-season friendlies, hardly the same as a term of Third Division fare. But it's a start!

Branfoot has already acknowledged the charisma of the Cottage ("Even when I came here as a full-back and was roasted by one of your wingers, Craven Cottage was somewhere special to come to play. The place has a special charisma."). We've had more than our share of bullshit in recent seasons. The new manager's remark was either bullish and honest or good-quality bullshit – either way, things are looking up! ⚽

Enter Ian Branfoot

Driving down to Woking for a pre-season friendly, the last thing on my mind was meeting the new Fulham manager. With our poor old Club having slipped into the bottom division for the first time, Ian Branfoot had been selected to succeed Don Mackay and right some wrongs.

While at Southampton, Branfoot hadn't exactly gone down a storm – dropping local hero Matt Le Tissier hadn't helped; no work ethic you see. Anyway, one of their fanzines, *On the March*, ran a front-page headline "Hope You Die Soon" (a Harry Enfield catchphrase of the time) underneath which they had Branfoot seemingly saying, "Bet I don't". This was supposed to mock the manager's legendary stubbornness, intimating that even if the Grim Reaper was on the way, Branfoot would tough it out and tell the Reaper where to go. Not hilarious, but it gave the Saints fans' "Branfoot Out" campaign national prominence (mainly because when the front cover was shown on the telly, "Bet I don't" had been airbrushed out, thereby suggesting much more sinister motives.)

In June 1994 Ian Branfoot was appointed FFC manager. I bumped into former Fulham Director Dave Gardner on the Kingfield Stadium concourse and, amid the pleasantries, he asked me if I'd like to meet the new boss, then led me into the bar. Branfoot positively bristled on being introduced

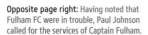

Opposite page right: Having noted that Fulham FC were in trouble, Paul Johnson called for the services of Captain Fulham.

Below: With Fulham sliding towards the bottom division, the Club turned to former Southampton manager Ian Branfoot to reverse the trend. It didn't quite go according to plan, although Branfoot did steady the ship somewhat by restoring a bit of pride in the squad and bringing in several key players.

to a fanzine editor. There was quite a pause. All very awkward. But our new team boss mellowed in the minutes that followed, even if his use of swearwords didn't.

He was engaging company, actually, and was more than happy to discuss his supposed love of route-one tactics. He called over his assistant Len Walker and positively enthused: "Come and say fookin' hello to a fookin' good bloke – he's the first fookin' sensible fanzine editor I've ever fookin' met." (Bear with me, this might not be verbatim; I may have left out a "fookin'" or five!) And we enjoyed a further ten minutes' chat before saying our farewells and heading off to watch the match.

Not long after our encounter, the first TOOFIF of that season came out. Not surprisingly it included much comment about Branfoot's appointment, a fair percentage of which was negative. In the week that followed the mag's publication I trudged home from work in a particularly lousy mood. I'd had to sack someone that afternoon, the only time I'd ever had to do this. To make matters worse, he was a pal of my brother and there were also mitigating circumstances, so I wasn't totally comfortable with how it had all panned out.

As I entered the house, ready to slump onto the sofa, the phone was ringing. It was Ian Branfoot. Purpose of the call was to bar me from the impending Club photocall – "It wouldn't be right to have the fanzine editor mixing with the players," he said, ignoring the fact that I'd been covering the

photocalls since my time on the Club programme and had supplied countless photos to the Club, free of charge, in that time (and since). Being already a little numb after the sacking, I wasn't as bullish as I should have been on the phone.

Later that night, however, I wrote to Branfoot (below). By chance, I saw him at the next home game and asked if he'd got my letter. He confirmed with a pleasant smile that he'd not only received and read it, but also that he thought it was fair. He assured me that he'd reply to it after the weekend. In the event, either he was lying or the Post Office let us both down. Nothing ever arrived. ⚽

Dear Mr Branfoot...

Dear Ian

Thank you for taking the trouble to phone me with your decision regarding the photo-call. Although naturally disappointed, I can understand your position. Also, knowing you've received possibly unparalleled flak from fanzines in the past, I'm sure you'd be wanting to keep any such magazine at arm's length (at least!).

I mentioned on the phone that I'd like to have ten minutes or so of your time in the near future. I was hoping to do this at the photo-call, and it was something I considered more important than the photo session itself. I'll attempt (briefly) to outline the sort of points I wanted to raise (even though I would still prefer to do so face to face).

* Love 'em or loath 'em, fanzines are now very much part of football.
* The magazine reflects the views of the fans – at least those who make the effort to write and who can be split into two camps: a) those who simply like to contribute; b) those who are hell bent on whingeing. That's the nature of the beast. All contributions from all quarters are considered for publication even if those views expressed are at variance with mine. Only those that are over-offensive (such as being racially motivated) or likely to land me in legal trouble are immediately "spiked".
* *There's Only One F In Fulham* attempts to portray an affectionate look at our favourite football club – warts

and all (as you acknowledged soon after your arrival, those warts have been all too obvious in recent years).
* On a personal front, no matter what happens under your guidance, there'll be no hint of a repetition of the unsavoury business at Southampton – that's simply not the Fulham way; and it's certainly not mine.
* Essentially, the only part of the magazine that I write is the editorial. The rest is all submitted. I am naturally keen to write a genuinely upbeat piece. Any hint of the team doing the business and the editorial will be singing it's praises. We want to be extolling our virtues at the expense of others, not languishing in the doldrums.

Here's to 1995/96 being our season.

There's only one F in
FULHAM
An alternative look at Fulham FC

**Which will
it be?**

£1

There's only one F in
FULHAM
An alternative look at Fulham FC

ROBERT HAWORTH (TOOFIF JUNIOR
OF LAST SEASON) LETS RIP...

INSIDE: More questionnaire results, plus, er, lots and lots of
other stuff, including one or two things that just might be of
possible interest...

Issue
35 *September/October 1994* £1

Fulham 1 Walsall 1
13.08.94   8th

Scunthorpe 1 Fulham 2
20.08.94   5th

Fulham 2 Wigan Athletic 0
27.08.94   4th

Doncaster Rovers 0 Fulham 0
30.08.94   6th

Torquay United 2 Fulham 1
03.09.94   8th

Fulham 0 Preston NE 1
10.09.94   10th

Fulham 1 Scarborough 2
13.09.94   15th

Walsall 5 Fulham 1
17.09.94   17th

Fulham 1 Hereford United 1
24.09.94   15th

Barnet 0 Fulham 0
01.10.94   17th

Rochdale 1 Fulham 2
08.10.94   16th

Fulham 4 Exeter City 0
15.10.94   12th

Chesterfield 1 Fulham 1
22.10.94   12th

Fulham 1 Carlisle United 3
29.10.94   15th

Northampton Town 0 Fulham 1
05.11.94   12th

League Cup

Luton Town 1 Fulham 1
16.08.94   Round 1

Fulham 1 Luton Town 1
23.08.94   aet Round 1 2nd leg
FFC win on pens

Fulham 3 Stoke City 2
20.09.94   Round 2

Stoke City 1 Fulham 0
28.09.94   aet Round 2 2nd leg
Stoke win on away goals

FA Cup

Ashford Town 2 Fulham 2 Round 1
12.11.94   Round 1

Auto Windscreens Shield

Leyton Orient 5 Fulham 2
18.10.94   Gp match

Fulham 3 Colchester United 2
08.11.94   Gp match

1st
2nd
3rd
4th
5th
6th
7th
8th
9th
10th
11th
12th
13th
14th
15th
16th
17th
18th
19th
20th
21st
22nd
23rd
24th

Bogged Down at Ashford

As we were sitting comfortably, if not prettily, in 12th spot in the basement division and unbeaten in four away League games, a trip to Ashford Town in the First Round of the FA Cup didn't look overly daunting.

Now a statement like that naturally comes with some caveats – of course we were nervous: this is Fulham we're talking about, and the previous year we'd succumbed (albeit unluckily on this occasion) to a last-minute goal at non-League Yeovil at the same stage of the competition. It was also only three years since we were humbled at home by Hayes, 0-2. Manager Ian Branfoot looked to have steadied the ship following our relegation to Division Three (we eventually finished 7th), so this first-round tie should have been viewed as a reasonable chance of reaching round two. All things being equal.

Sky TV must have sniffed an upset in the offing, however, as they had chosen to cover the match (if memory serves me right, the TV company were set to broadcast the full 90 minutes an hour after the final whistle). As we headed off into Kent (having made absolutely sure that we weren't facing Ashford, Middlesex), there was one indisputable fact: it was raining. In fact it was bucketing down. Our spirits weren't dampened though, especially as the sports coverage on the car radio gave no hint of any cancellation.

On reaching and squeezing into Homelands – the tie drew a capacity gate of 3,363 – it soon became apparent how bad things were. Not only was the rain still hammering down but the pitch was fast becoming a muddy mess. Not as bad as the pitch surrounds where we were herded perhaps, but bad enough. Unsurprisingly, with the home side eager to pick up Sky's dosh, the game went ahead. Had it been a Sunday League contest, the "parkie" wouldn't have even bothered getting out of bed, let alone entertained the idea of allowing 22-or-so herberts to ruck up his pitch, such was the incessant rain. And, for once, the herberts wouldn't have complained.

Opposite page: Fulham's 1975 FA Cup final team, minus the late Bobby Moore, play it one more time for Fulham 2000.

Below: In the mire at Ashford. At least until Micky Adams netted two late penalties

Welcome to The Homelands
ASHFORD TOWN FOOTBALL CLUB

Lucky Cottagers grab FA Cup replay in mudbath thriller

MUDLARKS: Striker Rob Haworth tries to make progress against Ashford. *Photo: NICK TOMEY*

Ashford Town..........2

Fulham........2

Ashford make a splash in a dash for cash

Neil Robinson

ASHFORD Town will soon receive £12,000 from the Football Association for allowing a game which Fulham thought should not have been played to be televised by BSkyB, who showed it as part of their highlights package yesterday. Torrential rain made for atrocious conditions but a postponement would have meant no cameras and no cash.

So the match went ahead and Fulham claimed a replay after the referee awarded them two late penalties in two minutes. Alan Cork, Fulham's veteran centre-forward, later revealed that the official works with his brother.

Hang on a minute. Doesn't all this suggest Zimbabwean affairs? Enough reporters thought so to barge into the referee's dressing room and pin him against the wall for after-match questioning. A man in his underpants is at an obvious disadvantage, but Andy D'Urso fought his corner with great tenacity.

He said that the decision to play was his — and his alone. No one had pressured him and he had not been filmed receiving a free satellite dish from "the short man" or even, since BSkyB's representative was Martin Tyler, "the tall man". D'Urso added that both the penalties were legitimate and looked forward to officiating in the replay tomorrow week.

Fulham remained insistent that the pitch, from which 600 gallons of water had been drained, was not fit. "If this was a league match it would never have been played," said their manager Ian Branfoot although his television conspiracy theory was undermined by the revelation that the visitors also receive a £12,000 appearance fee.

Fulham's chairman Jimmy Hill took another tack. "Both sides were risking injury out there," he said. "No one deserves to win on a surface like that. I still would have said that if we had lost but it would have sounded like sour grapes."

Certainly the quagmire pitch washed away any hopes of proper entertainment. It also

accounted for two TV vans which had to be rescued by a tractor after getting stuck in the mud.

Fulham's defence enjoyed no such escape route: on 18 minutes Dave Arter gleefully took advantage and Nicky Dent pounced for a second after the interval when he also hit a post.

And that would have been that had the referee not thrown the visitors a couple of unexpected lifebelts. Micky Adams grabbed both and Fulham, seemingly sunk without trace, were back on board.

The only compensation for Ashford was financial, with a bumper 3,363 crowd providing an extra £15,000 to go with the television booty. "We've waited 20 years for this game," said the

Ashford Town chairman Ernie Warren. "It's what the little clubs live for. Last year we made an overall loss of £1,500."

And where will the money go? Down the drain, actually. "We'd like a decent pitch," said Warren. "We don't like it any more than anyone else."

SCORERS: Ashford: (Arter, 19min), Dent (72). **Fulham:** Adams (81pen, 83pen). **Ashford:** Munden; Morris, Lemoine, A Pearson, R Pearson, Smith, Wheeler, Dent, Arter, Stanton, Ross. **Fulham:** Stannard; Finnigan (Jupp, 55), Herrera, Marshall, Moore, Blake, Mison, Morgan, Cork, Haworth, Adams. **Referee:** A D'Urso (Billericay).

Referee Andy D'Urso may have deemed the pitch playable, and yet to us lot getting more and more drenched by the minute it seemed a case of "see how we go": if it became dangerous to the players it was sure to be called off. With 20 minutes gone there was another factor to consider: Ashford were leading! They were still ahead at the break, at which point the home groundstaff had to restore the white lines to distinguish the pitch from a random mud heap. Any semblance of grass had gone the way of Fulham's hopes of a Cup run.

It got worse. With 20 minutes left Ashford went two-up in the sludge; our hopes now rested on a legitimate if improbable abandonment or divine intervention. In fact there was a third option. Step forward Andy D'Urso. With nine minutes to go he awarded Fulham a penalty, duly dispatched by captain Micky Adams. Once he'd located the spot that is! Two minutes later, another spot-kick, same taker, same result: 2-2. What a turnaround. Not that we were able to turn around on the sidelines: yes, we were cheering madly, but our thickly coated footwear had sunk too deep into the ever-worsening Kent quagmire

to allow us to move. Diplomatic draw attained, the players headed back to the dressing rooms, many complaining of skin burns from excess lime in the white lining. With considerable effort we sludged our way out of the ground and towards our cars. In my case I seemed to take a generous portion of the Homelands mud – and its astonishing stench – home with me. Despite getting a long overdue clean the following day, my Ford Sierra carried a whiff of Ashford for weeks afterwards. By that time, though, Fulham had squeezed past their valiant non-League opponents, winning the replay 5-3 after extra time, only to get knocked out by lovely Gillingham in round two. ⚽

1975 and all That

Only Fulham could celebrate the 20th anniversary of a Cup Final defeat, but, for all that, the celebratory dinner at the Heathrow Park Hotel was a resounding success. Fulham 2000, who organised the dinner – as well as the "Cup Final Replay" at he Cottage the previous evening, are to be heartily congratulated. Yet it was the appearance of our stars of yesteryear who made the occasion what it was.

It was, for example, good to see Peter Mellor and Les Barrett, who between them had won the Sixth Round game at Carlisle for us, back in tandem – even though Les demurred when it came to interview time with TV commentator Kenneth Wolstenholme.

The rest of the squad proved more forthcoming, with Jimmy Conway doing his "stage Irishman" routine to perfection, and dear old Alec Stock complaining about modern football in general and Arsenal in particular.

Then up came Les Strong. Until then Wolstenholme had been doing quite well, but Les managed to throw him completely by suggesting that everyone he worked with in the United States promptly died as soon as he had anything to do with him. And that included Peter Mellor! **Chris Mason**

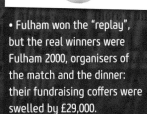

FULHAM 2000

F.A.CUP FINAL

1975

20TH ANNIVERSARY

Dinner

HEATHROW PARK HOTEL

FRIDAY 19th MAY 1995

• Fulham won the "replay", but the real winners were Fulham 2000, organisers of the match and the dinner: their fundraising coffers were swelled by £29,000.

Fulham 1 Lincoln City 1	
19.11.94	13th
Bury 1 Fulham 1	
26.11.94	11th
Fulham 1 Scunthorpe United 0	
10.12.94	8th
Wigan Athletic 1 Fulham 1	
17.12.94	10th
Gillingham 4 Fulham 1	
26.12.94	12th
Fulham 1 Colchester United 2	
27.12.94	13th
Hartlepool United 1 Fulham 2	
31.12.94	12th
Fulham 4 Mansfield Town 2	
02.01.95	12th
Fulham 1 Chesterfield 1	
08.01.95	11th
Darlington 0 Fulham 0	
14.01.95	12th
Carlisle United 1 Fulham 1	
28.01.95	12th
Fulham 1 Bury 0	
04.02.95	12th
Fulham 4 Northampton Town 4	
14.02.95	10th
Fulham 3 Darlington 1	
18.02.95	8th
Fulham 4 Barnet 0	
25.02.95	6th
Hereford United 1 Fulham 1	
04.03.95	8th
Preston NE 3 Fulham 2	
11.03.95	10th
Fulham 0 Doncaster Rovers 2	
18.03.95	11th
Fulham 2 Torquay United 1	
25.03.95	9th
Scarborough 3 Fulham 1	
01.04.95	10th
Fulham 1 Hartlepool United 0	
08.04.95	10th
Lincoln City 2 Fulham 0	
11.04.95	11th
Colchester United 5 Fulham 2	
15.04.95	11th
Fulham 1 Gillingham 0	
17.04.95	10th
Mansfield Town 1 Fulham 1	
22.04.95	10th
Exeter City 0 Fulham 1	
29.04.95	9th
Fulham 5 Rochdale 0	
06.05.95	8th
FA Cup	
Fulham 5 Ashford Town 3	
22.11.94	aet Round 1 replay
Gillingham 1 Fulham 1	
03.12.94	Round 2
Fulham 1 Gillingham 2	
13.12.94	aet Round 2 replay
Auto Windscreens Shield	
Leyton Orient 1 Fulham 0	
29.11.94	Round 2

1st
2nd
3rd
4th
5th
6th
7th
8th
9th
10th
11th
12th
13th
14th
15th
16th
17th
18th
19th
20th
21st
22nd
23rd
24th

Trials and Tribulations

The following was prepared for *Survival of the Fattest: an alternative review of the '94-95 football season.*

Following Fulham these past few seasons has been something of a trial. Personally I'm pleading insanity, and can only hope it's a temporary thing. Having been fortunate to have watched the Club perform in the lofty heights of the old First Division, produce a legendary England Captain in Johnny Haynes, a World Cup-winning right-back in George Cohen and, under the wily control of dear old Alec Stock, produce a skilful and entertaining (albeit Second Division) side that won through to Wembley in 1975, I can only applaud the Fulham fans who have stuck by the team in recent times.

Since 1983 when Fulham, managed by Malcolm Macdonald and Ray Harford, failed by the merest whisker to regain their First Division status, and the squad (which contained players of the calibre of Gerry Peyton, Paul Parker, Kevin Lock, Tony Gale, Ray Houghton, Ray Lewington, Dean Coney and Gordon Davies) was unceremoniously broken up, it's been pretty tortuous. Those fans who have joined the ranks since then have had very little to cheer. We've all had to endure some mind-numbing stuff as the Club has plumbed the depths, culminating last term in our first-ever season in the fourth tier.

Accordingly we were doomed to finish in the lowest position in our history, whatever the final placing. We'd have been more than satisfied (of course!) with a top two spot and automatic promotion, and happy with a Play-off berth with the prospect of a second Wembley appearance 20 years on from the first. But instead we languished in mid-table for most of the season and, in typical Fulham fashion, flirted with the upper placings in the latter stages only to fail miserably when the serious questions were being asked.

Still, at least the football was entertaining with tactical nous aplenty being displayed. Ha-bloody-ha! Much of it was turgid. On the worst occasions it wasn't even boring-but-with-a-semblance-of-a-game-plan long-ball tactics – rather a case of aimless "up and unders" in the hope that something might transpire. And yet at best we showed that we could play. With no

Top right: Terry Hurlock racked up a stack of disciplinary points in the 1994-95 campaign thanks to match officials who were seemingly all-too-eager to add his name to their collection.

Below: However, Hurlock broke his leg in a pre-season game with Brentford – and never played again – leaving Fulham, as this scribe suggests in the *Chronicle*, with a "gaping void".

Opposite page right: The ground saga continues to trundle on interminably, as the *Fulham Chronicle* reports here.

Pass-master Terry leaves Fulham with gaping void

The editor of Fulham fanzine There's Only One F In Fulham DAVID LLOYD reviews Fulham's pre-season and weighs up their prospects for the forthcoming Division Three campaign

There's only one F in FULHAM
An alternative look at Fulham FC

AN unbeaten run is always welcome (particularly if you're a Fulham fan - even in relatively meaningless pre-season friendlies).

The team kick-off the new season buoyed by an eight-match sequence which has seen them take on if not all-comers then all-sorts from either side of Hadrian's Wall.

After the customary trip around the Home Counties, the team went north. It was the club's first tour of note since the 1983-4 trip which took in Glentoran, Bohemians, Waterford Utd and Cobh Ramblers.

Hopefully the camaraderie and team spirit will have been enhanced just like the goals for column. Nine goals were rattled in against Cove Rangers and four against Deveronvale before a tidy single goal victory against Ross County continued the run - and set the scene for a real test against local rivals Brentford.

That match didn't take place as far as spectators were concerned. Terry Hurlock will be wishing it hadn't taken place at all. His broken leg must put a question mark on his footballing future. It has also put Ian Branfoot's best-laid plans to the test.

Hurlock's haul of disciplinary points last season made us think he'd taken one of Bruce Forsyth's catchphrase's a shade too literally. And anyway, who'd ever heard of a Fulham player winning prizes!

It's all very well saying that he didn't deserve half the bookings he received - he didn't - but it's no good having a player of such experience out for so long because of suspensions.

And yet various contributions to the current issue of TOOFIF (out this Saturday folks!) have demonstrated that for all his ability the team was more successful last season when El Tel was on the sidelines - in fact the difference was almost a point a game.

However, the veteran of many a skirmish was clearly central to the manager's plans - he's played in six of the eight friendlies and had looked a good deal sharper, too.

The Manager (sorry, General Manager) had gone on record just a few weeks ago to say he needed a wide player and a goalscoring centre forward to complete his jigsaw.

He duly signed Lea Barkus and Mike Conroy. With Hurlock now out of the frame Ian Branfoot will have to resort to Plan B - whatever that is. Let's not forget that Hurlock could pass the ball, a diminishing breed in our particular corner of SW6.

So who will get the call-up? And can he maintain our unbeaten run? Well, I've got my boots ready and waiting, but nigh on 39 I reckon I'm over the hill now... by just a month or two.

A Tenner for his thoughts

Fulham 2000 chairman Melvin Tenner offers a stoical voice of optimism as the club lurch into a new crisis. PAUL WARBURTON reports

HOPEFUL: Melvin Tenner believes Fulham can survive at Craven Cottage

Fulham 2000 chairman Melvin Tenner has forgotten what it's like to be surprised by news concerning Craven Cottage.

He said: "It's disappointing but true that nothing with regard to the development of the ground has ever worked out the way it should.

"After eight years you get used to dealing with the problems."

Tenner admits the heady cocktail of progress and setback does not have quite the same effect now as it once did.

In the week the board were reported as 'shocked' by the news of The Department of Enquiry investigation into the 110 year-old ground's development Tenner was half expecting the opposition to continue.

He said: "The local residents are quite clearly going to hang on to every last chance of ridding themselves of Fulham FC.

"If they are prepared to offer spurious claims that the ground development will 'increase crime in the area', whatever that means, they're prepared to come up with almost anything to stop the plans going through."

Fulham 2000 will meet for the first time since the news of the DOE's proposed enquiry on Saturday prior to the match against Torquay United.

One plan is to take supporters to Orient on September 2 by boat.

On board it is hoped club legends Johnny Haynes, George Cohen and Alan Mullery will lend their support.

Tenner said: "We also hope by the end of the meeting to have thought out how best to challenge the enquiry - or at least speed it on as quickly as possible."

"Naturally, we hope the Board, who are also Directors of '2000', will be present because we are as resolved as they to keep Craven Cottage what it is and where it is."

Outspoken

Tenner emphasised unity with the Board but found it hard to back the more outspoken thoughts of Chairman Hill that Fulham's coffin nails were already being hammered into place as a result of the enquiry.

He said: "I'm of the opinion that the club are unlikely to die - but will be merely delayed in getting approval."

"I appreciate the present board have had as as much as they are willing to take but I find it difficult to imagine the club folding having come this far."

Tenner sites one crucial area which is more important to Fulham's plans for developing the Cottage than anything local resident associations can throw at them.

He said: "The Royal Bank of Scotland are key to the whole thing.

"Hill has said the club enjoy a relationship that 'couldn't be better'. One wonders whether the Bank would consider re-evaluate the worth of the ground.

"Craven Cottage must surely be a millstone around their necks and I'm sure they would like to come out of the whole deal with some reasonable cash settlement or rent in the meanwhile than have on their hands 'an open space' which they can neither develop or sell."

"If banks are currently furthering images of being cuddly and co-operative it would not be in the best interests of the Bank of Scotland to pull the plug on Fulham.

"I rather doubt that the Bank are waiting for property prices to rise so they could please local residents in the same breath as getting a better price for the ground."

Tenner was looking forward to the day when he would earn the wrath of pressure groups who continue to pray for a repossesed Cottage with different owners.

SUPPORT: Johnny Haynes

"I'm quite convinced the Bank have finally acknowledged that Craven Cottage is a football ground - and nothing else.

"It's quite clear to me that when all this delay is sorted out local residents are are going to end up very disappointed.

"Unless, that is, they are Fulham supporters."

There's Only One F In Fulham editor DAVID LLOYD gives the fans' view

LAST week's article on the ground contained quotes from Jimmy Hill that were as punchy as anything the chairman has offered on that or any other matter.

The Department of the Environment's intervention is quite obviously a blow to the Fulham board.

Talk is that any any public enquiry could more than a year away - a critical time delay, since by then any fundraising efforts will in effect be nullified by the huge jump in rent.

Fulham fans remain largely confused however. Many have taken the club's advice and written to their local or Parliamentary Conservative MP. Others remain unsure of quite what to do.

In everyone's bad books, however, are Matthew Carrington for his 11th hour intervention and the minority of local residents who have rallied against Fulham's proposals on the grounds of more traffic and general hassle, but who supported the grander plans submitted by Cabra.

Strange how some locals are moaning about having a football club in close proximity - didn't they notice it when they moved in?

It's been there since the turn of the century, after all. And it's not as if the football club causes unnecessary grief - it has a well-earned reputation for friendliness and folksiness. But then as a friendly folksy Fulham fan I'm clearly biased.

A moneyed white knight remains elusive - as does a massive win on the lottery.

PUNCHY: Jimmy Hill

And the idea of changing the club's name to Fulham Football and Operatic Society to get a lottery grant isn't really on either.

The first move must be to renegotiate the leasing arrangements or even the purchase price with landlords The Royal Bank Of Scotland. No doubt the Fulham board have this at the head of their agenda.

Fulham 4 Mansfield Town 2	12.08.95	3rd	
Scarborough 2 Fulham 2	19.08.95	5th	
Fulham 4 Torquay United 0	26.08.95	2nd	
Darlington 1 Fulham 1	29.08.95	2nd	
Leyton Orient 1 Fulham 0	02.09.95	7th	
Fulham 3 Doncaster Rovers 1	09.09.95	3rd	
Fulham 1 Rochdale 1 3rd	12.09.95	3rd	
Exeter City 2 Fulham 1	16.09.95	7th	
Fulham 2 Preston NE 2	23.09.95	9th	
Northampton Town 2 Fulham 0	30.09.95	12th	
Plymouth Argyle 3 Fulham 0	07.10.95	12th	
Fulham 0 Bury 0	14.10.95	16th	
Chester City 1 Fulham 1	21.10.95	16th	
Fulham 0 Hereford United 0	28.10.95	17th	
Fulham 1 Colchester United 1	31.10.95	18th	
Wigan Athletic 1 Fulham 1	04.11.95	17th	

League Cup

Fulham 3 Brighton & HA 0	15.08.95	Round 1 1st leg
Brighton & HA 0 Fulham 2	22.08.95	Round 1 2nd leg
Wolves 2 Fulham 0	20.09.95	Round 2 1st leg
Fulham 1 Wolves 5	03.10.95	Round 2 2nd leg

Auto Windscreens Shield

Wycombe Wanderers 1 Fulham 1	10.10.95	Gp match
Fulham 5 Walsall 2	17.10.95	Gp match

1st
2nd
3rd
4th
5th
6th
7th
8th
9th
10th
11th
12th
13th
14th
15th
16th
17th
18th
19th
20th
21st
22nd
23rd
24th

little panache, actually. That's what hurt most – Fulham's was an above average group of players struggling to find their way. They'd have a couple of reasonable games and then we'd travel with a degree of hope to one of the basement's outposts, only to be beaten out of sight by an inferior side. Scarborough did the double over us for heaven's sake!

The attitude of the team unquestionably improved last season. The players, after a series of namby-pamby regimes, clearly respected the advent of Ian Branfoot's no-nonsense style of management. The improved levels of fitness, durability and resolve won us a fair few points as we launched several late comebacks, Two-four at home to Gillingham (Gillingham!) with two minutes to go became 4-4; 0-2 away to Ashford

(Ashford!) in the Cup with time running out became 2-2. Had we shown the same fighting qualities earlier in those encounters then we could have bossed – and won – the matches, rather than having to rely on late rallies.

That same fighting quality has nevertheless earned us an unwanted reputation. We may have found it hard to clock up League points at times, but had no trouble whatsoever in being pacemakers in the disciplinary standings. Terry Hurlock personally amassed 62 points - all from bookings – that's only a point fewer than the team's League total. Much sought-after full-back Duncan Jupp saw red a few times and was rewarded with the card of the same colour from the man in black. A couple of points are worth raising. The first concerns Hurlock. It would be very easy to don the rose-tinted (or in this case black and white) specs, and plead the midfielder's unequivocal innocence on the grounds that he's "one of ours". His type, and Hurlock in particular, are reckoned to be nasty, evil bastards until they join the camp at which point they are suddenly deemed "competitive" and "misunderstood". As a fair-minded football follower and one who is proud of Fulham's sporting (albeit too sporting over the years) reputation, I wouldn't condone having an out-and-out thug in our team. However – and please pass the soapbox – Hurlock's incredible collection of bookings was in the main wholly unjustified. Many's the time a bad tackle would be committed by one of the other 21 players on the park and would be "punished" with a finger-wagging or even ignored completely, but whenever Hurlock went anywhere near the action he was instantly yellow-carded. In one match it seemed he was "done" for smiling (not a pretty sight, I grant you!). Now, if they'd done him for being slow and overweight then fair enough, but smiling? In short, it seemed that many refs simply required "a Hurlock" for their private collection. Still, should we have the same officials control our games in the forthcoming season then Big Terry needn't worry, after all they've all ticked him off now!

Oh, and the second thing: the standard of refereeing generally. No doubt we've all got our views on the latest crackdown. (What will it be this season I wonder? Players who take four steps, dare to go near an opponent then pass the ball backwards – with or without smiling – will be penalised by an indirect free-kick, a booking and an evening out with Graham Kelly!) But whatever your views, don't you wish they'd be consistent? The last thing we want is some sort of robot in charge thereby taking away any common sense discretion, but some decisions given last season – both for and against – had to be seen to be believed.

Returning to the football, it's easy to forget that we were good enough to end Luton's interest in the Coca-Cola Cup over two legs. And Stoke needed extra-time to defeat us in the next round, again after two matches. The manner and style of those early season encounters promised much. We were privy to some terrific football, both in defence and attack. However, the real pointer, some would suggest, was the 1-5 loss at Walsall between those Cup rounds.

Top right: New signing Rory Hamill poses for the TOOFIF camera.

Below: *Time Out*'s review of a new addition to the list of football annuals.

Survival of the Fattest

DAVID JENKINS & JUDI HOLLY
RED CARD PUBLISHING, £9.99

Some 111 fanzines representing 83 clubs have contributed to this 'alternative review of the 1994-95 season', when football stumbled into the gutter and, completely addled by booze, cocaine and backhanders, lay there whimpering until the Premier Leaguers launched a clean-up campaign.

It's a good idea for a book, bringing together for the first time the views of those who make up 'fanzine culture'. After all, it's ordinary supporters whose health, wealth and happiness are constantly sacrificed for their team, while the increasing influence of corporate business on football makes it ever more difficult for fans to be heeded by anyone in power.

Jenkins (a Brighton follower) and Holly (Leicester City) noticed four main themes in the specially-written contributions: initial optimism leading to ultimate disappointment; lack of boardroom ambition; digs at bigger clubs; and season-saving wins against local rivals with general gloating over their misfortunes. Indeed, the vein of sleaze which was shown to run right through the game is seldom mentioned; as the editors put it, 'The vast majority of supporters only really care about what is going on at a local level'. A comprehensive introduction to the deeds and misdeeds of 1994-95 would, however, have placed parochial issues into a national context.

London clubs are well-represented: there's a typically splenetic piece from 'One-Nil Down, Two-One Up' about the goings-on at Highbury, while 'Leyton Orientear's contribution discusses the issue of 'celebrity crapness' as the worst team ever to shamble onto the Brisbane Rd turf plunged towards the Third Division. However, it's David Lloyd of 'There's Only One F in Fulham' whose words will strike a chord with most potential readers of this enjoyable, if monochrome, volume: 'Fans of top clubs are very quick to whinge about the crisis at their club when they've lost four games on the trot, or when their star striker has been carted off to a rehabilitation clinic. They should realise that a crisis (at least in footballing terms) is when your club is down among the deadbeats and when its existence is under genuine threat'. Spot on. *Andrew Shields*

The two highlights of the season came, however, after the last ball had been kicked in anger, and both had everything to do with the real battle at hand – the regaining of the freehold of the ground (and with it, many would say, the Club's very existence). The freehold, up for grabs at around £7.5m, is now held by the Royal Bank of Scotland following the collapse of the property market, without which the famous and much-loved Craven Cottage site had been earmarked for demolition to make way for a load of yuppie flats. Fulham 2000, a supporters-led fund-raising organisation crusading to keep Fulham at Craven Cottage, has done wonders (often with seemingly little assistance from the Club), but the battle is far from over. A major boost to the coffers came from an event that had all the hallmarks of Fulham's good old days. A fund-raising dinner was arranged by Fulham 2000 to mark the 20th anniversary of Fulham's lone Wembley appearance. All the players were tracked down and Jimmy Conway, one of three who flew in from the States, happened to remark it was a shame they couldn't have a bit of a kick-about beforehand. Within days that kick-about became a re-run of the final, with Pat Partridge again the man in charge.

It says much that the "gate" for a match between two sides of forty-somethings challenged Fulham's best of the season. The action, naturally, was a shade slower, but the ability was still very much in evidence and only served to remind us of what we've been missing in recent years. Peter Mellor again opened his legs to present the Hammers the opening goal but on this occasion Fulham responded and lifted the replica FA Cup with a last-minute winner. Glorious stuff.

The second victory came in the chambers of Hammersmith & Fulham Council, when the Club's planning application for a redevelopment of Craven Cottage was approved. At the time of writing this still needed rubber-stamping by the Department of the Environment but work could then start on a new 15,000 all-seater stadium. A glimmer of hope at last.

Fans of top clubs are very quick to call phone-ins to whinge about the "crisis" at their club when they've lost four games on the trot, or when their star striker has been carted off to a rehabilitation clinic. They should realise that a crisis (at least in footballing terms) is when your Club is down among the deadbeats and when its existence is under genuine threat. And when you're expected to travel from London to Hartlepool on New Year's Day for a noon kick-off!

New-season Concerns

If only Fulham were as accurate at putting the ball into the net as they are at shooting themselves in the foot. Somehow, some way, the powers-that-be and the PR machinery (or lack of it) at the Cottage have managed to overshadow what has been a promising start.

First the good news – we're on a roll: unbeaten in pre-season games that have covered the length and breadth of the country. And Ian Branfoot (who's General Manager by now) has been active in the transfer market. TOOFIF has steadfastly maintained it wouldn't pass judgement on the manager until he'd had time to wheel and deal, having been a ludicrously late appointment last close-season. Picking up Rory Hamill and Martin Thomas on frees was a good pointer. The manager went on record to say he was chasing a wide player and a goalscoring centre-forward. Since then he's signed Lea Barkus and Mike Conroy. Plus Tony Lange to replace Big Jim. So it seems he's delivered the goods.

Cream rises to the top. Yet at Fulham it's cack-handedness that generally comes to the fore. There'll no doubt be all the right noises to explain Emma Hawkey's departure. Probably something on the financial front. Here was a Fulham supporter

and trained journalist who'd produced a more-than-decent match programme, considering her hands were tied regarding the inclusion of "hard" information. Emma's efforts reaped two first prizes and a third in the annual Programme awards…and then the sack. It seems the tone of the programme wasn't upbeat enough. Well, get things upbeat FFC and even this mag will be singing everyone's praises! Emma's promotion to Press Officer coincided with an upsurge of media coverage – precisely what we'll require as and when the Fulham 2000 campaign goes into overdrive. Stability, it seems, isn't a virtue at FFC.

The departures of Richard Summers and Paul Cass left the Club without a drinks licence and, with weeks to go before any new application could be made, it looked like we'd be left thirsty and the Club out of pocket. Luckily for our palates and the Club's coffers a deal was struck with Cass to be at the Club on the days in question. Phew!

So to the Brentford game that was, then wasn't, then was again. What a fiasco! Apparently it all boiled down to another sacking. The by-now-former employee wasn't wildly enthusiastic about hearing the news so decided to reclaim what was his from beneath the Miller Stand. It could be that in so doing he exposed asbestos that had yet to be cleared from the area. In any case, there it was. And in a catering area, too. The Council promptly deemed it a no-go zone until work was complete.

The Brentford encounter (billed as a bonus match for season ticket holders) was called off. Or at least that was the line given by the Club – even to journalists. In fact it was played behind closed doors that afternoon (during which Terry Hurlock suffered a badly broken leg – TOOFIF has sent El Tel a card, 'cos we're big sweeties really). While many knew about the original match, and were keen to see brand-new signing Mike Conroy in the line-up, precious little effort appeared to be made to advertise the cancellation. The whole affair was a PR shambles, with the ordinary fan left in the lurch and the Club losing gate money. Wonder how many turned up?

Left: Martin Thomas joined Fulham from Leyton Orient

Below: Our below-par display at Northampton goes under the spotlight in the local *Gazette*.

There's only one F in FULHAM
An alternative look at Fulham FC

Only One F in Fulham editor David Lloyd casts a critical eye over Fulham's display at Northampton

"WHAT the hell do you lot get up to in training?" hollered a Fulham fan at Northampton's Sixfields Ground on Saturday. And he had a point. What indeed.

Faced with poor huff-and-puff opponents who made a succession of unforced errors, Fulham contrived to put on a show that would have put the average Sunday League team to shame.

Time and again a pair of players went for the same ball; flick-ons were cleverly directed into the space a team-mate had vacated; simple side-footed passes missed their intended targets by yards.

Above all, communication - the importance of which is drummed into any School XI - seemed to be virtually non-existent.

One of the main qualities of any side put out by Ian Branfoot is a never-say-die attitude. With one or two exceptions this was more of a never-say-anything performance. And it was clear that the home side, mis-kicks and all, wanted to win more than Fulham. They were certainly prepared to put in more graft.

Being beaten is one thing, but getting whipped by a below average side while displaying all the togetherness of Will and Julia Carling is another thing entirely.

In all it was a performance that tested even the most fair-minded of supporters and one that was a heaven-sent opportunity for the more fickle.

"Juppy, why don't you introduce yourself to that winger-by the way, he's that bloke out there you're supposed to be marking," suggested one wag. Another offered: "You're invisible Conroy." Then ten minutes later, after the player had been substituted: "Conroy, you're still invisible!"

Actually, too many were invisible for too long. An exception was the stout-hearted Terry Angus, complete with bizarre ginger rinse. Never one to miss a chance to gee up a team-mate, Big Tel had ample opportunity to speak his mind. Had all 11 played with his outlook we'd have won by a cricket score. Well, we'd have won, anyway... probably!

While not exactly in the Glenn Hoddle mould of ball-playing (in fact, not even in the Glen Thomas mould of ball-playing), you nevertheless get your money's worth from Terry Angus. And had he been able to convert that chance from almost under the bar...

Strange how Michael Mison, a natural scapegoat for some (particularly in the absence of Gary Brazil), was immediately blamed by a couple of half-wits for that miss. Mison, sporting a noticeably un-ginger coiffure, had a poor first half but worked hard to redress the balance in the second half.

He tackled back as effectively as anyone and even fired a 20-yard snap-shot just past the post.

At least he had a go, which escaped most of his detractors. More than anything, Mison needs to be coaxed through a game by his seniors rather than seemingly being left to sink or swim.

The players trooped off the field at the end without a glance at their supporters. Had they looked over they'd have noticed a new synchronised effect: the mass blowing out of cheeks and shaking of heads.

But the final word must surely go to a well-to-do gent sitting two rows back from me: "What a load of useless idiots! Most of them just didn't want to know!" Then he added: "But knowing this lot, they'll put up a good show against Wolves and it'll all be forgotten."

With so much resting on the Fulham 2000 campaign – which has been clearly defined by Board members as the fulcrum to regain the Craven Cottage freehold – it remains a mystery as to why the Club has been so slow to promote it.

A Load of Bull

On the day that Phil Stant scored four goals for Bury and Clive "Evergreen" Walker was hitting three for Woking, Fulham were failing to wear down nine men and find the net even once. It was as frustrating an afternoon as I've spent at the Cottage – and goodness knows there have been numerous other irksome occasions. It would have been much easier to take had the shots been raining in and the Hereford goalkeeper played a blinder. But no – we didn't really look like scoring, did we? Even though we used all 14 members of the squad, the nine men held out, comfortably.

The two sendings-off seemed to offer a heaven-sent opportunity of getting back on the winning trail. But as the game wore on it was painfully evident that we didn't have the necessary guile, ability or pace to break them down.

Ian Branfoot is quite right when he says: "These aren't the times for the faint-hearted." And it's also quite reasonable for him to state that the run of injuries has played its part in the loss of confidence, which was sky-high in August. However, the players that have been brought in as cover haven't been roped in from Fulham High Street, they're professional footballers for goodness sake. Yet we've seen schoolboy howlers from young and old players, which had nothing to do with complicated tactics but everything to do with football basics, such as fundamental ball control, simple passing and communication. ⚽

Cup of Cheer

Two Shrewsbury fans making their exit from the Riverside Stand after the Cup game on Saturday got it right: "How can they be so near the foot of the Third Division? They look a good side to me." "Yeah," came the replay, "we could have a struggle in the replay if they manage to keep 11 men on the park for the whole 90 minutes."

It's been a while since a game at the Cottage has kept us transfixed. Fulham had looked "in the mood" even before Gary Brazil's early dismissal. That decision, one of a string of inconsistencies from the referee, only served to strengthen the players' resolve. It remains a mystery as to why the team have produced such varied performances this season. After weeks of blowing cold, this was a much hotter effort.

In the thick of it until his legs tired, understandably, midway through the second half, was John Marshall. A few more strands of hair may have disappeared for good yet his commitment remained undiminished – and

he nearly marked his return with a goal. It took a lot of bottle to continually go in "where it hurts" after suffering such a bad injury eight months previously doing just that. Welcome back, John.

A replay was secured thanks to a silky, deft touch by Terry Angus seven minutes from time. Okay, the ball flicked him en route to the back of the net; but who cares? It was a magic moment. And it secured a place in the Fourth Round draw.

Tom Finney's aim was a true as ever on Sunday afternoon when he plucked out Fulham (or Shrewsbury!) with his very first dip. Nat Lofthouse, drawing the away teams, brought a smile to the face of Fulham's bank manager by offering the prospect of a sell-out game against Liverpool.

But if the impending Shrewsbury replay is a key fixture then so are the forthcoming League encounters, and none more that Saturday's home game with Scunthorpe. While we were focused on the Cup last week, Scarborough's draw with Hartlepool in the League meant that we slipped to 22nd spot; worrying to put it mildly! And even more so with the rumour that we could be docked points in the wake of the fracas at Gillingham. ⚽

Firing Blanks

It could, and should, have been Liverpool. Instead it was supposed to have been Darlington. As it turned out it was every football fan's dread: a blank Saturday. And as we weren't on the coupon, there wasn't even the heady excitement of waiting for the pools panel verdict.

Does any team flatter to deceive quite like Fulham? Time and again we've had our hopes raised, only to have them dashed. On the basis that "things even themselves out in football", we're due for a bumper payout. That defeat at Shrewsbury summed up so much about Fulham in recent times. It was no surprise, of course. Even before the first game a number of would-be Mystic Megs had forecast that we'd draw the game then get Liverpool or Manchester United at home, only to lose the all-important replay.

At the final whistle at Gay Meadow the frustration level among the considerable travelling Fulham contingent was high. A bumper pay day, so vital for the Club, plus potentially many column inches in the popular press that would have given the Fulham 2000 campaign a timely and generous boost, had been lobbed to one side by a sloppy, indifferent second-half showing.

As we trooped away miserably, it was easy to forget that we'd felt so different at half time. At that stage the team had done us proud. Having resisted a strong opening from the hosts, we'd

There's only One F In Fulham fanzine editor **DAVID LLOYD** reflects on the changes at the Cottage

SO now the truth can be told. The mystery businessman striving to take over Craven Cottage is none other than Del Trotter.

And his grandiose plans ("This time next year we'll all be millionaires!") include extensive use of the site. In will come all-year rugby with union side Peckham Irish playing in winter and Peckham Broncos scrumming down in the summer.

On alternate Sunday afternoons, Yankee football outfit the Fulham Monarchs will touch down and during the week provision is being made for hockey, lacrosse and stock car-racing among other pursuits.

When asked if all this would affect the state of the Fulham pitch, Mr Trotter said: "I shouldn't fink so – the ball's never on it much anyway.

"I can, however, refute all rumours that we're going to introduce high-diving into the Thames from the floodlight pylons, at least until the tide is out!"

It was illuminating to sit behind the dug-out at Cambridge to see and hear the managerial methods of Mickey Adams. With Ian Branfoot away 'sick', Adams geed up the team with an extensive use of a four-letter word. That the team responded was a credit to them and Adams. The word.....? PASS!

It may not have been the most flowing game, but there were more than glimpses that this team can play.

Pass of the night was surely McAree's 40 yard effort to Barber (who promptly lost posession!).

Jimmy Hill is quoted as saying after the draw at Rochdale: "We're not a bottom of the table side." So why are we one off the foot of the entire League? Wouldn't have anything to do with 'style' of play adopted for most this season, would it?

responded well. With Shrewsbury down to ten men we'd netted a flukey goal but, significantly, could have scored a few more.

All the players contributed to a half-hour spell that should have booked that Fourth Round spot. A deserved second goal would have killed off Shrewsbury in all likelihood, but we couldn't manage it and, inexplicably (but not surprising to us diehards, alas), only one team seemed to come out for the second 45 minutes. And it wasn't us.

Somehow this sums up our season. Ask most Fulham fans if this squad is better than others of late and they'd probably agree. However, the League table tells another story. Surely we can return from rock-bottom Torquay with something. Please!? ⚽

We Can Still Make the Play-offs!

Mathematically, the powers-that-be are quite correct, we can still reach the end-of-season jamboree, even now. What they seem to overlook is that we'd need to strike a particularly rich vein of form to do so; in other words, win a few games. In recent weeks we couldn't have won a raffle while holding the only ticket sold. So how is this remarkable change of form supposed to arise? More concerning, surely, has been our steady slide into the bottom two. And of the clutch of sides near the bottom, we're the only one not winning games. Play-offs? We look to have a real battle on our hands to stay in the League!

It's mighty difficult to say what our game plan has been this season – best described maybe as huff-and-puff tactics? – with confidence levels at an all-time low. I wonder if the manager knows his best line-up as, on top of the switches brought about because of numerous injuries and suspensions, the team has been

chopped and changed from game to game. We've used 28 players so far – and it's only early February for heaven's sake! – and many of these have played in more than one position. Hardly surprising that we've struggled to perform as a team at times, is it?

On top of everything else we've had a tendency to spoil our better showings (and rubberstamping the defeats in the poorer efforts) with crass unforced errors. How many times have we seen two players going for the same ball? And how many variations do we have in cocking up promising set pieces? Why do some crosses fly many yards beyond any would-be recipient? And has marking at key moments become an unnecessary trifle?

We looked to have done enough to beat Hartlepool, for instance. It was as spirited a performance as we'd seen in ages. But, having done the hard work and deservedly gone two goals in front, we crumbled in the last 15 minutes and, but for the crossbar, could have lost the match. Against Hartlepool! A team only two places above us; had we won we'd have dragged them back into the mire.

So it remains just one win in 21 League games; not the stuff that Play-off teams – and dreams –are made of. ⚽

Match	Date	Pos
Fulham 1 Barnet 1	18.11.95	17th
Gillingham 1 Fulham 0	25.11.95	19th
Preston NE 1 Fulham 1	09.12.95	20th
Fulham 1 Northampton Town 3	16.12.95	20th
Fulham 4 Cardiff City 2	19.12.95	16th
Lincoln City 4 Fulham 0	26.12.95	20th
Fulham 1 Scarborough 0	13.01.96	18th
Mansfield Town 1 Fulham 0	20.01.96	21st
Fulham 1 Scunthorpe United 3	30.01.96	21st
Torquay United 2 Fulham 1	03.02.96	23rd
Fulham 2 Hartlepool United 1	10.02.96	23rd
Cambridge United 0 Fulham 0	13.02.96	23rd
Rochdale 1 Fulham 1	17.02.96	23rd
Fulham 2 Exeter City 1	24.02.96	22nd
Doncaster Rovers 0 Fulham 2	26.02.96	18th
Fulham 1 Lincoln City 2	02.03.96	23rd
Fulham 2 Darlington 2	05.03.96	21st
Cardiff City 1 Fulham 4	09.03.96	15th
Hartlepool United 1 Fulham 0	12.03.96	16th
Scunthorpe United 3 Fulham 1	23.03.96	20th

FA Cup

Match	Date	Round
Fulham 7 Swansea City 0	11.11.95	Round 1
Fulham 0 Brighton & HA 0	02.12.95	Round 2
Brighton & HA 0 Fulham 0	14.12.95	Round 2 replay aet
		FFC win on pens
Fulham 1 Shrewsbury Town 1	06.01.96	Round 3
Shrewsbury Town 2 Fulham 1	16.01.96	Round 3 replay

Auto Windscreens Shield

Match	Date	Round
Brentford 0 Fulham 1	28.11.95	Round 2
Fulham 1 Bristol Rovers 2	09.01.96	Quarter-final

1st
2nd
3rd
4th
5th
6th
7th
8th
9th
10th
11th
12th
13th
14th
15th
16th
17th
18th
19th
20th
21st
22nd
23rd
24th

✱✱ TOOFIF BORED GAME ✱✱

Promotion! 40

39 Win a year's free listening to Clubline - *back 36 places*	**38**	**37** Free-kick ploy succeeds (at 37th attempt) - *forward 1 place*	**36**	**35** Opposition's players are tightly marked throughout the game - *no chance: miss a go*	**34** Chairman resigns - *sod this for a lark...go down the pub to celebrate!*	**33** Centre-forward seemingly has both feet nailed to ground - *back 2 places*	**32** Manager rates performance as "crap" - *back 4 places and forward 4 places*
24 Manager's name chanted followed by suffix "OUT" - *back 7 places*	**25** Board tell fans what is going on - *check it's not April 1 then go on 3 places*	**26** Manager's name chanted, with suffix "IN" - *no chance, but go on 5 places anyway*	**27** Ground problem solved once and for all - *cheer aloud then go on 9 places*	**28**	**29** Board do something positive on fundraising front - *faint, then forward 7 places*	**30** Youngster makes promising debut in back four - *forward 6 places*	**31**
23 Dealt with curtly when making routine call to Club - *back 2 places*	**22** One player highlighted for stick (as ever) - *back 5 places*	**21**	**20** Concede five goals at home (again) - *back 3 places*	**19** Receive reply to letter sent to Club - *forward 2 places*	**18** Concede five goals at home - *back 1 place*	**17**	**16** Dominate the midfield for majority of match - *forward 5 places*
8 Fail to beat nine men - *back 5 places (to the drawing board, presumably)*	**9**	**10** First choice keeper walks out after refusing to stick (as ever) to be a substitute - *back 3 places*	**11**	**12** Star full back believes his own press & suffers huge ego problem - *back 4 places*	**13** Board acts decisively - *watch out for flying pigs, then go forward 8 places*	**14** Abandon long ball policy - *forward 3 places*	**15** Ex-player comes back to haunt - *back 4 places*
7	**6** String four passes together ...on the deck! - *forward 3 places*	**5** Record an away win - *forward 2 places*	**4** Chucked out of Youth Cup after fielding ineligible player - *back one space*	**3**	**2** Win a Cup match - *forward 5 places*	**1** Matchday programme actually contains some news - *go forward 2 places*	**Kick-Off**

Meeting Micky (Twice!)

So, your favourite football club is in desperate straits (both on and off the pitch), the manager who had strengthened the squad but not halted the dreadful slide is moved "upstairs" and a replacement is appointed from within. And now the new man is keen to talk to TOOFIF. What could possibly go wrong?

Former Club Director David Gardner had heard that Micky Adams, who'd suddenly become Fulham's Player-Manager having replaced his mentor Ian Branfoot, wanted to get a message across to the fans; DG suggested that he did so via a chat with the fanzine. Still not entirely convinced, Adams agreed somewhat tentatively, having been reassured by DG that the mag's editor was, in fact, "reasonable and professional". Ah, that old chestnut! Anyway, armed with a clipboard of questions and a brand, spanking new tape recorder, I headed to the training ground at the agreed time.

Adams was understandably edgy. Was this idiot going to mess around with his words and make him look daft – or was he "professional" after all? In fact, we got on reasonably well and got down to the job in hand. After a little early sparring, both of us seemed happy with how it went. We exchanged smiles and firm handshakes when all was done and dusted; the start of a decent relationship perhaps? All of which made the phone call to the Club the following day a bit awkward. "Yes, of course I'd tested it beforehand. Yes I know it's hardly professional. Yes I realise it makes me look a total pillock…" Turns out my new tape recorder was one of a faulty batch – only our opening exchanges, about 45 seconds-worth, had been recorded and my notes were scant. And here I was pleading for a second chance.

It's fair to say Micky Adams wasn't best pleased. But he was prepared to let me have another go – especially as he was desperate to have the fans on his side. But if that phone call was awkward, it was nothing compared to when I made my sheepish return visit to the training ground. I was met by a torrent of derision and abuse; do you know, even Adams'

Below: Micky Adams took the first steps towards Fulham folklore by becoming the Club's Player-Manager. Almost at once he made it into the pages of TOOFIF – at the second time of asking!

sidekick Alan Cork had the slightest semblance of a smile, as the players, well primed, laid in to yours truly good and proper. Banter, some call it. Although that normally means it's a two-way thing; all I could muster was a meek "Er, has anyone seen the boss?" Cue further swearwords and then the ultimate insult: "You're even worse than Ken Myers, mate!" Might've been Morgs who spat that one out. Anyway, Micky Adams, who was sporting a knowing and slightly unnerving smile, saved me from further embarrassment. "Got your new tape recorder?" he asked pointedly, realising full well I was squirming. I nodded. "Okay, let's do it."

Was the elevation to team manager a surprise?
It was something that was discussed when I first came to the Club, in that I would eventually take over from Ian [Branfoot], and basically the Club were grooming me for the job. I've been involved in coaching at every club I've been at, and I learned a lot at Southampton, particularly with the School of Excellence. But the recent elevation to team manager has come sooner than I thought it would.

Had you had wind of the change of duties?
I was installed as manager for the game at Cambridge, although Ian had selected that particular team.

What's the precise relationship between you and Ian Branfoot?
Very good, I hope! Ian's classed as General Manager now, as you know, and he's involving himself with every aspect of running the Football Club, while my job is to be responsible for all the teams, the coaching, training and picking the sides.

Are things going well so far?
Yes; I've got my own ideas about playing the game, just as Ian had his – I would never dream of criticising him. Even though it's a team I've inherited from Ian, it's my team now. I have no problems in still having Ian around. I've got certain ideas about certain players, of course I have, but I don't want anybody left in any doubt that I am the boss now.

The fans clearly felt that something had to be done, and there was a certain sense of relief that a decision was finally reached. Was this also the case within the Club?
Not really, because I think the players, including yours truly, have a lot of respect for Ian. And that respect doesn't change. But certainly we were 91st in the League and obviously he wasn't happy. He

took a brave decision, but one made for the sake of Fulham Football Club. He knows what type of man I am, and how I think. So I am grateful to Ian for stepping aside and letting me get on with it.

It shouldn't go unremarked that, although we'd gone ever-downwards this season, Ian Branfoot had done much to stop the rot at Fulham and had instilled a fighting spirit at the Club. After what had gone on before we needed a strong individual to take charge. Would you agree?
Certainly. He did much to get us fitter, both mentally and physically, and he brought in some characters. We started this season very well and until we lost our first game at Orient it all looked pretty rosy. But of course football's not like that. We then got into something of a rut, and the more games we went without a win the harder it was to break that particular habit.

How have the players responded to you taking over the reins?
Quite positively really. I've changed a few things in training and a few things player-wise. They're certainly getting rewards for what they're doing, so yes, I've had a positive response.

Having watched a couple of training sessions, there seems to be quite a buzz about the place, and the players seem keen to take in what you're trying to get across…
I'm still a young man (I think!), so I just try to get the squad to do what I enjoy doing myself, with a theme.

Have you suffered any mickey-taking so far, or do they know you're the boss?
Oh, they definitely know who's the boss! You'd have to ask them about the mickey-taking. The biggest difficulty I've had so far is getting them to call me Boss or Gaffer and not Mick or Micky.

On the field, Simon Morgan looks back to his best in the centre of defence, with the by-product that Nick Cusack has more than settled into his new midfield role…
That's right. Simon went back there more by luck than judgement because Kevin Moore got a knock at Cambridge and Simon was the obvious choice to drop back to centre-half. He certainly enjoys it there, but the one thing you always get from Simon Morgan is 100 per cent effort – it doesn't matter where you play him. He was quite happy playing for the last manager in the middle of midfield, but for me his best position is centre-half from where he can organise people.

And Nick Cusack…?
I think it was my assistant Lenny Walker who first suggested that he could maybe play a midfield

role. I had my doubts – but his performances over the last few weeks have been encouraging to say the least.

He's been more than useful on the ball, as well as doing his fair share of grafting…
I like to people to pass and he's shown me he can pass the ball as well as being competitive.

He's played the "on" ball, whether short or long…
Yes, sure, but then I don't want players to pass the ball for the sake of passing it. I want it to be purposeful, to be played progressively forwards and Nick does that. I think why he can pass is that, having been a target man, he appreciates what kind of service is expected. I always have the luxury, too, of pushing him forward when needed.

Another midfielder, Rod McAree, looks a real find…?
Yes, we've been lucky with him, I suppose. He's still not the finished article. When he first came here he was well short of the required fitness, but I managed to put that right [gives knowing chuckle]. But then fitness has never been a problem with any of my teams, but sure the boy can play – you don't spend three or four years at Liverpool and not learn anything.

Scott and Conroy look to be linking well – and they grabbed three of the four goals at Cardiff on Saturday…
Micky Conroy's had his critics, but I'm certainly not one of them. I've told my lads to play to their strengths, and I think Micky is a good target man and he gets himself into good positions to score goals – he's unfortunate in that he's missed some, but I can live with that. As long as we're creating chances for him he'll put them away nine times out of ten.

Maybe his languid style, rather than being a "busy-busy" sort of player, plays into the hands of his critics?
I wouldn't say he was languid. I asked Micky to do a job for me and since I've been in charge he's tried to carry it out to the full. And as I've said before, I'll stick by my players as long as they're giving me what I asked for. The goals are a bonus.

At the other end of the field Tony Lange has done pretty well. Is he still on the transfer list?
Yes, but the previous manager sorted all that out. Tony's got a problem, and it's been well documented, that he lives in the West Midlands and it's not always possible, in fact it's not all that sensible, to bring him down for all the training sessions. So what I've said to him is, when you do

Fulham 2 Leyton Orient 1 26.03.96 18th	1st 2nd 3rd 4th 5th 6th 7th
Fulham 4 Plymouth Argyle 0 30.03.96 17th	
Bury 3 Fulham 0 02.04.96 17th	8th
Hereford United 1 Fulham 0 06.04.96 18th	9th 10th 11th
Fulham 2 Chester City 0 08.04.96 17th	12th 13th
Colchester United 2 Fulham 2 13.04.96 16th	14th 15th **16th**
Fulham 1 Wigan Athletic 0 20.04.96 16th	17th **18th**
Fulham 0 Gillingham 0 27.04.96 16th	19th 20th 21st
Barnet 3 Fulham 0 04.05.96 17th	22nd 23rd 24th

come in, you work hard – and he's done that. And anyway, I think he's one of the best goalkeepers in the League and I'm not just saying that because I want to keep him, but I understand his situation. But yeah, I do believe him to be one of the best.

He had a hard act to follow…?

That's right. Jimmy Stannard's a legend here, and rightly so. He gave the Club tremendous service, but Jim's gone and Tony's here.

What about those people who may yet come here – have you any plans to dip into the transfer market?

I've a few plans, yes…

Is there any cash available?

I've not asked for any yet! But I'm sure if the right person became available and is in our price bracket and would fit into our wage structure I'm sure the Board would, as they did with Ian, back the manager's judgement. I hope so, anyway.

You seem prepared to give the youngsters a go; after all you've worked with them for some time now. Will any of them figure between now and the end of the season?

Oh yes, I've had 18 months or so with them – I've been their coach, their "moulder", and at times even their mother and father, so yes, I know what they can do. And anyway I'm a great believer in youth. As far as I'm concerned if you're good enough you'll get a chance at this Club. As you've seen so far, I'm not afraid of putting the youngsters in if I think they can help us. Brooker, Williams and others have done well… The whole squad are responding to what I'm trying to preach at the Club.

What about Micky Adams – when are you going to pull on a Fulham shirt again?

I'm back running now, so it's just a case of building up my running work as well as my rehabilitation work. But I have to say that I've suffered in being the Club Coach.

Had I been "just" a player I may well have been nearer to playing a game by now, but I'm just not finding the time to do my own fitness work.

Would you find a place in the side?

Hey, listen, if the team's doing as well as I think it ought to be then I don't really want to play – I'd rather see them win.

And how do you stand contract-wise?

My contract runs out in the summer.

What about the other players' contracts?

There are about 13 or 14 contracts up, but until I'm absolutely certain what division we'll be in next season I can't really hold discussions with them.

You've been in the hotseat for a few weeks now, what are the immediate goals?

To get enough points, and to get them quickly, to ensure we can't go down. That's every manager's target at the beginning of every season. Once those points are in the bag you take whatever comes as a bonus. I think we're nearing that point now.

A by-product of your playing style is entertainment – we've seen bags of goalmouth action for example. How important is it to entertain the punters?

Yes, my philosophy is quite simple, pass the ball around (preferably to a colleague, not the opposition!), play forward, don't be negative with any sort of pass and get crosses and shots in. If that's entertaining, then great. And if we win then it's even better. But it goes without saying that I'd rather be less entertaining and win 1-0 regularly rather than losing a succession of games 4-3. But yes, I want us to entertain.

How can the supporters help?

The supporters have been different class to me so far. They can see what I'm trying to do. We're getting results, which helps, but they've been different class for sure. I need them to be patient, but then every manager who's been at this Football Club has said the same thing: "Please be patient, I'm looking for time" – I've got three months until the end of the season and if they want me to stay then I'll stay. But with that the fans must remember that it's not always going to go for us because I'm asking the boys to do different things and if I'm asking my players to pass the ball around, particularly towards the end of the season when the pitches are starting to deteriorate, it's important that the fans don't get on their backs and to encourage them just a little bit more than maybe they would have done in the past.

You've spoken pretty positively up to now. Has anything upset you in your short time in charge?

There's Only One F In Fulham editor **DAVID LLOYD** looks back at a poor season at the Cottage

SO it's farewell – and good riddance! – to yet another record-breaking season down by the Thames. For the third successive term (and the fifth time in seven seasons) Fulham recorded their worst ever final league placing.

And en route they slumped to their worst ever mid-term position – one off the foot off the basement division.

One measly win in 27 League games meant the unthinkable drop into the Vauxhall Conference became a real possibility, only 21 years after an FA Cup Final appearance.

The vultures came out in force for the visit of Hartlepool in February and the club received ample doom 'n' gloom exposure leading up to and immediately after what was to prove Ian Branfoot's last game in charge (officially at least).

And yet it was all so different back in August. Fulham stormed into the new season, seemingly making light of losing Terry Hurlock with a career-ending double fracture. The 'buzz' after the 4-2 win over Mansfield was almost tangible.

So many chances had been created that the 'goals for' tally which for a couple of weeks was the best in the country, could have been more than doubled.

By November, however, things wreaked of old boots. Injuries contributed, not least that of Mickey Adams.

But the persistence in a playing 'style' so unsuitable to the squad was surely the telling factor.

Several 'performances' plumbed new depths, including both encounters with Northampton. And the absence of guile or pace was pitifully highlighted in failing to beat nine-man Hereford at home.

Curiously, in amongst these showings came another record: the 7-0 destruction of Swansea in the FA Cup.

To Branfoot's credit he promptly offered Paul Brooker a longer contract.

Mickey Adams turned things around somewhat. His insistence that the team play the ball to feet obviously pleased the Fulham cognoscenti. Some decent results followed and hopefully the appalling effort against Cambridge – as bad as anything served up this season – was just a blip.

Much now will depend on Adams' close season activity. All Fulham supporters are hoping and praying that he'll be the one to get the club moving upwards at long last. But then haven't we long-suffering fans had similar hopes for years.

Well, Alan Mullery's had a pop at me on the telly, saying I don't care about this Football Club. He didn't mention me by name but he said that the management of this Football Club don't care about it. I can tell him that people who know me, and know how I work, know that I do care – passionately – about this place. I want to succeed. Just because I haven't played 200-300 games for this Club, does that mean I don't care for the place? I've worked really hard in the 18 months or so that I've been here to set standards, and I think that this Club will be better for me being in charge. So if he's saying that I don't care, he couldn't be more wrong. As far as I'm concerned Alan Mullery is part of Fulham's past; I'm Fulham's future.

So would you say that the past, and Fulham's revered tradition, has been something of a millstone…?

History and tradition – no matter how great – don't win you football matches. If you look around the graveyards of the world, to paraphrase the Leeds manager Howard Wilkinson (and I use him a lot!), you'll see a wealth of history and tradition but not a whole lot of life. But I'm telling you, there's plenty of life at Fulham. ⚽

Going Topless to Barnet

Manchester United did it. Even poxy Gillingham did it. So why not Fulham? Okay, we had nothing to celebrate save recording our worst-ever League position and ingloriously being hailed as London's worst team. But what the hell! So an open-top bus was booked for the season's final awayday. To Barnet of all places.

Fun and frolics were clearly high on the agenda. The bars of The Chancellor's Pub in Hammersmith were a sight – they were crammed full of face-painted, regalia-bedecked, balloon-blowing, alcohol-consuming Fulham fans. At 9.30am!

Top of the agenda, though, was the bus. However, cheers were in short supply when it turned up. As red Routemasters go it was splendid. But some clown had despatched one that was not so much deficient as complete – it had a roof, or, as one would-be traveller hollered, "Oi, it's got a bloody lid!" Another comment came from an off-duty bus driver and Fulham fan going with his wife and two children to the game (talk about a busman's holiday!)" "I'm not paying 24 quid to go to north London on that!" Yes, dear old London Transport had screwed us up good and proper.

Our departure time of 10.30 was already scuppered. And, despite a host of phone calls, we were getting nowhere until we insisted on a full reimbursement. As if by magic, we told that an open topper would pick us up at 12.15. The delay meant we'd have to hare northwards. The planned route, via Craven Cottage for a ceremonial drive past, via anti-FFC campaigner Roz Denny's abode for a tasteful, choreographed "moon" from the top deck, via several local markets for a bit of banter with the stallholders and via certain predetermined roads for salutes to family and friends, had to be ditched. Thanks LT!

The well-oiled choir was in great voice as we inched along Fulham Palace Road. Early favourites were "We're on our way to Barnet" (inspirational!) and "We love you Fulham" (a real tear-jerker), but these were soon eclipsed by "We're not very good" (ouch! But truth hurts!). In due course there was even a rollicking rendition of "There's Only One F in Fulham" (how sweet!).

As we approached Barnet someone remarked that he fully expected that Fulham would spoil his day by not coming to the party. How true. We had to endure a dreadful showing in which only Morgan, Herrera, Cusack and Brooker looked in any way bothered about putting in some effort for the cause. On the return trip (with the party understandably subdued after the 3-0 defeat) someone else opined: "If this is how Fulham celebrate when they've nothing to celebrate what will it be like if the Club gets its finger out and actually wins something?" How indeed. ⚽

There's Only One F in Fulham fanzine editor DAVID LlOYD salutes new Fulham boss Mickey Adams

MICKEY Adams is clearly doing things his own way – including giving an interview with the fanzine (out very soon, folks).

He was keen to get his views to the fans on how he feels the game ought to be played and his team are doing very nicely.

Having almost immediately sorted out one of Fulham's unwanted records, that of not winning an away game this season, he promptly lost a record, that of being at, just 34, the League's youngest manager – Jan Molby took the mantle only to be superseded by Adrian Heath.

At Ninian Park on Saturday Fulham's new management team of Adams and Alan Cork were considerably 'greener' than counterparts Phil Neal and Kenny Hibbitt. The 4-1 scoreline, however, said as much about the positive vibes and attention to detail from the away team's dug-out as it did about the players' efforts.

As the game progressed Neal and Hibbitt got increasingly ratty with the referee, the linesman and, seemingly, life in general. Adams, meanwhile, was forever cajoling his side and was quick to bark if he felt one of his players wasn't doing his job.

And yet when praise was due, it was just as fulsome.

Adams was the first in the ground to spot the opportunity of a quickly taken free-kick for the first goal. 'Take it, Macca,' he hollered four times.

As the moaning and groaning increased on the Cardiff bench so Fulham took charge on the field. Two more goals from Conroy prompted the travelling fans to sing 'Are you Swansea in disguise?'

Fulham are back – doing it the Adams way!

Record-breaking Woes

So it's farewell and bloody good riddance to yet another record-breaking season down by the Thames. For the third successive term, and the fifth time in seven seasons, Fulham recorded their worst-ever final League placing. And en route they slumped to their worst-ever position – one off the foot of the basement division. No wonder it's said that "There's only one F in Fulham". Come to that, there's only one f in "frustration" too, and we know that particular emotion only too well!

A grotesque sequence of 27 League games produced just one measly win and meant that the unthinkable drop into the Vauxhall Conference became a real possibility, only 21 years on from an FA Cup Final appearance. Following years of despair and decay, the rot had well and truly set in; this was surely the nadir (it couldn't possibly get any worse, could it?). No one knew where the next win was coming from. Fortunately Torquay had been having an even worse time of it and were adrift at the foot of the table. Plus, there was the added bonus that the ground of Conference leaders Stevenage Borough was deemed unfit for League status.

Nevertheless, after losing to Torquay, and with the Club languishing just above the trap-door, the vultures came out in force for the visit of Hartlepool in February. Fulham received ample doom 'n' gloom exposure leading up to and immediately after what was to prove Ian Branfoot's last game in charge. Officially, that is.

Branfoot had persevered with a long ball "style" to very little effect. The huff 'n' puff tactics were simply not conducive to the squad at his disposal. Mike Conroy, a £75,000-buy from Preston, and the latest in a long line of would-be 20-goal-a-season strikers, never looked like reaching that target. Clearly at his best looking for that vital last touch in and around the six-yard box, Conroy was instead asked to chase and harry. His lack of pace showed up alarmingly and you have to ask why he was brought in to play in a manner so alien to his strengths.

The squad members were fitter and, by and large, more determined than under previous regimes. But that's not much good if you don't have the ball. Or when a string of schoolboy errors ensured a steady increase in the "goals against" column.

Yet it was all so different back in August. On the back of a camaraderie-engendering Scottish tour, on which they were unbeaten, Fulham stormed into the new season, seemingly making light of losing midfield general and fervid collector of yellow cards Terry Hurlock to a career-ending double-fracture in a behind-closed-doors pre-season encounter with Brentford. The buzz after the 4-2 win over Mansfield on the opening day was almost tangible. So many chances had been created that the "goals for" tally, which for a couple of weeks was actually the best in the country, could have been more than doubled. It really was a much-needed breath of fresh air.

By November, however, things reeked of old boots. Injuries contributed, not least that to Micky Adams. But the persistence in sticking to a playing "style" so unsuitable to the squad was surely the telling factor. No sooner was the ball pumped upfield than it was back and our rearguard was again on the rack.

Several performances plumbed new depths, including both encounters with Northampton and a cowardly show at Lincoln at an ice-bound Sincil Bank (we lost 0-4). The absence of guile or pace was pitifully highlighted when nine-man Hereford held out with considerable ease for a draw at Craven Cottage.

Curiously, amid those showings came another record: the 7-0 destruction of Swansea – the best-ever FA Cup result by a team against another from a higher division. Swansea were pretty poor, it's true, but Fulham played it on the deck and created chance after chance. The much-maligned Conroy grabbed a hat-trick. To Branfoot's credit he promptly offered young winger Paul Brooker, the star of that show, a longer contract.

After the aforementioned Hartlepool game, which Fulham only drew after being 2-0 up going into the closing stages, Ian Branfoot marched into the press room and showed the larger than usual throng a clutch of "We hope you die soon" leaflets. He quite wrongly went on to blame a

Opposite page top: Ian Branfoot's long-ball game never paid off and, after being targeted again by Southampton fans, he "moved upstairs" and let Micky Adams take the reins.

Opposite page bottom: Young winger Paul Brooker – star of the show against Swansea in the FA Cup.

Below: Out with the old, in with the new – Micky Adams lines up with his squad hoping for a positive 1996-97 campaign.

voluble, mischievous, yet hugely supportive group of Fulham fans who were accordingly slated in the national press.

The fanzine was quick to lambast the leaflet's over-the-top sentiments – no one deserves such treatment – but also damned Branfoot's wild allegations. However, this was clearly a watershed. (The finger of blame for the leaflets was subsequently directed at Southampton fans by the powers-that-be at Fulham.)

Things were certainly getting to the manager. He was mysteriously "sick" for the midweek game at Cambridge (0-0, in which Conroy missed a late sitter) and was curiously "scouting for a striker in the north-east" the following Saturday while the team gained a 1-1 draw at Rochdale. Player/coach Micky Adams, who'd followed Branfoot from The Dell, took over the reins in his absence and was subsequently appointed to the hot seat the following week.

Adams turned things around somewhat. His insistence that the team play the ball to feet obviously pleased the Fulham cognoscenti. Hot on the heels of a bright win over Exeter, Fulham recorded their first away success of the season, at Doncaster. Some decent results followed, particularly the 4-0 trouncing of Plymouth, who eventually went up via the Play-offs. Hopefully the appalling effort against Cambridge – as bad as anything served up this season – was but a blip.

Much will depend on the new manager's close-season activity. He's been at pains to express that he wants to be judged on a squad of his own choosing – a squad that will do things his way. A summer clear-out is on the cards, but, with very little money to play with, it's unlikely that we'll get in any star names – although I've

heard that Tino Asprilla's grandmother is on the wanted list. But then we couldn't afford the airfare, let alone the signing-on fee!

All Fulham supporters are hoping and praying that Micky Adams will be the one to get the Club moving upwards at long, long last. And I'm prepared to stick my neck out and suggest that with a fair rub of the green Fulham could be among the front-runners in 1996-97. It won't be for the lack of trying on Adams' part, that's for sure.

The other good news will hopefully concern the ground. This particular saga has dragged on interminably, the latest chapter being a public inquiry into Fulham's proposed redevelopment of the Craven Cottage site, which they claim would raise the capital to buy back the freehold of the ground – currently held by the Royal Bank of Scotland after property developers Cabra Estates went into liquidation.

The inquiry was called after a small band of local residents, keen to see the Club go under and thereby increase the values of their properties, made enough noise to influence Matthew Carrington, MP for Fulham. Previously the green light had been given by the local Labour-led Council who have given steadfast support to Fulham (and Chelsea and QPR, the other clubs in the borough) throughout the struggle. Carrington, a Tory, begged to differ.

The current viewpoint is that the purchase price of the freehold is much nearer half the £7.5m previously demanded by the Royal Bank. It hasn't helped that the fund-raising efforts of Fulham 2000 have been baulked by all manner of in-house wranglings. The fans, meanwhile, have had to make do with just occasional strands of information from the Club rather than meaty bulletins.

Certainly no Fulham fan relishes the prospect of flats on two sides of the picturesque Craven Cottage site, but we're prepared to accept them as a necessary evil if it's the only way of ensuring that Fulham stay at the Cottage. October '96 marks Fulham's 100th year at the site: a successful outcome to this drawn-out saga would be the ultimate centenary present. Promotion would, as they say, be the icing on the cake.

Fulham 1 Hereford United 0
17.08.96   7th

Hartlepool United 2 Fulham 1
24.08.96   12th

Rochdale 1 Fulham 2
27.08.96   5th

Fulham 1 Carlisle United 0
31.08.96   2nd

Fulham 3 Colchester United 1
07.09.96   2nd

Exeter City 0 Fulham 1
10.09.96   1st

Swansea City 1 Fulham 2
14.09.96   1st

Fulham 1 Mansfield Town 2
21.09.96   1st

Darlington 0 Fulham 2
28.09.96   1st

Fulham 1 Torquay United 2
01.10.96   2nd

Northampton Town 0 Fulham 1
05.10.96   2nd

League Cup

Southend United 0 Fulham 2
20.08.96   Round 1 1st leg

Fulham 1 Southend United 2
03.09.96   Round 1 2nd leg

Fulham 1 Ipswich Town 1
17.09.96   Round 2 1st leg

Ipswich Town 4 Fulham 2
24.09.96   Round 2 2nd leg

Hopeful Signs

Micky Adams may not be a candidate for canonisation just yet, but he's on the right track. Forget the fact that we're among the pacesetters for a moment. The important thing is that he's developing a team with the right blend of attitude and attributes. It might not always be pretty – some of the performances have been more dogged than Lassie or Fred Bassett – but, given the opportunity, they can all play a bit as well.

Adams (and sidekick Alan Cork) has instilled a good team spirit – you can sense it's an all-for-one approach; his main trouble may be keeping the squad happy. There's a real competition for places, except at right-back, and it's clear that some players have been unhappy at being dropped or substituted. Great for that competitive edge, of course, but it all calls for careful man-management.

Those newcomers who've made the team thus far have proved good buys, with Danny Cullip looking the best bargain of the lot. Despite no League experience prior to joining Fulham, he's already slotted in admirably at the back, with hardly a blemish. Mark Walton has shared the goalkeeping responsibilities with Tony Lange and made some terrific saves. Darren Freeman has got stronger and stronger – on another day he would have won the man-of-the-match plaudits against Northampton for his all-round efforts and twinkle-toed skills, only for ex-Cobbler Terry Angus to put on a towering show. It was Freeman who hit the bar before that man Conroy reacted sharply to nod home the winner. Glenn Cockerill has proved influential in midfield despite missing the occasional training session to draw his pension. Cockerill's purposeful passing changed the course of the game at Swansea. When Glenn got injured going in where it hurts as ever, Richard Carpenter's arrival was timely. Chippy's debut at Darlington was a real eye-opener. ⚽

Super-Mick

The most remarkable transformation down Craven Cottage way this season has been the renaissance of Mike Conroy, now known to his legions of adoring fans as "Super-Micky". Our leading scorer turned out to be not just a personable Scot but also an incredibly modest footballer. He didn't want to highlight his own goalscoring exploits but wanted to focus instead on the team's all-round contribution.

You seem to be playing with a smile on your face again…
Aye, the one thing I've learned is that if you can enjoy your work then it helps. And as you can

see here at the training ground, all the lads are buzzing and we're all walking about with smiles on our faces. If we keep winning then the smiles will get bigger and broader.

We've clocked up a fair few victories already…?
But we let a lot of people down against Mansfield, and we let ourselves down. So we knew we had to lift ourselves and put that right against Darlington. We tore into them and came away with three richly deserved points…

…Which you may not have achieved in previous times…?
Last year we went there and got a one-each draw, but it seems that last year's draws are being converted to victories.

What are your specific strengths?
My strengths [slightly embarrassed chuckle]? If you look at my goalscoring record you'll see that I've hit the net on average once in three games… but I don't really like talking about my game, you'd be much better asking the manager! I just like to try to do the best for the team and if I score then that's a bonus.

Would you say the team is playing to your strengths this season?
Oh yes, definitely. We're creating chances now. If I miss them then people can have a pop at me, but, as they say, if you're not there to miss them you'll not be there to score them!

Second to bottom last season to, as we stand, top of the table. That's one helluva transformation?
The manager has brought in his own ideas and these have clearly been beneficial to the team;

> *"We're creating chances now. If I miss them then people can have a pop at me, but, as they say, if you're not there to miss them you'll not be there to score them!"*

Right: Micky Adams has overseen a decent start to the season – it makes a welcome change to be among the division's pacesetters.

Opposite page bottom: Micky Conroy, among the goals and enjoying the team's change in fortunes.

the results don't lie. We've got a great team spirit and we showed that grit and determination at Darlington. We've got plenty of ball players and those with pace to create problems, and it all seems to be coming together and paying dividends at the minute.

The team also seems to have the ability to mix and match the tactics to suit the opposition and occasion – even being able to switch things around during a game?

Aye, I've got to say that the formation the gaffer's playing just now is tremendous. He's told us what he wants and we've gone for it and we all believe in it. We've caught a few teams by surprise. He's also added Glenn Cockerill's experience to the squad – he's played at the top level don't forget. Only a few weeks ago Glenn changed the game at Swansea – his passing made a world of difference when he came on as a sub. And we have the pace of Darren Freeman and Rob Scott, so yes, we can chop and change.

You've already had more chances this season that in the whole of the last campaign. Might you be the 20-goals-a-season striker we've been seeking for years?

Every goal is a bonus for me. I don't set myself targets but the more you get the better for all concerned. I'll be doing my utmost to score as many as possible this season and the important thing is that we're creating those chances. Last year I felt we weren't getting the ball into the box enough. And, to be fair, I don't take long to tell the boys if it isn't being delivered, and neither does the manager. It's how you score goals, after all.

You look fitter and sharper…

I had a fantastic seven-week break in Melbourne

in the close season. My wife couldn't believe it because I usually put in a 7k run every morning before she'd even got out of bed. But I knew our pre-season would be hard but I wanted to come back in the best shape for Fulham. That's all paying dividends now.

What's it like to have the crowd behind you – it's been a dramatic turnaround?

I found last season quite traumatic to be truthful. It was the first time I'd had the crowd on my back. At both Preston and Burnley it was quite the opposite. But as I've said before, people are fully entitled to their opinions. I can only go out and do my best.

Would you say it was our adopted style that didn't suit you?

Well… [long pause] …possibly! Our current style certainly suits me a lot better.

Having the crowd behind you must do wonders for the confidence levels?

Oh, without a doubt. And we're all benefiting from the way we're playing and having the crowd behind us.

Micky Adams has got the team to "gel". The players are in it together – what's it like to be a part of such a set up?

It's great. Before each match the senior lads, especially, talk about the game – and we do get in among the younger lads and tell them we have to go for it. We're sitting top of the League and the longer we can stay there then the bigger the gap gets between the top three and the rest of the pack. So it's a question of getting that mental toughness and making sure that everyone is on their toes before each game. That's what pulled us through on Saturday [against Darlington] for sure.

It's clear there are quite a few "captains" out on the park these days…?

There's got to be. If someone's not doing it, it's up to someone else to tell them so he can take it in the right manner. You can shout and bollock each other now and everyone takes it in the proper way, whereas beforehand one or two might have taken umbrage.

It's early days yet, but do the boys think they can stay among the pacesetters?

Definitely, definitely. It's a matter of being mentally tough and physically strong, and we've proved we're okay on those scores so far this season. Nobody's really outbattled us up to now, and it's a case of getting your mind right and believing we can do it. Certainly this squad is good enough to maintain this good run. 🔊

Fulham 3 Doncaster Rovers 1	
12.10.96	1st
Fulham 3 Cambridge United 0	
15.10.96	1st
Hull City 0 Fulham 3	
19.10.96	1st
Brighton & HA 0 Fulham 0	
26.10.96	1st
Fulham 2 Scunthorpe United 1	
29.10.96	1st
Fulham 1 Lincoln City 2	
02.11.96	1st
Cardiff City 1 Fulham 2	
09.11.96	1st
Fulham 2 Barnet 0	
19.11.96	1st
Wigan Athletic 1 Fulham 1	
23.11.96	1st
Fulham 2 Brighton & HA 0	
30.11.96	1st
Chester City 1 Fulham 1	
03.12.96	1st
FA Cup	
Plymouth Argyle 5 Fulham 0	
16.11.96	Round 1

1st
2nd
3rd
4th
5th
6th
7th
8th
9th
10th
11th
12th
13th
14th
15th
16th
17th
18th
19th
20th
21st
22nd
23rd
24th

Thanks Micky!

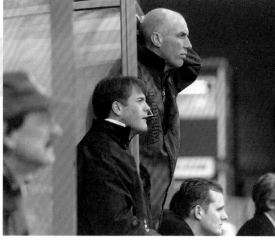

Christmas has arrived early for us Fulham fans. We're top of the table and our squad of players are quite capable of sustaining this terrific run given the rub of the green. At the risk of going into brown-nosed overdrive, Micky Adams deserves our thanks whatever the future holds. It'll be very easy, come May and with the Championship secured, to join all and sundry in lavishing praise on the manager (and number two Alan Cork). I prefer to offer my thanks here and now.

Adams has overseen a quite remarkable turnaround. No one needs reminding that only Torquay kept us off bottom spot in the division last February. On his appointment the new gaffer took us to the giddy heights of 17th by the season's end. During the close season Adams strengthened the squad, and you have to admire his judgement. With no money for superstars he had to opt for the bargain basement bracket: journeymen, freebies and veterans. They've all gelled admirably. Team spirit is high, and the collective will to win and the support for each other is almost tangible.

Without belittling Adams' achievement in the slightest, "all" he has done is what the average Fulham punter has been crying out for. He's taken a grip of the place, earned the respect of the players and done his very best with the squad and resources at his disposal. Had we been sitting in mid-table at this juncture, yet firing on all available cylinders, his efforts would have been just as special. But he's done brilliantly in the transfer market and it's no surprise – and particularly so at this level – that a truly concerted approach has been rewarded by putting so many points on the board.

Whenever we've suffered a rare hiccup we've bounced back, and in some style –

Top right: Micky Adams and Alan Cork – making the most of the players at their disposal

Below: There's been so much of an upswing that even Fulham captain Simon Morgan has been seen sporting a semblance of smile. Morgs says he's targeting promotion: "Great, isn't it?"

Bottom: The Two Stewards (by Goffe and O'Farrell) are bowled over by the transformation at FFC.

a sure sign of determination and resolve all round. There's still an awfully long way to go but Micky Adams' record to date suggests that he's growing into the manager's role rather well, despite his inexperience and young age. He's a winner whose focused approach, allied to good old-fashioned hard graft, has made it that much easier for us fans to go into work on Monday mornings. It's fun to be a Fulham fan again. ⚽

Captain of Industry

With the team still on course for that much-longed-for promotion, despite a recent wobble, the time was ripe for a trip to the training ground and a chat with our captain, Simon Morgan.

What does it feel like to be a part of a successful Fulham team after so many troublesome years?
Different! No, it's great, isn't it! Here we are in early March 11 points clear of the fourth-placed team – can't beat it, can you? The whole atmosphere has improved dramatically: we've got a great set of lads who mix together really well. We've had our bad times this year – in fact we've been bloody awful on occasions – but we've bounced back. That's as much to do with the team spirit as anything else – of the team, of the squad, of the whole Club. We gelled from the off, despite having a motley collection of lads. We've got some old sweats, some grumpy old men (I fall into that category as any of the others will tell you), some young lads, some free transfers with a lot to prove, but we all hit it off right away.

You were one of the first to refer to the feelgood factor back in August. Just how much difference does it make when all the fans are onside?
It's unbelievable. Some of it came from the end of last season with Micky taking over and the crowd responded. Then came the news about the ground, then we got some new players in. The supporters got to thinking there was something happening around these parts – they turned up for the Hereford game and they were all for us. We were crap that day too! But we got that important 1-0 win and went on to develop a system that works for us. We've had off days but have reacted to those well; in the past those off days ended with us being slaughtered. This time around we've toughed it out.

What do you make of the frenetic away support?
Great isn't it! You go to places like Scarborough and see the people who've taken the time, trouble and expense of going there and getting behind the team; it's fabulous. Most of the time we've rewarded the away fans by putting on some half-decent performances. I think they can see what we're trying to do. We know we're not necessarily the greatest football team and we don't always play the best stuff, but they've been behind us all the way.

What's been the high point of your time at FFC?
This season. The whole year, because it's been so enjoyable. Even during the low points our spirit has seen us through – we've had some great coach journeys home.

What about your low points?
That spell under Don Mackay. Not the relegation year – that was waiting to happen – but the year we should have gone up. That would have been his first full season and we were in the Second Division. We started well enough then had a bit of a wobble and he had the chance to bring in some players – and he brought in Mark Cooper! We finished ninth or tenth but given the players we had (who were in their prime) we should have gone up.

So what was the problem?
Him! He wouldn't say a word when it mattered. After a game he'd be quoted as saying, "I've told the lads this or that", but the truth is he'd said nothing to us at all. Ray Lew would be ranting and raving, but he'd just stand there. He wouldn't communicate with the players but did everything through the fans and the press. The fans loved him, naturally, and the press thought the world of him but he didn't have a clue. I regret those times – we should have improved ourselves; instead it all went downhill.

By that yardstick Micky Adams should take the credit for this season?
Without a doubt! Hey, when you're top of the division the manager's got to take the credit. The players have done their part too, but it's down to Micky that we're right behind him.

You won England representative honours while at Leicester. What was that like, and does it seem a long time ago now?
Oh yes, I'm over 30 now you know! I was reading The Traveller's article in the last fanzine – dear old Alex – and he listed an England Under-21 game in Östersund, Sweden, way up north. That was my England debut! It was in the middle of nowhere with barely 20 people watching. And one of them was The Traveller! He wrote that the match was notable for the first sighting of Anders Limpar. Well, guess who was marking him? And guess who was marking him when he scored?!

Do you ever regret joining Fulham?
No. There's no way I could in the situation I was in. I hadn't played for Leicester for 10 months, I had a bad knee and I was surprised Fulham were prepared to take a chance on me. Thankfully, they didn't do a proper medical. But I've played over 300 games since then.

You're regarded as someone who gives his all on the pitch. Has that helped you form a good rapport with Fulham fans?
I do have a decent rapport with the fans, but I've been here a while now and I get told by fans what they think of me – and I tell them what I think of them too!

What's it like to play alongside someone who doesn't appear to be giving 100 per cent?
Whoever do you mean?

Not this season, but in the past?
Well there's one obvious candidate: Mark Cooper. He was never really interested in the Club. But if you're generalising you must remember that different players have various ways of approaching a game. What does "100 percenter" mean anyway? Every player who's pulled on that Fulham shirt this season has given his all. As for me, if I'm having a bad time of it, my way of snapping out of it is to fly around to try to make up for it in some other way. I got out of jail last Saturday because I scored the goal that got us a point, having given away the goal that could have cost us the game.

What's your favourite position?
Everyone's got their opinion on that one, I'm sure! This is another subject that pissed me off about Don Mackay. He would move me about depending on the form or fitness of other players whereas, while I was willing to help out, I thought if I was playing well in one position then I should stay there. I have a good understanding with Mick Adams I'm glad to say. We've got a smallish squad and I know there'll be times when I've got to switch position.

Is it important that Fulham go up this season?
Having got this far, it's vital; vital for player morale and for supporter morale. And even for the future of the Club, you can put it that strongly. ⚽

Fulham 1 Leyton Orient 1	
14.12.96	1st
Scarborough 0 Fulham 2	
21.12.96	1st
Fulham 1 Exeter City 1	
26.12.96	1st
Fulham 6 Darlington 0	
11.01.97	1st
Colchester United 2 Fulham 1	
14.01.97	1st
Torquay United 3 Fulham 1	
18.01.97	1st
Scunthorpe United 1 Fulham 4	
25.01.97	1st
Fulham 1 Cardiff City 4	
31.01.97	1st
Lincoln City 2 Fulham 0	
08.02.97	2nd
Fulham 2 Swansea City 1	
11.02.97	1st
Fulham 1 Wigan Athletic 1	
15.02.97	1st
Barnet 2 Fulham 2	
22.02.97	2nd
Fulham 1 Chester City 1	
01.03.97	3rd
Fulham 4 Scarborough 0	
08.03.97	2nd
Leyton Orient 0 Fulham 2	
16.03.97	3rd
Fulham 1 Hartlepool United 0	
22.03.97	3rd
Hereford United 0 Fulham 0	
29.03.97	3rd
Fulham 1 Rochdale 1	
31.03.97	3rd
Carlisle United 1 Fulham 2	
05.04.97	1st
Mansfield Town 0 Fulham 0	
08.04.97	2nd
Auto Windscreens Shield	
Brighton & HA 3 Fulham 2	
17.12.96	Round 1

1st
2nd
3rd
4th
5th
6th
7th
8th
9th
10th
11th
12th
13th
14th
15th
16th
17th
18th
19th
20th
21st
22nd
23rd
24th

Carlisle Away

This was such a boozy blast that the day's events remain hazy. But a glance at the record books (and YouTube) confirms a very satisfactory outcome.

At the crack of dawn on Saturday 5 April 1997 we had a very long day ahead of us. And a potential dreary drag back to London if things went against us at Brunton Park. In short, we needed to get something from Carlisle. With six games left to play, Fulham, rejuvenated under Micky Adams, sat in third place in Division Three with 76 points, seven clear of fourth-placed Swansea who'd played a game more (41). Carlisle were a point ahead in second place (also with six to play), while Wigan led the way, just, on 77 points having played 41. This promotion race was going to the wire.

The train from Euston was crammed with Fulham fans. Just as crammed were our bags – jam-packed with sandwiches, newspapers and booze. But mainly booze. Camaraderie was high, as were the levels of anticipation and hope. This promised to be a good day out; as we pulled out of the station the big match was a while away – maximum effort today Fulham, please! Hours of discussion, debate, nostalgia, lots of ale, song and even a few crosswords later we pulled into Carlisle station and (bear with me…it's getting quite hazy now…) after a mélange of pub/long walk/fields/sheep/Brunton Park, suddenly it was almost kick-off time.

A season's best crowd of almost 10,000 – over a fifth of which were Fulham fans – created a cracking atmosphere. There was a real buzz, plus a stack of nerves. A 0-0 stalemate at Hereford and a 1-1 draw at home to Rochdale hadn't given us the expected boost going into this one. But here we go; game on. And the Third Division clash of the day certainly didn't disappoint.

Simon Morgan recalls: "The pitch was in excellent condition considering the incessant rain. Not so welcoming was the uncovered terracing behind the goal that would house the travelling Fulham fans. Our welcome on to the field for the warm-up was very boisterous, as the 2,000 Fulham fans made themselves heard above the bellowing Tannoy music. The players' ears pricked up: this was real football, a proper football match with a proper atmosphere."

And it was a proper blow when, after 20 minutes, Steve Hayward crossed from the left for Rory Delap to loop a header beyond Mark Walton. We were

still well in the game – particularly when Walton saved well from Warren Aspinall – but this wasn't going to plan. One down at half-time. Over to you Micky Adams…

The Whites began the second half with more belief. Within six minutes that paid dividends. From a Paul Watson short corner, Rod McAree sent a cross beyond the far post where Danny Cullip (having given his marker a sly nudge) headed the ball back across goal and Mick Conroy outjumped a ruck of players to nod home the equaliser from just under the bar.

That superb response heralded a classic FFC moment just four minutes later: Morgs picked out Christer Warren's run across the Carlisle area and the on-loan striker nodded the ball down into the path of McAree. It was begging to be hit. The lad from Dungannon did just that, belting the ball into the Carlisle net from 20 yards and propelling himself into Fulham folklore. The sodden Fulham fans behind the goal had barely calmed down after Conroy's leveller; now they went ballistic (I say "they" not "we" as I was nice and dry in the stand). The quality of the strike was one thing; the significance was something else entirely. Hold on to this lead and we'd be on our way out of this darned division. But hold on, there were still 35 minutes to play. Stay focused Fulham, stay focused.

As the minutes ticked away, the tension became almost tangible – with the home fans willing an equaliser (at least) and the voluble visitors desperate for their heroes to maintain their levels of determination and resolve. And that the ref would bloody well blow for full time sometime soon. We had a scare when Aspinall hit the bar and breathed a collective sigh of relief when Nick Cusack sliced a clearance onto his own crossbar. At the other end Conroy hit the post. At long last the ref blew for full time. We'd only gone and

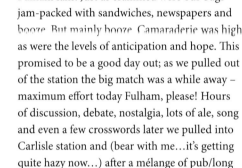

Top right: Carlisle United v Fulham, 5 April 1997 – game on!

Opposite page top: Rodney McAree fires home the matchwinner at Brunton Park in spectacular fashion.

Opposite page right: The *Fulham Chronicle* reveals that the Club were homing in on regaining the freehold of Craven Cottage.

Below: Who put the ball in the Carlisle net? Well, Mick Conroy got there first, equalising in front of the Fulham fans with a close-range header. After that, though, came the memorable howitzer from "the lad from Dungannon", Rodney McAree.

done it! Not mathematically certain (that would be resolved the following Tuesday with a weary 0-0 at Mansfield) but in our hearts we were up. Conga, anyone?

Morgs: "Our supporters were doing a mass conga along the terraces, celebrating victory, even before the final whistle. When the referee finally blew for time, the full range of emotions could be observed. As Carlisle trooped off in despair, our celebrations began, players and supporters together. The overwhelming feeling was of euphoria. Elated players openly hugged on the pitch, knowing deep down that our season's ambition had been achieved. We were up, perhaps not mathematically yet, but we were up. What a way to achieve it, with a 2-1 victory at the home of our main rivals. It was great to share a moment of triumph with the supporters. They were all soaked through, but didn't care. Their faces were alive with happiness."

If it was light-hearted and at times voluble on the way up, the return train journey was positively raucous. Oh yes; if it was all rather boozy going north, we were all pissed out of our heads coming home. And happy. Very, very happy. Engineering works resulted in a number of unscheduled stops that prolonged the party. But

that only allowed us to show off our questionable conga skills on station platform after station platform. What we lacked in style, we more than made up for in enthusiasm and volume. We made that stage our own. We nailed it. It was a million percent yes moment. Only for "moment", substitute "ruddy hours"

By the time our re-routed train lurched into Euston way after the last Tube trains had headed for their depots, we were a million percent knackered. It's fair to say that the party wasn't in full swing by then, a situation made worse when we discovered that Bradford Bulls and St Helens fans, in London for the Rugby League Challenge Cup final, had commandeered all the taxis. So, Shanks's pony then.... ⚽

FULHAM HOME IN

OURS AGAIN: The Fulham board is close to buying the ground back

FULHAM Football Club are on the verge of owning Craven Cottage for the first time in 10 years.

A deal worth £4 million is being hammered out this week between the Fulham board and landlords the Royal Bank of Scotland (RBS).

The club are desperate to thrash out a deal before May Day when they will have to pay £500,000 in rent to the RBS.

Fulham chairman Jimmy Hill and Director Andy Muddyman left a six-hour meeting with the bank on Monday and described their mood as "optimistic".

Hill and Muddyman refused to comment further but sources close to the negotiations revealed that a final cash figure was "closer to agreement than on any previous occasion between the two parties".

The source said: "It is expected a deal will be finalised within a matter of days."

If Hill, Muddyman and the bank can successfully negotiate the finer points of the sale then the freehold will return to the club before May 1.

With a deal virtually on the table by Tuesday night, the two sides were locked in dispute over the long-running rent wrangle involving a figure believed to be in the region of £200,00.

The rent was waived last August after the club had won their appeal with the Department of Environment to develop the ground.

By PAUL WARBURTON

But now the Bank are believed to have insisted on a pay-up policy which has forced the club's hand.

In February last year a rugby-based consortium attempted to buy the club for £6 million but were snubbed by the club who will now depend on the millions of Vice-chairman Bill Muddyman and his son Andy to secure the deal.

The Muddymans will be seen as the saviours

and they will have to dig into their own coffers as nobody has yet been found to redevelop Craven Cottage.

If Fulham prove successful it will be the final chapter of a saga that has run since former Fulham chairman Ernie Clay sold the ground to Marler Estates in 1987 for £6.25 million.

Marler Estates owner David Bulstrode wanted to merge Fulham and QPR under the banner of Fulham Park Rangers.

This was rebuffed and Bulstrode sold out to Cabra Estates. When Cabra folded in 1989 the freehold of the ground was returned to the RBS.

	1st
Fulham 0 Northampton Town 1	**2nd**
12.04.97 2nd	3rd
	4th
Doncaster Rovers 0 Fulham 0	5th
19.04.97 2nd	6th
	7th
Fulham 2 Hull City 0	8th
26.04.97 2nd	9th
	10th
Cambridge United 0 Fulham 1	11th
03.05.97 2nd	12th
	13th
	14th
	15th
	16th
	17th
	18th
	19th
	20th
	21st
	22th
	23th
	24th

Cockerill Crows

A few eyebrows were raised when Glenn Cockerill joined Fulham last summer. There was no doubting his pedigree but here was a veteran campaigner being released by Orient. What, then, could the old boy offer Fulham? TOOFIF's editor tackled the experienced midfielder after the Hartlepool game, and came out with his knees intact.

You're 37, and in the veteran bracket Glenn, but still enjoying your football?

Oh yeah, very much so. Enjoyment is the main thing now, as well as helping the other players through games. As you drop down the divisions the coaching side of your nature comes through and it's good to pass on what you can.

We've had a decent season here, so I guess that's given you a fillip too?

That's right, all the lads at the Club have helped me to enjoy it. It's not been a case of me getting old and seeing my time out, that's for sure.

So what lured you to Fulham?

I had two choices: Brighton or Fulham. At Fulham, Micky just wanted me as a player whereas Brighton's offer involved coaching and I didn't feel I was ready for that.

You must have felt at home right away with so many ex-Southampton players in the camp?

Yes, and that was another factor in coming to the Cottage. I knew it was the right choice once the pre-season games got under way. There was a great attitude to the pre-season training and to those early games. We had a tremendous start to the season and fortunately we've managed to keep it going. We were listening to the gaffer and doing exactly what he wanted us to do and we soon reaped the benefits. With that came a strong sense of belief.

Glenn Cockerill
A Fan's Appreciation

David Lloyd, Editor of *There's Only One F In Fulham* fanzine, gives a view from the Craven Cottage terraces

When I read in the press last summer the headline 'Cockerill considering move to Fulham', my first reaction was that the veteran of many a midfield tussle had designs on an old folks' home in the locality. I mean, where does a 37 year old go on being released by Orient? Not a go-getting club like Fulham, surely? A club whose player-manager had his on-field activities effectively curtailed by, err, Glenn Cockerill.

Okay, so he was probably Orient's best player in both games against Fulham last season – still tigerish in the tackle, as Micky Adams will confirm. And, okay, it's always handy to have an experienced and reliable old head in the ranks. But why were Orient prepared to release him?

Well, whatever the reason he's proved to be another of the gaffer's inspirational acquisitions. Glenn's high-pumping leg action has been prominent in more than 30 games; and his efforts have been sorely missed when kept out by injury.

He even managed to turn a game in our favour – at Swansea. We were one down at the Vetch and looking pretty ordinary when off the bench came Glenn. He acclimatised himself with a couple of tackles then set about orchestrating Fulham's recovery. As ever, nothing flash, just purposeful and to the point. He consistently chose the right options and was instrumental in both Fulham goals, scored by Conroy and Morgan.

The *Independent On Sunday* noted that 'Within minutes of the appearance of grizzled (grizzled!) 37 year old veteran Glenn Cockerill Conroy equalised. As Cockerill's influence grew so Swansea fell apart.' Grizzled or not, his influence led to one more away win, and three further points for the cause.

Then there was the boyish enthusiasm demonstrated at

Torquay. Although named substitute once again, Glenn was off the bench more than he was on it – chasing any overhit pass that went into touch like an over-excited ball-boy. When Tony Lange went down injured he shot to his feet immediately and promptly began to limber up. I'm sure he fancied his chances in goal.

Much more recently, Rod McAree's great strike in the tremendous win at Carlisle stole the headlines quite naturally. Yet when the home side launched their late offensive there was our Glenn picking up the pieces in front of our last line of defence. Where others would have been happy to despatch the ball towards Row Z of the stand. Glenn preferred to keep possession, tidily knocking the ball off to a team-mate amid the hurly-burly and being on hand for any possible return pass. That's pedigree.

Glenn's off-the-field contribution has been just as valuable. When asked for his top Fulham player in more than 300 games for the club, Simon Morgan was quick to nominate you-know-who as a gem of a midfielder. 'For overall effect on the squad, for respect and overall input it has to be Glenn – he's thirty-bloody-seven! He's been extremely influential and has had a great season.'

That input becomes a little more apparent when Danny Cullip, arguably the find of the season, made a point of thanking his much more experienced team-mate for his guidance and few quiet words of wisdom at the training ground.

The *Fulham Chronicle* reported recently that Glenn has shelved plans to retire and was hoping that his exploits this season have been enough to warrant a further one-year contract. 'This is the best season I've had in the last five years,' he told the paper, adding that he would consider a role that involved some coaching. 'Providing my legs are up to it, I think I'd have something to offer next season as well. I'd like to play for as long as I can, but we'll just have to see what Micky has in mind.'

I have a sneaking feeling that tonight will not be the last time we see Glenn Cockerill in a Fulham shirt. Or in those shoes.

The Fulham players are only too aware of Glenn's insistence at leading the singing on their coach trips. Well, as his singing mentor Rod Stewart might warble coarsely: 'Tonight's the night.' Enjoy it, Glenn...

22

You've just referred to him as the gaffer, but how long is it that you've known Micky Adams?
He came to Southampton in 1988 or '89, so about eight or nine years now. Mick had also played in the lower leagues so had done his homework along the way so to speak. Mick's a hard-working lad and I knew he'd do well.

What do you recall of that incident at Orient, which, as it turned out, effectively ended Micky's career?
I remember it very clearly, even though it was just another tackle in the life of Glenn Cockerill. I didn't realise it was Mick. The ball was there to be won, and that's been my game for 20 years now.

Was it a foul?
No. It was simply a 50-50 tackle. I went to see Mick after the game; by then he knew it was more than just a routine knock. I saw him a little later in the pub and then he came back to my house. By midnight we were both bladdered!

Your association with Ian Branfoot goes back even further…?
Branny was a player when I first joined Lincoln in 1976-77, and a good player, too. He packed up playing early and ended up coaching me at Lincoln. When he came to Southampton later as manager it was nice to see a friendly face and we had plenty of good times although, as it turned out, things didn't go all that well for us on the pitch.

You played in a much-documented game at Craven Cottage in 1981-82. It was the last time that Fulham clinched promotion and more than 20,000 watched Fulham draw 1-1 with Lincoln. What do you recall of that night?
We had to win it [to go up] while Fulham just needed a draw. We had Thommo [Steve Thompson] sent off and from the resulting free kick Brownie scored. We equalised about ten minutes from time then had a great chance near the end that was cleared off the line; that's football! ⚽

Above: Glenn Cockerill leads the singing at the Club's end-of-season shindig.

Below: Micky Adams salutes the Fulham fans from the Town Hall balcony in the wake of our promotion-winning season. Paul Brooker and Darren Freeman also enjoy the moment.

Hope Springs Eternal

Football relies on hope, whether your team is in the upper or lower spheres. At the start of each campaign, fans everywhere offer the same prayer: "Please let this be our season… Maybe, just maybe, we'll get it right this time." For fans of, say, Manchester United and Liverpool such prayers are directed at some grand aim, maybe another Championship or success in Europe. In Third Division terms, the hopes are much more basic, like avoiding the dreaded, and possibly terminal, drop into the Conference. A money-making Cup run would be more than welcome, as would striking a decent vein of form in the league. Then, if you're ever the optimist, there's the "P" word: promotion!

Of course, any dreams of a take-over by a mega-rich white (-ish) knight prepared to sink tens of millions of pounds into your lowly outfit would naturally be dismissed as wholly implausible. Get real!

When Micky Adams took over the FFC reins from Ian Branfoot in February 1996, the only way out of the bottom tier looked to be downwards and out of the League. At that point, only Torquay kept the Cottagers off bottom spot, but Adams was to lift the team to a relatively respectable 17th spot by the season's end. He rebuffed any congratulations at the time, saying he should be judged on what he'd achieve the following campaign. With *his* team.

Season '96-97 began with quiet optimism. The air of doom and gloom, so obvious in recent times, was replaced by a cheerier mood. It helped that Adams had been busy in the transfer market, even if his purchases had come from the Oxfam shop rather than Harrods. Pre-season friendlies gave little inkling of the tremendous months ahead, possibly because the squad had suffered a spate of injuries. But it was clear that the tour to Ireland had engendered a wonderful team spirit.

Sun, shirtsleeves and balloons – plus the hopes of Fulham fans everywhere – greeted the first match at home to Hereford. Balloons? Well, FFC had just received the long overdue OK for the ground development plans seen as critical in its quest to regain the freehold (but more of that later). It meant there was a definite feel-good factor around Craven Cottage, which even the players acknowledged after the match. And even if the game itself

was pretty poor, we managed a single-goal victory and slapped three points on the board.

The goalscorer against the Bulls was born-again Mick Conroy. Used by the previous regime as a "chase-that" merchant and, accordingly, voted a runaway winner of the "Not the Player of the Year" category by the fanzine readership, a leaner, fitter Conroy (soon to be dubbed "Super-Micky") was now being played to his strengths, chiefly as penalty-box predator. With Conroy supported by the tireless Scott and Freeman, Fulham suddenly had a forward line capable of scoring!

It was 18 games into the campaign before we failed to score – ironically against lowly Brighton – while First Division Southend were knocked out of the Coca-Cola Cup and only a couple of dodgy decisions (honest!) ensured Ipswich didn't go the same way in the following round. Conroy was, for a while, the country's leading scorer as he rattled up 18 goals by Christmas. Oh yes, and Fulham were top of the league. Yup, top.

It was really fun to be a Fulham supporter again. Away trips, always a laugh if discounted the matches themselves, were now a hoot. Wins were almost guaranteed and several off-licences close to the respective awayday railway station enjoyed bonanza sales when Fulham came to town. All in the cause of a celebratory tipple you understand!

Home form was never as assured. Points were stupidly dropped, notably against Mansfield, Torquay and Lincoln, but we remained top and all of us fans were self-adopted members of the "Adams family". Sky came to Craven Cottage in late January for the visit of Cardiff. A formality, surely? But if ever there was a reminder that this was Fulham we're talking about, this was it. Here was a great chance to strut our stuff, stamp our authority on the division and draw in a few more punters. Instead we were thumped 4-1; even our goal came courtesy of a Cardiff defender. A further lacklustre performance the following week meant we were knocked off top spot. Oh dear, an untimely wobble.

Adams later admitted that he thought the bubble had burst and, even though we'd been setting the pace for much of the season, he feared we might have to resort to the Play-offs to gain promotion. Some of the senior pros seemed to have "lost it" and Adams even abandoned one training session as he felt that most players were simply going through the motions. But to their credit the players were bothered and organised a few get-togethers in an attempt to cure the ills.

Meanwhile, even without being privy to these behind-the-scenes wrangles, there were numerous murmurings on the terraces prior to the following evening's home match. Had the Club's tremendous

Below: With so much happening over the summer months, TOOFIF produced a heavyweight "cuttings special" in time for the pre-season friendlies.

turnaround in fortunes been too good to be true after all? As it turned out Fulham's showing against in-form Swansea proved a real eye-opener. Fulham tore into the visitors with their rediscovered blend of skill and determination… only to find themselves a goal down! The hosts were up for the challenge, however, and, after Darren Freeman had levelled, Fulham completed a tremendous comeback when Paul Brooker struck a late winner.

Although knocked off the top perch, we were back in the hunt with renewed confidence. Fellow high-fliers Wigan were held to a 1-1 draw and another unbeaten run was set in motion. Promotion was all but secured at Brisbane Road where our raucous supporters found another cheerleader – injured centre-back Terry Angus was up and chanting with the best of 'em!

The 2-0 win against Orient set us up for the final stretch – which included a long trip to Carlisle, one of the three teams vying for the title. What a day (and night!) that was. The hosts opened the scoring, then Conroy – naturally – nodded home the equaliser before a scorcher from Rod McAree, out of the side since September, sealed the win. Cue another off-licence bonanza! Engineering works meant a meandering magical mystery tour back to The Smoke and numerous congas on platforms at one unscheduled stop after another. Worth recording, too, that BT Police commended our excellent, albeit boozy, behaviour. We eventually pulled into Euston well after midnight tired and exhausted and with no Tube trains to get us closer to home. Great; thanks a bloody bunch!

One more point needed. That came three days later at Mansfield. "A dour draw" said the papers. "Who gives a flying ****?" claimed those who were there. There was nothing dour about the emotions and celebrations. We were up. And farewell and good riddance to a dreadful basement division. Some decent clubs and supporters, it's true, but the pits as far as playing levels and most of the facilities go. And as for the standard of match officials…

With that we blew the chase for the title. Carlisle and Wigan were also faltering but we hit a barren patch, including a 1-0 home defeat by Northampton, in which Adams made two "tactical" substitutions inside the first 15 minutes, and a disappointing goalless draw at Doncaster.

But it was a great season, epitomised by Fulham's travelling supporters making up more than half the crowd at Cambridge on the final day. (One coach had a board on its back saying "Follow us to Colchester", a reference to the coach driver who in January insisted on taking his party of Fulham fans to Cambridge instead of Colchester, despite the pleas, and later threats, from his entourage.)

Decorum went out of the window as many turned up at the Abbey Stadium in weird fancy dress, and a host of fans had daubed black and white paint all over their faces. The ticker-tape welcome for the team, meantime, was almost claustrophobic in its density. Okay, so the title was Wigan's provided they didn't slip up at home to Mansfield. But we needed to win all the same, and miracles could happen, couldn't they? But they didn't. Freeman's strike ensured a Club record 12th away success of the season but it was a strangely subdued Fulham crowd that trooped away from the Abbey Stadium. Wigan had duly taken the crown by the narrowest of margins; how ironic that it was FFC's own Chairman, dear old Jimmy Hill, who had been instrumental in changing the rules. With both clubs on 84 points, Wigan were champions on goals scored; any other yardstick would have seen the title and the silverware coming south. But then rules is rules.

But the main shock to everyone's system was yet to come. No, it wasn't that the *London Evening Standard* (aka The North London Gazette or simply The Substandard) had suddenly woken up to Fulham's existence, neither was it the sudden news of Jimmy Hill standing down as Chairman after 10 years. In a move that astounded the world of football, Harrods supremo Mohamed Al Fayed was announced as the Club's new owner and he promptly pledged £30-60m ("or whatever it takes") to get FFC back to the big time. The sums were mind-boggling, especially for a club of Fulham's relatively lowly status. Al Fayed also promptly scuppered the hard-fought-for plans for a 15,000 all-seater stadium part-surrounded by flats. Instead his cash injection would resecure the Craven Cottage freehold outright and he had grandiose plans for the site: a state-of-the-art arena that would hold 25,000+. And, naturally, a team to match.

Oo-er! Things are never going to be the same again down by the Thames. ⚽

Under New Ownership

With us supporters still on cloud nine after Fulham had gained promotion, there were whispers that FFC were, at long last, on the verge of regaining the Craven Cottage freehold. The Fulham Board, under Chairman Jimmy Hill and Vice-Chair Bill Muddyman, had, for a decade, valiantly kept the Club going in the face of extreme adversity. But now things were seemingly coming to a head with regard to the famous old ground, at that juncture the property of the Royal Bank of Scotland.

The Board had agreed to the purchase, but were split. Hill's preferred route was to include a partial development – which, while a massive improvement on what we had at the time, would limit future expansion. (In the late 1990s, "future expansion" was but a pipedream.) Muddyman, who'd financed the Club during the recent dark days, had grander plans. Maybe he'd heard whispers of his own; either way, he was sticking out for a major investor.

With the pair failing to agree, it was exit Jimmy Hill, Chairman since 1987. Within days a new

Fulham 1 Wrexham 0	1st
09.08.97 6th	2nd
	3rd
Walsall 1 Fulham 1	4th
16.08.97 5th	**5th**
	6th
Fulham 0 Luton Town 0	7th
23.08.97 6th	8th
	9th
Wycombe Wanderers 2 Fulham 0	10th
30.08.97 13th	11th
	12th
Bristol City 0 Fulham 2	13th
02.09.97 9th	14th
	15th
Fulham 2 Plymouth Argyle 0	16th
09.09.97 5th	17th
	18th
Fulham 0 Grimsby Town 2	19th
13.09.97 9th	20th
	21st
Southend United 1 Fulham 0	22nd
20.09.97 11th	23rd
	24th
Wigan Athletic 2 Fulham 1	
27.09.97 18th	
League Cup	
Wycombe Wanderers 1 Fulham 2	
12.08.97 Round 1 1st leg	
Fulham 4 Wycombe Wanderers 4	
26.08.97 Round 1 2nd leg	
Fulham 0 Wolves 1	
16.09.97 Round 2 1st leg	
Wolves 1 Fulham 0	
24.09.97 Round 2 2nd leg	

Chairman/Owner rode into town: on 29 May 1997, in a gold landau carriage drawn by a string of white horses, the shy, retiring Mohamed Al Fayed made his grand entrance on the Craven Cottage turf. It was one of those surreal, awesome, "rub your eyes, is this really happening?" moments – the first of many such instances in the ensuing years. ⚽

How TOOFIF 52 Reported the News

The announcement was, quite simply, stunning. And the often-cynical press corps, out in force, were united in the view that the well-handled press conference offered genuine good news to the Club and its fans. One pressman said the mood was "buoyant". An apt description for a Club that had, until very recently, been sinking very fast.

The levels of shock and surprise among Fulham fans rocketed, as you'd expect, to stratospheric extremes – and yet they were also matched by the levels of cynicism. Our new Chairman's interesting past didn't suggest a serene future for FFC; neither had he demonstrated any obvious Fulham leanings

in the past. Would this be yet another chapter of Fulham's history to be filed under "misadventure" in the years to come?

Gloriously, Mohamed Al Fayed has, over time, ensured that his Chairmanship will go down in FFC folklore as the most remarkable in the Club's history. While it's important to stress that it was Micky Adams who gave the Club its vital kick-start under Hill and Muddyman, from May 1997 there was no doubting that Al Fayed was the man in charge. First to suffer was Adams, plus his sidekick Alan Cork. It was a surprise to Adams who'd announced at a press conference after a Cup game with Wolves that he was about to sign a clutch of players with the blessing of the new owner. Instead, he was shown the door. The official version at the time was that he was offered the chance to work with a "more seasoned manager", but that he'd turned down that opportunity.

In later years Adams admitted that he'd have probably benefited from such an arrangement. Only problem was, no such offer was ever made.

Below: Wow! It's all change at Craven Cottage as new Chairman and owner Mohamed Al Fayed, pictured here in this clipping with FFC Director Bill Muddyman, takes the reins.

Fulham cash in with £30m Al Fayed deal

By Richard Palmer

MOHAMED AL FAYED, the owner of Harrods, took control of Fulham yesterday and promised to invest £30 million in the newly-promoted Second Division club.

The Egyptian businessman signed an agreement making him the majority shareholder and chairman of the club.

He vowed to invest his money in getting Fulham into the Premiership and turning Craven Cottage into a state-of-the-art 25,000-seater stadium.

"I am a football fan, I am an admirer of Fulham and have supported Fulham for a very long time," said Al Fayed, who posed with a football beside a Harrods-liveried coach and horses on the pitch after completing five weeks of secret negotiations.

Al Fayed insisted he was not looking to invest in football simply to make a fast buck or raise his profile. "I don't need it, my profile is high enough," he said.

His aides said he considered the cash injection at Fulham a long-term investment. "I don't do business for the pleasure of making money but to enjoy it and see the football," said Al Fayed. "This is a great club really in desperate need of support."

His arrival follows the departure of Jimmy Hill, who announced last week that he was stepping down after 10 years as chairman to spend more time with his family.

Bill Muddyman, who briefly took over from Hill but will now become vice-chairman, said the BBC pundit had known nothing of the talks with the Harrods chief and would receive no payment as part of the deal. Muddyman, whose son Andy will also

remain on the board, said: "For Andy, myself and the other members of the board this marriage between Fulham and Mr Al Fayed is our dream scheme come true.

"It starts a new era. Fulham can get back to where they really belong and that's the top flight.

"We intend to rebuild Craven Cottage and challenge for the Premiership. Those are our ambitions."

Under the terms of the deal, Al Fayed has agreed to provide the cash to buy Craven Cottage for £7.5m and repay £2.5m which Muddyman had lent the club.

The Harrods owner, who now possesses three-quarters of the club's shares, is expected to invest about £15m on the new ground, leaving Fulham with about £5m to spend on players – perhaps five times as much as most Second Division sides.

Micky Adams, who won promotion in his first year as manager, said: "Before all this broke I was talking to agents about better quality players for next season and they were not even interested in talking to the club. They might have changed their minds now.

"I'm sure a lot of players we were interested in will have suddenly gone up in value. But I don't want players coming

here just for the money." Until the deal was signed yesterday, Fulham had intended to buy their ground and build a 15,000-seater stadium partly financed by 142 luxury flats to be constructed on part of the site.

The new stadium plans, which the club envisages will take a year to get through Hammersmith and Fulham Council and a further 18 months to build, will no longer need the flats.

Al Fayed, who previously expressed an interest in buying into Manchester United nine years ago, and Chelsea earlier this year, stressed that £30m was only an initial investment and more could follow. Other investors are also being brought into the club.

His two sons, aged 11 and 13, support Manchester United and Newcastle, but he said he had watched Fulham play many times. However, he could not remember when he had last seen them.

"I have been away on business for the last two months so I haven't seen them in the last two months of the season," he said.

Mark Griffiths, a senior aide to Al Fayed, said the deal had been put together after his boss and Muddyman were introduced by Mark Collins,

managing director of Harrods Estates and a vice-president of Fulham. Michael Cole, the former BBC royal correspondent who works as Al Fayed's press officer, is also a long-time Fulham fan.

Griffiths said the club, via a newly-created company called Fulham Leisure Holdings, would rebuild the ground and possibly create a club superstore and underground car parking.

They will not, however, be able to knock down the listed

cottage nor the Stevenage Road stand, which also enjoys planning protection.

"That's not a problem for us," said Griffiths. "Harrods is a listed building, we're used to working like that. We have an in-house architects department and fire and safety specialists and we will make them available."

The announcement stunned the world of football and delighted David Lloyd, editor of the fanzine There's Only One F in Fulham. He said: "It's

unbelievable. It's a different ball game now. Perhaps I'll have to change the fanzine's name to There's Only One H in Harrods."

Fulham have been in the doldrums for years. Their last moment of glory was in 1975 when they reached the FA Cup Final as a Second Division side, losing to West Ham.

But their heyday was in the Sixties when the side led by Johnny Haynes played in the old First Division before crowds of 40,000.

COACHING SESSION: Mohamed Al Fayed arrives in style at Craven Cottage   Picture: ALAN WALTER

Eccentric Harrods owner with rich past

By Kirsty Walker

MOHAMED AL FAYED was born and raised in Egypt, but moved to Britain in 1964.

The owner of Harrods, he is the 14th richest man in Britain, with a fortune of more than £1 billion.

Al Fayed, who, with his brother Ali, has been consistently denied British

citizenship, first hit the headlines in the early Eighties when his £615 million House of Fraser takeover was criticised by the Department of Trade and Industry. This led to a long feud and court battle with Tiny Rowland, then head of the Lonrho group.

Al Fayed, 64, has been heavily embroiled in the cash-for-questions scandal, after his claims that he gave

MPs money in brown envelopes to speak on his behalf in the House of Commons.

A friend of the Sultan of Brunei, he has amassed his fortune in property, oil, shipping and banking. He also owns the Ritz Hotel in Paris and Punch magazine.

An eccentric man, he is planning to have a pyramid built on the top of Harrods after his death.

FOOTBALL'S MOGULS

	Personal Fortune	Club
1.	Joseph Lewis, £3,000m	£40m Rangers
2.	Moores family, £1,000m	Liverpool shareholders
3.	Mohamed Al-Fayed, £1,000m	£30m for Fulham
4.	Jack Walker, £550m	Blackburn chairman
5.	Steve Morgan, £260m	Owns 5% of Liverpool
6.	David & Ralph Gold, £230m	£15m Birmingham
7.	Max Griggs, £220m	Rushden and Diamonds
8.	Sir John Hall, £220m	57% Newcastle Utd
9.	John Madejski, £200m	Chairman of Reading
10.	David Sullivan, £200m	co-owns Birmingham

"It was, rather like my supposed £1m pay-off, in that it was something concocted by the Fulham/Harrods PR department," he said. Anyway, with Adams likely to have spent the Chairman's money in football's Tesco (a step up, at least, from The Pound Shop), the new incumbents – Kevin Keegan as Chief Operating Manager and Ray Wilkins as Head Coach – were sure to head straight to Harrods. There was no doubting that Mohamed Al Fayed meant business and he unveiled a five-year plan to reach the Premier League.

It all seems so very matter-of-fact all these years later, but in 1997 this was a footballing bombshell, particularly to the diehard Fulham supporters who'd stuck with the Club despite the most appalling of footballing circumstances. Just a matter of months previously we'd been avidly counting and gratefully squirrelling away every penny to come in from the various fundraising drives in an attempt to keep the Club afloat. Now, after the wondrous uplift of having not only arrested a depressing nosedive down the League but having also clawed our way out of the bottom division, Fulham supporters could look forward to watching their heroes go onwards and upwards at a ground that was again in the hands of the Club.

As for reaching Premiership, as it was then called, well that still seemed a world away. But then, as Paul Johnson's cartoon strip in TOOFIF would say: "We Can Dream". ⚽

Strength of Character

May 29, 1997 may well go down in history as the day every Fulham supporter won the lottery. The fairy godmother we'd all craved for years finally turned up! ("A sleeping giant" he called us. Perhaps from here on in the giant in Jack and the Beanstalk will recite "Fee-Fi-Fo-F'lum"?) Next thing, loads of players… a brand new ground… and before you know it we'll be there – in the top flight.

This (apart from the Fee-Fi… bit!) was surely the reaction of all Fulham supporters when the news was announced. At last, at long last, Fulham FC were going to become what we all had been dreaming about for many, many years – a big noise in the football world. Look out, Chelsea, we'll be marching down the Kings Road again soon!

After the initial euphoria (by the way, well done Lloydie for getting more free publicity by wearing a TOOFIF t-shirt for your TV interviews!), it was time to sit back and take in what was happening, and what could happen to FFC. At the time of writing I've heard nothing bar the initial announcement regarding the ground purchase, the 25,000-capacity stadium and the fact that money will be made available should Micky Adams need it. Fine. All nice and neat and fairly low profile. And long may it remain so, because while I'd love to see a successful trophy-winning set-up at Craven Cottage, it should not be at the cost

of everything that we've built up over the years.

Character is an over-used word in football, but it's the one thing we have in abundance, and something we mustn't lose. In London, virtually every football fan has a soft spot for us and many "always look out for their results". There are, after all, no supporters of other clubs who really hate Fulham. There is something unique about our Fulham and, while we're eager for success, it must be achieved our way. The Fulham way: with style, panache and, no doubt, plenty of cock-ups!

I don't suggest we should carry on languishing in the nether regions of the Football League, but there's something about struggling and Fulham FC that have gone hand in hand. Even TV scriptwriters over the years have had good mileage out of us. In the *Minder* series, Terry's flat was resplendent with Fulham rosettes. Wolfy – *Citizen Smith* – and his Freedom for Tooting gang were always talking about the Hammersmith End, while in *Robin's Nest* Richard O'Sullivan was often seen sporting a Fulham bobble hat. But we loved them.

I also think there is the doom-monger and fatalist in every Fulham fan. Fulham are 3-0 up with 10 minutes to go… it's never a cert, is it? You can always see the opposition clawing their way back into it, right? Be honest, I'm right aren't I?

As I've always said, "Let's enjoy the dough, but let's always remember who we are and who we were." Let us go onwards and upwards in our own special Fulham style. Still, it's a lovely position to be in, isn't it? All that lovely lolly just waiting to be spent. But I am still cautious. After all, at one time I thought that Ernie Clay was the saviour of Fulham FC. I got that sadly wrong, didn't I? ⚽

Tim Rowley

NATIONWIDE LEAGUE DIVISION 2

Fulham
David Lloyd reckons it'll be *Promotion: The Sequel*...
Player To Watch: Darren Freeman – fast, forceful striker with straggly, permed hair. If only he could finish
Manager: Micky Adams 9/10 – promotion in his first full season can't be bad
Chairman: Mohammed Al Fayed 10/10 – so far, so good. But under constant review
Kit Sponsor: GMB Union
Style Of Play: Counter-attacking style based on an 'all-for-one' team spirit
Celebrity Fans: Hugh Grant
Mascot: 'Diddy' David Hamilton
Top Local Boozer: Well, there's this bloke called Badger… Oh, I see, probably The Crabtree on Rainville Road
Expectations: Even without the Al Fayed windfall, we would have held our own in Division Two as Micky Adams has shown plenty of managerial nous in his first post. His acquisitions, even with the new-found wealth at his disposal, seem sensible and, if the squad gels like last season, there's every reason to hope for another decent and highly enjoyable campaign.
Fan's Prediction: 2nd
TF's Prediction: 10th
Title Odds: 9/1

Micky Adams led Fulham out of Division Three on a shoestring. Now he's got Al Fayed's cash to splash.

Above: Positive pre-season predictions from *Total Football*.

Below: Tim Goffe and John O'Farrell reflect on the change of circumstances at Fulham FC via The Two Stewards.

TOOFIF salutes Jimmy Hill OBE   RIP, Jim - aka "Mr Football"

Jimmy Hill

H ere's a poser: how best to sum up one the most influential characters in Fulham's history and one of the most well-known faces in the world of football? One of the most difficult, stubborn men in the business, that's how.

To be perfectly clear from the outset, this opinion has nothing to do with a lack of respect – Jimmy's footballing track record is as phenomenal as it is unique. To coin a phrase: There's Only One Jimmy Hill. He deserves enormous respect for what he achieved in the game and for taking on – and succeeding, naturally – such an extraordinary range of roles along the way.

Without question, Jimmy Hill was a total one-off, and an incredibly forward-thinking and successful one at that. Even so, during his Chairmanship at Fulham, boy could he be awkward and bloody-minded. In short, he simply didn't trust football supporters. So, for all that he did for FFC, and that particular list of achievements is a long and illustrious one, he was still an awkward cuss – even when we were supposedly fighting for the same cause.

Probably the best tale to illustrate this involves a meeting of the Board of Management – this

was a group that served as a link between the Fulham FC Board and the Club's supporters during the difficult 1990s. On this occasion the FFC Chairman called the meeting for a weekday afternoon, meaning that most of us had to take leave from our day jobs in order to attend. With crucial Fulham business on the agenda, that's what we did.

Trouble is, early afternoon elapsed into very late afternoon – with us lot left to twiddle our thumbs in the Riverside Stand in the meantime – and when the great man eventually strode purposefully into the room he took his seat, plonked his feet up on the table and went directly into "When I was at Coventry…" mode. No doubt Jimmy had a perfectly valid reason for being late, although timekeeping wasn't his forte; that, in itself, wasn't the issue. No, there was barely an apology nor was there any sort of acknowledgement that we may have been inconvenienced in even the teensiest of ways.

Worst of all, though, he was extremely reluctant to get down to the business in hand. So much so that, having given JH a couple of chances to get the meeting back on track, an infuriated Allan Gould (the official Supporters' Club rep)

Above and opposite page: TOOFIF's homage to the ubiquitous Jimmy Hill – a couple of montages that reflect his huge influence on the game and his dedication to Fulham FC.

announced that he'd had enough of the continued prevaricating. As Jimmy Hill apparently couldn't recognise how important the whole issue was to the Club's supporters, and as he (JH) evidently wasn't prepared to treat the committee seriously, then it was a waste of time him (Allan) being there. With that, Allan got up, tendered his resignation and left.

There's no doubt that Jimmy Hill could be hard work. There's also no doubt that Melvin Tenner's remarkable patience won him around; eventually! Melvin, for the uninitiated, was chairman of Fulham 2000, the fans-led fundraising group tasked with raising life-saving sums of money for the Club in the mid-1990s; (it's incredible, really, that in today's footballing climate such sums would barely make an entry on the Club's accounts ledger].

In Jimmy Hill's defence he took an awful lot of flak, not least in the pages of TOOFIF, from supporters suspicious about his motives, or frustrated that he wasn't taking a tougher stance with the property developers desperate to make a financial killing by building on the Craven Cottage site. He also took a stack of unfair personal abuse for no other reason than being a famous person with a highly recognisable and easily lampooned face.

When push came to shove, though, Jimmy Hill was plain obstinate and bloody-minded – character traits that over the years had helped

him score numerous major goals during his various careers. But which could make him a nightmare to deal with, even if you were ostensibly on the same side of the argument.

What Jimmy Hill could never seemingly fathom was that among the sea of faces on the terraces were experts in their professional fields – he seemed to regard all football fans as idiots or louts. On one occasion I dared to ask him following one outburst based on such false assumptions that, as he'd probably watched more football matches than any of us, did that make him, by his own rules, a super-idiot or a mega-lout? Or might he be, by our yardstick, an expert in many fields? There's no doubt he considered himself an expert. But as to the comparison and to the question posed, JH simply didn't get it.

Melvin Tenner was certainly neither an idiot nor a lout. He was no pushover, either. With great forbearance Melvin managed to wear down Jimmy Hill over time until there was some much-needed mutual trust. And there's no denying that the survival of Fulham FC was as much down to Jimmy Hill as anyone – after all, it was Jim who put together the consortium, including Bill Muddyman, that saw FFC through such difficult years. Hill's support of Fulham 2000 was ultimately excellent and there's also no denying that without his input there would probably have been no club for Mr Al Fayed to purchase and take to far grander levels. ⚽

Above: Jimmy Hill doing what he does best – offering an opinion to the media!

Hey, this lad's a real prospect!

TOOFIF salutes Jimmy Hill OBE   A pictorial tribute to a Fulham legend

Respects Paid at the Cottage

Fulham's unremarkable 2-0 win over Plymouth Argyle in September 1997 was contested on a Tuesday evening. The match itself has long been forgotten, but the events pre-kick-off made for a surreal experience down by the Thames.

The match was Fulham's first at Craven Cottage since the appalling car crash in Paris at the end of August that claimed the lives of Diana, Princess of Wales, Dodi Fayed and chauffeur Henri Paul. Before the contest, tributes were paid to the Chairman's son with spokesman Michael Cole making a speech from the half-way line and the Chairman himself adding a few words. Supporters from both clubs impeccably observed a minute's silence – save a tinny mobile-phone ring-tone (whose owner was presumably suitably embarrassed) – and wreaths were laid on the centre-spot.

The sombre occasion was made all the eerier by the wailing tones of a lone piper offering a lament against a silent backdrop. All very unfootball-like

Rght: The main gates at the Cottage are bedecked with flowers and messages from Fulham supporters in the wake of the Paris car crash that claimed the lives of Diana, Princess of Wales, and Dodi Fayed, son of FFC's Chairman.

Opposite page, top: How TOOFIF covered the surreal pre-match events before Fulham locked horns with Plymouth.

Below: A letter of thanks from Kensington Palace after the TOOFIF readership chipped in to raise funds for the Princess Diana Memorial Fund.

KENSINGTON PALACE
LONDON W8 4PU

24 February 1998

Dear Mr Lloyd

I write as a Trustee of the Diana, Princess of Wales Memorial Fund to thank David Lloyd Publishing for its most generous donation of £430, raised from profits of the Fulham Football Club fanzine 'There's only one F in Fulham' for Issue 53.

There has been enormous support of the Fund by the public and companies both large and small, and it is extremely encouraging to know that so many wish the work of the Princess to continue.

We are overwhelmed by the generosity and numbers of those who are contributing to the Fund, from all walks of life, at home and abroad. It is a wonderful tribute to the life and work of the Princess.

Yours sincerely
Annabelle King
pp. Michael Gibbins

David Lloyd
11 Johnson's Close
Carshalton
Surrey   SM5 2LU

and yet very touching; here was "little" Fulham FC embroiled in a controversial incident that had reverberated around the world – and which would still be making front-page headlines for many years to come.

So surreal were the proceedings that it was something of relief when the referee blew for the start of the game. That shrill blast seemed to signal a total change in mood and all the pre-match pleasantries and homage were promptly forgotten as the teams tore into each other from the off, with the first free-kick being awarded for a bone-crunching challenge before 10 seconds had elapsed. Ah, the beautiful game!

When Issue 53 hit the streets shortly afterwards, a surcharge of 20p was added to the cover price to raise funds for the Princess Diana Memorial Fund. A small gesture, but it seemed the right thing to do – and £430 was ultimately raised. ⚽

All Change at FFC

The arrival of Kevin Keegan, Ray Wilkins and Arthur Cox heralds a new era for Fulham FC and with it comes the promise of an exciting, jet-propelled rise to the Premiership. After so many turgid years, the last 18 months or so excepted, it's a mouth-watering prospect and one that, if all goes to plan, will mark the most dramatic change in fortunes of any club in the history of the game. All Fulham fans must be wondering what other surprises are just around the corner as we embark on the (hopefully) magical mystery tour. TOOFIF welcomes our new footballing supremo, one of the most

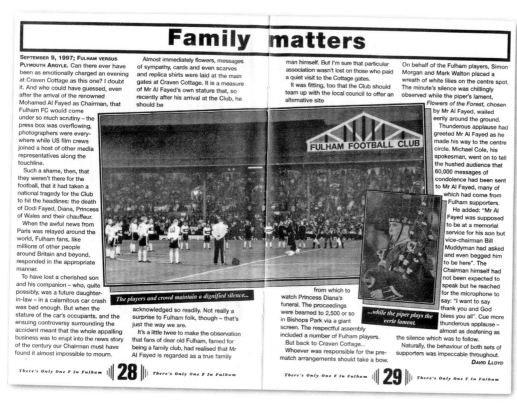

Family matters

SEPTEMBER 9, 1997; FULHAM VERSUS PLYMOUTH ARGYLE. Can there ever have been as emotionally charged an evening at Craven Cottage as this one? I doubt it. And who could have guessed, even after the arrival of the renowned Mohamed Al Fayed as Chairman, that Fulham FC would come under so much scrutiny – the press box was overflowing, photographers were every-where while US film crews joined a host of other media representatives along the touchline.

Such a shame, then, that they weren't there for the football, that it had taken a national tragedy for the Club to hit the headlines: the death of Dodi Fayed, Diana, Princess of Wales and their chauffeur.

When the awful news from Paris was relayed around the world, Fulham fans, like millions of other people around Britain and beyond, responded in the appropriate manner.

To have lost a cherished son and his companion – who, quite possibly, was a future daughter-in-law – in a calamitous car crash was bad enough. But when the stature of the car's occupants, and the ensuing controversy surrounding the accident meant that the whole appalling business was to erupt into the news story of the century our Chairman must have found it almost impossible to mourn.

Almost immediately flowers, messages of sympathy, cards and even scarves and replica shirts were laid at the main gates at Craven Cottage. It is a measure of Mr Al Fayed's own stature that, so recently after his arrival at the Club, he should be

The players and crowd maintain a dignified silence...

acknowledged so readily. Not really a surprise to Fulham folk, though – that's just the way we are.

It's a little twee to make the observation that fans of dear old Fulham, famed for being a family club, had realised that Mr Al Fayed is regarded as a true family

man himself. But I'm sure that particular association wasn't lost on those who paid a quiet visit to the Cottage gates.

It was fitting, too that the Club should team up with the local council to offer an alternative site

from which to watch Princess Diana's funeral. The proceedings were beamed to 2,500 or so in Bishops Park via a giant screen. The respectful assembly included a number of Fulham players.

But back to Craven Cottage... Whoever was responsible for the pre-match arrangements should take a bow.

...while the piper plays the eerie lament.

On behalf of the Fulham players, Simon Morgan and Mark Walton placed a wreath of white lilies on the centre spot. The minute's silence was chillingly observed while the piper's lament, *Flowers of the Forest*, chosen by Mr Al Fayed, wailed eerily around the ground.

Thunderous applause had greeted Mr Al Fayed as he made his way to the centre circle. Michael Cole, his spokesman, went on to tell the hushed audience that 60,000 messages of condolence had been sent to Mr Al Fayed, many of which had come from Fulham supporters.

He added: "Mr Al Fayed was supposed to be at a memorial service for his son but vice-chairman Bill Muddyman had asked and even begged him to be here". The Chairman himself had not been expected to speak but he reached for the microphone to say: "I want to say thank you and God bless you all". Cue more thunderous applause – almost as deafening as the silence which was to follow.

Naturally, the behaviour of both sets of supporters was impeccable throughout.

DAVID LLOYD

There's Only One F in Fulham ||| 28 ||| *There's Only One F In Fulham*

There's Only One F in Fulham ||| 29 ||| *There's Only One F In Fulham*

charismatic figures in football, and hopes he enjoys a long-term stay at Craven Cottage.

But before we get too carried away, we should remember the man who has been tossed aside, or "well shafted" as one fan so bluntly put it during a radio interview: Micky Adams. It is a mark of the Fulham fans' loyalty that, while acknowledging the massive pluses of Keegan's arrival, the treatment of Adams has been at the forefront of most of our minds.

It is true, as Kevin Moore told a gathering of Supporters' Club members, that Micky Adams will be all right once the dust has settled: he's had his contract paid up (he was in the first year of a five-year contract) and has an unblemished CV, which gives him a great chance of getting another post in due course.

But then that ignores the very nature of the man. Like Keegan, Adams wears his heart of his sleeve. He cared passionately about managing Fulham FC – indeed he looked on the task as something of a personal crusade. Previous managers have talked a good game at "Meet the Manager" nights while taking the Club ever downwards. Micky Adams frequently went way beyond standard manager-speak. And, unlike his predecessors who were allowed to stay at the helm way beyond their sell-by dates, he galvanised the place – lifting FFC from the ignominious position of one off the bottom of the entire League then righting the trend of recent years by leading the Club to promotion.

The fact that Fulham had regained their place in Division Two undoubtedly played a big part in attracting Mr Al Fayed to Craven Cottage. And yet Adams was to become the fall guy, in

many ways a victim of his own success. So, while it's true that he'll no doubt land on his feet, it's hardly surprising that he's feeling "disappointed and disillusioned".

By contrast Keegan was very upbeat about his new overseeing role. He told TOOFIF (and, seemingly, every press representative in the western world): "The quote of Fulham becoming the new Manchester United of the south never came from me. But the one thing we mustn't do is to aim too low. We've got to aim for the very best and that's always been my style. I can't wait to get started.

"Fulham is not a massive club. But it's a great club with a great tradition. It's a tremendous challenge. That's why it excites me, and that's why I'm here. Fulham supporters are in for a really exciting time. As for the Premiership, we've got a five-year plan. Then again there are many other clubs with the same dreams so we mustn't underestimate how difficult it's going to be.

"Then there's the redevelopment of the stadium. What we have here at the moment will, hopefully, not be good enough or big enough to hold all the fans who want to watch Fulham.

"I aim to take Fulham to the very top, and if we don't quite make it, it won't be for the lack of trying, I can promise you that. In due course we'll be trying to attract the best players to Fulham, too. But it wasn't all that easy to begin with at Newcastle, either. People forget that. But we got there in the end. Players want to be with a club if they think something is going to happen, and they're the players you want. If they're interested in the money or an easy ride then they won't be coming to Fulham Football Club." ◌

	1st
	2nd
	3rd
	4th
Fulham 3 Oldham Athletic 1	5th
04.10.97　　10th	6th
	7th
Fulham 1 Blackpool 0	8th
11.10.97　　8th	9th
	10th
Bournemouth 2 Fulham 1	11th
18.10.97　　13th	12th
	13th
Watford 2 Fulham 0	14th
21.10.97　　15th	15th
	16th
Fulham 1 Northampton Town 1	17th
25.10.97　　16th	18th
	19th
Fulham 1 Chesterfield 1	20th
01.11.97　　17th	21st
	22nd
Millwall 1 Fulham 1	23rd
04.11.97　　15th	24th
Bristol Rovers 2 Fulham 3	
08.11.97　　11th	
FA Cup	
Margate 1 Fulham 2	
16.11.97　　Round 1	

Ray of Sunshine

New team boss Ray Wilkins goes under the TOOFIF spotlight…

How surprised were you to get the call from Kevin Keegan?
Very surprised – especially as I'd been doing some TV work with Kevin that week but he'd mentioned nothing. On getting the call I dropped everything and flew to Scotland to meet Kevin who explained the Club's plans and asked if I'd like to be the manager. I must say that the plans are fantastic; it's now down to all concerned to make us successful on the pitch.

How are things going?
Taking an overview, I'm delighted – although I'm not happy at being in the wrong half of the table. The reaction of the players has been first rate. Despite being linked with a whole host of names we've only brought in three new players, don't forget. And I'm asking the players to modify the style of play; try as we might, these sort of changes don't slot perfectly into place overnight. But we're getting there.

What sort of changes?
Like Kevin, I like my sides to play the ball on the floor, and to play it about quickly. To get this working smoothly, all the players must have the confidence to get hold of and manipulate the ball; they mustn't be apprehensive. We played very well against Northampton, and had a particularly good 45 minutes when we moved the ball around with great purpose and made a host of chances. By half-time we should have been a few goals to the good.

So what happened against Chesterfield?
It was a frustrating afternoon, wasn't it? That vital spark was missing. Okay, so Chesterfield sat pretty deep and didn't make it easy for us to break them down, but we didn't have the necessary craft or guile to do so. I realise only too well that such showings play into the hands of the "Wilkins, the side-passer" crew, but that doesn't worry me. I'd be worried if we were still in 17th place at the end of the season – then I'd have to expect a degree of flak. I'm determined to get it right. The players are responding – I've noticed them trying different things and modifying their approach in training. The next step is instilling the confidence in them to make these moves on matchdays.

Micky Adams and co developed a great sense of camaraderie in the camp. Do you still sense this?
Oh definitely. There's a tremendous feeling throughout the Club. And you saw that from

> "I'm determined to get it right. The players are responding – I've noticed them trying different things and modifying their approach in training. The next step is instilling the confidence in them to make these moves on matchdays."

the players in the last 20 minutes or so against Blackpool. It might not have been pretty at times, but they all showed a terrific attitude to ensure that we held out. I have really been delighted with the players. When a new management team takes over there's always a period of uncertainty. This has been heightened here because of Mr Al Fayed's backing – is there any player we haven't been linked with? Yet all the squad have responded magnificently. I've had am excellent response from the players to my way of playing, and I've sensed their belief. They're a very fit bunch, too, thanks to Micky. And, while I'm at it, I'm delighted to say that the Club have a terrific physio in Chris Smith. He's working wonders with the lads.

Have you spoken to Micky Adams?
Yes I have. When he took over at Swansea he made an enquiry about two of our players. We had a pleasant chat – we're big boys and know the ways of the footballing world, don't forget. We both realise that once such decisions are made you have to get on with life.

Feelings have been running high among supporters – after all, Adams was our only successful manager in years before he was eased out. How has this affected you?
The whole business has been like a bombshell to the supporters; I know because of all the letters that have been written to the Club. Micky was clearly held in great esteem here, and rightfully so for winning promotion. It's my job to continue

Top right: On the ball – Ray Wilkins and Kevin Keegan face the cameras.

Opposite page right: Chairman Mohamed Al Fayed shows off his new management team of Wilkins (*left*) and Keegan.

that trend but, just as Micky did things his way, I'll be running things on my terms.

Money or no money, how big is the challenge here at Fulham?
It's an immense challenge. And the money tag brings its own problems. Selling clubs ask that little bit more for their players, opposing teams lift their game to try to get one over us, and, of course, expectations are that much higher, particularly among the supporters. But I accept all of this. I'm also aware of the depth of feeling here – and of the history, atmosphere and even the location of Craven Cottage.

As I've said, the plans for this Club are fantastic, but we're determined not only to fulfill these but also to maintain the Club's image along the way. Naturally there will be changes, and some quite grandiose ones if all goes to plan, but we're only too aware of the supporters' views.

What sort of views?
Well, one chap in the Enclosure at the end of the Chesterfield game suggested quite forcibly that I wouldn't be here at Christmas! We'll see [slight chuckle]! No, I was referring to the supporters' depth of feeling for Fulham and its sense of tradition.

You're not as demonstrative as some managers…?
If by that you mean I don't jump up and down if we score or concede goals, then you're right.

We're all made differently, but I can assure all Fulham fans that I've got the bit firmly between the teeth. I am totally committed, as is Kevin, to bringing the good times back to Fulham. Just because I don't rant and rave doesn't mean there's no burning in the gut when things aren't going to plan. Or, for that matter, [that I don't have] a sense of pride and delight when things go well.

How happy are you with the new signings?
I feel dreadfully sorry for Ian Selley. He had a quiet first game but was then very influential against Northampton before suffering that injury. Paul Bracewell's been there and done it and has slotted in well, as we all expected. As for Pesch, he was a very important signing. He's a busy player and I thought he sparkled on his debut. Pace is a commodity defenders hate, so I'm sure he'll surprise a lot of them.

We're currently hovering above the relegation places. Are you looking for consolidation this season or is promotion still a realistic aim?
The division's so tight that we're only three points off sixth place – so we've got to be looking for promotion. To do that, though, we'll need to put together a decent run of results. I haven't seen anything so far to frighten us, not even Watford who are ahead of the field. I expect us to be there or thereabouts next May. For now I hope that the fans maintain their excellent support for the team. Hopefully their patience will be rewarded. ⚽

Fulham 1 York City 1	
18.11.97	13th
Fulham 3 Gillingham 0	
21.11.97	8th
Preston NE 3 Fulham 1	
29.11.97	14th
Fulham 1 Brentford 1	
02.12.97	13th
Carlisle United 2 Fulham 0	
13.12.97	15th
FA Cup	
Fulham 1 Southend United 0	
06.12.97	Round 2
Auto Windscreens Shield	
Fulham 1 Watford 0	
09.12.97	Round 1

1st
2nd
3rd
4th
5th
6th
7th
8th
9th
10th
11th
12th
13th
14th
15th
16th
17th
18th
19th
20th
21st
22nd
23rd
24th

Get Well, Lewy

Going out of my way to fraternise with players and management has not been my thing. It's wonderful when such an opportunity presents itself, but, wearing the TOOFIF hat, I've always considered that the best approach is to keep things on a professional level as a rule, rather than chase their shadows and be some sort of unwanted, ubiquitous presence. However, I made an exception when I heard that Ray Lewington was in hospital, and in a fairly bad way.

By this time Ray was assistant manager to Alan Smith at Crystal Palace and required an operation. St Anthony's Hospital, Cheam, wasn't too far away, I had an afternoon off, and, to be honest, I never thought I'd actually get to see Ray anyway. But dropping him a get-well card seemed the least I could do.

I knew Ray fairly well in those days – during his early stints at Fulham, staff numbers were that much fewer, and of course the same could also be said about the number of regulars following Fulham during those less-than-rosy campaigns. In any case, chipping in with match reports for the local papers had called for numerous chats after games up and down the country during his various terms as manager. Now Ray was in hospital for a knee operation, but there'd been complications apparently.

I parked up outside the hospital and asked someone in uniform if they knew where Ray Lewington was as I had a greetings card for him. "He's just down that corridor," came the reply, and, amazingly, I was shown to his room. I knocked and stuck my head around the door. Ray looked to be asleep, but on the other side of the bed was the stocky MK Dons captain Dean Lewington, although back then he was decidedly unstocky. He was barely into his teens and decidedly slight in stature – almost obscured by the bed, in fact.

Young Dean's first words were: "Hey, I've seen you on the telly talking about Fulham," a reference to having recently been interviewed about the Club's continued perilous situation. That he'd recognised me was an unexpected bonus as it turned out, because Dean, clearly concerned about his dad's plight and wary about any old Tom, Dick or David strolling in, beckoned me towards a chair. With that, Ray opened his eyes, just about, and also invited me to sit down.

Lewy looked, quite frankly, utterly knackered. It transpired he'd drifted off into a woozy sleep at least twice not knowing if he'd still have both legs on waking up – gangrene had been doing its worst and his specialists had been hovering over one knee in particular, poised to take drastic action at any given moment if things didn't improve. Poor guy; what a torment. And now he had to talk to me; perhaps I'd better head off home after all.

Turned out, groggy or not, he was eager to chat. Former FFC midfielder Terry Bullivant – a former schoolmate of mine – had not long left Ray's bedside. Bully and Lew also went back a long way, and they would link up a few months later at Brentford, but their bedside conversation had ultimately done a flip – with the stricken Lewy consoling Bully. Terry was manager of Reading, but all was not going well and he feared the sack if the Royals lost at the weekend (they did, and he was, if I remember rightly). Big mates or not, a healthy dose of doom and gloom was probably not the best medicine for Ray at that moment.

Another visitor that day had been Ray Wilkins, another good pal of Lewy, but he too (if I've got the timeline right) was struggling to make things work as Fulham Coach alongside Chief Operating Officer Kevin Keegan. Matters weren't progressing as well as had been expected on the field, and the managerial duo had had numerous rows. Don't suppose gentleman Ray offloaded too much onto Lewy given the circumstances, but Lewy said that Wilkins certainly wasn't the life and soul of the party that day.

Opposite page top right: Ray Lewington – a marvellous servant to FFC.

Below: Ray Lewington in customary non-stop midfield action for Fulham at Huddersfield, watched by the comparatively statuesque Geoff Banton and Les Strong and a smattering of fans.

Opposite page bottom: Paul Moody, a hat-trick hero at Luton, could have had another three against Grimsby.

The most bizarre visit, though, was that made by Crystal Palace supremo Ron Noades. Apparently Noades spent most of his time with the stricken Ray not consoling his ailing employee but instead gassing on the phone to Mrs Noades. Apart, that is, from telling an already downbeat Ray that his personal bits and pieces at

Palace were at the front desk ready for collection. As if that was uppermost in Lewy's mind!

And so it transpired that a brief chat about old friends at Fulham and the mundane goings-on in the real world turned out to be a welcome change – just as the doctor ordered you could say. The fantastic, stop-press news delivered while I was there was that Ray's knees at last seemed to be responding to treatment, a prognosis that was confirmed over the next couple of days.

Many years later, when an obviously delighted Ray Lewington was involved with our charge to the Europa League final, he was level-headed enough to say in the media that the Club's Euro success was a reward to those fans who'd stuck with FFC when the going got really tough. It was also a massive reward to a loyal club servant who himself had overcome tough times personally and professionally. So it's wonderful to get the opportunity to say: "Thanks for all your sterling efforts in so many capacities over the years, Ray – and sincere congratulations on subsequently getting the England gig alongside Roy Hodgson." ⚽

The Power of TOOFIF!

There's been an astonishing transformation in performance levels and form since the Burnley game. Whether this has been solely down to switching from five at the back to four or the long overdue arrival of the mysterious gelling agent isn't clear. Whatever the reason – and spending more than £7m has got to be in there somewhere – it's been very welcome.

I rambled on last time out that: "Four or five wins on the spin would even apply pressure on the top two, but that sort of run is seemingly

beyond us." Well, since then the team has rattled off five League wins and two draws in seven games. Oh, the power of TOOFIF! Unfortunately, Watford, with their habit of nicking late goals, and Bristol City remain well clear.

It should have been six wins, though, as the draw with Grimsby was effectively two points lost as they are one of our nearest challengers. We had a stranglehold on the game only to concede a sloppy late goal. The stats reflect our dominance: in the first half we had seven shots on target to their none but couldn't put the ball in the net. Moods [Paul Moody], the hat-trick hero seven days earlier, could have had three in the first nine minutes. In the end we paid for trying to hold on to a slender lead (that came from a great finish by Kyle Lightbourne). Grimsby only had two shots on target all game, which had much to do with the form of Coleman and Neilson – the duo

are looking better and better by the game.

Our improved run has hinged on sparkling away form, which has been witnessed by fantastic travelling support. Away trips have always been fun, and the diehards have reaped the reward over the past couple of seasons. Recent levels of away support, both in terms of numbers and noise, have been better than ever. If only we could make the same sort of racket at home!

I don't know if it's because hundreds of newcomers, as well as many lapsed fans, have turned up just recently and don't know what to do, but the Cottage is hardly a pulsating or raucous place on matchdays, is it? We had a terrific gate for the Bristol City match, for instance but, compared with the volume at Wrexham, Spurs and Luton, we remained in mute mode. So, what about turning up the level at home, guys and gals? At times we're so loud we sound like Orient!

	1st
	2nd
	3rd
Fulham 1 Burnley 0	4th
19.12.97 10th	5th
Plymouth Argyle 1 Fulham 4	6th
26.12.97 10th	7th
Fulham 1 Bristol City 0	8th
28.12.97 6th	9th
Wrexham 0 Fulham 3	**10th**
10.01.98 4th	11th
Fulham 0 Wycombe Wanderers 0	12th
17.01.98 6th	13th
Luton Town 1 Fulham 4	14th
24.01.98 3rd	15th
Grimsby Town 1 Fulham 1	16th
31.01.98 4th	17th
Fulham 2 Southend United 0	18th
07.02.98 3rd	19th
Oldham Athletic 1 Fulham 0	20th
14.02.98 6th	21st
Fulham 2 Wigan Athletic 0	22nd
21.02.98 5th	23rd
Fulham 0 Bournemouth 1	24th
24.02.98 6th	
Blackpool 2 Fulham 1	
28.02.98 6th	

FA Cup

Tottenham Hotspur 3 Fulham 1
05.01.98   Round 3

Auto Windscreens Shield

Fulham 3 Wycombe Wanderers 1
13.01.98   Round 2

Fulham 1 Luton Town 2
27.01.98   Quarter-final

Priestfield Shame

My eldest son, Matt, was born on March 28. In 1998 he was six, and we had a birthday "party" arranged for teatime. March 28, 1998 is also the date that another Fulham fan named Matthew lost his life at Gillingham, just three days before his own 25th birthday.

I've never enjoyed matches at Gillingham. In November 1995 there was the infamous Battle of Priestfield; at the final whistle Fulham were down to nine men, one of the two sendings-off being a case of mistaken identity, and Gillingham's Mark O'Connor had suffered a broken leg. Both clubs were charged by the FA. The two sets of fans weren't exactly bosom buddies, and it didn't help that the Gills clinched promotion that season with a 0-0 draw at Craven Cottage in April.

In March 1998, the Fulham Supporters' Club was doing its best to spread the Fulham 2000 word, with committee members doing the rounds of other supporters' clubs to raise awareness of our Club's plight. Micky Roots, Siobhan Bowyer and I were invited into the Gills fans' bar before the 1998 game, and while the people we met were perfectly civil, the overall atmosphere was decidedly less cordial than the welcome we'd experienced at other grounds.

Below: The Craven Cottage gates are bedecked with flowers, messages and FFC memorabilia in the wake of Matthew Fox's untimely death at Gillingham.

But that was nothing compared to the atmosphere inside Priestfield. To begin with, our section of fans in the corner of the ground contained a whole host of new faces, and they spent the game spewing almost non-stop vitriol at Ray Wilkins. Chelsea weren't in action that day and QPR were at Norwich, but whether that and the previous statement are in any way connected I'll leave you to decide. Meantime, the home fans took great glee in lobbing bottles, poles, brollies, pieces of furniture, anything, over the divide patrolled by police officers and into our pen. A number of these items were accordingly lobbed back.

This is at variance with the comments subsequently made in a Review Report by the Kent County Constabulary: "On the day, the visitors' enclosure was at near capacity, holding approximately 1,320 spectators. Prior to the 89th minute of the match, the crowd had been orderly in watching what was an uneventful match." That's a very unusual use of the word "orderly" – the atmosphere had been bloody horrible throughout.

The report continued: "Following the second goal scored by Gillingham during the 89th minute, the mood and ferocity of the opposing factions located at the Gillingham end of the ground became immediately explosive. There was a barrage of coins being thrown from both factions, who were separated by a sterile zone, consisting of a metal-framed cage-walk. There were attempts to climb this structure to meet opposing fans who were spitting and shouting at each other, being very violent. Within three minutes of this unprecedented level of aggression the final whistle was blown and crowds immediately began to leave the stadium."

A subtext to matters on the pitch was that earlier in the month Ray Wilkins had tabled a bid of £1m for Gills forward Ade Akinbiyi, who'd rejected the offer stating that he thought "Gillingham have a better chance of going up, so I'm happy to stay." To the natural dismay of all Fulham fans, Akinbiyi netted both goals on the day. Given the hostile atmosphere, Akinbiyi's gleeful celebrations in front of the Fulham fans weren't at all helpful.

As the final whistle blew I legged it and scurried down that alley to get to my car. I just wanted to get home pronto, away from the odious Priestfield atmosphere and, I'll admit, eager to scoff some birthday cake. Up to that point, the most disturbing incident had involved a group of supposed Fulham fans chanting "Hope he dies" as a home fan was stretchered around the pitch before the end of the game. This was inexcusable behaviour, and hardly typical of our travelling fans – made that much worse when we learned that the fan in question did indeed pass away. So, you get the picture: it was a horrible afternoon on a number of levels. And yet I had absolutely no idea of the fateful post-match events.

TOOFIF stalwart Roger Scoon rang me around 9pm. Fully aware of what had occurred, Roger said how dreadful the afternoon had turned out. I simply responded by waffling on about the unpleasant atmosphere and a rotten result. As I droned on, my wife shouted from the other room that Fulham had made the lead item on the evening news. Shocked, but still none the wiser, I told Roger I'd call him back. The bulletin was grave: a fan had been killed. A Fulham fan. This was numbing news.

About 10 minutes later the phone rang again. Roger, perhaps. No, it was someone from one of the tabloids. I very nearly put the phone down. The reporter informed me that Fulham FC had prepared a general statement but were otherwise not taking calls on the matter. The reporter continued: "Can you tell me where the alley in question is in relation to Craven Cottage?" Okay, so this was a news reporter straying into sporting territory, but come on! I explained that the tragic incident had taken place at Gillingham, Kent, not SW6.

It was the first of stacks of calls between then and the following Tuesday afternoon; during that time the Fulham fan had been named as Matthew Fox. Probably the most stupid remark came from one poorly researched reporter who was setting the tone for his article by presuming that the aforementioned Battle of Priestfield referred to a violent clash between fans. I'm pleased to say that Fulham fans were acknowledged as fair and decent when that particular hack's report was published. Another one referenced the match at Craven Cottage with the Gills the previous November, "So this was the second leg, then…?" Hopeless!

I should own up here and say that I'd had several years' experience as a Press Officer (for London Transport), so wasn't in unchartered territory. It was "simply" a question of patiently going through the whole business with reporter after reporter so that facts and background details weren't mangled. I also insisted to all callers at the outset that I wasn't to be quoted in any way. The only newspaper to renege on this deal was, surprise, surprise, the *Evening Standard*, who used my description of Foxy, a guy I'd seen many times at matches but only knew slightly through sometimes being on the same train to away games. The description was innocuous, but it was still an underhand move

by a paper that had hardly been supportive of the Club when the chips were down, nor were they prepared to give it anything like proportionate coverage compared to other clubs in the capital. TOOFIF coined the paper's alternative name: the Sub-*Standard*. Hardly groundbreaking, but apposite.

Even so, while intensely irritating, that chat with the Sub-Standard wasn't the most uncomfortable phone call to TOOFIF Towers around that time. That came from someone purporting to be a Gillingham supporter, inviting me to a specific pub in the town where I'd be given "the same treatment as Matthew Fox." Needless to say the police were informed.

In amongst all of this, TOOFIF 58, which marked 10 years of the mag, was about to head to the printers. At the eleventh hour I decided to insert an additional stop-press "cover" inside the already prepared '88-'98 cover artwork in light of the whole appalling business. The more palatable breaking news was that the supremely gifted Peter Beardsley had signed for us that week (and had made his Fulham debut at Priestfield). Seeing that in a previous editorial years beforehand I'd referred to some outlandish event as being "about as likely as Peter Beardsley ever signing for Fulham," this was indeed significant news, even if the player's best years were behind him.

I went for the "Magic/Tragic" approach and, if truth be told, probably got a bit carried away with the angle taken. Under "Magic" I placed a picture of Beardsley, and under "Tragic" was a grainy shot of Foxy's body draped in a cloth. However, TOOFIF is a fans' mag not a tabloid paper. Even so, the supplementary cover provoked very few comments. Trouble was it offended those closest to Matthew Fox: his family and friends. While that was most definitely not the objective, the damage had been done. It was an error of judgement. As Foxy's father Ian soon impressed on me, a football fanzine shouldn't be printing pictures of a dead body, however distant and grainy, in its pages, let alone on the cover. That body is someone's son. In this case it was his son. I apologised there and then over the phone (and also later face to face, as well as via the next fanzine editorial). I'm pleased to say that my apology was accepted by Ian Fox right away, even if one or two of Foxy's mates have never accepted it for what it was – poor judgement; a mistake. It's a mistake that I've regretted ever since. Then again, that aspect of the whole sorry business is nothing more than a footnote to what was a terrible tragedy.

• In October 1998, having pleaded guilty to manslaughter, Gillingham fan Barry Cullen was jailed for four years.

Fulham 1 Bristol Rovers 0	
03.03.98	5th
Chesterfield 0 Fulham 2	
07.03.98	5th
Fulham 1 Millwall 2	
14.03.98	5th
York City 0 Fulham 1	
21.03.98	6th
Gillingham 2 Fulham 0	
28.03.98	6th
Fulham 2 Preston NE 1	
04.04.98	5th
Fulham 1 Walsall 1	
07.04.98	5th
Brentford 0 Fulham 2	
11.04.98	4th
Fulham 5 Carlisle United 0	
13.04.98	3rd
Burnley 2 Fulham 1	
18.04.98	3rd
Northampton Town 1 Fulham 0	
25.04.98	4th
Fulham 1 Watford 2	
02.05.98	6th
Division Two Play-off	
Fulham 1 Grimsby Town 1	
09.05.98	1st leg
Grimsby Town 1 Fulham 0	
13.05.98	2nd leg

1st
2nd
3rd
4th
5th
6th
7th
8th
9th
10th
11th
12th
13th
14th
15th
16th
17th
18th
19th
20th
21st
22nd
23rd
24th

Crazy Days

I t's been one surprise after another at Craven Cottage following the shock arrival of Mohamed Al Fayed as Chairman last summer. Whatever next? The Pope installed as spiritual advisor? George Michael recruited as unofficial Cottage guide? The whole World Cup-winning squad being bought en bloc? Or, crazier still, the Supporters' Club being allowed to have a pukka bar again?

Last season was, quite probably, the season no Fulham fan wanted. True, we made it to the Division Two Play-offs; on paper a creditable achievement having been promoted from the basement division only 12 months before. However, it was all so curiously unsatisfying. The euphoria and undoubted expectation following not only the appointment of Kevin Keegan and Ray Wilkins but also the very un-Fulham-like levels of spending led to problems, not least of which was the death of a supporter.

Keegan's unexpected arrival as Chief Operating Officer had been heralded as a major coup by the fans, although the jury was very much out as far as Wilkins was concerned. The replacement of the hugely popular Micky Adams – unquestionably the catalyst in the Club's latter-day change in fortunes – by a man with an unproven track record in management led to a heated exchange of views in the fanzine. And, although the season promised much, the feel-good factor and sense of togetherness, such strong features of the previous regime, came under serious threat.

The incredible change in circumstances, not least from being paupers to stinking rich, was something supporters found difficult to take in. This was Fulham, after all, where principles were still high despite (or maybe because of) the fact that just a couple of years previously the hard core of supporters had led the fight for the Club's very existence.

Suddenly, lapsed fans made their way to the Cottage once more, as did hundreds of inquisitive new ones. With no real period of transition, it made for an awkward mix at times. Although the bottom line was that every Fulham fan was delighted that their Club had been "saved" and the freehold of the ground re-acquired, people found it difficult to adjust. Some maintained Adams should never have been shown the door (as he effectively was); some maintained they preferred the down-at-heel existence; some feared for Fulham's traditional homely appeal; others shunned the new fans (where were they when the Club was in serious trouble?); while others didn't care much for the new "big business" approach, which included the Supporters' Club bar making way for a corporate hospitality lounge.

New players arrived almost weekly. With an ever-lengthening "gelling" period being demanded on the pitch, terrace "discussion" often erupted into arguments. Mind you, Fulham being Fulham, these were usually no more than lovers' tiffs. But there was a huge, and ultimately tragic, knock-on effect. You see we were no longer perceived as "Friendly Fulham" by most opposing fans. We were now considered the "Flash Moneybags" and not only the team they wanted to beat (fair enough) but ours were the fans they wanted to goad… and fight.

How different from a few years ago when we received such magnificent support from a host of other clubs when the ground issue was raging. Subsequently fans from all around the country chipped in to the Fulham 2000 fundraising appeal. Sadly, some of our new-found support,

Opposite page below: Peter Beardsley signs for TOOFIF!

Below: Another cut-and-paste special from TOOFIF Towers as Fulham FC continue to make the news.

and regretfully one or two stalwarts, were more than prepared to argue the toss.

Events on the park were doing little to appease the disgruntled. Millions of pounds were spent on players, yet apart from a purple patch in January it was all rather sterile stuff. A patient, steady passing approach is all very well but if there is no apparent passion, no final "killer" ball, no raising of tempo or, most importantly, no end product then the terrace troops will become restless.

That's not to say the new players weren't up to it. Far from it. In Paul Peschisolido, the Second Division's first £1m player, we had an energetic, pacy striker who suffered from a lack of decent service and later from a dip in confidence. Meanwhile Chris Coleman (blimey, two million quid for a defender!) was arguably the bargain buy. He offered style aplenty together with a superb attitude and was captain in all but name. The other new purchases were far from mugs either but many were plainly played out of position. With the balance all wrong, plus an apparent lack of heart, the team tended to stumble and stutter rather than purr as expected. It was all a bit Austin Allegro rather than Rolls-Royce.

The team needed to gel, we were told. Fine. (Goodness, how many times have we been asked to be patient?) Except that it never really happened. Sufficient points were being banked, though, to slip into one of the Play-off berths. But this was as much down to other teams dropping points as anything else. At one point Bristol City and Watford were wobbling and a decent run of results would have put real pressure on the top two. But a pretty successful policy of playing three up front was abandoned when loanee Kyle Lightbourne went back to the Potteries. And the chance was gone.

With all the money swilling about it was strange we had so little cover up front. The burgeoning squad contained midfielders in abundance, so much so that the £500,000 buy from Arsenal, Ian Selley, badly injured just as he was beginning to flourish in his second game, was barely mentioned for the rest of the season. Up front it was a different matter. Last year's goal machine Mick Conroy – who netted in spectacular fashion from the halfway line at Wycombe in August – picked up a long-term injury, as did Darren Freeman, Division Three's Player of the Season for '97-98, while Paul Moody spent much of the season trying to shake off a series of niggles. This left Pesky Paul, not the biggest striker the world has seen, to valiantly bear the brunt of the rugged Division Two defences. Oh for another forward, or at least someone who could open up the play and feed the front men.

Cue first Tony Thorpe from Luton and then Peter Beardsley on loan from Bolton. Thorpe, clearly out of shape, made his bow in a poor showing at a windswept Blackpool in February. But as his fitness improved so his penalty-box prowess increased; he was, after all, the division's top scorer. Yet the potentially predatory front pairing of Pesch and Thorpe (dubbed "The Krankies"!) never got going. The service was virtually non-existent! It was a sad indictment of the midfielders in particular that it took the reintroduction of the lofty but still only half-fit Moody to get us back on the rails. Moods, you see, could knock down the high balls and generally be a nuisance. A relevant tactic, but where was the guile?

When Beardsley arrived in mid-March, however, things changed somewhat. He went on to mastermind a terrific, gutsy 2-0 win against Brentford – Micky Adams, Glenn Cockerill, Danny Cullip, Paul Watson and all – at Griffin Park (where the first foul was committed after a mere six seconds!) then a 5-0 drubbing of Carlisle at the Cottage. Was it all coming together at the crucial stage after all? Not exactly, as it turned out, but we squeezed into the Play-offs nevertheless.

However, Beardo's Fulham debut (a pretty unforgettable encounter as, not for the first time, we were outmanoeuvred by a much less expensive outfit) was totally overshadowed by dreadful scenes off the pitch. Gillingham away on 28 March, 1998 will go down in the Fulham history books as one of the Club's lowlights: it was the day Fulham fan Matthew Fox was killed.

The press had a field day, making a swathe of wide-of-the-mark assumptions. Three things are patently clear, however: 1) Any fan attending a football match should be able to do so without the fear of being killed; 2) The ever-worsening

Macclesfield Town 0 Fulham 1
08.08.98   8th

Fulham 3 Manchester City 0
14.08.98   1st

Colchester United 0 Fulham 1
22.08.98   3rd

Fulham 0 Bournemouth 0
29.08.98   4th

Oldham Athletic 1 Fulham 1
31.08.98   2nd

Fulham 1 Stoke City 0
08.09.98   4th

Notts County 1 Fulham 0
12.09.98   7th

Fulham 3 York City 3
19.09.98   8th

Lincoln City 1 Fulham 2
26.09.98   6th

Fulham 2 Wycombe Wanderers 0
29.09.98   3rd

League Cup

Fulham 2 Cardiff City 1
11.08.98   Round 1 1st leg

Cardiff City 1 Fulham 2
18.08.98   Round 1 2nd leg

Fulham 1 Southampton 1
15.09.98   Round 2 1st leg

Southampton 0 Fulham 1
23.09.98   Round 2 2nd leg

1st
2nd
3rd
4th
5th
6th
7th
9th
10th
11th
12th
13th
14th
15th
16th
17th
18th
19th
20th
21st
22nd
23rd
24th

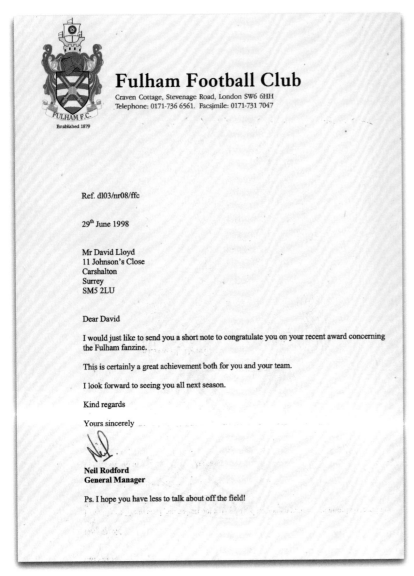

Fulham Football Club

Craven Cottage, Stevenage Road, London SW6 6HH
Telephone: 0171-736 6561.   Facsimile: 0171-731 7047

Ref. dl03/nr08/ffc

29th June 1998

Mr David Lloyd
11 Johnson's Close
Carshalton
Surrey
SM5 2LU

Dear David

I would just like to send you a short note to congratulate you on your recent award concerning
the Fulham fanzine.

This is certainly a great achievement both for you and your team.

I look forward to seeing you all next season.

Kind regards

Yours sincerely

Neil Rodford
General Manager

Ps. I hope you have less to talk about off the field!

Above: A "well-done" note from FFC General Manager Neil Rodford.

atmosphere between some sections of the crowd that day suggested that trouble was in the air (stewarding and policing left a lot to be desired); 3) All football fans should learn from this appalling tragedy – it's only a bloody game when all's said and done.

The atmosphere on the day was particularly unpleasant. Players and officials came in for a furious amount of stick as bad feeling that stemmed from a previous highly charged encounter resurfaced. Before long, some sections of the crowd became intent on out-abusing each other. In short, it was all set to "go off" – a fact seemingly overlooked by those in charge who had added to the problems by allowing opposing supporters to mix. Bloody crazy! One guy next to me spent the entire match hurling abuse at Wilkins. Towards the end, when he finally stopped to take a breath, I asked him what was the point of the sustained vitriol. "He buggered up my QPR," came the reply. He wasn't even a Fulham fan!

Anyhow, for the second time in an "unreal" Fulham FC season we had a "special" game as FFC and Preston fans honoured a minute's silence in Foxy's memory. It was impeccably observed.

Plymouth supporters had been equally respectful back in September when an eerie piper's lament wailed around an otherwise silent Craven Cottage to mark the awful Paris car crash that killed Dodi Fayed, son of the Fulham Chairman, and Princess Di. Although a tragedy of international significance, there was still the chance for Fulham folk to pay their respects in their own way and the main Cottage gates became engulfed in flowers, football shirts and scarves.

You'll gather this was no run-of-the-mill season, even if the end product probably was. Highlights included 4-1 wins at both Plymouth and Luton, a dalliance with the big time with a respectable effort at White Hart Lane in the FA Cup and a solid 2-0 win at Chesterfield where one of the "old guard", ex-captain Simon Morgan, was inspirational in a tremendous team performance. Behind the first-team scenes, the Youth Team under Alan Smith's guidance made tremendous strides and the Club were given the all-clear to set up an Academy of Football under the FA School of Excellence programme. The reserves have been elevated too, to the Football Combination.

Unfortunately there were simply too many lowlights. And ultimately Ray Wilkins – the ultimate nice guy – paid the price. The stats show we used 37 players and spent around £8m but only got into the Play-offs thanks, ironically, to Gillingham slipping up on the last day of the season.

KK couldn't steer us past Grimsby, who deservedly took the third promotion spot, but he subsequently confirmed himself as team boss for the new season. So what's in store for us lot now? Maybe the vision of Ronaldo as centre-forward and Zidane pulling the midfield strings is a little too far-fetched, but certainly the script suggests a roller-coaster season ahead. Things won't ever be boring at FFC again, that seems certain. C'mon you Whites! ⚽

We Are the Champions

TOOFIF has been lucky enough to reap a few accolades and awards along the way. Funny enough, getting three out of 10 from *The Sun* ranks up there somewhere. Rumour has it that someone at the Club contacted the red top to "arrange" a low score at a time when relations between one or two people at FFC and the fanzine were less than cordial (if so, what a sad state of affairs!). And yet that 3/10 remains a badge of honour for some reason.

About the same time, a young police constable, again possibly at someone's behest, wandered along to the TOOFIF sales pitch and threatened to confiscate my bag of magazines if I didn't "move on' or show him my street-trader's licence (not required as TOOFIF is a periodical; you *can* get done for obstruction, however). Now,

Left: The Ed, some silverware and, for the cameras at least, a smiling Richard Littlejohn.

Below: TOOFIF makes the news!

"Littlejohn was not only full of cold, and more than happy to let the whole bloody world know about it, but was also late filing copy for his Sun column, so was as warm and welcoming as a collapsed igloo."

not only was I on great terms with Inspector Ron Brooke from Fulham nick (who oversaw match-day policing) by then, but also, of the very few sales made that cold, rainy evening by the Thames, three had been to the obstinate young bobby's colleagues! Accessories to the non-crime? I patiently explained all this to the PC, but he remained oddly insistent, as if acting on someone's orders – so he was somewhat taken aback when I said he could help himself to the bag of mags, after all the bag itself was almost falling to bits and the mags were weeks old and getting wetter by the minute. A small crowd had gathered by now, chanting "Lloydy, Lloydy…" which hardly improved the bobby's mood.

The 10-minute stand-off ended with him stomping off towards the Cottage. In one of those wonderful quirks of fate, the following day I was heading into town on the District Line when who should I bump into but Inspector Brooke. I explained the situation before he got off at Fulham Broadway. He gave a knowing grin and simply said, most emphatically, "He was out of order; leave it to me." I had visions of a Hill Street Blues-type morning briefing at the cop-shop at which all those in attendance, and one bobby in particular, were told to leave that fanzine bloke alone! All very surreal.

By that time, the mag was sporting the "Fanzine of the Year" tag afforded by the *Sunday Times* (no less!) in 1991. That one was well-worth savouring. Some years later, the prize for winning

Teletext's Fans-scene Writer of the Year award in 1998 involved spending an afternoon at BBC HQ watching a World Cup match – England v Tunisia – alongside broadcaster/journalist Richard Littlejohn. As it turned out, this was worthy of a booby prize – Littlejohn was not only full of cold, and more than happy to let the whole bloody world know about it, but was also late filing copy for his *Sun* column, so was as warm and welcoming as a collapsed igloo. Coughing and spluttering all-too-openly, he snarled I could "watch the match if you like" but that he would be otherwise engaged. Charming! Then again given his wretched mood, watching the match was all the better for him not being there.

Much more recently, in 2009, the New Football Pools awarded TOOFIF the mantle of Best Print Fanzine (presumably because all the others were by then online). ⚽

Simply the best

REGULAR viewers of *Teletext* may be aware of the fan-scene pages that appear every Thursday of which *There's Only One F in Fulham* are among the contributors.

Well, *Teletext* have given out their regional award for the best contributors and the ever-brilliant *TOOFIF*, whose bumper issue went on sale last Saturday, has been voted best in the London and South-East category out of some 16 other fanzines.

They now go on to the national final, the winner of which will be decided by journalist and Spurs' fan Richard Littlejohn.

Champions

FULHAM fanzine *There's Only One F In Fulham* has been voted the best fans' magazine in the Nationwide League by Teletext.

Editor David Lloyd topped the pile of 40 other fanzines, which was whittled down to a final five before getting the decisive nod from TV presenter Richard Littlejohn.

Teletext ran a page on its news service last season called "fan-scene" where Lloyd's work was reckoned to be by far the best regularly seen by the weekly 4.6 million audience.

Taking the Pitch

In 1998 the fledgling ITV2 were trialling a new football quiz show and were touting for a famous ex-player, a celebrity fan and an imbecile to make up threesomes representing their football club. "Gentleman" George Cohen and "Diddy" David Hamilton made up two-thirds of the Fulham line-up. Seems I was I was a shoo-in for the other spot.

Hosted by comedian Bob Mills, the quiz featured the standard "fingers-on-the-buzzer" format as well as individual "specialist" questions – "Call yourself a fan, let's see what you really know…!" It also had a penalty prize round where you fired a spot kick at – or hopefully beyond – a noted goalkeeper.

At the time I was a sub-editor on a (very good) project called *Soccer Brilliance*, which built up into a coaching manual for youngsters. On top of a wealth of generic training information that came in the form of illustrated features and videos, the product included a topical monthly newsletter for which the TV company kindly gave permission for me to take photos backstage to illustrate a "behind the scenes at a football quiz show" feature.

In the event, TOOFIF stalwart Bill Plummer offered to take the pics and the pair of us headed to the London Studios in Wandsworth for the filming. I confess to being very nervous. Doing the show didn't overly faze me, but doing so in front of a sizeable gathering of Fulham fans definitely did. What if I couldn't answer the simplest of questions and caused us to crash out in the first round? What if I stumbled on the specialist fan question? Oh well, no pressure!

Bill and I were shown to a modest room where we were soon joined by a group of other supporters – the other "pillocks". Down the corridor a minor row was breaking out. Apparently some of the celebs, Fish (lead singer of '80s rock group Marillion) among them, were insisting that us makeweights be allowed to join the elite in their green room. Result! So, alongside such heavyweights as Gentleman George and Diddy David, Bill and I mingled with other luminaries such as Alex Salmond MP, *Soccer AM*'s Helen Chamberlain, boxer Steve Collins, *EastEnders* actor Dean Gaffney, Live TV's Weather in Norwegian presenter Anne Marie Foss, the multi-skilled Jo Guest plus footballers David Weir, Paul Buckle, Bryan Gunn and Rodney Marsh.

Every bit as interesting was the well-stocked table of food and booze conspicuously absent in the other room! When he wasn't tucking in to the hospitality, Bill was busy taking photographs with his digital camera (we'd explained to those present that we had permission to do this), then a "lively" Ann Marie Foss asked if she and her mate Jo Guest could have their picture taken with Steve Collins. Not on our remit, but to keep the peace we did so, and captured three sparkling showbizzy smiles.

Top right: Dean Gaffney (Robbie Jackson in *EastEnders*) goes into moody mode on being asked to go in goal so the Ed can practise his penalty taking.

Opposite page top: David Hamilton is first on the buzzer with a correct answer during the filming of Taking the Pitch. George Cohen (Far right) looks on in admiration, while the third member of the team is evidently in passive mode.

Below and opposite page: Backstage at *Taking the Pitch* (left to right): In make-up; with former England keeper Peter Shilton; meeting *Soccer AM*'s Helen Chamberlain; and making friends with media folk Anne Marie Foss and Jo Guest.

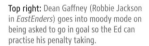

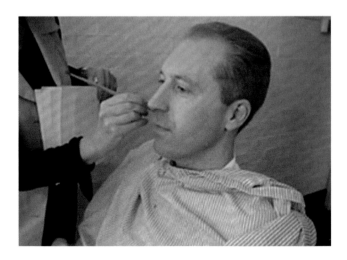

As the two women wandered into the corridor, Bill and I received a nasty shock – WBO middleweight champion Collins, who'd seen off Chris Eubank and Nigel Benn, suddenly grabbed the pair of us roughly by our throats. It's fair to say that Plummer and Lloyd weren't exactly Eubank and Benn. Collins had also cheated; he'd caught us completely off guard, and before any "bell"! But it really was no laughing matter – he was seething and insisting that we destroy the digital photographs there and then. Bottom line, as he told us most aggressively, was that he didn't want his wife seeing such a picture in one of the Sunday tabloids and getting the wrong idea.

Once our throats were released we did as we were told, deleting the pics, and sheepishly telling the boxer that we hadn't really wanted to take the photos in the first place. In a flash, Collins was as nice as pie again, thanking us from the bottom of his heart and laughing and joking as if nothing untoward had happened. Even so, we gave him a wide berth after that.

Nothing like having your nerves put at ease before making an appearance on the telly!

The quiz turned out to be a lot of fun. The questions weren't overly testing – although that didn't mean we got them all right! – and, pillock or not, I scored all my penalties. True, Peter Bonetti and Peter Shilton were past their prime, but then again they only had seven-a-side goals to defend. We won through to the semi-finals at which point we were shown the trophy ("Come and have a look at what you could've won…") that was ultimately lifted by Celtic.

On the way out of the studios a grinning Bill showed me some of the photos he'd captured for the newsletter feature… including one of Steve Collins and his two female admirers. "Hang on, I saw you delete those," I stammered, looking over my shoulder just in case Mr Collins was lurking somewhere in the Wandsworth shadows. "Ah, you have to press the "delete" button twice to make them vanish," said Bill knowingly. Hmm, now where's the number for that Sunday red-top…? ⚽

Fulham 1 Luton Town 3	
03.10.98	4th
Millwall 0 Fulham 1	
17.10.98	5th
Fulham 4 Walsall 1	
24.10.98	3rd
Blackpool 2 Fulham 3	
31.10.98	2nd
Fulham 1 Bristol Rovers 0	
07.11.98	2nd
Wrexham 0 Fulham 2	
10.11.98	2nd
Gillingham 1 Fulham 0	
21.11.98	2nd
Wigan Athletic 2 Fulham 0	
01.12.98	3rd
Fulham 4 Burnley 0	
12.12.98	2nd
Preston NE 0 Fulham 1	
19.12.98	1st
Fulham 2 Colchester United 0	
26.12.98	1st
Northampton Town 1 Fulham 1	
28.12.98	1st
Fulham 1 Macclesfield Town 0	
09.01.99	1st
Manchester City 3 Fulham 0	
16.01.99	1st
League Cup	
Liverpool 3 Fulham 1	
27.10.98	Round 3
FA Cup	
Fulham 1 Leigh RMI 1	
15.11.98	Round 1
Leigh RMI 0 Fulham 2	
24.11.98	Round 1 replay
Fulham 4 Hartlepool United 2	
05.12.98	Round 2
Southampton 1 Fulham 1	
02.01.99	Round 3
Fulham 1 Southampton 0	
13.01.99	Round 3 replay
Auto Windscreens Shield	
Torquay United 2 Fulham 1	
05.01.99	aet Round 2

1st
2nd
3rd
4th
5th
6th
7th
8th
9th
10th
11th
12th
13th
14th
15th
16th
17th
18th
19th
20th
21st
22nd
23rd
24th

Villans Nicked

e went for it on all fronts in 1998-99. Apart from the Auto-Windscreens Shield Trophy, obviously. Even so, it took an extra-time goal from Torquay to knock us out of that one. Cardiff (2-1, 2-1) and Southampton (1-1, 1-0) were dispatched in the Worthington Cup before Liverpool beat us 3-1 at Anfield. In the FA Cup, meantime, we overcame Leigh RMI (1-1, 2-0), Hartlepool (4-2) and Southampton (1-1, 1-0) before being drawn away to Aston Villa.

Villa, under John Gregory, were flying high in the Premier League, while we were making mincemeat of the Second Division with Kevin Keegan at the helm. I snapped up a match ticket as soon as they went on sale. Subsequently, the *Fulham Chronicle* asked me to cover the game; even better – I could get all the behind-the-scenes gossip courtesy of a press pass while my brother, Gareth, could have my ticket for the away end.

On arrival at Villa Park I'd been left two press passes. Result! And the first in what would be an extraordinary day. To begin with, the Villa corridors were full of conjecture about the whereabouts of one Stanley Collymore. And when the teamsheets were distributed as kick-off approached, sure enough, no Stan the Man.

I took my place in the press box, with Gareth assigned a seat in the row behind.

Press-box protocol dictates that while club allegiances are tolerated, any particularly overt displays are frowned upon. Eight minutes in and, just as the local radio reporter alongside me was doing a live piece, the ball reached the head of Simon Morgan, who duly guided it into the net. "GET IN THERE YOU BEAUTY!" yelled my brother, loud enough to be heard by the whole of Birmingham, with or without the aid of the local airwaves. I was just as overjoyed – and delighted for Morgs, a Brummie fan (and staunch supporter of TOOFIF) – but rather more restrained in my celebrations. The reporter tailed off his live report and swivelled sharply to suggest, with no hint of irony, that Gareth should refrain from such boorish behaviour or else he'd get an effing punch in the gullet.

A minute before the break Steve Hayward (a Villa fan) belted a free kick that flew into the net via a deflection – 0-2! And Gareth risked his swallowing mechanism with another joyous outburst, sensibly making himself scarce as soon as the half-time whistle blew, making a beeline for the coffee and nibbles. The pair of us shared a few giggles about his impulsive antics and raved over Fulham's outstanding first-half display.

Meanwhile in a nearby dressing room our captain Chris Coleman was lying unconscious on the floor having been knocked out briefly. Guilty party was Steve Hayward who'd stretched his legs rather forcibly just as Cookie was bending down to check his bootlaces. Morgs recalls: "Cookie was flat out. Then we realised it was his head and, of course, he got up without feeling a thing. No sense, and all that…". At least Gareth had managed to escape something similar, even though he was back in the press enclave as Fulham held out comfortably for a deserved giantkilling victory and gained an away tie at Old Trafford as their reward – hey-ho, an even bigger giant in need of a slaying…

In the post-match press conference at Villa, John Gregory had to field a barrage of questions about the non-appearance of Collymore (who bizarrely turned up on loan at Fulham within a matter of months). Kevin Keegan, in jubilant mood, was joined by Steve Hayward who was noticeably sheepish at getting so much of the attention even though he, like the rest of the team, had played extremely well. Fellow goalscorer Simon Morgan acknowledged: "I did a bit for the radio, but managed to escape most of the press entourage as I was eager to meet the family. Scoring that goal was a brilliant moment

Opposite page right: Chris Coleman and Gareth Southgate are pictured backstage at Villa Park. The former Palace team-mates are presumably placing bets on who would go on to become a national team manager first.

Below: Goalscorer Steve Hayward gets a playful slap from Fulham's delighted team boss Kevin Keegan during the post-match press gathering at Villa Park.

for Fulham and for yours truly. And all the sweeter for being a Birmingham fan. What a great day that was for the Fulham fans. People still talk of the match as one of the great away days on the journey up the divisions." ⚽

Double Trouble

It's a bit difficult penning a detached editorial in the immediate afterglow of that fantastic away trip to Villa Park. Suffice to say a League and Cup double remains firmly on the cards! Promotion from Division Two – any which way – must remain the sole priority, but a continued Cup run, if handled professionally, could actually give our promotion/championship push a timely boost. What we don't need, as a side issue to a glory, glory Cup chase, is a surfeit of injuries and suspensions, nor indeed a glut of League games in a short space of time. But, hey, the games against "superior" opposition have clearly given Kevin Keegan a boost – terms of performances, levels of support and the increased buzz around Craven Cottage – and he's re-emphasised his determination to see matters through here. That surely can't be a bad thing, can it?

That performance against Villa will have made many a long-in-the-tooth fan hark back to 1975. For Villa Park, substitute Goodison. A table-topping team from the top flight humbled on their own turf by underdogs from a lower division. And all done with style, panache, cohesion, no little grit, and a fabulous team spirit. It was all the more unexpected this time around as it came only a week after that hugely disappointing visit to Maine Road.

Realistically, most supporters would trade the Cup success for three points from that encounter with Manchester City. And lessons must be learned. It's one thing being the underdog and springing a surprise result by, perhaps, being more hyped up on the day. But that's exactly what we're having to face in the hurly-burly confines of Division Two. Until that Maine Road

effort, we've coped pretty well; even if the more recent showings have lacked a little invention. It's during this time, too, that Barry Hayles has been introduced. Whatever you think of the bloke, it's disgraceful that fights have broken out between Fulham fans over our £2m man. I'm all for free speech and yet the continued fury vented by some, which has been, perhaps understandably, met with resistance from others, should surely be put into context.

The Club is enjoying its most successful period in ages, just a matter of months since the darkest days in its history; and there we are bickering big time over the merits of a player!

That Hayles has failed to take the place by storm is in no doubt – his Cup winner against the Saints notwithstanding – but give the guy, and the team, a break! I agree his body language has been poor – not appearing to be too interested at times and always seeming as if he's about to burst into life without actually doing so. But then he's in a difficult position. He's trying to adapt to a new role at a new club, and with a huge price tag on his head. The latter point, of course, has nothing to do with him. I'd prefer to judge him on the back of a run of games in a settled side when he's upped his confidence. Hayles has a proven track record of scoring goals at this level, after all. That said, my favoured front two would be Horsfield and Peschisolido; but what do I know! ⚽

On the Up!

What a memorable few weeks. We've enjoyed a glorious sideshow to the League with a glamorous run in the Cup, have had our manager wooed by the FA for the England job (hmm, I don't recall that happening in the days of Dicks and Branfoot) and in so doing have ensured that we've had more media coverage than ever. Oh yes, and we've subsequently taken a grip on the division, rattling up the wins in the process. All a far cry from Torquay away in 1996, eh?

That awayday at Old Trafford was terrific. Okay, there were no real surprises on Valentine's Day (for a start, it rained in Manchester), but there was no massacre either. But for that miss by Salako we may even had earned a draw and a second chance at our place.

However, what a glorious sight to see so many Fulham fans enjoying themselves and outsinging the Old Trafford masses. We were able to see our boys more than hold their own, and at times strutting their stuff with good reason. It was only a deflected goal that beat us, after all!

Back in the league it's been win after win. When KK was being chased by the FA, our fans feared that if he went our promotion push might be affected. Ironic then that, as things have settled, we've stormed on. ⚽

Fulham 1 Oldham Athletic 0 26.01.99	1st
Fulham 2 Northampton Town 0 30.01.99	1st
Wycombe Wanderers 1 Fulham 1 06.02.99	1st
Fulham 2 Notts County 1 20.02.99	1st
Fulham 3 Reading 1 23.02.99	1st
York City 0 Fulham 3 27.02.99	1st
Bournemouth 1 Fulham 1 02.03.99	1st
Fulham 1 Lincoln City 0 06.03.99	1st
Luton Town 0 Fulham 4 09.03.99	1st
Bristol Rovers 2 Fulham 3 12.03.99	1st
Stoke City 0 Fulham 1 16.03.99	1st
Fulham 4 Blackpool 0 20.03.99	1st
Reading 0 Fulham 1 05.04.99	1st
Fulham 2 Wigan Athletic 0 10.04.99	1st
Fulham 3 Gillingham 0 13.04.99	1st
Chesterfield 1 Fulham 0 17.04.99	1st

FA Cup

Aston Villa 0 Fulham 2 23.01.99	Round 4
Manchester United 1 Fulham 0 14.02.99	Round 5

A Chat With the Chairman

Bristol Rovers away on a Friday night – 12 March 1999. And it was bucketing down. While heading down a drenched M4 the thought occurred that the game might be off. I was covering the game for one of the local papers so pushed on through the deluge and, upon arrival, picked up my press pass.

With not long to go before kick-off I made a mad dash to the stand – not altogether successfully. Getting to the press box involved crossing an uncovered part of the ground, so, despite a near-sprint, I was horribly wet on getting there. I squelched into my seat complete with sodden notebook and a sodding wet everything else!

Fulham's Communication Manager Mark Maunders approached; he'd got there before me and had dried out a little. "Wet tonight, isn't it?" said Mark with a smile, and you couldn't fault his eye for detail. His second remark, though, bowled me over. "Your request to interview Mohamed Al Fayed has been okayed by the Club. He'll see you at Harrods on Tuesday morning. Good luck." Hot news indeed; even so, I continued to shiver at the Memorial Ground as Fulham went 12 points clear at the top with a 3-2 win (our goalscorers were Kit Symons, Geoff Horsfield and Paul Trollope).

By the following Tuesday I'd not only dried out and got myself suited and booted but had focused on the job in hand. Thing is, I had absolutely no idea what lay ahead – a chat with the Chairman was a brilliant opportunity and it was marvellous of the Club, and the Chairman himself, to grant an interview to the fanzine. But who'd be there? Would I face a committee, one that might even not include the Chairman but which would represent his views? After all, Max Clifford, in his time as the Club's media guru, often circulated quotes on behalf of Mr Al Fayed.

After being ushered into a boardroom I waited more than a little nervously until who walked in but… the Chairman; alone. He greeted me warmly, resplendent in a typical shirt and tie combo. And he afforded me 25 minutes of his valuable time for a one-to-one chat. On his game-changing arrival at the Cottage he told TOOFIF: "The Muddymans had done wonders keeping the Club afloat but were now stretched financially and

weren't able to invest further. That's when I stepped in. Even then it was a near thing as it turned out – another 24 hours and, well, who knows…?"

On being asked about the dreadful events in Paris and the reaction of Fulham fans to the loss of his son, Mr Al Fayed said: "I received tremendous support, And yes, it helped, absolutely. Hundreds made sympathetic gestures, and these were ordinary people. Now I'm helping to bring a great Club back from the depths to where it belongs. In so doing, I feel I am giving something back to those people. I'm taking enormous satisfaction from that."

I took the opportunity to ask about the ground: "Do you then, like most Fulham supporters, feel that the Club is inextricably linked with the Craven Cottage site?" His answer: "Yes, definitely. You can't just take the Club away after it has been on the site for so many years." So, no major bombshells, but then that was pretty much a given.

On replaying the tape recently it was noticeable how the Chairman's passion shone through – with more feeling in his voice than one or two of our heroes on being interviewed. Perhaps his best line came when we discussed Second Division Fulham's 1-0 loss the previous month to mighty Manchester United in the FA Cup Fifth Round – when, you might recall, John Salako fluffed a decent chance to earn us a fully merited money-spinning second chance at Craven Cottage. "The Old Trafford pitch was very disappointing," he insisted, adding: "I am certain that had the surface been good then we may have won on the day, as we'd done at Aston Villa and against Southampton." Don't forget, this was the season that United won the Treble – Premier League, FA Cup and Champions League!

What drew you to Fulham in the first place?
I've been a fan for 30 years. I had a girlfriend who lived near the ground, and at weekends I'd stay with her and we'd go to the matches – just about all the home matches – so I've been following them for a long time. I confess, though, that I hadn't been in recent times, maybe for 15-20 years. Then an old friend told me: "You remember your club? Well, things are really going downhill and it looks as though it could end up as a block of apartments." I was shocked. And even more so when I discovered how desperate the situation had become.

It was complicated, wasn't it – the Club had long since lost the freehold of the site [latterly held by the Royal Bank of Scotland], the ground was in a ramshackle state and the only hope was a 15,000 all-seater stadium penned in by flats?
Things were tough. Having met the Muddymans, I asked to visit the ground to see it first-hand. It

---

"The first team has been built by Kevin, but he's had great help from others. Elsewhere, we've bought the University of London grounds and we have set up the Fulham Football Academy, completely dedicated to football."

Below: Fulham were crowned champions of Division Two in May 1999. Our Chairman, pictured here wearing part of the silverware as a hat, was eager to join the celebrations.

was in a very poor state. This was hardly surprising as it would have been foolhardy to spend money on a ground when its very existence was in doubt. Anyway, I got my people involved straight away to find solutions and to finalise a deal.

So, what were your impressions once you had taken over? There was clearly a lot to be done…
Number one was getting a really great manager. I met a real champion – Kevin Keegan – totally by chance. He came to see me for help with a "Football Circus" idea, a football theme park. I could sense that he'd fallen out of love with the game because of the way he'd been treated at Newcastle. Instead of me helping him, I asked if he'd help me, and immediately I felt that the "chemistry" was right.

Did it take long to feel part of the Fulham family?
Not at all. The supporters are ordinary people and they love the place. They appreciate what we've done and this gives you a lot of good vibes when you see all the smiling faces. The supporters are fantastic. I want to do more and more, and to deliver more, to make them happy. That is very important.

You seem to be enjoying things, highlighted by your walk around the pitch before kick-off?
A good football match can take your mind off other things. And it's good to mix with the people involved – that means the fans. Before that, I'm in the dressing room wishing the players luck.

If I can just touch briefly on the dreadful crash in Paris: the tragedy must have led to a difficult and very painful time for your family, and scenes of national and international mourning followed. On a less-grandiose scale, Fulham fans also offered their messages of sympathy at the Cottage gates. Did this help during your period of grief?
Oh yes! I received tremendous support locally. And of course it helped; absolutely. Hundreds made sympathetic gestures – and these were ordinary people. Now I'm helping to bring a great club back from the depths and to where it belongs. In doing so, I feel I am giving something back to those people. I'm taking enormous satisfaction from that.

Do you, like most Fulham fans, feel the Club is inextricably linked to the Craven Cottage site?
Yes, definitely. You can't just take the Club away after it has been on the site for so many years.

How are the plans for the new stadium going?
Fantastic! We have had tremendous support from everyone who's been involved.

Looking back to our Play-off defeat last season, were you frustrated (given your financial outlay) that things didn't quite take off as planned?
To build something can take time. When you

construct foundations you will sometimes find water, which results in an unexpected delay. But it's all about creating the right foundations. Football is a game as well as a business, and in both cases you don't automatically get things going your way.

You've mentioned him already, but what is it like to have Kevin Keegan in charge of team affairs?
It depends on what type of relationship you have with a guy. Can you trust him, for instance? With Kevin there is no problem – I simply let him get on with what he wants to do. I do not interfere.

…And that arrangement is working really well…?
Fantastic, yes. There is no hypocrisy or anything. He gets on with the job. If he wants a player, then he'll get that player, because he knows the game.

Are you worried that you might lose him to the England set-up – he's fiercely patriotic and ambitious, after all?
There's been plenty of speculation, hasn't there? Kevin's made his intentions very clear in the media. He's acknowledged that Fulham is part of him now.

Almost forgotten in the excitement of the first team's success are the numerous behind-the-scenes initiatives, not least of which is the vast improvement in the youth set-up. How important is getting a club's infrastructure in place, and are you pleased with the overall improvements so far?
The first team has been built by Kevin, but he's had great help from others. Elsewhere, we've bought the University of London grounds and we have set up the Fulham Football Academy, completely dedicated to football. It's an exciting development and we currently have 50 places for 12- to 18-year olds. We have teachers there and the youngsters can take their A-levels while learning their football. We're offering chances to youngsters who want a footballing career. We want to give more British players a chance so we don't need to import so many people. There are so many youngsters wanting a chance. Many have the talent, but not the opportunities – we are offering that chance.

Did you enjoy your recent trip to Old Trafford?
We came very, very close. The Old Trafford pitch was disappointing, however. It was a fantastic achievement all the same.

So, are we still on course for the Premiership?
We're moving full blast in the right direction.

As we currently fight it out with the Wycombes and Wigans of this world, is it fanciful to suggest that Fulham could be involved in European competition in the next few years?
Everything's possible. One thing's certain, we won't leave any stone unturned. ❖

Fulham 4 Millwall 1	
21.04.99	1st
Fulham 1 Wrexham 1	
24.04.99	1st
Burnley 1 Fulham 0	
01.05.99	1s
Walsall 2 Fulham 2	
04.05.99	1st
Fulham 3 Preston NE 0	
08.05.99	1st

1st
2nd
3rd
4th
5th
6th
7th
8th
9th
10th
11th
12th
13th
14th
15th
16th
17th
18th
19th
20th
21st
22nd
23rd
24th

Record-breaking Champions!

The following piece was prepared for *Survival of the Fattest 5: an alternative review of the '98-99 football season.*

How Fulhamish. We grab our first Championship for 50 years, doing so with a record points haul, only to have our last day of the season celebrations tainted by off-field matters

There can surely never have been so many flags and banners at the Cottage. Yet before the game, against Preston, most were being dragged along, or even held at half-mast, rather than thrust skywards and waved in jubilation. Why? Well, with immaculate timing, King Kev, who had steered the Club to the Division Two title and tremendous performances against several Premiership sides in the cup competitions, had decided in the previous 48 hours that he was off.

To be precise, it wasn't his leaving that left a nasty taste in the mouth – he was off to the England hot-seat after all, not another domestic post – but that he had pledged time and again that he would not be leaving Fulham. That's what grated. Massive media coverage of the Keegan-for-England campaign had consisted of rumour, speculation, jingoistic tub-thumping and incredibly patronising garbage, with an occasional well balanced, reasoned piece of reporting thrown in for good measure. What remained constant, however, were Kevin Keegan's quotes that he was remaining loyal to Fulham.

To be honest, it was no real surprise that he went. And, by and large, he did so with the good wishes of the Fulham faithful. It was the broken

promises that hurt, and the timing that stank. Plus the acute awareness that, not for the first time, a resurgent Fulham FC could possibly come off the rails. The main difference this time, we hope, is that the real key player in our future fortunes – Mohamed Al Fayed – is as ebulliently enthusiastic as ever.

To put everything into context, and to counter the relentless "Where were you when you were shit?" chants from opposing supporters, you must remember that's it's only three years since we sat one off the bottom of the entire league, then went to visit the bottom club – and lost. Those Fulham diehards at Torquay in February 1996 and the devoted stalwarts who did so much to keep the Club afloat during the dire decade when Fulham plunged from crisis to crisis (a "shoestring" was considered a veritable luxury in those dark days!) are now getting their pay-back. Big time.

But let's be honest, if anybody had then suggested that, three years on, we'd be bemoaning the loss of Kevin Keegan, but that at least we'd won the Division Two title in barnstorming fashion and had played the Premiership leaders off the (Villa) Park – not to mention having immense financial clout – then they'd have been deemed madder that a fusion of Collymore and Gascoigne.

Now would be an appropriate juncture to recognise and thank the assistance of non-Fulham fans. Our fundraising campaign, Fulham 2000, which wound up just recently with the balance of some £360,000 going towards ground improvements, received exceptional support from all over the country and abroad. Then we were perceived as many people's "second-favourite club" or simply "dear old Fulham". Odd then that once we were fortunate enough to receive an unexpected and massive cash injection, we became the Club that many loved to hate, with the appalling consequence of one Whites' fan, Matthew Fox, losing his life.

If a club is to get stronger it's vital that the gates go up. And yet in some ways we're as cheesed off at the bandwagon jumpers as anyone else. It's human nature for crowds to drift away when the team struggles and for attendances to rise as soon as things improve. But during those awful times when we begged for even the slightest financial assistance, the

Opposite page right: Dirk Lehmann (left) made an instant impact, scoring twice against Manchester City. Paul Peschisolido (*right*) netted our goal of the season at Anfield.

Below: Paul Moody (no 14) and Chris Coleman look to make inroads against Luton.

vast majority of the new Fulham "faithful" were nowhere to be seen. 'Nuff said.

If Micky Adams set the ball rolling in quite remarkable fashion, then history will record that Keegan's influence, especially once he took the hands-on role, was phenomenal (Ray Wilkins, you'll recall, was jettisoned as we scraped into the '97-98 Play-offs). His enthusiasm is boundless and incredibly infectious. He also helped to make Fulham newsworthy again. Keegan's talismanic qualities meant we were linked, often realistically, with a host of big-name players possibly prepared to drop down a division or two because KK was at the helm. So, all in all, and allied to an ever-increasingly professional approach behind the scenes, it was clear to everyone that the Club was going places.

On the field, the team amassed a record 101 points in winning the division, overcame Premiership side Southampton in the Worthington Cup before bowing out to Liverpool – where Paul Peschisolido netted our goal of the season. We enjoyed an even better run in the FA Cup, during which the Saints were again marched out. Aston Villa were outplayed 2-0 on their patch and it took all-conquering Manchester United to narrowly halt matters, 1-0, at Old Trafford. We were very nicely poised for a jump back into the big time.

For all the relevant pomp and majesty in the cups, however, it was very much bread and butter stuff in the league. Forget anything you may have read about "Keegan's cavalier Fulham'; it was much more formulaic than that. As spectacles, some League encounters were truly awful (not helped by team after team simply shutting up shop), but we ground out the all-important points. Forget, too, any thoughts of

big-money "fancy dans". It was great to see our team consistently turn in performances of terrific character. And it was all too apparent that there was a wonderful squad spirit. Yes, it's boring to prattle on about work-rate and application, but they're priceless commodities, even to a team with supposedly millions in the kitty.

One or two sparkling league showings stood out, including the early-season drubbing of Manchester City, when Dirk "German Porn Star" Lehmann thrust himself into the limelight. We enjoyed exciting encounters with Reading, 3-1, and Millwall, 4-1; won 4-0 at Kenilworth Road; defeated rivals and good friends Walsall 4-1; and had a cracking evening at home to Gillingham. The 3-0 scoreline flattered us that night, but who cared – promotion had been secured. Enter, stage right, our Chairman for a prolonged jig of delight.

Non-Fulhamites may be surprised to learn that the key contributors on the park were not "Super Geoffrey" Horsfield, the expensive Barry Hayles, or even Maik Taylor, whose goalkeeping performances from the turn of the year were hugely impressive. In fact John Gregory got it right (for once!) after our wonderful win at Villa Park. "Fulham's success was based on the form of their back three." And so it was for the whole season. Stand up and be counted Chris Coleman, Simon Morgan and Kit Symons.

Apparently Kevin Keegan had been keen to play with a flat back four but had his hand forced by these three – two of them full Welsh Internationals and the other, Morgan, an Englishman with the most Welsh-sounding name of all. Stoic, brave and utterly committed, the trio blended so well that they took it in turns to pop upfield to score. Symons, in fact, threatened the goalscoring feat of centre-half and war-horse

"The scene was set for Fulham to race past 100 points if we could beat Preston on the final day, by which time we'd been confirmed as Champions and a party atmosphere was guaranteed for the post-match trophy presentation."

Roger Brown, who scored an incredible 12 in '81-82. Kit finished one short of the record but treated us to some unexpected dribbling skills that dear old Roger could only have dreamt about! "Cookie" Coleman helped himself to five goals and earned the label "Best player outside the Premiership" from our now ex-leader. Slightly biased maybe, but more than slightly true all the same.

Then there is Simon Morgan. Where do you start? Successful author (his book *On Song For Promotion*, which recorded all the insider wheelings and dealings of our previous promotion year, '96-97, was lapped up by the fans); a great favourite for giving his absolute all for season upon season (and with a wholly deserved testimonial in the offing); labelled the "Moaning Minnie" by the fanzine for championing the cause of whingeing, whether at training or in the thick of the game… but supposedly finished as we kicked off the season.

Finished? Ha-bloody-ha! He scored eight times. But sod the goals. Even Keegan had to concede that "Simon Morgan has surprised me time and again," as he named him Man of the Match for the umpteenth time. If ever there was a player who deserved this season's success, it was our Simon. And if there was ever a moment to capture what he's all about, then it came in the first half of our final match. Determined to play in our "party day" game with Preston despite five stitches in his leg (courtesy of a really dreadful tackle by a decidedly rugged Burnley chappie), Morgs was our last hope as Preston breached our defence in the first half and homed in on goal. Morgan tracked his man and made his move. We all winced, and with reason. It was a bone-shuddering (stitch-splitting?) tackle, but one timed to absolute perfection and all carried out in his usual matter-of-fact fashion. The danger was cleared and, with spirits raised, forgotten man Paul Moody grabbed a second-half hat-trick to ensure we all went home smiling. Even Kevin Keegan.

Champions. Following a decade or more of despair, I could get used to this. More please… ⚽

Keegan for England

Once Kevin Keegan took over team affairs from Ray Wilkins there was no stopping us – even if his reign did finish on a flat note. In our 101st season in professional football we racked up 101 points as we cantered to the Division Two title, our first silverware for 50 years. Kevin Keegan did so well that when Glenn Hoddle talked himself out of a job as England coach in February 1999, the FA asked KK to step in, initially on a temporary basis to oversee four games. And that's when it turned a little sour. On the field the wins just kept coming; Fulham sealed promotion with a 3-0 win over Gillingham in April with six games still left to play, but for us Fulham fans the public promises made by Keegan were still ringing in our ears.

February 3, 1999: "I couldn't just walk away even though part of me does fancy having a go at the England job. I have made a commitment to Fulham and I will remain loyal. All of us at the Club are building something exciting."

Having continually insisted he would quit England after those four games and see out the 15 months of his Fulham contract, he did an about turn and became full-time England manager. You could hardly blame him, especially after enjoying that four-match stint; Keegan's folly was to announce so very publicly that he had unfinished business at Craven Cottage.

The scene was set for Fulham to race past 100 points if we could beat Preston on the final day, by which time we'd been confirmed as Champions and a party atmosphere was guaranteed for the post-match trophy presentation. Except that Keegan's presence had divided the Craven Cottage crowd. Many didn't want him involved at all. My own view was that he was perfectly entitled to be there given that he was responsible for our style of play and barnstorming success. Equally, though, I selfishly didn't want our big day tarnished. We weren't in the habit of picking up trophies; this was a party I was determined to enjoy and one that I didn't want spoiled. Only at Fulham, eh? ⚽

From the BBC:

Fulham have confirmed that Kevin Keegan will leave the Club after Saturday's match against Preston to become full-time England coach.

The Club's Managing Director Neil Rodford said that owner Mohamed Al Fayed had been formally approached by the Football Association in a bid to appoint Keegan on a permanent basis.

"Although Keegan remains under contract, it is obvious that he will not lead Fulham in their First Division campaign next season," said Rodford.

On ITV's *The Sports Show* on Thursday Keegan said it was not feasible to combine the two roles.

"I think what we've got to get back to is that you can't do the two jobs, that's what I've found, otherwise you jeopardise both parties and that includes Fulham Football Club," said Keegan.

In the event we beat Preston 3-0 in what was literally a Moody finale. Some of the crowd maintained KK was a "Judas" as he walked to the dugout while others gave him a standing ovation; on the pitch, substitute Paul Moody's second-half

"If the nation wants Kevin, the ordinary person wants Kevin and the FA wants Kevin then I will give him to England, no problem. The nation comes first, the glory of the country – and that's the sacrifice we will make at Fulham." – Mohamed Al Fayed

hat-trick wrapped up the victory that took our overall haul to 101 points.

In 2001, more than a decade after he'd quit the England job, Kevin Keegan admitted he now regretted leaving Fulham and taking the national job, claiming he did not enjoy his time in charge of the Three Lions. "The [England] fans were horrendous when I was walking off after the Germany game – fair enough. I was disappointed and thought 'they got me the job, it's time to go'.

"I suppose if I had my time again I would refuse it and stay at Fulham because I thoroughly enjoyed my time there." ⚽

Wot, no Craven Cottage?

As the new season beckoned, FFC unveiled plans for a new 30,000 all-seater stadium. The £55m project included 36 apartments, a restaurant, football academy and sports club, underground car parking, riverside pier, Roman-style arcade, the inclusion of the Stevenage Road frontage… but no Craven Cottage. David Lloyd spoke to FFC Managing Director Neil Rodford to discuss the scheme and gauge initial reactions.

How hopeful are you that the plans will become reality – and in what time-frame?
I believe it will go through. The scheme is a very good one and will hopefully be judged on its merits. But you, I and the fans all know the difficulty of the side issues we're going to face. We're trying to speak to all the pressure groups, some of whom have given us severe problems

in the past. That doesn't mean that we're going to win them all over but we're having an open dialogue. I'd say, so far at least, that things have gone as well as we'd hoped. The real test will come over the next three or four months. It's all likely to take two years to complete so we're looking at a possible 17 months away from the site, with the final touches being completed after that.

But the crucial question is how long might it take to get the plans passed?
Yeah, people are already asking when do I envisage work starting. It won't be next May even if the plans sail through, as there will be plenty of logistical, organisational and co-ordinating work to be put in place; so the earliest is likely to be May 2001.

Should we go up this season, what is the position regarding the Premiership's ground rules?
We can play with the stadium as it is for the next three seasons, so we could be in the Premiership for two seasons with terracing. The clock has started to tick on that score. You might be aware that we can make the current stadium all-seater, but that would bring the capacity down. It's relatively easy to do, too – rather like erecting scaffolding with seats on top.

Fulham fans need to show their support for the scheme (that's assuming they do approve of them!) via the local Council. But when?

Below: Neil Rodford, in white, displays his footballing prowess during a rousing encounter between the FFC Programme and TOOFIF teams at Craven Cottage. TOOFIF's Allan Gould (*left*) moves in to make a challenge, while in the background Paul Johnson (*right*) makes a mental note of the action for one of his *We Can Dream* masterpieces.

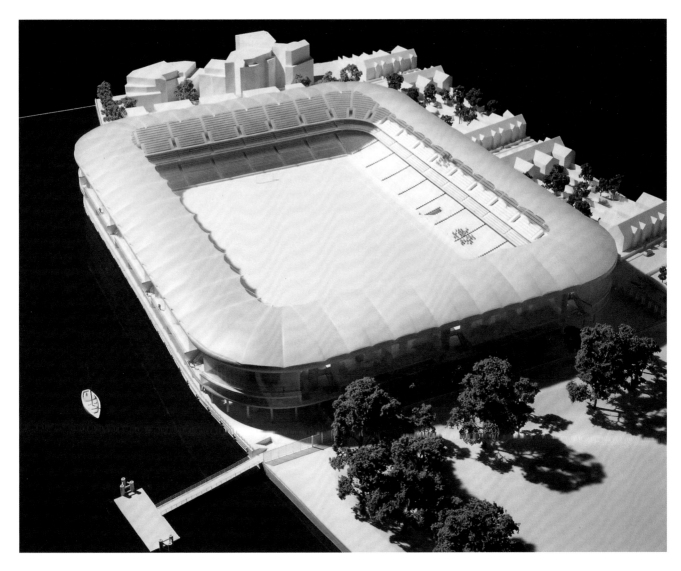

Above: An aerial view of the model of the new superstadium.

"We don't actively want our fans to come to games by car, and we're considering things such as residents-only parking on matchdays, but that'll be down to the local authority to decide."

First of all, the Council has to validate the planning application. We've submitted the scheme and we're also submitting specialist reports covering things like traffic, wind, light, impact on the river – they'll be considered in the next six months, but the validation of the application will probably be rubberstamped in late August or early September. Once that's publicised in the local press, as is the norm, then that'll be the time for supporters to send in their letters.

The new scheme doesn't include the Cottage. What's the latest position as to its relocation?
There's been relatively little debate with either the local residents or the local authority (since they haven't considered the application). There seems to be a mixed view: some people think it would be a great idea to relocate it and put it in Bishops Park, while some locals say that would be taking their public land. Our commitment is to relocate it somewhere subject to the local authority coming up with a site, and Bishops Park would seem to be one of the more obvious possibilities.

I've been about on a couple of occasions (the Fulham 2000 evening and the special open day) when the model and detailed boards have been inspected closely by fans and have yet to hear any rumblings of discontent. Have you received any criticisms?
Key to the application's success will be the local people, and whether we can demonstrate to them that it's a benefit to the area rather than a negative. The two issues that have come to the fore are the scale – that is, the height in relation to the existing stadium – and the traffic. My response to the traffic issue, and I know it doesn't answer their concerns, is that it's a society issue. We don't actively want our fans to come to games by car, and we're considering things such as residents-only parking on matchdays, but that'll be down to the local authority to decide. The scale of the stadium is clearly dictated by the capacity that we require.

What about any murmurings from Fulham fans? Any quibbles about the Cottage going?
A few comments, but that's all. I think people understand that if we want a unified stadium then the Cottage can't remain where it is. Also, it's not the fans' building, which I'd like it to be; it's used by admin staff and as changing rooms for the players. If it is the true ancestral home, it should be accessible to the fans.

Left: Has the Thames ever looked so tranquil, and so shiny and clean? Ah, it's just a model.

Below: An artist's impression of the proposed "Stevenage Arcade".

Three or four years ago, it would have been "over our dead bodies"… but people seem to have accepted the plans for what they are…?
Sure, I understand. But the scheme is a wonderful one – it makes me really proud to look at the model. Hopefully it has caught the imagination of all supporters and they will see that we haven't removed the Cottage for the sake of it. There's a need to do so, in order to create what we've presented.

Are there plans for Supporters' Club facilities in the new set-up?
Definitely! Clearly, details haven't been finalised as yet, but we'll have a number of areas that we can turn into supporters' facilities – and I'm thinking about Fulham 2000 rooms, Supporters' Club rooms, those for Riversiders, VPs, etc, but yes, there'll definitely be supporters' facilities.

All in all, you sound pretty excited…?
Oh yes – the pace of change is massive. Like the supporters, I sometimes have to remind myself

to take breath. The best day for me would be walking into the newly completed stadium, with the team in the Premier League where it can operate at a trading profit, and then we can say "Right, guys, it's back to the fans now." It was the fans, in conjunction with the Muddymans, that kept this place going for years, and that's why we can dream of undertaking all of this. If we don't get to the top flight and can't create this then we'd need a rethink – but let's not dwell on that! Things are really buzzing. We're heading for 7,000 season ticket holders for the start of the season, and I don't have to tell you what a significant leap that is. ⚽

Even the TOOFIF team's on the up!

Welcome back to another season of TOOFIFs. One thing's for sure, it's never dull following Fulham, and certainly not right now! Since we last hit the streets, Cookie Coleman and co hoisted the Second Division Championship trophy; we smashed the 100-points mark along the way; Kevin Keegan departed; we enjoyed a wonderful end-of-season "family day"; Paul Bracewell was named as KK's successor; Fulham 2000 was officially wound up; plans for the new ground were unveiled; we broke our transfer record once again; we've seen Stan Collymore in a Fulham shirt; and we gained a more than useful point at Birmingham. Oh yes, and the TOOFIF football team, bolstered by Jim Hicks, won a football match at long last!

Morgs Joins TOOFIF

Simon Morgan has kindly agreed to be a regular contributor to the fanzine in the hope that the special TOOFIF, in aid of his testimonial fund, will go easy on him; sorry, Morgs, no chance!

Ten years at Fulham! A reward or a life-sentence?
I was asked a similar question by Cottage Pie. I told them that after my first day at the Club I couldn't see myself lasting ten days or ten weeks, let alone ten years! That just shows how far the Club has come. Looking back, it really hits home how poor the team was and how badly things were being managed off the field – it's amazing that the Club is still around, never mind me! However, you can only recognise the vast difference in the standards when you see the job being done properly, as it is now.

Can you remember that first day at FFC?
In those days the Cottage walls were paper thin. I can vividly recall Janice [Baldwin] shouting through: "Oi, Dickhead, have you got those contracts signed yet?"

To whom was she referring?
I wonder! All the fans refered to him as "Dicks Out", but she was even more direct. My signing had

been delayed because the manager had been out to dinner with his wife, leaving me to sit around at the Cottage like a lemon. And when he got back he couldn't get into his briefcase because his glasses were inside, and he needed them to sort out the code for the lock. That pretty much summed things up. Then, on the first morning with the lads, I realised they'd all been out the night before. I knew of a few at Leicester who liked a drink, but never so close to a game. So there I was looking around the place on the Friday and it was a shambles…

…And wondering what you'd let yourself in for…?
Exactly! We had to do heading practice, but some couldn't do "heading" because of what they'd supped the night before. The thought, "What on earth am I doing here?" crossed my mind!

Ah, but if you thought that was a low moment in your career, here you are signing for TOOFIF!
Yeah, a bloomin' TOOFIF exclusive. Mind you, the fanzine and its correspondents have always been kind to me. I'm not saying I've not taken some stick, including a certain editor labelling me a "Moaning Minnie". But then, that's not far off the mark.

On that moaning theme, isn't it a remarkable coincidence that the word "testimonial"

Opposite page right: Simon Morgan, now on TOOFIF's "books"!

Below: The *Fulham Chronicle* reports on the threat of war in the Craven Cottage vicinity. Pictured are three "defiant" member of Fulham United: Ray Champion, Ian Gray and Dave "Nobby" Clark.

Telephone 0181 741 1622 for news and advertising   Thursday, September 23 1999   **5**

Stadium war hots up

BY SALLY GUYONCOURT

FULHAM fans living near Craven Cottage have formed their own organisation to fight another group of residents who are against the £55-million redevelopment plans.

Fulham United was set up last week by 40 residents and businesses after they learnt about the Fulham Alliance.

And as the temperature rises over the future of the Stevenage Road stadium a Tory councillor has said the club should think about leaving the area if it wants to expand its capacity.

The Fulham Alliance was founded earlier this month by residents who oppose the planned expansion to a 30,000 all-seater stadium.

Now Fulham United plans to highlight the importance of the club in the local community and why it should remain in the area.

The group plans to start a petition collecting signatures from residents living in the vicinity of Stevenage Road.

They will also be writing to the Palace ward councillors, Hammersmith and Fulham MP Iain Coleman (Lab)

and the council's planning department in support of the club's planned stadium.

Chairman Ian Coles of Greswell Street, said: "We want to redress the balance and make sure people who live in Fulham that support the club staying in Fulham have their voice heard.

"Otherwise there's a danger of a false impression being created. It's the same people who are trying to get the club out of the area.

"The danger is if we don't start saying what we think the powers that be might think the whole of Fulham is against the plans."

Fellow member Ray Champion of Stevenage Road, said: "We don't want anybody to be fooled into thinking everyone living in Fulham is as short-sighted as Cllr Emile Al-Uzaizi (Con) and his small group of friends.

"Nobody should be fooled by the words of a handful of people who have consistently campaigned over recent years to get Fulham Football Club out of the borough."

But Cllr Al-Uzaizi hit back claiming he is not against the football club – just the new development.

He said: "Unlike them we sent out a questionnaire to the local people – more than 80 per cent came back saying they

were opposed to this development.

"They are opposed to it on basic planning grounds. It's our democratic right to say we don't like what's being proposed.

"The only reason they want this 30,000 seater stadium is because

they can't become a Premiership football club without the 30,000-seater stadium.

"They ought to think about going somewhere else.

"It's a white elephant on the river."

DEFIANT: (l-r) Fulham United members David Clark, Ian Gray and Ray Champion

Photo: NICOLA RICHARDSON

Stockport County 2 Fulham 1	
06.11.99	8th
Fulham 1 Portsmouth 0	
09.11.99	4th
Fulham 1 Barnsley 3	
13.11.99	6th
Blackburn Rovers 2 Fulham 0	
20.11.99	8th
Fulham 1 Bolton Wanderers 1	
23.11.99	8th
Walsall 1 Fulham 3	
26.11.99	6th
Fulham 0 Birmingham City 0	
04.12.99	6th
Nottingham Forest 0 Fulham 0	
15.12.99	6th
Crystal Palace 0 Fulham 0	
18.12.99	7th
Fulham 0 Ipswich Town 0	
26.12.99	7th
Fulham 1 Tranmere Rovers 0	
03.01.00	8th
Manchester City 4 Fulham 0	
16.01.00	10th
Fulham 0 Grimsby Town 1	
22.01.00	10th
Fulham 1 West Brom 0	
05.02.00	8th
Portsmouth 0 Fulham 1	
12.02.00	8th
Charlton Athletic 1 Fulham 0	
15.02.00	8th
Fulham 2 Walsall 0	
19.02.00	8th
QPR 0 Fulham 0	
28.02.00	8th
Fulham 3 Port Vale 1	
04.03.00	8th
Fulham 4 Stockport County 1	
07.03.00	7th
Bolton Wanderers 3 Fulham 1	
11.03.00	8th
Fulham 2 Blackburn Rovers 2	
18.03.00	8th
Barnsley 1 Fulham 0	
21.03.00	9th
Ipswich Town 1 Fulham 0	
25.03.00	10th
Fulham 1 Crystal Palace 0	
01.04.00	10th
Tranmere Rovers 1 Fulham 1	
09.04.00	9th
Fulham 4 Sheffield United 0	
15.04.00	9th
Swindon Town 1 Fulham 0	
22.04.00	9th
Fulham 1 Nottingham Forest 1	
24.04.00	9th
Wolves 3 Fulham 0	
30.04.00	9th
Fulham 3 Huddersfield Town 0	
07.05.00	9th

League Cup

West Brom 1 Fulham 2	
12.10.99	Round 3
Fulham 3 Tottenham Hotspur 1	
01.12.99	Round 4
Leicester City 3 Fulham 3	
12.01.99	aet Quarter-final
(lost 0-3 pens)	

FA Cup

Fulham 2 Luton Town 2	
11.12.99	Round 3
Luton Town 0 Fulham 1	
21.12.99	Round 3 replay
Fulham 3 Wimbledon 0	
08.01.00	Round 4
Fulham 1 Tranmere Rovers 2	
29.01.00	Round 5

sounds like it contains the words "testy" and moany". They sit well alongside "Simon Morgan", eh? Oh 'eck; it's going to be a long 12 months!

That promotion season with Micky Adams was a good one, wasn't it (and you penned a certain book charting the campaign; copies still available presumably?)?
Copies certainly still available; in fact my garage is full of 'em! Micky motivated the players and the crowd; now I can look back and see when the turnaround at the Club all stated. Everyone was very close that season – the away support in particular was phenomenal. They followed us everywhere and were as happy and as loud and as fanatical (and as surprised come to that) in that period as they've ever been. That said, we've gone on to another level now under Mr Al Fayed and find ourselves within touching distance of the Premiership.

A decade ago that would've been the last thing on your mind, surely? What was the atmosphere like in the camp in those days?
There was discontent in the air, definitely. We were at the foot of the division and the Club were spending some of the Cabra money bringing in players for, at the time, quite a bit of money. There was myself, Stacey North and Gary Brazil. I wouldn't say it was hostile, but it wasn't a particularly welcoming dressing room. You could tell that the lads weren't too happy with the manager. Ray Lewington was carrying a lot on his

own back. I'd met Ray about eight months before when he'd tried to sign me, but now, from being the manager, he was the number two. It was a difficult situation all round.

You got the Fulham crowd on your side by scoring a "wonderful" goal on your home debut against Bury…?
It was a typical Fulham crowd; your name goes out on the speakers and you could sense them all saying: "Who the bloody 'ell is that!?" Then came the goal, given as an own goal in the papers, but credited to me in Dennis Turner's "Facts & Figures", and that's good enough for me thank you very much! It came from one of Stacey's long throws and I flicked it on. The ball was going nowhere but their great big centre-half decided to head it in. I remember we won 2-0, and recall Ivor getting a presentation for being Fulham's meanest-ever player – sorry, I mean the Club's all-time record goalscorer – before the game. It was obvious he was the big hero…

He didn't try to claim that goal for himself, then?
No, I got in first! But he was loved by the fans. I watched him in training over the next few days, and he was rather like me in training today: didn't move much, and generally walked around, but come a match situation and he'd come alive. He scored a few in my first batch of games and you could see how he'd netted so many over the years. He had that uncanny knack: a striker's intuition and the ability to react.

Ivor was nearing the end of his career; unfortunately the Club had no one to replace him. The only good thing about that season was that we somehow scrambled our way to safety.

You say "somehow" – was it more by luck than judgement?
Jimmy Hill came in for those last two months and did a lot to save us. Prior to that we were in a real mess. I remember going to Rotherham – for what would've been deemed a relegation six-pointer these days – in March, and we were shambolic. We were 3-0 down at half-time and we just didn't have a clue. Jimmy Hill came to see us the following Monday, with Bill Muddyman, and said "Look, we've got to sort this out, otherwise we're going down." From then he started coming in two or three times a week to take the training and, miraculously, since we didn't score many goals but we did keep clean sheets, we stayed up. Jimmy Hill never got the credit for that – in fact, while this was all going on the crowd were bellowing "Hill Out!"! One of the few good things about that season was

---

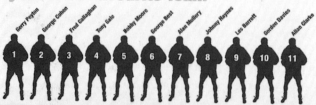
Right: The tables are turned as Gerard Lyons asks the questions on behalf of the Fulham programme.

4 Thursday, December 9 1999
Telephone 0181 741 1622 for news & advertising

Fans' show of support for Fulham development

By BERNARD GINNS

A LUMINOUS wall of nearly 10,000 yellow cards held aloft by fans marked the kick-off of the big sell out cup match between Fulham and Tottenham Hotspur at Craven Cottage.

The cards, handed out before the game by Fulham United, were marked with a simple message – "Fulham people say yes to a new stadium".

Fulham United, an independent group fighting for the proposed redevelopment of Craven Cottage, said the large display showed the real feeling of Fulham people.

But Fulham Alliance, which formed to oppose the £55-million 30,000-seater project, claimed the large number was irrelevant and people power alone would not be enough to force the controversial proposals for the new stadium through the planning process.

The cards were handed to fans outside the ground as they arrived to watch last Wednesday's Worthington Cup 3-1 vic-

tory over Spurs which attracted a crowd of 18,134.

Fulham United chairman Ian Coles said: "The whole ground was swamped with them and we are going to get coverage of the whole of Fulham and keep the pressure on.

"It showed how local people think and it won't be long before the Fulham Alliance get the red card."

But Fulham Alliance chairman Martin Smith retorted: "The planning authority grants planning permission.

"Hammersmith and Fulham Council will decide on planning grounds."

Fulham Alliance says the development will have a disastrous effect on the surrounding residential streets and neighbouring Bishop's Park.

But the campaigners are adamant they are not against the club itself.

Mr Smith added: "Fulham FC is a great club and many of our supporters are football fans and I watched highlights of the Tottenham match on television myself.

"But the club's application is harmful to the environment."

Twenty thousand cards were printed and published by Fulham United using

facilities of the GMB union which sponsors the group.

Around 100 people attended Fulham United's public meeting before Saturday's home game with Birmingham.

The meeting at the Crabtree pub in Rainville Road, Fulham, was heralded as a success by Mr Coles who added: "I think we got a positive response.

"People are starting to realise what is going on but some are still not sure what the situation is."

---

winning the local derby at Brentford, when Phil Stant managed to stay onside long enough to score in the last minute.

We stayed up then, and you might not have been the saviour, but I understand someone else was paraded to the players as such…
That's right. Alan Dicks was after a striker all season. We had Gary Blissett and Dave Regis down and, a little like today, we were linked with just about every striker going. Anyhow, one day Alan Dicks told us to have our showers and then go and sit down; he'd found the man who'd turn our season around. We were quite uplifted – another striker at last! So Alan Dicks came in and closed the door behind him. He said: "Right lads, I'm going to introduce you to our saviour now – the man who's going to stop us from being relegated." With that he opened the door and in walked… the Reverend Gary Piper! Oh dear!

Dicks was sacked the next season…?
Funny enough we had a reasonable run beforehand. We beat Bradford 4-3 away in a tremendous end-to-end encounter then beat Bolton away 3-0, with Gary Brazil and Andy Cole scoring, before defeating Preston 1-0 at home thanks to some bloke called Morgan scoring with a looping header. Not long after, on the train home from Darlington following a 3-1 defeat, Alan Dicks was sacked. I remember he and Mark Newson had a blazing row after the match. The old dressing room at Darlington had a big sloping wooden floor. Mark was at the higher end of the room

screaming away but, still in his studs, he slipped down the slope after which he was looking up at Dicks. It was crazy. Everyone soon joined in the row. Things were definitely not rosy in the camp.

From being top six, we slipped down a fair way – and we'd lost to Hayes at home in the Cup a couple of weeks before. We were so bad that day the crowd couldn't be bothered to boo us off the park. We came off the park fully expecting Dicks to have a right go at us, with justification, but he didn't. I was so frustrated. I simply got dressed, got in the car, drove home and, as I flung my car keys on the table, announced: "I'm giving up the game!"

So it was exit Alan Dicks and enter Don Mackay…
He didn't do too much to be honest. And yet at the end of the season he was chaired off the field by the supporters, who were desperate for any glimmer of hope. I'm still adamant that the squad of players in Mackay's first full season was a promotion outfit, and most certainly so had he signed another midfielder. We under-achieved by finishing ninth and 12th under his stewardship.

There were any number of characters in that set-up…?
Oh yes. We had big Jim, Mash, Pikey, Noose, Eckhardt, Thommo, Scotty, Garry Brazil and Gavin Nebbeling – all big characters and good pros who'd chip in and have their say. Perhaps what we were missing was the spark of youth, certainly when compared with the '96-97 side when we had players such as Freeman, Watson and Cullip to do the running for us old 'uns.

Above: Fulham supporters play their cards right, showing support for the new stadium plans, as reported in the *Fulham Chronicle*.

"From being top six, we slipped down a fair way – and we'd lost to Hayes at home in the Cup a couple of weeks before. We were so bad that day the crowd couldn't be bothered to boo us off the park."

Friendly With India

Back in the days when I'd get press invites from the Club, in came one to attend a media gathering ahead of the Club's pre-season friendly against India at the Cottage in July 2000. This would be new manager Jean Tigana's first home match in charge and India's first game in London since the 1948 Olympics. Might be worth a look, if I could get time off work. Might even get to chat to the new manager if there aren't too many people about.

When I strolled along to a gloriously sunny Craven Cottage I had a massive shock. I'd drastically underestimated things. There was an overwhelming attendance, so much so that the assorted media types from all over the world had to be divided into groups: TV, Radio, Magazine, National Press, Local Press, Others. This became normal practice once FFC reached the top flight, but unusual then. Each group was huge and there

Right: The front cover of the Fulham v India matchday programme.

Opposite page right: Jean Tigana, flanked by Christian Damiano (*left*) and Roger Propos line up for the TOOFIF camera. The new management team made an immediate impression.

Below: Close-season antics at Motspur Park as captain Chris Coleman does his bit for TV and (*bottom right*) the team don the shades for a publicity photoshoot.

was much jostling as everyone tried to get a piece of the action and get their specific angle covered.

In the spotlight, and in his element, was Mohamed Al Fayed, telling everyone in turn about Fulham's magnanimous gesture in hosting the fixture and explaining that the day's key picture opportunity would be happening before long. He was referring to the India football team, stuck in a coach the other side of a major traffic incident in Hammersmith. Not only was the weather warm, but so was our Chairman's welcome to all those present. Apart from the obvious glitch this was all going very well and Fulham FC were reaping the rewards with a whole raft of good news stories all set to be filed.

However, with the time ticking away and still no sign of the main guests, the Chairman started on a second round of interviews. Amid much shuffling of feet and glances at watches from most of those present, members of Fulham's PR entourage were frantically phoning around to

check on the whereabouts of the coach; news filtered back that it was apparently making some headway at last, albeit slowly. Meanwhile, near the centre circle, even the Chairman was getting a little agitated. No doubt his helicopter parked nearby was primed to take him to his next engagement – but this was a good photo-opportunity. Maybe hang on for a while longer. Then came the welcome news that the coach had made it onto the Fulham Palace Road. Phew, they'd be here in 10 minutes or so.

The Chairman, surrounded by a group of journalists and a clutch of FFC's press lackeys, cracked a joke to break the tension. It wasn't a belter, but everyone tittered graciously. "Did you like my joke?" he persisted, singling out a female reporter. When she half-smiled politely and gave the slightest of nods, he continued: "It was a big joke, right?" Which set him up for the climax of this particular exchange, one that took most of those in earshot somewhat by surprise: "It's a big joke, right? About a big as my willy, you know!" Cue much coughing and spluttering and the sight of all the FFC lackeys putting their heads in their hands. Nice one, Mo... ⚽

	1st
Fulham 2 Crewe Alexandra 0	2nd
12.08.00 2nd	3rd
	4th
Birmingham City 1 Fulham 3	5th
18.08.00 1st	6th
Fulham 4 Stockport County 1	7th
26.08.00 1st	8th
	9th
Norwich City 0 Fulham 1	10th
28.08.00 1st	11th
Fulham 5 Barnsley 1 t	12th
10.09.00 1s	13th
	14th
Fulham 3 Burnley 1	15th
12.09.00 1st	16th
Nottingham Forest 0 Fulham 3	17th
16.09.00 1st	18th
	19th
League Cup	20th
	21st
Northampton Town 1 Fulham 0	22nd
22.08.00 Round 1 1st leg	23rd
Fulham 4 Northampton Town 1	24th
05.09.00 Round 1 2nd leg	
Chesterfield 1 Fulham 0	
19.09.00 Round 2 1st leg	

John Collins Signs for Fulham

On the afternoon John Collins was officially unveiled as a Fulham player, TOOFIF caught up with the ex-Everton man...

What were your feelings once you were aware of Fulham's interest in you?
It wasn't a snap decision on my part. I had to think long and hard – it was a big decision to leave the Premiership, naturally. But it was the right move for me.

Why is it the "right move" – as you say, you've had to drop down a division?
I may be dropping down, yes, but my plans are to only be in this division for ten months after which, hopefully, I'll be back in the top flight with Fulham. It won't be that easy of course – there'll be nine or ten other teams that think they're in with a decent shout. It's a massive challenge. However, I believe the foundations are here at Fulham for the Club to progress this season.

Are you here as a player-coach?
The literal answer to that one is "No". I'm here as a player and to concentrate on playing. But

there's an option to join the coaching staff if and when I feel I am ready.

Did you have any other options? Or were you simply swayed by the lure of linking up again with Jean Tigana?
I did have one or two other openings, But neither was I in the position of having to get away from Everton. In short, it was only the move to Fulham that appealed.

Tigana's in charge now. And you worked with him at Monaco. What qualities will he bring to Fulham?
A great knowledge of the game for a start. He'll bring discipline to the playing side of the Club. He's been a winner in the past, so knows the winning formula. And he knows how to do so in a certain style – he's a great advocate of attacking football.

Wenger and Houllier have been successful in bringing French-style football to their respective clubs. Can Tigana be as successful

in the First Division?
There'll be tests along the way, but I think it's manageable and that he's the man to do it. Yes, he favours the French style, that's only natural, keeping the ball on the grass and adopting an "attractive" approach. I'm sure we won't be playing route one football anyway. And I believe that his way is the way that football should be played.

Sounds like there'll be a lot of involvement for midfielders!
Of course! I don't want to see the ball flying over my head all the time. If fans like watching good, passing football then they should be in for a treat.

Demon Internet

Gobsmackingly Good

What a scintillating start to the season! And that's not simply referring to our run of victories but more so to the manner in which they've been achieved. You know things are going well when the players have broad smiles on their faces. It's good to learn from Simon Morgan that there are no egos in the dressing room. It all goes back to the Micky Adams ethic of hard work, commitment and sound squad spirit – and very little to do with "moneybags Fulham". The only obvious difference between the Adams set-up and that of Tigana is that the current crop of players are infinitely better. And there's Morgs still hanging on in there!

Ray Lewington was at the Cottage for the Barnsley match. Ray was gobsmacked by our performance – he remarked on not only how good and streamlined it was but added that the 5-1 trouncing had been carried out in a style he didn't think was possible in the First Division. A number of fans near me in the Hammersmith End thought it was a perfect showing, in that the whole line-up contributed massively to the win.

The 3-1 victory over Burnley a couple of days later was arguably just as convincing. In this match we had to outfight a dogged, hardworking side and to do so after conceding an early goal. Having leveled through Bjarne Goldbaek's brilliant free-kick, we went on to win it in style – and frustrated our opponents to such a degree that they had a man sent off. It wasn't the first time that had happened this season, and it probably won't be the last.

We made it a record-breaking seven from seven at Nottingham Forest. The stats will show that we could have been out of sight by the break, but that it took a couple of late goals to rubberstamp our victory. It wasn't our most fluid display of the season by a long way. But we still notched three goals away from home and, unlike many a Fulham side of the past, won an important game when the fans had turned out in force. How long can all this continue? And can we continue to steamroller teams into submission with confidence but without arrogance? We hope so! ⚽

High Hopes of a Positive Verdict

Amid a further batch of victories, genuine promotion aspirations, accusations of arrogance from some green-eyed quarters and typical over-reactions from sections of the media comes the news that we should get a decision on the ground issue before Christmas. If approval is given then, apart from sighs of relief all round (well, nearly all round) and a further boost to the feelgood factor around Craven Cottage at present, the Club is assured of a much

rosier future. The alternative doesn't bear thinking about of course and, as Fulham MD Michael Fiddy explains, should a public inquiry be called that, too, could be just as devastating.

Clearly this mag – and this editor – is biased on the issue. The proposals depict a state of the art stadium light years away from some of the soulless Meccano types that have sprung up in recent times. While such factors as scale, traffic, and impact on the vicinity including the river needed to be considered, the fact remains that a great deal of time, effort and money has gone in to ensure the plans are appropriate. From what's been presented, the Club has behaved properly throughout and has taken on board whatever adverse comments have been coming their way (plus the many favourable ones) – and have been seen to do so. All appropriate bodies

have been consulted in an attempt to steer through proposals that are worthy, workable yet impressive.

Amid the hornet's nest stirred up by a few it's hard to get away from one fundamental fact – that Fulham Football Club has existed on the site for more than one hundred years. No local – whether supportive, in opposition or indifferent can match that. Anyone moving in to the immediate area did so knowing there was a football club on their doorstep. And anyone with a grain of sense would realise that over any period of time a club's fortunes could fluctuate dramatically. In Fulham's case the last 15 years or so have been really turbulent. Presently, thank heavens, we're on the up. And how! Accordingly Fulham FC needs a ground that befits its status and aspirations. The plans currently before the Council reflect that. As Yuletide grows ever nearer, long-suffering Fulham fans could possibly have the best Christmas present for many a year: a secure future at Craven Cottage in a brand new stadium. Oh yes, and with the distinct possibility of Premiership football to boot.

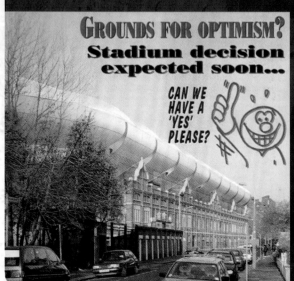

GROUNDS FOR OPTIMISM?
Stadium decision expected soon...

CAN WE HAVE A 'YES' PLEASE?

Fiddy Sense

It's been seven months since Michael Fiddy was appointed FFC's Managing Director – so it's high time he came under the TOOFIF spotlight. The Ed popped down to Motspur Park for a natter...

You've been MD for just over half a year. Has the job thrown up any surprises and, overall, have things gone to plan?

I was asked on my first day what I'd be focusing on. The Club needed to get into a position where it was making a challenge for Premiership football; the other main issue was the ground. In the meantime we've appointed a new manager and it was vital we not only made Jean Tigana and his team welcome but that they were properly integrated. This included such fundamentals as learning the language and ensuring he was aware of the British way of football club management. When Jean arrived we were running about the place like headless chickens, concerned with matters such as bolstering the squad. The cultural difference was immediately highlighted as Jean couldn't understand the urgency until we explained to him that there was no early-season transfer deadline in this country.

You came to Fulham from a legal background. What's it like to be in the world of football – it's something of a change for you, especially as it's rumoured that you're a Leeds fan?!

I haven't been paying any attention to Leeds, I can assure you...! The whole nature of the operation is different – and the people are far more interesting than lawyers! Within a football club you have so many different people with different needs – that's an obvious distinction. In the football world things can happen with extraordinary speed; take player transfers for example when you can also be dealing with huge amounts of money...

So here we are at Fulham in a key phase of our regeneration – pushing for a Premiership place and awaiting a decision on the ground.

It's a key phase for all sorts of reasons. Yes, we're pushing hard for promotion, but also on the footballing side we're developing the whole of that structure. Among other things, this embraces the style of play as well as the French philosophy on how you develop young players. They have a very well-thought-out process, and that developing someone means throughout their career, not just until they're 18 and on the fringes of the first team. We're also developing the training ground facilities – we have a new gym, for instance. We have to keep pace with new technology – Roger Propos has bought in heart-monitoring equipment – so you see we're striving for the very best. The same goes for the new stadium. As things stand our stadium isn't suitable for First Division football. Compare ours with Sheffield Wednesday or Wolves, say...

"Homely" is one description for Craven Cottage. "Ancient" is another...

Exactly. As the Club's ambitions grow we want our visitors to be welcomed, our home fans to be in an environment that is appropriate and safe. In short we want a stadium and facilities fit for watching football in the modern era and one that reflects the Football Club's success. So it's crucial the planning application gets approved – if not it's difficult to see what happens next.

You've recently made modifications to the planning application – the apartment block being reduced from six storeys to four and the reduction of flats to 16, for instance – why?

After we initially submitted the application, the Council and a number of statutory consultees came back asking for clarification of some of the technical information contained in the Environmental Statement. Over the last few months we've gone through a process of guiding people through the Statement showing that the issues they'd mentioned were actually covered by information already included in this report. We also had to consider a couple of further matters and in so far as possible we've done our very best to reach positive solutions regarding these.

I suppose the real question is "When are we going to hear something?"...

We're hoping it'll now be December. Everyone's worked ludicrously hard on this for a very long time. It's an enormous project all said and done, but we think we've approached it in the right way – we consulted everyone and listened to their views.

If it's a yes, what happens then, and how quickly?

If, as we hope, we get to a position where we can progress, much will depend on timing. It's well documented that it'll take us two close seasons and a full season to get the stadium built. The later planning permission comes, the shorter time we'd have to negotiate contracts and, of course, there's only a certain amount of people in the world who can take on a job of this sort, and we'll have to check that they'd be available at the time that we'd need them. We don't want to put any carts before horses, however. The key thing has been concentrating upon getting the proposals accepted.

There could be another inquiry, though?

We're hoping it won't get called in – that could have the same effect as a rejection. As things stand we have one more year under the Taylor Report before Craven Cottage has to be an all-seater ground.

Can you not apply for an extension?

I think it's Barnet who've set the precedent. If you have planning permission or are well down the process then you can get an extension. But for

	1st
Fulham 3 Gilingham 0	2nd
23.09.00 1st	3rd
Bolton Wanderers 0 Fulham 2	4th
30.09.00 1st	5th
Fulham 2 Blackburn Rovers 1	6th
15.10.00 1st	7th
Fulham 3 Crystal Palace 1	8th
18.10.00 1st	9th
Wolves 0 Fulham 0	10th
21.10.00 1st	11th
Fulham 0 Preston NE 1	12th
24.10.00 1st	13th
Sheffield Wednesday 3 Fulham 3	14th
28.10.00 2nd	15th
Fulham 3 Huddersfield Town 0	16th
04.11.00 2nd	17th
Wimbledon 0 Fulham 3	18th
11.11.00 1st	19th
Fulham 3 Portsmouth 1	20th
18.11.00 1st	21th
Sheffield United 1 Fulham 1	22th
21.11.00 1st	23th
Fulham 2 Grimsby Town 1	24th
25.11.00 1st	
Preston NE 1 Fulham 1	
02.12.00 1st	
West Brom 1 Fulham 3	
09.12.00 1st	
Fulham 3 Tranmere Rovers 1	
16.12.00 1st	
Crewe Alexandra 1 Fulham 2	
23.12.00 1st	
Fulham 5 Watford 0	
26.12.00 1st	
Stockport County 2 Fulham 0	
01.01.01 1st	

League Cup

Fulham 4 Chesterfield 0
27.09.00   Round 2 2nd leg

Fulham 3 Wolves 2
01.11.00   Round 3

Fulham 3 Derby County 2
29.11.00   Round 4

Liverpool 3 Fulham 0
13.12.00   aet Round 5

how long the Licensing Authority would allow that to go on, I don't know – it would be at their discretion. It's a situation we clearly want to avoid.

So let's be positive – where might we play as and when we have to move out?
I realise this is a talking point among the fans, but it's also a highly delicate matter. Focus at the moment centres totally on the application, and when we receive the positive result there will, no doubt, be another stage of furious activity, including discussion of where the team might play, along with securing contracts for the planned work.

Okay, on to other matters – are you disappointed in the number of Fulham fans attending games so far this season?
Not disappointed; more surprised, I guess. Considering the attractive football, I'm surprised we haven't picked up more "passing trade" popping in to be entertained and hopefully hooked. Some of this season's displays have been magnificent. But all said and done the level of support has been fantastic in the last few games – we're moving in the right direction. After all, we want "trends" rather than "blips" – we want people coming to Fulham to support the team on a regular basis.

Your predecessor, Neil Rodford, frequently said that Fulham would only sign players who'd fit in the "right for Fulham" category and who "wanted to play for Fulham". This has been borne out by the good squad spirit and apparent lack of egos. Can you confirm that's still the philosophy?
Very much so! The decision-making process involves Jean Tigana, the Chairman and myself, and certainly Jean is very focused on the need for it to be a team effort. He wouldn't be interested in anyone who might upset the equilibrium. And any player, no matter how flamboyant or otherwise, must have the work ethic...

Since Neil's departure, things have taken a Gallic course. How has this affected your role – apart from frequent trips to France and having plentiful supplies of Jean Tigana's wine...?
I suppose the difference would be that in a European structure the manager is more of a coach and is less involved in the decision-making on player-buying and direct negotiations, which is the English way. Jean and I have to work on a partnership on that basis and the emphasis might be a bit different, but the end product is exactly the same. And yes, I guess there are more trips to the continent now than to, say, Rotherham!

Much has been made of the innovative changes introduced by Tigana and his staff. Have you been surprised with how well things have gone?
I'm not surprised in the slightest! If anyone came to watch how they operate you'd realise there and then that they are doing the right things...

You mentioned the word "focused" earlier but "detailed" and "meticulous' are other words associated with our manager...
Oh yes. We have a great squad of players but the introduction of a training programme for each player to maximise their performance has made a huge difference. Getting each of the players to their maximum fitness level and to give of their best puts us in the best position to win football matches. If you're going into a Grand Prix you want your car highly tuned – okay so occasionally someone might crash into you and force you into the rails, but that's down to luck on the day. The systems that have been put in place give the players the best opportunity to win matches.

And levels of confidence have rocketed, too?
That's right. They've felt fit and confident in their ability of lasting 90 minutes at full throttle.

Can the Club maintain its "Friendly Fulham" image while pushing towards the very top?
It's vitally important that we retain our friendliness – and it's not an image, we *are* friendly!

Fans have been well looked after just recently what with the "pegged" prices on away travel and season ticket offers, but how keen are the powers-that-be that the good relationship between the club and its fans is maintained? Can you confirm that ticket prices won't go through the roof in order to pay for the new stadium, for example?
The business plan for the new stadium includes plans to keep ticket prices at an accessible level – that's the ethos and policy of the Chairman. I'm sure as and when we reach the Premiership prices will rise a bit but we have to retain the accessibility for the ordinary fan.

You can understand the fans' unrest considering the prices set down the road at Chelsea…?
Yes, but then Mohamed Al Fayed's our Chairman, not Ken Bates.

What do you see as the main challenges ahead?
The single main challenge is promotion to the Premiership – and the Club is geared up for it. Hopefully, if promotion is secured then some of the other hurdles may well be overcome. The impact of it all will lead to other issues being addressed right across the board.

In closing, what about an exclusive? When's the next big-money signing coming in; and who is he?
Good try! All I can say is that our vision is to see the Club as a power in the Premiership and when the right players come along that can help us

"Getting each of the players to their maximum fitness level and to give of their best puts us in the best position to win football matches. If you're going into a Grand Prix you want your car highly tuned – okay so occasionally someone might crash into you and force you into the rails, but that's down to luck on the day."

TIME RUNNING OUT FOR STADIUM PLAN

All-seater ground decision is sidelined after talks are delayed until New Year

By SALLY GUYONCOURT

FULHAM Football Club's new stadium remains in limbo after a meeting to decide whether the site's redevelopment can go ahead was delayed until the New Year.

As the club vie for promotion to the Premiership they must face the fact that unless a decision is made soon on the new stadium they could be homeless by August 2002.

Under the rules laid down in the Taylor Report, Fulham had three seasons from their entry into the first division to bring make Craven Cottage an all-seater stadium.

But the town hall has postponed the planning committee making a decision on the new £60 million 30,000 all-seater stadium plans until the New Year after amendments to the plans were submitted to the council last month.

Deadline

The delay also means the prospect of a costly and lengthy public inquiry looms larger which would delay the completion of the stadium still further.

Now time is running short to provide a new stadium to meet the deadline.

Fulham FC managing director Michael Fiddy said: "It is disappointing. We wanted it to be heard as soon as possible.

"We want the council to give the amendments we have submitted the necessary time and full consideration.

"And what we genuinely want is that anyone involved is given enough time to view them properly.

"The key fact, however, is under the Taylor Report we only have one year to go before we must become all-seater.

"We can't see how there can't be any positive resolution – there's nowhere else the club can go.

"The current stands at Craven Cottage are very old and falling down. They need to be replaced to meet modern safety standards."

In a concession to residents, the block of flats next to the development in Stevenage Road has been lowered from seven storeys to five and the number of flats reduced to 16 from 30.

And the supporting wall beneath the upper tier of the stands will now be clad in green copper rather than stainless steel as requested by English Heritage.

A council spokesman said: "Following the final changes to the planning application, there will be a short period of consultation for local residents, interested parties and fans to make their views known. We are anticipating that the application will be heard early in the New Year."

Fulham United spokesman Tom Greatrex said: "In one sense it's disappointing but support for the new stadium is very strong.

"I'm sure when the council planning committee meet to determine they will take that into account."

Consultation

Fulham Alliance spokesman Paul Mitchell said: "I'm not at all surprised it's taking as long as it is taking because the application is complex and highly controversial.

"We are quite content to move at the pace dictated by the council on this."

Six thousand letters of consultation have been sent out to interested parties from the council and the deadline for comments or objections is December 20.

DISAPPOINTED: Michael Fiddy

Above: More from the *Fulham Chronicle*, detailing further delays in FFC's ground plans – and the Club's "disappointed" Managing Director, Michael Fiddy.

---

deliver that then we'll be out in the market striving to bring them to Fulham Football Club. We have the advantage of being sited in west London, which is deemed a fashionable part of the world, and then there's the Tigana factor – incoming players will, I'm sure, believe he'll improve their game. The Chairman's backing is crucial, too. So the ingredients are right to attract players here. It'll be that much easier once we're in the top division. ⚽

All Right my *Sun*? No, Actually

With Fulham and their wonderful new brand of "total football" sitting proudly at the top of Division One under Jean Tigana's stewardship, it's surely time to look forward, not back. However, TOOFIF editor David Lloyd takes a quick peek over his shoulder now that former boss Kevin Keegan has relinquished his England duties…

So, Kevin Keegan has done the right thing/a runner/us up good 'n' proper (delete as appropriate). Whatever your view, it's interesting to note the tabloids' stance on KK's resignation, particularly that of the "red-tops". Keegan was simply not the man for the job, they all trumpeted – he's patently been tactically naïve and out of his depth.

Oh really? Are these the very same red-tops who piled the pressure on KK not so long ago by clamouring for his appointment. Of course they are, the ruddy hypocrites.

Whatever you think of him now, Keegan was at the time doing a great job at Craven Cottage, but was pressurised by the media and the FA into totally severing links with Fulham Football Club. For us long-suffering fans it looked as if outside influences had conspired to burst the bubble. And at the vanguard was the super, soaraway *Sun*.

To recap, following our FA Cup tie at Old Trafford in February 1999, Keegan was appointed part-time England coach for four matches, kicking off with a friendly against France. He turned down the job on a permanent basis, preferring to push on with the "day-job" at Craven Cottage.

"I'm really enjoying what's happening at Fulham," he said. "It gave me a huge boost to see 8,500 Fulham fans at Old Trafford. On the one hand you've got that emotion, but on the other you've got a pull that every Englishman should have which is to manage your country."

The Sun who, remember, reckoned KK was never fit for the task, blasted forth with these headlines:

KEV BREAKS OUR HEARTS (when Keegan insisted on retaining his Fulham job);

COME ON KEV (when the FA made a move for their man);

KEEGAN IN ENGLAND TALKS TODAY (when Al Fayed let the FA talk to Keegan).

Good eh? No sign of any "COME OFF IT, KEV", is there?

At the time Fulham fans were rightly bemused, acknowledging that a decent appointment was necessary and that Keegan had every right to be interested. Anyway, like today, there was hardly a long list of candidates. Yet we truly believed he'd stay (his words, remember) in some capacity to oversee our continued improvement. That was the script.

The Sun, meantime, remained bullish:

MY WAY OR NO WAY – Kev will boss England if FA clear Fulham link

KEV GETS HIS WAY – Keegan is part-time boss

Acting FA Chairman Geoff Thompson said: "We've had to respect the fact that he was under contract to Fulham – and contracts need to mean more in football." Yeah, right Geoffrey!

The Sun (anti-Keegan don't forget) used its *Sun Sport* leader to proclaim on Feb 17: "Can you believe it? The FA have got something right. Kevin Keegan is the England manager".

A day later their back page headline was: **KEEGAN BREAKS ALL OUR HEARTS AGAIN**, adding "Kevin Keegan is the new England boss – but only until June. People's favourite Keegan has broken the nation's hearts by insisting he does not want the job beyond the summer.

All Fulham fans probably felt a warm glow – despite everything, Keegan was still committed to Fulham. Selfishly or otherwise we could still consider ourselves on track for better things. Then, after promotion was secured against Gillingham, Keegan famously announced: "I could never give this up – not even for England. The FA understand my situation. They are not putting pressure on me. We've seen tonight how wonderful Fulham is. This makes me even more convinced that Fulham has to remain part of my career." *The Sun* ran the headline **KEV: I WON'T QUIT FULHAM**.

But by the end of March the pressure was back on. Without a doubt Keegan was being steered towards taking the national job on a full-time basis. The man himself was keen to retain at least a hand-holding role down by the Thames. "Fulham have been good to me and I would like to stay in some capacity" he told the *Standard*. A day later his number-one fans at *The Sun* declared **IT'S YOUR JOB FOR LIFE, KEV**.

The bombshell news came as the domestic season drew to a close and with runaway Division Two champions Fulham preparing for a jamboree

final day and possibly breaking the 100-points mark against Preston. After everything that had been said before, and with desperately bad timing, an uncomfortable Keegan revealed on a televised sport programme (and with a clutch of Fulham fans in the audience) that he was leaving Fulham. Even though the total severing of links was thought to be on the FA's orders, the announcement left KK with egg on his face.

His final matchday programme notes, written earlier in the week to meet printing deadlines, gave no hint of his decision. But as we read his words an unhealthy atmosphere was threatening to spoil our first championship in 50 years.

Rumours were rife of a row at the training ground between Keegan and the FFC powers-that-be and speculation that "the nation's favourite" would be barred from the Preston game and the ensuing presentation ceremony. Brilliant – this was supposed to be a carnival occasion!

In the event Keegan – so responsible for a great season – did turn up, but remained very much in the background. Fans were understandably miffed – one or two even booed – that their champagne day had been blighted. (Mind you, by 5pm Paul Moody's second-half hat-trick had done much to instill a wonderful buzz.)

Keegan may well have made a massive U-turn, the timing of his "final" announcement may well have been appalling, but there's no doubt the desperate FA were hell-bent on getting their man. The media, meantime – and the red-tops in particular – had been more than happy to lap it all up – and apply the pressure in a big way. *The Sun*, incidentally rounded the whole thing off with **NOW FAYED WANTS GULLIT AS NEW BOSS**. ⚽

Meeting Morgs

The Ed spoke to Simon Morgan a couple of days before our match with Wimbledon...

FFC have reportedly made a £6m bid for a player. What would Alan Dicks have made of that?
Good grief! Can you imagine who he'd have bought for £6m!!? Naturally the lads were talking about this – we agreed we could've got gangly Ian Ormondroyd for only £50,000, whereas we've offered that huge sum for his double! Jan Koller's his name…

Dicks would've called him "Coca" no doubt…?
That or "Pepsi"! But it remains an indication of how far this football club of ours has come. Whether or not it comes off remains to be seen, but I suppose now that we've declared our hand most supporters will be coming up with ideas of how to spend £6m.

What about a younger Simon Morgan?
Six million lira, more like – and there'd be a stack of change!

Below: Looks like Kevin Keegan has fallen asleep and is already dreaming of getting the England job. In the end our magnanimous Chairman let KK leave FFC, saying it was his "gift to the nation".

You must know The Fizz and Roger Propos quite well by now. How's are things coming along – are they steering you back towards full fitness?
The Fizz has disowned me; he knows me too well! No, they're doing their bit. To be serious for a minute, it's all very professional. The rehabilitation is excellent. The good news is that the knee I damaged in April is in fantastic shape; it's just the other one now. But judging how things have gone so far I'm sure I'll be as good as new in due course.

They've been working you hard?
Well we don't call Roger "Forrest Gump" for nothing. He likes to run! Mind you I'm not at that stage as yet. But I'm really looking forward to it…

What, Morgs looking forward to training…!!?
Okay, so running's not one of my passions – I tell the lads that the first ten yards are in your head, anyway – but it's a must to get back to full fitness. It's great, really – Roger gives you a weekly schedule, or [in mock French accent] "skedool", and you can see how you're building up. Every day you're loading a little bit extra through the knee.

You said last time that you're enjoying watching the game. Is that still the case?
Oh yes. I was in the commentary box for the Blackburn game, covering it with Paul Thorpe for the new Internet section. I enjoyed it, but I can't have done all that well as Thorpey hasn't asked me back! It was a good game to commentate on, plenty happened especially in the first half and there was a great atmosphere. Trouble was, I was a bit biased; but then why not! I certainly screeched down the headphones when we scored the winner.

This "arrogant" label has been pinned to us just lately. As with your reaction there, the fans are merely enjoying the good times, and why not!?
Of course you're enjoying it – we certainly are. The fans aren't arrogant. Being hypercritical, that chant of "You'll never play us again" as we stormed out of the Second Division under Kevin Keegan – although quite funny first time out – smacked more of arrogance than anything said this season. To label the players or fans "arrogant" is just daft. The players have been careful to stick to the facts: we've said we're playing really well and that it's a pleasure to play in such a manner, that we're enjoying training and also that there's a long way to go.

The media have, as usual, been a little mischievous, one week labelling us as world-beaters and then, days later, trumpeting that the Fulham bubble has burst…
After the Palace game our friends at *The Sun* ran a report saying they were taking odds on us winning every League this season. A week later there was a serious crisis at Fulham as we'd lost and were

off the top of the table. The truth is Preston did a very good job – they were excellent on the night – we had some half chances that had been flying in during other games but not that night. The manager's philosophy hasn't changed, it's "pass, pass, pass" whether we've won, drawn or lost.

It's true to say, though, that by the highest of yardsticks set in those first ten games we've not been as fluent recently, even if this is also down to the approach of the opposition, too…
The other teams have maybe approached things a little differently and possibly one or two players have had less influential games, but I think they've come through that. It was telling that even when we weren't at those high standards we were still trying to pass the ball around and do the right thing. The crowd responded to that – they realised we weren't resorting to just humping it upfield. Mind you, if we buy a 6ft 7in centre-forward we might!

The short passing game has given us many exciting moments and created no end of chances, but a long pass – as opposed to an aimless punt – is still an important tactic…
We favour the diagonal ball to switch the point of attack, it's certainly not all short passing. As for the aimless punts, you'll have to wait until I'm back to see the famous humps into row Z again! All this playing out from the back – pah! – it'll have to go!

Did the players consider the dropping of points a "blip"?
They laughed it off really. To go from "world-beaters" to "chumps" in a matter of days was daft. They'd never got carried away during that winning run either, there was a far more realistic mood to be honest. They were disappointed that two points were dropped at Sheffield Wednesday probably because it was a downer to concede that late, late goal. They knew how well they'd played in the second half, scoring three goals…

The manager apparently chipped in with more than three words at half time on that occasion…?
Yes that's true – he let the lads know he wasn't too happy. When something like that happens, what the manager wants is a response, and he got it. ⚽

"To label the players or fans 'arrogant' is just daft. The players have been careful to stick to the facts: we've said we're playing really well and that it's a pleasure to play in such a manner, that we're enjoying training and also that there's a long way to go."

Morgs' Magic Moment
I must comment on the legendary scones available at half time in the press room. In all these years this was my first tasting session – and they were fabulous! Well I say "they" – in fact there was just the one left on the plate by the time I got there because Tony Gale had scoffed the rest. On the playing front the magic moment must go to the French Connection against Huddersfield. Fabrice [Fernandes] whipped in a quality cross and Louis Saha did the rest with a bullet header. Absolutely fabulous – as was the well-deserved England Under-21 call up for Sean Davis.

Wide Boy... Ultimately

All long-in-the-tooth Fulham fans will have fond memories of Les Barrett darting along the wing, chalking up 491 appearances for FFC in all. Like any long-term Fulham player, he had his ups and downs at the Club. Les kicked off his rollercoaster career in the mid '60s when playing Liverpool, Manchester United and their like was the norm (as was the annual battle to avoid relegation!), and he made an FA Cup Final appearance in 1975. In between times, life at FFC wasn't as rosy, and he probably wished Bobby Campbell hadn't come anywhere near Craven Cottage. Not that Les, as self-effacing and discreet as ever, would ever contemplate saying as much...

You played through a number of eras and squads, Les, but what was it like in those early First Division days?
They were the best days, without a doubt. It was an incredible time – I was only about 18 and we were playing top teams and performing before packed crowds. Everything seemed like a dream.

Did you appreciate it all then, or more so as time passed?
I certainly took in all the excitement at the time. But I suppose I only really put it into perspective when we were subsequently relegated and the crowds dwindled. The 1975 Cup run was great, of course, as it rekindled all of that. You can't beat playing in front of large crowds and the terrific atmosphere that's generated.

You made your debut against Blackpool, then faced Chelsea and scored in your third game, a 3-4 reverse at Spurs – a good moment, presumably, despite the defeat?
It was great. There was a packed house at White Hart Lane, so the adrenaline was flowing. You can't compare the feeling to turning out for the reserves before a hundred or so people as had been the case in the previous weeks. The step-up to the big stage is unbelievable and the impact is difficult to put into words.

It wasn't just the big stage, though, was it – you were playing alongside, and against, some genuine star players?
In the Fulham side at the time were Johnny Haynes, George Cohen and Bobby Robson, and I found it hard to take in that I was on the same pitch as them. You might say that I felt like a schoolboy daring to be on the field with the masters of the game.

You've mentioned three "masters", but there were many more besides (towards the end of your time at the Club came the Best and Marsh roadshow). Were any of these influential in any way? I bet Haynes was pretty useful at pinging a pass out to the left wing...?
Johnny was a class player and yes, he'd knock some fantastic balls out wide into space and I'd have to get on the end of them. George Cohen was another great guy – he took the time to help me out with my crossing. The funny thing is, I'd never really been a left-footer; previously I'd always played down the right or through the middle, so George used to coach me a little – even before I'd made my mark on the left.

So, Les the flying left-winger was really Les the nifty inside-forward, at least in your schooldays...?
To tell you the truth, when I played at Putney Vale when I was about 11 I was played at right-wing, before that I'd been centre-forward for my primary school side. I always preferred the role down the middle – a little in the Jimmy Greaves mould, I suppose. In those days it was simply a case of the ball being knocked forward, I'd get on the end of it and dribble it towards the goalkeeper and knock it past him. Sound easy,

Opposite page right: Les Barrett – a firm favourite with Fulham fans.

Below: Les Barrett controls a difficult ball at full stretch against Aston Villa in March 1969. The match ended 1-1, and Fulham were closing in on a second successive relegation.

There's Only One F In Fulham
An alternative look at Fulham F.C.
WHEN ONLY THE BEST WILL DO
...Les Barrett interview inside
www.TOOFIF.com
POWERED BY PASSION
£1.50
Issue 73   Jan/Feb 2001

Fulham 2 Norwich City 0	2nd
13.01.01 1st	3rd
Watford 1 Fulham 3	4th
20.01.01 1st	5th
	6th
Fulham 0 Birmingham City 1	7th
27.01.01 1st	8th
QPR 0 Fulham 2	9th
31.01.01 1st	10th
	11th
Fulham 1 Sheffield United 1	12th
04.02.01 1st	13th
Barnsley 0 Fulham 0	14th
10.02.01 1st	15th
	16th
FA Cup	17th
Fulham 1 Manchester United 2	18th
07.01.01 Round 3	19th
	20th
	21st
	22nd
	23rd
	24th

right? And, to be honest, it was. I did it time and again – but I was still stuck out on the right wing.

You found the net against both Liverpool and Manchester United in the spring of 1967. Both matches ended 2-2 – can you remember anything about those games?

Not a thing! Actually, I do have a hazy memory of my goal against Liverpool. I think I was being marked by renowned hardman Tommy Smith and I was on the edge of the area. The ball was played in – maybe by Graham Leggat, or maybe not! – and I took it on my thigh and hooked it on the turn. And in it flew! When I think about it now, I suppose I'd say "that wasn't a bad goal", but it was all down to pure instinct. Some might ask what was I doing in the centre of the pitch. Well, at the time we were playing a system of three roving forwards, Stevie Earle, Jimmy Conway and myself. Once Allan Clarke was established in the side, I was pushed out to the left with, as I recall, Jimmy on the right.

Clarkie had a reputation as a greedy so-and-so in front of goal…?

That's right. But he was paid to be greedy, and he certainly got his share of goals. He was headstrong for sure. We were a stepping stone for Allan, and that's fine. If you're going to get to the top that's the way you've got to be.

You won an England Under-21 cap in 1967…

It was all part of my euphoric baptism. There I was just breaking into the first team, we were facing the top sides, and it goes to show that if you're in the spotlight and doing reasonably well then other things can follow. We were on the telly every few weeks – and this was before the seemingly blanket coverage offered nowadays by the likes of Sky – and it all became a rollercoaster ride. And yes, I got the England Under-21 nod.

Who were your contemporaries?

Gerry Francis was on the tour, as was Frank Sibley, plus Clarkie. What happened was at the end of the season they had a Young England v England match at Highbury. I got in because one of the "youngsters" pulled out through injury. It must have helped that I was based in London. So I played in that game and the tour came a week or two later. I suppose the other young lad must still have been "out" since I was called up for the mini-tour. I played in the match in Greece, which finished 0-0.

Back to Fulham matters, then! You had great players around you, but what about great characters?

I have to mention Tosh [Chamberlain]! It was the time when several of the old faces were being replaced and Tosh wasn't around for too long once I'd made my mark, which was a shame. Vic Buckingham was changing things around – he dropped Johnny Haynes for the first time, I remember; Steve Earle was brought in. Terry Parmenter was another to come through, while Fred Callaghan had taken over from Jimmy Langley at left-back. Graham Leggat had been playing on the left, so Tosh's days seemed numbered.

In general, though, it's reckoned that Fulham was a fun place to be at the time?

Oh yes! We had Keetchy [Bobby Keetch] – what a character and what a ladies man! It's very difficult to describe how I felt. I was really in awe of everything that was going on. Even going into the dressing room was something of a struggle in that I couldn't believe I was part of it all – possibly because it all happened so quickly.

Would you say that Steve Earle was your main foil, even though he wasn't a traditional big centre-forward?

Yes, I suppose he was. Although not a giant, Steve was good in the air. He seemed to be there whenever I was crossing the ball – and that's the mark of a good player. Jimmy Conway, too, often made a habit of turning up at the far post.

The Club's fortunes nosedived when the annual escape from the relegation berths didn't materialise in 1968. In fact, we shot straight through Division Two, downwards. Was that a time of despair?

It wasn't too clever! The nucleus of the First Division squad remained, so we should have done much better.

From the terraces, there didn't seem to be too much spirit about the place. Is that a fair assessment?

139

"Johnny Haynes was put in charge for a few matches. Then Bobby Robson came in, when he was only just learning about management. To be blunt, the Board didn't have what was necessary to halt the slide."

It wasn't so much that, more that the managers they brought in, and the players that were signed, were terrible. It was never going to work. Many were panic buys. When we were struggling it was a case of having to get someone in – anyone! – to try to rectify matters. Signing Budgie Byrne typified things. He'd been a great player in his time but there was no spark at Fulham. Cliffie Jones was another – an all-time great, but unable to do too much for us. Nice blokes but the circumstances were all wrong, with the wrong guys in charge. Johnny Haynes was put in charge for a few matches. Then Bobby Robson came in, when he was only just learning about management. To be blunt, the Board didn't have what was necessary to halt the slide.

During our First Division days there was talk about you being linked with Manchester United…

Yes, there was talk! But you see I was still young and really in awe of the whole playing situation so it never entered my head to go in and see what was happening and demand this or that. Of course in retrospect, I think "what a stupid idiot!". Then again, I've always been backward in coming forward.

Things started to get back on track when Bill Dodgin took over – the flying wingers and all that…?

As I've said, we still had the nucleus of the First Division squad, but we were now in the Third. Bill was so easy going, with Terry Medwin – another lovely bloke – as his number two, and I can't recall them coaching us too much. What they did do, though, was to get us playing football again. For some reason things started to click and – surprise, surprise – we found ourselves winning football matches once again. Confidence was an important factor, as was the fact that the various departments within the team were doing their jobs once again.

Some years later came the Best and Marsh roadshow…

It was a great shame that didn't last longer. I was asked about the whole showbiz aspect back then. My view was that if they were going to do the business for Fulham and make it a better club then I was all for it. But if they were just coming along to muck about and disappear before long – which is what I suspected would happen – then perhaps it wouldn't be such a great idea.

Thames Bank Travelling

Eager to get to away grounds sooner that the official coaches (in order to sell you-know-what!) I signed up for the Thames Bank Travellers, whose aim since the early 1970s, was even more specific: to get to away venues for when the pubs opened. Bearing in mind that in TOOFIF's early days, trips to away games were almost guaranteed to be marked by a customary defeat, there had to be something to make the regular outings worthwhile. While the mists of time might add a certain rosy over-affection to these jaunts, they remain remarkable nevertheless. In an age when trouble was a footballing byword, the regular travellers somehow bucked that trend, managing to rid pubs up and down the land of copious amounts of alcohol yet never causing any bother. Plenty of trouble walking in a straight line afterwards, maybe, but never any out-and-out hassle.

On one occasion we made an unscheduled stop at an out-of-the-way rural hostelry as one of our number was desperate for a pee. "While you're there, see if it's okay for us to come in for a few pints," suggested one of our ever-thirsty party as our ever-more-agitated one

shuffled out of the coach and towards the door. The main obstacle was the impossible-to-miss giant sign between us and the building; it read: "ABSOLUTELY NO FOOTBALL COACHES ALLOWED". Something of a stumbling block perhaps. Not a bit of it. Our by-now frantic, cross-legged charmer not only managed to relieve himself in the appropriate place and manner but also gained us entrance, possibly suggesting that we were a group of church dignitaries en route to a special service, and that the assorted collection of black and white scarves and hats were simply a sensible answer to the cold weather. No matter, we were in – even if the gazes of the staff and locals were, to say the least, as suspicious as they were unwelcoming.

Some 90 minutes and many quids into the till later we filed back onto the coach – waved away by most of the pub regulars who'd come out to see us off. The sight of the locals standing adjacent to the "No football coaches" sign, waving us off with their hankies was bizarre, and yet summed up the TBT. We'd been loud, full of fun (and full of beer) but still on the right side of the line. "Don't forget to call back on your way

home," they implored, an indication of our decent behaviour as well as their healthy bar takings. Unfortunately for them, we stuck to the motorway network on the return journey.

Aboard the coach, it was a case of Groundhog Day most weeks. The fundraising raffle, to part-subsidise the coach travel, was organised by Graham "Get yer money out" Duke. Alex "The Traveller" Ferguson would always go for "half a bar" (50p-worth). The prizes, always reasonable, invariably included a chocolate bar that was perpetually "won" by Podgy Paul. The predictions book always made its own steady journey up and down the coach as the TBTers filled in their guesstimates of all the day's League fixtures.

Until Micky Adams stopped the rot, such awaydays also invariably included our heroes succumbing to yet another defeat. At least the Thames Bank Travellers went out on a relative high: the final jolly boys' and girls' outing was to Cambridge in May 1997, where a 1-0 away win confirmed our runners-up spot to Wigan, despite finishing level on points (87) and having a superior goal difference.

Was it a treat or a frustrating time?

For me it turned out to be the latter I'm afraid. To be perfectly honest, when George and Rodney played you were just there to make up the numbers. You knew half the time you weren't going to get the ball, that sort of thing. It wasn't a great time for me personally. I got injured at Sheffield United – by Ernie Howe of all people! I was trying to clear the ball and Ernie tried to clear me – giving me a boot in the back of the knee. It was also my testimonial year and, unfortunately, that season and the one after were disastrous for me.

The 1975 Cup run – all the way to Wembley – was a much happier time…?

When Steve Earle and Paul Went left I thought we were losing our way. I felt they were our mainstays. But then Alec Stock brought in a few new faces and we started to get going – all right, it wasn't brilliant in the League but that Cup run was something special. It's often forgotten how good some of those early games against Nottingham Forest and Hull City were – they were tight contests as evidenced by the number of replays! They were certainly great to play in – I felt I'd done well and had contributed to the team. And it got better and better as we went along. It was brilliant to play at Everton – a big occasion and in front of a bumper crowd.

Bobby Moore was imperious at Goodison…

He was. But then everyone played their part during that cup run – that was the beauty of it. Everyone had their day along the way.

Can you explain how you felt when John Mitchell's last-gasp goal crept over the line against Birmingham in the semi-final replay? You'd made it to Wembley!

Numb! We hadn't played well, but then neither had they. That goal came out of the blue. I can't even remember where I was on the pitch. All I know is that the ball was played across from the right – was it by Alan Slough? – and it ricocheted in off Mitch. It's true that things go into slow motion in such circumstances – or maybe the ball really was travelling that slowly! But the realisation gradually sank in: "Hello, we're in the Final!". The final whistle went almost immediately and I saw one of their wingers loping off, crying his eyes out. I think I said "Sorry" – although I wasn't sorry at all!

Was there a sense of elation, Les?

Not really. It only started to sink in that we'd made it to Wembley in that week beforehand, what with all the interviews and stuff. But no real elation, not for me anyway. Throughout my career I only got a buzz when I felt I'd contributed

Above: Les Barrett, Fulham's very own Roadrunner, goes up the gears against Luton.

– either through scoring a goal or beating a few players and putting in an important cross or two. Although we'd earned our right to play at Wembley through our effort over the course of the matches, I hadn't directly affected things in either of the semi-finals. That's just me, I guess.

But it was still one hell of an achievement to have got to Wembley, especially having played all those matches?

Definitely – and I'm proud to have got there. Fact is, though, we didn't win, did we? We were right in it during the first half and West Ham certainly weren't giving us too many problems. John Lacy's header went just over the bar for us, but otherwise it was all pretty much nip and tuck.

Wembley's pitch should have suited you…?

It should have! The whole occasion is hard to describe. The only thing I can say is that it was like a dream. I wasn't bothered by the crowd because they weren't there, or so it seemed. Must be down to it being your visit to the place, I guess. You walk down the tunnel at the start to be greeted by this tremendous roar, but it doesn't seem real. Had I got back to Wembley, as I very nearly did with Woking in the FA Trophy, then it might have been a different experience. In saying that, the whole day was very exciting and I'm so glad I had the chance to play there. ⚽

Paul Johnson

Paul Johnson's cartoons have been a mainstay in the mag since Issue 4. His longrunning, whimsical *We Can Dream* series has been backed up by a host of others, including the *All Washed Up*, *Those Were The Days* and *In A League Of Their Own* mini-series – a selection of which are displayed here. So what prompted Paul to contribute in the first place (and to do so unfailingly since then)?

"The inspiration (if that's the right word) for the first *We Can Dream* cartoon – 'Cavalry Charge' – came after watching a particularly mind-numbing 0-0 draw against Northampton Town. To be fair to the Cobblers, they weren't the only team employing a tedious offside trap in their away games, but this match, and this cartoon, originally submitted simply as a one-off gripe, clearly struck a nerve.

"It became the template for a series of strips, and these have featured ever since. There were only a couple of rules: a) the cartoons should hopefully raise a smile, whatever the subject matter; and b) they should avoid litigation. (Cue caveat: any resemblance to persons living or dead is purely coincidental, and likely to be rather poorly drawn anyway.)"

Ah, but which of all your offerings is your favourite, Paul? "I suppose that's the one from Issue 31 (November 1993). I could only imagine what the players would be saying in the wake of yet another defeat, so I tried to put into words and pictures how elaborate and far-fetched their excuses might be. 'Ley Lines' was the result, and remains something of a favourite." ⚽

Right: Paul Johnson presents Simon Morgan with a personalised drawing. (And that's even though "any resemblance to persons living or dead is purely concidental!")

Below: An updated version of the first We Can Dream that appeared in Issue 4.

This page: A small selection of Paul's considerable input to TOOFIF over the years is showcased here. It includes an almost obligatory reference to our visit to Torquay in 1996 (*below left*), as well as Paul's own personal favourite – "Ley Lines" (*below*) from November 1993.

Get Well Soon, Cookie

The last issue had just gone to the printers when the awful news came in about Chris Coleman. Those pictures showing the mangled wreck of what was once his sleek motor demonstrated that he was very fortunate to survive at all. Cookie faces a long haul back to fitness, and really the issue of whether he'll play again is totally irrelevant at present. What is certain is that he'll get the best possible care and attention, together with a wealth of support from us, the fans.

The whole business brought out the best and worst in people. Football fans from all over the world contacted the various Fulham websites with goodwill messages. Those that were posted on the TOOFIF site have been passed on to Cookie, incidentally. The press, meantime, had a field day – many reports were fair, if speculative, but others were unnecessarily spiteful in the extreme. Talk about kicking a guy when he's down.

Word is, Cookie's due to attend one of the next Fulham games. The very least we can do is to give him a thunderous welcome back to Craven Cottage. Here's to a speedy and complete recovery, Chris!

The accident happened in the lead up to a important contest against some team called Manchester United, reckoned to be better than most (I have impeccable sources!). What has been amazing is that something as catastrophic as a dreadful car smash involving your influential captain, who's been as responsible as anyone for our rise through the divisions, has been absorbed by the club with barely a ripple.

We remain firmly on course for the Premiership and, as a little taster of what's hopefully to come, gave Man Utd arguably their sternest test of the season. With a weakened side! What a great afternoon that was. All season we've been saying how wonderfully well we've been playing and all season we've had to endure put-downs from certain sections of the media and ill-informed or jealous fans. But this match was beamed all over the world. Suddenly it was "official" – this Fulham team can play a bit. Even the "moneybags" tag was briefly shelved. ⚽

Jean Tigana's Destiny

The meet-the-manager evening hosted by the Supporters' Club was a real success. Jean Tigana came across extraordinarily well – witty, honest, determined and very, very professional. Amid the jocularity came a real sense of purpose and depth about what is happening at the club.

As well as suggesting it was his "destiny" to manage Fulham, JT fielded questions on topics as diverse as his toothpicks [a legacy of quitting smoking], his tenure [he's on a three- to five-year contract and expects this to be his final job in football], the British way ["It's a different way of working over here, but it's up to me to change"], young players ["Sean Davis has the potential to be a great player"] and his hopes ["I want to build the club. Not just the first team but also the academy and things like the medical system too"]. In short, he had all those packed in the George Cohen lounge spellbound. We've come a mighty long way since the Dicks/Mackay years. ⚽

Big, Bad Bazzer

A Bristol Rovers fanzine wanted a few lines on Barry Hayles for a feature on ex-Gasheads scoring goals elsewhere these days. This is what they were sent...

Hmm, Barry Hayles? What can one say? Big Bazzer (aka Harry Bayles) is the darling of the Fulham crowd. At the time of writing he's tucked in behind Louis Saha in the goalscoring charts – and is one half of the country's most effective strike force. So doing very nicely, thank you.

There's no doubt Barry is enjoying himself just now. Given the freedom to express himself by Jean Tigana, and with new-found zest and confidence, Bazzer is playing like a man possessed. And, invariably, sporting a broad smile on his face.

It hasn't always been so. The £2m price tag, and a change in tactics and responsibilities to what he'd been used to with Rovers, meant that he took a while to settle. In some Fulham fans' eyes he was surplus to requirements during his first season (under Kevin Keegan). Even Keegan himself was thought to consider the purchase an expensive ricket as Hayles struggled to make his mark.

When Barry eventually broke his scoring duck KK was seen dancing with glee by the dug-out

Below: Influential captain Chris Coleman, who suffered a catastrophic car smash.

144

– maybe there was something there after all. Gradually he found favour with the majority of fans. Important goals followed – although he wasn't exactly banging them in at that stage.

One lasting memory came on the day we faced the mighty (and as it turned out, all-conquering) Man Utd at Old Trafford in the FA Cup fifth round.

Fulham had a considerably weakened side. Despite this, they were possibly unlucky to lose 1-0. Japp Stam, for one, knew he'd been in a game, all right. The big, indomitable Dutch defender was dumped on his backside twice as Bazzer decided the direct route to goal was through his marker! Quite incredible.

But it's not until this season that we've seen the best of Barry. Fitter, leaner and with a brimful of confidence, the man who was expected to be shown the door by the new regime was now terrorising defences with his footwork, pace and considerable strength. But more than that, the guy was even chasing back to make to make bone-crunching tackles! And yes, the goals have flowed – including a Boxing Day hat-trick against Watford.

I've always thought he was a good player – and luckily I've got previous TOOFIF editorials to back that up! Also, truth be told, some of the barracking even when he was doing a good job over the last couple of seasons had racist undertones I'm sorry to say. But even I have been surprised – and maybe Barry has, too – at just how big a change there's been in his all-round effectiveness. It's there for all to see – the sullen striker with the worries of the world on his shoulders has been superseded by a lively, goal-hungry attacker sporting a beaming grin. And he could well be scoring goals for fun in the top flight next season. ⚽

Fulham 1 Nottingham Forest 0 17.02.01 1st	1st 2nd 3rd 4th
Burnley 2 Fulham 1 20.02.01 1st	5th 6th
Gillingham 0 Fulham 2 1st 24.02.01 1st	7th 8th 9th
Fulham 1 Bolton Wanderers 1 04.03.01 1st	10th 11th
Fulham 2 QPR 0 10.03.01 1st	12th 13th 14th
Crystal Palace 0 Fulham 2 17.03.01 1st	15th 16th
Tranmere Rovers 1 Fulham 4 30.03.01 1st	17th 18th
	19th–24th

Morgs on Cookie

Simon, how's the battle for fitness coming along?
I'm winning at the moment. It's been a long haul, with a number of ups and downs along the way but I think there's light at the end of the tunnel now.

One the field, the promotion drive remains firmly on track…
Hasn't it all been fabulous! I can't describe how much I've admired the way it's all gone. We gave Manchester United their hardest game of the season in the Cup, no doubt about that. In fact, in United's own words, we "ran them ragged for half an hour". It has been an unbelievable season.

With still plenty of points to play for, the squad spirit remains very high…?
Oh yes, it's still there. And it was given a boost when Cookie came back. It's brilliant to have him around the place again. The banter's still there — even if, at times, the foreign players can't understand a word we're saying! There's a terrific calibre of characters at the club — when you have the likes of Kit, Cookie, Mel and Rufus around you're never going to struggle.

What was the reaction when Cookie returned?
He got a chorus of "you tart!"! And "what the hell's the matter with you?" "Get out there training, you wimp!" A lot of banter, obviously — which he no doubt expected, but which will do him a power of good. It's important to keep involved and to feel part of the place — mind you I think Kit may have been stretching things when he threatened to visit him… dressed as a flippin' pheasant!!! My overriding memory of the Cookie business goes back to about ten days after the dreadful accident. He was in Parkside Hospital at the time. About a dozen of us had gone to see him. Only two were supposed to be there at a time, but we all piled in as you'd expect. Poor Cookie wasn't in the best of states but for about half an hour he was in top form, giving as good as he got, if not more so. He was like a stand-up comedian (and that's not a piss-take!), laying into everyone. He was so funny and mentally strong, despite everything — which led us to think he'd be strong enough to see it all through.

He'll have some inner demons to see off, won't he?
He will. And the lads are going to have to help him. He's certainly been completely overwhelmed by the response he's had from the fans…

…From Fulham and all around the country, I gather…
But the messages from Fulham fans, in particular, demonstrated what a special man and player he is, and what everyone thinks of him.

Is there anything the fans can do to help him at this stage?
Give him a huge cheer and a clap when he turns up for a game — I understand he wants to do that pretty soon. Keep asking him how he is whenever you see him. I know from experience that even such a small gesture can help a lot. When you're out for any length of time you can quickly become the forgotten man if things aren't handled properly.

But presumably we should add "you tart" at the end of every question…?
D'you know, he'd probably appreciate that!

145

Green Light for the Cottage

As TOOFIF 75 went to press, FFC were given the green light to redevelop the Craven Cottage site by the Government Office for London – the Secretary of State having decided not to intervene following Hammersmith & Fulham Council's approval a month earlier.

Grounds for a party!

Last night's walk through Bishops Park was very enjoyable. It's a walk I always take home from work and many have said great things about the stroll from Putney Bridge to the home of Fulham FC.

And I took this walk knowing the battle was over. Fulham FC had been granted permission from the Government to build its fantastic new stadium. The Fulham Alliance had lost. And it was just what they deserved, for conducting such a pathetic NIMBYist campaign in an attempt to force our historic Club out of its home. The gutless Alliance, who earlier in the day had bottled out of a debate over their sleazy accusations against Fulham United; The shameless Alliance, whose supporters conducted a website messageboard hate campaign on the official FFC site; The lying Alliance, who have always stated that they are not anti-football, but admitted that by forcing a Public Inquiry they could delay the matter to such an extent that Fulham FC could go bankrupt.

Oh, the Alliance might mount a legal challenge, but they'd have better luck trying to mount Godzilla. Any move of this nature would see them humiliated, make no mistake about that. Take it from me, we've won. It's over.

What makes the whole thing even more satisfying is how we beat the media as well, who curiously were quite clearly in the Alliance's camp from day one. I've heard that a story that was planned to go into the *Evening Standard Magazine* was pulled as it showed our campaign in a reasonable, balanced light. That's just one example of many. The Alliance's professional lobbyists (based in Southwark, not Fulham) clearly worked all night and day to get their own way. Victory in the face of all of this is extremely pleasant.

But enough of the Alliance. They're nobodies, and will now be consigned to the dustbin of history, a disgrace to our local community. This is fantastic news, of course, for the real Fulham community, especially the thousands of community-conscious residents that have wished us luck throughout our campaign. You see, 70 per cent of Fulham residents said yes to the new stadium, and if the Alliance don't like it, well tough. All the good Fulham people out there (and there are many) who recognised the excellent role the Club plays in the area, from its award-winning community work to its charitable activities, pensioners clubs and youth schemes, will be delighted. This is their victory, and they should be proud that they all played their part in keeping "old Fulham" alive.

This is, of course, also a great result for Fulham's tremendous supporters. We could not have hoped for better support during our campaign than that received from you folks. You should be proud of yourselves. Fulham supporters are made of solid stuff, the best in the land. How you handled yourselves when labelled by the Alliance as thugs who charge around Bishops Park and urinate in people's front gardens was a credit to the community. And who could forget that night at the Town Hall when you turned up when it really mattered and supported the new stadium with such dignity and respect. Also, your messages of support have really made a difference when things were tough. Our heartfelt thanks go out to all of you.

You see, we had one thing the Alliance could never understand. We had right on our side. Spirit, passion and determination to achieve our aims, with a team spirit that was second to none. We fought the good fight, and we won the good fight.

Below, and opposite page right: Fulham supporters show their support for the new stadium.

Opposite page bottom: Blackburn away, 2001 – we won it at a canter!

The other winners are, of course, everyone connected with Fulham FC. The amazing vision that led to the tremendous stadium scheme, and the non-stop dedication of all involved in the project are to be highly commended. These are the people that did the real work, to face the challenges of the site and create a new stadium that will be one of the best in Britain. Our independent role was to rally local support behind the plan, the Club's was to design and implement that plan in the first place. So it's hats off to Fulham FC and its Chairman for dreaming the dream that is now set to become wonderful reality.

I will walk through the park many times in the future. Only in the future the view will be enhanced by a tremendous state-of-the-art stadium of which we can all be proud. The dream is true; long live the dream! ⚽

Ian Coles

Tigana's Sprint Finish

Jean Tigana's Fulham took Division One by storm in 2000-01, gaining promotion to the top flight in record-breaking circumstances and doing so with extraordinary style and panache. And yet the key fixture in the run-in was decided more by great character and resolve – and provided one of those delicious footballing moments when, despite being up against it, we were able to ram some pre-match hype firmly back down the instigator's gullet.

Blackburn away: a tough test at any juncture. Their manager at the time, Graeme Souness, had insisted that despite Fulham's dominance of the division – we were 13 points clear of second-placed Rovers in April 2001, had already racked up a dozen

away wins and had netted 81 league goals by that point – his Blackburn outfit were really the division's top dogs. In truth, we could afford to lose this game; however, a win in the rescheduled encounter at Ewood Park would all but guarantee a long-awaited return to the top flight.

So it didn't help our cause when (after good work by Damien Duff!) Matt Jansen put the home side in front after just five minutes. That goal spurred on Blackburn even further and, unusually that season, it was our opponents who had the larger share of the ball.

Worse followed with half-time in sight. Rufus Brevett, already cautioned, was shown a straight red card for kicking out at Garry Flitcroft four minutes before the break. It was the culmination of some aggressive stuff by the home side, particularly on Barry Hayles, that had gone unpunished. Rats! This wasn't going to plan at all and, for all our endeavours, the sub-plot regarding Souness's comments was playing out in his favour thanks to the dubious interpretation of the rules.

On came Alan Neilson at left-back (for Hayles) and a switch to 4-4-1; damage limitation seemed the order of the day. But hold on folks, Tigana's impending half-time talk was given a positive twist when a Brad Freidel fumble allowed Louis Saha to score his 28th of the season mere moments before the interval. That came from nowhere, but we'll take it. On the restart, Rovers were evidently determined to regain the upper hand. Fulham, however, were just as resolute.

The second half became a proper slog between two heavyweights – with our 10 men not only turning in a gritty performance but looking reasonably assured too. As the

147

Right: Sean Davis savours his late winner at Ewood Park.

Opposite page: Jean Tigana oversaw a brilliant season. We scored 90 goals, racked up a record-breaking 101 points and went up to the top flight as worthy champions. Merci, Jean!

minutes ticked away so slowly, the contest seemed set for a stalemate, and with it a well-earned away point. Come on guys, see it out!

With 91 minutes on the clock, a Blackburn attack was halted on the edge of Maik Taylor's area by Lee Clark who strode clear and fed Bjarne Goldbaek on the right. The winger carried the ball 15 yards, moved infield and slipped a great return pass to Clarkie, by now homing in on the Rovers penalty area. Four home defenders were between him and goal but Clarkie remained positive, made a yard and tried a shot. It didn't look likely to trouble Freidel, but the ball took a very welcome deflection and dropped into the path of Sean Davis, and the midfielder made no mistake from 10 yards. Get in! Discipline then gave way to barminess. Our fans went loopy; Davis performed his memorable dance routine – and the normally phlegmatic, toothpick-chewing Jean Tigana went tearing down the touchline, such was his delight. Up yours Sourpuss! Our "inferior" team now stood 16 points clear of your world-beaters. What a result; what a finale!

Lee Clark picked up on the Blackburn manager's pre-match assertions by saying: "I thought we did brilliantly in the second half when you consider we were down to 10 men and up against the best team in the league. There was always going to be a bit of hype, but we just tried to do our talking where it mattered, out in the middle. Let's just say we showed Blackburn a bit more respect than they showed us. People have wondered whether we have got the bottle and heart to go with our class, and we surely answered that tonight."

Nice one, Clarkie. And nice one Sky: work commitments meant I couldn't get to the Wednesday night fixture so instead I spent the evening glued to the box in the company of eldest son Matt, then aged nine. Our maniacal movements when the winning goal went in may not have matched the style of Sean Davis's fancy hip-swaying nor the directness of Jean Tigana's touchline sprint, but were every bit as crazy as the mayhem in the Ewood Park away end.

Three days later I was at Huddersfield to see Luis Boa Morte score the goal that rubber-stamped our promotion as Fulham recorded another 2-1 away success. Two days after that came a further late show from Davis – his 90th-minute volley rescued an all-important point following a tired-looking display against Sheffield Wednesday. But who cared? We were Champions. And we'd rattled in 90 goals. And finished with a record 101 points. Not bad, eh Mr Souness? ⚽

Below: Here we go again – a further delay looks likely as the *Fulham Chronicle* suggests a possible judicial review.

LEGAL CHALLENGE TO STADIUM PLAN

Fulham Alliance seek judicial review into football ground development

By MARTIN HILDITCH

THE FULHAM Alliance has written to the High Court to apply for a judicial review into the re-development of Fulham Football Club.

Residents who support the development to transform Craven Cottage said they were "not surprised" by the news, and added the objectors represented a "very small" group of people who were effectively trying to force the club out of Fulham.

The Alliance will base its case on

Secretary of State John Prescott's decision not to hold a public inquiry into the 30,000-seater scheme which was passed by Hammersmith and Fulham Council.

It submitted the challenge, along with members of Ranalagh Sailing Club, Bishops Park Co-ordinating Group, the Putney Society, and Hammersmith and Fulham Agenda 21, to the High Court last Tuesday.

Mr Prescott will be given time to submit a response. A High Court judge will then decide if there is a case to be answered.

Alliance chairman Bill Adlard said he expected a result by July.

He said: "The first ground [for a

review] is that the Secretary of State has to give reasons for his decision, which he has refused to do.

"Part of it depends on the Human Rights Act which came into force in October last year.

Quality of life

"The developer has been given permission to build a development which will have a significant adverse affect on the area's homes and quality of life both on this side of the river and the other side.

"That much is acknowledged in the planning officer's report.

"We should get a decision whether a judicial review can go ahead by July. It

is then usually six months before it comes to court."

But Tom Greatrex, a member of Fulham United which supports the development, said: "Bill Adlard said in the *Chronicle* on May 10 he thinks the planning committee acted within the law and there was no impropriety in the decision.

"Any judicial review has to provide evidence of impropriety. They themselves confirm they have no case at all.

"At their last meeting they themselves the majority of funding they have comes from 10 individuals.

"They may try to claim there are loads of groups taking part – but it is the same people in all of the groups."

Mr Greatex claimed the Alliance submitted an application for a judicial review earlier in the year and then removed it – an allegation the Alliance denied.

He added: "They are obviously confused about what they are doing. This is the last desperate throws of an organisation that has lost the arugument. They are speaking on behalf of a small group of people who want the club out."

Fulham FC's managing director Michael Fiddy said: "I heard the news on Friday. I am due to consult with my legal advisers.

"I will deal with all the issues under consideration and will take advice before planning our next steps."

The French Revolution

To this day I don't think Fulham FC received enough credit for their superlative exploits in their first season under the enigmatic Jean Tigana.

The quality of football displayed was consistently brilliant (at least until January or thereabouts, and it wasn't at all bad after that) and a young French striker by the name of Louis Saha made a blistering start to his career in English football.

Tigana was announced as the full-time replacement for Paul Bracewell in April 2000, taking the reins from caretakers KarlHeinz Riedle and Roy Evans. Tigana, supposedly recommended to Mohamed Al Fayed by none other than Eric Cantona, brought in fellow Frenchmen Christian Damiano as his assistant and Roger Propos as fitness coach. The trio oversaw a revolution.

In came early morning training sessions, at 7am! Plus further sessions in mid-morning and early afternoon. This was all a wake-up call to players used to strolling in at 10.30am. Tigana also instigated an alcohol ban, plus dental check-ups to monitor general health patterns. This was the norm in France, but novel in British football at the time.

"A few of the old pros found it a bit of a shock," admitted Andy Melville. I bet they did. "Yeah, we moaned at the time," revealed Sean Davis. "Days off were very rare and we weren't exactly happy with the long hours and double training sessions. But all the work we did on things like core strength and injury precaution certainly did us good. We were unbelievably fit. And the moaning soon stops when the results start coming in!"

Simon Morgan concurred: "I remember when pre-season training was Micky Adams standing at the top of a hill with a stopwatch and saying 'go', now we have people from the British Olympic Medical Centre giving us time trials and all sorts of tests. The training is completely different and I think it's the first time we've had to be in for a 7am start." Players are notoriously wary of new regimes; yet when those methods bear considerable return – especially in the form of win bonuses! – they can be persuaded to conform.

Jean Tigana's Fulham didn't merely hit the ground running in 2000-01, they took the First Division by rampaging storm, romping to 11 successive wins during which they rattled up 31 goals and conceded just six. The movement, pace, flair and teamwork on show was breathtaking. Amazingly, Watford were keeping pace at this point (although they tailed away to finish the season in ninth spot) and when Fulham drew game no.12 with Wolves and then lost at home to Preston, Watford even had the temerity to take over at the top of the table. But only temporarily. Ten sparkling wins and two draws in the next dozen games – including a 5-0 swatting of the Hornets – established Fulham not only as Champions-elect but also the team to watch.

It was scintillating stuff as Club records tumbled: new markers were set for the most wins, fewest defeats, the highest points total, best goal difference and the highest individual scorer (Saha). And for the most part, at least until January, it was a swaggering brand of passing football that swept them to the title – and into the Premiership. Us Fulham fans had to rub our eyes on several occasions, hardly able to take in the astonishingly consistent levels of brilliance.

Meantime, Jean Tigana, for the most part, simply chewed away on his toothpick as his charges racked up 101 points to finish 10 points clear of Blackburn. ⚽

Stunning Transformation

The following piece was prepared for *Survival of the Fattest 6: an alternative review of the '00-01 football season*:

I'm rather looking forward to going to Highbury. Not only have the majority of Fulham fans not seen us play there, but Arsenal Vice-Chairman and FA bigwig David Dein is sure to get a few catcalls. Unbelievably he sided with property developers when Fulham's very future (and certainly the Club's existence on the Craven Cottage site), was in grave doubt not so long ago.

At a public inquiry hearing, Dein suggested that there was no hope for struggling clubs like Fulham and, while privately many of us might have feared the worst, we never actually gave up hope. Neither did we wilt in the face of ever-mounting problems – no ground, no money, no training facilities, no reserve team, no structure and no management to speak of. What we had was a would-be homeless, hopeless team seemingly destined for the Conference. It was bad enough that property developers were seeking permission to build luxury flats on a much-sought-after riverside site. But inexcusable that a football man, in the shape of Dein, was prepared to back them.

Opposite page top: Going up as champions – Fulham celebrate at the Cottage and (*below*) Chairman Mohamed Al Fayed gets his hands on the silverware.

Below: Jean Tigana, *sans* toothpick!

Kit Symons didn't let success go to his head. When asked how he celebrated winning the Division One title, Symons replied: "Having played for Manchester City and been relegated twice, I wasn't sure what to do, so I just went wild and had a packet of pork scratchings." (From *The Standard*)

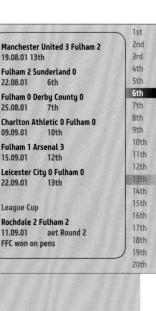

	1st
Manchester United 3 Fulham 2	2nd
19.08.01 13th	3rd
	4th
Fulham 2 Sunderland 0	5th
22.08.01 6th	**6th**
Fulham 0 Derby County 0	7th
25.08.01 7th	8th
Charlton Athletic 0 Fulham 0	9th
09.09.01 10th	10th
Fulham 1 Arsenal 3	11th
15.09.01 12th	12th
Leicester City 0 Fulham 0	**13th**
22.09.01 13th	14th
	15th
League Cup	16th
Rochdale 2 Fulham 2	17th
11.09.01 aet Round 2	18th
FFC won on pens	19th
	20th

Yet here we are only weeks away from a Premiership fixture in which dear old Fulham, 91st in the Football League in February 1996, will take on the mighty Arsenal on equal terms. On merit. The transformation has been stunning – so much so that there's a danger that many supporters will automatically expect a good season in the top flight. Certainly, those who've swelled the ranks during our exciting rise through the divisions have experienced little other than win after win. We've notched 100+ league points twice in three seasons, and it'll be curious to note their reactions should we not get off to the by now customary flying start.

However, despite the previous guarded comment, there's no doubt that we will be well equipped to take on the very best, and should Lord Luck's other half give her blessing, then who knows…?

So, on what basis does this long-in-the-tooth Fulham fan pass so favourable a judgement? Why should a set of supporters who'd more than earned the oft-used "long-suffering" tag expect FFC to at least hold their own against the likes of the Premiership Uniteds – Manchester, Leeds and Newcastle – when it's not so long ago that the "big" United fixture was against Carlisle? A review of the season just gone offers many a pointer.

Fulham versus Crewe was viewed as a perfect opening fixture for our new boss Jean Tigana's "revolutionary" new system. With several friendlies out of the way, here was a chance to test the more relaxed passing game for real. Keeping possession was the key, interspersed with sudden, dagger-like thrusts into the heart of the opposition's territory. That was the plan, anyway. Dario Gradi's men didn't disappoint, offering decent footballing opponents rather than rugged route one merchants or 11 men behind the ball. While not a vintage performance compared with what was to come, the Fulham die was set. Every player was encouraged to pass his way through the game, whether that be out of trouble in the tightest of areas or when opening up play. Most markedly, players such as Andy Melville and Rufus Brevett, who'd appeared so limited under the safety-first Paul Bracewell, were looking comfortable on the ball and were consistently finding team-mates rather than Row Z. Time to sit up indeed.

On top of that, our new striker from Metz, Louis Saha, about whom little was known save that he'd had a brief, uneventful spell with Newcastle and who was a straight swap financially for "Super" Geoff Horsfield, was forming an electric partnership with a rejuvenated Barry Hayles. Hayles had previously looked as if he was carrying the world on his shoulders, but unburdened of that and a fair few pounds from around his midriff, he looked a different player. His beaming smile amply demonstrated that something was going right.

Above: Nice touch – Andy Melville hoists the trophy with injured skipper Chris Coleman.

"*Confidence oozed from the Fulham players, and their speed of thought and movement, plus general workrate, was exemplary. Big Bazzer almost scored a wondrous goal with a clever, jinky run that relied on strength as well as trickery, only to be denied by the inside of the post.*"

In fact it was going more than right. We were on a roll. Victory followed victory in the League, with the only real surprise being that Watford were keeping pace. "Super" Geoff himself got his come-uppance in our first away game, a televised Friday-nighter at Birmingham, when we left with maximum points and Geoff on a stretcher following a clash with buddy Maik Taylor. But it was the style as much as the points gathering that took our breath away. The players were super-fit and super-confident. It all made for an amazing series of performances. True, we squeaked a win at Norwich in a contest that we had to tough out. Otherwise it was mesmeric.

And with Luis Boa Morte gradually making his mark, we had the choice of any two from three livewire forwards capable of terrorising opposing defences. Superb interplay ensured that chance after chance was created via the midfield orchestrated by the tireless Lee Clark and Tigana's lieutenant John Collins. Saha clocked in with 32 goals, Boa Morte with 21 and Hayles with 19 – in the past these would have been career records for our forwards, not seasonal returns!

At this stage, some vanquished opponents thought it possible that we'd go the whole season unbeaten (a notion that was laughed at from within the Craven Cottage walls), whereas a number of media critics proved just as wide of the mark. Rather than study the quality and depth of what was on show, some preferred to suggest that it would all blow up in Fulham's faces once the heavy pitches came along. It was also suggested that Tigana's pretty-pretty football wouldn't stand a chance on a murky winter's evening up the M6.

These five-minute experts couldn't have been more wrong. One of the early highlights was

the away game – up the M6 – at Bolton. Okay, so it wasn't winter and neither was it an evening fixture – but much-fancied Bolton offered a stern test, surely. In the event, had we taken all of our chances then Bolton's promotion quest may have been blown away that day. Otherwise, it was just about the complete performance. An early goal (after 13 seconds – now that's early!) set things up nicely to leave the home side chasing the game as well as the Fulham shadows.

Confidence oozed from the Fulham players, and their speed of thought and movement, plus general workrate, was exemplary. Big Bazzer almost scored a wondrous goal with a clever, jinky run that relied on strength as well as trickery, only to be denied by the inside of the post. Yet even that would have been eclipsed had John Collins' fizzer gone in near the end – his effort followed an extensive period of Fulham possession in and around their opponents' box that caused Bolton to unsuccessfully try fair or foul means to retrieve the ball. Superiority had long been established but victory was only confirmed in the latter stages when Boa Morte added our second.

Bolton managed to maintain their promotion drive, but the same could not be said of Watford. The only team to be ahead of Fulham during the season, albeit briefly, the Hornets were swatted twice as they fell away alarmingly. Graham Taylor was to suggest only three of Fulham's squad were of Premier League calibre. By his yardstick our 5-0 and 3-1 victories would imply that he had few players worthy of Division One status. Neither was it the last time a rival manager would open his big mouth. But more of Mr Sourpuss later.

We enjoyed a decent run in the Worthington Cup. Tigana adopted a pick'n'mix policy as we overcame first-leg deficits to beat Northampton and Chesterfield. Our second string then saw off Wolves and Derby in the straight knock-out stages before we had a fascinating tussle with Liverpool at Anfield. Not surprisingly Le Gaffer fielded Le First Team that more than held its own for 90 cagey minutes, only to succumb in extra-time. Fulham fans consoled themselves with the thought that had it been a league encounter we'd have gained a point.

One of the most incredible factors of the season was that halfway through we lost the services of our most influential player on and off the pitch, and yet carried on virtually seamlessly. Chris Coleman, "Captain Cookie" to the fans and colossus at the heart of our defence, suffered appalling leg injuries in a dreadful car smash. One glance at pictures of his smashed up Jag and you realised football was secondary. The big fella was lucky to escape with his life. Genuine football fans from all over the country responded with hundreds of goodwill messages, something for which Cookie was extremely grateful.

But the show had to go on, with the small matter of Manchester United to face in the FA Cup. "United Given Tough Draw" reckoned the tabloids. Times had indeed changed… first Liverpool and now Man United! Cookie Coleman was one of several absentees for Fulham, while the battle for midfield superiority between rugged Roy Keane and fey Fabrice Fernandes could only possibly have one winner. But, blow me, we gave them one hell of a fright and little was seen of their superstars. However, it was Fernandes, whose disdain for defensive duties is on a par with Gary Lineker's, who scored with a peach of a free-kick to bring Fulham level. ("It arced in a lazy parabola," suggested one learned fan.) And for a while we actually outplayed the mighty Reds. It was gripping stuff until a late Teddy Sheringham strike relegated us into the "gallant losers" category.

We had played well, extraordinarily so, with a weakened team – a point put to Jean Tigana afterwards by the Sky reporter. "But we didn't win!" was the Frenchman's firm but polite response. No resting on one's laurels at Fulham, then.

Defeat did allow us to (ahem) concentrate on the League. Something we did rather well. Okay, so the truly magical pre-Christmas displays weren't as prevalent by now but the work ethic was just as sound. The points total moved ever upwards as the season neared its conclusion. Even so, the most significant victory came off the park. Following years of uncertainty, the latest plans to revamp Craven Cottage were finally given the green light by the local Council after no end of wrangles and local bickering. A state-of-the-art 30,000 all-seater stadium should now be in place in time for the season after next. Yippee!

Meantime, Blackburn now looked favourites for the other automatic promotion spot. Accordingly, our Wednesday night fixture – up the M6 – at Ewood Park in April was a massive test. In truth we had the luxury of knowing we could probably afford to lose the game. But it wasn't as simple as that. Lovely, cuddly Graeme Souness had suggested Blackburn were the best team in the division. Right, game on!

We suffered a wretched first 44 minutes without playing at all badly. Blackburn opened the scoring but not the floodgates. The referee opened his notebook but not his eyes. Brevett received his marching orders for one foul too many – a yardstick that apparently didn't apply to Flitcroft. Then Berg floored a rampaging Hayles at thigh level, yet wasn't even pulled up for a free-kick. Oh dear, one of those games.

In fact, it transpired it would be one of *those* games, not that you'd know it when we scrambled an equaliser right on half-time thanks to a goalkeeping error. The home side piled on the pressure in the second half but we simply soaked it all up and counter-attacked whenever possible. It looked like a brave and worthy 1-1 draw for the 10 men. But hang on a tick, we've engineered an opening, the ball's fallen to Sean Davis (what the hell is our defensive midfielder doing as the furthest man forward?) and he's nonchalantly knocked the ball home on the half-volley with seconds to play. We've only gone and won the ruddy game! Good old Lee Clark; interviewed afterwards he said the victory for the 10 men away from home "against the best team in the League" was pretty special.

Victory at Huddersfield the following Saturday would clinch promotion. And when Boa Morte latched on to a terrific curling pass from Steve Finnan five minutes from time, the end of the rainbow – the top-flight – had been reached. However, there was still the Championship to play for. One more point would do it. Sheffield Wednesday should have been easy prey. But we failed to break down a determined defensive outfit. Goalkeeper Marcus Hahnemann had a sad full debut, gifting the visitors a goal from a corner. But nowhere near as sad as the Fulham fans who trooped away from the ground as the drab game drifted into injury-time. Out of nothing Davis lashed the ball into the net and we were Champions. The adrenaline surge was amazing. Poetic, too, that the home-grown lad (and recent England U-21 cap) should steal the headlines once again. What a moment! Cue glorious delirium, plus a fair few tears.

With the trusty Morgs (a genuine FFC hero) offloaded after more than a decade of sterling service, Sean Davis is set to become the first Fulham player to play for the Club in all four divisions. It's all happened that quickly. Fifty years without any Championship silverware and then two come along in swift succession. Considering the current set-up, who'd bet against a third? ⚽

"We suffered a wretched first 44 minutes without playing at all badly. Blackburn opened the scoring but not the floodgates. The referee opened his notebook but not his eyes."

Below: FFC's players and staff wave to the fans during their open-top tour of Fulham.

We Have Lift-off!

The following piece was given an airing in *FourFourTwo* in the autumn of 2001.

Five years ago Fulham were 91st in the league. Now they're doing battle with Manchester United in the Premiership. How times have changed…

Crisis. Now there's an over-used word in football. Fans are quick to call phone-ins and whinge that their team has lost four games on the spin, but that's not a crisis. A real footballing crisis is when you're down among the deadbeats, when you've all but lost your ground and your very existence is under threat.

Believe it or not, just five years ago Fulham FC was a club in crisis. It may be the stuff of dreams down by the Thames right now, but the nightmares are fresh enough to induce the shakes in long-standing fans.

The nadir came on 3 February 1996. After years of mismanagement and decline, Third Division Fulham faced a trip to the English Riviera. With just two wins from 19 games, The Cottagers had plummeted from third place to join Lincoln and Scarborough on 26 points, nine clear of bottom club Torquay. The Gulls themselves had won just three league games all season, conceding eight goals twice, so, despite Fulham's predicament, a win at Plainmoor was a reasonable bet.

Around 200 fans made the journey, nervously hoping that the worst was over. It was bad enough being in the bottom division, but there was now a real possibility that the Club that had graced the FA Cup final only 21 years before could fall through the trapdoor and into the Conference. Fulham had no ground, no money, no reserve team (and arguably no first team!), no youth policy to speak of and very little hope. But at least Torquay were acting as a buffer. However, after just 70 seconds Paul Baker fired Torquay ahead and although Mike Conroy levelled, eight minutes from time Simon Garner grabbed the winner for the Devon side. Now only six points separated Fulham from the bottom of the Football League.

There was no hiding place for manager Ian Branfoot. As soon as Torquay's second goal hit the net the visiting dugout was bombarded with comments from the travelling fans. At the final whistle, in a display of "Fulhamish" behaviour, supporters formed an orderly queue to express their annoyance.

Branfoot had "led" the Club to its lowest-ever position, 91st in the League, and not surprisingly he bore the brunt of the supporters' frustrations. But he wasn't entirely to blame. Fulham were already in Division Three when he took over.

In fact, the origins of The Cottagers' agonising decline could be found farther back, in the days of former Chairman Ernie Clay.

Clay, a bullish Yorkshireman, came to the fore as a Fulham Director in July 1976. Within a year he was Chairman having ousted music-hall comic Tommy Trinder, but he was faced with a Club heavily in debt. One early innovation was to introduce Fulham Rugby League Club (now the London Broncos) to the Cottage, but while that provided little more than novelty entertainment, it was two other decisions that would ensure Fulham fans cast him as the villain of the piece.

In 1986, Clay sold the freehold of Craven Cottage to property developers, a move that would haunt the Club for another decade (see sidebar). By then though his iron grip on the Club's purse strings had already led to a decision that many Fulham fans believe cost the Club almost as dearly.

During the 1982-83 season, Malcolm Macdonald's young squad had racked up the points in Division Two with a fluid, passing style that won plenty of admirers – not unlike today's set-up. But unlike Jean Tigana, Macdonald could not call on a Chairman willing to dip into the coffers when the need arose.

In a rousing start to the season, Fulham scored four at home to Bolton and at Middlesbrough, Grimsby and Wolves. Newcastle, too, were blitzed 4-1 at St James' Park, despite Kevin Keegan's best efforts. The top flight beckoned, but by the turn of the year the goals were drying up. Striker Gordon Davies and 19-year-old Dean Coney needed a breather. Macdonald duly brought in Andy Thomas on loan from Oxford, but Clay refused to sanction a permanent move; Thomas scored twice in four games. Without him, Fulham were left to stutter towards the finishing line lacking firepower and confidence when it mattered most.

There were two key fixtures in the run-in. Leicester, who had gradually eaten away at Fulham's 12-point cushion in the promotion battle, snatched a single-goal victory at Craven Cottage

"Around 200 fans made the journey to Torquay, nervously hoping that the worst was over. It was bad enough being in the bottom division, but there was now a real possibility that the Club that had graced the FA Cup final only 21 years before could fall through the trapdoor and into the Conference. Fulham had no ground, no money, no reserve team (and arguably no first team!), no youth policy to speak of and very little hope."

Top right: Goodness! Fulham's Louis Saha makes it onto the cover of November 2001's *FourFourTwo*.

leaving Macdonald's side needing victory from their final fixture at relegation-threatened Derby at the Baseball Ground.

When Bobby Davison gave Derby the lead the atmosphere hotted up. Stewards did nothing as home fans strode onto the pitch perimeter. Fulham's all-time record goalscorer Gordon Davies remembers the occasion all-too clearly. "For the final quarter of the match Derby fans were gathered all around the pitch. Robert Wilson actually got kicked in the thigh as he went down the wing! I hit a shot wide and as I ran to get the ball I was surrounded by skinheads – in colourful language they told me if I scored a goal they would break my legs. It was a really intimidating atmosphere."

When the referee blew for an infringement near the end, the crowd surged onto the pitch thinking the game was over. Jeff Hopkins was attacked as the teams struggled to get back to the dressing-rooms. "Had the ref asked us to go back out we wouldn't have had a complete side," recalls Davies. "We were all badly shaken and Jeff was hurt. The whole episode was a shambles. As far as I'm concerned it's the longest-running game in history – the final whistle still hasn't gone."

Two days later the Football League turned down Fulham's appeal for a replay and Leicester went up in third spot behind QPR and Wolves. For Fulham it was the start of a dreadful slide. "It cost the Club dearly," says Davies. "After that everything went downhill. Inside 18 months a dozen players had left and Fulham were on the way down."

Macdonald left the Club in 1984, a result of his tangled private life. Coach Ray Harford took over, but, with too many senior players being sold, relegation in 1985-86 was inevitable. That summer one of the mainstays of Macdonald's side, Ray Lewington, returned to become Fulham's first Player-Manager. During the next year he witnessed the Club change hands, be all but closed down and narrowly avoid relegation to the bottom division. Oh, and Fulham were whipped 10-0 at Anfield in the Littlewoods Cup.

Lewington steadied matters and even guided the side to the Play-offs in 1989 but, with the team slipping again, in 1990 Chairman Jimmy Hill and the Fulham Board turned to Alan Dicks, who had been out of the game for some time. Simon Morgan joined Brighton at the start of this season after more than a decade at Craven Cottage. Ask him to react to the oft-heard chant of opposition fans during recent glory seasons at the Cottage – "Where were you when you were shit?" – and he'll reply, "I was there… in fact I was the bloody captain!" He also recalls his first exchange with Dicks: "My contractual documents were in his briefcase, but he needed his glasses to open the coded lock. Guess where his glasses were? In his briefcase! It was an introduction to his lack of organisation. He was a

lovely person, but not cut out for the hurly-burly of management."

More poor performances followed – giving vent to those infamous "Dicks Out" chants – and a gutless FA Cup exit to non-league Hayes in November 1991 led to the hapless Dicks being replaced by the equally ineffective Don Mackay. "He'd talk a good game," says Morgan about Mackay, "often telling the supporters what they wanted to hear, but the players could see straight through this football phoney. We used to laugh about his media statements portraying himself as a strict disciplinarian because the reality in the dressing room was very different. There was no discipline at all."

With relegation to Division Three on the cards, the Board dismissed Mackay, virtually at half-time in a game at Orient. Jimmy Hill marched into the dressing room to reorganise a side who found themselves 1-0 down and they recovered to salvage a point. By the Monday Mackay was out and Lewington was recalled, with nine games left to escape the drop. "The extent of the decline under Mackay was awful," admits Morgan. "The playing staff hardly spoke to each other; the supporters seemed apathetic; the atmosphere around the Cottage was funereal; there was nobody trying to entice sponsors while the ground looked tired and dilapidated."

A 2-1 reverse at Swansea on 7 May 1994 confirmed Fulham's relegation. In pathetic fashion we'd sunk into Division Three. Amazingly it would get even worse before it would get better.

Despite taking Fulham to 91st place in the League, Ian Branfoot was, according to Morgan, instrumental in turning around the Club's fortunes. "He was very much a players' manager," says Morgan. "He paid very little attention to public relations, but the fans should be aware of how much he did. When he arrived we had absolutely nothing. Everything was second rate, the training facilities, the kit and the general organisation, all of which was reflected in low morale among the playing staff. He managed to restore professional pride in the players."

Branfoot also introduced players who would provide the backbone of the following season's promotion-winning side, not least his successor, Micky Adams. What rankled for the fans was the determination to stick to a long-ball game with a set of players patently unsuited to such tactics. Mick Conroy, a £75,000 purchase from Preston, was neither the tallest nor quickest of strikers but was asked to chase lofted "passes" and struggled to make an impact.

Branfoot wasn't helped by an incredibly unlucky string of injuries. Terry Hurlock and John Marshall suffered broken legs while Mark Blake, Gary Brazil, Terry Angus and Adams all had long-term injuries. Morgan recalls: "Rip the heart out of any team and

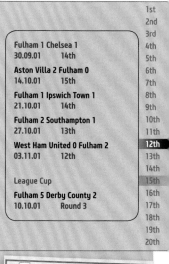

Fulham 1 Chelsea 1	1st
30.09.01 14th	2nd
	3rd
Aston Villa 2 Fulham 0	4th
14.10.01 15th	5th
	6th
Fulham 1 Ipswich Town 1	7th
21.10.01 14th	8th
	9th
Fulham 2 Southampton 1	10th
27.10.01 13th	11th
West Ham United 0 Fulham 2	**12th**
03.11.01 12th	13th
	14th
League Cup	15th
Fulham 5 Derby County 2	16th
10.10.01 Round 3	17th
	18th
	19th
	20th

We have lift-off!

Words David Lloyd

Five years ago Fulham were 91st in the league. Now they're doing battle with Manchester United in the Premiership. How times have changed...

CRISIS. NOW THERE'S AN OVER-USED word in football. Fans are quick to call phrase- like and whinge that their team has lost four games on the spin, but that's not crisis. Real crisis is when you're down among the dead-beats, when you've all but lost your ground and your very existence is under threat.

Believe it or not, just five years ago, Fulham FC was a club in crisis. It may be the stuff of dreams down by the Thames right now but the nightmares are fresh enough to make the stakes in long-standing fans.

The nadir came on February 3 1996. After years of mismanagement and decline, Third Division Fulham faced a trip to the English Riviera. Two wins from 19 games had seen The Cottagers plummet from third place to join Lajos and Scarborough on 26 points, nine clear of bottom club Torquay. The Gulls themselves had won just three league games all season, conceding eight goals twice so despite Fulham's predicament, a win at Plainmoor was a reasonable bet.

Around 200 fans made the journey, nervously hoping the worst was over. It was bad enough being in the bottom division but there was now a real possibility the club that had gutted the FA Cup had only 21 years before could fall through the trapdoor and into the Conference. Fulham had no ground, no money, no reserve team (and arguably no fans team), no youth policy to speak of and very little hope. But at least Torquay were acting as a buffer. However, after just 70 seconds Paul Baker fired Torquay ahead and although Mike Conway levelled, eight minutes from time Simon Garner grabbed the winner for the Devon side. Only six points separated Fulham from the bottom of the Football League.

There was no hiding place for manager Ian Branfoot. As soon as Torquay's second goal hit the net the visiting dugout was bombarded with comments from travelling fans. At the final whistle, in a display of 'Fulhamish' behaviour, supporters fanned an orderly queue to express their annoyance.

Branfoot had 'led' the club to its lowest ever position, 91st in the league, and not surprisingly he bore the brunt of the supporters' frustrations, but he was not entirely to blame. Fulham were already in Division Three where he took over. In fact, the origins of The Cottagers' decline could be found further back, in the days of former chairman Ernie Clay.

Clay, a bullish Yorkshireman, came to the fore as Fulham director in July 1976. Within a year he was chairman having ousted much-loved cornic Tommy Trinder, but he faced a club heavily in debt. One early innovation was to introduce Fulham Rugby League Club (now the London Broncos) to the Cottage, but while that provided little more than novelty entertainment, it was two other decisions that would see Fulham fans cast him in the villain of the piece. In 1986, Clay sold the freehold of Craven Cottage to property developers, a move that would hasten the club for another decade (see sidebar). By then though, his iron grip on the club's purse strings had already

results will suffer, But where the top clubs go out and spend millions on replacements we had only young lads to draft in. It was asking too much of them."

Two games after the Torquay disaster, Branfoot had "flu" for the trip to Cambridge, while he was "away scouting" as Fulham picked up another useful point at Rochdale. In fact, he'd moved upstairs and Micky Adams was installed as Player-Manager with Alan Cork his sidekick. As is often the way, performances picked up. Wins against Exeter and Doncaster plus a thumping 4-1 success at Cardiff made Adams an instant hero.

Simon Morgan remembers the new manager's first few days in the hot seat: "Micky Adams spoke from the heart and told us everything he expected from us. He showed vitality, eagerness and energy, qualities that helped inject enthusiasm into the squad. His training methods were inventive and he introduced a new, shorter passing style plus a new tactical formation."

The following season, Adams brought the smiles back to Craven Cottage. On a shoestring budget he put together a side – famously referred to as "more Woolworth's than Harrods" – that made being a Fulham fan fun again. Adams engendered an atmosphere of pride and passion and Fulham were soon making the running in Division Three.

The goals flowed. Conroy re-emerged as "Super-Mick" as he rattled in 23 League and Cup goals. "It was a transformation," says Morgan. "The lads were in awe of him. We were prepared to give him the Player of the Year trophy by September. I even let him pick my lottery numbers."

Conroy provided the goals, but it was very much a team effort. A win at promotion-chasing Carlisle with six games to go provided a timely boost and

left Fulham needing just a point at Mansfield to guarantee promotion. The rot had stopped. Fulham were back... as far as Division Two at least.

Since then it's been mainly good news for the Fulham faithful, starting with the announcement in May 1997 that Harrods owner Mohamed Al Fayed had bought the Club. Although the promotion year was a truly galvanising one for the players and supporters, the Club's future was far from clear. So while some fans may have wondered about Al Fayed's designs for the Club, having prayed for a moneyed "white knight" for the previous decade, the immediate reaction was simply a very loud "hallelujah".

In fact the bond between the fans and their eccentric Chairman has become strong. When, not long after Al Fayed purchased Fulham, his son Dodi died in Paris with Princess Diana, a mass of scarves, shirts and flowers appeared at the Cottage gates as a tribute. Al Fayed was genuinely touched and has said he wants to repay the fans for that measure of respect.

Nevertheless, it was a massive disappointment for the fans when Adams became an early casualty of the Al Fayed regime. That his replacements were Kevin Keegan and Ray Wilkins, however, showed the new direction of the Club. Another notable newcomer, in December 1997, was Chris Coleman, Fulham's first £2m player. His willingness to drop two divisions and believe in the Club's drive to reach the Premiership would be the catalyst for other big-name recruits.

Wilkins was axed after seven months despite steering Fulham to the Play-offs, after which Keegan took over and guided Fulham to the Division Two title. It was the Club's first silverware for 50 years (unless you count "Best Street Carnival Float" under Alan Dicks), won with a record 101 points. Crucially the squad spirit installed by Adams remained and it was hard work rather than "cavalier Keegan" tactics that won the day.

Yet the superb season was soured by the manner of Keegan's departure when, despite repeated

Above: Fulham's return to the top is celebrated in *FourFourTwo*.

Fulham timeline 1983-2001

May 1983 Fulham just miss out on promotion to the top flight

May 1986 The Cottagers are relegated to Division Three

Jul 1986 Chairman Ernie Clay sells the freehold to Craven Cottage to property developers Marler Estates

Feb 1987 A merger between Fulham and QPR is proposed. Craven Cottage is earmarked for development

Apr 1987 Jimmy Hill takes over as Fulham Chairman, appointing a new Board

Aug 1989 Hammersmith & Fulham Council propose placing a compulsory purchase order (CPO) on Craven Cottage

Oct 1989 Marler Estates is sold to Cabra Estates. A public inquiry is set up to decide on the CPO

Jan 1990 On the eve of the inquiry, Fulham and Cabra strike a deal that will see the Club leave Craven Cottage

Nov 1991 Fulham lose 2-0 at home to non-League Hayes in the FA Cup

May 1992 The home League game against Bradford City is billed as the last ever at Craven Cottage

Jun 1992 Cabra Estates goes bust and the Royal Bank of Scotland step in as principal creditors

Mar 1993 A new 10-year lease on Craven Cottage is agreed, with an option to buy

Nov 1993 Non-League Yeovil Town grab a last-minute goal in the FA Cup to sink Fulham 1-0

May 1994 Fulham are relegated to the basement division

Aug 1994 A clutch of fans sail a coffin down the Thames to remind Jimmy Hill that he carried a coffin after the Club's 1968 relegation from the top flight

assurances to the contrary, he quit to become England coach. Paul Bracewell filled the void and started season 1999-2000. "Paul is fantastic," said Al Fayed midway through Bracewell's term in charge. "Everybody says bring in an Italian, bring in a Frenchman but hey, give the young man a chance to prove himself." The team failed to sparkle, however, and as they slipped out of promotion contention so Bracewell slipped out of the door. The young man was sacked.

Craven Cottage did not have to wait long for the next bombshell. In April 2000 former Monaco boss Jean Tigana was unveiled as the new Manager. The French revolution was immediate. Using the same nucleus of players, Tigana transformed Fulham into an eye-catching, goal-grabbing side. Between them, Louis Saha, Luis Boa Morte and Barry Hayles hit 63 goals and the Division One title became a formality. For the second time in three seasons Fulham topped the 100-point mark, but more importantly they were back in the top flight for the first time since 1968.

Having until then spent more money on the Club's infrastructure than the team – including purchasing and upgrading a training ground, introducing an Academy and even launching a professional women's team – Al Fayed went on a spending spree in August 2001. The Club transfer record (just £150,000 until his arrival) was smashed twice more in a matter of days. Holland goalkeeper Edwin van der Sar arrived from Juventus for £7.5m before Steve Marlet signed from Lyon for £11.5m. Steed Malbranque, Jon Harley and Sylvain Legwinski also arrived for big fees. "We are not in the Premiership to make up the numbers," claimed Al Fayed defiantly. "I have a determination to turn Fulham into a great club that is known worldwide and I have great faith in Jean Tigana and his proven talent as a manager and coach."

It would seem that this particular U-turn, as dramatic as any in football, is a long way from being over yet. ⚽

How Fulham Nearly Lost Craven Cottage for Good

In May, Fulham's famous old ground will be knocked down... but it's amazing it has survived this long.

In 1986, then-Chairman Ernie Clay sold the freehold to Craven Cottage, Fulham's home since 1896, to property developers Marler Estates for £9m. Marler already owned Stamford Bridge and soon acquired QPR's Loftus Road proposing a merger. Fulham Park Rangers would play at Loftus Road and the Cottage would be redeveloped.

Naturally, the two sets of fans fought the plans, while the football authorities, the PFA and MPs lent their support. Fulham fans staged a peaceful half-time protest during a match with Walsall, gaining plenty of media coverage – football fans behaving well? In the 1980s?

Out of the chaos emerged Jimmy Hill, asked by a group of fans willing to fund the Club to become Chairman. The new Board, with Bill Muddyman as Vice-Chairman, took control of the Club, but Marler still owned the ground.

The Board admitted its main aim was to protect the Club rather than keep it at Craven Cottage, but the vast majority of fans were intent on keeping the Club on the site. They found support from Hammersmith & Fulham Council who not only refused planning permission but also proposed a compulsory purchase order (CPO) on the ground.

In 1990 a public inquiry was called to decide on the CPO, but on its eve Fulham agreed a staged deal with Cabra Estates (who'd bought out Marler) worth up to £13m. The Club played out the three-year lease and, in May 1992, staged what was billed as the last match at the Cottage, against Bradford City. Cheers of relief greeted the half-time announcement of a further stay of execution.

Fulham 2000, a supporters fundraising group with Johnny Haynes, George Best and Gordon Davies as figureheads, was formed with the aim of repurchasing the freehold. More than £400,000 was raised.

Nevertheless a long-mooted move to Chelsea's Stamford Bridge was looking imminent – a second "home" dressing room had even been planned – but in a stroke of luck the recession claimed Cabra Estates as one of its victims. In June 1992, the Royal Bank of Scotland stepped in; as main creditors they now owned Craven Cottage. A 10-year lease was arranged, during which Fulham had an option to buy the site.

In May 1997, with the team on the up, Bill Muddyman, in a brief period of Chairmanship, reclaimed the ground for £7.5m. Within days Mohamed Al Fayed was the Club owner complete with his five-year plan for Fulham to play in the Premiership in a 30,000 all-seater stadium.

Nov 1994 Two late Micky Adams penalties salvage an FA Cup draw at non-League Ashford Town

Feb 1996 Fulham hit an all-time low, 91st in the League – and lose 2-1 to bottom club Torquay

May 1997 Under Micky Adams, Fulham are promoted to Division Two

May 1997 Chairman Bill Muddyman reclaims Craven Cottage for £7.5m; Harrods owner Mohamed Al Fayed buys the Club

Sep 1997 Kevin Keegan arrives as chief operating offier, Ray Wilkins takes over as team boss

Nov 1997 Chris Coleman signs for a Club record £2.1m from Crystal Palace

Apr 1999 Michael Jackson visits Craven Cottage for the League match against Wigan

May 1999 Keegan becomes full-time England manager just before Fulham secure the Division Two title with a record 101 points

Mar 2000 Manager Paul Bracewell is sacked with his side mid-table in Division One

Jun 2000 Jean Tigana arrives as Fulham Manager and signs Louis Saha from Metz

Oct 2000 Fulham start the season with a record 11 successive league wins

Mar 2001 A £70m stadium redevelopment is given the go-ahead

Apr 2001 Division One rivals Blackburn Rovers are beaten 2-1 en route to the championship with 101 points

Aug 2001 Fulham twice take the lead in the first Premiership game, against Manchester United at Old Trafford, but lose 3-2

Aug 2001 Steve Marlet arrives from Lyon for a record £11.5m, just weeks after Edwin van der Sar's £7.5m signing from Juventus

Barry Tones it Down

A TOOFIF chat with our swashbuckling striker Barry Hayles.

You have recently earned an extension to your Fulham contract – does that mean you've cracked it as a Premiership player?

I don't know about that! But I am very pleased it's all settled – I'm really delighted to have signed a one-year extension to my current deal.

It's all a long way from being a carpenter and turning out for Stevenage Borough – and yet it's all happened very quickly?

It's like a dream come true. I sometimes can't believe I'm mixing it with the big boys in the top flight. Five years ago I was a chippy. To be honest, I never dreamed all this would happen to me.

When Kevin Keegan signed you, did you really believe the Club would make it into the top division, and that you would get there too?

Obviously I realised the Club was going places and the goal was reaching the Premier League. But my first obligation was to justify myself to Fulham and the fans. I thought I had the ability, but I'd be lying if I said I always thought I'd make it. I hadn't had the chance to learn the ropes as a YTS player for example; instead I'd made it via the back door. Even on signing Fulham for £2m I had my doubts.

You took a while to settle in – and it's fair to say that pockets of Fulham fans weren't convinced. How tough was it to acclimatise?

It was a big move for me. It came not that long after I'd left Stevenage for Bristol Rovers and there I was a £2m player, the second most expensive signing in Fulham's history. Kevin Keegan had faith in me – and I gradually got going.

Jean Tigana is very different to Kevin Keegan. Is it fair to say the current manager has unearthed a new dimension to your game?

Yes, he's different, and yes he probably has. Jean's made me leaner and fitter. You could say I'm a five-a-side footballer at heart. Not only do we do plenty of that in training but he's encouraged us to take those ways onto the pitch. The manager wants me to curb my aggression, but then much of my game is based on that. I guess he's looking for me to cut down on the verbals and not get involved... and I suppose he's right! Mind you, I only picked up four yellow cards last year – not bad for an "aggressive" player and not bad compared to others. But I'm only trying to make up for lost time, you know. I'm hungry to do well – that's why I'm aggressive on the pitch, I'm determined to do well. The manager

wants me to cut out the backchat, but to be honest I'm not sure I can. But there again, I'll have to try!

During last year's romp to the First Division Championship and now during this season's Premiership campaign we've been treated to a couple of smiles. You're enjoying things...?

[Laughs] If you say so! We played so well last season. We were fitter, more confident and the goals were flying in. You couldn't help but enjoy it. Scoring in the top flight is a lot more difficult – it's all a lot more organised and the players are that much better. But I must give the Club more goals. I've set myself a target of around 13-15 this season. I've come from nowhere to the Premier League in five years, and so haven't the footballing culture and background of others that have been playing regularly in the top flight. But I'm catching up!

Just how much does confidence play a part?

You'd be surprised. You all saw how well we started the season – we might not have won at Old Trafford, but we pushed Manchester United all the way – and yet we then had a slight dip. It was no big thing really, just a question of slotting in new players and coming to terms with the top division, but we weren't really firing. Once we got that next win it was a real shot in the arm and you've all seen the difference in the last few games.

How would you react to the criticism that the team are trying to walk the ball into the net?

I'd say it was spot-on! We're playing some great stuff, but we've got to shoot more – if you don't have a go at goal you don't score.

There are a number of French people on the staff and our lead striker is French: have you picked up the lingo?

The foreign players are all expected to talk English around the camp, which is just as well as my French is on a par with my Portuguese, Dutch and Danish! Occasionally they forget and lapse into a discussion in French, but that's only natural – and I don't think they're talking about me anyway! There again, I've picked up enough of the bad French words to chip in now and again!

Is there plenty more to come from you, Barry?

I'd like to think so. It won't be for the lack of trying. The manager's trying improve my all-round awareness. It's a big step-up into the top division – you have to be that much more aware and on the look-out for those half-chances, which aren't cropping up as often as last season. You need to make split-second decisions in and around the

> *"The foreign players are all expected to talk English around the camp, which is just as well as my French is on a par with my Portuguese, Dutch and Danish!"*

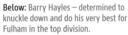

Below: Barry Hayles – determined to knuckle down and do his very best for Fulham in the top division.

opposition's penalty box. Take the right option and there might be a chance on goal, take the wrong one and the whole move breaks down. Having been a late developer I'm having to think on my feet, literally. I know there's lots to learn, but I also think I have plenty to contribute.

What are your ambitions?
Before this season the answer to that would have been to play in the top flight with Fulham. Now I suppose it's got to be playing in European competition. We've got a good squad here now, good enough to stay in the Premier League – which is the bottom line – but we're confident we can push on for a top-half finish.

You've developed a good partnership with Louis Saha – and getting a decent run through Steve Marlet's absence?
The manager has always been prepared to switch things, but it's true that Steve's injury has probably meant more time on the pitch for me. It's up to me to make the most of that.

With Fulham progressing so quickly, did you ever think you'd fall by the wayside?
The Club have high ambitions – anything seems possible! – and there's plenty of money available so you've got to stay sharp. There have been one or two uncertain times but it's simply a question of knuckling down and doing your very best. I've never doubted my ability although, as I've said, everything has happened so quickly and you've got to keep pace with the changes. I've certainly not doubted my determination to succeed. ⚽

Nearly, but not quite

The following review of the 2001-02 campaign was prepared for *Fultime...*

A visit to the Theatre of Dreams, aka Old Trafford, was the perfect way to kick-off our first season in the Premiership. The travelling fans were guaranteed a day to remember, while the team had a glorious stage on which to announce their return to the top flight. Oh yes, and it was a chance to get "Man Utd (away)" out of the way. Fulham fans travelled probably more in hope and in the spirit of adventure rather than expecting any serious shocks. But then again, it was the opening day; could we catch the mighty Man Utd cold?

We lost, of course, after being ahead twice. And it took a dodgy decision to bring the home side back into the game. But it wasn't the onfield action that captured the attention. Neither was it the fact that FFC's wonderful fans comfortably outsang the enormous home contingent. Instead it was a couple of comments from the normally

taciturn, camera-shy Jean Tigana. Pressed for a third time by the persistent Sky reporter to praise his side's efforts, JT conceded slightly, admitting: "Yes we played very well", only to immediately add with a typically Gallic shrug of shoulders, "but we lost". (There would, alas, be several more such shrugs as the season transpired.)

Commenting upon the free-kick award against Steve Finnan that was superbly despatched by you-know-who, JT quickly agreed that any free-kick should have gone Fulham's way since Giggs was doing the shirt-pulling. He went on to say that big teams in big stadia and before big partisan crowds often get awarded the big decisions. However, just as the press gang sensed that it was degenerating into standard blinkered or rose-tinted manager-speak he quickly added: "And I should know – I played for big teams throughout my career and benefited from such decisions." Brilliant!

That enthralling encounter with Fergie's lot, which should have earned us at least a point, rather summed up Fulham's season: able to live with the very best but not able to score enough goals to be up there with the elite. With more than the odd dodgy decision thrown in for good measure.

The press made a lot of Saha's brace at Old Trafford – and he netted again next time out. Maybe Louis believed all the rave reviews and thought he'd truly "arrived". Whatever the reason, he only showed his true abilities intermittently in the following months. And yet on-form and with good levels of confidence and determination he is a supremely gifted player.

The solid 2-0 home win over Sunderland earned us our first Premiership points. Maybe Fulham had "truly arrived" too. And maybe our ebullient Chairman's proud boast that we could win the title wasn't all that over-the-top either.

However, that win wasn't the springboard for a stack of further victories – in fact we didn't win again in the League until the end of October. Mind you, if we weren't winning points, we were winning all sorts of plaudits for our playing style. And we were making chances.

However, there was already a worrying tendency to try to walk the ball into the net. It was almost as if every goal had to be near-perfect – there'd be no in-off-the-defender's-backside efforts here! Malcolm Macdonald may have played (and managed) in a different era but surely his

Fulham 3 Newcastle United 1	1st
17.11.01 10th	2nd
	3rd
Bolton Wanderers 0 Fulham 0	4th
24.11.01 11th	5th
	6th
Fulham 0 Leeds United 0	7th
01.12.01 13th	8th
Fulham 2 Everton 0	**9th**
08.12.01 8th	10th
Liverpool 0 Fulham 0	11th
12.12.01 9th	12th
Tottenham Hotspur 4 Fulham 0	13th
15.12.01 10th	14th
Fulham 0 Charlton Athletic 0	15th
26.12.01 10th	16th
Fulham 2 Manchester United 3	17th
30.12.01 12th	18th
Derby County 0 Fulham 1	19th
02.01.02 10th	20th
Fulham 2 Middlesbrough 1	
12.01.02 9th	
Sunderland 1 Fulham 1	
19.01.02 9th	
Ipswich Town 1 Fulham 0	
30.01.02 10th	
Fulham 0 Aston Villa 0	
02.02.02 10th	
Fulham 2 Blackburn Rovers 0	
09.02.02 9th	
Middlesbrough 2 Fulham 1	
19.02.02 9th	
Arsenal 4 Fulham 1	
23.02.02 9th	
Fulham 0 Liverpool 2	
02.03.02 10th	
Chelsea 3 Fulham 2	
06.03.02 11th	
Everton 2 Fulham 1	
16.03.02 12th	
Fulham 0 Tottenham Hotspur 2	
24.03.02 14th	
Southampton 1 Fulham 1	
30.03.02 13th	
Fulham 0 West Ham United 1	
01.04.02 15th	
Newcastle United 1 Fulham 1	
08.04.02 16th	
Leeds United 0 Fulham 1	
20.04.02 14th	
Fulham 3 Bolton Wanderers 0	
23.04.02 11th	
Fulham 0 Leicester City 0	
27.04.02 11th	
Blackburn Rovers 3 Fulham 0	
11.05.02 13th	
League Cup	
Fulham 1 Tottenham Hotspur 2	
29.11.01 Round 4	
FA Cup	
Wycombe Wanderers 2 Fulham 2	
08.01.02 Round 3	
Fulham 1 Wycombe Wanderers 0	
15.01.02 Round 3 replay	
York City 0 Fulham 2	
26.10.02 Round 4	
Walsall 1 Fulham 2	
16.02.02 Round 5	
West Brom 0 Fulham 1	
10.03.02 Round 6	
Chelsea 1 Fulham 0	
14.04.02 Semi-final (Villa Park)	

*"Best buy
was probably
Steed. He'd just
about come
to realise that
the crowd were
not booing
him whenever
he touched
the ball in
time to net
twice against
Southampton."*

philosophy of "If you don't shoot, you won't score" still holds true. Also, if defenders are able to assume you're always going to play that extra pass they can anticipate the lay-off and intercept or make a telling tackle. By mixing it up, though, they're in two minds and the attacking team has an "edge".

All this meant that while most people's relegation favourites Bolton were blazing a trail, Fulham, who'd been streets ahead the previous season, were at the wrong end of the table, even though only Champions-elect Arsenal had caused us major problems.

Okay, so we were bedding in some new players. Edwin van der Sar, Jon Harley, Abdes Ouaddou and Steed Malbranque had arrived during pre-season while Sylvain Legwinski and Steve Marlet took the manager's spending spree to new heights (we had to replace Simon Morgan somehow!). Ironic then, that the most eye-catching debut came when home-grown Zat Knight literally towered above the rest in a drab scoreless encounter at Filbert Street.

Best buy was probably Steed. He'd just about come to realise that the crowd were not booing him whenever he touched the ball in time to net twice against Southampton. The win looked to have put us back on course as it was followed by excellent performances at West Ham and at home to Newcastle. These back-to-back victories in November should have been the benchmarks for the season. At the Boleyn Ground we totally outplayed an improving West Ham, working really hard when the home side were in possession then counter-attacking purposefully and in numbers..

Against Bobby Robson's Newcastle, Louis Saha played as if he had a point to prove to his ex-teammates. Sporting the latest of his hairstyles, Lightning Louis was everywhere and weighed in with a glorious curler – his first goal since August. Steed then set up Monica and it was Fulham deux at half-time. Les garçons done good, n'est pas?

Gary Speed and Barry Hayles traded goals in the second half before Alan Shearer, of all people, missed a penalty. 3-1 it finished: superb entertainment all round and several talking points. Not least surrounding that spot-kick – the award had looked generous in the extreme but when van der Sar tipped the shot onto the post Shearer was then baulked for what looked a "dead cert" foul in the box. The ref, on the other hand, thought otherwise and waved play on.

Cue one or two whinges: why didn't we get a penalty at Charlton when Saha was poleaxed? By rights their keeper should have been red carded, too. Why was Boa booked more than once for diving when it was clear he'd been upended? And what on earth was going through the referee's mind when Hayles, looking to add to Marlet's goal at Middlesbrough, was upended by the already-booked last defender? To his credit

Bazza bounced back up to be left with a one-on-one with the keeper, only to be halted again – this time by the ref's whistle. No yellow/red cards just a free-kick to our lot with all the home side now behind the ball. Unbelievable! And to add salt to our wounds Boro's two goals should have been chalked off for offside. I've said it before and I make no apologies for repeating it here, had those incidents involved any of the perceived big guns they'd have been replayed and analysed at great length. But as it was "only" us and Boro… virtually nothing! But hey, I'm racing ahead of myself!

General concensus as the New Year approached was that we deserved a few more points in the bag. And, with the division unusually tight, that would have meant a more-than-okay League placing. But there were also signs that, for all our possession, we could be as toothless as old man Steptoe; Leicester and Bolton away being prime examples.

It has been brilliant these past few seasons to see Fulham – our Fulham! – playing such brilliant football. Playing to feet, maintaining possession and then with a rapier thrust homing in on goal. Even allowing for the fact that Premier defences were, by definition, much more organised and miserly, we seemed to be playing possession football more for the sake of it rather than to create openings. In short, we seemed to have been found out, and our players became less and less willing to go for half an opening, whether that meant taking a shot or making a telling pass. We had the ability for sure but maybe not the required confidence levels – and it goes to show what a fine line there can be between success and failure at this level.

Still, there was the magic of the Cup. Mind you, we were less than magical in slipping out of the Worthington Cup at the Fourth Round stage. Spurs did enough to overcome our reshuffled XI and so a valuable pathway to Europe became a cul-de-sac. Considering the teams left in the competition at that stage it was a chance missed.

It's worth reflecting upon our opening round in that competition. We squeaked through at Rochdale thanks in the first place to Rufus's late leveller and then by holding our nerve in the penalty shoot-out. It was a surreal encounter, however, as the horrific images from the US earlier that day were still fresh in our minds [this was nine-eleven-2001]. Football: a matter of life and death? Hardly.

The trials and tribulations of Wembley stadium pale into insignificance when compared to the (still) ongoing saga of Craven Cottage. But with Wembley still out of action it was time to consider our chances of making it over the Severn Bridge and on to the Millennium Stadium, Cardiff for the FA Cup final. A number of our fans fancied our chances in the competition, including yours truly, the eternal optimist.

Okay, so it fell apart in Brum – a bizarre venue for an all-London semi-final – but as the minutes

Below: Midfield schemer Steed Malbranque became a firm favourite of the Fulham faithful after arriving from Lyon.

ticked away at Adams Park in early January, a Cup run looked as likely as Barry Hayles scoring a 30-yard screamer or Andy Melville pipping Ryan Giggs in a 100m dash. But with Wycombe ready to celebrate another Cup shock up popped "Bob" Marlet to nod the ball home.

In the replay Louis Saha narrowly escaped being beheaded and Bazza ensured our passage to round four, where another potential banana skin awaited us. Cash-strapped York, 91st in the League… away. Been there, done that, flogged the ruddy t-shirts, of course. One off the bottom with ever-dwindling resources and hopes – it brings a shiver back to the spine just thinking about it. Those were pre-Mo days, but our Chairman's gesture to hand York our share of the gate receipts was touching nevertheless. And naturally the travelling fans dipped into their pockets for the day's bucket collection. That's where the generosity ended, though; 2-0 to Fulham and on to Walsall. Away again.

That many potential banana skins and we weren't even sponsored by Fyffes! Our Fifth Round game at Bescot Stadium was the first of six away games out of seven (the piggy-in-the-middle being Liverpool's 2-0 win at Craven Cottage). If our first goal, a scrambled effort by "Oggy", was scrappy, our second, and the worthy match-winner, was a peach. Steve Finnan crossed the ball towards Barry Hayles and although it fell slightly behind him, big Bazza, who was otherwise very subdued, cleverly despatched a low volley into the bottom corner.

It was away again in round six, and parallels were now being drawn with our journey to Wembley in 1975 when we traipsed up and down the country to reach the Twin Towers. West Brom, hard working but one-dimensional, were a tough nut to crack but we always had the edge and Bob's decisive header was, er, decisive.

The shame was we were now something of a Jekyll and Hyde side. Despite the Cup run, confidence levels had dipped and if we didn't settle into our rhythm early on and, hopefully, grab a goal, we tended to play well within ourselves. There was very little width in the side and we were creating fewer chances. Games best forgotten are Ipswich away and the home games against Spurs and West Ham. Six consecutive League losses meant that instead of looking at a comfortable top-ten finish and the possibility of a coveted place in Europe we were being drawn into the relegation battle. The worry was genuine – did we have the necessary mettle? Thankfully enough players stood up to be counted at Southampton, Newcastle, Leeds and, ultimately, at home to Bolton, to make sure we survived.

In amongst those losses, however, was a very narrow 3-2 defeat at Stamford Bridge; the only difference between the sides on the night was probably that the Blues had the in-form strike force. We played very well ("But we lost!" as JT would no doubt have said). But it did mean that we had no real need to fear playing Chelsea at the semi-final stage of the FA Cup. Results elsewhere meant that we'd qualify for Europe as long as we made it to Cardiff. So there was everything to play for.

At least the all-capital clash would be staged in London. Wrong! As ever with such decisions it was the fans who'd be shafted. Forget London, Villa Park would be the venue, and with TV dictating a 7pm kick-off it meant that motorway snarl-ups were almost inevitable afterwards. And so it proved. The majority endured a nightmare return journey with the respective teams apparently not making it back to the capital until after 3am. Many children who went to the game didn't get home until way past midnight – with school a few hours away. Quite ludicrous and so avoidable.

In saying all of that we probably wouldn't have cared a hoot had we won. However, not for the first time, a Fulham team failed to turn it on when it really mattered. There was plenty of effort, but very little end product. The enduring memories are of a tentative chess-like encounter between two sides that largely cancelled each other out, settled by a single scrambled effort that on another day might have been cleared.

We bounced back brilliantly to win at Elland Road and then, inspired by Bjarne Goldbaek, to thump Bolton 3-0 in what was billed as the last night match at Craven Cottage. Days later, in one of those strange footballing quirks, our "last-ever" game at dear old Craven Cottage would be against a side managed by Micky Adams, responsible for turning around Fulham's fortunes in the mid-90s. The game itself, against already-relegated Leicester, was dreadful. The atmosphere was nostalgic and wistful, with many a spectator unashamed to spill a tear or three. However, with the Fulham Alliance employing yet more delaying tactics to our grandiose but approved ground plans there were as many rumours flying around the ground as there were former Fulham players there on the day. Yet again we were ending a season with a question mark. It was announced that one season's tenancy at QPR has become two. How there can be so many twists and turns in this particular saga defeats me.

Finishing in 13th spot, getting to the FA Cup semi-final and qualifying for the Intertoto Cup isn't a bad return for our first Premiership season. It all rather depends upon whether you're the sort of person who thinks a glass is half empty or half full. Many would have settled for that back at Old Trafford in August. For what it's worth, I just happen to think that there was a little more in the tank at times. But then we now know what to expect and, who knows, our second season in the Premiership might well see us springing some major surprises – after all, recent history has shown that we've had a consolidatory season before each of our title successes! As I said, ever the optimist… ⚽

Above: Left-back Jon Harley arrived from Chelsea in August 2001. He's best remembered for a howitzer of a goal against Aston Villa in 2003.

"We bounced back brilliantly to win at Elland Road and then, inspired by Bjarne Goldbaek, to thump Bolton 3-0 in what was billed as the last night match at Craven Cottage."

Adapting to the Top Flight

The following appeared in *Survival of the Fattest 6: an alternative review of the '01-02 football season...*

When you've got a larger-than-life Chairman you have to expect an outrageous comment or two. "Fulham will win the Premiership" – blurted out before the cameras as we celebrated our runaway success in the First Division – was one of his choicest. Several months on and with Fulham hovering mostly around mid-table before flirting with the relegation trapdoor, that TV clip was replayed with glee by one presenter. Almost weekly!

However this scribe isn't knocking Chairman Mo for two reasons: a) I wouldn't dare!; and b) What's wrong with aiming high? Last time we were in the top flight (many moons ago) we lurched from one perennial relegation battle to another, finding title-winning form from somewhere to escape the drop. The annual struggles of way-back-when arose because the Club had very little ambition; simply being in the top division was enough. The eventual payback was devastating – a double relegation from which we've only really just recovered.

By contrast, Mohamed Al Fayed has not only put his money where his mouth is (and you can insert "considerable" as appropriate in that last phrase) but his overall stewardship has delivered the goods to date. He pledged the Club would be in the Premiership inside five years of him taking over, an almost laughable target at the time. Any sane football fan knows that a stack of cash guarantees nothing (although it certainly helps!). And in any case the bulk of the initial spending went on the infrastructure of the Club rather than the first team.

But by 2001-02 FFC were a Premiership outfit and Jean Tigana, fully aware of his Chairman's lofty ambitions, was now prepared to spend to make Fulham a force to be reckoned with. Bettering the Club's previous best finishing position of 10th (in 1959-60) was seen by many as the least we should achieve. Qualifying for Europe via the League would be a bonus.

Well it didn't quite go to plan, did it? The team that had scored for fun the previous season and which had attacked so brilliantly now struggled against much tougher opposition. The super-slick passing and electric movement didn't quite come to the fore this time around despite a spending spree that would have been classed as obscene in our penny-pinching days of the mid-nineties.

We had our moments, not least on the opening day of the season when we twice led the mighty Manchester United at Old Trafford. The turning point was a free-kick awarded against Finnan when TV replays showed it was Giggs doing the shirt-pulling. Up stepped Golden-bloody-balls to do what he does best and an under-the-cosh United were back in the game. We gave them a mighty fright; it wasn't the script anyone expected although the eventual home win certainly was.

As the season progressed we fans were rather more opinionated, of course, particularly as a string of poor decisions went against us. There was also, truly, a sense that we weren't getting the run of the ball, and conservatively we felt Fulham could/should have been up to a dozen points better off by Christmas. We managed an impressive unbeaten run of eight games, though, including a fine 2-0 win at Upton Park and a 3-1 home victory over Newcastle. We had finally cracked the Premiership code – or so we thought. Up to this point, only Arsenal had given us the run-around (and even in that game we hung on well and might easily have escaped with a point), otherwise our patient passing game looked sound even if the goals were not exactly flying in.

As the season wore on, however, we became ever-more predictable. We rarely used a wide player, preferring a narrow point of attack. Our passing was rarely penetrative and shots from outside the box were as rare as a politician giving a direct answer to a pointed question. Then, with the very real threat of relegation, came some sterling efforts to save face and also some reputations. It was like a throwback to the '60s! So we're back for more next season.

In amongst all this was the FA Cup. There seemed a genuine chance of a trip to Cardiff as we survived one "banana skin" after another. Until, that is, our great mates from down the road did just enough to pip us at the semi-final stage. Chelsea were the slightly better of two ordinary teams on the day. But why the hell did the FA insist the all-London encounter was played in Birmingham? And at 7pm on a Sunday evening! And then they had the nerve to declare the arrangements a success when thousands of shafted fans were still on congested motorways in the early hours of the following morning. So much for sweet FA!

That semi-final defeat meant another European route was severed. But what's this? We'd applied for entry to the InterToto Cup. And it was all down to the final day of League fixtures to see if FFC or Everton would qualify for this hugely prestigious event. So, a fortnight after our "final" game at the Cottage (don't be too sure about that "final" tag ladies and gentlemen) we showed how up-for-it

"Chelsea were the slightly better of two ordinary teams on the day. But why the hell did the FA insist the all-London encounter was played in Birmingham? And at 7pm on a Sunday evening!"

we were by playing a stinker at Blackburn, going down 3-0, and still getting the nod thanks to Everton's narrow defeat at Highbury. That means an early July start to next season...yippee!

So, as we look forward eagerly to a couple of seasons at Loftus Road, TOOFIF offers it's own unique end-of season awards: *Player of the season:* Alain "uninjured" Goma, so consistent the Newcastle fans couldn't recognise him; *Best buy:* "trusty" Steed Malbranque, a snip at £4m; *Most improved player:* Rufus Brevett, few FFC fans ever believed the words "Brevett", "measured" and "panache" could ever be used in the same sentence; *The so-near-so-far award:* Louis Saha; far fewer goals this season but, apparently, the Premiership player who struck the woodwork most times; *Gary Sprake award for goofing:* Edwin van der Sar, brilliant much of the time but then...oops!; *Greg Louganis award:* Luis Boa Morte, considered a top diver by match officials; The *Dermot Gallagher award:* no surprises here – it's Dermot Gallagher for his, er, almost surreal "handling" of our game at Middlesbrough; *The lump in the throat moment:* a dead heat between a) Micky Adams' return to the Cottage for the "final" game along with a host of other former players; and b) the news that Chris "Capt Colossus" Coleman should be ready for a return to first team action next season – it'll be like signing a multi-million pound player for free... Chairman Mo will be pleased. ⁘

Boredroom Blues

As another close season bites the dust so it's a warm welcome to a further season of TOOFIFs. And, rather than easing our way into it gently, we're doing so on the back of a little turmoil. The team may well have progressed into the InterToto Cup Final, leaving us tantalisingly poised to enter the UEFA Cup, but it's still unclear what the precise relationship (if any!) is between Jean Tigana and Franco Baresi. However, even that particular internal wrangle pales in comparison to the latest reports on the continuing ground saga.

Just prior to the Leicester game we learned that our tenure at Loftus Road would be two seasons rather than a single term. Since which time, of course, we've played a further two "last-ever" games at the Cottage in the InterToto competition. Now reports suggest we may never return. Whatever the ins and outs of all this, it's clear that Fulham fans are being kept in the dark by the Football Club. There may have been a couple of low-key statements on the official website, but there has hardly been a clamour to confirm or deny what's been touted in the media. Unusually, I'm going to hand over the bulk of this column to a fellow Fulham fan this time around. Tom Greatrex, a leading light in Fulham United, posted the following on the TFI messageboard and has okayed its use in this mag. Tom makes the points

far better than I could – yet it's also important to take in his very first sentence, as at the moment we don't actually know all that much officially.

I hope this turns out to be the most pointless posting ever written, but I have a very bad feeling about all of this…

As Ian Coles would no doubt testify, during the whole Fulham United time I was positive that the Club was 100 per cent behind the plan to rebuild on the Cottage site and do not think that changed until about the tail-end of last season. My opinion now, however, is that we have been used since May and that there is a carefully co-ordinated drip of information on the ground to present a fait accompli with Adlard, Mitchell, Martin Smith and the rest [Fulham Alliance] as a convenient smokescreen. I do not consider that I am normally a conspiracy theorist, and I very much hope that my fears are completely unfounded, but there are very real grounds for concern over whether we will ever play at our own stadium in Fulham again.

First, just before the last game of last season, the fact that the Alliance are saying that they will petition the House of Lords for an appeal prompts the Club into saying that they will not now sell seats, turf, etc., and that due to the time-delay involved will now be sharing at QPR for at least two years. Contrast this with Arsenal, where although the planning process has pretty much followed the course of events at Fulham, including a similar anti-football group of gentrification profiteers posing as residents, they have already begun preparatory work and issued information in the local area about what works will be done when. And their change involved building a whole new stadium.

Second, Bill Muddyman makes oblique references questioning the viability of a new stadium on the Craven Cottage site at an end-of-season dinner when a large number of the audience, he knows, will have been celebrating… hoping to plant the seed. From what is later to emerge in the press, at the very same time the Club was in the bidding process for a site in White City to (perhaps) build a new stadium altogether.

Third, the *Fulham Chronicle* reports on authority from sources close to the Board that the cost of the new stadium has risen to £100m. I don't believe that the practicalities regarding access of the site and London prices make that level of difference. It seems more likely that £100m is a handy figure to pluck out of the air to use for justification at a later stage.

Fourth, after the last league match is safely out of the way and so unhelpful publicity is possible, *The Times* sports pages (not business or property pages) report in detail that FFC have failed in their bid to buy a site in White City for a new stadium. Owen Slot is a senior sports writer on

	1st
Fulham 4 Bolton Wanderers 1	2nd
17.08.02 1st	3rd
Middlesbrough 2 Fulham 2	4th
24.08.02 3rd	5th
West Brom 1 Fulham 0	6th
31.08.02 13th	7th
Fulham 3 Tottenham Hotspur 2	8th
11.09.02 8th	9th
Sunderland 0 Fulham 3	10th
14.09.02 5th	11th
Fulham 0 Chelsea 0	12th
23.09.02 6th	13th
Everton 2 Fulham 0	14th
28.09.02 8th	15th
	16th
InterToto Cup	17th
Fulham 0 FC Haka 0	18th
06.07.02 Round 1 1st leg	19th
FC Haka 1 Fulham 1	20th
14.07.02 Round 1 2nd leg	
(FFC win on away goal)	
Fulham 1 Egaleo 0	
20.07.02 Round 2 1st leg	
Egaleo 1 Fulham 1	
27.07.02 Round 2 2nd leg	
Fulham 1 Sochaux 0	
31.07.02 Semi-final 1st leg	
Sochaux 0 Fulham 2	
07.08.02 Semi-final 2nd leg	
Bologna 2 Fulham 2	
13.08.02 Final 1st leg	
Fulham 3 Bologna 1	
27.08.02 Final 2nd leg	
UEFA Cup	
Hadjuk Split 0 Fulham 1	
19.09.02 Round 1 1st leg	
Fulham 2 Hadjuk Split 2	
03.10.02 Round 1 2nd leg	

There's Only One In Fulham
An alternative look at Fulham F.C.

BYE- BYE... ...FOR GOOD?

Issue 82 Aug/Sept '02 £2.00

The Times. This announcement is dismissed as a "contingency" and our priority is still to redevelop the Cottage site.

Fifth, on the same day as our first game as tenants at Loftus Road, Leo Spall of *The Standard* reports that we are still looking at alternative sites and that legal cost problems are making redevelopment of the Cottage likely. I do not believe a journalist puts an interpretation on stories such as that one without asking certain questions and, by the reading of it, being given off-the-record unattributable briefing about the potential consequences. The Club did not rush to rubbish the story.

Personally, I do not believe that these are unconnected or unplanned events. The focus is not the Alliance, as the judgements both from the High Court and the Court of Appeal make very clear they are engaged in nothing but a time-wasting exercise. This could be very convenient, however, in justifying an unpopular decision that may be taken for other reasons.

So what's the plan from here? As the Club have not made any definitive or convincing comment, then it is little surprise that there is a lot of speculation. At the Supporters' Club AGM there was a very clear feeling expressed by members that they wanted the committee to find out on their behalf. Of those members who'd responded to the FSC survey, and amongst most members present, there was a feeling that they wanted to return to the Cottage in due course. There were also those present who seemed to be less bothered.

I know if I had the chance I would be keen to put the following eight questions to someone in the know at the Club (the replies would make very interesting reading)…

1. Is it the Club's intention to not sign any contracts, make any arrangements or begin any building or demolition work until all possible legal challenges are exhausted?

2. Is it the Club's view that there is no reason at all why work cannot start when planning permission is in place, and there is no injunction to prevent it?

3. How far from Fulham are the Club willing to look at potential sites for possible relocation?

4. Have any preliminary plans been drawn up for the alternative uses for the Craven Cottage site in the event of relocation?

5. Have any scoping exercises been done for the value of the Craven Cottage site with planning permission for residential development?

6. Does the Club or any subsidiary company have plans to put proposals for residential development on the Craven Cottage site to Hammersmith & Fulham Council?

7. Do the Club intend to continue with plans to build a new stadium on the Craven Cottage site?

50 THE SUN, Wednesday, August 28, 2002   ·3M

MIGHTY MOTO IS IN TOP GEAR

Junichi's cup hero

FULHAM 3
BOLOGNA 1
(Fulham win 5-3 on agg)
By DAVE KIDD

JUNICHI INAMOTO won instant hero worship with a hat-trick to send Fulham rolling into the UEFA Cup for the first time.

The Japanese midfielder, in his first start for the Cottagers, grabbed a stunning treble to defeat a cynical Italian side in a red-hot Intertoto Cup final second leg.

Inamoto, on a year's loan from Gamba Osaka, had conjured up an amazing solo strike after coming on as a sub in Italy two weeks ago so Fulham boss Jean Tigana opted to hand him a place in the starting line-up.

His heroics meant Fulham's great gamble of playing eight intertoto games this summer paid off with a place in the European big-time

Plus it was the club's first cup success in 125 years.

Party

Showing their inexperience at all this trophy-lifting, Fulham could not decide who would hold the cup aloft.

Rufus Brevett, skipper for the night, and regular captain Andy Meville, who had been dropped, both tried to cling on to the tiny bauble while chairman Mohamed Fayed barged his way to the front of the celebration party.

Tigana said: "All the rest of it doesn't bother me, I just love working with players on the pitch. When I arrived here two years ago, nobody would have dreamt we would be playing in Europe.

"Now I want to go further. This is just a step towards what we want to achieve.

"It was important we kept calm in this match. I told them at half-time it was not their job to fight with Italians who cheat all the time."

After a year without a Premiership appearance at Arsenal last season and five substitute appearances for Fulham, it was no wonder

World Cup star Inamoto, 22, looked so impatient.

Tigana added: "Inamoto played very well. I think the chairman wants to keep him."

And Inamoto added: "I will do my best to earn a permanent move here. I would like to stay at Fulham for longer."

He fired Fulham into the lead with a low 13th-minute shot after a slick one-two with recalled Argentine striker Facundo Sava.

And then, after Tomas Locatelli had equalised with a shot that deflected off Zat Knight, Inamoto demolished Bologna with two goals in the first five minutes of the

second half. A sweet move involving Luis Boa Morte, Sean Davis and Steve Marlet appeared to have broken down when the ball cannoned off a Bologna defender.

But Inamoto, 22, needed only a split-second to thump home from 20 yards.

Three minutes later, he brought Fulham's adopted Loftus Road house down when he smashed in the rebound after Marlet's shot was blocked by keeper Gianluca Pagliuca.

FULHAM: Van der Sar, Finnan, Brevett, Knight, Goma, Davis (Collins), Legwinski, Boa Morte, Inamoto (Malbranque), Sava, Marlet (Saha). Subs not used: Taylor, Melville, Ouaddou, Hayles.

THREE CHEERS . . . hat-trick hero Junichi Inamoto fires Fulham ahead against Bologna

GLORY . . . Fayed and Tigana celebrate

A triumphant Junichi Inamoto holds the InterToto Cup after his brilliant hat-trick at Loftus Road last night earned Fulham a place in Europe

8. Have the Club made any approaches to Hammersmith & Fulham Council about the possibility of sharing at Stamford Bridge?

Phew, it's difficult to follow that little lot from Tom. However, as he suggests, hopefully we've all been wide of the mark. But if we don't pass comment now then, who knows, a chance to have any say at all on the matter may be missed. ⚽

"We Won it One Time"

One of the highlights of our time at Loftus Road was winning the InterToto Cup, and with it passage into the UEFA Cup for the first time. A gritty 2-2 draw in Bologna set up a grand opportunity in the return game at our temporary home. Junichi Inamoto, on target in the first leg along with Sylvain Legwinski, ensured it was a night to remember by grabbing a wonderful hat-trick.

Fulham took the lead after 12 minutes when Inamoto swapped passes with Facundo Sava then shot low into the far corner. Bologna dished out some rough stuff in return, and scored an undeserved equaliser with a shot that took a deflection off Zat Knight before flying past Edwin van der Sar on 34 minutes.

Level on the night, but ahead on away goals, our nerves were eased by Inamoto netting his second early in the second half, making the most of a poor clearance and sending a wonderful strike beyond Pagliuca. Three minutes later it was 3-1 – Inamoto was in the right place to tuck the ball home from close in. ⚽

Programme Notes

It's that time of year when aspirations of footie fans from all over the country are at their highest: will it be our year this time around, maybe in the league or possibly a decent run in one of the cups. And it's no different down Fulham way, except that we've got the bonus of a European sortie already under our belts. Fulham in Europe – hey, times certainly have changed, eh?

As has our ground, in case there's someone out there who hasn't noticed! The cosy confines and grand riverside location of Craven Cottage have been swapped for the, er, shall we say, compact Loftus Road stadium. At least it's not a Fulham Park Rangers scenario – that unpalatable suggestion was roundly vetoed by the two sets of fans as much as anyone back in 1986. Since those terribly uncertain days the fortunes of the respective clubs have yo-yo'd dramatically. At one end of the scale Rangers flirted with Premiership glory while at the other Fulham sailed perilously close to the League trapdoor. Years later it's ironic that with Fulham now on the up our tenancy at Loftus Road is giving Rangers a much-needed financial fillip. Times have indeed changed!

But whoa, hold on, what's the fanzine editor doing offering his two-penn'orth in the proggy – sorry, matchday magazine – anyway? Hasn't he got a scurrilous journal of his own in which to spout his inane drivel? Questions, questions. In answering the above (i. 'Cos I was asked; and ii. Yes, thank you) maybe it's worth giving one or two other answers. After all, it's a heck of a long time since the first issue of TOOFIF appeared back in February 1988 and there's an awful lot of you newcomers who have yet to give it a once-over (hint, hint!).

What's the point of a fanzine? It gives the ordinary fans a chance to air their views. The game is famously all about opinions and, while I don't have to agree with the sentiments, as long as the offerings aren't libellous, racist or just plain nasty, then they have a strong chance of inclusion.

Yes, but what's the point? It's true that fanzines operate most effectively when there's a campaign afoot. TOOFIF has, I think, done its bit to keep various issues alive and out on the streets, not least when the club was precluded by the deal with would-be developers of Craven Cottage, Cabra Estates, from referring to even the most basic of the goings-on at the time. The fanzine, which has always been independent of the Club (but naturally fanatically supportive of it) was able to keep fans in touch as best as possible.

So, the point? Okay, one of the main points of a fanzine is not to take anything (or itself) too seriously – in fact, to have plenty of laughs along the way – until a point of principle comes along. Then the mag sobers up as necessary. It wasn't a happy mag to edit during the years of FFC's near terminal decline, that's for sure! But even the most belligerent contributions of the time came from the heart. And that's the point! A fanzine is an outlet for heart-felt missives or even pleas from the fans. It's there for YOU!

Why write for the programme, then? Don't forget that I wrote regularly for the programme for many years before Jimmy Hill decided on a random cull of contributors (to cut down on the free match passes). I jumped at the chance to do so again, if only because it might be my last chance of getting a back-door pass into the staff football team.

My brief is to be alternative. Whatever that means. However, it's true that the traditional British football proggy is relatively bland these days. Often this is of necessity, but I shall try to get what I can past the red pen and dreaded "spike" of the editor.

In the meantime, let's raise the roof in support of the team. That's why we're here, after all. Who knows, a significant rise in volume might equate to an increased number of shots on goal! We can dream... ⚽

From FFC v Bolton Wanderers programme, 17 August 2002

> *"Fulham took the lead after 12 minutes when Inamoto swapped passes with Facundo Sava then shot low into the far corner. Bologna dished out some rough stuff in return, and scored an undeserved equaliser with a shot that took a deflection off Zat Knight before flying past Edwin van der Sar on 34 minutes."*

Groundless Fears

Give us some news please and don't fob us off, was the thrust of a letter sent to FFC by disillusioned Fulham supporter Tristan Poturic.

I am writing to you as a lifelong fan to discuss the furore surrounding our current position concerning the ground development:

I've been a Fulham fan since the late '70s/ early '80s and know nothing other than my heroes in black and white. Throughout the past 15 years when our wonderful club has been at a horrendous low I have stood, side by side, with the same hardy group of fans in hellholes such as Doncaster, Bury, Scarborough and Darlington, watching Fulham sides – surely the worst in living memory – lose heavily. I have watched us climb out of those depths, and have seen us play our fiercest rivals on an even footing for the first time in 17 years. However, give me the choice of going to Craven Cottage to see us take on Bury or to Loftus Road to see us play Chelsea and I'd rather see us against the Lancashire club every time.

You see, for me, as with most Fulham fans, the ground *is* the Club. Without football at Craven Cottage, there is no Fulham FC. I was never keen on leaving the Cottage, and in fact I wrote a letter to Neil Rodford at the time asking why,

E-mail to Bruce Langham

Good afternoon Mr Langham,

This is the first time I've contacted you this way but felt I had to do so following today's announcement. Here we are in the Premiership, progressing superbly in the UEFA Cup (having won the InterToto), still in the Worthington Cup and with the FA Cup yet to come. All pretty much according to the FFC script. And a very good time to be a Fulham fan.

On the down side, the fall-out following the move to Loftus Road and the ongoing ground business is confusing many and causing unnecessary frictions among the supporters. That said, it should be a time for celebrating rather than moaning.

And yet, I couldn't believe my ears on hearing that our return game with Hertha Berlin has been shifted to a 5pm kick-off. What a severe kick in the teeth for some fans. Those fortunate enough to be able to switch working arrangements will clearly be the lucky ones. But why, oh why, should fans have such obstacles placed before them for what could be billed as the most significant/important game for FFC since the 1975 Cup Final? Fulham ought to be moving heaven and earth to enable as many Fulham fans as possible to attend, not put such barriers in their way. As it is it could result in a very small crowd, although I (and the players, surely!) hope that won't be the case, with pictures of the empty spaces beamed around the world courtesy of German TV.

Everyone will have a different tale to tell of course, but my working arrangements mean that, within reason,

I can juggle things so I can attend home games. I am a seasoned away traveller, but my current situation means I am unable to get to midweek aways at the moment, while I have had to forego the joys of following Fulham abroad. However, I may well have trouble getting time off for this particular HOME game.

The Club's statement says the kick-off time will encourage families to attend. How the hell can that be the case? My eldest boy (aged 10), a season ticket holder and who's only missed one home game to date this season, doesn't get home from school until 3.45. Please enlighten me as to how, practically, I can get him from Carshalton to White City in time for a 5pm start when I'm in central London and unlikely to be at the ground to meet him in any case?

Had it been, say, a 6pm start then I may well have been able to get out my Pied Piper's penny whistle and "lured" a clutch of family and friends' children along (especially considering the very attractive admission prices) – but 5pm makes it impossible logistically. Or are you contemplating printing a stack of "Let this child go early this afternoon" notes for us to hand to head teachers?

I am sincerely sorry to go on the attack like this. But for all the wondrous times we've had on the park during these last few years I see this as a massive own goal by the club. At a time when FFC have been struggling to draw Fulham fans in sufficient numbers to attend games at Loftus Road, and criticising the stayaways, this move can

only hit a sizeable number of those who DO attend regularly.

Patently the sum of money from German TV is a significant amount. Clearly, too, the Club will welcome such unbudgeted income. And certainly, whoever had to make the decision had a difficult choice to make. But please don't forget that the Club is built on its fans. Club administrations come and go, but the true diehard fans are there week-to-week, year-on-year, decade-upon-decade.

We should be cheering from the rafters at what the Club has achieved in recent times. It's been a truly wonderful transformation of fortunes. And yes, I was one of those who not only steadfastly stuck it through the bad times but actively helped the Club in whatever way I could to keep it ticking over. So I can make such comments with some justification. But instead of it being one long party, these days the whole atmosphere is muted. I'm thoroughly fed up of hearing moans and groans from our lot, although it's a clear indication that all is not well – or rather, all is not perceived to be well.

I'd go as far as to admit that some of the moaners, dare I suggest, are set in their ways. However, there have been enough cock-ups even this season (with regard to ticketing/stewarding/ merchandising issues for example) to make many a grievance totally justified. The majority of these can't simply be swept under the "teething troubles at Loftus Road" mat (some of the Ticketmaster cock-ups have been truly horrendous) and on the back of these, the 5pm kick-off looks to be another PR mistake.

if Man Utd, Liverpool, Villa, Chelsea and others can develop their grounds without leaving, then why couldn't we? Even though part of me still considers this to be a reasonable option, I accept that the state-of-the-art stadium that Mr Fayed has planned needs us to be elsewhere during the rebuilding, and that Loftus Road was always going to be the best "local choice".

This was never a huge problem to me. I was willing to overlook the huge hike in season ticket prices and go to Loftus Road for two seasons, but as the reports of searching for alternative sites emerged from the Club, my mindset changed. I can now, as a matter of principle, not go to QPR to watch Fulham until positive news comes out of the Club.

This isn't a travelling issue. I now live in London and could easily make the journey to Shepherds Bush, whereas for the past three years it's been a case of making a 150-mile round trip to see a home game. Here we are in late 2002 and the last home match I'd missed was against West Brom in August '91. You see, I will always support Fulham. My family has stood on the Cottage terraces for generations and I couldn't support anyone else.

However, the feeling that I and many other loyal supporters are being fobbed off disturbs me. Our Club had been in its death throes for years and found a white knight in Mr Fayed, and for that I am grateful. Yet I feel that it is gravely possible that various Club executives and senior backroom staff could misjudge the strength of "fan feeling" on this issue, and leave themselves without a large chunk of core support which, in any business, is surely the most important. ⚽

Tristan Poturic

Hold the Back Page!

A fair few Fulham fans boycotted our spell at Loftus Road, feeling that the Club was being less than open with regard to its plans for the future, specifically, those of Craven Cottage. Not unnaturally, the Club made repeated appeals for more supporters to turn up and get behind the team at our temporary home. However, in the same breath they then announced that our Thursday evening UEFA Cup third-round tie with Hertha Berlin was being brought forward to 5pm for the benefit of German TV. Well, that's a sure way of packing 'em in!

Right away, I knew I'd be affected; I'd be at work so would have to miss out. As soon as the late afternoon kick-off time was announced I emailed Fulham CEO Bruce Langham (*left*). This missive was pinged on its way well before I was contacted by a couple of press reporters.

The morning after the new kick-off time was announced I took a call from the *Evening Standard* at 8am; they wanted a fan's comment for their website. With lots of stuff about the future of Craven Cottage bubbling under at the time I'd agreed with Bruce Langham to his request to call him "at any time, day or night" if contacted on any contentious issues. The Club were keen to ensure that I knew the "full picture" before making any comments to the press.

Clearly I didn't have to go along with this, but in the interests of harmony I promised to do so. Accordingly I told the *Standard* reporter that I needed to make a couple of checks before I could talk to him, and we agreed to a 90-minute hiatus. In that time I made at least 20 calls to the Club, to several numbers, leaving messages about the subject matter where I could and stressing the urgency of any response. The couple of voices I spoke to promised me someone would call back "within minutes". No one rang back. Well I'd done my bit.

So the chat went ahead. I told the fella that I appreciated the Club had taken the controversial decision to boost their coffers, but the fact remained that many long-standing fans wouldn't be able to see Fulham's most important/prestigious match in years. And it was a kick in the teeth to those who had followed FFC through the tough times and were continuing to do so at their temporary home – at the very least they'd be inconvenienced, at worst they'd not be able to make it at all. (At that stage it looked like I'd have to miss my first "home" game in decades until a planned meeting at work was thankfully switched and I was able to slap in a request for an early departure.) The irony of all this was that the matchday programme imploring more fans to turn up was read by those that had, not the absent minority.

Oh well, this'll simply be much ado about nothing. Actually no. It turned out to be a quiet news day and the "small piece for our website" became the back page lead in the newspaper. And of course suddenly my phone became red hot with calls from the Club asking why the hell I hadn't contacted them. Thankfully I'd logged most of my calls so was able to put them right on that one.

In one of those subsequent conversations it was pointed out that the tickets for the match were only £5 and that children could get in free. My reply was that it didn't matter what special prices were in place if you couldn't get there. My eldest son, for example, was at school in Carshalton until nearly 4 o'clock and couldn't get to Shepherds Bush (on his own) in time. Incredibly I was informed: "I come from that neck of the woods and can make it down the A3 in 30-40 minutes." All well and good, but my 10-year-old son neither owned a car nor was able to drive. Financially expedient, maybe, but this was a PR own goal as far as the fans were concerned. To make matters worse, a 0-0 draw resulted in our

Fulham 1 Charlton Athletic 0	1st
06.10.02 5th	2nd
Fulham 1 Manchester United 1	3rd
19.10.02 7th	4th
Fulham 0 West Ham United 1	**5th**
23.10.03 8th	6th
Southampton 4 Fulham 2	7th
27.10.02 11th	8th
Fulham 0 Arsenal 1	9th
03.11.02 11th	10th
Aston Villa 3 Fulham 1	11th
09.11.02 12th	12th
Birmingham 0 Fulham 0	13th
17.11.02 10th	14th
Fulham 3 Liverpool 2	15th
23.11.02 12th	**16th**
Blackburn Rovers 2 Fulham 1	17th
30.11.02 13th	18th
Fulham 1 Leeds United 0	19th
07.12.02 12th	20th
Fulham 0 Birmingham City 1	
15.12.02 14th	
Newcastle United 2 Fulham 0	
21.12.02 14th	
West Ham United 1 Fulham 1	
26.12.02 15th	
Fulham 0 Manchester City 1	
28.12.02 16th	
Bolton Wanderers 0 Fulham 0	
11.01.03 16th	

League Cup
Fulham 3 Bury 1
06.11.02   Round 3
Wigan Athletic 2 Fulham 1
04.12.02   Round 4

UEFA Cup
Dinamo Zagreb 0 Fulham 3
31.10.02   Round 2 1st leg
Fulham 2 Dinamo Zagreb 1
14.11.02   Round 2nd leg
Hertha Berlin 2 Fulham 1
26.11.02   Round 3 1st leg
Fulham 0 Hertha Berlin 0
12.12.02   Round 3 2nd leg

FA Cup
Fulham 3 Birmingham City 1
05.01.03   Round 3

European campaign coming to a juddering halt as we went out 1-2 on aggregate. And who knows, a more numerous, raucous "home" crowd may have inspired the team to a win and an even more lucrative spot in the fourth round? ⚽

Fraud Focus

An anonymous poster (whose identity I know all too well) decreed I was way off line in making the above comments. I've no problem with that. I did, though, have a problem at being referred to as "that fraud David Lloyd", plus one or two other accusations. In due course I received a weasly private "apology" by email, not via the public website where he'd made the remarks. Regarding the difficulty of getting to the game for the new kick-off time, the guy in question suggested: "We've all thrown a sickie or got a dental appointment". Point taken, but now who's the fraud? Anyhow, I took sufficient umbrage to respond:

So let's get this right. You make an outrageous remark for all to read on a public messageboard then come and apologise, sort of, on the quiet. I suppose I should be grateful for the apology. What the hell did you mean by "fraud" anyway? I'd like to hear your definition. You made a whole load of slurs in your postings that aren't mentioned in the apology. But of course, you've

always allowed yourself to be hugely opinionated without giving a toss about the opinions of others (whether they be "right" or "wrong"). That's massive arrogance in my book.

Of course I'm angry. Angry about the whole episode actually. ...Angry that you've selected bits of newspaper coverage and implied that it was all down to me. I did not say it was a "sell-out" by the club or tell the *Standard* (or more accurately their website) that all Fulham fans were outraged. Neither was I on the offensive in the couple of telephone conversations to the press that day. I was simply cheesed off that the Club are one minute asking more people to attend (I've been to every "home" game by the way) and then the next are putting obstacles in the way of a sizable number of regulars. As a regular fan I expect to be able to make home games. Seems reasonable to me. Still on the "reasonable" theme, I do also realise that the lump of money was far too good to turn down.

...Angry that despite going through the official (and unofficial) channels on the day in question to get Fulham's take on proceedings before opening my gob – something I didn't have to do since I'm not on this planet to do their job for them but which, in recent times, has become the accepted practice – I got no response. You, of course, were not aware of this. But I can promise

Fury Over Fulham Early Kick-off

Fulham are facing a backlash from their fans after moving next month's UEFA Cup third-round tie at home to Hertha Berlin to a 5pm kick-off to accommodate German television.

Next week's away leg has already been brought forward 48 hours to Tuesday, but it is the decision to change the second leg at Loftus Road on Thursday 12 December that has infuriated supporters.

Fulham have slashed ticket prices to £5 in an attempt to mollify angry fans, but that will cut no ice with those unable to watch the match because of work commitments.

The switch has been made entirely for financial reasons.

A club statement read: "This unusual step has been triggered by the offer of substantial TV revenue to the club from the German broadcaster, ARD.

"In the current financial climate this is an offer that we are not in a position to refuse.

"This is not a decision we have taken lightly and we trust the substantially reduced prices will compensate Fulham fans for the early kick-off time."

Many Fulham supporters may interpret

the decision as a sign that the club value finance above the feelings of their fans.

David Lloyd, editor of the fanzine *There's Only One F in Fulham*, said today: "Potentially, it's a massive own goal by the club for a game that will be billed the biggest since the 1975 FA Cup Final. Instead of going into the game all marching together, it's going to be overshadowed by another squabble.

"I am one of the lucky few who is still hoping to make it, but there's no way I can take my son. The Club are saying it will give an opportunity for kids to go along, but only those that go to school locally. They're ignoring the fans that turn up week in, week out.

"It's not an away game, but a home game that should have been fairly easy to get to. Given how patient everybody has been over the Loftus Road move, you'd have thought the Club would have tried to keep us happy. The fans have been short-changed."

Fulham could feel a reaction in the form of an embarrassingly low attendance in a competition that has yet to capture their fans' imagination. Only 7,770 watched last week's win over Dinamo Zagreb at Loftus Road.

**Matt Hughes, *Evening Standard*
20 November 2002**

you that I aim to do things professionally. I'm aware of many of the pitfalls but not arrogant to believe that I'm anywhere near perfect.

All those who are able to switch around their working arrangements are obviously unconcerned about the whole thing, indeed they'll be able to go to a match on the cheap. I guess you're in that number. And good luck to them and to you. To my knowledge, scores of FFC fans are not so lucky (these have made themselves known to me) and that number may well run into hundreds.

But, as I subsequently posted on the board, I am delighted it's looking like it'll be a decent crowd (I've bought five tickets myself and redistributed them!) as the key issue is for the team to do well.

My comments on FFC matters, if included at all, are normally tucked away at the foot of a story – and quite rightly too!!! On this occasion, though, they were used at length on account of it being a very quiet news day. So the back-page "splash" was as much of a surprise to me as it was to you. ☺

david lloyd TOOFIF editor

Our recent run of 'unlucky' own goals simply demonstrates that we're not getting a decent rub of the green, right? Or that Jean Tigana gave a black cat a hefty kick on the way to the training ground one morning. Well, maybe not. You see it's just possible that Steve Marlet, Facundo Sava and Rufus Brevett were aware of what occurred in that hot-bed of football, Madagascar, last month and that our three heroes were actually staging a bizarre protest against general refereeing standards. Unlikely? Well it becomes slightly more plausible when you consider that two of our trio have been shown red cards in recent weeks, while the other's masked celebrations have reportedly come under scrutiny.

Naturally we're biased, but if you asked the average Fulham fan if we've seen fair and consistent refereeing so far this season then the answer would be an emphatic 'no'. Different interpre- tations seem to apply from week to week while it's curious that so many 'big' decisions seem to favour the so- called big teams. Er, allegedly! Fulham's management have schooled the squad not to talk themselves into trouble on the park, while you can hardly accuse us of being a dirty side. And yet, thanks to a series of 'interpretations' we stand at the wrong end of the fair play league with four sendings-off in all. Amazing! Over in Madagascar, meantime, one team decided to make their point.

Stade Olympique l'Emyrne's coach Ratsimandresy Ratsarazaka, an obviously far-from-happy chappie, decided to orchestrate a protest from the stand, instructing his side to put the ball into their own net...149 times in all! New champions AS Adema (and their goal difference!) were the beneficiaries as SOE, the previous season's champions, deliberately netted oggy after oggy in protest over refereeing decisions that had gone against them during the four-team play-off to decide the national championship.

The blue touchpaper was ignited by an incident in the previous game. SOE, 2-1 up, were pegged back to a 2-2 draw by Domoina Soavina Atsimondrano when referee Benjamina Razafintsalama (hmm, not even a distant relative of any of the premiership whistlers then!) awarded a late, hotly disputed penalty against

SOE. The result meant Adema were champions with a game still to play. Cue SOE 'protest'.

Unfortunately, it is not recorded if any of these own goals included an almost impossible to execute slice at the near post from a corner, a well-struck volley into the top of the net or a bundled-in effort from an attempted goalkeeping clearance. It would seem unlikely, however, as SOE's opponents weren't allowed near the action. Kick-off after kick-off saw the ball go all the way back and into the net. What a humdinger of a match it must have been to watch! I wonder what the Malagasy equivalent of "Can we play you every week?" is... I wonder, too, if they were trying to make it a round 150? Who knows, perhaps the ref miscounted!! Or maybe it was a Mr Dudek in goal, and he accidentally saved one!!!

Above: Someone gets to have his say in the FFC v Hertha Berlin matchday programme. All very enlightening, I'm sure! The front cover of the programme (*left*) features Steve Marlet.

Right: Our European adventure comes to to a halt "with a whimper" according to the *Daily Mirror*. The report also mentions the backstage grumblings about the £11.5 transfer fee paid for Marlet.

TIGANA'S ACES GO MISSING

By MARTIN ROGERS
Fulham 0 Hertha Berlin 0
Hertha Berlin win 2-1 on aggregate

JEAN TIGANA last night blamed his attacking flops for Fulham's depressing UEFA Cup exit.

The French coach saw his side squander a series of chances, despite the best efforts of striker Steve Marlet.

"I'm sure we were the better side," said Tigana, "and we should have gone through. But it was an experience and, hopefully, we have learned from playing at this level.

"I hope my players now know that you get only one chance at this level and you have to score from it."

Afterwards French striker Marlet broke his silence on his controversial transfer last

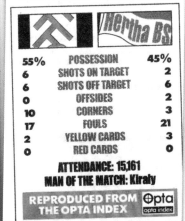

55%	POSSESSION	45%
6	SHOTS ON TARGET	2
6	SHOTS OFF TARGET	6
0	OFFSIDES	2
10	CORNERS	3
17	FOULS	21
2	YELLOW CARDS	3
0	RED CARDS	0

ATTENDANCE: 15,161
MAN OF THE MATCH: Kiraly

REPRODUCED FROM THE OPTA INDEX ●pta opta index

year. He confirmed that he had waived a £2million fee to join Fulham.

The club have launched an investigation into what happened to the £11.5million they paid Olympique Lyonnais. Marlet said: "It is true that I gave up the fee that I was entitled to under my contract with Lyon.

"I knew if I didn't, I would not be able to move to Fulham. This affair has not affected my game."

But something seemed to affecting fellow-striker Luis Boa Morte. He wasted two clear chances as Fulham saw their European adventure end with a whimper.

FULHAM: Taylor, Finnan, Melville, Goma, Brevett (Goldbaek 71), Djetou (Legwinski 45), Davis (Inamoto 62), Malbranque, Wome, Marlet, Boa Morte.
HERTHA BERLIN: Kiraly, Friedrich, Simunic (Van Burik 8), Rehmer, Nene de Brito, Goor, Marcelinho, Neuendorf (Schmidt 72), Hartmann, Dardai, Luizao (Preetz 81).

Mission Mostly Impossible

When applying for a new job you're often asked for examples of your work. In my case, there's one set of articles that never get an airing in such circumstances: my efforts for the Fulham programme penned while we were at Loftus Road. I was delighted to be asked by the then editor Patrick Mascall to write a regular column from the TOOFIF viewpoint. However, it soon became clear that it wouldn't be the column either of us wanted. Comments were fine, but only if they were positive. Any run-of-the-mill terrace opinions of our heroes, if deemed in any way negative, would be omitted.

I'm not daft. You're not going get away with trashing a player in an official Club publication, and neither would I wish to do so. You naturally hone your words to suit the particular publication; so in a Club magazine you'd understandably be expected to toe the party line by and large. Fair enough. But it soon became evident that you couldn't even refer to, say, an own goal, however unlucky, in a match round-up, even if that was a turning point in a game you'd been asked to cover.

Such a reference would have carried no criticism, implied or otherwise, of the player concerned, just a factual mention of what happened. But it wasn't my place, apparently, to highlight such incidents. For "highlight" read "make a mere mention". So my offerings were often terribly anodyne (no change there, some might say!). To be fair, Patrick insisted that his hands were tied. Apparently there was no room for any manoeuvre on this editorial stance so, despite being recruited to provide a terrace talk angle to the matchday pages, pretty much anything that was the talk of the terraces was off limits.

So why didn't I tell them to sling it? The fact that I was getting paid a few quid was, admittedly, a consideration – I was out of work at the time – but that in itself wasn't worth the hassle of supplying regular watered-down copy. No, the key reason was being able to channel the Back to the Cottage news.

During our Loftus Road tenureship, some sections of the fanbase were suspicious of the Club's motives with regard to where we would call home in due course (it subsequently came to light that FFC seriously considered a U-turn or three) to the extent that a good number voted with their feet and stayed away from QPR. The Back to the Cottage crew, brilliantly fronted by Tom Greatrex, were striving to steer us back to SW6. It was worth a few paragraphs of frothy nonsense to ensure the date of the latest Town Hall meeting, or whatever, was included too. At least that way there was a guaranteed mention of any upcoming days of action. However, even this became a problem when contributors were barred from commenting on the whole ground issue. ⚽

So's You Know (From Issue 85)

FFC have banned me (and others) from referring to the ground saga in the matchday programme. I argued you can't expect to have a fan's column with no reference to the recent Club statement, but was told it was a taboo subject. The notes supplied for the Birmingham proggy (6 Jan 2004) were therefore not only short but also lightweight (standard fare then!). Joking apart, the censorship makes you wonder what's the point of having such a column. The following passage – written, necessarily, in particularly diplomatic tones (and a first draft at this point) – was therefore cut:

The pre-Christmas announcement that FFC are not now going to pursue the approved plans for redeveloping the Cottage unfortunately came as no surprise. It's pretty apparent that the Club are not exactly flush at the moment – we've been limited to loan deals in the transfer market for example – and the £100m figure supposedly required is particularly high. Two points on that, however: a) how can costs rise so much in such a short space of time?; and b) it wasn't us fans that wanted or put forward such expensive plans in the first place.

In fact, the statement actually says very little, apart from asking the fans for more patience. Fair point, although we've been showing saintly degrees of patience (and unstinting support) for years now. The statement certainly allows for a return to Craven Cottage in some shape or form. But, sadly, reading between the lines I get the impression that we'll never go back there now, which flies in the face of umpteen previous statements from the Club. Whatever you think of the whole issue – and I can confirm that there are no end of opinions and suggestions right across the spectrum – there is no doubt that the vast majority of Fulham fans are confused and not a little upset, about the way things have turned out.

A redeveloped Craven Cottage may well not be seen as the answer by the powers-that-be. But seeing as the old place was kept ticking over by thousands of decent fans, many of whom turned out in force to support the ultimately approved plans, the Club must realise we're more attached to our spiritual home than fans of the average club.

Any rational supporter would readily agree that no major decision should be taken via "irrational or emotional thinking" but the Club should also note that it's those same emotions that keep us tied to our Club. It's the not knowing that's so frustrating, but then at least the Chairman acknowledges that.

No one's doubting for a moment what Mohamed Al Fayed has done for the Club to date – that's not the issue at all. It's just that we'd love to turn up to our home ground and have nothing to be concerned

> "I'm not daft. You're not going get away with trashing a player in an official Club publication, and neither would I wish to do so. You naturally hone your words to suit the particular publication; so in a Club magazine you'd understandably be expected to toe the party line by and large."

about save the team's on-pitch fortunes. I realise I'm not the one holding either the purse strings or the nitty-gritty "inside knowledge" but, for me, that home should be at Craven Cottage. ⁘

Dein's Dirty Deed

In the Chelsea v Middlesbrough match programme last Saturday, Ken Bates savaged the Arsenal Vice-Chairman and virtual chief executive David Dein, accusing him of being hired for a £40,000 fee to facilitate the dire plans of Cabra Estates who in the 1980s wanted to merge Fulham with QPR, call them Fulham Park Rangers, and get them playing at Loftus Road, while Stamford Bridge and Craven Cottage were sold for building development.

Bates, as he recalls, dug his heels in and the plan fell through. Next time he saw Dein at a meeting he told him to "sod off". It's been interesting to see the evolution of Dein from entrepreneur to elder statesman, holding the ring at the Crozier and post-Crozier FA. That clearly isn't how Bates sees him. Ken won't, one imagines, be too pleased if Arsenal abandon their idea of building a new stadium near to Highbury to play at Wembley, where he foresaw a conflict of interest. Meanwhile, Fulham won't be playing at Stamford Bridge.

When that great comedian Tommy Trinder was Fulham's "president" he used to rule it out, saying "I don't want to move in with my mother-in-law."
Brian Glanville in *World Soccer*, November 2002

In the 1980s Fulham and QPR fell into the hands of a property company, Cabra Estates plc (headed by John Duggan), which also acquired the freehold of Stamford Bridge from the Mears family. The grand plan was for Fulham and QPR to merge into Fulham Park Rangers and groundshare with Chelsea at Loftus Road. This would have released both Stamford Bridge and Craven Cottage for residential development. This collapsed because I helped to block that merger and I also refused to move Chelsea to Loftus Road despite the offer of substantial financial inducement and David Dein's uninvited intervention and self-appointed "honest broker" in the dispute between Duggan and myself. After some minutes of ear-bashing I told him to sod off and not interfere in Chelsea's affairs.

I don't know if Dein was on a success fee had he persuaded me to groundshare, but he received over £40,000 to appear as a so-called expert witness on behalf of Cabra at the Public Inquiry that was part of Cabra's scheme to throw Fulham out of the Cottage. When I popped into Fulham Town Hall unexpectedly to watch proceedings, Dein scuttled out like a frightened rabbit when he saw me. ⁘
Ken Bates, Chelsea programme, 16.11.02

Why do we do it?

Following your club up and down the country during exceptionally trying times isn't an especially sane thing to do. So why bother? I'd say it's because we've all been in it together – the fans, the Club, the players. Anyway, there's something different about FFC. Have you ever tried explaining to workmates the phenomenon of turning up in Carlisle, walking into a random pub, and finding 20 familiar friends? Friends, that is, whose surnames, even first names, you're not sure of, but who you see week in, week out? By comparison, Manchester United away must be like a trip to the theatre – a decent performance each week, but watched alongside total strangers.

Have you ever noticed the blank looks when you casually mention to Spurs, Liverpool and Chelsea fans at work that you were drinking with the Club's groundsman, or that you're mates with the bloke who runs the Club's Internet site, or that you went to a player's testimonial do and chatted to him like an old mate? This Club is different. It's OBVIOUS.

If we're not in it together, if the Fulham Football "Club" doesn't comprise everyone – its supporters, and its officials, and its players, and its characters, old and new – then it's nothing at all; just another small club in the shadow of bigger ones, rotting away while the game is sold down the river to the big few PLCs. That bond, that togetherness, is why we go to such lengths, and such expense, to pursue an interest with no guarantee whatsoever of reward.

This is where the Club has gone badly, terribly wrong this season. The cooperation has gone. The fans aren't being respected, so the trust is falling to bits. We're not 25,000 stereotypical ignorant football plebs. Fulham fans are bright and intelligent and thoughtful. We've got lawyers, and planners, and engineers who can understand the ground scenario, and who know where to look for the information that the Club chooses not to share.

We've got immensely football-aware people, with contacts at other clubs who've experienced the same and worse. We've got politicians, journalists and media-savvy folk – people who recognise spin when they see it. The spin is intolerable. Perhaps our wage bill necessitated a large season ticket price rise. These things happen. But releasing the details on the day before a Cup semi-final weekend doesn't pull the wool over anyone's eyes. Since then, we've been subjected to a drip-feed of information on the ground as, sentence by sentence, we're gently being informed of what we'd already been suspecting.

So, I implore the people running the Club to remember that FFC isn't just its management. It's the team, too, of course, but most of all it's the fans. The fans were here first, and they'll be here long afterwards, as will the rich history and heritage. These guys are the best pals I've ever had; it breaks my heart to watch as they talk sadly and seriously about drifting off to assorted non-League clubs.

Stop treating us like sheep. For the sake of Fulham Football Club give us the facts; give us the respect we deserve, and GIVE US A VOICE! ⁘
Ormondroyd

Fulham 1 Middlesbrough 0	1st
19.01.03 15th	2nd
Manchester City 4 Fulham 1	3rd
29.01.03 15th	4th
Arsenal 2 Fulham 1	5th
01.02.03 15th	6th
Fulham 2 Aston Villa	7th
08.02.03 15th	8th
Fulham 3 West Brom 0	9th
19.02.03 14th	10th
Tottenham Hotspur 1 Fulham 1	11th
24.02.03 15th	**12th**
Fulham 1 Sunderland 0	13th
01.03.03 12th	14th
	15th
FA Cup	16th
Fulham 3 Charlton Athletic 0	17th
26.01.03 Round 4	18th
Fulham 1 Burnley 1	19th
16.02.03 Round 5	20th
Burnley 3 Fulham 0	
26.02.03 Round 5 replay	

An Editorial Rant

Sorry, but I feel a rant coming on! That's not my way as a rule, but here goes... We've enjoyed a decent inaugural run in Europe, winning a tiny "pot" in the process, and look sure to retain our top-flight status. So why is the overriding feeling one of a misspent season? In school report terms: "could do better". A whole lot better, in fact.

These are not the witterings of a fan who's become accustomed to success in recent seasons and who arrogantly demands more of the same, but one who instead suspects the wheels have been allowed to come off the Fulham bandwagon big time. I desperately hope I'm wrong but the signs are ominous. While there have undoubtedly been several highs we've had to endure many disappointments both on and off the field. That, in itself, is nothing new to us diehards, is it? But it's the sense of negativity surrounding just about all things Fulham that's hard to take, particularly when much of it would seem to have been avoidable.

The uncertainty regarding Jean Tigana's position has been tangible from the early months of the season and you can't help but feel he's been forced to operate with at least one hand tied behind his back. Things hardly got off to a good start with the tactless (if well-meaning?) appointment of Franco Baresi, as Director of Football, and fingers of suspicion pointing at JT for the unnecessarily expensive Marlet. I'm told there have even been occasions when, on the back of certain incidents or blows to the manager's pride, FFC staff have taken bets on whether or not he would turn up for training the following morning – thereby turning his back on the job. If true, that's not exactly the basis for training ground harmony, is it? If untrue, why is it yet another example of the "bad vibes" allowed to circulate unchallenged around the place?

Other sources, not backed up by newspaper quotes just recently mind you (a number of players have been quoted saying they like the Tigana regime...good grief, a "positive vibe"!!), suggest JT "lost" the confidence of the players in the Autumn. By then, the scale of the Marlet fee, and alleged "missing millions", made for an anything-but-sweet relationship between Manager and Chairman it would seem. Even so, surely JT should have been allowed to get on with his job. If, as now expected, he leaves at the end of the season, he'll have been, in effect, a lame duck manager, especially more recently – he wasn't pleased about having to play those two games in three days, but seemed to have no say in the matter; he apparently wanted to enter the InterToto Cup again, but others decided against it. I've said previously that if he remains 100 per cent up for the job and he knows where he stands then I hope JT, a class act, stays, but...

Now, much of this is based on conjecture – but serves to point out that there's hardly a good news tale to be seen, whether in the form of fact or Club "spin". The management of the Club has, in my humble view, been dreadful, while the handling of its image has been just as bad. Accordingly the fun, and certainly the charm, has evaporated from FFC. There's no warmth to the place, no sense of togetherness or trust. In fact the overall impression for a while now has been that the Club just want this season over as soon as possible.

But at least we were going back to the Cottage as promised. (Cue, in best panto tradition, a cry from the back: "Oh no you're not!") The much-longed-for House of Lords decision regarding the proposed new stadium at CC came just before the Hertha Berlin game. FFC needed to get a goal (at least) to maintain our Euro hopes; the fans turned out in force despite the ludicrous kick-off time. What better way to get the crowd roused – and to lift the team – than by making them aware of the good news. It would have been worth far more than a goal start, surely. Only...nothing! Not even a "spun" message of part-intent. Okay, decision made, not my call. And in the weeks that followed it became clear that the Club were unable to go ahead with the approved scheme. Meantime back out on the park, though, we're struggling to get things together while the crowd (a UEFA Cup crowd for a match involving FFC for goodness sake) remained as silent as gagged, throat-infected dormice! Oh, and we slipped out of the competition: not only was the European Tour over, but with it went our hopes of both further glory and financial income. Hey-ho.

Much was discussed then about the Club's need to take a sizeable chunk of TV money in return for the 5pm start. More recently a similar money-grabbing decision was made. JT's spoken out in the past about having a decent rest period before games. So, of course, FFC went ahead with two matches in three days. Handsomely paid for, naturally. Or was it? With the Spurs game out of the way (which had presented the bulk of the money on offer), did we really have to play Burnley so soon after for the sake of a reported £250,000? A tidy sum, but not a lot when put into the context of the players' weekly wage bills (and their signing-on fees!) and the hefty salaries of the many working behind the scenes.

Two points: a) who has presided over the decisions that have decreed that we're in such an apparently parlous financial state?; and

> "The uncertainty regarding Jean Tigana's position has been tangible from the early months of the season and you can't help but feel he's been forced to operate with at least one hand tied behind his back. Things hardly got off to a good start with the tactless (if well-meaning?) appointment of Franco Baresi, as Director of Football."

b) the decision to take the money for the Burnley game clearly jeopardised our chances of getting to the Cup Final and, who knows, even beyond into Europe. Financial spin-offs would have brought in far more than £250,000, I'd suggest (although there was still the small matter of beating Burnley on whatever date the game was played!). On paper, at least, we'll never have a clearer path to a final.

So another disappointment! And the bad vibes continued. Whereas only a couple of seasons ago we were the fittest squad in the land, nowadays we're a poor tired bunch. Same club, same regime, but different outlook perhaps. I'm not actually decrying the tiredness aspect, even honed athletes should be a little knackered after giving a flat-out 100 per cent in matches (hmm, I feel another discussion point in there somewhere!) but more the fact that the excuses are made, and publicly. From being a world-beating force – in the First Division admittedly – confident, fit and ready for anything (and displaying marvellous levels of team-work and general spirit, which unsurprisingly translated into one sparkling display after another and a stack of League points) we're now hiding behind negative excuses. Where's the drive, leadership and squad spirit?

There have been genuine reasons to cloud some of this, though, not least the appalling run of injuries, to our front men in particular. But it's all too clear to see when a bunch of players are "up for it": all pulling together and playing flat out, and when they're not. That doesn't necessarily mean winning matches either – the Spurs away game is a good example. What a great effort that was! The same could be said of both Arsenal games, from which we somehow finished pointless.

I mentioned earlier that there have been high-points, and you've only got to look at our decent performances to see what could have been possible. When we've played well we've been as good as anyone in the division, displaying all the qualities of a successful side in all respects apart from having a prolific goalscorer. The performances against Bolton and Bologna, back in August, set an early yardstick, but then we had that storming comeback against Spurs. What a finish to a game! We seemed to be getting the hang of the Euro business with a 3-0 win at Dinamo Zagreb, beat Liverpool (and the ref!) and, more recently showed we could still turn it on with a great show against Villa. Set against those there have been dreadful, disjointed and seemingly heartless efforts at home to West Ham, away to Wigan, Newcastle, both games against Manchester City and of course at Burnley to name but a few. What a disparity!

I'm far too long in the tooth to expect perfect performances every week. Coming from the generation who came along week in week out

in the lower leagues hoping that this week it would somehow be different, I couldn't be happier that we're back in the big time. And while I crave success like any fan, I don't demand it. But what I do expect from any team I'm involved with – playing, watching or even in a works/office environment – is all-round effort and commitment every week. And a positive approach. Having forked out considerable sums of money to follow and passionately support the club/team, that's surely the least we deserve.

We could be in for a big shake up very soon: a new manager, new backroom staff and wholesale changes in the playing squad. Already it's strongly hinted that Steve Finnan is off, that Sean Davis may be upping sticks, too, and that any number of others are set to leg it if JT goes. We'll see! A shake-up might prove a good thing, but the worst-case scenario is that the heart is ripped out of our squad and that we'll be relegation material this time next year. I sincerely hope the bubble hasn't burst.

I'd better take a deep breath...I'm getting "ranted out"! You may or may not agree with me – I've been known to be wrong many a time – but I'm cheesed off at the way it's become something of a drudge to follow the Club. And that's something I never, ever thought I'd say or write in these pages. Even in the awful times we made sure there was plenty of Fulhamish fun around. Bring it back please!

In closing, I wish to make it clear this shouldn't be seen as a "pop" at the Chairman – although I'd be delighted if he took it upon himself to ensure some positive news (what about a return to the Cottage for a start, Mo?) but more at those responsible for making decisions on his behalf. So what's achieved by such a rant? Well I guess it's a roundabout plea for an injection of goodwill and commonsense. I feel it is essential that fans and Club are united at this time more than ever, and that only serious and well-intentioned dialogue will ensure a rosy future for this wonderful football club of ours. The Chairman personally hasn't let us down to date (far from it!). Hopefully we'll be saying that for years.

Stop press: At a recent open meeting the decision was taken to form the Fulham Supporters Trust, but still to operate under the Back to the Cottage campaign name for the time being. The trust will be formally launched at a public meeting. BTTC hope to present workable plans for a return to Craven Cottage to the Club and Council by the end of March. ❖

	1st
Fulham 2 Southampton 2	2nd
15.03.03 12th	3rd
	4th
Manchester United 3 Fulham 0	5th
22.03.03 13th	6th
Fulham 0 Blackburn Rovers 4	7th
07.04.03 13th	8th
Liverpool 2 Fulham 0	9th
12.04.03 15th	10th
Fulham 2 Newcastle United 1	11th
19.04.03 14th	**12th**
Leeds United 2 Fulham 0	13th
22.04.03 16th	14th
Chelsea 1 Fulham 1	15th
26.04.03 15th	16th
Fulham 2 Everton 0	17th
03.05.03 15th	18th
Charlton Athletic 0 Fulham 1	19th
11.05.03 14th	20th

Get Back!

TOOFIF'S David Lloyd meets Tom Greatrex of Back to the Cottage (BTTC) and asks if the campaign has any chance of success.

What prompted the formation of the Back to the Cottage group?

It came about through a combination of the Fulham Supporters' Club ground sub-committee – those elected or who volunteered at the public meeting last October – and a group of people who were doing leaflets and stuff anyway. We all wanted the same thing, to get Fulham Football Club back to Craven Cottage. We joined forces and were supported by, and received financial support from, the Supporters' Club. But it's a wider group than that; the idea is that we develop this into a Trust, to give us accountability and real authority – and which would have the support of the government-funded Supporters Direct. We'll then be able to represent the views of the Fulham supporters at a time when, yet again, the issue of our home ground is high on the agenda.

Where do you fit into all this, Tom?

I've been going to see Fulham play for the last 24 years, having been dragged along my by dad, who had previously been taken there by his old man who owned a shop in Fulham. My very strong view is that Fulham FC should play in Fulham. I lived locally and, with the likes of Ian Coles became involved with Fulham United. Things have really gone on from there. Long-term sustainability and viability of FFC, which is, frankly, a medium-sized club, should depend on it developing proper community roots and being a proper community club at its proper home.

So BTTC was formed. What are its aims – and are they realistic?

The name's pretty self-explanatory! But FFC have to play somewhere and there aren't any alternative sites in Fulham. If there were we'd be in an entirely different situation. If we were in a similar situation to some of the examples cited by Bruce Langham, such as Southampton, Sunderland and Middlesbrough, where they were able to build new grounds locally, then things wouldn't be as fraught. There isn't a site available nearby, as we know, and if one were to become available the cost of the land would be prohibitive anyway. Really, to get FFC playing in its own ground, it's got to be back to Craven Cottage – the area of its origins and where it's played for more than a century. It's the only place in Fulham or the surrounding area where you could build a football stadium.

Remind us, briefly, what the BTTC campaign isn't about – there have been one or two misconceptions along the way...

Certain people have tried to suggest that BTTC is a rallying point for just a handful of folk who want to whinge and moan about the Premiership and the experience of the Club and the Chairman and this and that – it's not! Back to the Cottage is a broad group of people – with 750 closely involved, and that figure ever-rising – who support FFC and love to see FFC in the Premiership and doing well generally. I never thought I'd see Fulham play in the top division and I think everyone is immensely grateful for that and appreciates the contribution of the Chairman, in particular, in steering Fulham back into the top flight. But there is an important line – the Club must be sustainable. The Chairman himself said, when he took over, that his desire was to see Fulham Football Club being self-sustaining in the top division. To do that you need your own stadium. And to do so successfully you need to have a stadium in an area where you can attract support. So even if we can't have the super stadium envisaged at Craven Cottage because of rising costs then we should look at ways of building a stadium that doesn't cost as much. Looking at the fortunes of some other London clubs, I feel we're at a crossroads – we can either go the Charlton route or the Wimbledon route. Let's get back to our historic home, build up the community involvement and sense of ownership that Charlton supporters have with their club and build a stadium up around it gradually. We know the Council are sympathetic to that aim – as we've been in discussion with them as to what would and what would not meet with their officers' likely approval. This has to be preferable to the Wimbledon way: tenants somewhere until a mythical site turns up.

Surely all Fulham fans would want to return if all was well?

There's plenty of mixed views on the ground situation. There are lots who don't like Loftus Road and some who aren't even going to Loftus Road. There are also fans who say "if we're groundsharing at Stamford Bridge then I won't go anywhere near the place", whereas others will say, "I might go to the Bridge." But what every single Fulham fan, I think, would be absolutely delighted with is going back to Craven Cottage. So if we can find a way in which we could do it, that isn't financially prohibitive, that is a realistic proposition and would get the backing of the local authority then isn't that the sensible route to take?

BTTC has been busy leafletting, holding peaceful demos and open meetings: how pleased are you with the response to date and how would you say things are going?

"I never thought I'd see Fulham play in the top division and I think everyone is immensely grateful for that and appreciates the contribution of the Chairman, in particular, in steering Fulham back into the top flight."

I can only say that when Mohamed Al Fayed was announced as the new Chairman and owner of FFC my immediate concern was "Is this something to do with the ground?". I'm sure I wasn't alone in that thought. But I was very, very pleased when they put some serious plans together for a new stadium and got the required planning permission. Now, if the economic situation within football, or within Harrods and associated businesses, makes that particular dream impossible then it doesn't mean you can't do something else, such as come up with a cheaper option. It might not be a unified stadium as previously proposed, it might have four separate stands, it might be that you'd have to do one stand at a time, and it might be that we'll have to live with the existing Riverside Stand for a while longer, but I don't think any of that would bother too many people if it meant getting back to Craven Cottage.

But do you think such a nuts and bolts scheme would bother the powers-that-be at Fulham who've been thinking in more grandiose terms all round...?
I can't be only one to have noticed a change in the way things are being handled at Fulham. As football was expanding, thanks to the general economic state of the sport, there was the real opportunity of building up a club and constructing a super stadium, but the financial climate has changed. The collapse of ITV Digital was really the catalyst and people are taking a step back now. You just have to look at what has been happening at Leeds to see that people are reassessing things. But by following the example of clubs like Charlton you can make the whole thing viable and sustainable. I certainly think that if there's a will to do it then we can find a way.

Are you in discussions with the Club?
We have spoken to the club, and very soon

They're going well. There's been a certain amount of activity of which most fans would be aware, but what many aren't as aware of is the scale of work undertaken behind the scenes: talking to the local council – including extensive talks with council officers – and local MPs and working very hard on plans to get the Club back to the Cottage. These activities clearly won't attract the attention of the press, neither will they be apparent to the fans turning up to games. It shows, though, that there are different strands to the BTTC campaign – some of it is very public, some of it far less so. But overall I've been pleasantly surprised by the amount of dedication and commitment among lots of Fulham fans, many holding different views on various things FFC, but all united behind the fact that we all want to get back to Craven Cottage. The challenge is there.

What would you say to those who suggest that returning to Craven Cottage simply isn't viable?
I don't think anybody's presented any evidence to show why it isn't viable. It might not be viable to construct a 30,000 all-seater stadium on that site costing £100m or more and then make income out of it. That may or may not be the situation regarding the present planning permission. Now if the Club have made the decision not to build it then we, as fans, have no influence on that decision. But that doesn't preclude any number of other options on that site. You could easily build stands one at a time, and for less. If the cost is lower therefore the amount of capacity and the commercial revenue required won't need to be as high to make it viable.

It wasn't as if the fans themselves put forward the grandiose plans anyway...?

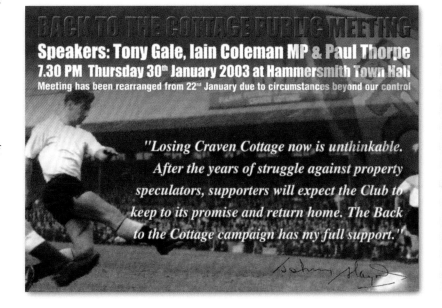

"Back to the Cottage isn't about protesting and moaning, it's about using the expertise available from within our fanbase to present a way of ensuring FFC have the chance of playing at Craven Cottage for another hundred years."

we hope to be able to put new plans to them. These plans are currently being put together with the help of experts from within the Fulham support and some of the people involved at Charlton. That's the challenge that was set in the Chairman's recent programme notes – "you show us a way, and we'll have a look at it" – we've taken that up at face value and very much hope that the Club will be in the right frame of mind to sit down with us constructively and see we can all find a way forward.

These are highly professional plans, of course (I was talking to a Brentford fan who opined that football club directors consider as a rule of thumb that football fans know bugger-all about anything)...?
I can only talk about Fulham supporters, but we know of a huge range of expertise, experience, abilities and contacts. Back to the Cottage isn't about protesting and moaning, it's about using the expertise available from within our fanbase to present a way of ensuring FFC have the chance of playing at Craven Cottage for another hundred years. It's worth emphasising that football can't be categorised as being one particular social economic class or, to put it crudely, that they're all flat-capped people who come along to watch football but have no understanding of how the world works. That's not the case. Back to the Cottage is about getting Fulham supporters working together just as the whole idea of a football trust is about getting supporters understanding the bigger picture and using their expertise. Directors, chairmen, players and managers come and go – most fans, though, will stay with their Club for most of their lifetime. As the long-term people involved it's important to engage with them and ensure their contributions are taken into account.

And fans add a level of devotion to that expertise too...
Absolutely! But the point I'm trying to make is that BTTC is no "Blind hope, devotion-led exercise" with nothing to back it up.

You might not want to answer this if things are at a delicate stage, but how do you think the Club have handled things up to now?
I am prepared to answer it, and I'll be as frank as I've been throughout this business: The Club have handled this appallingly. There's been a level of duplicity, and inconsistency in the statements they've made publicly. We've seen things happen at the same time as they've been making comments to the contrary. None of this has done

them any good – Fulham fans want to trust the club they support. I don't think there's any Fulham fan who wants to be in an argument the whole time. I would love to be able to go to watch my football team every other week or whatever and talk to my mates at football about football – that should be my release from the pressures of work and everything else. I don't want to have to spend hours involved in a campaign. I'm sure the others don't want to spend time, effort, money and commitment involved with a campaign that might be at variance with their football club. I think it's been a mistake for FFC to have treated their fans in the way they have. The level of goodwill is there if it's harnessed properly. But to treat people with a lack of respect is, in my view, foolhardy.

Do you think this might be because there are so few "football people" at FFC or is it more sinister than that?
Clearly I don't know what the motivations of various people at FFC are. But I think those people who think you could somehow sell Craven Cottage and then an ideal solution or site would become available are mistaken. I do think there is an extent to which people at FFC don't understand football, don't understand football fans and Fulham fans. There's much talk these days of football being a business. Well if you're a decent business you make sure you respect your customers, and you communicate with your customers – you don't hide things from your customers. I've noticed that the general atmosphere this season isn't as good as it was last season – and at least part of that is down to the fact that the way the Club has treated its fans hasn't been up to the sort of standards you'd expect.

Trust needs to come from both sides..?
Oh yes, and that's why I think it's in the interests of the Club and us (however you want to label a group of fans!) that there's a proper dialogue between club and fans. If there is, then there's far less chance of disharmony. If there's no disharmony then you're all bound to be pulling in the right direction – and I'm sure that's what all Fulham fans would want.

So bridge-building is the order of the day?
Absolutely – I don't want to be in conflict with the Club.

That fabulous season under Micky Adams came on the back of a good news announcement about the ground which, as Simon Morgan wrote in his book, played no small part in us having that wonderful year. A good news announcement, such as a move back to Cottage,

Below: Tom Greatrex: "Let's see if we, as a responsible group of committed Fulham fans, can persuade the Club to get back to Craven Cottage."

would surely recreate that feelgood factor and bring back the fans in their thousands...?

That was a great season wasn't it? And a springboard for what followed. I don't think it's any coincidence that where clubs have difficult situations off the pitch it affects what happens on it. Because even if it isn't that tangible I think the overall atmosphere has an impact. I think it's quite realistic and quite feasible for Fulham Football Club to be able to announce relatively soon that they are going back to Craven Cottage and it may well be that it's done with reformation of terraces and with seats bolted on behind both goals and it might be that the capacity isn't much higher than it is at Loftus Road initially but I think that would give us all a huge lift. Just look at how Charlton was transformed after they got their club back to the Valley. And look at them now, banging on the door for a European place! They're performing very well in the Premiership, with a capacity in the mid-20,000s, selling out every week and with a real sense of ownership among the fans of the Club.

So what can the fans actually do?

Back to the Cottage has evolved as a group and we now wish to set it up as a Trust so that it has proper lines of accountability. We want it to be a representative group of Fulham fans, initially based around the stadium issue so getting involved with the Trust is an important first step. Any Fulham fan who has the inclination to get involved, even slightly, will be warmly welcomed. Let's see if we, as a responsible group of committed Fulham fans, can persuade the Club to get back to Craven Cottage.

Bruce Langham recently said: "We are looking at Craven Cottage to see if there's a way we can build a more affordable stadium" – that statement must give you some heart?

I'd be interested and pleased to see what the Club are looking at! Which is, of course, why we're so keen to show the Club what we've managed to put together. It can be done, it is relatively simple to do, and doesn't require difficult planning permission. I really do hope the Club are serious about this and are not just offering some PR-speak during the season in the hope that it'll keep everyone quiet, and then in the close season announce something completely different.

A positive announcement would make sound business sense with regard to season ticket sales?

I think a piece of good news will have a significant impact on things like season ticket sales. More bad news or lack of news might mean that up to half of the current season ticket holders may choose not to renew them. ⚽

A Trip to Poundland

David Lloyd fires some questions at Steve Pound, MP for Ealing North and fervent Fulham fan.

Above: Steve Pound MP: "We're umbilically linked with Craven Cottage. We must go back."

Steve, should Fulham go back to the Cottage?

God yes. Yes, yes yes! We're umbilically linked with the Cottage. We ARE Fulham FC, the riverside team – we could move back next week, we put in temporary "stands" at the Putney and Hammersmith Ends, giving us something like a 16,000 capacity – and we'd sell it out. Instead of which we're selling 13,000, at the most, at Loftus Road. We must go back, and I just hope to God we do.

You're very emphatic on the subject...

The Chairman has said we're going to stay within Hammersmith & Fulham – I know every inch of the Borough, you tell me where the alternatives are... Bishops Park? I don't think so!

Do fans have a right to be concerned?

Of course. I don't like criticising the Chairman – I'm a Fulham loyalist in a way. But we've had some awful Chairmen in the past, some of them we've got shot of (or they've done it themselves!) but where would we be without Mohammed Al Fayed? You can't argue with the fact that everything we've achieved after famously getting out of the bottom division with Micky Adams has been down to our Chairman. If I live to be 100 I'll never cease to be grateful for that. But why can't he simply say, "Hey we're never going to be a 40,000-fanbase club" – we never are! – let's go back, sell a stack of season tickets, get some money coming in, consolidate in the Premiership and then push on from there.

What should fans do?

The first rule of politics is that the squeaky wheel gets the oil. Fans must make themselves heard – I don't mean aggressively, as that's not the Fulham way. Fans should form a united group (as we did with Fulham 2000), speak with one voice, argue the case logically and meet with the Chairman who, after all, is a football fan, and then see what happens. Tom Greatrex and the BTTC boys have actually worked out the costings, how much money we could generate if we went back. The Chairman loved all the adulation that came his way during those pre-match walkabouts at the Cottage. I'd love to see all that again. And I'm sure he would, too! ⚽

Heading Home!

It was wonderful to learn that (should planning permission be granted as expected) we're heading back to Craven Cottage in time for next season. It's also terrific to see the team playing with such heart, team spirit and determination – basic requirements, surely – and no little skill. The gritty win over Leicester propelled us up to fourth place (cue nosebleeds) and rubbished the so-called experts' views that we'd be one of the push-over teams, and that rookie Chris Coleman was a favourite for the sack. Obviously it's very early days as yet, and in football it's foolhardy to take anything for granted, but the die has been well and truly cast. If the same playing attitude can be maintained then a top ten finish, let alone mere Premiership survival, might not be out of the question!

Those pundits – with Mark "Lawro" Lawrenson one of the biggest doubters – may have done FFC a big favour. If the squad spirit wasn't good enough already as the season neared, then the doom-and-gloom merchants may well have helped to instill a dogged backs-to-the-wall approach. Although our playing record, as I write is, pretty similar to this time last season, there's much more consistency and overall drive in the performances under Chris Coleman and Steve Kean and a visible willingness to work for each other and within the team framework.

Fulham CEO Bruce Langham's monthly updates via the official website are to be welcomed, too. This seems part of a genuine attempt by the Football Club to be more open with the fans. From the outside looking in, this should surely be a fundamental approach of any club – and most particularly one that is looking to shore up its support. In the relative juggernaut that is Fulham FC these days, perhaps that is something that has been inadvertently lost along the way. Can't think how and why myself, but then I've always tended to see things in black and white.

I must, though, take issue with some of Bruce's recent comments regarding the Craven Cottage announcement and the ensuing lack of impact in new season ticket applications. On the face of it I'd have expected more of an upswing, too. However, not only do I think it will prove to be more of a gradual thing (since it's still relatively easy to buy home tickets match by match) but also I don't think the real surge will come now until next season. Had it been a close season announcement then a few more might have been tempted this time around.

However, my main bone of contention centres on the announcement itself (much of which is shown alongside this piece). There may be all sorts of reasons and implications as to why FFC made such a muted fist of it. But there was hardly a drum roll to be heard, was there? Can you imagine the announcement of a Harrods sale without the accompanying press and PR blitz (including an eye-catching megastar being feted by the Chairman himself)? All done to ensure maximum publicity and to bring in the punters.

All right, there was never going to be a Kylie or whoever involved in the breaking Cottage news (shame!) but you get my drift. And, although the news itself was very eagerly received, the manner of its delivery meant it proved something of a damp squib for the ardent Fulham fan. From the Club's perspective it was an open, fulsome news release – but, with the inclusion of so many perceived negatives, it wasn't one to necessarily send the fans' pulses into overdrive. Hardly surprising, then, that the ticket office wasn't immediately inundated – even though we ARE delighted to be going back.

There is still plenty to be debated on the issue but it really could come down to simply taking it one stage at a time. A case of getting back to

Opposite page top: That scoreboard at Old Trafford makes mighty fine reading!

Opposite page right: No wonder Junichi Inamoto is smiling. He's not only scored against Manchester United but (along with fellow goalscorers Lee Clark and Steed Malbranque and their team-mates) has condemned United to a 3-1 defeat at the Theatre of Dreams.

Cottage Return

Fulham Football Club's chairman, Mohamed Al Fayed, today announced that the Club has launched a formal bid to return to its Craven Cottage stadium from the start of next season.

The proposed return to Craven Cottage will be a temporary move since the Club remains committed to building a larger stadium elsewhere in the borough. Last night Mr Al Fayed said: "I am delighted to take this step towards fulfilling the fans' dearest wish to take us home, albeit temporarily".

The Club turned its attention to buying a plot of land within the London Borough of Hammersmith and Fulham for the purpose of building a new stadium. A suitable plot was identified at White City, which the Club is still actively trying to acquire to build an appropriate stadium together with modern leisure facilities (including a swimming pool) for the local community.

The Club is grateful for the help and support it is receiving from Hammersmith and Fulham Council. The local authority is working closely with club officials to assist in finding the best solution for Fulham Football Club, the fans, and all the residents of the borough. The Council is prepared to consider all alternatives to keep the Club in the borough and secure the appropriate site.

"Like all Fulham fans, I was bitterly disappointed when our plans to build a state-of-the-art stadium on the Craven Cottage site became impossible to achieve," said Mr Al Fayed. "I still believe that if we are to fulfil our long-term dreams of making Fulham a major force in football we need a larger stadium than it is possible to erect at the Cottage and I continue to be entirely dedicated to working towards that end."

"I am doing everything that I can to find a commercially viable long-term solution," said Mr Al Fayed.

the Cottage and, if you'll excuse the pun, see what develops. In the meantime, though, we should welcome the Club's open approach and make the very most of it.

There's no doubting that the team's inspirational performances together with the welcome news about returning to Craven Cottage has lifted the fans' spirits. After drifting along indifferently for a while, it's so welcome to have so many positive matters to discuss – and hopefully the feelgood factor will grow and grow. Season ticket, anyone? ⚽

United Approach

It's not going too badly, is it? Fourth in the table; winning away at Old Trafford (and doing so very comfortably by the final whistle!); reports that the local council are set to approve FFC's return to Craven Cottage; and the understanding that there's money available for some additions to the squad come the January transfer window – I think we'd all have settled for that little lot at the start of the season!

That magnificent 3-1 triumph at the Theatre of Dreams is hard to take in – what a performance, and what a way to achieve the dream result. When United squeezed home that equaliser just before half-time only the most optimistic of Fulham fans would have dared to suggest that we'd take 'em to the cleaners (again) in the second half. It wasn't a case of Fulham pessimism to fear that our chance had gone, merely long-in-the-tooth realism that the "customary" script would now be played out. We'd seen it all before, so many times.

But it was no hard-luck tale on this occasion – despite Mike Riley (and his assistant) inexplicably ignoring that two-handed push on Boa in the penalty area; instead, it went on to be one of the all-time great away-days. The warm glow lasted well beyond the weekend as fans all over the land realised that it wasn't a just case of United being beaten at home but that they had been outplayed and outmanoeuvred.

The draw at Highbury and the win over Bolton were gained in very different circumstances to the heady champagne showing at Old Trafford. I felt we were hanging on grimly during the first half at Arsenal as the home side consistently turned us inside out. The backs-to-the-wall tactics could

well have backfired big time but, having settled rather more during the second half, we continued to work hard and, in the end, hung on for a rare point at the Library thanks, largely, to a fantastic, unshowy display of dominant goalkeeping by Edwin Van der Sar.

The Bolton game was something of a slog, too. Even Cookie agreed that the visitors had the edge for much of the match. But full credit where it's due, we changed our tune, got more involved in the nitty-gritty aspects and two goals in a minute or so sent us wild and Big Sam apoplectic. So that's all right then! And we're in fourth spot – that'll do nicely! ⚽

Fulham 3 Middlesbrough 2		
16.08.03	3rd	
Everton 3 Fulham 1		
23.08.03	11th	
Tottenham Hotspur 0 Fulham 3		
30.08.03	7th	
Birmingham City 2 Fulham 2		
14.09.03	9th	
Fulham 2 Manchester City 2		
20.09.03	10th	
Blackburn Rovers 0 Fulham 2		
28.09.03	6th	
Fulham 2 Leicester City 0		
04.10.03	4th	
Fulham 0 Wolves 0		
18.10.03	5th	
Fulham 2 Newcastle United 3		
21.10.03	6th	
Manchester United 1 Fulham 3		
25.10.03	5th	
Fulham 1 Liverpool 2		
02.11.03	6th	
Charlton Athletic 3 Fulham 1		
08.11.03	7th	
Fulham 2 Portsmouth 0		
24.11.03	5th	
Arsenal 0 Fulham 0		
30.11.03	4th	
Fulham 2 Bolton Wanderers 1		
06.12.03	4th	
Leeds United 3 Fulham 2		
14.12.03	4th	
Fulham 0 Chelsea 1		
20.12.03	4th	
Fulham 2 Southampton 0		
26.12.03	4th	
Aston Villa 3 Fulham 0		
28.12.03	5th	
Middlesbrough 2 Fulham 1		
07.01.04	7th	
Fulham 2 Everton 1		
10.01.04	6th	
Newcastle United 3 Fulham 1		
19.01.04	7th	
Fulham 2 Tottenham Hotspur 1		
31.01.04	7th	
Southampton 0 Fulham 0		
07.02.04	7th	
League Cup		
Wigan Athletic 1 Fulham 0		
23.09.03	Round 1	
FA Cup		
Fulham 2 Cheltenham Town 1		
04.01.04	Round 3	
Everton 1 Fulham 1		
25.01.04	Round 4	
Fulham 2 Everton 1		
04.02.04	aet Round 4 replay	

Positions table: 1st, 2nd, **3rd**, 4th, 5th, 6th, 7th, 8th, 9th, 10th, 11th, 12th, 13th, 14th, 15th, 16th, 17th, 18th, 19th, 20th

Ready, Steady, Cookie!

Much has been made of the poorish home gates recently. Chris Coleman issued a rallying cry before the West Ham FA Cup tie. Time for a chat with the big man...

Preparations for the next game have been disrupted by a round of International matches...?
I don't like the Internationals week as we lose 20 or so players and, yes, it disrupts training, but that's today's Fulham. I was very pleased to see Wales win, mind you! And I thought Luis Boa Morte did well against England. Luis is quick, he's direct and he had a lively 20 minutes or so. It was good to see him come on and cause a bit of havoc. It was good to see Louis Saha get a goal for France, too.

Do you think Saha would have been selected if he was still at Fulham?
Maybe, maybe not – he'd been banging in goals left, right and centre for us and he looks like he's set to do so at Manchester United. That's not harmed his International chances at all. I wasn't happy about the way his transfer came about but I can totally understand Louis wishing to play for Man United – it's just that the timing was all wrong. I wanted to wait at least until the end of the season. But that's history now – he remains a nice guy, he's still a great player and I really hope he goes on to achieve something as that will reflect well on Fulham. We've had a big say in making him the player he is today; he's blossomed this season and a lot of people at this Club can take a lot of credit for that.

How would you deal with another such instance?
We're not a big "top six" club – that's the reality, not me being defeatist – and when a really big club comes knocking it causes a problem. We've not had a decade in the top flight; in our case it's more like two minutes, so we've yet to establish ourselves. It was perhaps inevitable that we'd lose Louis in the end, I just didn't want it to happen halfway through a season; it gave me precious little time to replace him. We don't want to lose our best players and, in most circumstances, there's no reason why we should. Steed Malbranque, Sylvain Legwinski and Lee Clark have all just signed contract extensions, which is great for the Club. We've got good players here and we're doing well. If I had a bunch of unhappy players that might be different, but we've done pretty well and are eighth in the division as we speak – higher than the Club has ever finished.

We're not in the big top six, but we're surely in a better position than last season to attract players to Fulham? If nothing else, the Saha situation has shown that a move to FFC could

be a springboard to better things, at this Club or ultimately elsewhere...
I'm much more positive about attracting players to Fulham than I was in the summer – it's much more stable here now, and we've more than held our own in the top flight. The players have been different class – okay, our last couple of games have been disappointing – but, yes, on the back of the way things have gone I'd be very hopeful of being able to attract quality players here in the summer.

What's the score on your contract situation?
The Club have started the ball rolling on that one – I'd love to sign a new contract, obviously. Hopefully it won't be too long before I put pen to paper.

Things have moved on from pre-season when you were the media's favourite for the chop!
There were a few comments, weren't there? One or two fellas now managing in the Premier League said a few things which were a bit, how shall I put it, "slippery", but that's all right, the game's all about opinions, isn't it? Mind you, it's nice when we go to play their teams and turn them over – you can't blame me for sporting a big smile! We're still in the Cup and have a great chance of achieving a decent finish in the top division. But whatever happens it'll be down to me to at least match things next season. I may have proved a few people wrong up to now, but I've achieved nothing as yet.

You've made mention of the poorish gates of late – how influential are the fans during a game?
Players love to run out at a packed stadium where the atmosphere is good. We clearly play a part in the atmosphere; it takes the players to set a standard on the pitch by getting involved and so giving the crowd a lift, but the influence of a lively crowd is massive. I was disappointed in the FA Cup crowds for the Everton replay and West Ham games. I know the Everton encounter was a night game but the West Ham match was the FA Cup Fifth Round at home on a Saturday afternoon and I was surprised to see so many empty seats. I'm not in any way criticising those who were there and certainly not those who regularly follow us away from home; they're absolutely brilliant. It's just that I can guarantee that when Manchester United roll into town we'll be playing to a full house. I just wonder why – finances and commitments allowing – a few more don't turn up every week.

The only demurrals regarding your rallying cry have been on the grounds of cost (a run of games in a few weeks) and ticketing problems. It also might suggest that we've got a fairly limited

Below: Chris Coleman: "It was perhaps inevitable that we'd lose Louis Saha in the end. I just didn't want it to happen halfway through the season."

fanbase and that some find the circumstances of playing at Loftus Road a little uncomfortable?

We do have a limited fanbase compared to some, but we were regularly attracting 18-19,000 to the Cottage during our first season in the Premiership. We're heading back to the Cottage next season, but what I'm trying to say is that we really need the fans – all the Fulham fans – there with us for the rest of this season. If we're not doing the business, or they're unhappy with me, I don't mind fans voicing their opinions, but we really do want them there for matches.

These days players are earning thousands of pounds a week and yet a few more fans in the ground can make a critical difference…?

Absolutely! And the money makes no difference come matchday! When you're playing football all you want to do is to play before a noisy full house. I realise fans are longing to be back at the Cottage, but even at Loftus Road we've had some great occasions and whipped-up atmospheres. I can't stress enough how important the fans are; they've played a massive part in what we've achieved so far this season. As a former player myself I can confirm that if the fans are singing your name or singing their hearts out for the team it gives you and all your team-mates a massive lift and can frequently help you to find that extra gear.

The Aston Villa and West Ham games weren't our best performances – is it fair to say that there's even been a degree or two of showboating?

That's a fair comment, although God knows why we've been showboating because we've achieved nothing as yet. In fact having got ourselves to a certain level, now is the time for the whole Club – and I include the players, management, staff and fans – to see if we can take things up another notch. Do we want to take things forward? Are we ambitious enough as a club?

I told the lads after the West Ham game that I could sense an air of cockiness. We huffed and puffed, but we're a better side than that. I told them not to forget where we've come from and to realise too that we're at a critical stage of the season; if we can dig some decent results out then we've got a good chance of finishing quite high up the division. It'll be a shame if it all fizzles out now, we've come this far and we need to get on to the next level, but we'll only do so if we show the same levels of desire, togetherness and commitment that we showed in the first six months of the season.

Do you take a lack of those qualities personally?

If you don't take it personally and get upset when your team underperforms then you're in the wrong game. Let's not forget that we're talking about human beings here not machines and they're going to have off-days – but it all boils down to the fact that it's down to me to see that they're all properly prepared and motivated.

The Club's ambition has been questioned by some in the recent past. Are you still convinced the Club is making positive strides?

The future of the Club is more important than any one person involved with it. Much of the money we received from the sale of Louis Saha went on securing our return to Craven Cottage. But I've still got some money to spend, and I'm sure money would have been found had the right player become available during that last transfer window. There's plenty of ambition here and I'm certain I'll be able to bolster the squad in the summer without having to sell anyone, but the days when Fulham Football Club can splash £10m or more on a single player are long gone. That's not a lack of ambition, it's the reality of the situation.

Was the whole Louis Saha affair disruptive?

Definitely. And the press continue to fan the flames even after he's left Fulham – he's scoring for United, he's scoring for France, we're not a big enough club to hold on to him and all that. If I'm honest, it has been disruptive on the playing side. We've lost a bloody good player – it's up to us to close ranks and march on.

We have Manchester United coming up, Saha and all. And we've got the chance of achieving a rare double. Is it simply "just another match"?

Someone told me the only team we've managed to secure a double against in the Premiership is Spurs. If we were to grab another win against United – and that'll be a tough ask – it would be incredible, with the added spice that Louis is likely to be in their ranks. It'll be a great game – and if we're not "up" for that one then I'll have something to say!

You're a managerial new-boy who's faced all manner of unexpected hurdles – it's been a steep learning curve, hasn't it?

I've learned a hell of a lot in the first few months. And quickly! Even Bobby Robson says he's still learning, so there's plenty to come my way as yet! You can do as many football courses as you like, but there's nothing like getting the first-hand experience and, hopefully, learning from it.

Fans like to get a sense that their club is evolving – onwards and upwards – rather than drifting. You must feel the same?

Yes. And that's why it's so important that we finish the season strongly. The better the finish, the more attractive a proposition we are to any new players. We've also got the carrot of going back to Craven Cottage and all the good vibes that should entail – and we want to do so with a good platform for our first season back by the Thames. ⚽

Fulham 1 Aston Villa 2 11.02.04 8th	1st
	2nd
Wolves 2 Fulham 1 21.02.04 8th	3rd
	4th
Fulham 1 Manchester United 1 28.02.04 8th	5th
	6th
Fulham 2 Leeds United 0 13.03.04 8th	**7th**
	8th
Chelsea 2 Fulham 1 20.03.04 9th	9th
	10th
Manchester City 0 Fulham 0 27.03.04 9th	11th
	12th
Fulham 0 Birimgham City 0 03.04.04 10th	13th
	14th
Leicester City 0 Fulham 2 10.04.04 8th	15th
	16th
Fulham 3 Blackburn Rovers 4 12.04.04 10th	17th
	18th
Liverpool 0 Fulham 0 17.04.04 10th	19th
	20th
Fulham 2 Charlton Athletic 0 24.04.04 7th	
Portsmouth 1 Fulham 1 01.05.04 7th	
Fulham 0 Arsenal 1 09.05.04 9th	
Bolton Wanderers 0 Fulham 2 15.05.04 9th	
FA Cup	
Fulham 0 West Ham United 0 14.02.04 Round 5	
West Ham United 0 Fulham 3 24.02.04 Round 5 replay	
Manchester United 2 Fulham 1 06.03.04 Round 6	

181

The Craven Cottage Story

All football fans have a special affinity with their club's ground. But given the seemingly never-ending problems surrounding Craven Cottage from the mid-1980s until fairly recently, Fulham fans have a particularly close bond with the Cottage. The following is a TOOFIF take on the whole saga – how it developed and how, wonder of wonders, it all came to a fabulous conclusion. For the time being, at least!

The sight and sound of a packed Craven Cottage rocking on all sides as we progressed ever-further on our 2010 European Tour not only belied the turmoil of previous years but also underlined how right and proper the various campaigns to keep Fulham FC at the Cottage have been. The Club moved to the site in 1894, and played its first match there, a Middlesex Senior Cup encounter with Minerva, in 1896 (meaning that any local resident has moved in to the area knowing that they had a professional football club down the road – but more of that later!). However, from the mid-1980s, an interminable saga developed with regard to the future of the ground and even, at one point, the continued existence of London's oldest football club.

In the very early days of the fanzine, the Club was under the new stewardship of Jimmy Hill, Bill Muddyman and co, struggling to come to terms with the fact that Ernie Clay, Chairman from 1977 to 1986, had sold the ground to property developers Marler Estates for £9m. Clay had hatcned plans to part-develop the ground, but these were bulldozed into touch so he sold out, for a handsome profit naturally.

For decades before Clay's involvement Fulham had paid a peppercorn rent to their Church Commission landlords, but when the blunt Yorkshire businessman purchased the ground in late 1984 for £900,000 (with no stipulation about maintaining the playing of football on the site) it set off a chain of events that virtually crippled the Club and almost saw it and the ground disappear for good. A vigorous rearguard action by supporters (actually a series of campaigns) was pivotal – but the road to success was as long as it was winding.

Clay's sell-out resulted in Marler Chairman David Bulstrode becoming FFC Chairman. In February 1987 his proposed merger with QPR – Fulham Park Rangers for heaven's sake! – was staved off thanks to fans' protests, indignant public

Above: A dramatic shot of Craven Cottage given the "extra-moody" treatment by the photographer, Julian Newton.

opinion, the sale of Paul Parker and Dean Coney to QPR and the arrival in April 1987 of Jimmy Hill and his new Board of Directors. (The Fulham fans made their views on the would-be merger very clear with a peaceful on-pitch demonstration at half-time in a match against Walsall; it should be remembered that Walsall's players and fans were hugely supportive too.)

Even so, Craven Cottage was still owned by the developers and, while the respite was welcome, it was only temporary. The local Council stepped in with the aim of securing the ground via a compulsory purchase: this called for a government-sponsored public inquiry, arranged for January 1990. Yet on the eve of the inquiry Fulham FC struck their own deal with the developers – a new lease for a further three years at the ground but, with it, an agreement to leave quietly in due course in return for staged payments that could ultimately total £13m.

The deal horrified most supporters, most of whom believed the Club and the ground were inextricably linked. Sure, the future of the Club came first, but the CPO inquiry offered a realistic means of regaining the Craven Cottage site. A key argument for the pro-Cottage supporters was that there was no real Plan B. Groundsharing – with Stamford Bridge the obvious candidate – was a hot potato locally, while the only other "option" at the time was a mythical purpose-built "Legoland" stadium somewhere within the M25. What the hell was going on?

The Club argued that they couldn't take the risk of losing the CPO and so took the property developers' money – by now Marler had sold out to Cabra Estates – which included an upfront payment of £2m for withdrawing their support for the CPO. A further £3.5m would follow when the Club vacated Craven Cottage, while the remaining hand-outs were subject to various conditions being met. The new arrangements also included provisions for FFC's lease on the ground, due to expire on May 31, 1990 extended for a further three years.

The controversial deal, however, did provide the fledgling TOOFIF with an unexpected bonus: within the small print lay a clause that barred anyone from Fulham FC from commenting on the deal via its own outlets, i.e. the programme and Clubcall. Remember, this was way before the Internet, swish Club magazines and the wall-to-wall media coverage offered nowadays. The independently run TOOFIF, though, was free to carry on unhindered and probably established itself by trying to keep the magnificent diehard supporters fully in the picture (or at least as far as was possible!).

These were crazy times. A clutch of local residents, seemingly hell-bent on seeing the Club go to the wall, and with it an ensuing rise in their property prices, became highly vocal. Every syllable written at the time was closely monitored by all parties. One word inadvertently out of place could easily have led to disaster. (This was underlined when various passages from TOOFIF and FSC magazine *Cottage Pie* – I edited both at the time – were subsequently read out and discussed at the public inquiries… leaving yours truly on tenterhooks.) Thankfully no damage was done. Phew! Even so, with the Football Club having withdrawn its support, the Council's CPO was ultimately rejected; crucially, however, so were the building schemes put forward by the Council and Cabra.

At the time, the prospect of Fulham ever playing in the top flight again was nonsensical. Our cash windfall from Cabra, far from securing (or improving) our third-tier status was negated by rank bad management. Fulham FC, once of Division One (yesteryear's Premier League), and proud producers of a magical England captain in Johnny Haynes and an England World Cup winner in George Cohen, were on the wane and, unable to secure the necessary points on a miserable afternoon in Swansea, they slipped into the basement division in 1994.

The ground issue rumbled on and on. Every time the supporters thought they had engineered a winning goal, either the goalposts were moved or further time was added to the clock. But with Cabra's hopes of building luxury flats on the site taking a daily nosedive, along with their share price, this particular episode had a happy ending. The property developers' dreams went down the divisions even quicker than Fulham! Unlike Fulham, Cabra did not survive. How we cheered!

Even so, by 1996 things looked bleak indeed. The visit of Scunthorpe in January to a by-now dilapidated Craven Cottage, attracted a mere 2,176, the lowest-ever attendance at the ground for a first-class game. By February we were one off the foot of the basement division, and lost to the bottom club Torquay, 2-1. Horrible times indeed, and a true test for those supporters who still made the effort to attend.

Things could only get better, surely – the alternative was no ground, no money, no future, no hope – and, thank goodness, they did! First piece of good news came in August 1996: the Football Club's plans to part-develop the Cottage had

Below: A classic shot of the Cottage from Finlay Street.

Above: Back to the Cottage they demanded – and, in due course, back to the Cottage we went.

Below: The lights go out at Craven Cottage! Down come the floodlights in preparation for the Club's return to a plush all-seater stadium.

finally been given the go-ahead. (Earlier approval in June 1995 had been challenged by local residents and local Tory MP Matthew Carrington, which had led to another public inquiry; now the Government's Environment Secretary had given the longed-for thumbs-up.)

With that came some breathing space. And we were still at the Cottage. Now, though, we had to deal with bankrupt Cabra's principal creditors, the Royal Bank of Scotland (RBS). Fulham supporters hadn't sat idly by during all of this. In February 1993, and with Fulham's lease on the Cottage ticking down towards the May 31 deadline, the supporters unveiled their "Fulham 2000" scheme, inviting supporters from all over the land to join for £10. All monies raised would go towards the cost of a high-profile campaign to persuade RBS to deal with Fulham FC – at the time RBS were refusing to discuss either a lease or a buying option.

The first person to join Fulham 2000 was the great Johnny Haynes, followed by George Best; not a bad first pairing on the "teamsheet"! Some £20,000 was raised in the first couple of weeks – then came the news that the Royal Bank had agreed to a new 10-year lease, with Fulham FC having first option to buy.

Tantalisingly "our" Craven Cottage could indeed be ours again, but at a price. However, it was money the Club didn't have. As for the lease, little or no rent was to be paid to the Bank to begin with, as long as Fulham sought planning permission for partial development to add value to the site. The downside of this would be a scaling down of the stadium capacity to 15,000, and with it any hopes of once again competing with the big boys. Crucially, these agreements also allowed the Club to buy the freehold from the bank for around £7.5m. The Fulham 2000 group accordingly stepped up their fundraising.

It made for an upbeat atmosphere on and off the pitch. In his book *On Song For Promotion* Fulham legend Simon Morgan says: "We were starting on the right note…this was the plan, masterminded by Director and former Fulham full-back Tom Wilson, which offered Fulham the chance to own the freehold of the ground, the prospect of a substantially modernised stadium and the opportunity to pay off past debts. The long battle to save the illustrious home of Fulham Football Club from the grasp of avaricious property developers had come to a successful conclusion. It was news that the real supporters had only dreamt about in the long years of struggle."

Under Micky Adams, Fulham FC – still virtually penniless – began to make great strides and, following a fantastic squad effort, clawed its way out of the division – upwards! It was a move that heralded probably the most significant few days in the Club's history.

The Board now agreed to purchase the Cottage but could not agree on the best method. Jimmy Hill wanted to go ahead with the partial development; Vice-Chairman Bill Muddyman, though, was looking for a major investor. Suddenly it was exit Jimmy Hill… and hello Mohamed Al Fayed who rode into town promising (and in due course delivering!) Premiership football. It was also exit Micky Adams, not a big enough "name" in football for the new Chairman's grand plans. In his place came Kevin Keegan and Ray Wilkins. By then Craven Cottage had been purchased – yippee! – although it wasn't too long before it became a thorny issue once again!

The money raised by Fulham 2000 was sunk into the ground's repurchase and the £750,000 refurbishment of the Stevenage Road Stand's splendid Edwardian façade. By now, though, a grandiose new wonder-stadium was in the offing and, after yet another series of public meetings and consultations, it finally received approval… only to get dropped by FFC on the grounds of increased costs and viability. During this time, Fulham were making tracks towards the Premier League. By the time they got there in record-breaking style under Jean Tigana in 2001, post-Hillsborough rules required all top-flight clubs to have all-seater stadia. Having risen so rapidly, Fulham were allowed a 12-month period of grace, but were unable to settle anything in that time.

So, after several supposed "last-ever" games at the Cottage over the years, there was indeed a last one this time. (More than one, in fact! The final League game was a fixture against Leicester City in April 2002, but further InterToto matches, against Egaleo and FC Haka, were staged there in July.) After that off we went... to Loftus Road. A one-season stay became two as it became clear that the Club were pursuing a site at White City. With little or no information being passed to the fans, the age-old tensions and concerns resurfaced.

Before we'd even left Craven Cottage a supporters campaign, "Back to the Cottage" (BTTC), had been developed. What started off as a small group of like-minded fans distributing leaflets and engaging the media to seek answers to a number of pertinent questions, soon developed into an umbrella organisation initially within the Fulham Supporters' Club. Following a well-attended meeting at Hammersmith Town Hall, fans decided to establish the 'Fulham Supporters' Trust', emulating the successful model in place at more than 100 clubs across England, Scotland and Wales. The key aim was to encourage the Chairman and his advisers that Craven Cottage was the only viable option for Fulham FC.

One of the BTTC statements included the following: "Throughout the last six months, there has been a lack of clear information and comment and a number of contradictory statements coming from the Club on this most significant of subjects. This has undoubtedly contributed to the level of suspicion amongst many fans over the intentions the Club has for the Craven Cottage site. Fulham Football Club must correct that error to prevent the further diminishing of trust between fans and Club." Amid this confusion a number of fans decided to boycott games at Loftus Road and the Club seemed oblivious to the strength of feeling. The BTTC group forged on, though, and even (during a memorable evening at Hammersmith Town Hall) outlined in incredible technical detail how a return could be feasible.

In the summer of 2004 Fulham FC and it's ever-swelling band of supporters did indeed return to a refurbished Craven Cottage – a move that, with shades of the transfer of Paul Parker and Dean Coney to QPR in June 1987, was part-financed by the sale of Louis Saha to Manchester United for £9m. It was a move that brought relief and delight in equal measure.

Club historian (and latterly a Club Director) Dennis Turner took up the tale brilliantly in his 2007 book *Fulham The Complete Record*: "By adding all-seater stands behind the Hammersmith and Putney goals, Craven Cottage became, at a stroke, a modern football ground (thankfully, still not yet a 'stadium'), yet one which

retained its old-style charm. The 1905 Stevenage Road stand and the Cottage were still in place and untouched, the oldest surviving examples of [Archibald] Leitch's work and as such a throwback to the pre-1914 era. They are, moreover, listed buildings. But the addition of the two stands behind the goals in 2004 (the responsibility of Fulham Director and supporter Mark Collins) was done extremely tastefully and they have blended in very comfortably with the more traditional surroundings. The atmosphere with a full house (and there are quite a few these days in the top flight) is much better than at many more palatial grounds."

In July 2012 Hammersmith & Fulham Council gave the Club the thumbs-up to build a plush two-tier structure to replace the Riverside Stand, thereby increasing the ground capacity to 30,000. Those particular plans, alas, went the way of our top-flight status. Before that relegation in 2014, Owner/Chairman Al Fayed sold FFC to US business tycoon Shahid Khan in July 2013, since which time various other revamps to the riverside portion of the ground have been mooted. However, in March 2018, as we extended our promotion push, Hammersmith & Fulham Council approved the Club's plans to expand Craven Cottage. The Riverside Stand is to be redeveloped, raising the stadium capacity from 25,700 to 29,600, while a riverside walk will be opened up. Work is expected to begin on the project in the summer of 2019.

The Craven Cottage saga has been one of innumerable twists and turns. With things having looked so bleak for so long, it's wonderful that we're still able to watch our beloved football team ply their trade at their traditional home. Fulham FC and Craven Cottage remain intrinsically linked – for the foreseeable future at least! The tortuous tale also demonstrates that Boards, Managers and Players come and go over time but that the Fans – at least the Club's diehard supporters – remain constant. ⚽

Above: After two seasons as tenants at Loftus Road, Fulham returned to a wonderfully refurbished Craven Cottage in the summer of 2004.

Home Sweet Home

You may recall "Back Home", a ditty recorded (not all that tunefully!) by the 1970 England World Cup Squad. Now that we're back at Craven Cottage, perhaps we should put together an FFC 2004 rendition? It's great to be back, isn't it? And especially good to have a place we can really call home once again. And now that we are back, you have to say that the old place really looks the business.

Having been embroiled with the ground saga since the very early days of TOOFIF, it's as heartwarming to be back at Craven Cottage as it is essential that we enjoy a period of stability. All in all, it's little wonder that we've been hankering for the place. While the football set-up has made giant strides – enjoying a decent run in European competition, cementing our Premiership berth culminating in that magnificent ninth spot last term – the heart of the Club hasn't kept pace. For all the practicalities of adopting Loftus Road once the Cottage became unable to host Premiership football, it was never Home. The continuing uncertainty made the tenure that much more unbearable. Rumours and counter-rumours circulated freely while the emphasis from within the Club was switched from a grandiose, state-of-the-art complex at our historic site to another supposed set-up "somewhere in the borough". Thankfully the acquisition of the Dairy Crest site in White City never materialised. Thankfully, too, there was a further switch and the emphasis now is on Fulham Football Club plying its trade at Craven Cottage once again. Of course, it remains to be seen if it will be a long-term state of affairs.

The fans may not have had their hands on the tiller but all those concerned in the BTTC movement, now the Fulham Supporters' Trust,

should be congratulated for diligently, and with plenty of expertise, pressing the point that we should – and could – return home. Clearly sincere thanks, too, should go to the powers-that-be at the Club – not least the Chairman for rubberstamping the move and footing the bill.

Considering we were up in fourth or fifth spot for much of the opening half of last season, and that a number of the perceived "top" teams continued to drop points, it could be argued that a final placing of ninth in the Premiership was a little disappointing. Having regrouped admirably after the much-publicised and protracted departure of Louis Saha, it would only have taken another few measly points to have finished even higher, and to have claimed a Euro spot.

We'd all have settled for a top ten finish at the season's start, though. And it was certainly very pleasing to ram the predictions of many so-called experts back from whence they came. With knobs on. It's been a continuing theme in TOOFIF over the years that, whatever the division and whatever the circumstances, we've been largely overlooked by the media (except when Sir Red Nose wants your star striker) and patronised as a club whose raison d'etre is more to make up the numbers rather than actually take on the big boys.

True, it's probably preferable to make blindside runs, and to use those media put-downs as a gee-up (while sticking two-fingers up at the blinkered/biased individuals – but being Fulham, doing so very politely!). Better than being in the spotlight and playing with a huge weight of expectation on the shoulders.

Chris Coleman and co proved a lot of people wrong last year but, as Cookie himself says, that was last season and we've got to aim just as high this time out. Certainly the new acquisitions have bolstered the squad, with Claus Jensen reckoned by many to be the pick of the signings. Shame, then, that Boa chose to head off to Greece and that fellow maverick Steeeeed (is it five e's or six, I'm never sure?) is out for a few weeks. While nothing's guaranteed in the top division, we have a reasonable set of games to begin with – much like last season when we did well in terms of racking up points as well as confidence. Surely the return to the Cottage will be a beneficial factor – and reason alone to raise the noise levels.

So what have the pundits predicted this time around? Well, the following is purely a toe in the water (or in other words just from those journals I was able to scrounge!). *FourFourTwo* notes that "Despite being marooned at Loftus Road and denied the riches lavished upon his predecessors, Coleman presided over the

Opposite page: A couple of cartoons by Steve Bishop capture some of the sentiments doing the rounds as we headed back to the Cottage.

Below: The players show their appreciation to the fans after our last game as tenants at Loftus Road. Now let's get back to the Cottage!

THE GREEN POLE DOESN'T SEEM TO HAVE THE SAME MAGIC!

BISHOP

most successful season in Fulham's history." But the mag reckons that "unless they find a cutting edge to finish moves off, they're more likely to repeat last Spring's post-Saha plod than the blazing form of Autumn."

Gary Lineker's middle of the road comments in the *Sunday Telegraph*'s Premiership Guide are, well, unremarkable. "Now they're back at Craven Cottage, there's no reason why they should not do well. Steed Malbranque and new-signing Andy Cole will be a key to their campaign." Lineker also tips Collins John as our "next Wayne Rooney". Pretty remarkable, 'cos he's not what I'd call ugly!

The People's Frank Wiechula tips us as his surprise package: "I'm still chewing my way through the plate of humble pie sent to me by Mohamed Al Fayed after tipping their demise last season. A Euro place and I might get an invite to dine at Harrods." The same paper's Lee Clayton, however, puts Cookie in the sack race frame, saying that "Chris Coleman of Fulham could find the heat too much second time around."

In the *Daily Express*, David Pleat, that wise old football sage, tips Fulham to finish in eighth spot. "We will once again this season enjoy watching Steed Malbranque twisting and manoeuvring the ball to great effect for Fulham. With Andy Cole hopefully motivated again following his move to the Club, Tomasz Radzinski quick in the box, Brian McBride strong and Luis Boa Morte surging, boss Chris Coleman can continue to sleep relatively easily. Another advantage for Fulham will be being back by the Thames again – but watch out for the breeze." Ho-ho – and you watch out for those flashing blue lights, David!

The *Sunday Times* suggest that if Fulham "were a cartoon character" they'd be "The Jetsons" – 'cos we "never quite caught the public's imagination." Very droll. As for a prediction, they tip us to finish

11th "slipping a bit, but nothing terminal". *The Guardian*, meantime, are way off the mark in describing Cookie as having "deathly pale skin" and Facundo Sava as his worst buy. Whatever you think of the Argentinian, he wasn't bought by CC! The paper says "if they were a biscuit" Fulham would be "Ritz Crackers – [they] offer an immediate explosion of taste but they have been known to crumble readily." Hmm, let's see, shall we? ⚽

Back at the Cottage

Tom Greatrex, BTTC Chairman, on our return home…

A friendly football match between Fulham FC and the honest toilers of Watford may not sound to everyone like the best way to spend a Saturday in July. However there were thousands of us who were unable to wait until the start of the new football season to see a match at the newly refurbished Craven Cottage – even if it did involve 40 substitutes!

The feeling on Saturday was sheer joy, after a bleak two-year period away, Fulham were back where we belong – in Fulham. Many of us, myself included, sometimes doubted we would ever see Fulham back at Craven Cottage again. After all, there had been plenty of worrying revelations sufficient to dishearten even the most optimistic of Fulham fans – the abandonment of the original plans for redeveloping Craven Cottage, the secret conditional sale of the ground to a shadowy group of property developers and leaked news about an attempt to secure a site for a new stadium in White City.

However the announcement, at the end of 2003, that we were returning home marked a turn in fortunes. The summer months have proved even more pleasing – it became increasingly clear that the Club have not spent the minimum and constructed a "quick-fix" solution, but have gone the extra mile and built something far

Manchester City 1 Fulham 1	1st
14.08.04 5th	**2nd**
Fulham 2 Bolton Wanderers 0	3rd
21.08.04 2nd	4th
Fulham 0 Middlesbrough 2	5th
25.08.04 8th	6th
Portsmouth 4 Fulham 3	7th
30.08.04 13th	8th
Fulham 0 Arsenal 3	9th
11.09.04 15th	10th
West Brom 1 Fulham 1	11th
18.09.04 15th	12th
Fulham 1 Southampton 0	13th
25.09.04 11th	14th
Crystal Palace 2 Fulham 0	15th
04.10.04 14th	16th
	17th
League Cup	18th
Boston United 1 Fulham 4	19th
22.09.04 Round 2	20th

I'M 4 A COTTAGE RETURN

LOFTUS ROAD

GOOD BYE.

BISHOP

There's only one F in Fulham
1988 2004
16 YEARS
£2.50
72 PAGES!!!

We're back... YIPPEE!!!

Inside:
Craven Cottage photo-file; Supporters' Trust latest; Commemorating O'Farrell and more at the Cliffie; chat with the Chairman; and much, much more...

Issue 91   August-September 2004

AN ALTERNATIVE LOOK AT FULHAM F.C.

187

"Ashford away in the Cup was the most ludicrous, awful football experience I've ever endured. It was pouring with rain, and the ground was completely unsuitable for anything other than mud wrestling."

better. Perhaps most striking are the changes to the Putney End. Where previously a crumbling open terrace had been located, the new Putney End is now a modern roofed stand, with neat seating. Seen in context, with the Cottage intact to one corner, the protected tree by the Thames still peeking out at the other and FULHAM confidently emblazoned in the black and white seats is a splendid sight: the old blending in with the new beautifully.

As Chairman of the Fulham Supporters Trust, the organisation that has coordinated the "Back to the Cottage" campaign, I can confirm that things really don't get much better. Fulham fans are rightly grateful to the Chairman for listening to their concerns – he should be congratulated for having the foresight and wisdom to recognise Fulham should return to Craven Cottage. The Club must never again consider half-baked plans to move from our historic home. It is no exaggeration to suggest that such a move could place the very future of the Club we love in jeopardy. It is clear that in recent times Mr Al Fayed has been particularly poorly advised by some of those around him. He was told it was impossible to have a Premiership-compliant stadium at Craven Cottage without spending more than £100m – the reality is that we have returned for a fraction of that price.

However, Saturday was not a day for inquests. While there remains much to be done, the sight of a Fulham team running out onto the pitch from Craven Cottage was a wonderful way to demonstrate the progress that has been made. The Club has made the practical, prudent and popular decision to come home. Put simply – we are back, and on behalf of all Fulham fans everywhere, thank you Mr Al Fayed for making it happen. ⚽

Below: The Jimmy Hill puppet from *Spitting Image* is pictured apparently catching up on the goings-on in and around Craven Cottage.

Have You Got Views For Us?

A chat with author, comedy scriptwriter and Fulham fan John O'Farrell...

So John, why Fulham?
Good question! When I moved to London I made a conscious decision to find a club that suited me. I went to Spurs when they were pressing for the championship in '85 but, squashed in the terraces there, hated it! I went to see Wimbledon at Plough Lane and it was a case of "Hmm, yeah all right" but it didn't really grab me. I even went to Chelsea and, well,

enough said. Then I went to Craven Cottage and it was virtually empty, the match was dismal, the players were rubbish and thought "Hey, this fits perfectly!" If anyone needed my support it was this club!

So that was your introduction to Fulham – and you were hooked…?
It was the place as much as anything. It was so nice being able to enjoy a pint alongside the river afterwards. It all felt comfortable and right. I decided to stick with them and hoped that with my support they'd go up a division. Of course we were relegated.

Was it life changing?
Well there'd be times that I'd book the family a weekend away in, say, Devon and, once there, would say with enormous surprise, "Oh look, Fulham are playing down the road at Torquay." (And we managed a 1-0 win, too – I was right behind the goal, although I can't remember who scored [Udo Onwere!]).

Any other awayday memories?
They say you weren't a soldier in the Second World War if you weren't at Dunkirk. I'd say you can't call yourself a Fulham fan if you weren't at Ashford. Ashford away in the Cup was the most ludicrous, awful football experience I've ever endured. It was pouring with rain, and the ground was completely unsuitable for anything other than mud wrestling. The "ground" was simply a field in the countryside that was, wet or not, unable to cope with thousands of Fulham fans. We could barely see any of the so-called action and were getting soaked through and caked in mud.

Fulham are heading back to the Cottage for the new season. Has the whole ground issue affected your support for the Club?
It saddened me greatly when I thought we were never going to go back to the Cottage. I really had a bad feeling about the move to Loftus Road. It's really important to fans to be able to identify with something and, while Chairmen, directors and managers may sometimes have different priorities to those of the fans, a club's name, the ground, the kit and the history is so very important. Had we been hauled off to some new bloody stadium in Tolworth or wherever, then it would been another MK Dons scenario for me. So yes, I care passionately about the ground and I'm really delighted we're going back. I was there for the Watford game and think the ground is just perfect – I wouldn't want it any bigger, I wouldn't want to lose the Cottage in the corner, and I think the black and white seating looks fantastic.

We're riding high now, but what was your abiding memory of life at the wrong end of the League?
Going out to Hayes in the Cup! That was dismal. And what about drawing 0-0 with Hereford, when they played much of the game with just nine men? I remember Scarborough doing the double over us. Alan Dicks, oh dear. There was a real masochism about going along in those days, and the moaners were given plenty of scope! We seemed to play game after game without getting the ball anywhere near our opponents' penalty box. Going out to Yeovil was also pretty grim.

You mentioned moaners; there were plenty of *Grumpy Old Men* moments in those days.
Oh yes! Part of the joy of supporting a football club is having something to moan about – and we had a field day back then. Some people can drive you mad – I mean there was one guy who screamed abuse at the players when we missed a chance against Swansea many moons ago, even though we were 7-0 up at the time! But even these days, when you're one-all with Manchester United, are awarded a penalty, and bloody Bartez spends ten minutes cleaning his boots and Steed is sufficiently distracted to fail with the spot kick, then you're not going to sit there in silence, are you?

Your CV's impressive, but just how important in the grand scheme of things was your involvement with TOOFIF all those years ago?
When people ask me what I've done in the past, they're not interested in *Spitting Image*, *Have I Got News For You* or *Chicken Run*, I always say I used to co-write a cartoon strip, called the Two Stewards, for a few issues of TOOFIF, or that I wrote a cod interview with Jimmy Hill – and these are the main things that stand out on my CV obviously. I did the cartoon strip with my friend Tom Goffe – who I still go to Fulham with. Tim did the drawings and I did the bulk of the text. Funnily enough, of all the writing that I've written over the years it's what I've received the least feed-back on. I used to watch people reading it around the ground and they'd never say anything to the person next to them or dwell on it in any way, it was more a case of flicking over to the next page! The Club's fortunes were on the change then – once Al Fayed had come in there was much less to make jokes about!

Spitting Image is rumoured to be making a comeback. But whatever happened to that Jimmy Hill puppet?
I don't know to be honest! I've not seen it since we dug it out to do the photo-shoot for the TOOFIF interview.

You're an experienced writer these days, and you've incorporated the names of Fulham

Above: Author and comedy scriptwriter John O'Farrell, pictured in front of the famous Fulham FC gable.

players in your books... what's that all about?
When I was putting together my first novel I soon realised that you can waste a lot of time trying decide on the names for your characters. So I thought I'd pick a Fulham squad as a database of names and pluck one out as and when I needed it. The Fulham set-up under Micky Adams was fairly obscure nationally, so it wasn't as if too many people would sit up and notice. In fact, I made my lead character Michael Adams; you'll also find a Darren Freeman and references to pretty much most of the squad. Oh, and there's a Mrs Morgan...

...You got that one about right...!
...plus an Angus, and just about all of that promotion squad. It turned out to be a very efficient way of short-cutting that particular problem and it was also my way of saying thanks to that team for hauling us out of the bottom division. Heady days. ⚽

Haynes, a Maestro? Tosh!

So, who's the most appropriate person to ask to sum up Johnny Haynes? Look no further than Tosh Chamberlain – himself a Fulham legend – a long-time teammate and left-wing foil, but an even longer friend of John. If you're still not convinced, consider the following tale recounted by Alan Mullery...

"I was given a ticket to sit on the track round the pitch and watch the first team. There was an empty seat next to me and, with the game going on, the Fulham No. 11, who I only later learned was called Tosh Chamberlain, came and sat next to me. He said: 'I haven't seen the ball for 20 minutes!' With that he crossed his legs, grabbed a cigarette from a nearby fella and started to have a smoke. Next thing, Johnny Haynes hits one of his inch-perfect 60-yard passes to where his winger should have been. Haynesy gave him the biggest rollicking I've ever heard. So Tosh stands up and takes one last drag, stubs out the fag and shouts back: 'When I'm standing there you don't want to pass it, and when I'm having a fag, you give me a pass'. That was Fulham. And that was when I knew I had to join this football club."

Tosh, of course, was also the reason Johnny Haynes came to Fulham...

When did you first meet Johnny Haynes?
I was playing for Islington against Edmonton, when we were 13 or 14. John played for Edmonton – and I did my very best to kick him!

You became mates right away?
We got friendly after we played against each other a couple of times – in fact our friendship blossomed because of his mother and father, who treated me like a son. Great people.

You went to Fulham before John?
In 1948, when I was nearly 15, I joined the Fulham groundstaff. Tottenham and Arsenal both tried to poach John, but I told him: "Why go to either of those clubs – come with me to Fulham". It was, and is, a great club. I said, "You'll get in the first team and get the same wages as elsewhere." So he joined Fulham.

Did he ever regret that?
[Laughs] You'll have to ask John that! No, he was well looked after by Fulham. I don't think many other clubs would have given him £100 a week once it became possible. But I'd like to have seen John

win something. When Whitey [John White] of Tottenham died, I wondered why John didn't have a couple of years at White Hart Lane. With no disrespect to Fulham, he had more chance of winning an FA Cup medal or whatever there, but he was content where he was. John said to me, "I've got all I want here and I'm playing for England, so why go?"

What was he like as a player?
Superb. We were having a technical talk at the Club one day and a young kid asked Ron Greenwood about John. He said he was blessed with "peripheral vision". The kid asked, "What's peripheral vision?" Another player butted in, "It means he's got eyes up his arse"! Which was about right!

You scored with your first kick on your Fulham debut. Johnny Haynes didn't – doesn't that give you an edge over him?
Too bloody right! He didn't have everything, you know! No, I just hit the ball that day and in it went. Great feeling, though.

But for the benefit of those who didn't see him play, how good was John?
Beckham gets all the headlines today, but John had a far superior range of passing. He could pass the ball anywhere. And, don't forget, we were playing with leather footballs, not balloons. John could hit a wonderfully weighted pass and had such vision to see the moves as they developed. He was a moaning sod at times – but a top-drawer player!

He was given the nickname "Narky", wasn't he?
That's right, but that was only because of the perfectionist in him. If I have a slight criticism of him, it's that he should have scored more goals. He scored plenty, I know, but he had such great technique and mastery of the ball – he could strike a wonderful half-volley for instance – that I feel he should have gone for goal a bit more often.

What's your favourite memory of John the player?
Oh, every game! He seldom played badly. John was totally dedicated and drove himself to reach consistently high standards. A number of his performances for England rank very highly, naturally, but the mere fact that I played outside-left to him for a number of seasons is a sound enough memory.

You had some cross words from time to time?
Not really. As I said, John was a perfectionist who was as tough on himself as he was on those around him who, sometimes, weren't on his wavelength.

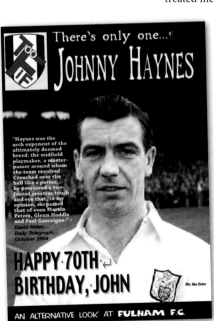

Above: Johnny Haynes (*left*) lines up for a team photo alongside his pal since schooldays, Trevor "Tosh" Chamberlain.

Below: Issue 92 included a 70th-birthday tribute to Johnny Haynes.

He had a nark at Cooky [Maurice Cook] or me or whoever – but it was always instantly forgotten (at least it was once I'd had my say, too!).

You were very different players and it was a different era?
John was a superb passer of the ball and a gifted midfield schemer. I knew what I could do – I could hit the ball hard and I could run. I also did plenty of crazy things and got on his nerves. In one game I was given an overhit pass from someone that knocked me right over the touchline. John called me a choice word for not controlling the ball. The ref went to John to take his name, yet John was insistent: "But that's his name – it's what we always call him!" The ref went off laughing. Another time I gave John some verbals back and the following Monday I had to report to Frank Osborne for swearing at John! By then, of course, we were laughing about the whole affair. It was all spur of the moment stuff. The truth is, we got on so well – and still do. The beauty of when I played is that it was the spectators who paid the players' wages – there was little or no advertising. So I went out to give my all for Fulham, naturally, but also to entertain those on the terraces. I did some things that, in today's climate, they'd probably sack me for – like sitting on the line and having a chat to the spectators. Johnny, meantime, would do his conkers. But that was me. I'd have to adopt a different approach today. It's a business these days, pure and simple.

You and John put in a fair few years for FFC – how would you sum up the Club?
Oh everything about Fulham was lovely. It was a super club. And there were no nasty players either. It was a friendly club, make no mistake about that. The comradeship amongst the players in my day was tremendous – and we're still big mates. And there was real quality there, too – one year we had Macedo, Cohen, Langley, Mullery, Bentley, Lowe, Stevens, Robson, Jezzard, Haynes and I got in too, somehow. That was just after Charlie Mitten finished. But for all those wonderful names, John was the Club's kingpin. The crowd loved him. The players loved him...

...and of course you loved him to bits...?
[Laughing mischievously…] No, not really!! ⚽

A Mark Halsey-induced Rant!
I'm writing to TOOFIF about some rumours that have started to circulate as a result of the Arsenal game and the matches that followed. First, I think we can dispel the theory that there was a second shooter behind the grassy knoll when Andy Cole went down – or that Chris Coleman hypnotised Mr Halsey into saying those things

about the reaction of the players making him change his mind. And also that Collins John's life-threatening challenge rightly forced him to disallow that "goal". No, it's the ensuing game that I'm hearing all kinds of conspiracy theories about.

I've heard it said that that nice man Mr Purse should have been sent off for his challenge on Papa Diop. Now, surely we all know what a nice man Mr Purse is, and it couldn't have been that bad a foul as the BBC didn't think it was even worth showing in their highlights package. Instead they homed in on that heinous crime of sitting behind the dugout (in a quiet and humble manner) once sent off. Good old Auntie Beeb – that'll stop him from being so nasty, eh? It was even suggested that nice Mr Purse deliberately stepped on nasty Mr Diop's foot. Surely not! The referee did not see it and the BBC did not bother to look at that aspect of the incident, so it must be a rumour – and simply another excuse to make Fulham out to be the new Crazy Gang.

Then our Andy, the naughty boy, got involved. It's been said that he was stamped on. The BBC cleared that one up, too: Neil Clement probably did not realise Cole was there when he put his head into Andy's and then subsequently grabbed his throat. No one mentioned this, so it couldn't have happened. My friend says that nice Mr Purse threw a punch. Surely not, our Andy did, for all the world to see. It will be interesting to see if, once the dust has settled, Mr Clement receives another red card to go with the yellow and red he'd already accumulated. But his role was barely mentioned, so he's bound to escape. After all, nasty Andy started it all, didn't he, so he must get a lengthier ban.

Oh, and another friend, who keeps up with all the latest nuances in football law interpretations, asked: "Is there not meant to be daylight between attacker and defender for offside to be given?" Not at West Brom, apparently. So another goal chalked off then. And that psycho John makes it into the ref's post-match talk when the official tells anyone who'd listen that Fulham are a bunch of moaning minnies and he's going to report us, citing more charges than the Light Brigade, and that he's never heard the like in all his years. Probably didn't tune in to the Arsenal match that was, what, a whole one week before.

Funny, one week we don't moan enough, but the next week we moan too much and have the book thrown at us. No coincidence, then, that at Boston one player collects two yellows, the second a bit harsh. Before that, though, 15 minutes to go and a Boston player takes our player out. No booking, only a few minutes to go after all; it's 4-1 and not worth the hassle. Then in the dying seconds Mr Rosenior, the cheating little tyke, takes a dive ('cos we desperately needed a fifth!) and the referee gives him a second yellow, which meant that the scallywag had to leave the field. I heard that nice Mr Craig Brown on the radio later, and he

<table><tr><td>Fulham 2 Liverpool 4
16.10.04 16th</td><td>1st
2nd
3rd</td></tr><tr><td>Aston Villa 2 Fulham 0
23.10.04 17th</td><td>4th
5th</td></tr><tr><td>Fulham 2 Tottenham Hotspur 0
30.10.04 15th</td><td>6th
7th</td></tr><tr><td>Newcastle United 1 Fulham 4
07.11.04 12th</td><td>8th
9th</td></tr><tr><td>Fulham 1 Chelsea 4
13.10.04 13th</td><td>10th
11th</td></tr><tr><td>Everton 1 Fulham 0
20.11.04 13th</td><td>12th
13th</td></tr><tr><td>Fulham 0 Blackburn Rovers 2
27.11.04 14th</td><td>14th
15th</td></tr><tr><td>Norwich City 0 Fulham 1
04.12.04 14th</td><td>16th
17th</td></tr><tr><td>Fulham 1 Manchester United 1
13.12.04 14th</td><td>18th
19th
20th</td></tr><tr><td>Charlton Athletic 2 Fulham 1
20.12.04 15th</td><td></td></tr><tr><td>Arsenal 2 Fulham 0
26.12.04 15th</td><td></td></tr><tr><td>Fulham 2 Birmingham City 3
28.12.04 16th</td><td></td></tr><tr><td>Fulham 3 Crystal Palace 1
01.01.05 15th</td><td></td></tr><tr><td>League Cup</td><td></td></tr><tr><td>Birmingham City 0 Fulham 1
27.10.04 Round 3</td><td></td></tr><tr><td>Nottingham Forest 2 Fulham 4
10.11.04 aet Round 4</td><td></td></tr><tr><td>Fulham 1 Chelsea 2
30.11.04 Round 5</td><td></td></tr></table>

said there had been contact – but then again he's Scottish so what does he know about football?

The ref was right. As was Mr Halsey. And Mr Dean at West Brom. And look, we've got that nice Chelsea-supporting Mr Poll for the Southampton game. As OJ Simpson told me, conspiracy theories can get you into trouble – look what happened to him (luckily justice saw through in that case). Yes, it's all a whole load of trumped-up charges and merely coincidence that it all brewed up after Halsey made such an arse of himself in that Arsenal game. Paranoid? Aaarrrggghhh! ⚽

Jim Cox, "The Hammy End Wag"

You Are The Ref!

Hi there all you budding referees. Described here are everyday footballing circumstances, but you're in charge. How well do you know the laws of the game? If you're a bit vague on all of this, don't worry, you're in very good company! So, read the circumstances very carefully and have your whistles at the ready. What would YOU do?

1 A player runs goalwards but, as he cuts into the penalty area, he's tripped by a defender. The offence warrants a card. However, not only has the attacker been denied a clear goalscoring opportunity, the defender is the last man bar the goalkeeper. You are perfectly placed and can tell that the tripping incident takes place three yards inside the area. So, would you:
a) Automatically award the spot kick and send off the defender;
b) Consider other factors, e.g. "might it affect the defending team's chances of success?";
c) Phone your mum for advice;
d) On no account give the penalty if the defending team is Man. United or Arsenal;
e) Go to check with your assistant to see if the manager of the defending team has passed word to him about what you should do. Note that this is something of a trick question – if Luis Boa Morte is the attacking player, you should automatically simply smile and wave away all claims of a penalty and, of course, caution the cheating scumbag for diving as soon as the ball goes out of play.

2 After blowing your whistle for an infringement you are surrounded by a pack of players moaning and whinging at your decision. Do you:
a) Give them a final warning that the decision's been made and that your decision is final and – if they continue to bleat – caution them as necessary;
b) If it's a non-glamour side, book the lot of 'em straight away and subsequently report the team to the authorities;
c) If it's Gary Neville and co. involved, stand your ground for a little while longer (they might just self-implode, which would be a giggle) before remembering that you'll only get the hair-drier treatment from Fergie later. Best course in this instance is to reverse your decision and to make a mental note to add at least five minutes at the end of the match to more than make up for your own time-wasting.
d) If it's Arsenal, take into account their extraordinary unbeaten run, apologise most humbly and reverse your decision right away (after taking a gentle stroll to your nearest assistant to ask him where he's going for a beer afterwards).

3 Player A commits a dreadful foul on player B. Do you:
a) Send player A off right away;
b) Wave your finger at player A giving player B the chance to take retribution – thereby giving you the opportunity to send him off, the nasty piece of work;
c) Send off both players (as long as player B is Robbie Savage);
d) Brandish the red card at player A but then turn your back on affairs, so allowing all hell to break out. This, of course, allows you to get rid of more players. It means there's more paperwork involved, but it guarantees your picture in the tabloids and Auntie Bessie will see that her favourite nephew has got an important job at last. She'll be pleased to note that the days of being the playground bully are long gone.

4 Player A, sandwiched between two burly defenders, rises well under pressure to head the ball into the net. Do you:
a) Award the goal (noting the time in your notebook and mentally consider that, with only seconds to go before the break, it's a "great time to score");
b) Realise how damaging it is for the defending team to concede a goal so close to the half time and, as it's Arsenal, give the poor luvvies a break;
c) Let the young striker think he's scored for a moment. As he and his team-mates set off on their celebrations, tip Arsenal the wink and let them restart – thereby taking full advantage of the other team being completely out of position;
d) Realise, with a start, that you'd been daydreaming about a string of previous nightmare decisions, so much so that you hadn't noticed any of the recent action. Best to disallow the goal and allow everyone to regroup for the second half. It's only fair. ⚽

Below: Under the spotlight in *Zoo* – TOOFIF and Ask Cliffie!

'Zine Zone

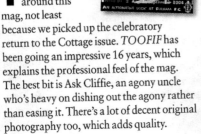

We're back... YIPPEE!!!

ZOO has a read of football's funniest fan rags This week: *TOOFIF* – There's Only One F In Fulham

There's a feel-good factor around this mag, not least because we picked up the celebratory return to the Cottage issue. *TOOFIF* has been going an impressive 16 years, which explains the professional feel of the mag. The best bit is Ask Cliffie, an agony uncle who's heavy on dishing out the agony rather than easing it. There's a lot of decent original photography too, which adds quality.

The Curious Diddygate Saga

Fans Restore Diddy David

Many of you might not be aware that our own Mike Phillips is a fanatical Fulham fan and has supported them from a young lad. We relate this because I was very disturbed to hear from Mike that Diddy David Hamilton had been relieved of his on-the-pitch duties at Craven Cottage. The Board of Directors had decided to "do away" with this very professional broadcaster who has been a Fulham fan for many years. He was on the Board at Craven Cottage for a while. Well, together with *The Sun* newspaper, the fans of Fulham have brought pressure to bear on the Directors to reinstate the wee man.

This is a great result for someone who is heart and soul behind the Club and does not expect a whacking big fee for going on the pitch. Suddenly you have someone not very knowledgeable about the Club paid to produce some overblown build-up for a Premiership club playing to a full house of supporters who want to voice their own approval. No wonder there is only one F in Fulham.

Alan Hutchison, writing in the Wycombe matchday programme

Diddy David's no Whipping Boy

Not a good Wednesday night for Fulham. Not only were they dreadful in a 2-0 loss to Middlesbrough but the Club's glamorous PR team were left feeling small by Diddy David Hamilton. The Fulham spin team vehemently denied claims that former Radio One DJ Hamilton had been axed as the Club's PA announcer and were especially scathing about claims that he had been dumped for not being "good enough at whipping up a crowd".

Yet minutes after their briefing, Hamilton – having been given his job back by Fulham owner Mohamed Al Fayed – strode onto the pitch and declared: "They sacked me because I was not good enough at whipping up a crowd! I want you all to prove them wrong."

Daily Mirror

David Explains all. Well, nearly all...

"It's been a funny few weeks. I was told shortly after the end of last season that my services were no longer required as I didn't fit in with the new 'Fortress Fulham' image. Apparently it was considered that I was unable to 'work the crowd' in the way that was now required. After having to put up with Loftus Road for two years and all the rigmarole that went with it, I felt more than a little let down. Like everyone else, I'd been thoroughly looking forward to our return to the Cottage. I have to say that, having compered hundreds of pop shows, I didn't quite understand what they were on about.

"But here I was shunted out of the match-day job. If that was a shock, what followed really surprised me! First there were a whole host of messages on the various FFC-related Internet sites – mostly complimentary, for which I'm very grateful – then *The Sun* got in on the act. Reporter Dave Kidd – a Fulham fan – ran his "Diddygate" piece. Mind you, I think he was stretching things a little bit when he suggested Chris Coleman had a hand in the decision!

"It was great that 87 per cent of people who took part in the *Sun* poll voted for me to be re-instated. But the real reason I got the job back was down to the Chairman.

"On the Monday after the Bolton match one of our directors, Mark Collins, phoned me during my morning radio show to ask if I would call in to Harrods to see Mr Al Fayed that afternoon. I had no idea what was in store. When I got there, the Chairman walked into the boardroom and plonked on the table two presents for me – a bottle of Scotch Whisky and some Viagra tablets!

"As you can imagine, I was more than a little bemused – and unsure as to what might follow. But he simply asked me what had happened and, after I'd told him, he declared emphatically, 'Right, I want you back on Wednesday'.

"Lots of other things were said, which, I'm afraid, must remain private. Suffice to say, much of it was highly amusing – and yet enough of the serious stuff convinced me that this is a man who cares deeply about the Club and whose heart is very much in Fulham."

Fulham's midweek match was against Middlesbrough. "By the Wednesday I was back on duty – for what turned out to be a thoroughly miserable game. It was a real shame that I wasn't on the mike for the curtain-raiser, that terrific victory over Bolton to mark our Premiership return to the Cottage, but that's all water under the bridge now.

"I can tell you that the ground not only looks great but it sounds great too! The enclosed nature of the revamped ground means that things sound a lot noisier now. It really does bring a tingle to the spine when the crowd is cheering – and that's only when I oversee the Fulham Flutter draw, so imagine what it's like for the players with the crowd in full voice! Keep it up!!

"Now that we're back where we belong, you've got to say that the Chairman has kept his promise and it's up to us, the fans, to make sure the ground is full every week. I'm not suggesting that everyone is compelled to make it to every single match (I'm not that insensitive – people cannot always attend for a variety of reasons) but broadly speaking now is the time to show our support to the Chairman and to the team by ensuring that our return is backed up by the numbers of bums on seats.

"Oh, and the other piece of good news is that the Viagra is working!"

In the Relegation Mix, Alas

Enduring countless sterile performances has been a depressing experience this season. All the while we've been expecting our season to kick-start into life with the talent available, yet here we are going into the final batch of games facing a genuine threat of being relegated. Throughout the campaign there have been a clutch of clubs in a worse state than us up to now, but, while we should still have enough about us, we've not only failed to pull clear but have been dragged into the mix. On top of that, plenty of us are now doubting whether we have the wherewithal to keep our heads above water.

This is no overnight knee-jerk assessment but is based on what we've had to watch and on our perilous position in the table. Some of our performances have been shambolic – devoid of heart, wit and even competence. The stifling formation – preferred by so many in the top flight – has hardly been a rip-roaring success. And yet

if we do stay up, a prerequisite from day one, I suppose it will be deemed worthwhile.

The much-debated line-up – intended as 4-3-3 but effectively 4-5-1 due to the seeming inability of some of the players to conform or even, at times, to join in – is something of a red herring. Had it been seen to be working (as it did remarkably well for most of last season) then there'd be few complaints from supporters. Even the purists would be generally supportive if points were being racked up and some progress made. And even this season, a decent League placing would override the mind-numbingly ordinary performances. But that hasn't happened.

We made giant strides last season, of course, with Louis Saha spearheading our attack – a far more mobile player than Andy Cole and far more suited to the lone central attacking role. So why stick to the formation if it doesn't work? Maybe, in the Manager's eyes, because it should have. Say what you like, we were making plenty of chances earlier in the season. But it helps if the ball is passed somewhere in the vicinity of the intended recipient. Seventy-yard punts over Cole's head are simply hopeless. Is this down to a lack of confidence or inability? If it's the former, it's hard to understand how confidence can be allowed to get so low – this is a professional Premiership footballing set-up, after all. Why hasn't this been sorted out? Beats me!

Crucially, our defence, which was so tight in '03-04, has been anything but this time around. Some of the basic errors seen have belonged to Sunday Parks football. How many times have we seen two players going for the same ball apparently without calling, for instance? And what about the occasion when we won a corner and no one went over to take it! In other circumstances that would be funny; the way things have been going, though, it's been embarrassing to witness.

Sure, mistakes are there to be made, that's not the point (this is a pressure sport and we're generally supportive of rickets – if not always at the time! – if players are seen to be giving their all). But we've got a reasonable squad, one that was by general consensus bolstered by pre-season signings, and yet it has looked at times as if they've never met before. So is it down to tactics, lack of confidence or inability? Or all three?

One mitigating factor is the number of injuries picked up – losing playmakers Steed Malbranque and Claus Jensen from our fairly thin squad for most of the season has proved a great loss. And it's certainly true that for much of the season Chris Coleman's been unable

Opposite page right: Lee Clark, who's reckoned to be "Classic Captain material and inspirational on and off the field."

Below: A letter of thanks to TOOFIF from the Dandelion Trust after the fanzine raised £815 for the Sri Lankan Tsunami Appeal.

THE DANDELION TRUST

41 The Limehouse Cut, 46 Morris Road, London E14 6NQ
Tel: 020 7538 5633   Email: mail@dandeliontrust.org   Fax: 020 7537 7099

David Lloyd
11 Johnson's Close
Carshalton
Surrey
SM5 2LU

15th March 2005

Dear David

Thank you so much for your donation of £815.00 which we received on Friday. This is a fantastic fundraising achievement and has significantly increased the funds available for Mr. Perera's project. Please pass on our gratitude to everyone who contributed through TOOFIF.

Please find to follow an update on the Dandelion Trust Sri Lanka appeal. If you know of anyone who might be willing to offer us further support we would be most grateful if you could circulate this report to them.

Thank you again for supporting this appeal. We would like to wish you the best of luck with your excellent fanzine (and that's coming from an Arsenal supporter!)

Yours sincerely,

Caroline Glitre
Office Manager

The Dandelion Trust Sri Lanka Appeal
- Report on Progress so far -

"The villages still exist, just the buildings have been destroyed, but the communities remain"
"Local people need a say in recovery and reconstruction"
"We need to rebuild livelihoods based on sustainability"

- **Uchita de Zoysa** - Executive Director CED (The Centre for Environment and Development). Facilitator of Peoples' Task Force during Disasters and Alliance 2020. Also presents the most comprehensive assessment of the situation in Sri Lanka we've found so far available at www.suscom.org

Registered Charity Number: 328159
Patrons: David Shepherd OBE, FRSA   Sir Peter Maxwell Davies   Keith Critchlow FRCA, FDIH   Professor Paul Robertson ARAM
Dr Rupert Sheldrake MA   Frederick Franck DMD, LDSRSC (Edin) DFA (hon) (Pittsburgh)   Ernest Hall O.B.E., D.L.

to field a settled side. But why persevere for so long with square pegs in round holes? No one's doubting Carlos Bocanegra's will and general ability but he's not a natural left-back. Apart from pace, what does Tomasz Radzinski give us wide on the right? He's not exactly one to have beside you in the trenches, is he? (Or if he is, there's not been much evidence of that so far.)

The most frustrating aspect is that we've proved we can play a bit. We were tremendous in the opening match of the season against Bolton; we more than matched "invincible" Arsenal for an hour; we even bounced back from that horrendous showing against Blackburn to push Chelsea all the way in the Carling Cup just days later. But, by and large, we've settled into a negative rut and now need to pick up points pretty quickly to avoid being caught by the teams below scrambling for their Premiership lives.

It shows the state we were in that it took the return of Lee Clark to see what we've been missing. That's not a double-edged comment, just acknowledging that Clarkie's in the twilight of a terrific career and that he's never been considered either a ball juggler or speed merchant. But he's a top-class player, classic captain material, inspirational on and off the field and someone who's prepared to stand up and be counted. If the rest of the team had collectively stood up and been counted this season we'd not only be much higher up the table but have bagfuls more confidence, too.

A quick look at the most recent games highlights our inconsistencies. Our second half improvement at Bolton was not enough to keep us in the FA Cup. We were absolutely appalling going forward against a very beatable Tottenham, and yet the defence (with Goma back to his best) was resolute until those closing minutes. Against Charlton we played some decent stuff in the opening half hour – but should still have been two down by the break. After that, it became a dreary stalemate. At Old Trafford, we nearly grabbed a point with a late flurry. But didn't.

And there's the rub. No one expects us to go to the likes of Old Trafford and Highbury and attack naively, leaving us wide open to trademark counter-attacks. There has to be a modicum of control. But isn't our trademark supposed to be lightning counter-attacks? Aren't we supposed to spring into attack with at least three forward players, with the midfielders backing up? And perhaps more pertinently, why haven't we been the team to set the pace at home,

particularly against those considered our inferiors or equals?

That infamous Arsenal home game was pivotal in my opinion. It all spilled over into the following game at West Brom – a match we should have won – and then an alarming brittleness set in. Further points were dropped after playing so well to go two-up at home to Liverpool. How vital will they prove to be?

We enjoyed a decent January during which we made our own luck thanks to a welcome tenacious streak (and big Bouba deservedly hitting the headlines). Have we got the bottle to stay up? We'll see. At least we've tended to be up for the big games – well, there are plenty of big games coming up! And time to give an indication of what's in store for next season. Meantime, it's down to us "mutes" to make a right din – whatever the formation on show! ⚽

Southampton 3 Fulham 3		
05.01.05	15th	1st
Fulham 1 West Brom 0		2nd
16.01.05	15th	3rd
Birmingham City 1 Fulham 2		4th
22.01.05	13th	5th
Fulham 1 Aston Villa 1		6th
02.02.05	15th	7th
Fulham 0 Charlton Athletic		8th
05.02.05	15th	9th
Tottenham Hotspur 2 Fulham 0		10th
26.02.05	15th	11th
Fulham 0 Charlton Athletic 0		12th
05.03.05	14th	**13th**
Manchester United 1 Fulham 0		14th
19.03.05	16th	15th
Fulham 3 Portsmouth 1		**16th**
03.04.05	14th	17th
Bolton Wanderers 3 Fulham 1		18th
09.04.05	16th	19th
Fulham 1 Manchester City 1		20th
16.04.05	16th	
Chelsea 3 Fulham 1		
23.04.05	16th	
Fulham 2 Everton 0		
30.04.05	15th	
Fulham 1 Newcastle United 3		
04.05.05	16th	
Blackburn Rovers 1 Fulham 3		
07.05.05	16th	
Fulham 6 Norwich City 0		
15.05.05	13th	

FA Cup

Watford 1 Fulham 1	
08.01.05	Round 3
Fulham 2 Watford 0	
19.01.05	Round 3 replay
Derby County 1 Fulham 1	
29.01.05	Round 4
Fulham 4 Derby County 2	
12.02.05	Round 4 replay
Bolton Wanderers 1 Fulham 0	
19.02.05	Round 5

Johnny Haynes (1934-2005)

I was lucky to see Johnny Haynes play, albeit not at the peak of his powers. Fulham fans of greater vintage can testify to his supreme passing ability while at his imperious best for Fulham and England. If the younger element cannot take that at face value, his former Fulham team-mate and lifelong friend Tosh Chamberlain described him as "a superb passer of the ball and a wonderfully gifted midfield schemer – he was everything to me, a good mate and a great footballer", while world greats George Best, Bobby Moore and Pele readily referred to him in similarly glowing terms.

Bestie called him "a sublimely gifted playmaker"; Mooro (who succeeded Haynes as England captain) said: "Once you get used to watching that perfection you realised the rest

of the secret. John was always available, always hungry for the ball, always wanting to play. I loved watching the player. Later I learnt to love the man." Pele referred to the Maestro as "the best passer of the ball I've ever seen".

So you get the picture: John Norman Haynes was rather good. And he stayed at Fulham for 18 years, clocking up a record 658 appearances in all competitions and netting 158 goals from midfield; he even had a spell as the Club's Player-Manager. The Maestro played 56 times for England, 22 of which were as captain. Not a bad CV!

And yet when Johnny Haynes lent his support to the Fulham 2000 campaign you'd be pushed to meet a humbler ex-superstar. Superstar isn't overdoing it: an England captain, World Cup performer, brilliant midfielder, supreme passer of a football, handsomely paid sportsman and the face of Brylcreem – that's a description of David Beckham to the modern generation. In fact that was Johnny Haynes at the height of his game. And a much better and more complete footballer than Beckham!

Haynes had plenty to crow about but instead, in his latter years, he was happy to melt into the background and make the most of his close circle of true friends. Not for Haynes a reinvention as media pundit; no, he chose to run a dry-cleaning business with his wife Avril in Edinburgh. Can't see Becks ever taking that route somehow. When the Fulham 2000 committee came a-calling in 1993 Johnny was eager to help out, travelling down from Scotland on a regular basis. His appearances at press calls, along with fellow patrons George Best, Gordon Davies and Simon Morgan, ensured a good attendance and vital media coverage. But the man himself remained bemused that he was in any way the centre of attention, famously batting back Club historian Dennis Turner's suggestion of putting together a biography with the words: "Why would anyone want to read about me?"

When Johnny Haynes died in 2005 the obituaries were fulsome in their praise for his abilities. Some were truly marvellous reads, the big shame, of course, being that Johnny Haynes never got to see them. Neither did he get to know about the Stevenage Road Stand being renamed in his honour nor the superb statue that now graces Stevenage Road. Naturally, he'd have shunned the limelight had any such grandiose notions been suggested while he was still alive, but wouldn't it have been so much more fitting if his standing could have been acknowledged during his lifetime?

Below, and opposite page: Flowers and tributes to Johnny Haynes at the Cottage following his untimely passing in 2005.

At least TOOFIF celebrated his 70th birthday in 2004. Okay, so this hardly ruffled the publishing world at large, but Johnny was pleased to receive his copy of the mag all the same. Reaching 70 years of age seemed to be a decent milestone and it occurred that the fanzine had never really celebrated his time at FFC – and his birthday seemed a good time to remind and inform contemporary Fulham folk just how good he'd been back in the day. And that, as in his heyday, he was still a hero to Fulham supporters everywhere.

The *London Evening Standard*, that worthy publishing bastion covering all things connected with the capital (except our corner of SW6, naturally), did pay homage to Johnny Haynes, holding a gala presentation dinner in his honour in March 1993 at the Café Royal. Genial TV commentator Brian Moore was the host as football stars past and present took their turn to pay tribute to the guest of honour.

We heard countless anecdotes from George Cohen, Rodney Marsh, Terry Venables, Ian St John, Jimmy Greaves and others. Then came the main presentation, and onto the stage teetered a phenomenally drunk George Best who, after a cursory nod to the guest of honour, promptly vented his fury at Michael Herd, the *Standard's* Sports Editor, who, with impeccable timing, had that week penned a less-than-

flattering review of Best and Marsh's impending roadshow.

We'd barely had a "bloody" up to that point; Bestie proceeded to turn the air bluer than blue with an outpouring of vitriol that left Herd squirming in his seat on the top table. It blew the cobwebs away and the shock value stirred all of us from our post-meal lethargy. The outburst was initially quite funny but, rather like a trademark Best dribble, he didn't know when to stop and it became terribly embarrassing until he reverted to the script by remembering the recently departed Bobby Moore, saying that Mooro would undoubtedly have been there to add his own tribute to Johnny Haynes had he been able. Remarkably, when a smashed Bestie subsequently posed with Johnny Haynes for the presentation pics, that glazed look had all but been replaced by a fairly sober visage.

A car crash in 1962 brought an end to the Maestro's England career; he was out of action for a year, and damaged knee ligaments not only blunted his genius but also meant he was never on Sir Alf Ramsay's radar as England approached the 1966 World Cup. In October 2005, another car crash had even more devastating consequences; on this occasion Haynes suffered a fatal brain haemorrhage that caused him to veer into traffic. Edinburgh had lost its adopted son whereas the football world at large had lost a true superstar. In SW6, meanwhile, we mourned the loss of our Maestro, our finest-ever player, our Mr Fulham. We had the chance to pay our respects both at the next home game, against Liverpool, and at a memorial service at St Paul's Church, Hammersmith. In due course a breathtakingly brilliant statue was unveiled outside the Cottage gates in October 2008 (design: Bill Mitchell; sculptor: Douglas Jennings). ⚽

	1st
Fulham 0 Birmingham City 0	2nd
13.08.05 7th	3rd
Blackburn Rovers 2 Fulham 1	4th
20.08.05 13th	5th
Arsenal 4 Fulham 1	6th
24.08.05 16th	**7th**
Fulham 1 Everton 0	8th
27.08.05 14th	9th
Newcastle United 1 Fulham 1	10th
10.09.05 12th	11th
Fulham 1 West Ham United 2	12th
17.09.05 15th	13th
Tottenham Hotspur 1 Fulham 0	14th
26.09.05 17th	15th
Fulham 2 Manchester United 3	16th
01.10.05 18th	17th
Charlton Athletic 1 Fulham 1	18th
17.10.05 17th	19th
Fulham 2 Liverpool 0	20th
22.10.05 14th	

Wigan Athletic 1 Fulham 0
29.10.05   15th

Fulham 2 Manchester City 1
05.11.05   14th

Middlesbrough 3 Fulham 2
20.11.05   14th

Fulham 2 Bolton Wanderers 1
27.11.05   14th

West Brom 0 Fulham 0
03.12.05   14th

Birmingham City 1 Fulham 0
10.12.05   15th

Fulham 2 Blackburn Rovers 1
17.12.05   14th

Chelsea 3 Fulham 2
26.12.05   15th

Fulham 3 Aston Villa 3
28.12.05   14th

Portsmouth 1 Fulham 0
31.12.05   15th

Fulham 2 Sunderland 1
02.01.06   14th

Fulham 1 Newcastle United 0
14.01.06   12th

West Ham United 2 Fulham 1
23.01.06   13th

Fulham 1 Tottenham Hotspur 0
31.01.06   13th

Manchester United 4 Fulham 2
04.02.06   14th

Fulham 6 West Brom 1
11.02.06   14th

Bolton Wanderers 2 Fulham 1
26.02.06   14th

League Cup

Fulham 5 Lincoln City 4
21.09.05   Round 2

Fulham 2 West Brom 3
25.10.05   Round 3

FA Cup

Fulham 1 Leyton Orient 2
08.01.06   Round 3

George Best (1946-2005)

George Best's demise couldn't have been in more different circumstances to that of Johnny Haynes. Whereas our very own Maestro had all but been forgotten by the media beforehand, George Best had lived all his life through the tabloids. His latter years provided a series of lurid headlines very much at variance to the glory, glory headlines of the 1960s. And his final days were charted almost obsessively by the broadcast media.

We were "treated" to farcical reports of the "he's-not-dead-yet, but-soon-will-be, we'll-be-right-back" variety. Astonishing really – but then Georgie Best was an astonishing footballer whose gradual descent via the ravages of alcoholism was as pitiful as it was inevitable.

I am not suggesting that Best was anything other than a Manchester United legend. Had he not fallen from his extraordinarily high levels, we wouldn't have had a sniff of seeing him in a Fulham shirt. But see him we did, and his 40-plus games for the club represent a significant chunk of his footballing career.

And it's a case of "speak as you find" – comparatively out of condition at the start of his spell at the Cottage, Bestie nevertheless made an immediate impact, scoring after just 71 seconds of his debut. Now that's how to make headlines! And, past his peak or not, he continued to do

Above right: George Best presents Johnny Haynes with a special award from the *Evening Standard* at a Gala Dinner at the Café Royal in 1992.The former footballing superstars passed away within weeks of each other in 2005.

Below: George Best, seemingly taking on Chelsea on his own, scores a beauty to help Fulham to 3-1 victory in April 1977.

things with the football that surprised even his team-mates.

TOOFIF 96 documented his brilliant goal at Peterborough from just outside the penalty box and he served up many moments to savour. Most pertinently, whatever he may or may not have been getting up to off the field, Best couldn't be faulted for his efforts on it.

Best said many times that he loved his time at Fulham Football Club. So much so that he was prepared to help the Club and its supporters when the going got tough. George Best not only lent his name to the Fulham 2000 fundraising campaign – along with FFC legends Johnny Haynes and Gordon Davies – but also attended the press launches when his reputation suggested he'd more than likely be elsewhere. His presence – along with the other Fulham icons – gave the whole campaign a tremendous lift, for which we should be eternally grateful. I was fortunate to be involved in the campaign and can confirm that ALL those involved were fully committed to the cause. In Bestie's case, we should be grateful that the Man. Utd legend had enjoyed his time at the quaint club down by the river sufficiently to lend his considerable name to our cause. ⚽

Mitch and the Big Top

John Mitchell recalls when George Best signed for FFC. "I was expecting to feel hacked off. I was our top goal-scorer the season before. We played with three men up — Viv Busby, Les Barrett and myself — and somebody was going to be left out. But the impact that George brought to Craven Cottage was extraordinary.

"The very first training session after George arrived was the most memorable I've ever known. George had to wait for Football League

Left: Fulham striker John Mitchell – who loved the circus coming to town.

permission to make his comeback. But we soon discovered he was magnificently fit. Bestie and Marsh were trying to outdo one another in the session. I remember thinking to myself, 'If I am dropped, I can't really moan.'

"George loved it at Fulham, he really did. That old cliché about playing with a smile on his face definitely applied to George. Before games, he'd deliberately see how many times he could ping the ball against the crossbar rather than warm the keeper up.

"It might have been different if they just came back for the money, or if they couldn't hack it. But the real shame was that George was still only just 30, and was light years ahead of everybody else at that level, the Second Division. You knew that you could give George the ball and he could just go and score a goal on his own.

"But from day one, we didn't treat him as if he was an icon. We gave him so much stick. Les Strong and I were the two who'd wind up George and Marshy, take the mickey out of them. It was a fabulous time – every week was like the circus coming to town." ⚽

Farewell Mary and Jim

In summer 2005 Fulham FC lost two stalwart fans, Mary Doughty and Jim Sims. Sandra Coles, FFC ticket office manager and a close pal of Mary, penned the following. "A member of the Fulham family, a true legend to many Fulham supporters, Mary Doughty was known to the fans for her work at Fulham FC, helping to organise the away travel and working tirelessly over many years, always with a smile on a face and a helping hand. She loved this Club and Craven Cottage was her second home."

Jim, for whom the phrase "lovable eccentric" was surely coined, had been poorly for a while and, sadly, hadn't seen his beloved FFC return to the gloriously revamped Craven Cottage. Jim had been a contributor to the programme and TOOFIF, always aiming to squeeze in a mention of his all-time hero Ronnie Rooke. ⚽

The Traveller's Wings are Clipped

FFC stalwart Alex Ferguson, aka The Traveller, tells TOOFIF about his recent health scare...

You had something of a close call in the close season – but being The Trav, you just had to have a Fulham connection...!
In short, Tony Gale saved my life. I was on the plane from Rome to Heathrow on the return leg from a trip to Mauritius and Tony said: "Al, you've turned blue!" As you know, I've got a natural aversion to that colour, so I knew something had to be done! Tony called a steward and he arranged for me to be given oxygen; water was then slapped all over me and I perked up a bit. After landing at Heathrow, I was walking out and I saw a chap standing to one side with a wheelchair. "That can't be for me," I thought (it was!) – and I marched off.

What had you been doing in Mauritius in the first place?
I was watching Walton Casuals play out there. Tony Gale is their Director of Football, and his son plays for them. Anyway, luckily for me the wife of the Casuals chairman was picking him up and he lived local to my place and they kindly gave me a lift home. By early the next morning I felt rough so I dialled 999.

From what I gather. things moved very quickly from that point...
Quicker than Les Barrett in his prime! Especially when I was being moved from West Middx A&E to St Thomas', and we had to go through "filthy blue land" with the siren nee-nawing at full blast. I kept my head down, naturally! Somehow I didn't feel in the mood to wave two fingers at the buggers!

I've been overwhelmed by the good wishes and support received from the Fulham camp. One particular batch of cards took my breath away – which in my current state isn't too advisable – there was one from Simon Morgan, another was from Tosh Chamberlain, while the third, which I'm placing on a slightly higher pedestal than the very high pedestals reserved for the previous two names, was from The Maestro himself, Johnny Haynes. Get well cards to treasure!

What happens now, Alex?
I've an assessment at Harefield coming up with a view to having a double lung transplant. Not much fun, I don't suppose, but it's got to be done. Survival, that's the number one objective. Not far behind is getting back to Craven Cottage as soon as is practicable – well, you've got to have goals, haven't you? Let's just say that '05-06 is my "gap" year.

Watchoo Talkin' 'Bout, Arnie?

Millions watched England's 1990 World Cup semi-final with Germany, when Andreas Brehme's shot struck Paul Parker and looped into the net over Peter Shilton. "Arnie" helped England back into the game, setting up Gary Lineker's equaliser, before the almost inevitable penalty shoot-out defeat. But what's he up to these days? TOOFIF caught up with him a week after Fulham played at Old Trafford...

What did you make of Fulham's recent game at Old Trafford, Paul?
It was similar to the game at Craven Cottage – Fulham could easily have got two points from those matches. It surprised me, but Fulham played really well on both occasions and were unlucky to come away with nothing. Man. Utd were perhaps even more fortunate to claim maximum points this time around. Somewhere along the line Fulham have got to win away from home – it's a mystery as to why they haven't done so already this season. Maybe they shouldn't be quite as open; they should possibly keep things a little tighter. Teams like United rely on the opposition playing open attacking football so they can counter-attack. But with the attacking options offered by Malbranque, Boa Morte, Helguson, McBride and with John in reserve, it's difficult not to play to your strengths.

We've done well at home. Maybe there's a *really* good team in there somewhere...?
I was surprised when Chris Coleman got the job but you've only got to look at what he's done since – you can't deny that he deserves to be Fulham's manager and you can see him going on to bigger things. Fulham aren't the most fashionable of Premiership clubs and the finances are very different to Old Trafford, for instance, so he's done a great job. His team has certainly deserved a few more points from their efforts this season.

Put your pundit's hat on firmly and talk us through that goal by Van Nistelrooy. Slightly offside? And a turning point?
A huge moment. Fulham had just got back into it with that great header from McBride and yes, Van Nistelrooy was two yards offside – and I can fully understand Chris Coleman's annoyance.

Playing for Fulham juniors must seem ages ago?
That's because it is! Terry Mancini was in charge; he said I was too small, too lightweight. Terry was a great guy, so full of enthusiasm and motivation.

You made your full Fulham debut at just 16...

Yes, against Reading. The average height of their front line was over six-foot – it was all pretty scary, but thankfully my pace got me out of trouble!

You became a regular in 1983 under Malcolm Macdonald and Ray Harford, when we nearly made it to the top flight. How good was that side?
It was a fantastic side that could only have got better. Ray Houghton was a free – *free!* – from West Ham and was a fantastic player. Tony Gale improved a lot under Malcolm: Galey could play, but he became hungrier and had more desire once Malcolm was in charge. Robert Wilson and Sean O'Driscoll blossomed, too; then there was Roger Brown, who loved to smoke cigars before a game. He was an incredible character who'd eventually made it back into the team after getting a nasty injury on his debut. He was awesome.

How do you rate the Macdonald/Harford era?
Ray was a father figure to me (and a number of others), while Malcolm was the potentially volatile one. He could holler and scream for sure! Ray tended to put his arm around you and explain what was required and generally chivvy you along. But they both knew their football. I was very young at the time and looked on Malcolm as being a good deal older – but, looking back, he was very young himself in management terms.

Are you in touch with anyone from those days?
I speak to Ray Houghton, and I see Tony Gale now and again, too. Tony may have got older but his mentality's still the same! It's nice to bump into former Fulham players and contacts, and I'm always sure of the Fulham connection because they call me "Arnie" (after the lad from *Diff'rent Strokes*). Funny enough, I don't turn around so readily if someone calls me "Paul" as it's more likely to be someone who doesn't know me that well! I relate to nicknames; "Arnie" was during my Fulham period, and I ended up as "Parks".

You and Dean Coney were sold to QPR in 1987. What do you recall about the transfer?
I didn't really have any say in it. But then we'd seen so many good players offloaded that it seemed only sensible to try our luck elsewhere. Ray Lewington was manager by then, and the whole thing wasn't fair on him as he was trying his best in a situation that he had no control over. Whatever he had was constantly being taken away from him, and that's not simply the players but even things like us being able to look reasonably smart in training. Ray, to be fair, tried to hang on to Dean and me for as long as possible as he knew that whatever we'd be sold

Below: He went thataway! Paul Parker's second spell at the Club was as brief as it was unsatisfactory.

for, he wouldn't get a sniff of that money. So, not only would he lose two first-team players but he'd not get the finances to replace us.

It was an extraordinary time. Most fans became aware of the bigger picture, doing so much to keep the Club alive. At the time, it was difficult for them to relate to what they were seeing, so soon after having a great side storming towards the top flight.

The fans banded together to keep the Club afloat – were you aware of the scale of the problem?
Now, yes. But then – not at all. I only realised that Dean and I had to be sold when former Club Director Dave Gardner told me we had to be sold so that the Club could raise money to buy back the players' contracts. All right, so they couldn't get the ground back but at least they were then able to put out a team and stay in business.

You went on to bigger, better things?
Fulham was my life from the age of 11. The move to QPR opened my eyes a little. They were then a top club – they finished fifth in the top flight in 1987-88, after leading the way for a time. I'd been used to just a few people behind the scenes at Fulham, such as Janice [Baldwin], Yvonne [Haines] and Sandra [Coles], but there was a bigger set-up at Rangers. Then United came in for me.

Just like that?
After the 1990 World Cup I was told that several clubs, including Everton, Arsenal, Tottenham and Sheffield Wednesday were interested in me. The chance of signing for Spurs really appealed – I'd followed them as a lad – but then United came in at the last minute.

It wasn't such a bad career move...
I enjoyed many a highlight at Old Trafford – winning that first championship in 26 years, and doing the double the following season. By then I'd had many a thrill playing for my country as well; getting to the World Cup semi-finals was a great achievement. All in all I've been very lucky.

Did you ever get the Fergie "hair-dryer" blast?
Once or twice! But the one thing you should never do is respond. I still talk to him, of course, and I'm full of respect for him. But then I had respect for most of my managers. Take Malcolm Macdonald – I'd have loved to have played for him and Fulham for a lot longer as I genuinely believe he could have gone on and really done something in the game. He had the respect of the players and, like Sir Alex, had a real hunger for the game. Don't forget that, with Ray Harford as his trusty sidekick, Malcolm stirred things up at the Cottage; he transformed a small set-up into a reasonably big one. Fulham suddenly became a club that was poised for great things – and

he ensured that the football world was taking notice. Here we are talking about Fulham in the Premiership, but older Fulham fans will be thinking that the Club should have made it into the top flight in 1983. And we'll never know how significantly that would have changed history – would the subsequent years have been quite so turbulent for instance?

You did make it back to Fulham – albeit briefly – in January 1997, but it didn't go to plan. Did that experience sour your memories of the Club?
No, it was nothing to do with the Club. It soured my opinion of the manager at the time. I found it sad that he had to "use" my friend and ex-team-mate John Marshall, someone who I'd grown up with. Marshy was there in the room with Alan Cork and Micky Adams as I was told what I consider to be a pack of lies. It seemed the manager needed to have cover in there with him and that he couldn't speak to me on his own. I don't think he enjoyed me being around and he, perhaps, underestimated my popularity.

I hope that doesn't sound big-headed. Bill Muddyman had offered me a short-term contract but I turned it down as I didn't want to put the Club in that position. I wasn't sure of my overall fitness and appetite so, in the meantime, I was only on travelling expenses. After getting through the game against Darlington, in which we got a great result [6-0], I was then selected to play out of position at wing-back, a tough call for someone who was feeling his way back into the game. It seemed something of a ploy, given my fitness levels, to get me out. Whereas I'd been told they were looking for a sweeper and someone to organise things, now I was expected to race up and down the field as a wing-back.

There was also an incident at training. We were playing Cardiff on the Friday night and had a training session that morning. I'd probably been spoilt at other clubs, but I'd been used to relaxing on the day of a game. Anyway, I realised that if I had to hike over from Essex to Fulham's training ground in Surrey, I wouldn't have time to go home before the match. I packed a tracksuit for training and, once there, put it on – only to see the other players looking at me with fear in their eyes. I asked, "What's wrong?" and was told that only the manager was allowed to wear bottoms. There's me more concerned about keeping my body warm and in reasonable nick – after all you only generally go through set plays at such sessions – but I had to take them off. I had no shorts, so I couldn't train! All very petty. It was something I'd never heard of or seen before. As I say, perhaps I'd been spoilt but, all said and done, all my other managers respected their players as to how to prepare themselves on matchdays. It was all so unnecessary. ⚽

Arsenal 4 Fulham 0	1st
04.03.06 16th	2nd
Everton 3 Fulham 1	3rd
11.03.06 16th	4th
Liverpool 5 Fulham 1	5th
15.03.06 16th	6th
Fulham 1 Chelsea 0	7th
19.03.06 14th	8th
Aston Villa 0 Fulham 0	9th
25.03.06 14th	10th
Portsmouth 3 Fulham 1	11th
01.04.06 15th	**12th**
Fulham 2 Charlton Athletic 1	13th
15.04.06 15th	14th
Fulham 1 Wigan Athletic 0	15th
24.04.06 14th	16th
Manchester City 1 Fulham 2	17th
29.04.06 13th	18th
Sunderland 2 Fulham 1	19th
04.05.06 14th	20th
Fulham 1 Middlesbrough 0	
07.04.06 12th	

Farewell, Alex

One of FFC's most stalwart fans, Alex "The Traveller" Ferguson, lost his long-term battle with lung cancer on Friday March 10, aged 59. A lifelong fan and my best mate, Alex started travelling to games, often hitch-hiking to ensure his presence, in an age when those making cross-country journeys to watch their team were very much in the minority. In the early 1970s, as away travel became more of a trend, Alex and a group of like-minded fans formed the Thames Bank Travellers. The group travelled together to all games outside London, with Alex organising the arrangements.

An ardent England supporter, Alex was featured in the 1966 film *GOAL!* celebrating in the fountains of Trafalgar Square wearing a Mod's Parka with "Fulham" on the back. He attended eight World Cup tournaments in total, including Mexico 1986 and Japan and Korea in 2002.

He is the only fan to have seen all of Fulham Football Club's games in Europe, including the Anglo-Italian matches and he – naturally! – attended all of the InterToto and UEFA Cup games in 2002-03. He also supported the Fulham Ladies on their UEFA Cup campaign.

Alex wrote for the programme and, more recently, for TOOFIF; he also penned two books – *Pandora's Fulhamish Box* in 2003 and *A Fulhamish Coming of Age* in 2005. A third title, a second *Pandora's Box* is sadly left unprinted.

At one point Alex hadn't missed a Fulham game, home or away, for 25 years until a clash of fixtures arose between his beloved Fulham and England.

Graham Blackman

> "*In the early 1970s, as away travel became more of a trend, Alex and a group of like-minded fans formed the Thames Bank Travellers. The group travelled together to all games outside London, with Alex organising the arrangements.*"

Above: Alex is pictured in perfect surroundings – beer in hand and in the company of fellow Fulham supporters.

I had the pleasure of knowing Alex for about 25 years and was privileged to be asked to say a few words at his funeral service…

When the arrangements for today's service were circulated we were advised that although the venue is known as Hanworth Crematorium its official title is something else. That would have tickled Alex, always a stickler for detail. So, if you don't mind, I'll just make an official note of things in the old stats book... just for the record... just for Alex.

Venue: South West Middlesex Crematorium
Event: Alex Ferguson Trophy: The Final
Date: Thursday March 30, 2006
Kick-off time: 12.15pm
Attendance: 300 … APPROX!

On hearing the sad news that Alex had died I rattled off a few words for the fanzine website and it seems appropriate to read these out today…

The Trav: an FFC legend, but more importantly a mate. I went to see Alex after the Arsenal game. Although the famous Fergie sparkle was dimmed (we *had* lost 4-0!), I hoped it was just a below-par day. His resilience had been astounding, his bravery in the face of ever-increasing odds and ever-demeaning circumstances, second to none. But it wasn't to be. Hearing that he'd died a few days later set off a load off mixed emotions. The most obvious was a sense of relief – that it was a release for a brave trooper. At the other end of the scale was a degree of incredulity; our Fulham and England veteran had seemed nigh-on indestructible. During his brave fight for life, he'd made more comebacks than Paul Gascoigne. Only without the comedy breasts. And with far fewer tears.

So, what springs to mind when I think of Alex? Well, in no particular order:
• the often raucous Thames Bank Travellers away trips (for the uninitiated, the TBT were the unofficial away travellers who left Putney at dawn in order to stop at an hostelry or three en route. Copious amounts of alcohol were consumed but, being Fulham, there was never any trouble. As the Club hit rock bottom and performances became ever-more depressing, the match became almost incidental. Meanwhile, the camaraderie amongst the motley crew became ever stronger. At the helm, of course, was Alex – even then he was the doyen of the group. After all, he'd already crossed off the Workingtons, Southports and Hartlepools before we'd even realised such places existed. Some referred to him as The Bombardier…)

Now where was I… oh yes…
• his trusty stats notebook;
• being somewhat worse for wear and dancing with a chair in a football clubhouse in Amsterdam;
• his incredibly smelly trainers on the same trip (to cheer on the Fulham Juniors);
• walking from Craven Cottage to Brighton with Cap'n Beaky Billing to raise funds for an ailing FFC;
• the cross of St George;
• telling my too-young-to-be-listening son a string of decidedly un-pc jokes!;
• his unflinching loyalty to FFC;
• his "as-seen-on-TV" Fulham flag;
• heading off to all parts of the globe to see a game of football (especially if Fulham was one of the teams involved) and taking in the local sights wherever possible;
• his anguish when Fulham looked to be going out of existence…;
• …but determination to see the Club survive;
• his bullish insistence that if the bulldozers ever moved in, they'd have to trundle over him first;
• disgust at the new souped-up regime ignoring core Fulham values;
• his utter delight at returning to the Cottage;
• savouring what turned out to be his last Fulham match – the 6-0 trouncing of Norwich;
• his resolve and sheer bloody-mindedness that he'd beat the odds once in hospital;
• finding the last dregs of energy, when in dire straits on the ward, to raise a middle finger on hearing there was a Chelsea fan in the bed opposite.

Oh yes, and his devotion to TOOFIF.

Yes indeed, Alex was very much a TOOFIF man. He was unceremoniously released from the FFC programme team, made up of volunteers in those days, at about the same time I was, in the mid-1980s. But here's not the place for a political rant… even if dear Alex would rather have enjoyed it – with that inimitable twinkle in his eye. Instead, TOOFIF was born and Alex was promptly offering

his highly individual and idiosyncratic views on all things FFC and his legendary footballing travels. Almost immediately there was a running gag on the TBT coach that his pages should come with a cut-out-and-lob-away scissored dotted line. Others mischievously suggested they relied on his travelogues… if ever they were struggling to get to sleep! But he often scored a glorious bullseye – has there been a better article than the one Alex penned about his visit to Auschwitz while on England duty in Poland? But for all of that, you couldn't knock his pieces, because he was there.

And that's the crux of it. He was ALWAYS there. Anywhere Fulham were playing. Anywhere to see his beloved England in action. And, on the TOOFIF front, always there to lend support – whether by supplying articles or helping to flog the flipping thing. For these past ten months I've missed the eve-of-matchday calls to my home, the bottom line of which would always be: "What time do you want me there, Dave?" And my answer would invariably be the same: "Look, just get there when you can, any help is gratefully appreciated". And invariably he would be spotted trooping up Stevenage Road on Saturdays at about midday. With a broad smile on his face. It was Fulham, wasn't it? That was his life. That was Alex.

Bloody-minded? Too darned right. Idiosyncratic? For sure. (And he'd be delighted that I managed to get such a word in twice in the same article!!) But immensely loyal too? Hey, there's no debate on that one. He was fiercesomely loyal, as well as a true mate.

TOOFIF is sometimes referred to as "One F"; well, Alex was a one-off. We think we're a special lot at Fulham. Well, there was no one more special or more loyal than Alex Ferguson. And so the Traveller's making his final journey. No passport required (as he might have put it). ⚽

Above: Alex takes a much-deserved breather at the Goldstone Ground, Brighton, in November 1992. He had just completed a fundraising walk for his beloved Fulham FC with fellow madcap fan Gary Billing. Having set off from Craven Cottage the previous evening, the intrepid duo were rewarded by seeing their Fulham heroes secure an away win.

Letter for Alex Ferguson…

Frances and I remember the time during the Falklands crisis when Sammy McKay drafted a spoof letter on MOD headed paper calling Alex up for active service. He had briefed Colin Kempster, Fulham's matchday announcer, of the wind-up and Colin made an announcement five minutes into the match: "Would Alex Ferguson please report to the Cottage immediately?" We all watched as Alex marched from the Hammersmith End, via the enclosure so that he didn't miss too much of the match, to the Cottage; then back again through the enclosure reading the MOD letter

that explained why he, as a senior calligrapher, was required to report to the Cottage after the game where he would be taken by taxi to Northolt Airfield and flown directly to Port Stanley. The letter was signed by A. Wynder.

The old fella came back to his place at the Hammersmith End solemn faced to tell us that he had had his calling. Thirty or so scallywags waved a copy of the letter at him saying: "Yeah, we know". He took it well – responding with a usual retort of "You bastards!"

Allan and Frances Gould

A Chat With "Mullers"

Alan Mullery made his Fulham debut aged 17 versus Leyton Orient. After playing more than 200 games for FFC, he signed for Spurs in 1964 for £72,500 and went on to win the FA Cup, League Cup and UEFA Cup. He also earned 35 England caps, one of which was gained in the epic 1970 World Cup quarter-final against West Germany where he scored the opening goal. A final spell at Fulham featured an amazing FA Cup run to Wembley in 1975, alongside his great mate, Bobby Moore.

Right, Alan, where shall we start? Johnny Haynes, Bobby Moore, Alec Stock, Alf Ramsey, Fulham, Spurs, England…? I know: fish manure...!
That awful stuff! My first summer, along with the other groundstaff boys, was spent aerating the pitch with forks. We'd wheel out barrowloads of the evil-smelling manure for groundsman Albert Purdy to put onto the aerated pitch. As Albert flung it about, it would drift all over us. Albert lived in the Cottage, so he could get a shower whenever he wanted, but us kids stank like hell. I got some funny looks when I went home on the bus.

Johnny Haynes made an immediate impression on you – but just how good was he?
There was barely any football on TV. Wembley had no floodlights, so any Internationals were shown in the afternoon. As a consequence, when any Internationals were played during the school term, I was "ill" that day. Johnny Haynes' ability shone through the grainy TV images. He was an amazing footballer, the best passer of the ball that I've ever seen. He had a great touch, wonderful natural ability, was a superb striker of the ball, and he could "drop his shoulder" one way and opponents would go the other – he played football the way football should be played. If he were playing today he'd be rated in the top three in the world.

Allowing for his legendary intolerance, John must have been a dream to play alongside?
He could be bloody awful! John was great if he thought you were doing your job. He was a footballing genius, that's indisputable, but he expected everyone else to be the same and on a similar wavelength. His best pal in football was Tosh Chamberlain, but the amount of stick he'd give Tosh was outrageous. The boyhood pals loved each other like brothers – even so, how Tosh took that stick week in, week out, I'll never know.

I copped it a couple of times, when instead of giving him the ball I passed it to somebody else. Johnny wanted the ball all the time – in fact, I remember Brian Clough saying that when you played with Johnny Haynes and Jimmy Greaves you needed three footballs, one each for those two and one for the rest of the team! Anyway, when John let rip on this particular occasion, I grabbed him by the throat and gave him a few words of my own. I was sorry at once – he was the England captain – but from that day on, he accepted me for what I was, someone with far less ability than him, but someone who'd run all day for the cause.

I think if a few more had stood up to him and said things face to face, he'd have taken it – he was a big man and a lovely fellow all said and done – but they didn't. People were frightened of him because of his stature within the Football Club.

On the other hand, you must have enjoyed a load of laughs and larks with Tosh around...?
I've not met a funnier person in football. That was established the very first time I met him – I had two tickets to watch a game and he left the pitch to come and sit right next to me on the touchline to smoke a cigarette – while the game was going on! Johnny Haynes wasn't best pleased. Now here we are about 50 years later, and Tosh is exactly the same. Always a laugh, and ready with a choice turn of phrase. Everybody loves him and – along with Johnny of course – he was one of the reasons I joined Fulham. The fun element was tangible, and I thought: "I want to be a part of this."

So, how did 17-year-old Alan Mullery make the breakthrough to the first team?
I was confident in my own ability. I liked a tackle and I'd got a bit of a reputation for that. I wanted to make use of the ball once I'd got it and, having watched Johnny Haynes practising his passing on his own, time and again after training, I thought, if I'm to improve I'm going to have to do the same. So I used to practice 40-50 yards passes – never as accurately as John, naturally – but I improved. I had terrific energy; I could run all day and didn't feel tired at the end of games. So I guess that added up to an energetic, mobile, combative midfielder who could pass the ball quite well. A few years ago, one of the papers described Steven Gerard as "a young Alan Mullery", and I was extremely proud of that.

At the end of your first season, '58-59, Fulham got promoted to the top division. Great timing!
I had 14 games that first season; then it was up to the First Division. It was fairy-story stuff really.

We've mentioned the fun aspect, but there were a host of good players at Fulham...
When Fulham were struggling during the '90s, I'd be talking to people and the same question would

> "I had terrific energy; I could run all day and didn't feel tired at the end of games. So I guess that added up to an energetic, mobile, combative midfielder who could pass the ball quite well."

Below: Alan Mullery recalls the many laughs and larks he enjoyed at Fulham.

come up: "What was it like in your day compared to modern-day Fulham?" My answer was simple; I'd just rattle off: "Macedo, Cohen, Langley, Mullery, Bentley, Lowe, Leggat, Hill, Cook, Haynes and Chamberlain." Tony Macedo played more times for the England Under-23s than any other keeper – he couldn't play for the full International side because of his Gibraltan background, but he was good enough. George Cohen won the World Cup, so had terrific pedigree; Jimmy Langley also played for England and was fantastic; that Alan Mullery chap also ended up an international footballer; Roy Bentley was the ultimate professional, playing for England at centre-forward and then converting to an outstanding centre-half; Eddie Lowe may only have got one cap, replacing Billy Wright, but England hit ten against Portugal, in Portugal, so that's not a bad average, is it?; Graham Leggat was a top Scottish International; Jimmy Hill was an England B International; Maurice Cook didn't get such honours but would run all day for you; Johnny Haynes was England captain; while Tosh had played for the England youth team. Not a bad line-up, is it!?

Looking back, do you wish things had been a bit more professionally run (you're quoted as saying it was much more business-like at Spurs)?
Absolutely not! That's how things were. I don't think Tommy Trinder could've made FFC "professional" – he was a full-time comedian and he had fun with us. When the FA Cup came around, we'd go for a "Cup training" week at Worthing. We'd play golf on Monday afternoon, go back to the hotel for an unbelievable meal; the following day it would be golf in the morning and afternoon, and back to the hotel for another great meal. This went on until the Thursday, when we'd have a five-side game and, yes, another great meal. After a little light running along the Worthing seafront on Friday morning, we'd head off back to London for the Cup game. I can't recall us losing a game after a trip to Worthing! It was outrageous – we were all probably half a stone heavier, but that was Fulham. It all changed when I got to Spurs: Tottenham was business, but Fulham was fun. But to be brought up in that environment as a teenager was simply fantastic – I couldn't have wished for anything better.

You went on to play with and against the world's top stars. Can you explain to us parks footballers what it's like to play at the top of the profession?
I *never* took it for granted. I played against Pelé at Rio's Maracana Stadium before nearly 150,000 spectators. Alf Ramsey told me to do my best to stop him playing. I was nervous, but also focused on doing well. If I could do well against the world's best player then my prestige would go up enormously. So that's how I went about it; I had no fear, even though I knew Pelé was blessed with pace, control, awareness... everything really. He could drop a shoulder and in doing so send half the crowd out of the ground! I was lucky to play against Pelé three times; there was another famous occasion in the Mexico World Cup, and then later for Fulham when we hosted Santos at the Cottage, but that was much more of a fun evening. Many years later, when I was on *This is Your Life*, Pelé was gracious enough to say that I was the fairest player that ever played against him. I'd like to think that was the truth! I felt ever so humble.

You let him slip once – leaving Gordon Banks to make a reasonable save...
What a header that was, but what a save by Banksy! Jairzinho went down the line, crossed it to the far post above Tommy Wright (we'd all shifted across, marking-wise, so that's why Tommy Wright was on him!) and Pelé was already rising. Banksy somehow goes from covering the near post to the far post, but Pelé had made a great contact and was already shouting "goal", only for Banksy to finger-tip the ball away. A wonderful, wonderful top-class save. I patted him on the head and couldn't resist asking politely: "Why didn't you catch it?" He gave me a right verbal. Perhaps that was my Fulham upbringing coming to the fore once again! It was always a privilege to be playing at the top level.

After some glory years at Spurs you returned to Fulham, at first on loan: was it a home-coming?
That might have been the perception, but it was very different when I came back. I had numerous offers, from clubs like Nottingham Forest, Stoke and Crystal Palace. I was offered a huge sum of money to go to Palace, but things took a real twist when I was in Alec Stock's office. I took a phone

Manchester United 5 Fulham 1		
20.08.06	20th	1st
Fulham 1 Bolton Wanderers 1		2nd
23.08.06	18th	3rd
Fulham 1 Sheffield United 0		4th
26.08.06	9th	5th
Newcastle United 1 Fulham 2		6th
09.09.06	7th	
Tottenham Hotspur 0 Fulham 0		**7th**
17.09.06	8th	8th
Fulham 0 Chelsea 2		9th
23.09.06	11th	10th
Watford 3 Fulham 3		11th
02.10.06	11th	12th
Fulham 2 Charlton Athletic 1		13th
16.10.06	10th	14th
Aston Villa 1 Fulham 1		15th
21.10.06	9th	16th
Fulham 0 Wigan Athletic 1		17th
28.10.06	9th	18th
Fulham 1 Everton 0		19th
04.11.06	8th	20th
Portsmouth 1 Fulham 1		
11.11.06	10th	
Manchester City 3 Fulham 1		
18.11.06	11th	
Fulham 0 Reading 1		
25.11.06	11th	
Fulham 2 Arsenal 1		
29.11.06	10th	
Blackburn Rovers 2 Fulham 0		
02.12.06	10th	
Liverpool 4 Fulham 0		
09.12.06	13th	
Fulham 2 Middlesbrough 1		
18.12.06	11th	
Fulham 0 West Ham United 0		
23.12.06	12th	
Charlton Athletic 2 Fulham 2		
27.12.06	12th	
Chelsea 2 Fulham 2		
30.12.06	12th	
Fulham 0 Watford 0		
01.01.07	12th	
West Ham United 3 Fulham 3		
13.01.07	12th	
Fulham 1 Tottenham Hotspur 1		
20.01.07	15th	
Sheffield United 2 Fulham 0		
30.01.07	15th	
Fulham 2 Newcastle United 1		
03.02.07	14th	
Bolton Wanderers 2 Fulham 1		
11.02.07	14th	
Fulham 1 Manchester United 2		
24.02.07	14th	
Fulham 1 Aston Villa 1		
03.03.07	14th	
Wigan Athletic 0 Fulham 0		
17.03.07	13th	
Fulham 1 Portsmouth 1		
31.03.07	14th	
Everton 4 Fulham 1		
06.04.07	15th	
Fulham 1 Manchester City 3		
09.04.07	15th	
Reading 1 Fulham 0		
14.04.07	15th	
Fulham 1 Blackburn Rovers 1		
21.04.07	15th	
Arsenal 3 Fulham 1		
29.04.07	16th	
Fulham 1 Liverpool 0		
05.05.07	15th	
Middlesbrough 3 Fulham 1		
13.05.07	16th	

League Cup
Fulham 1 Wycombe Wanderers 2	
20.09.06	Round 2

FA Cup
Leicester City 2 Fulham 2	
06.01.07	Round 3
Fulham 4 Leicester City 3	
17.01.07	Round 3 replay
Fulham 3 Stoke City 0	
27.01.07	Round 4
Fulham 0 Tottenham Hotspur 4	
18.02.07	Round 5

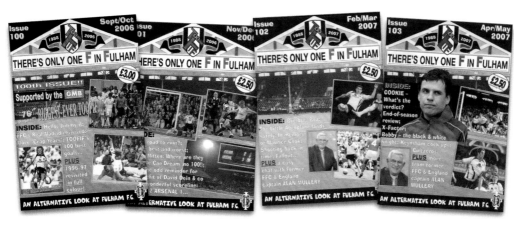

"Nobody ever thought that Fulham could get Mooro. I was doing more and more for Alec by then, attending meetings, going to functions with him, even being his chauffeur and confidant. On this occasion, he called me back from training and asked: 'Do you get on with Bobby Moore?' I replied cheekily: 'I've slept with him for five years.'"

call from Aston Villa, who were offering me a coaching post. Alec said something there and then that made up my mind: "If you sign for Fulham for four years, you'll be given the manager's job." Bert Head at Palace had offered to double my weekly pay to £300 and £25,000 to sign on. That was a lot of money in 1972, and very tempting. But Stocky had unexpectedly offered me something I'd always dreamed about, being manager of Fulham, and that swayed it. So that's why I went back – not simply the love of Fulham Football Club, even though I loved the Club then and still do today. It was the chance of a reasonable contract and the promise of the managership in due course.

Having signed, you made it to the Cup Final with Fulham, with a little help from Bobby Moore...
Nobody ever thought that Fulham could get Mooro. I was doing more and more for Alec by then, attending meetings, going to functions with him, even being his chauffeur and confidant. On this occasion, he called me back from training and asked: "Do you get on with Bobby Moore?" I replied cheekily: "I've slept with him for five years, Alec." He went "Whaaat?" so I quickly added: "We roomed together for England." He then said: "We're thinking of bringing Bobby Moore to the Club – would you have any problems with that?" I said: "No, none at all – go and get him!" But Stocky countered, "No, you go and get him!" So off I went with [Club Secretary] Graham Hortop with the transfer forms in the hope of signing Bobby. Alec's parting shot was that it was far from a done deal.

We met Ron Greenwood and the club's directors. Bobby wasn't convinced. As a former England captain and national icon, it was his call. He'd be welcomed with open arms at almost any club, and even the journey time from his Essex home for daily training was an issue. In the end I suggested that he had two or three years left in the game, he'd given so much to football, why not come to Fulham and have some fun? I warned him that we might not win anything, but that he'd like the people there and all the lads, and that it was a friendly, fun place. And that was it, Bobby Moore came to Fulham. It turned out to be a very good move for him – and a great one for the players around him, such as Les Strong and John Lacy.

So there were two strong captains in the side. Was that ever a problem?
He never once disputed that I was the captain of the Football Club. Yet he'd been a captain all his career; and what a career! But what a great person, too.

And he managed another Wembley appearance, this time for Fulham. But what about his performance at Everton in the Fifth Round...?
That was Bobby, the master on the big stage. Everton were top of the First Division and were

expected to see us off. But he was in his element. We played very well that day and Viv Busby took his two goals well, but that was a master show from Bobby; it was just like an England captain performing for his country. He was imperious.

Shame it didn't all come together at Wembley...?
It was the first Cup Final I'd got to and lost! It was a real shame for Bobby to lose to his former club. I couldn't hack it, I must admit, but Mooro masked his own disappointment, put his arm around me at the end and said: "Did you ever expect us to do this so late in our footballing lives?" I replied: "No, mate – but we lost!" His response was simple: "Maybe so, but we weren't really supposed to be here."

Many Fulham fans felt that way too, but in hindsight it was a winnable game, wasn't it?
Oh yeah! If you recall, that season we'd already beaten West Ham in the League Cup at the Cottage, so we thought we'd beat them at Wembley. We had chances to score in the first half, but then Peter Mellor, who'd done as much as any of us to get us to Wembley – he played Carlisle virtually on his own in the Sixth Round – made a couple of mistakes, and that was that

The Fulham hierarchy have been making noises about finishing in the top ten of the Premiership. Do you think now's the time for the Club to move up a level and aim for the upper half of the table rather than avoiding the relegation places?
That's going to be very difficult, but it has to be the aim. I can't envisage anyone else coming to Fulham and spending the way Mr Al Fayed has done to secure the ground and to back Fulham's climb through the divisions. What he's overseen has been nothing short of marvellous. I've seen Fulham at their very best this season. For example, against Arsenal at Craven Cottage they were absolutely fantastic. Really wonderful. But I've also seen them at their worst, and you start to think where's the next win coming from. So I don't think we've reached a level where we know how we're going to perform. It would be really great to see a level of consistency from the players.

And Alan Mullery the manager wouldn't condone anything less than that, would he?
We're struggling for a leader, to be fair. For me, Luis Boa Morte was not a captain. He was always something of a maverick – and a potential matchwinner of course – but not a leader. It comes down to that word "consistency" again. Mavericks tend to blow hot and cold; a captain should be consistent in what he does and how he behaves.

What are the best qualities of the current side?
Fulham have become very resilient. We have a very hard-working team. And let's not forget that

Jimmy Bullard has been missed enormously – he looked outstanding in those first three or four games. I hope he comes back fully fit. McBride and Helguson will battle for goals, and Montella looks able to offer something different, but I don't think we'll ever be prolific in goalscoring terms.

Do you think Cookie's grown into the job?
I find it difficult to answer that one. There seems to be a fair few people on the fringe that have a lot to say at Fulham. I know Chris has the final say on this and that. But I haven't really seen Chris Coleman come out as Chris Coleman. By that I mean that as a player, Chris dominated people on the pitch and in the dressing room because he was a terrific leader. I don't think I've seen Chris do that as a manager. Having said that, I think he's done a tremendous job, with the resources at his disposal. But I'd really like to see him being his own man a bit more, rather than have others coming up and whispering in his ear and passing him notes. I think if you're the manager you should be seen to be in total control over the 90 minutes. Taking advice is fine, but only at the appropriate times.

There was a suggestion, especially in his early days as a manager, that Chris should have had an "elder statesman" as his assistant and mentor. Would you agree?
I think it would have done him the world of good.

Could that have been you?
I would have done it, yes. And willingly so. I like Chris. He's still very much a young man, and you know how young people tend to think they know it all – I've seen it with my young children! I look back at the time Louis Saha was linked with Manchester United and Chris went on the telly and in the papers saying "He leaves this Football Club over my dead body." Chris was being forthright, but it really needed an experienced head to suggest he said something like "Of course we want to keep the lad, but that depends on..." whatever. And get round it that way. In the event, within 24 hours Saha had gone. It was just inexperience. There are so many other factors; it's normally football club chairmen who have the final say over players staying or going. That's the way it is.

The promise of the Fulham hot seat at the end of your playing days never materialised – the episode with Alec Stock is well documented in your autobiography. But is it something that has rankled?
Yes. I always thought Stocky was a nice guy, and someone who was true to his word. What actually happened was that June and I had a holiday booked in Majorca at the end of the season. We bumped into Joe Harvey, the ex-manager of Newcastle. We were enjoying a glass of beer by

the pool and he asked me what I was going to do the following season. I said when I got back, I was going to be the manager of Fulham. He was very interested, asking me "Has that been in the papers yet?". I said no, but that after my four years at the club, Stocky was going to hand over the reins. Joe wished me well.

We returned home and I went into Fulham the following Monday. I was sun-tanned and fit, and Stocky was in his chair. He turned and said that I looked in good shape and that I'd no doubt come back to get another playing contract. I said I'd come for the job as promised. Alec spun on his chair so that he had his back to me and stared out of the window. He said: "I don't want to give it up. I don't want to retire. I don't want to go upstairs. If you want to play, you can play, but I'm not going to give you the job." I was fuming. I stormed out, slammed all doors as I came to them and met Strongy at the bottom of the Cottage stairs. "Do we call you boss now?" he asked. I told him briefly what had happened and got into the car and came home.

I mulled things over on the drive home and considered eating humble pie and playing on for a bit longer. But no sooner did I get home than the phone went and it was Brighton Football Club, offering me the manager's job. So my career went in that direction instead. But I must admit that missing out on the Fulham job does still rankle with me today. If I give my word to do something, I do it. And I believed that of Alec Stock at the time. He was a gentleman – okay, so he knew how to bullshit on occasions – but he was very, very good at his job. The funny thing was, Bobby Campbell became Fulham manager about six months later, so they did end up getting rid of Alec after all. Had he given me the job as he promised, he could have stayed on as Director of Football. Bobby's arrival meant the end of Alec, which was very sad.

You're still very much a passionate football man...
I hope I never lose my affection for the game. Football's been my life. Alongside my family, of course. But even they've had to become football folk; it always seemed to be the topic of discussion. Reporters and television have always been a part of my life. I genuinely still love to be involved, whether it be watching a game or talking about it on Sky. I still get a great thrill out of people asking me for my autograph. In fact, when I see some of today's players declining a polite request, I shudder. I think players should be instructed to not only sign autographs but to meet their club's supporters a lot more. Okay, they might have to deal with a minor bit of flak now and again, but in general it would do wonders for building bridges between supporters and players. ⚽

"Fulham have become very resilient. We have a very hard-working team. And let's not forget that Jimmy Bullard has been missed enormously – he looked outstanding in those first three or four games. I hope he comes back fully fit."

Lawrie Driven Out!

Just a few months into the job or not, the axe had to come – it just wasn't working out, was it? So it's goodbye Lawrie Sanchez and hello and welcome not to hot favourite John Collins but Roy Hodgson, formerly Roy of the (Blackburn) Rovers. Our new, vastly experienced gaffer has the task of righting the wrongs of the previous regime and, hopefully, maintaining our Premiership status.

So what went wrong, then? And why sack a bloke half-way through a season and just before Christmas? Well, I think most of us regulars have plenty of opinions about how and why it all went pear-shaped. Bottom line, of course, was that we weren't winning football matches. And perhaps, even worse, that we were looking more and more unlikely to do so. After a bright opening few weeks to the season, during which we suffered a number of setbacks, we simply started to fall apart, and the body-language on the pitch and from the management began to tell its own story.

Below: Hello and a warm welcome to new team boss Roy Hodgson after Lawrie Sanchez (*pictured opposite*) was shown the door.

We were seriously struggling and, as a consequence, had slipped into the bottom three. So much for "pushing for a European place"!

With the transfer window looming, and further surgery obviously needed, the board had to decide whether to back Sanchez – and possibly entrust him with further millions – or to make a clean start. A no-brainer, really! Funny how, once he went, the players found a bit more confidence. Okay, so they didn't transform into wondermen overnight,

but given licence, first by Ray Lewington and subsequently Roy Hodgson, to play the ball through midfield, we saw that there was a bit more to one or two players than we may have thought. Tellingly, both Lewington and Hodgson promptly went on record to say that we have a reasonable squad of players but that the balance is wrong – precisely what was expressed in TOOFIF 105! Not that it really needed a nuclear physicist to work that one out!

Our midfield has been consistently outmuscled for a start. Hardly surprising given that most of our midfielders could easily get subsidiary jobs as garden gnomes! Not so much for the ability to remain static, maybe with a fishing rod (Jimmy Bullard?), but for their pint-sized physique. In fact, you cannot accuse the players of not trying – there's been plenty of huff and puff – but there's been a lack of quality, a terrible imbalance and poor tactics.

Once the confidence started to wane, goalscoring chances became fewer and fewer, while at the other end we've been conceding goals for fun, especially from set pieces. That's a recipe for relegation! As we all know, we have let slip countless points this season – I make it 22! – being unable to hold on for wins or draws when the going got tough.

As well as not showing too many signs of becoming a top-class Premiership manager, Sanchez was certainly not a lucky one, either! And having assembled virtually a new squad for the season, spending countless millions doing so, the buck stopped fair and square with him. Sanchez's sacking prompted much comment from the media. Most of which was wide of the mark as usual – there really is a good case for saying that some sections of the media don't care much for FFC! Those with most to say clearly hadn't seen

Universally Challenged

You know how it is, you get home a little later than usual from work and have missed the family meal. So instead it's a case of warming up the bangers and mash, grabbing a tray, turning on the telly and, with brain switched to neutral, munching away while absent-mindedly taking in the evening fare on the box.

Jeremy Paxman came into view, threatening me with a bout of pre-meal indigestion. *University Challenge* was in full flow; not my favourite viewing to be honest,

mainly because I can hardly ever answer a question. I did on this occasion, mind, as Paxo, just as I sat down to eat, aired a bonus question on the subject of acronyms.

"To what, in the world of football, does the acronym TOOFIF refer?" A mouthful of hot bangers and mash was very nearly spat out in the direction of Paxo's sneering features as the team on the telly struggled to make sense of the question. Did he really say TOOFIF? On University Challenge? I suddenly became the goody-

two-shoes at the front of the class, with hand up, straining like mad to get teacher's attention. "I know, I know, Mr Paxman" – and I should flipping well know – "It's 'There's only One F In Fulham'." And I'm the editor actually. No one in the studio knew the answer and Paxo, by now in sneering overdrive, seemed particularly perplexed as he read out the answer, adding that he'd not heard of the magazine either. Shame on you, Jeremy. With that, it was off to the next "starter for 10"…

us play too often, but were all too eager to opine that the decision was at best premature and at worst unjustified. Interesting to see that Allardyce getting the boot from Newcastle after an almost identical length of time in the hot seat was seen as a bold move whereas getting rid of Sanchez was deemed sheer folly! However, I didn't see any of the same hacks suggesting that the unfortunate Sanchez should replace Allardyce. Funny that!

Roy Hodgson has slipped into the job with quiet authority and great dignity. No tetchy sound bites, so far at least! For all his experience, he has yet to really do the business in the top flight of the British game. Now's the time to start, Roy! As this issue went to press, the transfer window was ajar. Quite what we can expect is anybody's guess, but please no more "possibles" from the Championship. It could well be that Hodgson (and us lot) will get a massive boost through the return of Jimmy Bullard and Brian McBride, as well as our most invisible of wingers, Lee Cook. If Bullard and McBride return in anything like the form they showed before their respective injuries then we'll be in for a treat! And even if they feel their way for the first few matches, surely their inclusion will give us all a boost.

The spine of the team needs the most attention (a minor detail!) – it was foolish not to have any cover for the honest toil of McBride. Kuqi, for all his similar endeavour, has no end product at this level. Dempsey, when played up front, has worked really hard and won more than his share of aerial battles but there's been no one there to benefit. Healy, with an obvious eye for goal, is desperate for a taller partner while Kamara has been the most disappointing of all the new players.

At the heart of the midfield, Murphy, after a sluggish start, has got stronger and stronger. Against Bristol Rovers at home he was outstanding in terms of determination, ability and end-product. The fact remains, though, that he's not that big in stature, and can hardly be expected to carry the midfield alone (step forward Jimmy B…?).

At the back, we've leaked goals galore, and have switched centre-backs at will. Get that department sorted and we'll be on the up. We've even been forced to shuffle keepers; it's good to see Antti Niemi back (even though

Kasey Keller was warming to his task before getting injured), although he must be much more authoritative. He's a top shot-stopper, but tends to stay rooted to his line.

The defeat to West Ham – yet another game in which we took the lead only to ultimately succumb – leaves us perilously poised five points from safety. The visit of Arsenal is hardly a "gimme" so the scale of the job is now clear to us all. I seem to recall saying this last time out: "A flurry of wins can send any team up the table." We were 12th at the time, but since then have played nine games without winning a single one. Three draws and six defeats is lousy in anyone's book – thank heavens for Derby's even-worse plight! The other teams around us nine games ago did the ungentlemanly thing and got on the winning trail. So it's vital that we turn the corner, and soon. Some winnable games are coming up – let's get behind the team and do our bit!

It was great to hear that the local council had approved plans to increase the stadium capacity – but it doesn't take a genius to work out that we'll need to maintain our top-flight status in order to fill the extra seats. Good luck, Roy! ⚽

		Pos
		1st
Arsenal 2 Fulham 1		2nd
12.08.07	9th	3rd
Fulham 2 Bolton Wanderers 1		4th
15.08.07	9th	5th
Fulham 1 Middlesbrough 2		6th
18.08.07	13th	7th
Aston Villa 2 Fulham 1		8th
25.08.07	18th	**9th**
Fulham 3 Tottenham Hotspur 3		10th
01.09.07	15th	11th
Wigan Athletic 1 Fulham 1		12th
15.09.07	16th	13th
Fulham 3 Manchester City 3		14th
22.09.07	17th	15th
Chelsea 0 Fulham 0		16th
29.09.07	16th	17th
Fulham 0 Portsmouth 2		18th
07.10.07	18th	19th
Fulham 0 Derby County 0		20th
20.10.07	13th	
Sunderland 1 Fulham 1		
27.10.07	14th	
Fulham 3 Reading 1		
03.11.07	13th	
Liverpool 2 Fulham 0		
10.11.07	13th	
Fulham 2 Blackburn Rovers 2		
25.11.07	12th	
Manchester United 2 Fulham 0		
03.12.07	14th	
Everton 3 Fulham 0		
08.12.07	14th	
Fulham 0 Newcastle United 1		
15.12.07	18th	
Fulham 1 Wigan Athletic 1		
22.12.07	17th	
Tottenham Hotspur 5 Fulham 1		
26.12.07	18th	
Birmingham City 1 Fulham 1		
29.12.07	19th	
Fulham 1 Chelsea 2		
01.01.08	19th	
West Ham United 2 Fulham 1		
12.01.08	19th	
Fulham 0 Arsenal 3		
19.01.08	19th	
Bolton Wanderers 0 Fulham 0		
29.01.08	19th	
Fulham 2 Aston Villa 1		
03.02.08	19th	
Middlesbrough 1 Fulham 0		
09.02.08	19th	
Fulham 0 West Ham United 1		
23.02.08	19th	
Fulham 0 Manchester United 3		
01.03.08	19th	
Blackburn Rovers 1 Fulham 1		
08.03.08	19th	

League Cup

Shrewsbury Town 0 Fulham 1
28.08.07   Round 2

Fulham 1 Bolton Wanderers 2
26.09.07   aet Round 3

FA Cup

Fulham 2 Bristol Rovers 2
06.01.08   Round 3

Bristol Rovers 0 Fulham 0
22.01.08   aet Round 3 replay
Rovers win 5-3 pens

Squeaky Bum Time

What a waste of a season! What a catalogue of errors!! As I write, our Premiership status hangs in the balance – but at six points adrift of 17th place, the Championship is well and truly beckoning. Whether the welcome point gained late in the day at Ewood Park will prove vital, we'll have to see. Either way, Jimmy Bullard's fantastic late leveller against Blackburn was more than welcome.

Although we're looking more solid under Roy Hodgson, there's the small matter of scoring goals and picking up sufficient points. But whatever happens between now and the end of the season, there's no doubt the Club has been poorly controlled these past few months, and we've all had to suffer. So much for the Club's oft-vaunted top-ten ambitions!

For all of his plus-points as a player, captain and, ultimately, manager, I think we all agreed that Chris Coleman's tenure had run its course this time last season and, with a similar spectre of relegation, something had to be done. The records show that we just about retained our top-flight status, but we remained uninspiring in those last few games under Lawrie Sanchez as temporary boss. Whether we needed as brutal an overhaul as Sanchez demanded once he lost the "caretaker" tag is debatable. What we didn't need was an influx of broadly similar players who, although fairly capable, could best be described as "Championship-class". Now there's planning for the future!

Being Fulham folk, we got behind the new manager and hoped (prayed?) for the best. And, to be fair, we enjoyed a fairly bright start and were genuinely unlucky on a number of occasions. But, with no real spine to the team and no obvious leaders, it all started to fall apart. Sanchez's cause wasn't helped by the cruel injury to Brian McBride – but surely we should have had an adequate replacement as cover for a veteran striker anyway?

Millions of pounds were squandered on a virtually brand-new squad that was probably inferior to the previous group of players. That takes some doing! Little wonder that just a few months into his stewardship Sanchez was booted into touch. The scary thing is, had we managed to pick up those half-a-dozen points or so that we probably merited early on, he'd probably still be in charge! And how interesting to read his recent comments that we're in a far worse predicament than when he was in the hotseat. There's hardly been a stampede from other clubs for his extraordinary "talents" has there?

So, with ten or so games remaining, it's hardly surprising that there are grumblings of discontent about the whole Premiership package. I must confess that I grew out of love with the whole money-raking, warped enterprise ages ago. Mainly because at this level the fans are often an after-thought to the whole over-hyped business. However, if you want continual evolvement and improvement for your club, then it's the place to be, like it or not.

Should the trapdoor open, I don't dread dropping into the Championship, in fact it'll probably be like returning to the real football world once again, where supporters count for something and the games kick off at 3pm on Saturdays – and where the whole shooting match isn't apparently run for the benefit of a perceived Big Four. The major worries about relegation are the financial implications, which could prove calamitous for our Club, and the probable exodus of some of our favourite players.

But that's all being a bit presumptuous! First off we've a run of potentially winnable games to deal with, and there's enough quality in the squad to do something about our perilous position. The question is – have we the belief? And will we go for it with a modicum of passion? ⚽

So, Where *is* Ara?

Cyprus, actually! TOOFIF regular and all-round good egg Dave Johnson tracked down Ara while on business on the island and set up this interview, conducted by the Ed.

So remind us Ara, how did you end up at Fulham in the first place, and what were your first impressions…
I was trialling at QPR, although still technically attached to Apoel in Cyprus. Ray Wilkins, being good friends with Ray Lewington, got Lewy to come down to watch me play in a reserve game. George Armstrong was there too, and after the game he offered me a three-week trial at Arsenal while Ray, on behalf of Don Mackay, offered me a two-month contract – until the end of that '93-94 season – with Fulham. Arsenal was tempting, but it was better for me at the time to have some money coming in rather than go for a trial period.

Opposite page top: Ara Bedrossian stalks Exeter's Danny Bailey, who also had a spell at Craven Cottage.

Below: Ara loved his time at Fulham and had a genuine bond with the fans.

Hmm, Arsenal in the top flight or Fulham struggling in the third tier of the Football League – was that a wise decision in retrospect…?
[Laughing] Obviously in due course things went downhill for me and certainly for Fulham, but you can't look back with any regrets. It was the right decision at the time. I broke into the first team and I really enjoyed those two months at Craven Cottage.

You made your debut as a sub at Bolton and, after a second appearance from the bench, you played seven games on the spin…
That's right, I came on as sub against Bolton then again against Huddersfield – we lost both games 1-0! – then the next game was at Rotherham and Don Mackay put me in the starting line-up. We drew that one, but we won the next five before finishing the season with a 1-1 draw at home to Exeter.

You must have thought, "This ain't so tough…"?
I really enjoyed that run of games – and of course all that crazy stuff started with a section of fans chanting my name and the fanzine *Where's Ara?* starting. Amazing! I must have done quite well during those games as both Middlesbrough and Birmingham City came in for me. I had trials with both.

So what was happening on the Fulham front?
In what turned out to be my last couple of days with Middlesbrough, Don Mackay called me and asked what I'd been offered. When I told him, he said Fulham couldn't offer me terms that good, but might come reasonably close. My answer was simple – just make me an offer and, as long as it wasn't something silly, I'd come back like a shot. So he and Jimmy Hill promised my father, who looked after my affairs, that they'd do the honours. All that my Cypriot club, Apoel, wanted was £10,000 to ensure I was totally free from any ties. I'd been through Uefa previously and won my case but I had to find £10,000 to pay liability damage or such like. Jimmy Hill and co promised that they would get the money, so that was that – it was back to Fulham for another two-and-a-half years.

A quick roll call of the players that you played with around then included: Jim Stannard, Simon Morgan, Martin Pike, Mark Newson, John Marshall, Udo Onwere, Glen Thomas, Julian Hails, Sean Farrell, Mark Kelly and Gary Brazil – do you have any specific memories of them?
All of them! It's so very different in Cyprus. There, when a newcomer arrives on the scene, he's treated a little indifferently, the onus is on him to mix. But at Fulham everyone was so welcoming. Especially Gary Brazil, Simon Morgan and Sean Farrell – the

handshakes were warm and welcoming and I was really glad to be "home". I must single out Julian Hails – what a great lad and probably my best mate at Fulham while I was there.

Your silky skills in midfield made quite an impression on the fans, especially in those early games, hardly surprising as we went on a winning run! And there was that fanzine named after you. Did you appreciate all of that?
It was a brilliant boost initially. The warmth of feeling from the terraces was almost tangible. But it made things difficult when I came back, I guess. I wanted to do so well, but I wasn't really fit. I'd missed pre-season training after all, and here we were into October and I was trying to play "catch-up". I should've made things clearer to Don and Ray, but it was just a case of me not wanting to upset the applecart by appearing too forward. I'm shy by nature and thought it best to just get on with things.

Your second debut was against Reading…
They were top of the table, if I remember rightly, and Fulham were near the bottom having won only twice. So with the side struggling I was thrown in, not necessarily as a match-winner but more because I was a new, if familiar face. And, false modesty aside, I had such a great first half – you know when you've played well, and I was pleased and proud to be back in a Fulham shirt – but I should have told him at half-time that I was really tired and that I should be a candidate for being subbed. But my shyness took over – I was never as strong in character as the British players were – and I stupidly kept quiet. And of course I flagged in the second period. We went down 1-0.

Not as strong in character as, shall we say, Glenn Thomas and…

"What an awful afternoon. It was really depressing. I loved being at Fulham so much, and yet there was the Club, and us players, heading for the bottom division. And no one wants to be down there, do they?"

[Laughing] …and Jim Stannard! No, you're spot on there! I guess I had a few good games in that second spell, but I could have done so much better – although it's easy for me to say that now. All I can say is that I never stopped trying, in whatever position I was selected. And when Ian Branfoot subsequently came in, he said he didn't think I was the kind of player he was looking for; he said he wanted me to be more of a midfield hustler. So I said, "No problem" and I vowed to really go for it. I can remember the pre-season training under Branfoot – we used to go on 45-minute runs and I was winning most of these very easily. (I was lucky in that I was always good at pre-season stuff, whereas some guys had to re-acquaint themselves with all of that every summer.) I was desperate to make the right impression on the new manager and I thought I was doing okay; in fact he played me in all the pre-season games and I was selected to play in the first match, at home to Walsall. We went one-down but I put the pass through for our equaliser, so I thought things were going fairly well. I started another couple of games in October, the second one at Rochdale being settled by a goal from Terry Hurlock, but that was it.

Nipping back a season, Simon Morgan has gone on record as saying that the '93-94 squad had been good enough to push for promotion, but we ended up getting relegated. So, what went wrong?
He's right, we shouldn't have been at that end of the table. But I do recall that when we managed to win four games on the spin in January and February, all the other teams in trouble won as well! That did nothing for the confidence, I can tell you. Possibly we'd got rid of some players that we shouldn't have – I always thought Mark Kelly was a great player, capable of beating a player and making things happen. And yet Don Mackay let him go.

It all came down to the game at Swansea…
It all rested on that game, that's right. Win or go down, pretty much. We had a free-kick routine that we'd worked on long and hard in training a couple of days previously and, as luck would have it, we earned a free-kick against Swansea at 0-0, I think, and the routine worked a treat. I can't recall who it was, but the move left one of our guys in a one-on-one with the keeper and, had we scored, I'm convinced we'd have gone on to win the game. Honestly, I can remember that moment clearly to this day (just as I remember that I probably had my worst game ever!). But what an awful afternoon. It was really depressing. I loved being at Fulham so much, and yet there was the Club, and us players, heading for the bottom division. And no one wants to be down there, do they?

Let's lift the mood pretty sharpish. If I mentioned 12 February, 1994, would that ring any bells?
[A pause] I confess I'm struggling…

…What if I said "Blackpool"…?
[Excitedly] Blackpool, oh yeah… my goal! My only goal for Fulham! I know the fans appreciated me for trying to get the ball down and play, but I didn't get enough goals, did I? Those diehards – and I know you're one – might well remember that I hit the woodwork in seven consecutive games. Against Brentford I hit the bar twice – and I knew what it meant for Fulham to beat their neighbours – but the ball just wouldn't go in. Against Bournemouth, I think it was, we scored three times at their place to win the match, but I hit the woodwork twice that day, too!

Your one and only goal proved to be a match winner…?
Yeah, it was the only goal of the game. I really put myself about against Blackpool, it was one of my better games, and I was really proud to score. I remember Julian [Hails] coming up to me after the game and saying "At last!" Funny thing is, I remember that day for another reason. They used to do bets and stuff under the old stand and, what with me hitting the bar and post so often, my odds for scoring were getting longer and longer. Against Blackpool I was 33-1. Anyway, the manager of one of the junior sides put a tenner on me, so he made a tidy profit on my only Fulham goal! But to score was a terrific highlight for me. Another genuine highlight was being selected to play for the TOOFIF side some time later. In a funny way it gave me a chance to have one last game at the Cottage. And that meant so much to me. It might only have been a friendly, but I really loved the place and it was a thrill to be able to play there one last time. I had such fun and it meant a lot to be invited to take part.

Not quite so jolly was the game at Orient when, with Fulham a goal behind at half-time, Jimmy Hill effectively relieved Don Mackay of his duties. What happened?
Jimmy Hill came in to our dressing room, and he didn't look too happy. He asked: "Who's not playing in their right position?" I'd been pushed out to the wing that day so I put my hand up. Jimmy reshuffled the team slightly, putting me back into the middle, and we managed to get a 2-2 draw. I have to say here and now that Don Mackay was a lovely man and always treated me and my family well, but his knowledge of football was, shall we say, somewhat lacking at times. Ray Lewington used to do much of the training, even if Don had the final say in selection.

So what happened after you left Fulham, Ara?

I went to Sweden. I played in their First Division for a while for a team called Skövde then heard that my old team were interested in me so I went back and we did the League and Cup double that year and so qualified for the Champions League, where we beat Bangor City before going out to Paris St Germain. In time I moved on to another Cypriot club, Olympiakos, before hanging up the old boots at the age of 35.

Do you still look for Fulham's results?
Always! I watched the Adams and Keegan years unfold, from a distance unfortunately, and it's been brilliant to see the team scale the footnalling pyramid. I was so pleased to sign for Fulham all those years ago. I thought Queens Park Rangers would sign me, and then Glenn Roeder, at Gillingham, spoke of an 18-month contract. But by then I'd already spoken to Ray Lewington so I was hoping something would work out.

All these years later and Ray Lewington is back at Fulham.
I was watching the Aston Villa game on the TV and when Fulham scored, the camera homed in on him celebrating. I couldn't believe it! I said out loud: "That's Ray, that's Ray!" He is such a good guy. Him and Ray Wilkins were the two biggest influences on my career in England. Okay, I may not have achieved that much over there in truth, but whatever I did manage was down to those

guys. And possibly Ray Lewington shades it as the top dog. He put me so much at ease when I went out to play. He'd simply say: "Just go out and play your game" – of course I'd have responsibilities to the team too, but Ray did so much to take off any pressure. I wasn't going onto the pitch with a book-full of the manager's demands swirling around in my head, I was free from all of that. And I'll always be grateful.

Do you have a message for the Fulham fans from the mid-'90s who still remember you with great affection?
I really do, actually. I was at Fulham for 22-23 months in all, hardly a lifetime, but – apart from when I met my wife! – they were the best months of my life. And the fans were wonderful. Every time I stepped onto the pitch I just took a look around and appreciated everything about Fulham. The crowd was always very genuine towards me. It was great to be able to go into the bar afterwards and mingle with the supporters. Most were shy about approaching me, but the joke was I was the shy one! The fans were truly fantastic – I even remember the name of my kit sponsor, Bob Howes, and I'd like to say a thank you to him, too. I'll never forget the Fulham fans – in fact, my wife is bored of me saying time and again how great my time was at Fulham! It didn't really matter what division they were playing in – just to put on that white shirt was all that mattered. ⚽

Portsmouth Away – The Great Escape

A vital game for Fulham, and I didn't have a ticket! I hadn't applied in the usual way because of work commitments, but a change of circumstances a couple of days before the main event meant I was now free to go. Unsurprisingly the vital game was a sell-out. Despite making a host of phone calls, the best I could manage was one "might" and two "maybes".

Things looked bleak for Fulham – we needed a win, an away win for heaven's sake, to stay up. Things also looked bleak for yours truly, too; after all, who'd have a spare for such an important encounter? Then came an extraordinary lucky break: who should I bump into at a crowded Victoria Station but Gary Double, who'd not only overseen the PR for Michael Heatley's book *Match of my Life: Fulham* for which I'd contributed three chapters, but was by then, wait for it, Portsmouth's Director of Communications. He confirmed that not only was the game a total sell-out but that

all the press places had been allocated too. However, he might, just might, be able to squeeze me in somewhere as a favour to a fellow Fulham supporter.

The next morning he came up trumps – bless you, Gary! – even if it certainly was a tight squeeze in the press box and the rest of the ground on the day. Fratton Park was heaving and, to our right, the travelling supporters were in good voice. So to the big question: could we possibly pull off what had seemed mission impossible in the closing weeks of that season and somehow maintain our place in the top flight? Of course we could! Mind you, the clock was ticking away as we adopted a measured rather than gung-ho approach to the massive task. Roy Hodgson's methods paid dividends when Danny Murphy, that well-known target man, timed his run into the Pompey area 14 minutes from time to meet Jimmy Bullard's flighted free-kick and send a header (a header!) beyond the reach of keeper Jamie Ashdown.

The remaining few minutes took weeks to elapse but, finally, Mark Clattenburg gave a shrill blast on his whistle and we'd done it – an unbelievable result and an emotionally draining afternoon. Down in the press room afterwards Roy Hodgson had the media cynics eating out of his hand with a classy display of his own. No sound bites, that's simply not his style, but immediate words of consolation to the managers of the relegated sides: "For much of the game I was contemplating this post-match interview and dreading the fact that we could well be facing life in the Championship, so my thoughts are with the managers and players who have not been so fortunate this afternoon."

You had the feeling that afternoon down on the south coast that after this there might be a few more intriguing chapters to the Fulham story with Hodgson at the helm. Then again, no one could have truly foreseen the incredible adventures that were to follow...

Perfect Working Order

Forget Roy Hodgson. And Jimmy Bullard. You can even dismiss Danny Murphy and Brian McBride. Okay, they played significant bit-parts during the run-in, but in fact it was New Order wot done it! With a little help from a clutch of Fulham fans and Emma Jones, from Radio London 94.9, perhaps. You see, heading along the M4 towards Reading, my eldest son Matt and I decided to whack on some New Order, which, if nothing else, put us in a toe-tapping mood. It was an even better drive back home having secured three precious points (an away win at last!).

A few weeks later, Matt put on the same CD as we drove to the Cottage for the game with Birmingham – and, having got there, it was then we realised we were bumping into the same mini-groups of Fulham supporters, as well as Emma Jones. We remarked on it on the drive home, with another three points in the bag. With everything riding on the trip to Pompey, you can guess the preparations. Based on the aforementioned scientific evidence, our humble people-carrier was positively rocking on the drive to the south coast and, once there, we began to tick off the required Fulham faces. I was fortunate enough to get a seat in the press box, where, to my relief, Emma Jones was on duty. Everything was in place!

The match itself was terribly tense, every minute seeming to last four or five. Fulham struggled to get going in the intense heat and rarely troubled the home goal. Portsmouth, on the other hand – and Kranjcar in particular – looked lively early on. Thank heavens for Hangeland's man-of-the-match performance. The longer it remained 0-0 we had a chance, but to be truthful, we were looking leg-weary after the heroics of the previous weeks and, as the home side ran out of ideas, the game looked sure to remain goal-less. For no apparent reason, I started to hum the opening bars of "Blue Monday". Almost at once we had a goalmouth skirmish. Now, I'm not the superstitious kind, but, as a noted advertising slogan exclaims, "Every little helps"!

So I continued humming, and even tapping my foot. With that, Bullard's well-flighted free-kick headed towards the penalty spot, the Pompey defence went walkabout, Murphy rose majestically (what's he doing there? And unchallenged!?) and nodded the ball home. An instinctive glance towards the linesman confirmed no offside; cue delirium pretty much everywhere. And much, much relief. We weren't there yet, but, bloody hell, we'd only gone and scored!!! Just need to hold on for 13 or so minutes...

If the early stages had dragged, time now seemed to stand still. But standing still was not on the agenda for Fulham's terrific away following. They were going barmy to my right. However, that was nothing to the explosion of delight when the final whistle was heard about three weeks later. I leapt in the air right away – sod pressbox protocol – we were safe! Directly in front of me "Gentleman" Jim McGullion was, seemingly, set to explode, screeching with glee to all those listening to his commentary. Me, I was utterly knackered. I simply sat back and took in the wild scenes of delight on the field and to my right where the Fulham awaydayers were a mass of movement and noise. The Pompey fans, with their own big day a week away, were generous in their applause, too. Before heading downstairs for the press gathering, I realised I was humming/tapping the opening to "Bizarre Love Triangle" (the extended dance mix!). Yep, New Order had done the trick all right and the drive home was a good 'un!

Reflecting on our Great Escape, several images remain vivid, not least Danny Murphy's header. And yet the one that sticks out is not a Bullard free-kick, a McBride header, Kamara's late winner at City, or even our wild celebrations at Pompey. No it's Ray Lewington totally "losing it" when Bullard's belter finally put paid to Villa. The camera was seeking a reaction from our Roy. But up popped Ray instead, going berserk with joy – we know just how you felt, Lewy! Now there's a guy who's seen a host of changes at FFC!

Thanks, Ray. And, of course, thanks Roy. A true gent. And mastermind of a truly Great Escape. ⚽

Bully for us

The 2007-08 campaign was, ultimately, quite a season for Jimmy Bullard. Having fought back courageously from a career-threatening injury, our much-missed, tousle-haired midfielder returned to the action for the final months and played a significant part in our dramatic survival. That magical, hard-fought win at Fratton Park obviously meant a great deal to him. Immediately after the Portsmouth game, I managed to grab a few words with our talismanic (some might just say "manic"!) midfielder...

"When I was injured, I simply never thought a day like this would come around. I feel on top of the world right now. After a brilliant result like that, it makes it all worthwhile to come back. All that hard graft in that gym – which I really hated! – seems worthwhile right now.

"Having been injured, I owe the Club loads. They've been right behind me the whole way. They didn't rush me – they just said, 'when you're back, you're back'. I can't thank them enough – they've been awesome. I'm just so happy that I was able to

Above: Our "Tousle-haired midfielder" Jimmy Bullard – the man who puts the "manic" in talismanic"!

play my part in keeping Fulham in the Premiership.

"Hey, four wins in the last five games – it's crazy really... unbelievable! And it's kept us out of the Championship! We've chalked up three away wins out of three. But no one amongst us ever said that it was over and we were as good as down. And the gaffer believed in us loads.

"That Reading game away was a really massive result for us – and it gave us extra belief. As you know, we hadn't won an away game for God knows how long, but we came away from there believing, and it sort of snowballed after that great win.

"We've played awesome in the last three games. Not like a team deep in relegation trouble, and we've thoroughly deserved to stay up. I know it's a bit early to talk about it, but if we can start next season in the form we've finished this one, who knows what might happen!

"The great thing is that we can relax now. We all know that we're Premier League players so we can go home and have a holiday, and it will definitely be that much sweeter because we've stayed up in the top flight.

"The manager has been awesome – as have all the coaching staff. I'm sure he'll look to buy players now. His organisation is immense – he's been absolutely awesome. But then you've just got to look at his CV – he knows his stuff, obviously, and he's a real football man and his belief is massive.

"When we came back to the dressing rooms at Manchester City 2-0 down, he believed more than any of us that we could still do it. He just said, 'Okay, go out and win this half.' We went out and won it 3-0 and picked up three points which was another massive turning point." ⚽

A Few Words From the Gaffer

Calmest man in the press room – seemingly at least – after the vital victory at Portsmouth was Roy Hodgson. Our experienced manager was, unsurprisingly on great form.

"A relief? Of course! We were aware throughout the game that the other results weren't going for us and only a win would suffice and we were playing against a Portsmouth team that were very well organised defensively, but I'm very pleased with the way the players kept their shape. They kept plugging away and were trying to do all the right things, hoping that would bring its reward, which, at the end, it did. I don't really feel we were lucky to get the result here today, I feel a draw here would also have been a decent result [under normal circumstances], but luckily we who needed the victory the most got it! And I'm really delighted for everybody at the Club.

"Everyone at Fulham Football Club – from the Chairman and the staff to the fans – has been magnificent since I arrived and it's been a really good four months. I've often been quite saddened

by the fact that I haven't been able to wave a magic wand and transform us from a bottom-three club to a top-six club, but I can feel a lot of satisfaction today with the job that everybody's done – but at the same time I feel a lot of sympathy for the two managers who have got relegated this afternoon. Alex McLeish and Steve Coppell are friends of mine – both are excellent managers and, having had a long time to contemplate that it might be us going down, I know exactly how they are feeling. My thoughts go out to them in all the jubilation that we justifiably feel. I'm fully aware that in this game if we win, someone else loses.

"People say that I looked reasonably calm during the closing stages – well, all I can say is that it must have been the valium! I always felt that it was important for us to keep playing the right way. I was a bit worried that we were going to go a bit "gung-ho" just because we knew we had to win. By that I mean, trying to do too much individually or to fly forward – in truth, there were one or two long shots that didn't please me too much, as that wasn't what we were trying to do. But really I always had that thought that if we could ensure that they didn't score and so keep us in the game, that something would come our way. And it did! Danny got in there for a good header before the goal and there were a couple of exciting moments close to their goal-line when it looked like we might score, and so in that respect I suppose I could stay fairly calm. Not that I was calm in those last few minutes after we'd scored I must say! If the game could have stopped the very moment Danny's header went in, I'd have been the happiest man in the world!

"We left it late, both in this game and in terms of the season generally, and we certainly gave ourselves a mountain to climb. But I think that in the course of the last two months, even in those games we lost – against Sunderland and Liverpool – it wasn't because we played exceptionally badly, we just got punished for defensive mistakes in those games. So I think we've had quite a long spell where we've played reasonably well, and we've been picking up the points.

"My biggest fear was that we were running out of games; had we had a few more games to go, I would have been confident that we had enough football quality to get out of the situation. But here we are, we're safe. Am I going to celebrate tonight? Probably not. When you've had such a great day as we've had today, that's celebration enough. I might even watch *Match of the Day* this evening – and I don't do that very often!

"We'll enjoy this result for two or three days, but then we've got to start making certain that next season we've got a stronger platform so that we don't find ourselves in the bottom three. A lot of hard work needs to be done in the summer to make sure that a platform is built." ⚽

Result	Pos
Hull City 2 Fulham 1	
16.08.08	15th
Fulham 1 Arsenal 0	
23.08.08	11th
Fulham 2 Bolton Wanderers 1	
13.09.08	6th
Blackburn Rovers 1 Fulham 0	
20.09.08	10th
Fulham 1 West Ham United 2	
27.09.08	13th
West Brom 1 Fulham 0	
04.10.08	16th
Fulham 0 Sunderland 0	
18.10.08	17th
Portsmouth 1 Fulham 1	
26.10.08	16th
Fulham 2 Wigan Athletic 0	
29.10.08	14th
Everton 1 Fulham 0	
01.11.08	15th
League Cup	
Fulham 3 Leicester City 2	
27.08.08	Round 2
Burnley 1 Fulham 0	
23.09.08	Round 3

1st
2nd
3rd
4th
5th
6th
7th
8th
9th
10th
11th
12th
13th
14th
15th
16th
17th
18th
19th
20th

More Tosh...

osh Chamberlain, a chum of Johnny Haynes since schooldays, recalls the impact the former England captain made on FFC and the game in general, and savours the unveiling of the statue of his much-missed pal...

Walking into the foundry, a few days before the unveiling, I was a little apprehensive. But I needn't have worried – a few steps in and, well, I couldn't believe how lifelike the statue was. It wasn't on any base at this point, simply on the floor, and so I was walking more or less directly towards Johnny's face. It took me back for a moment – in that instant I thought it was Johnny, that's how lifelike it was to me. What an incredible job!

The sculptor was a bit frightened of me – or at least of what my reaction might have been. One or two early sketches hadn't been right. But, after taking it all in, I said: "There's nothing you could have done to have made that statue any better."

I phoned Avril (Johnny's widow) before she set off for London, to put her mind at ease – I think she thought I was exaggerating how good it was. On the day, she and everyone else present were amazed.

The ceremony was lovely. It was great to meet up with so many of the lads again, who were all overawed by the brilliance of the end result. I'm lucky in that I'm still in touch with a lot of the fellas, but seeing so many there on the day, all having come down to honour "our kid" Johnny, was wonderful. It was a pleasure and a privilege to be in their midst.

I must remark on the many supporters who had made their way to the Cottage up to four hours before the game. That in itself says so much about Johnny, and his loyalty to the Club, even though it's nearly 40 years since he last played for Fulham.

Right: The impressive statue of Johnny Haynes was unveiled in October 2008

Below: Tosh Chamberlain is pictured with the "incredible" likeness of Johnny, his close pal since schooldays.

As Jimmy Hill said, you had to see Johnny in action to really appreciate him. You can rave all you like today about your Beckhams or whoever, but there's no real comparison. Honest. Johnny's passing was supreme. And he did it with a leather ball that, if wet, weighed about half a ton! Kicking those footballs with so much accuracy and with the right pace was just unbelievable. And, don't forget, we often played in inches of mud! Most people would be happy with managing one such pass a season; with Johnny it was simply routine.

Yes, he was a great player. And yes, he was a perfectionist. Johnny never looked down on anybody – he classed everyone the same. He didn't expect you to be as good as him, he thought you were as good as him. And when you made a mistake, he'd have a right go. But he was every bit as tough on himself. We were big mates, of course, but Johnny could be a proper miserable so-and-so on the pitch, to himself and to others. If he made a mistake, everyone knew about it – but, equally, if someone else messed up, then watch out!

I knew Johnny from when we about 12 or 13. I saw him grow into this beautiful footballer. At 14 or 15, even though he was tiny, I'd realised he was going to be some player, so all that followed didn't surprise me. Every club in the country wanted him back then. And yet he said he wanted to stay with me – I must have owed him a few bob!

That he did so all seemed very matter-of-fact back then. Now, of course, I class it as an honour. He could have gone to Arsenal or Tottenham, two of the finest clubs in the country at the time, but no, he came to dear old Fulham – because of me. I've gone on record as saying that, after a few years at the Club, I tried to persuade him to leave Fulham for a while because I thought he was worth a Cup, a League winner's medal or whatever, but he was adamant. He didn't want to leave Fulham because Fulham was his club.

Leggat Likes it!

Former Fulham sharpshooter Graham Leggat, now based in Canada, admires the statue from afar:

"The recent unveiling of the Johnny Haynes statue brought back many vivid memories of my enjoyable years at Craven Cottage, especially as a teammate of Johnny's. His attributes were innumerable. As the skipper, he was a true leader – a perfectionist. If he didn't play up to scratch, he stewed over it and he'd let us know if we had made a mistake!

"Being a perfectionist, he would have loved the statue. It's perfect – in every single detail.

"Johnny's loyalty has, at last, been so fittingly honoured by his loyal fans. Congrats to the artist, congrats to the fans. The Maestro stands once again in the perfect place – Craven Cottage."

And now we've got a beautiful statue to remember him by. I know people are saying it's overdue, but, knowing Johnny as I did, I can tell you that if you'd tried to get one done 20 years ago he'd have said no, as he never wanted that type of fame. But I do agree that now it's up, the only downside is that Johnny's not here to see it.

Johnny Haynes was my best mate. Johnny was a great player, the best. He was the hardest trainer, his passing was unbelievable, and he was a terrific captain. All Johnny ever wanted was to play the game for his club and for his country to the best of his ability. I reckon he did all right, didn't he? ⚽

Roy's Team Takes Shape...

With Johnny Haynes taking centre stage at the Cottage once again, much of TOOFIF 109 has a nostalgic feel. And there's nowt wrong with that! However, and with Micky Adams' words ringing in my ears ("Nostalgia's all well and good – but it doesn't win you any bonus points on the field!"), the focus of this column is firmly on the matches played so far this season. [Micky's quote is from 1996-97, by the way. Aah, the nostalgia...!]

Following that euphoric end to last season and subsequent galvanising of the squad by Roy Hodgson, there was real expectation of a solid start to this campaign. But it's all been a bit hit and miss, hasn't it? Ironically, one of our three successes to date came in a fixture that many would have written off beforehand. Okay, so Arsenal were below par – and that's not me slipping into lazy hack mode! – but we thoroughly deserved our success by harrying the visitors, pressing them back as much as possible then making the most of the possession that came our way.

It was a terrific team performance that not only fully merited maximum points but also promised much more of the same. The talk after that "bonus" win was that it was all very well raising our game collectively against Arsenal's artisans, but would we be ready, willing and able to mix it with the likes of Bolton, next on the fixture list, and a side we're obviously hoping to finish above come next May. In the event, and thanks to another really polished show, we pinned back Bolton for most of the game, launching wave after wave of well-constructed attacks. Things were looking mighty good. The only downside on the night was the number of chances missed; early alarm bells for the games to follow. As we all know Bolton nicked a goal towards the end and, although we weren't truly tested, it became a case of hanging on when we should have been trumpeting about a four- or five-goal winning margin. Typical Fulham!

Since then, though, it's been a case of flattering to deceive. And it's been fascinating to read the wide-ranging viewpoints on the messageboards in the meantime. My own view is that while I don't think the balance has been quite right up to now,

it's time for us to acknowledge that summation, rather than go into full panic mode.

Starting from the front, we've not yet had a run of games from the Zamora/Johnson combo, although there are hints of a rosy future. By rights, this "little and large" duo should provide enough goals to keep us in the top flight with points to spare. But, with few strikes on goal between them to date, the partnership's clearly not firing as yet. Johnson's silly sending off against West Ham and subsequent suspension did nothing for continuity. And up to now, the supply to the forwards has hardly been something for them to savour, has it?

The midfield quartet is something of a worry. We have four highly talented players as Roy's first choices. And they should be imposing themselves more on games than they have so far, collectively and individually. Gera, probably our best close-season signing, would probably favour playing infield rather than on the flank. For all his tricks and industry, he hasn't the pace to get round defenders so is continually having to check and play the ball back to a supporting player. Not being naturally left-footed inhibits him too on that flank. (And he's developing into a something of a "nearly-man" in front of goal!) Davies, so very worthy of his player-of-the-season award for '07-08, hasn't been as influential up to now. He, too, isn't the paciest of wide players. Murphy, as committed as ever, has looked to be flagging in the closing stages of games (although less so recently) and Bullard, whom I'll return to in a moment, isn't pulling the strings all that emphatically either. This talented quartet should be providing the front two with many more openings than we've seen thus far. That said, these criticisms are from the attacking point of view and it seems they're having to stifle their natural attacking tendencies for now in order to do their collective bit defensively. And we're not exactly leaking goals are we?

For the first time in ages the defence isn't looking porous! Hangeland, surely our best purchase in ages, is looking more and more at home. While not error-free, he's put in several towering performances, being prepared to throw his body at the ball when necessary and looking to play the ball with no little pedigree as often as possible. Hughes is the less-dominant partner (understandable given his size) but has also acquitted himself well – and was my man-of-the-match at Everton. Crucially, the pair do seem do be forging a respectable partnership. In the full-back berths, both Pantsil and Konchesky are adequate defenders and aren't likely to be given the total runaround by most opposing widemen. Neither player, though, has the out-and-out acceleration to inject the necessary pace when lending their support to our attacks – although that was great link up play by Konchesky to set up Andy Johnson's first for the Club, against Wigan.

Fulham 2 Newcastle United 1	1st
09.11.08 10th	2nd
Fulham 2 Tottenham Hotspur 1	3rd
15.11.08 9th	4th
Liverpool 0 Fulham 0	5th
22.11.08 9th	6th
Aston Villa 0 Fulham 0	7th
29.11.08 8th	**8th**
Fulham 1 Manchester City 1	9th
06.12.08 9th	10th
Stoke City 0 Fulham 0	11th
13.12.08 10th	12th
Fulham 0 Middlesbrough 0	13th
20.12.08 8th	14th
Tottenham Hotspur 0 Fulham 0	15th
26.12.08 8th	16th
Fulham 2 Chelsea 2	17th
28.12.08 9th	18th
West Ham United 3 Fulham 1	19th
18.01.09 10th	20th
Sunderland 0 Fulham 0	
27.01.09 10th	
Fulham 3 Portsmouth 1	
31.01.09 9th	
Wigan Athletic 0 Fulham 0	
07.02.09 10th	
Manchester United 3 Fulham 0	
18.02.09 10th	
Fulham 2 West Brom 0	
22.02.09 8th	
Arsenal 0 Fulham 0	
28.02.09 8th	
Fulham 0 Hull City 1	
04.03.09 10th	
Fulham 1 Blackburn Rovers 2	
11.03.09 10th	
Bolton Wanderers 3 Fulham 1	
14.03.09 9th	

FA Cup

Sheffield Wednesday 1 Fulham 2	
03.01.09 Round 3	
Kettering Town 2 Fulham 4	
24.01.09 Round 4	
Swansea City 1 Fulham 1	
14.02.09 Round 5	
Fulham 2 Swansea City 1	
24.02.09 Round 5 replay	
Fulham 0 Manchester United 4	
07.03.09 Round 6	

Schwarzer, another canny signing, looks comfortable between the sticks (and so he should, given his "veteran" status!) and, while perhaps lucky to keep a clean sheet against Sunderland, he also showed in that match that there's more to it than luck, pulling off several fingertip saves.

So, overall, no major negatives, but it's also very clear that the sum of our individual parts doesn't equate to the team we thought we'd be watching. If I knew the reason why I'd be in football management somewhere, not penning this bilge. But a few observations… I'm all for knocking the ball around, but aren't our midfielders a bit "samey"? Maybe Etuhu, as and when he's fit, would give us another dimension – we could certainly do with a ball-winner – but, if so, who to drop?

Then we come to the enigma that is Jimmy Bullard. Before I kick off, I remain a fan and his call-up to the England squad was refreshing. Had Fat Frank not recovered from that knock, we may well have seen him in an England shirt (and, given the tempo of International matches, it may well have been to his liking – rather like our game against "continental" Arsenal, against whom Bully shone). However, is he attempting to do too much for us in Roy of the Rovers fashion? That's not a crime, of course – indeed it's great to see someone who is so "up" for the cause, who's obviously blessed with almost as much natural ability as exuberance, and who's as likely as anyone on the pitch to come up with a match-winning spark. Trouble is, it's not really happening, is it? That splendid run of man-of-the-match performances seems a while back now. Is it simply a case of trying too hard? Playing too deep? Demanding too much of the ball and thereby slowing the play down? Conversely, despite seeing much of the ball – he remains the hub of the team – is his disciplined approach, demanded of by the manager, inhibiting his natural inclinations? It's a conundrum Roy Hodgson needs to figure out. Then again, we've seen that even when subdued or off-form, he can still come up with something special – the late goal against Leicester being a prime example.

Another puzzler for us lot is why Erik Nevland has barely figured. Okay, so Zamora and Johnson are first choice, but Nevland has proved a decent finisher and would surely be worth a punt late on if things aren't going our way. Then again, Roy's not been one to mix it up a bit up, subs-wise, up to now has he? He made an interesting comment after one game that he didn't think what he had on the bench was better than what was on the field of play. That's fair enough, I suppose – if there was someone outstanding on the bench, the question would have to be asked, "Why wasn't he playing in the first place?" To use Nevland as an example, I wouldn't suggest that he's better than either Zamora or Johnson, but if it ain't happening out there for whatever reason (and

there's a host of obvious ones: tiredness, injury, off-day, lack of confidence, etc.) then why not take a chance? Interesting to note that two subs, Nevland and Dempsey, were directly involved in our late leveller at Portsmouth.

I think most of us would have thought we'd have a few more points on the board up to now. Our discontent is possibly heightened by the way that the promoted teams have made a decent fist of it so far, and that teams such as Sunderland and Blackburn seem to have bought well and are pushing on. And in general it seems a tighter division all round.

And yet, as stated above, we've not played all that badly either – certainly the effort's there, and there's a clear team structure. But for a mad three or four minutes against West Ham (who looked a poor side) we would surely have gone on to win that game. And, even though we had the woodwork to thank (what was it, five times?) against Sunderland, we could easily have nicked that on another day had Gera been wearing his shooting boots. I think our main complaint is that it's all a bit sterile at times. And, given our propensity to flirt with the bottom places in recent seasons, it's hardly a surprise that we're a bit nervous about doing so again, even if it's still very early in the campaign. Another viewpoint, though, is that we're almost deliberately sterile. Or at least very deliberately going through certain motions in a disciplined way – with each player doing his vital bit within a structured framework. Blimey, this is getting professorial, so let's switch to stating-the-bleedin'-obvious: if we can maintain our miserly ways at the back (we're conceding less than a goal a game) and get going on the goal trail, then it's job done! Easy, eh?

As ever, a couple of good results will probably not only change the whole mood but also our league position as well as the all-important confidence levels. Thank goodness, we have the players in the camp to move us up the table – we are surely a better outfit than last season. But it's no good appearing better on paper, we need to prove this on grass. And, to quote the Hammersmith "poet" James Cox, we need to look bothered, and be prepared to "rip some bloody spleens out"! A tad over the top, perhaps – but I know what he means. ⚽

On the up, Slowly but Surely

Last time out, I wittered on about how things weren't quite right on the field, but suggested that we were heading in the right direction. A long unbeaten run later and here we are sitting snugly, if not securely, in the top half of the table and in the Fifth Round of the FA Cup. Okay, okay, I know we're not that many points away from the relegation places either, but let's enjoy it while it lasts. And there's no doubt that, putting the lousy showing at West Ham to one side for a moment, we're looking a decent, resilient unit these days. It just shows what can be done with a little footballing nous. Actually, in the case of Roy Hodgson, a lot of footballing nous!

Not that our move up the table has been championed by the tabloids. On the one hand, I'm perfectly happy that we've been allowed to regroup and move onwards and upwards in a softly, softly manner. In the real world, we've only just turned the corner anyway so fawning or lurid headlines could only rock the boat. But it still narks me that we're not getting the credit we deserve for having pushed on so splendidly.

Isn't it amazing how many teams have had an off-day when facing us this season? Nothing to do with our input to the proceedings, naturally! An article on Chelsea's failings at the Bridge highlighted the teams with superior home records to the Blues: as well as good old Fulham FC, they included Liverpool, Aston Villa and Stoke. We managed to dent those records by getting points there on our travels. And yet the tabloids have steered clear of highlighting our renaissance, preferring to home in on stories such as John Terry Picks His Nose, Rooney Picks His Spots, or Gerard Picks A Fight as, sadly in this day and age, such tales sell more newspapers. We only get the tabloid spotlight when they trumpet the supposed imminent departure of our top players.

At least some of the broadsheets have cottoned on, and their articles offer some uplifting insights. It makes a terrific change to see Brede Hangeland being quoted as saying: "For me, this Club is perfect", rather than being linked to any club who might possibly need a commanding centre-half.

Most of us are realistic enough to know that if one of the perceived big clubs comes a-calling, waving their wads and promising regular European football, then it's hard for a player at a club like ours to be anything other than interested. And, given that we're so attached to our club, it's often difficult for some to realise that players rarely feel the same way. It's a mercenary world and a short-lived career; contracts count for nothing when it suits – especially with all the caveats and small print hidden from the public. In short, money talks!

On the other hand, players appreciate a well-organised set-up and can generally feel when things are on the up. Roy Hodgson and his staff have instilled a tremendous club spirit and it's only very recently (with the transfer window beckoning!) that we've detected whispers of discontent from a few of those not playing regularly.

You've only got to look at how the team has improved defensively to recognise the manager's input and influence. The acquisition of Hangeland has been an enormous factor, but it's still taken the back four (plus a reliable goalkeeper and the extra cover afforded by the midfielders) working as a unit to limit the goals-against column to well under a goal a game.

At the start of the season many (including yours truly) doubted that the midfield partnership of Danny Murphy and Jimmy Bullard was the way forward. Murphy's legs were on the way out, it was suggested. A ball-winner was essential, right? But with a new disciplined approach to the whole team, Murphy has positively blossomed. No one doubted his work ethic or abilities but the games generally tended to pass him by. Yet he's had a stormer of a season to date and has worn the captain's armband with distinction.

Bullard, meanwhile, has hopped off to Hull in exchange for £5m! Good deal or bad? Was he our best player or not even our best midfielder? Indispensable or too often flattering to deceive? Vibrant personality or pain in the arse? Hub of the team or greedy bastard? Playing far too deep or playing to orders? I'm not privy to how he was perceived at training (mind you, turning up in a Borat mankini, according to the *Daily Star*, would suggest that he hasn't always conformed to Roy Hodgson's old school, gentlemanly approach!), and so can only comment on what he's done on the field. As I've hinted above, of the two players hawked about in the press, Hangeland would be the greater loss, given that he's the linchpin of our defence and is improving with each game. We'll get by without Jimmy Bullard. Even so, I was firmly in the pro-Bullard camp. His first touch was excellent, meaning he could be trusted to collect the ball and move it on; his obvious confidence in his own ability meant that he was always ready to receive a pass or throw-in even when shadowed by an opponent. He often provided an "out" ball to those around him, especially at the back, and, generally, was able to keep possession and keep the move going with a decent variety of passing.

Of course, when it went wrong he stood out like a sore thumb, but he still didn't hide, preferring to play himself back into form, and yet was always likely to come up with something special even on an off-day (remember Leicester in the Cup?). But that's all history now and while the deal is clearly good for the player, it remains to be seen just how good it is for FFC. £5m is great on paper, but the real test is how we adapt from here and whether we can bolster the squad. ⚽

Above: That statue unveiling according to Paul Johnson, *We Can Dream*-style!

Simon Morgan

I f ever a Fulham player deserved a testimonial it was Simon Morgan. Despite his consistently valiant efforts, his decade at the Club included our very worst seasons. "Where were you when you were shit…?" was often chanted by opposing fans as we made our subsequent climb up the divisions. Morgan's answer, given the chance, was always the same: "I was not only there but I was the bloody captain!"

What was sometimes forgotten as he hurled himself into one ludicrous challenge after another in the thick of an often losing midfield battle while taking the art of complaining to a whole new level, was that Simon Morgan could play. He joined FFC in October 1990 as a former England Under-21 International with the intention of helping Fulham to go on to greater things. That he did eventually, but only after the

Club's disastrous and almost terminal drop into the basement division.

In 1993-94 his team-mates included Peter Baah, Lee Tierling, Martin Ferney and Mark Cooper, but back in 1986 his England colleagues included Perry Suckling, Tony Dorigo, Garry Parker, Stuart Pearce, Tony Adams, Des Walker, David Rocastle and Nigel Clough. There's no doubting that Morgs became very attached to FFC and its supporters, and, once he'd hung up his boots, was proud to head up FFC's Community scheme. But what really kept Morgs at Fulham were his dodgy knees. As we slumped towards football's plughole, had he been offered a decent move elsewhere he'd have gone. We were the lucky ones in that his knees were, to use professional parlance, effin' knackered; he'd never have passed a proper medical. The poor state of Morgs' patellae mirrored the plight of our beloved club, so he'd have been utterly mad to turn down any potential move. Even Pulis at Gillingham!

As it was, though, he not only lasted the course but was a shining beacon in a quagmire of shite. He looked bothered, was bothered and was prepared to fight for the cause week in, week out. And if things didn't go his way (which they invariably didn't for a few seasons) he'd moan with as much ferocity as his tackles. TOOFIF labelled him a "moaning minnie", which, while not as derogatory or plain filthy as many a nickname, did make it into print several times, including Morgs' excellent *On Song For Promotion* (his diary of the '96-97 campaign).

As well as doing more than his share of duties on the field, he was also a staunch supporter of

Below: Rum goings-on – Captain Morgan with Captain Morgan.

Below right: The Ed presents Morgs with a framed TOOFIF front cover.

the fans' activities. For example, when Alex "The Traveller" Ferguson and Gary Billing slogged their way to Brighton on a fundraising walk for the FFC coffers, Captain Morgan made it his business to be at Craven Cottage to see them off and to greet the by-then gruesome twosome at The Goldstone Ground the following day.

Morgs' reward was to enjoy the Club's resurgence, first under Micky Adams, then forming a formidable centre-back triumvirate with Chris Coleman and Kit Symons under the stewardship of Kevin Keegan. As the reasons for whingeing became fewer by the week, we were all reminded of what a good player he was – and the Brummie Bluenose even grabbed the national newspaper headlines by heading home a beauty as third tier Fulham stunned Premier League high-fliers Aston Villa 2-0 at Villa Park in the FA Cup in January 1999. Even so, Morgs' crowning glory was getting a regular column in TOOFIF and, subsequently, his very own testimonial fanzine (*There's Only One Simon Morgan*).

After finally recovering from a long-term injury and with Fulham charging towards the Premier League, Morgs was given one last hurrah by Jean Tigana (who apparently called "Mr Fulham" into his office the day before the game to ask him what position he played!). Morgs was given 15 minutes or so against Wolves and was not only cheered every time he went near the ball but was adjudged man-of-the-match for taking an effective throw-in!

Fulham stalwart Phil Mison, writing on the ESPN site in 2010, captured the moment

superbly: "Who can forget our win (against Wolves) in April 2001? Our 2-0 victory came courtesy of two Saha penalties, and the victory pushed us past the 100 points mark as we roared towards the top flight. The performance was not one of our most scintillating, but there was a cheer that night that would have done Wembley proud. Inside the last 20 minutes Tigana allowed Simon Morgan some game time after a 15-month injury lay-off. He touched the ball maybe five times... but when David Hamilton announced 'Simon Morgan is Man of the Match' close to the end, the roof came off! It was his last-ever appearance for the Club." ⚽

Above: Ken Coton's fantastic image of Simon Morgan in celebratory mode.

Below: More celebrations – with Morgs, as you'd expect, leading from the front.

Fulham 2 Man United 0

What a performance, what a result! To beat Manchester United was one thing. To do so deservedly, having pinned them back for much of the first half at least, was another thing entirely. And to bounce back from two lame defeats against them makes this latest result all the more remarkable and, of course, as enjoyable as it was unexpected.

To those defeats first. It's no disgrace to lose to Man United. We cannot compete with either their financial or playing resources. However, we gave them far too much respect and seemed to wave the white flag all too early in both encounters. But what a difference third time around!

With only seconds gone on the clock, though, it appeared to be the same old script as Paul Scholes dived in with a trademark "rash" tackle – his umpteenth foul at Craven Cottage – and yet again escaped a "regulation" yellow card. Cue lots of murmurings of "special treatment". And you couldn't argue.

But neither could you argue with our determined approach. Someone near me suggested: "We've been by far the better team for the opening four minutes." The remark was met by a swift, droll riposte: "Yeah, but there's 86 minutes left. Plus whatever Fergie needs for 'added time'."

Before the game, much of the talk was fairly resigned rather than bullish. A nice day for watching football... Doesn't Craven Cottage look splendid in the spring sunshine...? Dempsey's had food poisoning, but I'm shitting myself...! [Nice!] Let's hope we give them more of a game this time... Understandable, I guess. But as the minutes ticked away, the air of resignation gave way to the more usual matchday nerves. Hell, we were giving them a good game. In fact, we had them on the back foot. If only we could score – that'd make it interesting... bloody hell, we've got a penalty. And they're down to ten men!

Phil Dowd had a good game. His first big decision was routine, however – as long as he or his officials saw it. Handball almost on the goal-line. Scholes off. Things were getting more interesting by the minute. Now, come on Danny, keep your cool, don't be put off by Edwin's usual antics... We needn't have worried. GOOOAAAL!!! A wonderful penalty kick; 1-0. Game on!

And we continued to press. By half-time there was an air of wonderment. As good a half of football as we could have dared to hope for; quite magnificent. From the steady authority of Schwarzer in goal, via the calmness and focus of the ever-brilliant Hangeland, the leadership, toil and ability of Murphy to the much-maligned Zamora leading the line in rumbustious fashion and giving the visiting centre-halves a torrid time. And that was just the team's spine – the others were just as effective and revelled in a terrific all-round performance. Up yours, Fergie!

Trouble was, it was just half-time. With a little more care with the final pass or shot we could have been more than one goal to the good. Without doubt, on the balance of play we could have been two or three goals up – hardly the expected script – yet with typical Fulham humility, we were happy with what we had. Could we maintain the high-energy tactics after the break, though? Please, Fulham, don't sit back!

Rooney's introduction made a huge difference. Suddenly we had a whole set of new challenges. And we very nearly rued those earlier missed openings. However, a brilliant double save from Schwarzer preserved our lead and brilliant mopping up from Hangeland and Hughes helped to steady the ship.

All the while we had been treated to a disgraceful cameo from Ronaldo. Showing ever-increasing petulance, the talented Portuguese fancy-dan preferred to histrionically show his displeasure to his teammates, opponents, referee and assistants rather than help his side get back into the game. What a twat. But great for us, of course. It was a very public demonstration that the mighty Reds were rattled.

As the clock ticked away (slowly!) and the scoreline remained unchanged, so the petulance levels rose. Dowd had his work cut out. Every decision was questioned by someone in a red shirt. So much for the much-vaunted Respect campaign – but then we've known for ages that different rules apply to Manchester United, haven't we? And the whingeing winger was finally booked. Having lost the ball, Ronaldo lunged at Murphy. It was an awful tackle, if not, ultimately, a leg-breaker. Murphy, of course, simply picked himself up, ready to get on with the game.

Can you imagine the scene had the roles been reversed? Ronaldo would probably still be rolling over and over even now in an attempt to get his opponent sent off! As the whingeing continued Dowd gave a very public "final" warning to you-know-who. With Scholes already off, you could sense that the referee was desperately trying to

Below: John Pantsil laps up the applause after our tremendous win over United. His post-match circuit of the Cottage pitch, arms aloft, acknowledging the fans, was a regular thing, though. Reckon the smile's a bit broader on this occasion, mind!

keep his red card in his pocket. In truth, Ronaldo should have been sent off twice over.

Once Gera doubled our lead with that acrobatic effort minutes from the end, the points were safe. But Rooney was far from finished. Already booked, his notoriously short temper erupted again and Dowd was left with no choice. His red card was given a second airing – and by doing so there was a real danger that our magnificent show would be overshadowed by the unsavoury headline-making antics of Fergie's spoilt brats. The scowling Rooney's total lack of respect and lack of control continued unabated as he took on the corner flag as he exited the field. It's worth noting that the corner flag won the contest (and stayed on the field for 90+ minutes!). Sadly, it's also worth noting that Fergie defended his players afterwards. No surprises there, then.

In fact, the newspapers were fulsome in their praise of Fulham's tactics and application, and several snippets are reproduced below. Having proved that we can mix it with the top teams, there's every reason to suggest that we can push on next season. At least last season's desperate escape from the dreaded drop is but a distant memory! Clearly one big result doesn't make everything all right, in the same way that disappointing reverses, such as those against Hull and Blackburn, don't necessary signal disaster. The table doesn't lie, though, and it's abundantly clear that we're moving in the right direction. And full credit goes to Roy Hodgson, Ray Lewington and Mike Kelly for overseeing the transformation.

Okay, so it's been fairly steady progress thus far, and there's still lots of work to do – not least in the low return of points gained on our travels. But given the relative chaos previously, it's been wonderful to see the vast improvement in the levels of basic organisation. Good, old-fashioned coaching has seen us tighten up dramatically at the back and, in essence, defend from the front. Players have been fully aware of the roles in the team, and it has shown.

Credit, too, for the controlled way they've gone about their business. No toys hurled out of the pram unlike the so-called superstars mentioned earlier. Far from it. While acknowledging that we've had a few insipid showings, in general we've competed with the best of them and yet we are clear leaders of the Fair Play table. Very laudable. And all very Fulhamish, wouldn't you agree? Here's to much more of the same. ⚽

Fulham 2 Manchester United 0		1st
21.03.09	8th	2nd
		3rd
Fulham 0 Liverpool 1		4th
04.04.09	9th	5th
Manchester City 1 Fulham 3		6th
12.04.09	8th	**7th**
Middlesbrough 0 Fulham 0		8th
18.04.09	8th	9th
Fulham 1 Stoke City 0		10th
25.04.09	7th	11th
Chelsea 3 Fulham 1		12th
02.05.09	9th	13th
		14th
Fulham 3 Aston Villa 1		15th
09.05.09	7th	16th
Newcastle United 0 Fulham 1		17th
16.05.09	7th	18th
Fulham 0 Everton 2		19th
24.05.09	7th	20th

What the Papers Said...

Through the carnage of United's defeat we must not overlook the job Roy Hodgson has done at Fulham. He saved them from relegation last season and has lifted his club into the top half of the Premier League.

Hodgson has done it without losing his principles of playing attractive football. Tactically he is astute and outfoxed Alex Ferguson.

He called the win a red-letter day and this was the only time he has beaten his friend Fergie.

Brian Woolnough, *Daily Star*

Fulham were so dominant they could have gone in at the break at least three goals up. Not long ago Edwin van der Sar was unflappable. Yesterday he was forced into saves from Zamora that prevented another humiliation.

Steve Bates, *The People*

The truth was that Fulham outpassed, outscored and, for long spells, outplayed their opponents. Their performance in the opening 45 minutes was the best, according to Hodgson, they have played under him. Almost unnoticed, the club have reached 40 points with eight games to spare. At this rate, Hodgson should be on any shortlist for manager of the season.

Daniel Taylor, *The Guardian*

Zamora, in particular, was transformed, a man possessed. In the first half he did a passable impression of Zlatan Ibrahimovic, and United could not get close to him as he battered three shots that forced Van der Sar into emergency action, and a fourth that Patrice Evra blocked.

Amy Lawrence, *The Observer*

Fulham were quicker to the ball, sharper in the tackle... It was a tranquil setting for an ambush. The passion [at Fulham] is refined rather than raw, but, for one afternoon only, the most polite fans in the Premier League turned rabid. Roy Hodgson's team responded in kind. Hodgson, and his unsung assistant Ray Lewington, have undertaken a quiet revolution. This was the day an impeccably organised set of players came of age.

Michael Calvin, *Sunday Mirror*

Murphy was the most composed man on the field for much of this frenetic game and – amidst Rooney's rage, Ronaldo's amateur dramatics, Berbatov's indolence – we mustn't forget an astonishingly vibrant Fulham display. They hammered United in the first half like no team has hammered them in recent memory. Not even Liverpool eight days ago.

Andy Dunn, *News of the World*

Seventh Heaven

With the bar now set at an all-time high, what will this campaign bring, I wonder? What an astonishing achievement last season, given our comparatively meagre resources. But it was hugely deserved for the fantastic way we set about the challenge. Having escaped the dreaded drop by a matter of minutes 12 months previously, anything better than fifth from bottom would rank as an improvement. What we got was the stuff of nosebleeds: seventh spot, our highest-ever finish, and with it a ticket to Europe – and one that didn't mean a pre-season friendly in Ireland.

Regular readers will know that this column has banged the "could've done better" drum on a number of occasions in recent times. Never from a wholly unrealistic or overambitious perspective, but based purely on what's been on view for us all to see. It's all a matter of opinion anyway, but there have been occasions when, having seen what the other teams in the division have had to offer, it's been all-too-apparent that a little bit of basic coaching/management to, say, limit the silly errors or to bolster the team ethic would have earned us a few more points. Call it the Brian Clough factor if you like – on more than one occasion he (with sidekick Peter Taylor) moulded a set of reasonably good players into table-toppers and, subsequently, European champions. Okay, I've never suggested a leap of those proportions, but you get the drift.

Ask anyone who's played in a well-drilled outfit and they'll say that winning (or at least not losing) becomes a habit and a fair few extra points can be eked out by playing and working for each other, and reducing the number of basic errors. In our case over the seasons, this may only have resulted in a moderate rise, maybe three or four places up the table, had we got it together a bit more. And yet given the standard of the opposition outside the top seven or eight clubs, quite feasible and within our capabilities.

But then along came Roy Hodgson to demonstrate the point brilliantly. He transformed "doomed for the drop" to "heading towards the top" in a matter of months. It was rarely scintillating, never cavalier, but always controlled and focused. Key signings helped, notably Mark Schwarzer, but the overriding impression of last season is of a bunch of players improving before our eyes. The defence, marshalled superbly by Hangeland and Hughes, not only cut out the errors but forged into a niggardly quartet. And they were shielded at every opportunity by a hard-working, disciplined midfield. Although we sprang forwards with genuine purpose, if not always with numbers, the emphasis on defence meant the forwards were hardly spoon-fed chances and it was imperative that they remained as patient and diligent as they were hardworking.

With the much-discussed Bobby Zamora firing blanks with as much regularity as his workrate was high, we were hardly scoring goals for fun, and this will need to be addressed if we are to push on. Given Zamora's poor goal return, it was commendable that the crowd didn't get on his back en masse – probably due to his evident work ethic and the fact that we generally looked a more solid outfit with him in the line-up. (Mind you, I can recall several other Fulham players over the years whose overall contribution outweighed their "faults" but who weren't so lucky!) Worth watching to see if his "rapport" with the fans improves this season!

It's been interesting to note the steady transformation of Dickson Etuhu from lumbering passenger to defensive midfield marauder as the season progressed. The messageboards were certainly alive after his first few showings, suggesting he should lumber off elsewhere. He came good, and, tellingly, has several times been quoted in the press praising our coaching set-up and general know-how behind the scenes.

Etuhu's gradual integration, coming as it did after the departure of the effervescent Jimmy Bullard, highlights the fact that it's not always easy to slot into a well-honed system. Even if that system looks a relatively simple one – belying all the hard work done on the park and on the training field. And, if you cast your minds back to the last campaign, several others struggled too when thrown into the mix, whether as occasional starters or substitutes. Stoor and Kallio spring to mind, good players both, while even the popular Eric Nevland found it tough when pitched in against Swansea. Word has it that the training is all about drumming in the Hodgson way of things, week in, week out. Practice makes perfect.

It wasn't always perfect, of course. Think back to the Sunderland home game, for example, when only the woodwork denied the visitors a thumping win. (Actually, to be accurate, it was their lack of accuracy that denied them the win; the woodwork's there for a reason!) And we were hardly fluent in the cup game at Swansea, either. On the other hand, we went to both Arsenal and Liverpool and earned deserved draws. And we

---

"Then along came Roy Hodgson to demonstrate the point brilliantly. He transformed 'doomed for the drop' to 'heading towards the top' in a matter of months. It was rarely scintillating, never cavalier, but always controlled and focused."

Below: Mark Schwarzer's arrival from Middlesbrough in May 2008 was key to our subsequent success under Roy Hodgson.

tore into Man United at the Cottage and should have been more than one goal to the good at the break. We held off a Rooney-inspired United comeback before making sure of the victory with Gera's acrobatic effort near the end. A superb result, gripping entertainment and a red face for Ferguson. A good day all round, wouldn't you say?

And yet maybe the game that announced the arrival of "new" Fulham was the one at Newcastle. By now comfortably placed in the table, we were facing a relegation-haunted outfit who, by then, had Alan Shearer at the helm. They'd just beaten Middlesbrough and were expecting a routine win against our southern softies to move out of the drop zone. Our away record was hardly inspiring, after all! But we got into the groove, never allowed Newcastle to threaten and banked an invaluable extra three points in the European account. Oh, and it was great to give Big Al the elbow for a change!

When Bullard hopped off to Hull, Danny Murphy was given the chance to play a more prominent role, and it's been wonderful to see him step up to the plate so effectively and to revel in the role. He's never been the speediest of players (indeed many were suggesting this time last year that his legs had gone – "good player, but he'll never last the season" was a typical sentiment). But he's got great speed of thought, terrific technique plus an eye for a pass. Add to that his tenacity and leadership qualities and you have a top player. Where was that player at Spurs and Charlton, I wonder? While I'm at it, Murphy has been exceptional off the field, too, talking a good game as FFC captain and being a fine ambassador for the Club.

Towards the end of the campaign, even the media began to sing our praises. That's the same media that gave Hull more column inches than Peter Andre. And look where they finished up! But it was probably to our benefit that we were left to our own devices and could gradually flourish under the media radar. Even so, it still rankled when match report after match report centred on the failings or plight of our opponents rather than the way we'd blunted their advances or taken the game to them.

Still, the plaudits were many come the campaign's finale – with Roy Hodgson being many a pundit's choice as manager of the season. We also finished top of the Fair Play League. Rather like Cloughie, Hodgson has managed to instil a fantastic work ethic while cutting out the histrionics. To return to Murphy, his annoyance is plain to see if things aren't going to plan, but can you imagine him losing it in the way £80m Ronaldo did at our place (he wasn't worth 80p that day!)? No one wants or expects a whiter-than-white group of players, and it's always a morale booster to see the tackles going in, but the fact that we've managed to compete, harry and tackle in a controlled way (while winning a fair few points along the way) speaks volumes for the management approach. It might even sway match officials now and then!

All of which brings us back to the original question: "What does this season hold?"

I suppose we should be prepared for not hitting such dizzy heights between now and next May. For a start, the other clubs may well be a little more prepared for us this time around. In fact, we could easily have an even better campaign – at least in terms of progression and seeing the team continuing to evolve – in 2009-10 yet end up a little lower in the table. Although not too much lower, hopefully!

Much will depend on keeping the vast majority of the current squad while doing the necessary bolstering to underpin the European Tour. It's crucial we hang on to Hangeland – to preserve our defensive strength and also to demonstrate that we can (subject to out-of-our-league financial "bribery" from the big boys) retain our top players. For a while, at least.

The European malarkey, so eagerly awaited by the knot of travelling fans who racked up the air miles on our previous InterToto/UEFA jaunt, may yet blow up in our faces. The priority must be to retain our Premiership berth. But as things stand, the European Tour is another adventure and, probably a valuable learning experience – while the prospect of a domestic cup run remains as appealing as ever. We can dream! ⚽

Portsmouth 0 Fulham 1 15.08.09	7th
Fulham 0 Chelsea 2 23.08.09	12th
Aston Villa 2 Fulham 0 30.08.09	15th
Fulham 2 Everton 1 13.09.09	10th
Wolves 2 Fulham 1 20.09.09	14th
Fulham 0 Arsenal 1 26.09.09	17th
West Ham 2 Fulham 2 04.10.09	15th
Fulham 2 Hull City 0 19.10.09	12th
Manchester City 2 Fulham 2 25.10.09	13th

Europa League

Vetra 0 Fulham 3 30.07.09	Qual Round 3 1st leg
Fulham 3 Vetra 0 06.08.09	Qual Round 3 2nd leg
Fulham 3 Amkar Perm 1 20.08.09	Play-off Round 1st leg
Amkar Perm 1 Fulham 0 27.08.09	Play-off Round 2nd leg
CSKA Sofia 1 Fulham 1 17.09.09	Gp stage (Group E)
Fulham 1 Basel 0 01.10.09	Gp stage (Group E)
Fulham 1 Roma 1 22.10.09	Gp stage (Group E)

League Cup

Manchester City 2 Fulham 1 23.09.09	aet Round 3

1st / 2nd / 3rd / 4th / 5th / 6th / 8th / 9th / 10th / 11th / 12th / 13th / 14th / 15th / 16th / 17th / 18th / 19th / 20th

TOOFIF joins the list of victors

Roy and the boys weren't the only winners for their exploits in 2009. Seventh place, manager of the year claims, fair play winners, goal of the month... the list goes on. But credit also goes to FFC fans for retaining the best-behaved supporters crown. Last year's winnings (£20,000) went towards the superb Johnny Haynes statue. What about putting this year's award towards a Supporters' Bar at the Cottage? After all, we've not had a proper focal point at the Club since leaving for Loftus Road.

Oh, and TOOFIF got in on the act, too – those awfully nice people at the New Football Pools judged this humble mag as the Best Premier League Print Fanzine for 2009. Yippee! "Packed with content... more content than most fanzines and maintains a very high standard throughout" said the citation.

Roma Rocked

Having despatched last season's bogey team, Hull, 2-0 we're handily placed in 12th spot. Beating The Tigers was the crucial result of the week – but, job done, now for the glamour of European competition. Yes, next up Roma – a far cry from Rochdale not that many seasons ago! Prior to the game the talk was about the prestige of staging a cracking European game against world-renowned opponents. And all without the "must-win" tag. Then the game kicked off... and all that nonsense went out of the window. Bloody hell – we were outplaying the visitors. Better than that, we'd only gone and taken the lead. Deservedly. Hey, we "must win" now!

What a heartbreaker! Having dominated for so long (in fact, until Zamora was taken off) the visitors, spurred on by the tiny Pizarro, began to push us back. Still we held on. All of the above, though, became overshadowed by the penalty incident 12 minutes from time. Hangeland, whose towering header had looked to be the matchwinner, was shown the red card when Riise fell in the box. Presumably for being the last defender or "denying a goalscoring opportunity", only for the ref to change his mind after a long lull. The dark-haired Kelly was now deemed guilty of the crime – itself far from clear-cut – and not the much taller, blond-haired covering player. Yeah, clear as mud, right? All the while standing (as he had like a lemon for the duration) a few feet from the incident was one of the phalanx of officials. His contribution was merely to highlight the stupidity of the whole episode and with it the worthlessness of the experiment. Between them all, no one could correctly ascertain who did what and who was positioned where. Ah, but a Roma player had gone down in the box. Had to be a penalty, didn't it? (Whereas their routine shirt-pulling was allowed to go unpunished all night long.)

Schwarzer saved the spot-kick superbly but that cruel sending-off came back to haunt us with a measly five seconds remaining. Andreolli was left unmarked at the far post and crashed home the leveller via Pantsil and the crossbar. Devastating.

Here's a portion of Henry Winter's excellent report in *The Telegraph*. It began: "So near and yet so farcical. This was so nearly a famous victory for Fulham, their inspirational manager Roy Hodgson and their wonderful fans, who had Craven Cottage rocking on its ancient riverside foundations. This was so nearly a humiliating defeat for Roma and Claudio Ranieri. One outcome was beyond question: this was an embarrassing setback for Michel Platini's Europa League experiment with officials behind the goal."

Oh well, we'll just have to win in Rome...!

> *"Managers, players, directors and chairmen all come and go but for the supporters it's a lifelong thing. For me, it's the supporters who make the Club, and in the case of Fulham it's a wonderfully unique set-up. They've even managed to keep the ground more or less as it was..."*

Below: Les Strong, a Fulham legend and staunch supporter of TOOFIF.

Strong Points

Right, here's a quiz question. In 1992, who were the four Englishmen managing national teams? Well there was Graham Taylor with England, Jackie Charlton (Republic of Ireland), someone called Roy Hodgson with Switzerland (whatever happened to him?) and then there was Les Strong – manager of Anguilla.

Les, it's 40 years since you started with Fulham – with a little time off for good behaviour at Brentford, Crystal Palace and five minutes at Rochdale. Does it seem like 40 years?
No, it doesn't! Mind you, I had ten years out of the country, too – three in the Caribbean and seven in America. I was coaching in Anguilla and looking after terminally ill people in America. Quite a contrast. I kept in contact with Peter Mellor and Jimmy Conway while we were all in the States. But no, it doesn't seem like 40 years ago... We came back in 1995, when we had the "replay" of the Cup Final and it was great to see the players again. But then I've got so very many wonderful memories of my time at Fulham.

FFC's fortunes have yo-yo'd in that time...
It was all pretty steady when I was at the Club; 13 of the 15 years were spent in the old Second Division – we were relegated once but came back under Malcolm Macdonald. After that it went a bit wobbly, didn't it? I missed much of those awful years as I was in business by then. It looked dodgy when we were second from bottom of the old Fourth Division and the crowds were well down – but fast-forward to today and the Club have just enjoyed their best-ever season, which is brilliant.

Is there really something special about Fulham?
Without a doubt. But then I've been involved off and on anyway. There was the catering after I finished playing and now there's the corporate side of things. But of course the Club's special. And much of that is down to the supporters. I'm friendly with a lot of them – in fact, I think you'll find that most of my friends are Fulham fans, so there's no escape! Managers, players, directors and chairmen all come and go but for the supporters it's a lifelong thing. For me, it's the supporters who make the Club, and in the case of Fulham it's a wonderfully unique set-up. They've even managed to keep the ground more or less as it was...

It's good to see the Cottage full to the brim...?
It's fantastic and a sign of how far the Club's come. I can remember the ground before the Riverside Stand was built. When I came to Fulham as a kid

we'd walk around the pitch to be at the end Fulham were attacking – no chance of doing that today!

Who was responsible for bringing you to Fulham?
Most south London boys when I was 13 or 14 went to Crystal Palace and I was no different. I trained with them and was a ballboy there. One day Arthur "push-and-run" Rowe, who was in charge of the youth team, patted me on the arse and said "It doesn't look like it's going to be your game, son."

Which bit couldn't you do – "push" or "run"?
Don't know. I hadn't played a game there, so I've no idea how he came to that conclusion! Anyway, I was off. I wrote to Fulham and got a trial. I recall walking in and asking the coach: "'Scuse me, mate, could you tell me where the geezer is who takes the training?" That "geezer" was him – Ken Craggs! Anyway I trained and didn't do anything special, after which he said, "Sorry mate, can't help you." So I joined a Sunday team, Tulse Hill. One day we played a cup game against a team that included George Cohen's brother, Peter (Ben Cohen's dad), and he thought our team of mainly 16-year-olds were decent. George was running the Fulham youth team then and Peter tipped off his brother, the upshot of which was that the whole team went for a trial. I got picked by George and Ken Craggs to return for more training; my Fulham adventure had begun. I was picked to play for the youth team against Arsenal on October 7, 1969; the score was Arsenal 4 Fulham 2, and I scored the first goal!

John Fraser was an early team-mate wasn't he?
Yes, as were Barry Silkman, Dave Carlton and McAndrew Johnson, to name but a few. I thought I was a midfielder back then, but George took a look at me and said: "Why don't you try left-back?" I played there for a year with the youth team and signed pro in 1971 and continued there for the reserves under Bill Dodgin. He saw I liked to overlap and suggested I play on the wing. So that's what I did, alongside "Mitch" [John Mitchell].

Before long came your first-team debut. Jimmy Conway had picked up an injury and his brother, John, had stood in for five games, only for John to break his arm at Bristol City...
I got the call on September 30, 1972! It was against Orient and, yes, it was on the wing. On the right. I played there for about 20 games, then Alec Stock said: "Do you know, given what you've done as a winger, I think you'd better go back to full-back!" So that was it – full-back for the rest of my career.

Full-back or winger, you were always close to the crowd. Did you hear what they were saying? And did you get much stick?
Absolutely! The lower the attendance, the more you'd hear, funnily enough. I used to have fantastic

banter with the crowd, especially with those in the Enclosure. But that's all part of it. And a real part of Fulham. You have to accept it when they shout at you – and give a quip back when you can.

I got on well with the supporters. I always tried to give 100 per cent for the team and for the Club, and I think the crowd recognised that. We've all seen players – some of them much better players than me – not looking bothered, and I don't think supporters accept that, do they? It sounds a bit cheesy, but I simply loved the Club. I had absolutely no desire to go anywhere else.

By this time you were playing alongside Alan Mullery and Bobby Moore. That must have been one hell of an education...?
Whatever relative success I had at the Club was down to those two. To play alongside Mooro was fantastic. People would say that I was terrific going forwards, but that was down to Bobby. Generally, full-backs shouldn't be in advance of the centre-half when he gets the ball; most centre-halves are stoppers and not necessarily comfortable on the ball. Full-backs are there as cover. With Mooro I could stand on the halfway line! One ball from him and off I went! When he retired, I had to go back 20 or 30 yards. He was a footballing genius.

Then there was Mullery – what a captain! I've not seen anyone like him. He was an inspiration. You look at the game today and not many players say that much – you'll see poor passes go without a murmur and also a lack of effort at times. Mullery wouldn't stand for that – he'd virtually grab you by the throat and drag you through the game. He was a brilliant player, too, and he worked as hard as he talked. You couldn't help but learn from those two. Such a shame that Mullers didn't get the manager's job at Fulham as expected.

Bobby Moore reckoned you were good enough to play for England...
He did! And I've got that in print in one of his books. Our coach Bill Taylor was also the England coach at the time and he told me, "Don Revie's had a good look at you and you've got a chance of making the England Under-23 team next time out, but you've got to practice a bit more with your left foot." I practiced for hours and hours with my left foot and I remember being really disappointed when the squad was announced and I hadn't made it. That was as close as I ever got.

In 1975 came that marathon Cup run. At what point did you realise that Second Division Fulham might actually play at Wembley?
We had three nondescript games with Hull. No thought about Wembley then, for sure. What an insane decision it was to play that third game at West Brom. There were barely 1,500 there, it was a grim evening, pissing down with rain; we just

	1st
Fulham 3 Liverpool 1	2nd
31.10.09 11th	3rd
Wigan Athletic 1 Fulham 1	4th
08.11.09 11th	5th
Birmingham City 1 Fulham 0	6th
21.11.09 11th	7th
Fulham 3 Blackburn Rovers 0	**8th**
25.11.09 10th	9th
Fulham 1 Bolton Wanderers 1	10th
28.11.09 10th	11th
Fulham 1 Sunderland 0	12th
06.12.09 8th	13th
Burnley 1 Fulham 1	14th
12.12.09 9th	15th
Fulham 3 Manchester United 0	16th
19.12.09 9th	17th
Fulham 0 Tottenham Hotspur 0	18th
26.12.09 9th	19th
Chelsea 2 Fulham 1	20th
28.12.09 9th	
Stoke City 3 Fulham 2	
05.01.10 9th	
Blackburn Rovers 2 Fulham 0	
17.01.10 9th	
Tottenham Hotspur 2 Fulham 0	
26.01.10 9th	
Europa League	
Roma 2 Fulham 1	
05.11.09 Gp stage (Group E)	
Fulham 1 CSKA Sofia 0	
03.12.09 Gp stage (Group E)	
Basel 2 Fulham 3	
16.12.09 Gp stage (Group E)	
FA Cup	
Fulham 1 Swindon Town 0	
02.01.10 Round 3	
Accrington Stanley 1 Fulham 3	
23.01.10 Round 4	

wanted to get home, let alone go to Wembley. Then we had four games against Nottingham Forest. Cloughie had just taken over, and I had a torrid time against their winger, Miah Dennehy. In the first game at Fulham I was taken off at half-time. But by the fourth game I'd mastered him. Just. It wasn't until the Everton game that we started to look ahead with any conviction. Everton were top of the First Division and we did really well to win there. Mooro was magnificent – what a player he was! But he was just as excited as the rest of us.

Let's be fair: Bobby Moore was really, really slow. And to be as good as he was showed what a complete player he was. He could read the game so far in advance that he'd simply drift into the right positions. He'd played in so many big games – he'd lifted the World Cup for heaven's sake – yet here was the chance of another one.

We eventually made it, but for you it was a case of double disappointment. We lost and you missed the game through injury. It could be argued that it was that injury that cost us the Cup?
I'd have been marking Alan Taylor. I've always said that had I played we wouldn't have lost 2-0. At least Taylor wouldn't have scored twice. And Tony Gale has always agreed with me. He says, "No, Taylor would've scored four!" What I will say is that we didn't play anything like the way we had in getting to Wembley. I've watched it since, and you can't point fingers at any specific player, but in retrospect I think there were some who were just pleased to get there, and because of that we didn't function in the way we should have.

You were a busy bunny on the morning of the match. A boot boy again after all those years!
That's right. I went to court in the morning. I was privileged to read a eulogy at Ron Woolnough's funeral recently and much of it centred on the business in court. Months before, the Club had signed a contract with a boot company safe in the knowledge – or so we thought! – that we'd never get to Wembley. And now we'd been reminded that we'd have to wear those boots, which wasn't an option, hence the court appearance. As I wasn't playing, I had to go along. One of the stipulations from the judge was that there should be no markings on our boots – which meant blacking out any white bits. But the judge also pointed out that the physio – Ron – couldn't have any markings on his bags. You see Ron had signed a deal worth two grand with Adidas and this decision meant he lost his money. Ron loved a pound note so, as I said at the funeral, Ron blamed me for the judge's decision when I was simply the messenger!

A win against West Ham would have meant a European Tour the following season...?
Funnily enough, I always remember thinking that

playing in Europe would be a huge "plus" for me after realising that I'd have to sit out the Wembley game. Fulham in the European Cup-Winners Cup, what a bonus that would have been!

Our European Tour was therefore put on hold for a fair while. However, you did subsequently score the winning goal in a cup final...?
I did – and what a wonderful goal, I left Peter Mellor with no chance! That was against Middlesbrough in the Anglo-Scottish Tournament. And it was the only goal in the two-legged final.

And you DID play in Europe...?
Yes we did, in the Anglo-Italian competition. We played Como, AS Roma, Bologna and Torino, drawing all four games. And I scored twice – against Roma and Torino.

You knew the great Johnny Haynes from your early days at the Club...?
I suppose you could say I took an interest in Fulham mainly because of Johnny – and that's going back to the late sixties. You talk to any player of stature – Mullery, Cohen at Fulham and plenty more around the world – and they all say he was one of the best players, ever.

And yet he didn't crave the attention, even though he was recognised as a genius within the game, albeit from a bygone era...?
No he didn't. And you're right, he WAS that good. He was, without a doubt, a truly wonderful player. But something in his personality meant that he shunned publicity. I found him extremely shy – not during games, maybe – but certainly so away from the pitch and ever more so as time went by. I run the Johnny Haynes lounge on matchdays and he came along to open it officially. Yet it was all he could do to pop his head around the door – he could see there were 40-50 people waiting to see him. He wasn't being rude, he was just that shy that he found it very difficult to simply walk in. And we're talking about the Club's greatest-ever player.

There's a great picture – by Ken Coton – of Johnny in the Wembley dressing room trying to cheer me up before the 1975 FA Cup Final, when injury meant I had to sit out our big day. A lovely man: Mr Fulham, always will be, and such a pleasure to have known him.

Johnny made a big impression on you, as did George Cohen, Alan Mullery and Bobby Moore. But then came George Best and Rodney Marsh...
Ernie Clay strolled in one morning and said we'd signed a couple of players; someone said that he'd heard one was George Best, so I went "Yeah, right". But the Chairman confirmed that it was Bestie and Marsh. We all went "Bloody hell!" Or words to that effect! I'd got used to having Bobby Moore and

"Ernie Clay strolled in one morning and said we'd signed a couple of players; someone said that he'd heard one was George Best, so I went 'Yeah, right'. But the Chairman confirmed that it was Bestie and Marsh. We all went 'Bloody hell!' Or words to that effect!"

Alan Mullery around the place by then – Bob was just one of the lads by this point. But then Bestie pops up and, well, it was fantastic. Playing with someone like him was magnificent.

We had the impression that whatever went on off the field, Best never shirked on it – is that fair?
It's well known that he did go missing, he did miss training – as did Peter Storey, and a lot of people forget that. While I'm at it, Pete was a great player, too; everyone knows he played it hard, but he wasn't just a cruncher, he had a lot of skill as well.

Those two never got on, did they?
No! They had their differences – something to do with the fact that when they'd faced each other in the past Peter had simply kicked the shit out of George, which Bestie hated! But as they were never at training together, it was hardly a problem! That's not to say George didn't train – he did. His problem was not being able to get up in the mornings – for well-documented reasons! He'd come along in the afternoons and, more often than not, train twice as hard as we'd done earlier in the day. The downside, of course, is that he wasn't training with us. Even so, it was great playing with George – he could do things that would make you marvel – that brilliant goal at Peterborough, when, crowded by defenders, he flipped the ball up just outside the box and volleyed into the top corner. Unbelievable. The only trouble with George, though, was that if you passed the ball to him, it tended to be the last you'd see of it! I must have gone on a thousand overlaps, but he'd go inside and do his bit – he'd always give me the thumbs-up and say "Great run, Les" but I didn't get the ball.

Bestie is a Man. United legend; his time with us was fleeting and after his heyday. He supported the Club, though, during the Fulham 2000 days, turning up whenever asked, ensuring a few extra columns of much-needed publicity for our plight.
Bestie loved Fulham, as did Marshie. They'd say the other players – us! – would try to emulate what they were able to do. We'd all try the flicks and tricks – especially in training. I used to say Johnny Mitchell couldn't trap a bag of cement, but you'd then see him doing things he'd picked up. For all my joking, Mitch was a terrific centre-forward for us. Another who'd try stuff was Teddy Maybank; many players improved their technique thanks to Bestie and Marshie.

Okay, who made you Club Captain?
Bobby Campbell had just got sacked and Ted Drake and Ron Woolnough took over in the interim. Ron called me in – I'd known him for about eight years by then – and said he was going to make changes, just to show that there was a transition. He was going to drop six players, make

Dave Clement the coach, and he wanted me to be captain. Tony Gale was captain at the time, and he and I were great mates. I told Ron it probably wasn't a good idea; chances were he wouldn't get the job and so such disruption was unnecessary. Ron was adamant. He insisted he'd be making the changes and he'd offer the captaincy to someone else. So I said: "I'll take it." And when Malcolm (Macdonald) took over, he asked me to carry on. Regardless of who gave me the job, I considered it a great honour – I loved every minute of it.

You skippered the team to promotion in 1981-82...
I did! And I remember it all so well. We had a good team. We'd been relegated with a good team...

The team that came up boasted players considered Fulham legends – Gerry Peyton, Roger Brown, Ray Lewington, Paul Parker, Gordon Davies...
I've been lucky to play with some wonderful players during my time at Fulham. Not all were in the "world class" bracket, but you tell me two finer wingers at Fulham than Les Barrett and Jimmy Conway. Then there'd be some who didn't get the praise their play deserved. One was Alan Slough, a great professional; he'd do so much of the unsung work. And in our promotion season there was another who dipped under the radar of many fans – Peter O'Sullivan. He was one of the best midfield players I've played with. Sully took a lot of stick, but he was a great player and by far the most effective player I've played behind. No one ever got through to me! He was brilliant.

When my time at Fulham was coming to an end Malcolm told me that I wasn't playing particularly well and that he was going to replace me with Paul Parker. I said: "You're having a laugh! Paul Parker? He can't tackle, he can't head a ball, he's slow and his passing's atrocious. And on top of that, he's a midget! You haven't got a clue what you're talking about!" We all know what happened to Paul – after some good years with Fulham he played loads of games for Manchester United and got to the World Cup Semi-Finals with England. Years later, I told Malcolm he'd made a bloody good decision! Paul had been my boot-boy at Fulham (I used to give him a fiver at Christmas – quite generous of me, eh?!) and was a great lad and a terrific player.

Having been relegated the year before, what galvanised the team into promotion candidates?
Malcolm wasn't a great coach, but he had a genuine personality. People liked him; the players would have run through a brick wall for him. After the previous 18 months when we'd had a poor run of things, he brought a bit of fun back to the place. Roger Thompson was the same, and he was also a good coach. It was like Fulham of the old days – lots of smiles and it all helped people to relax. As you pointed out, we also had some very good

Above: Strongy challenges Wally Downes of Wimbledon using the classic back-to-back method not found in any coaching manual.

players and, compared to what had gone on before, we breezed through to promotion.

The squad was that good you very nearly made it a double promotion and back to the top flight?
I only lasted about six games in '82-83. But the squad was very good and, with Malcolm as manager, they played great football for most of the season and deserved to go up. We all know about the disgraceful scenes at Derby, but to be truthful the results hadn't gone for us in the run-in. From my perspective, I felt it was time to move on. I wish I'd handled things a bit differently, though. I'd bought a business and, with, an eye to the future, I was trying to juggle that and the playing side of things. I let the business distract me a little bit and I ended up retired at 30. Who knows, had I been truly focused, I could have had at least another season or two with Fulham.

You played under a fair few managers. How would you rate them?
Bill Dodgin, my first manager, was very easy going (rather like Malcolm); he gave me my chance. Alec Stock was brilliant – a great manager. He never took the coaching but was a fabulous man-manager and knew how to win games. Bobby Campbell used to get a lot of stick from fans, but, for me, he was probably the best coach I've played under. His man-management probably got up a lot of players' noses. He changed things around very quickly and got rid of a lot of players and staff – I was the only one to escape the cull, according to Bob, "because no one would have me". I don't know how true that was! Malcolm I've already discussed, but he was a good man-manager in the mould of Alec Stock. All different in their ways, but all part of the rich tapestry of FFC history.

And they all tolerated you...!
They did! Funny thing is, they'd all say things like: "Mitch: great centre-forward; Les Barrett: fantastic winger; Alan Slough: great workhorse; Les Strong... great in the dressing room." No one ever said "Les Strong – good left-back": seems I did all my good work in the dressing room! (Cue those left-back-in-the-dressing-room jokes! I've heard 'em all!)

We've reminisced about how Mooro thought you might have played for England. You never did – but you did end up playing *against* England...?
I did – that was my Testimonial match. Malcolm Macdonald was quite magnificent; he arranged for the full England team to come along to Craven Cottage for what, in effect, was a World Cup warm-up. For them, that is, not me! It was a truly fantastic occasion for me – and I treasure the memories of that night. I look at the programme every now and then just to look at the roll-call of names that came along. My only regret was that

we couldn't announce the game too far in advance. Ron Greenwood didn't want the game advertised, maybe because other clubs would've tried to jump on the bandwagon, so we were only able to say a couple of weeks beforehand that England were coming to the Cottage. We may have got more people to come along had we been able to flag it – but, hey, I played against England.

You were – and still are – known as the master of the quick quip. But what are the funniest incidents you can remember at Fulham?
How long have you got? My mum used to live in Roehampton – the house backed on to the training ground. One day Mike Kelly had set out all the training cones but we couldn't find Bobby Campbell anywhere. So there we all were shouting out: "Where's Bob?" and, rather than getting us lot ready for training, Bob was by the fence munching away on a bacon butty and a cup of tea... prepared by my mum. It's alright for some!

One day I'd had a really bad training session when Malcolm Macdonald was in charge. When we'd finished, he called all the lads together – apprentices, everybody – and said: "I want you all to witness this." He continued by saying: "Les, that was the worst training performance I've seen from any professional at any time in my footballing career as a player and manager. Your passing was atrocious, you missed every tackle, you couldn't head the ball, every player breezed past you when they got the ball, your attitude was terrible – you're an absolute disgrace... anything to say?" He was scowling. It all went very quiet. I said: "Now come on Malcolm, you're being totally unfair – I've been a lot worse than that!!" And everybody fell about laughing. There was always a joke to be had, even when things weren't going so well – but the bottom line was that every day at Fulham was a joy to me. Sounds corny when you say it, but it's true!

Which opponent caused you most problems?
Fulham fans may well disagree with this, but I think I only ever had about half-a-dozen truly disastrous games when I'd be taken to the cleaners. And they were all similar types of player – in the mould of little Willie Johnson. Those wingers who dropped deep and then had a run at me were nightmarish to play against. If I could get up tight to a player then I don't think that many got past me too often (as I remember, anyway!).

On leaving Fulham the connection continued...?
Near the end of my time at Fulham, Fred Callaghan gave me a call. He asked, rather than play for the reserves, did I fancy going to Brentford, initially on loan. Fred got me in front of the squad and really talked me up – there was Stan Bowles, Terry Hurlock, ex-Man United keeper Paddy Roche and Ron "Chopper" Harris as Fred's coach – and said:

"I got a call out of the blue from Vic Halom. He said, 'I'm at Rochdale – would you be consider playing for us?' I just said: 'Where the hell's Rochdale?' I went up, trained for a week, negotiated a bit of money and played one game. But they never paid me. So I never went back."

"I'm signing Les Strong, he can play left-back, right-back, left-wing, right-wing, midfield – he's gonna help us get promotion." Brentford were sixth in the old Third Division at the time. So I played seven games for them over that Christmas period; we lost six and drew the other one! By the time I left, they were six from bottom! Do you know, every time one of us played a back pass to Paddy Roche you'd turn away to get into position only to hear a roar as the ball had gone through his legs! Nightmare! So it was back to Fulham for me.

Fulham released me at the end of that season and Mullers called to see if I'd like to join Crystal Palace. I jumped at it – going back to the club where I started as a kid seemed right. I had a season there, although I only played about 12 games – I had a row with the chairman (easily done with Ron Noades!) over payment so that was that.

Then, after I'd started running a pub, so I wasn't playing or training, I got a call out of the blue from Vic Halom. He said, "I'm at Rochdale – would you be consider playing for us?" I just said: "Where the hell's Rochdale?" I went up, trained for a week, negotiated a bit of money and played one game. But they never paid me. So I never went back.

But you did go on to enjoy a spell in management yourself – in the Caribbean?
I'd been running a pub in Richmond for about nine years, and it was exhausting work. Really knackering! I went to the Caribbean to visit a friend in Anguilla and enjoy a (deserved!) holiday. I only planned to be out there for six weeks or so. There were only six football teams on the island and I'd often go to watch the games. At one game, the President of their Football Association came up to me and said: "I lived in Slough for a while and used to watch you play – would you be interested in coaching the national team?

I asked how they'd been doing and he said: "We've never won or drawn a game in our history." My reply was instant: "I'll take that job!" I stayed for three years, restructuring their footballing set-up. I took them from bottom of the world rankings, about 185 I think, to about 165 – and Scotland were at about 160 at the time – so it went rather well. I took them on tours (funnily enough to other Caribbean islands I'd never visited!) and it was great fun and a brilliant experience. Then the Football President went into politics, gave up the football, and it all came to an end.

So what do you make of the current Fulham set-up then? It's changed a bit from "your day"!
You say that, but the supporters are the same – the hardcore supporters, that is, not the new "prawn cocktail brigade". I'm full of admiration for those who worked so hard to keep Fulham alive during those dark days of the late '80s and early '90s. But in saying that, everyone's welcome

at Fulham – and, all said and done, the newcomers are now paying my wages, aren't they?

Have you had much to do with Roy Hodgson?
I've known Roy for about 35 years. When he was in charge of Malmo, we used to go there pre-season with Bobby Campbell and Mike Kelly, and Roy would arrange pre-season games for us. Roy lives about 50 yards down the road from me so I bump into him every now and again. He's very much in the mould of Alec Stock, and he speaks so very well, doesn't he? He's doing a superb job here. It was pretty miraculous how he saved the Club from going down the season before last. I'll be honest: I couldn't see it happening. But from then we've gone from strength to strength. Roy, for me, is very much a Fulham man.

We're looking pretty tidy, aren't we? And Roy's steered us to wins against Liverpool and Manchester United...?
We're looking an improved team to last year, which is an amazing achievement. We're a compact and well-organised set-up. I went to that Liverpool game, and it was brilliant. I went to the Roma away game too – we really deserved more from those two games with the Italians. In fact, I'd say we did well enough to have won both of them. The key thing is that we're not out of place now in that sort of company. And when it came to that Manchester United game we thoroughly merited the win – we were fantastic on the day. It's hard to think of a better all-round Fulham performance.

A little birdie tells me Roy Hodgson had a smile on his face for a totally different reason recently. Something about a recent TOOFIF front cover with a certain Leslie Strong playing a part...?
I thought that last front cover was hilarious and, knowing that Roy, Ray Lew and Mike Kelly have a great sense of humour, I made sure they saw a copy – just in case they're not on the regular mailing list! It really goes to show the way things are going at Fulham – the Club's doing really well and they're all taking their jobs very seriously, but without losing their sense of humour or perspective. It's important that we keep that traditional Fulhamish way of doing things.

Roy and his staff are as knowledgeable as they are approachable, and they invariably like a laugh. I was at the training ground recently and thought it was brilliant that they've given Ray, not the tallest of guys as you know, the topmost locker so that he has to jump up just to get his training kit out every day. Brilliant stuff. Very Fulhamish!

Above: Strongy made sure that Roy Hodgson, Ray Lewington and Mike Kelly saw the "hilarious" *Last of the Summer Wine* spoof cleverly fashioned by TOOFIF stalwart Bill Plummer.

Mugged Up North

Had these notes been written a few weeks ago as planned, we'd still have been basking in the glow of that wonderful performance against the mighty Manchester United.

As I write, however, the last pair of League games were at Stoke and Blackburn – so the mood's not quite as euphoric! For all our imperious football against United at the Cottage, we let ourselves get mugged up north. Twice! Roy Hodgson said after the Blackburn encounter that we'd perhaps lost our edge. No "perhaps" in my book. Anyway hopefully he'll ensure that we bounce back in style.

But that wasn't all we lost, was it? Having been unlucky with injuries this season already, we fell foul of several robust challenges at Stoke and Blackburn. For "robust" read "dirty" and "unpunished"! Our injury list duly got longer and more serious. To give Stoke credit, they really got at us from the start, being very quick to pounce on Danny Murphy in particular and limiting our possession. They were pumped up and ready to tough it out, legally or otherwise. All the while we gave a brilliant impression of a team of southern softies not relishing a cold, unwelcome Tuesday night up north.

I've admired the way we've gone about our business without causing the ref too many problems – much like Brian Clough's Nottingham Forest did – but maybe we're too meek at times. That clear handball in the box near the end at Stoke could have given us a point (while the tug on Nevland at Blackburn should have brought us a penalty and a red card for the already-booked Samba) but the officials shied away from the obvious. Possibly because it's just those jolly nice Fulham lads.

The point about both the Stoke and Blackburn games is that we lost to inferior opponents. Our comeback at Stoke – which included that super strike from Clint Dempsey – served to highlight just how brittle they were, but the damage had been done. We played better at Blackburn but didn't attack the ball and gave away two soft goals. We've become accustomed to our defence shutting up shop in recent months. Alarmingly we've not only put up the "open" sign again but also one that says "help yourself"!

I suppose in the context of the whole season those two defeats, while maddeningly frustrating, aren't so bad. We're picking up enough points to be midway in the league, having taken the notable scalps of Liverpool and Manchester United, and have progressed in the Europa and FA Cups. That night in Basel was one of the special Fulham occasions. Naturally, the two ties against Cup holders Shakhtar Donetsk, with the prize of facing Ajax or Juventus, could top that.

But before we get ahead of ourselves, it's vital that we get back to what we're good at. And hopefully with something like our first-choice line-up. I've got this far with barely a mention of Bobby Zamora. Given the tendency over the years of some of our crowd picking on a scapegoat (think Peter O'Sullivan, Paul Trollope, Andy Melville, etc.) Zamora has been given generous backing during his time here. Sure, the goals weren't flashing in, but his workrate and value to the side have long been recognised.

Things came to a head with those gestures to the crowd after he'd scored against Sunderland. In my opinion, it wasn't pretty and it wasn't clever. On the other hand, you almost want to thank BZ's one or two voluble critics given his outstanding form prior to that injury at Stoke. If they had a hand in geeing him up then I'd say "keep on moaning"!

Zamora has looked a far more complete striker. Once the goals started to flow, his confidence levels went up accordingly. Opposing teams have struggled to handle him – or rather, they've often resorted to handling him (Jamie Carragher, to name but one) – as he's put in one powerhouse performance after another. Against Man Utd, it was all too easy to suggest that the "Zamora for England" cries mightn't be so outrageous as they first appeared. Especially given the anonymous showing that day by Michael Owen. It's not overstating the situation to say that how we fare over the rest of the season may well depend on how quickly a fully fit Bobby Zamora is back leading our attack.

> *"We're picking up enough points to be midway in the league, having taken the notable scalps of Liverpool and Manchester United, and have progressed in the Europa and FA Cups."*

A word from the manager

1. Vestiges
Meaning: A small amount or trace
Usage: "Diomansy Kamara has spent a couple of weeks in France in the clinic he goes to get the last vestiges of the problem with his knee sorted out…"

2. Balm
Meaning: Anything that heals, soothes, or mitigates pain
Usage: "We played well enough to get something but all these factors are balm to the wound – but the wound is still the problem…."

3. Jiggle
Meaning: To move up and down or to and fro with short, quick jerks
Usage: "I told the chairman I might jiggle about with the team, use different players, give a guy like Chris Smalling some games."

4. Fundament
Meaning: A theory, principle, or underlying basis
Usage: "But we must be careful not to constantly raise the barrier because to do that we would have to change the fundaments of how we work."

Roy Hodgson has, of course, signed a new contract since the last issue. (He had a good chuckle over the cover of Issue 113, apparently, so maybe he's staying to see what else we can dream up!!) This can only be good news. Not only does it offer us further stability but also every chance to maintain our steady improvement. With his wealth of experience, Roy has stamped his authority on the Club and it has to be said that Roy Hodgson and Fulham FC make the perfect match right now.

Hangeland, too, has decided to stay. It's a mark of how far we've come that we're able to keep a major player happy. Clearly there's a close bond between manager and player but that on its own is not always enough. That said, the big fella's been less than secure in recent weeks and will need to overcome the injury niggles to ensure the Hughes/Hangeland partnership rediscovers its "thou shalt not pass" approach. ⚽

Fulham 0 Aston Villa 2 30.01.10 11th	1st 2nd 3rd
Fulham 1 Portsmouth 0 03.02.10 10th	4th 5th
Bolton Wanderers 0 Fulham 0 06.02.10 10th	6th 7th
Fulham 3 Burnley 0 09.02.10 9th	8th
Fulham 2 Birmingham City 1 21.02.10 9th	10th 11th
Sunderland 0 Fulham 0 28.02.10 9th	12th 13th
Manchester United 3 Fulham 0 14.03.10 10th	14th 15th 16th 17th

Europa League
Fulham 2 Shakhtar Donetsk 1
18.02.10   Round of 32 1st leg

Shakhtar Donetsk 1 Fulham 1
25.02.10   Round of 32 2nd leg

Juventus 3 Fulham 1
11.03.10   Round of 16 1st leg

Fulham 4 Juventus 1
18.03.10   Round of 16 2nd leg

FA Cup
Fulham 4 Notts County 0
14.02.10   Round 5

Fulham 0 Tottenham Hotspur 0
06.03.10   Round 6

Pressing the Point

When Fulham spring a surprise result, it's customary for the media to put the vanquished team under the spotlight — you see we didn't win the game, they lost it. So it was brilliant to see so much decent coverage after Man Utd were humbled at the Cottage...

The striker christened "For England" Zamora by prehistoric DJ Diddy David Hamilton is in the form of his life. Zamora's fifth goal in four games pushed Hamilton, Fulham's celebrity cheerleader, to the verge of spontaneous combustion.

"Look forward to *Match Of The Day*" he screamed. "We might even be first on."

Once again, the tranquility of the setting, and the nature of the executioner, belied the nature of the threat. Losing at Fulham is a little like being mugged at an art gallery. It's so civilised you don't notice the blood on the carpet. United were warned. They were ambushed at the Cottage last season, when Wayne Rooney's sparring session with the corner flag was the highlight of a dispiriting defeat.

His latest impression of an angry young man was almost an afterthought, as United were overwhelmed by a Fulham side that played fluid, intelligent football. The champions were not merely beaten. They were embarrassed, dismantled with alarming ease. It was a convincing measure of Fulham's progress, and further confirmation of the impact of Roy Hodgson.

Sunday Mirror

Hodgson is revelling in a warm front of publicity at the moment. Good on him. Anyone who manages to get Zamora linked to an England call-up deserves all the accolades that come their way. But Zamora's winter coat has a confident sheen to it. I've never seen anyone chest as many passes. He must have heartburn after a game. One of them was so well weighted, Zoltan Gera could do little else but to welcome it with a sweet volley. Tomasz Kuszczak's camera-friendly aerobatics hardly hinted at more laboured efforts to follow.

For Hodgson, it was a seminal result. Fulham look like they belong. That Hodgson was able to take off Duff, Murphy and Zamora — individually to guarantee their rousing ovations — showed how far they have come. And how utterly comprehensive this defeat was for United.

News of the World

"We want four," crooned the Craven Cottage faithful. Hodgson was thrilled, in that understated way of his, by a performance as vibrant and statement-making as any during his spell with Fulham. "We beat Manchester United and Liverpool this year and we've got to be really proud of that," he said. "I told the players, it is a sign of how far we have come. The result was not because we got fired up for one particular game, but the reward for the work the players have put in for the last year or two."

He urged some caution, though, to prevent the euphoria from setting them up for a fall. "It's like the story of the elastic band. Stretch it too far and it breaks."

The Observer

Hodgson's Fulham represent the best value for money in the country. They have the best organised team, bar none, and the best attitude to the game.

When Hodgson's Fulham return from Europe, as they did last week with the triumph over Basle that sent them into the Europa League's knockout stages, they do not harbour excuses for a diminished performance on Saturday, as even the elite do; they just go out and play again. With what Mark Schwarzer, their goalkeeper, described as "an extra spring in our step".

This, Fulham's biggest win over United in 69 matches going back to 1908, was just another footnote in a wonderful chapter in the Club's history. Where the story is leading, no one knows. Hodgson tries to be sensible, identifying an ambition to keep the club at the present level, but his Fulham keep making progress and the supporters would not swap this experience for anything.

Nor would most of the players. What a good professional footballer craves most is a clear understanding of what the manager wants from him, coupled with confidence that he can do it. Long may the likes of Murphy and Hangeland enjoy life at the Cottage.

The Times

Bill and Andy Muddyman

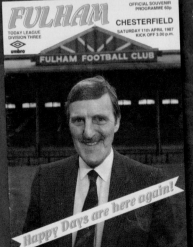

In April 1987, the front cover of the Fulham's "official souvenir programme" for the match with Chesterfield trumpeted: "Happy Days are here again!" as a new Board of Directors, fronted by Chairman Jimmy Hill and Vice-Chairman Bill Muddyman took charge. At that stage, the Craven Cottage site was owned by property developers eager to make a financial killing. Fair to say that a lot has happened since then, and Bill, whose son Andy subsequently joined the Board, has seen the lot. The Ed caught up with Bill and Andy to discuss the Club's incredible change of fortunes.

A little over 30 years ago, you and Jimmy Hill spearheaded a new Board of Directors that effectively saved Fulham FC. It must give you huge satisfaction to see the Club not only still at Craven Cottage but also back in the Premier League?
BILL: It does. And when we were at Wembley for the Play-off Final, the whole occasion was very emotional for Andy and myself. The last time we managed to gain promotion to the top flight was with Jean Tigana in charge – and that was quite a journey. As far as saving Fulham

Football Club, well that's true but it was really down to the considerable efforts of so many people. The Board members were the figureheads of that particular drive.

How did you get involved in the first place?
BILL: I was living abroad at the time and started to pick up stories of Fulham being taken over by developers. I knew David Emery, then sports editor of the *Daily Express*, and, during a phone call with him, he said that the only person who could help Fulham was Jimmy Hill. So David arranged a meeting and I flew over to meet Jimmy. After that came the meeting at the Wig and Pen club, just off Fleet Street, convened with a select group prepared to invest in the Club. Andy

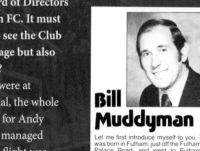

Bill Muddyman

Let me first introduce myself to you. I was born in Fulham, just off the Fulham Palace Road, and went to Fulham Palace Primary School, which I understand is now called Melcolme School. From there I moved on to St. Clement Danes School and continued to live in Fulham until I was married.

I attended my first match at the tender age of five, persuaded by my brothers, and have kept up an interest in Fulham Football Club ever since. The last thing I ever imagined was that I would become involved in the way that I have, and even when I agreed to attend the historic meeting at the Wig and Pen Club I still thought it was an uphill battle. However, the enthusiasm for Fulham Football Club that was generated at that meeting, led by Jimmy Hill who finally agreed to be Chairman, convinced me that not only had I a part to play, but that in some way it was fate.

I was very impressed with the attitude of those who will be my colleagues, and together I can promise you that we will do our best for Fulham Football Club in the future. We certainly won't fail through lack of ambition or hard work by everyone involved. All we need now is your support!

BILL MUDDYMAN

joined me for that. I vividly recall telling Andy beforehand: "We are not buying a football club. Anyway, we agreed to match pound for pound what those present would be able to contribute. Ultimately we had a figure of around £300,000 on the table – not an enormous sum in today's terms. That's what Fulham FC had in the kitty at that moment. Plus a wave of enthusiasm.

One of those present was David Dein, but Jimmy didn't want him on board. Subsequently we were very pleased about that decision as spoke against Fulham at the Compulsory Purchase Order (CPO) Inquiry. In fact, he took money to do so.

That Inquiry was one of a number of key issues you had to deal with. [The local Council stepped in with the aim of securing the Craven Cottage site via a compulsory purchase; this called for a government-sponsored Public Inquiry in January 1990.] On the eve of that Inquiry you struck a deal with Cabra Estates that included an upfront payment to FFC of £2m in exchange for leaving the site quietly in due course and withdrawing your support for the CPO…
BILL: We also secured a three-year extension to our lease – due to expire at the end of May 1990. That £2m payment proved to be the last straw for Cabra, who were already in financial difficulties. It sounds very straightforward all these years later; back then, though, it was anything but. They were interesting times! A little earlier in the tale, I was taken to lunch by a friend of mine in the building industry. We'd helped each other out in the past but now my friend was asking me: "Do you know what sort of people you're dealing with here?" It dawned on me that he was trying to warn me off when he talked about bombs under cars. I stress that nothing happened – and this was before Cabra got involved, actually – but it just added another layer to what was already a very complex situation.

Things are much healthier at Fulham these days. And there were "ups" while you were on the Fulham Board – promotions gained by Micky Adams, Kevin Keegan and Jean Tigana. Even so, you went through a hell of a lot: was it worth it?
BILL: Absolutely; yes!

I'm asking because you – the Board – and specifically Jimmy Hill took an awful lot of flak and personal abuse…
BILL: When we finally got control of the Club in 1987 I walked into the ground with Alistair Spencer, another Fulham fan who worked for our company, and surveyed the scene. This was my first time in the ground after we'd taken charge. Alistair never swore, but he turned to me and said: "Bill, I know you love this club, but this is effing ridiculous!" We knew things wouldn't be easy.

One area that brought us a little negative press

was our tightening of the Club's purse strings. You'd get players complaining that they'd only be allowed fish and chips on away trips, for example. What wasn't appreciated was how much we were having to spend on legal fees – we're talking hundreds of thousands – and in addition cashflow support for the Club on a monthly basis. That figure reached £50,000 a month, so balancing the books was a real challenge. During that time we found many cash drains, which we plugged and ran the Club as a proper business.
ANDY: People also weren't aware of our strategy that had been put in place after that meeting at the Wig and Pen. We had to get into a position of being able to apply some leverage on Marler [owners of the ground at that juncture]. We bought the players' contracts and the operating business with the view that, once we were in, we could get tough with Marler. We were then able to renegotiate a five-year lease, which gave us a platform on which to go to work behind the scenes. The goal, of course, was to get into a position where we could acquire the freehold to protect the Club's long-term future.

Your strategy called for a huge financial outlay, and yet surely the main thing you had to buy was time?
ANDY: You're right. Buying time was essential. We had no crystal ball to give us advance warning of the property crash; that was a bonus further down the line. However, once we'd received that £2m from Cabra, that's when we thought there was a chance they might go bust. As part of that deal, though [which also meant having to withdraw our support for the CPO], we couldn't say anything publicly.
BILL: Tom Wilson [former Fulham full-back, a Club Director from 1987 steeped in property surveying experience] had given us very good advice from the very start. He advised us that if we took the £2m and then subsequently lost the CPO Inquiry, we'd still be able to appeal. So it was a calculated decision.
ANDY: It was a bit of a roll of the dice. But it wasn't without careful consideration of what we thought the outcome would be. As we know, Cabra did go bust, and the ownership of the ground transferred to the The Royal Bank of Scotland. What you might not know is that RBS then paid John Duggan (previously Cabra's CEO) to be their consultant to sort out their bad-debt property book.
BILL: Once the RBS owned the ground it was far easier to deal with

Below: A fabulous photo of Andy (*left*) and Bill Muddyman savouring our Play-off success at Wembley in May 2018.

"We truly believe Fulham FC would not have survived but for that deal and the efforts of so many. And it made our recent trip to Wembley that much sweeter. We stuck our necks out and took a substantial risk back then, and, had we not done so, I'm convinced the Club would not exist today."

them, initially at least, because of the bad publicity we could generate against them. In fact, owning Craven Cottage became a hot potato for the Bank.

You must have welcomed such a shift in balance?
BILL: Oh yes. But they were frustrating times all the same. Jimmy and Tom Wilson were giving the Bank more credibility – by considering they were the good guys – than we were. I went to the RBS in Edinburgh so many times and just felt that things weren't quite right. The Bank had been saying there'd be a discount if we could do the deal for the ground quickly; they were eager to wrap things up as soon as possible. And yet we, the Muddyman family, were being asked to come up with £10m – not in securities or pledges, but in hard cash. After negotiations, that figure became £7.5m, but only if signed and sealed in 10 days.
ANDY: The Bank's strategy, on the advice of John Duggan, was for us to fail. They'd be seen to be offering us the ground, and we'd be perceived as the fall guys – unable to do the deal (because of such penal conditions). And, yes, they insisted on a cash-only deal.

In all of this, did it help that Chelsea had been in the same position; Stamford Bridge had also been owned by Cabra?
ANDY: Not directly. In retrospect, though, it helped that people became greedy along the way. Had the property companies focused on one of the three sites – they owned Fulham, Chelsea and QPR – they may have got away with it. By going for the jugular with their grand schemes, they came a cropper.

Back in 1990, three members of the Supporters' Club Committee, Allan Gould, Andy Dance and myself, were at Craven Cottage the day after the deal with Cabra was announced. We were surprised to be invited into the Cottage for a lengthy chat…
ANDY: We did our best to put out enough road signs to indicate our intentions. But there still had to be an element of trust, as we couldn't say much on the record because of the terms of the deal. It was a case of hoping that, even though there was much we couldn't say, people would judge that we were operating in the Club's best interests. Despite that, we still felt a bit awkward knowing that Fulham supporters would simply have to fill in the gaps themselves and trust us.

BILL: Other factors fell into place in due course, but we truly believe Fulham FC would not have survived but for that deal and the efforts of so many. And it made our recent trip to Wembley that much sweeter. We stuck our necks out and took a substantial risk back then, and, had we not done so, I'm convinced the Club would not exist today, and there would have been no Wembley this year.
ANDY: Do you know, we took the Club from losing £750,000 a year to breaking even within three seasons; that was no mean feat given the bigger picture.

Your appointment of Ian Branfoot as Team Manager helped to stabilise things on the football front, even if the results on the field weren't too brilliant…?
BILL: It was at this time that we took direct control of running the Club as a business following our 2-1 defeat at Torquay when we were 91st out of 92 Football League clubs. Ian brought in Annie Bassett, among others, who did much to help us run the Club properly, as Andy's just outlined.
ANDY: Ian's contribution to the Club's resurgence isn't really recognised. He brought in Micky Adams and several other key figures, and established a decent squad spirit.
BILL: Ian Branfoot had a tough time at Southampton and a group of their fans came up from the south coast and stirred things up again. Ian wasn't prepared to put his family through all that again, so he resigned. I was in New York at the time, but asked him to call me. We invited him to be our Director of Football and to install Micky Adams as the team manager.

How did you feel when – albeit at a price – the freehold of Craven Cottage was within your grasp?
BILL: It was the Holy Grail. And, once we'd acquired it, it was a fantastic feeling. In fact, the feelings of relief and pride were extraordinary. But it was simply the start of another chapter.

The next announcement came as a bombshell to most supporters: Mohamed Al Fayed was the new owner…
ANDY: Al Fayed was one of three targets – another was the Sultan of Brunei (stalwart Fulham fan Peter Thomson had links) and the third was a commercial businessman. At that juncture we'd put a lot of work into a three- to five-year Premiership plan in order to find someone who could oversee the ground refurbishment and the player acquisitions necessary to take the Club forward. That plan had a whopping £70m price tag. Today you can barely buy a goalkeeper for that price! By the time Al Fayed became our focus (although he paints it that he targeted us!), we'd already achieved one promotion thanks to Micky Adams. We then

delivered the Premiership plan in four years – a year ahead of schedule.

BILL: Al Fayed has rewritten that period, and that irks me, and it irks my family. The deal was £30m contracted and a further £30m non-contracted. And then he'd put in a further £40m should we reach the Premier League; which he did. We told him that every penny he put in to Fulham Football Club would stay there; and it did.

ANDY: He told the newspapers that he'd paid us that £30m personally. That did that generate some bad PR for us and disquiet among the fans.

With Al Fayed at the helm, Fulham charged towards the top flight, having first sorted out the Club's infrastructure…

ANDY: There's no doubt he had some excellent people working for him – and I mean commercially and as individuals. They helped to ensure that the plans were implemented, and that included the purchase of the Motspur Park site. My favourite season was Jean Tigana's promotion season. Not only was the football breathtaking, but it was all backed up by a fantastic set-up behind the scenes; off the field we were absolutely singing. Al Fayed was simply the figurehead at the time and never chaired a Board meeting – that was left to Dad – and he left his people and us to get on with it. And it worked – superbly! You can tell when a football club is being run correctly; it's a tangible thing. When everyone's pulling together for the common cause, on and off the field, it's a fantastic feeling. After that, though, Al Fayed couldn't help himself. Instead of just taking the applause – justified applause for overseeing such a marvellous period – he had to tinker with things. And he got very jealous of Jean Tigana.

BILL: I must mention one of Al Fayed's appointments: Tim Delaney, of creative agency Leagas Delaney, was appointed to the Board. We got on with him extremely well and he was bloody good. Tim was instrumental in doing so much behind the scenes to ensure Jean Tigana had every chance of taking the Club into the top flight.

You both stepped down as Directors in October 2003. What that a voluntary decision?

BILL: Not exactly. When we did the initial deal with Al Fayed we ensured we had a lot of vetoes, and the big veto pertained to the building of a new stadium. In time, we decided to veto the grand super-stadium because we'd discovered that all the Chairman's expenditures on the project were not considered as equity but structured as a debt on Fulham. So, in due course, we stood down as share-holders and directors under threat of Al Fayed putting the Club into liquidation.

That meant you were "regular" supporters again! And there was a trip to Hamburg in the

pipeline on the back of being an established top-flight club…

ANDY: We took great pride in that, having been so involved in getting Fulham to a position of strength.

So what was it like to see us crumble and suffer relegated in 2014? You said earlier that it's tangible when everyone at a club is pulling the same way; was this the reverse of that?

ANDY: After the Club was sold things went badly awry; that was evident to almost everyone. We even offered our help at the time. We were in no way trying to be confrontational or disruptive, but at the same time we could sense where it was all heading. All the effort that so many people had put in to raise the Club from a perilous position in the basement division to a stable footing in the Premier League was simply being tossed to one side. And, as was proved, within two seasons that was all flushed away.

BILL: We arranged a meeting and said that we could deliver Jean Tigana, Christian Damiano and Roger Propos. While nothing's ever guaranteed in football, these three were eager to get back to "their" football club and to raise its profile again. However, that proposal went nowhere. due to the management of the Club not accepting our offer of help.

Did that day out at Wembley help to put all that on the back burner?

ANDY: So many people were going crazy with delight when that final whistle went, and we were no exception. It was a superb afternoon and it's magnificent to see Fulham back where they belong. There's a much better feeling about the whole set-up, too.

BILL: I agree. However, I don't sense much of a soul in the Club. It's great to be back in the Premier League, but I'd love to see the Club have a bit more heart and soul. The supporters displayed plenty of that, most notably in those end-of season P lay-off games, and I'd like to see Fulham FC embrace the supporters more. ⚽

Opposite page left: Former Fulham 2000 Chairman Melvin Tenner's witty note to Bill Muddyman in June 1997 celebrating the Club reclaiming the freehold of Craven Cottage. Very Fulhamish!

Below: Mohamed Al Fayed is flanked by Andy (*left*) and Bill Muddyman. The Club's plan to reach the top flight was well and truly on track!

The Euro Tour Gathers Pace

Be honest, who saw that one coming? I'd dosed up on realism in readiness for the second leg against Shakhtar. Which made what followed all the sweeter – even if the 90 or so minutes seemed to take three weeks to elapse. Enthralling and yet gut-wrenching; a must watch, but daren't look; exhilarating, yet exhausting! Big Brede's brilliant header from Duff's beautifully flighted cross did calm the nerves for a minute or two (or was that down to the mad arms-flailing "embarrassing dad" dancing/singing session that ensued the moment the ball crossed the goal-line?). But then it was back to the twitchy clock-watching.

Dave Kidd recounts a recent chat with Simon Davies who said that much of their training centres on the team's shape. *After the magnificent first-leg victory over Shakhtar Donetsk, Simon Davies gave some intriguing insights into life under Roy Hodgson. The secret of Fulham's success, announced another journalist, is that they "keep their shape" better than pretty much anybody else. At this, a wry smile crossed the eloquent Welshman's lips as he tells us it's all down to practicing the same old drills, day after day after day.*

I ask him whether this is all rather boring and he tells us that, yes, the players do have a laugh about the tedium of it all.

But then Davies shook his head in disbelief and mentioned the fact that we have just beaten the UEFA Cup holders – a team who dress like Barnet but play like Brazil – and that this is quite a contrast to the first few years of his Fulham career, when we were merely battling relegation.

Well, all that "repetitive" work under Roy Hodgson was never better brought to fruition than in this encounter. Hardly pretty at times given the expected onslaught from Shakhtar, but effective. Damned effective.

I think it's fair to say that Brede Hangeland hasn't really hit the heights of last season, whether due to niggly injuries or a slight loss of form; in fact he's been eclipsed at the back by Mr Reliable, Aaron Hughes for much of this season. But this was a towering performance. Sure, the goal meant he was guaranteed the headlines, but just as noticeable were his awesome defensive qualities and sheer determination to see the job through. That dogged streak ran through the whole team, meaning we not only repelled Shakhtar's repeated attacks but were able to counter ourselves, and looked more and more menacing as the clock wound down.

Shakhtar's equaliser on the night briefly threatened the overall result, but noticeably it didn't knock us out of our stride. We simply reset the internal computers. Not only were the previous levels of concentration and defensive determination found again in an instant but we also had the nerve to be dangerous on the break. Two or three times we breached their rearguard, with the best opportunity falling to Gera. But, in heroic fashion, we made it and Sir Roy's CV just got that little bit more impressive. What a game plan! What a result! And what a mouth-watering clash now awaits. Fulham v Juventus. Rolls off the tongue quite nicely, don't you think? ⚽

Fulham v Juventus: March 2010

My younger daughter, Carys, isn't what you'd call a football nut, hardly bothering with games shown on the telly, even when Fulham are playing. But whenever we've managed to get an extra ticket for her at the Cottage she's been utterly enthralled, doing her level best to see every single second of the action in between the heads and shoulders of those much bigger supporters in front of her. She's also been something of a lucky mascot, having a 100 per cent win rate.

On the way to the Europa League return game against Juventus I did my best to prepare her for potential disappointment, telling Carys, then aged 12, that at 3-1 down against one of the great names of European football, Fulham would do very well to just get back into the tie. Actually, optimist that I am, I was still clinging to the hope that our away goal might prove to be somehow useful. Elder son Matt, usually so cynical, was also hopeful that Fortress Craven Cottage might affect the visitors; he was insistent that we'd win on the night. A rose-tinted outlook perhaps, but we were clinging to the faint hope that a 2-0 home win wasn't completely beyond us; we can dream!

Having nabbed a ticket for the Putney End, Matt kindly gave up his Hammersmith End season ticket berth to Carys and watched the game alongside TOOFIF stalwart Roger Scoon. Little did we know as we took our respective seats for the 6pm kick off that we were all about to witness the most amazing night of footballing drama at the famous old ground – with an unbelievable atmosphere to match.

When David Trezeguet did the unthinkable and scored an away goal for Juventus at 6.02pm I gave Carys a hug and, in full stating-the-bleedin'-obvious mode, mumbled: "That's made it awkward for us; we'll struggle to get back into this now." The swearwords I kept to myself. At 6.09 there was a glimmer of hope as Bobby Zamora chested the ball down and fired home a leveller

Above and below: A couple of programme covers from the famous Europa League run. First we took on the dazzling skills of defending champions Shakhtar Donetsk, whose line-up included Fernandinho and Willian. Fortunately our line-up included Gera, Zamora and Hangeland who scored as we won the tie 3-2 on aggregate. Then came Juventus at the Cottage!

on the night. Oh well, we're giving them a game at least. Let's enjoy the spectacle.

In fact, Big Bob was giving Juve's defenders all sorts of problems, so much so that Fabio Cannavaro (and others) made repeated attempts at taking the shirt off his back. With the referee seemingly turning a blind eye to the rough-house tactics, it was turning into of those nights. But hang on, that's a red card! One of Cannavaro's more innocuous tugs has received the ultimate punishment. He's off. Hmm, I wonder…? Meantime, we're all going berserk – and even more so when Simon Davies and then Dickson Etuhu hit the woodwork. Still 1-1 on the night, but what a game; this is extraordinary stuff, we're giving them a real test and the excitement levels are rising by the minute! I'm indebted to *The Guardian* for giving me a breather here; this is how they described what happened six minutes before the break:

GOAL! Fulham 2 Juventus 1 (Gera, 39) HOLY CRAP! Am I allowed to say that? To hell with it. Zamora drops deep, flicks the ball over Juve's defence, Davies just stops it from going out of play, crosses low and Gera, two yards out at the near post, converts. Zamora is destroying them single-handed. Honestly, this is incredible. Genuinely astonishing. When Trezeguet scored to put Juve 4-1 up on aggregate, it was over. Since then: Two goals, two woodwork-thwackings, one red card and my eyebrows raised so high I'll need scaffolding to get them down again. I'm off for a drink. Maybe I'll make it a double.

In the Hammy End we were buzzing during the interval; everyone was. Carys was beaming and all those around me were being carried along on the wave of whatever was doing the rounds. Astonishing, intoxicating stuff. Whatever the end result might be, Fulham were giving it a right go and Juventus were rattled, no doubt about that. The extent of their shirt-pulling was testament to their unease! One more goal and we'd be level overall. Dare we dream?

As the teams came out for the second half those around us were bemoaning the fact that we should have been awarded two or three penalties for the visitors' various misdemeanours. They were right, but we'd witnessed a red card and, given that the game was on a knife-edge, any penalty would surely have to be a stonewaller. And yet three minutes after the restart the referee pointed to the spot, right in front of us at the Hammersmith End. Un-bloody-believable.

It was a poor decision if I'm totally honest; ball to hand from a couple of yards, but 95 per cent of those present at Craven Cottage couldn't give a flying fig. No Danny Murphy, of course, after his silly injury-time dismissal at Shakhtar Donetsk. Who'd have the balls to take this one? Step forward Zoltan Gera. There's a hush. Talk about nervous

tension! Zolly starts his run-up. He makes decent contact… it's in for 3-1! A nanosecond later Craven Cottage erupted with a roar that could surely be heard by the Old Lady of Juventus herself. "Thank God you brought Carys with you," said two or three of those in the know around us.

Like us, Carys herself was on cloud nine, we were all dancing around with a strange mixture of raw excitement and utter bewilderment, and we were all sporting smiles of face-busting proportions. (If every game was as pulsating as this one your health would suffer serious consequences – but then again, what a way to go!) So, 4-4 on aggregate, and still plenty of time on the clock: Fulham had 40+ minutes to conjure a winner against 10 men. We were in the driving seat, no question; don't mess it up now, guys. (And yet how many seasoned Fulham veterans had at least a passing thought at that juncture that, having come so far, it would be just like us to dip out due to a silly slip-up? No heroic failures this time, Fulham, please!)

We continued to press, but perhaps not with quite as much purpose; the frequent glances at the watch confirmed that those 40 minutes were slipping away rather too quickly. Roy Hodgson sent on Clint Dempsey for Stephen Kelly, but with 10 minutes left on the clock not even that attacking substitution was giving Juventus any major problems – Italians keeping things tight defensively, not an unheard of occurrence, right? We were knocking the ball around well, true enough, but not making any incisive in-roads. Another glance at the watch. Extra-time was nigh. And then penalties. You just know what'll happen if we take it that far, right?

Meantime, Fulham went for another pass-and-move attack down the right and the ball was passed back into midfield where Dickson Etuhu knocked it forward to Clint Dempsey, whose run into space outside the box from a point level with the penalty spot had not only given him three or four yards on his marker but also lulled the visitors into a false sense of security. After all, what could he possibly do with his back to goal, 25 yards out and to the right of centre – and with four Juve defenders within five yards? Make the whole of the flipping footballing world take note of "little old Fulham", that's what.

It was footballing poetry in motion as Deuce gathered the ball, turned and, with barely a glance at the target, chipped a shot towards the far top corner. Everything went into slow-mo – keeper Antonio Chimenti, apparently well positioned for anything to his right, could only shuffle his feet slightly and look upwards in despair as the ball arced its path oh-so-perfectly up and over him before dropping just under the bar and into the net. Was it a cross? Was it a shot? Does any Fulham supporter give a damn!?

	1st
Fulham 1 Manchester City 2	2nd
21.03.10 10th	3rd
	4th
Hull City 2 Fulham 0	5th
27.03.10 12th	6th
Fulham 2 Wigan Athletic 1	7th
04.04.10 12th	8th
Liverpool 0 Fulham 0	9th
11.04.10 12th	**10th**
Fulham 0 Wolves 0	11th
17.04.10 10th	**12th**
Everton 2 Fulham 1	13th
25.04.10 12th	14th
	15th
Europa League	16th
Fulham 2 Wolfsburg 1	17th
01.04.10 Quarter-final 1st leg	18th
Wolfsburg 0 Fulham 1	19th
08.04.10 Quarter-final 2nd leg	20th
Hamburg 0 Fulham 0	
22.04.10 Semi-final 1st leg	
Fulham 2 Hamburg 1	
29.04.10 Semi-final 2nd leg	
FA Cup	
Tottenham Hotspur 3 Fulham 0	
24.03.10 Round 6 replay	

What a moment! Chimenti, utterly mugged and rooted to the spot, simply shrugged at his defenders. Deuce was anything but motionless, grabbing the badge on his shirt then haring behind the goal with arms pumping and looking up at us in the Hammersmith End with a triumphant stare; he might well have run right into the Thames had a beaming Paul Konchesky not checked his charge by leaping on him.

How do you portray euphoric delirium? All around me normal, perfectly reasoned human beings were going stark-raving bonkers. And I was every bit as bonkers as any of them. There were hugs, kisses, handshakes, cheers, yells, screams, tears, pushes, shoves – all while jumping up and down as best as the limited space between the seats allowed. The scene was one of mass hysteria and maniacal movement. What a goal; what a moment; what a football match. And it wasn't over. There were six or seven minutes still to play.

After that mass eruption of emotion, we were all pretty drained and willing the intervention of that final whistle; the players, though, were still standing firm. Not only did they deny Juventus any chance of a party-pooping equaliser but they were looking strong as the board went up for three extra minutes. Surely the game was up for the visitors, wasn't it? Well it was when the referee

TOOFIF football matches

Sometimes, just sometimes, along comes a game of football that ticks all the boxes. One that's a joy and privilege to play in; one where the result is almost incidental (almost!). For such an encounter to be contested on the hallowed turf of Craven Cottage only adds to the magic of the occasion. In fact, a motley crew playing under the TOOFIF banner has played a clutch of games at the Cottage. We've been fortunate to play alongside or against Jim Stannard, Simon Morgan, Ara Bedrossian, Jim Hicks, Gerry Armstrong (ex-Northern Ireland), Jeff Eckhardt and Ray Lewington.

Ask TOOFIF's co-editor in the early days, Dave Preston, what he thinks of Jim Stannard and you'll get an expletive-filled response. (Actually, that's pretty standard, come to think of it!) DP was in goal for the Fanzine No-Stars and Big Jim, turning out for a Programme XI, decided he was a rampaging forward intent on playing the hero before a gate of, er, 50 or 60. DP made a routine low save and was rewarded by taking an unnecessary late lunge from Big Jim to the face and upper torso. Winning mentality or brutish behaviour? You decide. And no, that particular incident wasn't from the dream encounter alluded to above.

The first TOOFIF game at the Cottage was a fundraiser for the Club. And we very nearly had Hugh Grant in the ranks, but any chance of seeing him (or Liz Hurley!) in our line-up went up in smoke as soon as *Four Weddings and a Funeral* went stratospheric.

Being on the same pitch as Ray Lewington was a privilege as well as an eye-opener. We faced each other in central midfield. And it went as you might expect – I hardly touched the ball, and why would I? Lewy was everywhere. Playing at the Cottage might have been a major occurrence for most of us that day, but this was a two-bob game for Lewington. Or so you'd think. However, in an encounter that comprised participants of widely ranging standards, physiques and ages, the future England coach was having none of that.

Not only did Lewy never stop moving, taking a fully motivated part in the match, he never stopped speaking either. Always cajoling, forever encouraging, bringing people into the game, offering advice, making himself available, cracking the odd joke (usually at my expense!), but always – always! – positive. He inspired people around him to play when one or two may well have stayed in their shells, especially the younger element. Most importantly, by getting so many around him involved, Ray ensured that they all thoroughly enjoyed themselves.

As someone on the opposing side it may not have been so enjoyable, but it was one heck of an education. And what a vivid demonstration of how much Ray enjoys his football, from grass roots level to the very top. You only had to look around to see the sky-high enjoyment levels. An occasional piece of genuine skill here and there, plenty of running, players of all standards/fitness/ages getting a decent share of the ball; people feeling that they belonged. The tackles flew in to remind the players that it was a "proper" game, but everyone was mindful too when a couple of younger lads joined the fray in the second half.

A reshuffle in the closing stages resulted in Ray Lewington dropping back into central defence, a move that not only gave my ears a bit of a rest but also enabled me to see the ball once or twice. And yes, I managed to stick one into the goal at the Hammersmith End, a rather pitiful gesture of defiance. Quiet for a nano-second, Ray let his raised eyebrows do all the talking; there's no way he'd have allowed that to happen had he not moved back. Those eyebrows weren't wrong.

sidelines
scoops & snoops

Four weddings and a Fulham

When Hugh Grant stepped up to claim his BAFTA award the other night, it was the closest Fulham FC have come to winning anything for years. For good old Hughie is, it seems, is a fan. He proudly selected Fulham's 1975 FA Cup Final disc, the appalling 'Y Viva El Fulham', on 'Desert Island Discs'. 'I'm right behind the campaign to repurchase Craven Cottage,' says Hugh, 'although I'm unable to help the club as much as I'd like.' Grant has a season ticket and has sponsored goalkeeper Jim Stannard. Hugh may even get to meet the portly custodian. 'Hugh's invited to the sponsors' evening on May 9,' said Fulham's Emma Hawkey. However, Grant *is* likely to attend a twentieth-anniversary replay of the '75 FA Cup Final. Hollywood forget it. Hugh's ambition is to play on the Craven Cottage turf, and he has been offered an awfully big adventure in a pre-match friendly for fanzine *There's Only One F In Fulham*. If Hugh and Liz Hurley continue to prosper, could Hugh become Fulham's own version of Blackburn's Jack Walker? Rumours that under chairman Hugh the club theme will be Beatrix Potter's 'The Flopsy Bunnies', another of Hugh's 'Desert Island Discs' choices, remain unconfirmed.

6 Time Out April 26-May 3 1995

flashed another red card, this time for a kick at Damien Duff. "Extraordinary" barely covers it: here we were, 5-4 up on aggregate against nine men, having been 4-1 down two minutes into the second leg.

Ninety seconds later it was all over. The European tour remained very much on track following the most momentous of comebacks. One for the history books; one for the Fulham hall of fame. As we left the ground the impression was of the Fulham supporters simply floating away from the scene of the incredible action; it was all so surreal and relatively quiet – there was just a general "hum" – as if the supremely happy throng disappearing into the night couldn't quite take in what they'd just witnessed. Bottom line though was that we'd reached the quarter-finals, where Wolfsburg lay in wait. Could we keep this magical cup run going? Don't know about that, but best make sure I get Carys a ticket… ⚽

April 2010

Our incredible Europa League adventures continued with a 3-1 aggregate win over Vfl Wolfsburg at the quarter-final stage. Bobby Zamora and Damien Duff put us two-up at the Cottage before Alexander Madlung threatened to undo things with an 89th-minute header. However, a mere 21 seconds into the return leg at the Volkswagen Arena it was Zamora again; 3-1, an away goal and we were back in the driving seat and en route for the semi-finals.

Just as incredible is the fact that I'm glossing over that victory given what was to follow. Next up were 1983 European Cup winners Hamburg, who, if they won, would enjoy home advantage at their Nordbank Arena in the final. In the first leg a typically resilient showing by Fulham in Germany earned a goalless draw, meaning it was all still to play for in the return game at the Cottage.

Hard to believe, but Fulham were just one game from reaching a major European final. Don't balls it up now, fellas.

Understandably, there was something of a surreal atmosphere at Craven Cottage on that Wednesday evening. The final was within touching distance and, for all the underlying excitement, it was all rather tense, and we hadn't even kicked off as yet. It soon became evident that this wasn't going to be easy. In fact, things weren't going to plan at all. Hamburg were no mugs and they held sway in the first half. That superiority was rewarded with a goal – a potentially critical away goal – after 22 minutes, thanks to a superb 25-yard free-kick from Mladen Petric which rocketed past Mark Schwarzer. With our own talismanic frontman Bobby Zamora – awesome and often unplayable during our epic cup run – hampered by injury it looked like being one of those nights. Not tonight, Fulham, please!

We needed something special, not least when Zamora limped off the Cottage turf about ten minutes after the break.

Despite that big blow, we were indeed treated to something special but not from the players; not to begin with, at least. Here's how David Hytner of *The Guardian* recorded the events: "As Fulham were trailing at the beginning of the second half it was impossible to foresee their latest comeback. It was then that the home support on all four sides of Craven Cottage took to their feet and bellowed their defiance. "Stand up, if you still believe."

It was a genuine "hairs on the back of your neck" moment. Craven Cottage, never the noisiest of football stadiums and more recently renowned for its poor acoustics, was bucking the trend loud and proud. Out of nowhere, the famous old stadium was reverberating to an astonishing, unrehearsed and oh-so-apposite chant. It was a phenomenal wall of sound, and underpinned by an extraordinary demonstration of support. Such a call to arms deserved an equally rousing response.

The Guardian continued: "The chorus was repeated 10 minutes later, with Hamburg still in the ascendancy from Mladen Petric's 30-yard free-kick, which counted double for his team…"

With that, we grabbed two goals in seven minutes from Simon Davies and Zoltan Gera. Danny Murphy played in Davies with a clipped pass and Davies equalised with a sublime 69th-minute finish. Then, when Gera pounced to stab home what proved to be the winner the celebrations all around the ground, on and off the pitch, were raucous. Belief and relief in equal measure! As rousing responses go, this was pretty damned special.

More from *The Guardian*: "The Fulham support struck up the chorus for the third time but now, everybody had been converted, everybody believed."

Of course we believed; we were 2-1 up and heading for the final. ITV's Peter Drury added his own spontaneous commentary: "There's a tidal wave on the Thames! How about that?! A night beyond compare. Old Father Thames has never seen the like. Hamburg will host the final; Fulham will play in it! What an achievement for Roy Hodgson – what an extraordinary achievement for Fulham. A level of success that this lovable, once-quaint club could never previously have dreamed of. This is special. This is Fulham. This is the team that knocked out the holders, Shakhtar Donetsk; this is the team that knocked out the competition favourites Juventus; this is the team that has now knocked out two major German forces in a row; this is the team that has played 18 games in Europe in a campaign that began ten months ago. And now they'll play a 19th game – in the final of the Europa League. This is Craven Cottage's greatest night!" ⚽

> *"It was a genuine 'hairs on the back of your neck' moment. Craven Cottage, never the noisiest of football stadiums and more recently renowned for its poor acoustics, was bucking the trend loud and proud."*

The Europa League Final

Only at Fulham could a momentous Europa League campaign be threatened by an enormous cloud of volcanic ash emanating from somewhere unpronounceable in Iceland (Eyjafjallajökull, if you must!). Having played 16 matches in the competition, and with Wolfsburg dispatched 3-1 on aggregate in the quarter-finals, it was back to Germany for the first leg of the semi-final. With all flights grounded due to an over-abundance of ash, the Fulham team weathered a 17-hour cross-European road trip to secure an excellent 0-0 draw against Hamburg. Crikey, things were looking good!

However, a return to the same venue for the final looked in doubt when Hamburg opened the scoring – netting a potentially pivotal away goal – in the second leg at the Cottage. With Bobby Zamora finally giving in to his injury and limping off just before the hour mark, our unlikely quest to reach a European final looked well and truly doomed. But Simon "Digger" Davies netted a beauty to offer real hope with 21 minutes left, then Zoltan Gera broke Hamburg hearts and sent all at Craven Cottage into a burbling mass of delirium by slamming home the winner from close range. Dunno about "Stand up if you Still Believe", I think most of us were flying at that point. We've only gone and made it to the final of a major European competition! Surreal, and yet richly deserved.

Almost at once our attentions turned to getting tickets for the main event. The "special edition" matchday programme for the semi-final second leg made no reference at all to the not-insignificant ticketing information. And, would you believe it, "Diddy" David Hamilton's on-pitch microphone chose that night to give up the ghost, so no details came our way once the final whistle went. Luckily for me, my next-door-neighbour in the Hammersmith End Allan Gould said he'd do his best to get something sorted via the Internet as soon as he got home. Allan, good man, duly delivered. Loads of regulars lost out, however. Turned out the tickets were only available via the Internet and season ticket holders were allowed to book four tickets each. Our 12,500 allocation was snapped up inside four hours.

I was at the Cottage the following morning and saw people being turned away by the dozen at the ticket office, simply because the key information hadn't been communicated properly and as a result supporters who weren't regular users of the Internet were penalised. John Aitken said his piece on the *Daily Mail*'s website: "Many of the fans who have spent a lot of money and taken time off work to go to other Fulham Euro away games were not given priority for tickets at all; many fans who turned up to the ticket office were told to go home and phone in, when they did all the tickets were sold out. Many, many long standing season ticket holders are not able to get tickets unless they go on ebay or other sites where tickets are many times the cost of the tickets the Club has sold. It's very poor management by the Club [officials who are] busy patting themselves on their own backs for the success of Roy, but it's typical Fulham."

That evening there was a knock on my front door; it was the legendary Cliffie Dean, well away from his local manor, asking if I happened to have a spare ticket. I'd have loved to have been able to pluck one out of my top pocket for the clearly distraught Mr Dean, but instead had to say no. I'm pleased to report that Cliffie did eventually go to the ball – something I came perilously close to not doing!

Come the week of the big event, four of us were lined up to make the journey in Allan's car, setting off the night before for an overnight stay in Folkestone before heading onto the Eurotunnel train at dawn. However, any chance of some reasonable shuteye before the long drive ahead were banjaxed when the fourth member of our party suddenly realised he had a meeting after work so would follow us down to Folkestone by train – only to then somehow mislay his one bag containing his passport at Waterloo East, causing a partial station closure as the "suspect baggage" was inspected.

We eventually picked him up from Folkestone station near midnight. I was sharing a room with the late arrival. Fair play, he went to sleep immediately. Not so grand was that he snored at a truly phenomenal volume. Added to that, his watch chimed every 15 minutes. Turned out the volcanic one had taken a sleeping tablet, so I couldn't rouse him. The snoring continued, as did those bloody chimes. Wake-up time was 4am – except I'd had no sleep. The biggest match in Fulham's history was just hours away and I had a humongous headache. Oh well, it'll wear off…

Turned out that the drive was a nightmare. Allan did the bulk of the chauffeuring; he did a

UEFA EUROPA LEAGUE

HAMBURG 2010
UEFA EUROPA LEAGUE FINAL
HAMBURG ARENA 12 MAY 20.45

PRESENTED BY

brilliant job and was as phlegmatic as ever. But even his patience began to wear thin as, despite racking up the miles, Hamburg seemed as far away as ever. Road works, detours, wrong directions, traffic jams – these all put us behind schedule, even though we'd allowed plenty of leeway.

Frances's exhortations became ever-more pointed. What began as a jovial "I'm looking forward to spending some time (and money) in the town's markets" then became a slightly more threatening "If I don't get to Hamburg to have a few drinks in the Fanzone area there'll be trouble…" But that graduated to "If I don't get to the stadium to take in the atmosphere…" to "If I don't get to see Danny Murphy leading out the lads…"

Ultimately we reached our hotel a mere 45 minutes before kick-off, checked in, then squeezed onto a packed train to the stadium. We were cutting it fine. The floodlit Hamburg stadium looked impressive; ten minutes before kick-off we were still making our way through the park, with Frances insisting: "I'm not bloody running" – as we began to jog a weaving path towards the vibrant arena. And it was as well that we did hotfoot it, reaching our seats with barely a minute to go before the big match kicked off.

We'd missed all the pre-match revelry (let alone a drink in the fanzone area), the fanfare, cheering the team onto the pitch and even David Hamilton getting stuck on the raised gantry. But at least we'd made it. My humdinger of a headache was now of migraine proportions (wimp!) and, very much out of character, as I got to my seat I started belting out several Fulham songs (with no bearing to what was being sung en masse) in an attempt to conjure a rush of adrenaline from somewhere. Fulham's biggest-ever game and I was properly out of sorts.

Alas, after all the heroics of getting to the final, "out of sorts" was a description that could also be applied to both Bobby Zamora and Damien Duff. The pair had been passed fit to play, but both looked below-par and were struggling to shake off Achilles (Zamora) and calf injuries (Duff) picked up en route to the final. Ominously, a shot from Diego Forlán hit the post, before the same player capitalised on a mishit effort by Sergio Aguero. Half an hour gone and one-down. Oh boy.

Five minutes later came that welcome surge of adrenaline. Zoltan Gera's cross was turned in past David De Gea quite brilliantly by Simon Davies. Oh yes, the dream was back on. Without reaching the heights of previous rounds we had more of an edge after the break, especially once the peripheral Zamora was replaced by Clint Dempsey. Davies had a shot saved, but the game moved into extra-time. Our patched-up team were in defensive mode by now, but were holding on without too many scares.

Penalties were looming when we lost it in a cruel fashion. Just three minutes before the end of our 63rd game of the season, Forlán's effort took a decisive deflection and crept past Mark Schwarzer's despairing dive. Brede Hangeland sunk to the floor. As did I up in the stand. It was hard to describe how tired and emotional I felt at that point – and without having touched a drop! Talk about a low blow.

What a mixture of emotions: proud that we'd got so far, proud of the players, proud of the fans who'd decked out the stadium with flags and who'd supported the Club's magnificent effort superbly; proud of the way that Roy Hodgson and co had put Fulham on the European map – and yet totally gutted to have got so near to unlikely Euro glory with a depleted team before succumbing to such a soft goal so late in the day. What a sickener.

But what an achievement! As we headed out of the stadium most were insistent that we'd have won the penalty shoot-out had it ended 1-1 – and with Mark Schwarzer in goal, that was a definite maybe. But these weren't the usual "we wuz robbed" or "if only…" sentiments. This was uncharted territory and we'd almost landed a biggie. The peculiar mix of pride and despair felt throughout the Club would surely serve as a launchpad for a repeat attempt. To paraphrase Oliver Twist: "More please"! ⁙

	1st
	2nd
Fulham 3 West Ham 2	3rd
02.05.10 10th	4th
	5th
Fulham 0 Stoke 1	6th
05.05.10 12th	7th
	8th
Arsenal 4 Fulham 0	9th
09.05.10 12th	**10th**
	11th
Europa League	12th
Atlético Madrid 2 Fulham 1	13th
12.05.10 aet Final	14th
HSH Nordbank Arena, Hamburg	15th
	16th
	17th
	18th
	19th
	20th

Brilliant, Fulham, you deserved a night of glory

ONE winter's day in 1987, I stood at Craven Cottage watching a peaceful pitch invasion protesting at a developer's plans to knock down that beautiful old ground and merge Fulham with QPR.

Another time, when they were in the old Third Division, I saw the supporters carrying a coffin across the centre circle, demonstrating against some other dastardly scheme which would have killed their desperate, near-bankrupt but much-cherished team.

Last night they beat Juventus 4-1 there. Rarely can there have been a more uplifting – or unlikely – story of reward for a group of people who kept a wonderful club of the people alive out of sheer, old-fashioned love. Football, bloody hell? It applies here in fabulous fashion, too.

Hughes Next

After last season's euphoria we've come back down to earth with a big bump. The highs (and, ultimately, that horrible low three minutes from the end of extra-time) of that magical night in Hamburg seem a distant memory now that Roy Hodgson has been lured to Anfield, leaving Mark Hughes (of whom more in a mo...) to pick up the pieces.

I say "lured" – but once the Anfield finger beckoned, Roy was racing up the M6 faster than Jensen Button in a Bugatti Veyron! As expected, the media's coverage of his departure was almost wholly based on the Liverpool angle, with barely a nod as to where this left FFC (the UK's most successful club in Europe last season and, unbelievably, in joint sixth place in the world club rankings – according to the International Federation of Football History & Statistics). But that's the point: where *has* it left us?

Hodgson's departure was to be expected I suppose. His two and a half year tenure at Fulham was longer that most of his many managerial stints. Even so, most of us mistakenly thought that he'd stay a little longer seeing as how it seemed the perfect arrangement for both sides: the Club loved Hodgson and Hodgson seemingly loved the Club. His eloquence, humility and old school charm was in stark contrast to the brash, ego-led ways of the big-money Premier League. His genial ways suited Fulham brilliantly – and the gradual turnaround that led to success in the League and then in Europe was eagerly received by all concerned. It also made football folk away from SW6 sit up and take notice. By the time we went to Hamburg for the Europa Final, "little" Fulham were well and truly on the world map and it was fantastic to see the good guy coming out top for a change.

Hodgson had developed the squad with a mix of old-school methods and an encyclopedic knowledge of today's game and, critically, had a set of players keen to play to his tune. Yes, much of the training was repetitive but, as evidenced by the telling improvements in all of the players and in the team framework, it was also wonderfully effective. Confidence levels soared accordingly and, along with thumping Liverpool and Man. United, we very nearly claimed a major European trophy. Hodgson and his staff performed wonders. But he's history now: Mark Hughes, welcome to Fulham FC (and welcome to TOOFIF!) – you've a hard act to follow. ⚽

> "Hodgson had developed the squad with a mix of old-school methods and an encyclopedic knowledge of today's game and, critically, had a set of players keen to play to his tune. Yes, much of the training was repetitive but, as evidenced by the telling improvements in all of the players and in the team framework, it was also wonderfully effective."

Opposite page right: Bobby Zamora – victim of a crunching tackle by Karl Henry.

Below: Fulham's ticketing issues are covered by *The Independent*.

Fulham fans wait for Uefa verdict on extra final tickets

By Thomas Keppell

UEFA IS expected to announce in the next couple of days whether Fulham have been successful in their application for extra tickets for Wednesday's Europa League final against Atletico Madrid in Hamburg.

The club sold out their allocation of 12,650 tickets within hours of them going on sale last Friday morning. Fans have been angered by the decision to allow the club's 10,000 season-ticket holders to buy four tickets each, which has left many other supporters without a chance to go to the game.

"A lot of disgruntled fans have come up to me asking if I have any tickets because they are that desperate to go," said David Lloyd, editor of fanzine *There's Only One F in Fulham*. "I think that the club's lack of experience has caught them out here. To give season-ticket holders four tickets is a bad decision. It was a knee-jerk reaction. The club put the tickets on sale at 7am in the morning straight after the match.

"They didn't take any steps to talk to the fans and some of those who have followed the club across Europe this season have now been left with

out. It leaves a bad taste in people's mouths ahead of the biggest game in the club's history."

Fulham's request to bring forward their final league game of the season against Arsenal, to give them extra time to prepare for the final, was turned down by the Premier League yesterday. The Cottagers made a formal request to have their game at the Emirates moved from Sunday to Saturday.

However, the Premier League cited the need for all last-round matches to kick off at the same time as the reason for denying their request.

The club is monitoring the fitness of Damien Duff and Bobby Zamora ahead of the final. Duff will be checked by the club's medical staff after he was forced off at half-time of Wednesday night's defeat to Stoke.

He is likely to miss Sunday's game, while Zamora is struggling to overcome the Achilles injury which has kept him out of Fulham's last two games. "Duff was taken off because he took a kick and we thought one of his muscles was cramping up," said manager Roy Hodgson. "We hope it's not too serious and I hope he'll be fit for the final."

Just the ticket? Not exactly

Our astonishing progress in the Europa League was somewhat soured by the ticketing arrangements in the latter stages. An allocation of up to six tickets per season ticket holder for the home semi-final leg seemed incredibly generous. The touts were out in unbelievable numbers between Putney Bridge and Craven Cottage on the night in question – and only the people involved know how they got their hands on so many tickets.

Before the Final itself, things got pretty desperate. As the final whistle beckoned as we brilliantly overhauled Hamburg in the semi-final, what we wanted was some audible precise information about the tickets for the grand occasion. What we got was a muffled David Hamilton on a dreadful microphone telling us... well, the sound was so bad that poor Diddy could have been giving us the shipping forecast.

As we all ultimately found out – some the hard way – tickets were NOT on sale at the Cottage. It was an Internet-only deal, from 7am, although I gather some sales were done by phone too. And, in the determination to sell out, season ticket holders were allowed up to four each – seems Club officials (not the ticket office staff) were anxious not to be stuck with many quids'-worth of unsold tickets. Although a reasonable thought process, it was so wide of the mark as to be laughable. But it proved no laughing matter as, in the early morning clamour and confusion, many diehards, some who'd traipsed all around Europe, were left without. Thankfully, by the time of the Final, most of those wanting to go had scavenged a ticket by various means (including a further wave of tickets made available to FFC) so not too many missed out on "going to the ball". Hopefully lessons have been learned – just in case there's a next time! ⚽

Flattering to Deceive

I remember taking stock after our opening few games and being genuinely excited. We'd rounded off our pre-season friendlies with a 5-1 trouncing of Werder Bremen, sealed a decent point at Bolton then more than matched Man. United at the Cottage. The extra positivity called for by Mark Hughes seemed to be a brilliant augmentation to the supreme teamwork and understanding developed by Roy Hodgson. Our ex-gaffer may have done wonders for our Club, but he wasn't faultless – and the Hughes outlook seemed set to give an extra edge thanks to our pressing further up the pitch and the new manager's willingness to change things by lobbing on a substitute or three far more readily that his predecessor. Hey, we might well chalk up a few away wins, too!

Everything clicked against Port Vale. Yeah, yeah, the visitors are from a lower division but Micky Adams' side – League Two leaders – aren't complete mugs. However, they were utterly overrun. A sparkling effort earned us a 6-0 win, but it could have been many, many more. At that stage it all looked rosy.

Fast forward to November. We were insipid against Villa and then dreadful in the first-half against Manchester City, who took full advantage; 0-3 at the break, 1-4 by the final whistle. So much for that "hard to beat" tag. Surely if there was one game that would see us fight our corner for the manager it would be against his former employers. As it was, we meekly surrendered the midfield, the football and the match. Playing high balls to Andy Johnson (or rather to Kompany!) was daft. There was a marked improvement all round after the break; then again, the game was all but lost by then.

Against Birmingham we gave away a dreadful goal and our brittle confidence levels took another blow. A resurgence after the break brought a deserved equaliser (set up by the superb Gera), but we didn't have the nous to push on for a winner, and nearly lost it when the visitors hit the bar.

Whereas we had a measure of control last term and pinged the ball about with confidence and pace, the same players are looking laboured this term. With the ball given away so often the defence is under more pressure and those silly mistakes that had all but disappeared are now back in evidence.

There *are* mitigating circumstances for this alarming dip in form. Not long after that Port Vale fiesta Bobby Zamora fell victim to Henry's crunching tackle. One man doesn't make a team, but there's no one else like Zamora in our squad. You could argue that for bustling effectiveness there's barely anyone to touch an in-form, confident Zamora in the country. And he was England's centre-forward at the time, don't forget!

And it's not just been Zamora, a glut of injuries have affected the team – Schwarzer, Stockdale, Baird, Salcido, Senderos, Etuhu, Duff, Murphy, Davies, Dembélé and Kamara are among those to have joined Big Bob on the sidelines. At West Brom we had our entire first-choice midfield absent — hardly a recipe for consistency, is it?

That said, we've recently been able to field line-ups akin to our Euro sides but have looked a shadow of that set-up. Jittery at the back, hesitant and ponderous in midfield and unconvincing up front. It's often been a case of hoping for something to happen rather than having the skill or nous to make it happen.

Thanks heavens, then, for the game at Arsenal. It's a mark of how things are going that I'm taking solace from a defeat! There were encouraging glimpses of the Fulham we'd become accustomed to seeing during the cut and thrust encounter, We showed great character to withstand a barrage from Arsenal and no little skill and determination to not only get back into the game through Kamara but also to slug it out with the Premier League leaders. Once we'd levelled, we looked the likelier side to score the all-important second goal before the break. With Arsenal playing a high line, we had several "nearly" moments, but needed one cute pass, one skilful piece of control, or one clever run to stay onside… Then Kamara was through one-on-one with the keeper. A key moment. Alas, Joe couldn't tuck the ball beyond Fabianski and, to be blunt, our chances of a shock result went with that slack finish.

That it took a further piece of brilliance from Nasri 15 minutes from time to defeat us only emphasised our much-improved showing. Until then, it seemed the draw specialists might well notch another – and in my view we were well worth a point on the day.

On a general note, Sparky may or may not prove to be the right man for the job, but now's the time to get behind him and the team and show that we're not your typical Premier League big-time Charlie supporters. ⚽

Bolton Wanderers 0 Fulham 0	14.08.10	8th
Fulham 2 Manchester United 2	22.08.10	13th
Blackpool 2 Fulham 2	28.08.10	11th
Fulham 2 Wolves 1	11.09.10	5th
Blackburn Rovers 1 Fulham 1	18.09.10	6th
Fulham 0 Everton 0	25.09.10	6th
West Ham United 1 Fulham 1	02.10.10	9th
Fulham 1 Tottenham Hotspur 2	16.10.10	11th
West Brom 2 Fulham 1	23.10.10	16th
Fulham 2 Wigan Athletic 0	30.10.10	8th
Fulham 1 Aston Villa 1	06.11.10	12th
Chelsea 1 Fulham 0	10.11.10	15th
Newcastle United 0 Fulham 0	13.11.10	16th
Fulham 1 Manchester City 4	21.11.10	17th
Fulham 1 Birmingham City 1	27.11.10	17th
Arsenal 2 Fulham 1	04.12.10	17th
Fulham 0 Sunderland 0	11.12.10	17th
Fulham 1 West Ham United 3	26.12.10	18th
Stoke City 0 Fulham 2	28.12.10	17th
Tottenham Hotspur 1 Fulham 0	01.01.11	18th
Fulham 3 West Brom 0	04.01.11	13th
Wigan Athletic 1 Fulham 1	15.01.11	15th
Fulham 2 Stoke City 0	22.01.11	14th
Liverpool 1 Fulham 0	26.01.11	15th
Fulham 1 Newcastle United 0	02.02.11	12th
Aston Villa 2 Fulham 2	05.02.11	12th

League Cup

Fulham 6 Port Vale 0	25.08.10	Round 2
Stoke City 2 Fulham 0	21.09.10	Round 3

FA Cup

Fulham 6 Peterborough United 2	08.01.11	Round 3
Fulham 4 Tottenham Hotspur 0	30.01.11	Round 4

1st
2nd
3rd
4th
5th
6th
7th
8th
9th
10th
11th
12th
13th
14th
15th
16th
17th
18th
19th
20th

Getting it Together Again

Had this load of old nonsense been written after the Boxing Day debacle against West Ham, the tone would have been downbeat and the forecast gloomy. That lacklustre showing against a very poor side was the worst example of how a decent unit had sunk from European finalists to Premier League relegation candidates. We looked ordinary at best, and our gradual decline has been painful to watch.

Yet here we are, just a matter of weeks later, pushing up the table and with designs on further progress in the FA Cup. And, along with this welcome dramatic upswing there's suddenly a real competition for places.

From being jittery and pedestrian, we've rediscovered that vital edge and now look confident and positive – and, crucially, we look like scoring goals once again. Having bemoaned his loss for most of the season, we now have the amazing prospect of Bobby Zamora finding it hard to regain an automatic starting place – which is not only a peach of a problem for Mark Hughes but possibly also a good thing for Zamora, too.

Whatever happens, we've got to give Big Bob a chance to re-find his feet. After suffering such a nasty injury it's vital that he's given a chance to rediscover that powerhouse form without having to endure extra pressure from the supporters. Had the team still been performing poorly there would have been a real temptation to throw him in at the deep end and rely on him to get us out of the mire. With Zamora no doubt champing at the bit it could have been a risky strategy. Luckily we're looking in much better shape just now and the big fella can be eased in gently.

Zamora's enforced absence together with that of Mousa Dembélé, caused us severe problems given that Andy Johnson was already on the long-term injured list. In the meantime, Clint Dempsey performed wonders up front, but the American is much happier and more effective operating from

> *"Zamora's enforced absence together with that of Mousa Dembélé, caused us severe problems given that Andy Johnson was already on the long-term injured list."*

Below: It's a Pretty Young Thing, and It's Got to Be There, our Chairman (might have) said when this monstrosity was unveiled in 2011. It's Bad, we thought. But, as we didn't Wanna Be Starting Something we didn't actually Say, Say, Say too much at all.

a little deeper. Unlike the mega-rich clubs we had no top-class cover for the injured players, and boy have we paid for it. We've sorely missed Zamora's powerful hold-up play and his pivotal role in our attacking moves – his potential like-for-like replacement, David Elm, for all his honest endeavours, simply wasn't Premier League material. Of the other candidates, Eddie Johnson has been willing but largely ineffective and Diomansy Kamara has a tendency to blow hot and cold.

Things improved when Andy Johnson made a welcome return and his goal at Wigan gave his confidence and match fitness a timely boost. Also back is Dembélé, and his strength, ball control and trickery are there for all to see now he's returned to full fitness. (Rumour has it, he was the subject of a cheeky 11th-hour bid from Tottenham in the transfer window.)

Without these guys we were, at worst, one-paced when going forward and punchless in the final third. And, as the weeks went by, the confidence levels suffered and we looked anything but a tight cohesive unit – hardly a recipe for success! However, we now have the lively Gael Kakuta – who sparkled on his debut as a second-half substitute against Newcastle – and Eidur Gudjohnsen to throw into the mix. Things are looking up.

These new names are, along with Steve Sidwell, the result of Mark Hughes' transfer dealings; astute signings it would seem. The only point of debate is whether Sparky's low-budget policy was by circumstance or design; did the Chairman keep a tight rein on the purse-strings in January, I wonder? No one's expecting us to compete with the mega-million-pound outlays of clubs such as that lot down the road, but we did bank a healthy €10,010,114 (about £8.5m) from the road to Hamburg while the sale of Chris Smalling to Manchester United realised a reported £10m.

A modest outlay for Steve Sidwell and the two loan signings has hardly broken the bank. Sidwell was at the heart of our decent performance at

Villa Park. Looking to impress against his former club (it was the same script for Damien Duff a few days earlier against Newcastle), it was Sidwell's fierce shot that led to Andy Johnson's leveller. Mind you, Sidwell's lack of pace was highlighted when Walker eased past him to score Villa's second from distance – and there's a concern that he and Murphy aren't the quickest. That said, we tend to let the ball do the work and Murphy, in particular, has more than carried his weight this season. Sure, one or two passes have gone astray, but he's always prepared to step up to the plate and so much of our play goes through him that the odd error is sure to be highlighted. Some of his passing has been a delight – and to see that excellent through ball to Duff against Newcastle described as a hoof upfield, or words to that effect, was insulting. The great Johnny Haynes would have been proud of that inch-perfect delivery and it simply demonstrated Murphy's vision, quick-wittedness and range of passing. With Duff making the most of the opportunity (then going bananas at scoring against his former employers!), it turned out to be the match-defining moment.

AJ's clever effort at Villa Park cancelled out yet another own goal from John Pantsil; three in a season is going some. Maybe he'd received some pre-match tips from Richard Dunne, who's netted eight own goals up to now. JP, alas, is catching him up fast.

One guy who's not playing as much as he'd like is Zoltan Gera, so prominent during our Europa League run last season. For the moment he seems set to see out his contract from the bench. The crowd favourite, who started the season is such good form, isn't, it would seem, a favourite with the boss, but he remains a top player to bring on when necessary. And a look at our bench highlights the improvement in the squad. As well as having terrific cover for the key positions, there are now several potential game-changers ready and waiting for the call. If we stay free of further serious injuries we might yet surprise a few people between now and May. Optimistic? Of course! ⚽

Michael Jackson Statue

Oh boy did this become a thorny issue for a while! Michael Jackson's visit to the Cottage in April 1999 was a surprise in itself, so much so that even the majority of the supporters present on the day were fairly nonplussed for while, assuming that our world-famous special guest was a lookalike – at least until he went on that pre-match umbrella-protected stroll in the sunshine around the hallowed turf. What on earth would Michael Jackson be doing at Craven Cottage, after all? Preparing himself for statuehood, evidently.

When the news emerged 13 years after his one and only visit that we'd be getting a likeness (and I use that word loosely) plonked at the Cottage, the media had a field day – and the coverage, full of inaccuracies, prompted a barrage of mickey-taking from all parts of the country and beyond. Overlooked by many was that the statue wasn't commissioned for FFC. Apparently our esteemed Chairman, who'd recently befriended Jacko, had decided to put a statue of the pop superstar in his world-famous corner shop, Harrods. Trouble was, by the time the statue was ready for delivery, Harrods had been sold.

One Craven Cottage wag suggested that the Chairman then put it to his wife that it might look good on his private estate, but that she said he should stick it where the sun doesn't shine – so he did, on a shady spot on the far side of the Hammersmith End structure!

Unsurprisingly most Fulham fans were aghast at its eventual unveiling. Not only was it a poor representation but, with no direct connection to FFC, there seemed no reason having for a Michael Jackson shrine at the Club. However, while most fans stuck to the above views, some more vehemently than others, the majority were also very quick to acknowledge that the Chairman's generosity and superb leadership gave him the trump card: he could, within reason, do what he damned well liked.

If the previous years of success and continued improvement, all under-pinned and rubber-stamped by Mohamed Al Fayed, were weighed against having to tolerate an irrelevant statue tucked away on the far side of the ground, then it's no contest. That didn't mean we had to cherish such a curious embellishment to our traditional home, it was just a measure of how highly we valued the Chairman's contribution. There's no getting away from it though, the Jacko statue was…BAD! ⚽

Fulham 1 Newcastle United 0	1st
02.02.11 12th	2nd
Aston Villa 2 Fulham 2	3rd
05.02.11 12th	4th
Fulham 0 Chelsea 0	5th
14.02.11 12th	6th
Manchester City 1 Fulham 1	7th
27.02.11 13th	**8th**
Fulham 3 Blackburn Rovers 2	9th
05.03.11 11th	10th
Everton 2 Fulham 1	11th
19.03.11 12th	12th
Fulham 3 Blackpool 0	13th
03.04.11 10th	14th
Manchester United 2 Fulham 0	15th
09.04.11 11th	16th
Wolves 1 Fulham 1	17th
23.04.11 13th	18th
Fulham 1 Bolton Wanderers 1	19th
27.04.11 9th	20th
Sunderland 0 Fulham 3	
30.04.11 9th	
Fulham 2 Liverpool 5	
09.05.11 10th	
Birmingham City 0 Fulham 2	
15.05.11 8th	
Fulham 2 Arsenal 2	
22.05.11 8th	
FA Cup	
Fulham 0 Bolton Wanderers 1	
20.02.11 Round 5	

Kevin Keegan:

"You could write a book full of anecdotes about Mr Al Fayed's reign. In 1999, for example, we had none other than Michael Jackson visiting the Cottage. I took the King of Pop into the players' lounge, and down a very small corridor that was decorated with photos of Fulham's squad in the 1920s. All the men pictured were donning old-fashioned hats and he was fascinated, not with the game that day, but with these dusty old pictures chronicling the distant past of Fulham Football Club. "Look at the hats," he said. "They are the same as my hat!" That's the kind of unexpected event that would happen in my time with Mr Al Fayed."

Safety First

You could argue that our performance at Manchester's Theatre of Dreams mirrored our whole season. After all, we enjoyed a promising opening before we were brought down to earth with a dodgy decision, one from which we were never really able to recover. Sure, we flattered to deceive – and at Old Trafford we saw a decent Fulham team put on a decent performance without really getting anywhere. In the grand scheme of things staying safe in the Premier League for another season must rank as some sort of achievement, however there's the nagging feeling that, despite all the obstacles, we could have done better..

Bobby Zamora's importance to the squad was unfortunately highlighted by his prolonged absence. We're no one-man team but with no other conventional target man in the squad, and certainly no one as on-form as Big Bob was before being hacked down by Karl Henry last September, the absence of one man was to prove critical.

The pre-season managerial turmoil – losing Roy Hodgson, then his apparent replacement Martin Jol before appointing Mark Hughes as the season approached – hadn't stood us in good stead as far as transfer dealings went. Losing Zamora, after we'd made a highly promising start to the campaign, highlighted that shortcoming and meant we had to mix and match.

Last season's European exploits, as unlikely as they were welcome, very soon became history. The real shame was that the head of steam built up by all around the Club in terms of progress and excellent publicity had been allowed to dissipate. Few Fulham fans expected such highs this time around, but there was every reason to hope for further evolution. Until the defection of the manager (who left with a resounding vote of thanks, if also a brickbat or three for the manner of his departure) we'd been set fair – key players such as Hangeland and Dempsey were happy to stay at the Club and even the potential loss of Schwarzer was overcome. We'd even managed to recruit a promising player in Mousa Dembélé.

Okay, so new gaffer Mark Hughes hadn't had much time to probe the transfer market, but his less defensive outlook compared to his predecessor suggested that we'd more than hold our own. If the new man "clicked" perhaps we might do better than that – no Euro glory this time perhaps, but a domestic cup run would be nice! (Be fair, pre-season's all about hopes and aspirations!) Instead, after an excellent start, it's been rather humdrum.

Of the lowlights, losing at home so meekly to Man. City stands out, as does that abject home defeat to a very poor West Ham. But in general we often played quite well without posing too much of a threat up front – for all the efforts of the stand-in strike force.

The FA Cup demolition of Spurs and Zamora's return suggested that we might enjoy a bright finale – only for Bolton (and referee Stuart Attwell) to put paid to any hopes of reaching Wembley. In the League, with points being shared around in crazy fashion all season, had just a few of the 14 draws been turned into wins then we'd have been heading for a really healthy final berth rather than looking over our shoulders at the relegation skirmish. A fit Zamora would surely have seen to that. ☙

Fair Play, Chris

When Chris Baird hared after the Bolton winger during our FA Cup contest and "took him" cynically as the pair entered Fulham's half of the field, it was a clear demonstration that the Fulham players are no angels. In fact no one would accuse a squad that includes Sidwell, Etuhu, Zamora and Baird of being soft touches. And yet we sit proudly at the top of the Fair Play table (alongside Chelsea) – at the time of writing we're the only Premier League side not to have a man sent off and we've had the fewest yellow cards (37). (As a comparison, Newcastle have amassed 69 bookings this season, while both Arsenal and West Brom have had six red cards so far.)

A closer look reveals Fulham lead the way for respect towards their opponents and respect towards the referee. The conclusion is clear: Fulham attempt to play to the rules and compete while showing a marked level of respect. Not for them the surrounding and haranguing of match officials every time a decision goes against them; not for them the high levels of cheating employed by others; not for them the habitual shirt-pulling and off-the-ball obstruction ingrained in others. And full marks to the past and present management teams for setting the bar so high – for heaven's sake, we very nearly lifted a major European trophy last year playing to the rules. That would have been something of a first!

Thing is, though, does it count for anything? Going into March, the media was chock-full

Below: More statue reaction, this time from the Football Supporters' Federation.

of articles bemoaning refereeing howlers and players' indiscretions. Yet in successive home matches, against Bolton and Blackburn – and in another stand-out home game earlier in the season (v Wolves) – we've stuck to the rules while our opponents' constant fouling has tended to go unpunished. Amid the frenzy, we have a much-admired ever-present centre-half who's not been yellow-carded at all this season – congrats, Aaron Hughes.

But this is no holier than thou bleat. When Baird took out Petrov he was booked. Fair enough. When, for example, Murphy's fouled an opponent in a midfield skirmish or Hangeland's baulked an opposing forward, they've been yellow-carded. That's to be expected. And, on the basis that it's still supposed to be a physical game, there's no better sight than a well-timed, thumping tackle. But by the same token you expect clear-as-daylight fouls to be punished – and yet we've seen a run of desperate, cynical shirt-pulling and off-the-ball blocking be routinely ignored. I remain convinced that had Bolton's persistent fouling (especially of Dembélé whenever he moved into a dangerous position) been properly dealt with by the match officials then we may well have come a whole lot closer to winning on the day. Of course we'll never know now, but a couple of yellow cards and a clutch of free-kicks in decent positions could well have proved decisive.

It's worth stating that in the matches mentioned (Wolves, Blackburn and Bolton) the fouling was, at worst, rugged rather than nasty. Zamora was particularly unlucky, the victim of an especially meaty challenge rather than the nasty sort that felled Dembélé at Stoke for example. No, the games were ruined by weak refereeing; a lack of control and appropriate action meant the protagonists were simply allowed to carry on unchecked. And it's so frustrating to watch!

So where does that leave Fulham? One would have thought that their good behaviour should in some way be rewarded. In the same way that over-physical teams and individuals have their cards marked over the years so Fulham's combative yet respectful ways should also have been acknowledged by match officials. If two teams obviously want to scrap it out and are prepared to maim each other, there's a case for saying "let 'em get on with it"! When one team is toeing the line and the other is obviously transgressing then it should be a given that the referee steps in – it's what they're there for, after all!

Against Wolves, the cry went up: "Disgrace to the Premier League". It was targeted at the visitors for their concerted fouling, but it should also have been aimed at the referee who could have nipped it all in the bud, but for some strange reason chose not to, at least not until the second half. We

Melvin Tenner Reflects

Melvin Tenner was Chairman of the Fulham Supporters' Club when the Football Club was on its uppers. Before long, he also found himself heading Fulham 2000, the fans'-led fundraising group.

You were very involved at Fulham for a number of years, Melvin – coming along to watch the games was almost incidental…?
Yes, it was all rather intense! When Fulham 2000 was formed we spent a lot of time putting together the material necessary for the launch. However, the main launch was delayed because we had to persuade the Club that, between us, we'd raise a greater sum if the money was held by the supporters rather than the Club itself. That was the climate of the time. Resistance was quite fierce from some Fulham Directors on that point. Dates of our meetings were arranged by the Club, so whereas we were eager to get cracking, we had to wait for the meeting to be set, then go along to, among other things, put our case time and again. But eventually we launched as we wanted to. Ultimately, we raised around £550,000 – the bulk of which came from within the Fulham supporter base – and I'd say that was a pretty good effort.

Fundraising was essential, but so was publicising Fulham's plight?
Yes indeed. Before pressing any fundraising buttons we'd concentrated on getting Fulham's position across to as many people as possible. However, this had to be done without breaching the legal contract with Cabra, owners of the ground. We had to be the Club's voice, and we raised the issue via the House of Commons, adverts, newspaper articles and all manner of avenues.

It was difficult to gain the trust of the Board, then?
They had taken so much abuse from supporters that they didn't feel sympathetic towards them. So I tried not to be antagonistic while earnestly making our points; gradually we got there. The Board members were impressed with our efforts when the money started to come in very quickly.

It was all so time-consuming and, as you've said, intense. But a worthwhile exercise all the same…?
They were tough times, but yes I'm quite pleased. Had things remained antagonistic then there may well have been a different result. So diplomacy won the day in that respect and in the end everyone pulled together famously. And the extensive efforts of the supporters had a major effect on the Club's wellbeing.

may well have recovered to win the match, but we were the losers on the day with Zamora being booted onto the long-term injury list. Had any number of earlier niggly fouls been punished and one or two cards produced, Karl Henry might have thought twice about making that tackle.

I suppose FFC have been rewarded, in as much as we've been consistently awarded good marks, but that's not the same as getting the bog-standard decisions right on the day, is it? However, those good marks may yet offer a convoluted back door route to Europe. (Although you need a degree in advanced mind-boggling to understand how this is calculated.) If England remain in the top three slots in the Euro Fair Play rankings (quite a big "if") then Fulham are in pole position to be awarded a Europa League first qualifying round spot. So, who knows, that Thursday/ Sunday routine may well be reintroduced next season!

Off the Mark!

So farewell then Mark Hughes, who's walked out on Fulham after a matter of months in the managerial hotseat. And, rather like last pre-season, it's a case of where do we go from here? It's clear that Hughes used FFC as a stepping-stone – although at the time of writing his next stop-off point isn't clear! And that always seemed the way of things – mind you, I thought he'd hang around for a bit longer before diving off somewhere else.

Unlike last summer, when first Roy Hodgson dallied and then Martin Jol kept us waiting before deciding to stay at Ajax, we should be able to get a decent replacement in place well before the real action starts. The question is: "Who?".

The delay in appointing Hughes last pre-season meant there was little time for him to bolster the squad and we suffered big time when Bobby Zamora was crocked against Wolves in September 2010. With Andy Johnson still a long-term absentee it was left to Clint Dempsey to manfully step into the breach.

Just how much we missed Zamora became clear on his return this spring. We looked a more complete side and worked our way up the table to finish a creditable eighth. A lot of credit should go to Hughes for ultimately steering the ship in the right direction. Our eventual surge up the table showed what might have been. We're a good side. And, without falling into the trap of wishing for something that's unattainable, there's more to come from this squad if everyone's pulling the same way and if we get the breaks.

Our position as established Premier League top-tenners might well highlight the deficiencies of the other "middling" clubs, but it also demonstrates that we've got a damned good set-up at Fulham. Ever since Hodgson shuffled the pack and instilled magnificent defensive qualities together with a terrific ability to retain possession and counter-attack with menace, we've been able to give anyone a game.

Hughes added a slightly more attacking thrust and, at least until Zamora's injury, we began to look the business. In amongst all of this was the fact that the key personnel were happy to stay at Fulham (sure Schwarzer was pursued by Arsenal but he was persuaded to stay – and in any case we have a ready replacement in David Stockdale). I hope that Hughes walking out does nothing to rock the boat.

The one downer about us treading water last season rather than push on is that the players are all one year older. Danny Murphy, so influential (and with the record number of touches of the ball in the Premier League last term) in terms of play and direction, is in the latter stages of his career while Duff, Davies and Greening, also influential in the closing months, are no spring chickens either. So it remains to be seen if the new man is going to maintain the status quo or take things in another direction. If it's the latter, here's hoping it's upwards!

If Hughes wanted out, then he's best out of it. It's fair to say that we didn't exactly warm to him. He was extremely fortunate to have a great set of players at his disposal and was unlucky at having so little time to effect matters at the start of the season. It looked as if he was putting his mark on the set-up – Mousa Dembélé and Steve Sidwell, his purchases, have enhanced the squad, while our bench at the end of the season emphasised the general improvement.

So farewell, Sparky. Despite leading us to eighth, I can't see that you'll be remembered as one of the greats. Buggering off so soon into your tenure has blighted that achievement and your standing at FFC. Now it's a case of "what happens next?".

Anyone got Ray Lew's number…? ⚽

Jolly Replacement

Welcome, Martin Jol – albeit 12 months late! Mark Hughes' abrupt departure once last season finished caught us by surprise, even if few of us thought he was here for the long term. But to walk out just ten months into what was a successful tenure only served to emphasise the "fit" wasn't right.

Sparky's comments on closing the door behind him that the Club didn't match his ambitions weren't likely to win him any extra friends. Our ex-boss then found the apparently open doors at Villa closed in his face and, for the moment at least, he remains out of work. But now it's down to Martin Jol to lead us onwards and upwards.

Our season's well under way already thanks to our somewhat squeaky inclusion in the *Coronation Street* of football competitions, the Europa League (does it ever end?). And the general reshuffling of the pack hasn't helped us make the most fluid of starts. As last season drew to a close, with our squad pretty much back to full strength, I was confident that we'd do well this season. In fact I reckoned we were just a few key signings away from being a genuine force in the Premier League. (Can this really be Fulham FC I'm writing about?!) Before I get too carried away, much of that show of confidence is based on the poor quality of most of the top-flight teams and the fact that we had a squad spirit, playing system and a perm-any-11-from-15 first team playing to their strengths and capable of beating any team in the division. In short, our sound defence and

> "So farewell, Sparky. Despite leading us to eighth, I can't see that you'll be remembered as one of the greats. Buggering off so soon into your tenure has blighted that achievement and your standing at FFC."

improved attacking style meant that we were potentially every bit as good as any team outside the top five.

As we all headed off for, as it turned out, a very short end-of-season break, it didn't take a genius to work out that as well as a general bolstering of the squad, the key acquisition would be another striker. The loss of Bobby Zamora for so long last season highlighted how much we've come to rely on him, as well as just how little cover we had. A proven quality striker – even if it took, say, £10m to get him – would be money well spent in my humble opinion. While nothing's ever guaranteed in football, surely this would be a worthwhile expense and ensure not only that we stayed in the Premier League but that we might make a few waves at the upper end of the table.

Hughes, it was said, was after a co-forward but (reading between the lines) was denied the cash and this may have led to his haughty departure. (That, or he'd wrongly surmised he was a shoe-in for the Villa job. Hmm, perhaps they didn't share his ambitions...)

Either way, it seems that Martin Jol is shopping around. Left-back John Arne Riise is a great signing, giving us an instant improvement in that position as well as our first set of first-team brothers since the Conways, Jimmy & John (Andy and Eddie Johnson don't count!). Of the others, Pajtim Kasami's already made a good impression, while Marcel Gecov has upped the Club's ginger quota and Csaba Somogyi provides goalkeeping cover now that David Stockdale is on loan at Ipswich. But no extra striker – either for "£10m" or from the bargain basement. There's still time yet!

The fact that the new manager's blooded a few of the youngsters already this season suggests that he's of the opinion that if they're good enough, they're old enough. Or that he's listened to trusty lieutenant Ray Lewington, now back in the first-team dugout after being virtually ignored by Hughes last season and left to look after the kids.

But despite all the general optimism it remains to be seen if we'll carry on where we left off. Hughes tinkered very little, apart from adopting a more positive style to that of Roy Hodgson, and benefited from the "if it ain't broke, don't fix it" approach. Jol is keen to do things his way, and if it works we'll all be delighted. If not, then there'll no doubt be a few grumblings as we've become accustomed to a gradual improvement in our lot. Much of our success has been based on the Hangeland/Hughes partnership at the back with Chris Baird at right-back, for example, but in pre-season he's tried Senderos alongside Hangeland with Hughes shifted out to full-back. Only time will tell if this was an experiment or the proposed way forward. We'll also have to see if Jol's ways sit happily with the players.

Get the Picture?

Whenever I'm asked the question: "What's your relationship like with the Club?" I always reply "Generally good".

Obviously the Club can't be over-enamoured about having an independent publication offering its views for 20+ years right on its doorstep – it's not part of Brand Fulham, is it? – but then, unlike many such mags, TOOFIF is hardly the most vindictive or aggressive of publications, is it? The advantage of such an approach is that the occasional printed criticism or airing of a point of principle should be afforded a greater degree of credibility. Well that's the idea!

Also, when I'm asked to air my views to the media I'm always mindful of not simply being their fodder and an automatic critic of the Club. That said, I've always being prepared to stand up on a point of principle – such as the cack-handed distribution of tickets in the latter stages of our last Europa League foray, for example.

Since the early days of the mag I've made it my business to meet any incoming CEO at FFC: no real agenda, merely a chance to share a polite hand-shake and underline that if I could help in any way then I would – basic good manners, really. FFC has moved on massively in the couple of decades that TOOFIF's been around and the chances of the Club wanting any assistance nowadays – I've experience in press office as well as editorial dealings – has nosedived. However, these days it seems that my TOOFIF affiliations have led to me being blackballed in some quarters!

I've tried to get in touch with the current CEO Alistair Mackintosh for some time. It's quite possible that he's oblivious to this. It's also quite possible he's far too busy to see me, or that he

Fulham 0 Aston Villa 0 13.08.11 7th	1st
	2nd
	3rd
Wolves 2 Fulham 0 21.08.11 14th	4th
	5th
Newcastle United 2 Fulham 1 28.08.11 16th	6th
	7th
Fulham 1 Blackburn Rovers 1 11.09.11 18th	8th
	9th
Fulham 2 Manchester City 2 18.09.11 18th	10th
	11th
West Brom 0 Fulham 0 24.09.11 17th	12th
	13th
Fulham 6 QPR 0 02.10.11 10th	14th
	15th
Stoke City 2 Fulham 0 15.10.11 12th	16th
	17th
Fulham 1 Everton 3 23.10.11 17th	18th
	19th
Wigan Athletic 0 Fulham 2 29.10.11 15th	20th
Fulham 1 Tottenham Hotspur 3 06.11.11 16th	
Sunderland 0 Fulham 0 19.11.11 16th	
Arsenal 1 Fulham 1 26.11.11 15th	
Fulham 1 Liverpool 0 03.12.11 15th	
Swansea City 2 Fulham 0 10.12.11 14th	
Fulham 2 Bolton Wanderers 0 17.12.11 11th	
Fulham 0 Manchester United 5 21.12.11 13th	
Chelsea 1 Fulham 1 26.12.11 13th	
Norwich City 1 Fulham 1 31.12.11 13th	
Fulham 2 Arsenal 1 02.01.12 12th	
Blackburn Rovers 2 Fulham 1 14.01.12 13th	
Fulham 5 Newcastle United 2 21.01.12 12th	
Fulham 1 West Brom 1 01.02.12 13th	
Manchester City 3 Fulham 0 04.12.12 14th	
Fulham 2 Stoke City 1 11.02.12 12th	
QPR 0 Fulham 1 25.02.12 11th	
Fulham 5 Wolves 0 04.03.12 8th	
Aston Villa 1 Fulham 0 10.03.12 10th	
Fulham 0 Swansea City 3 17.03.12 10th	
Manchester United 1 Fulham 0 26.03.12 13th	
Fulham 2 Norwich City 1 31.03.12 11th	
Bolton Wanderers 0 Fulham 3 07.04.12 10th	
Fulham 1 Chelsea 1 09.04.12 9th	
Fulham 2 Wigan Athletic 1 21.04.12 9th	
Everton 4 Fulham 0 28.04.12 9th	
Liverpool 0 Fulham 1 01.05.12 9th	
Fulham 2 Sunderland 1 06.05.12 8th	
Tottenham Hotspur 2 Fulham 0 13.05.12 9th	

HERE'S A CLUE!

The publishers of *FulTime* asked TOOFIF for a favour – they wanted an image previously used in the fanzine of Les Strong on Anguilla beach (left). This was duly supplied. What appeared, though, and without any thanks or credit, was a doctored version (right). Bit of a cheap shot!

Above: Trust Les Strong to be the focus of some FFC skulduggery. He's pictured reading the fanzine on an Anguillan beach, only for the pic to have been mysteriously doctored by the time it appeared in *FulTime*.

Below and opposite page: Here's how the Riverside Stand may look in the next few years if the latest proposals are given the thumbs-up and actioned.

simply doesn't want to. Fair enough, that's not the point at issue – more so that it's fast becoming a one-way channel of communications between FFC and yours truly.

My telephone request to Mr Mackintosh's secretary some time ago didn't get the promised "call back". Instead, when I followed it up over a week later I was given the message that a prominent figure at the Club had said that I couldn't see the CEO – but that I'd be invited to an imminent Fans' Forum instead; I could see Mr Mackintosh there. Not quite the same thing, but it would do. Several forums have been staged since then, but I'm still waiting for that invite.

In the meantime I've had numerous requests from FFC to help out in various ways – whether that be with contact details of ex-players (you'd think the Club would have a log of such info), confirmation of historical facts and figures or supplying photographs. I've assisted the Club on every occasion, because that's what you do.

The latest request took the biscuit, though. I took a call from *FulTime* asking for a specific picture of Les Strong. They were including an interview that covered his time as boss of Anguilla and were keen to use a TOOFIF picture of Les sitting on the beach in Anguilla. No problem. I dug out the relevant pic from the archives and *FulTime* had it within the hour.

So, imagine my surprise when *FulTime* arrived to see that the picture had been doctored. The copy of TOOFIF that Les was reading

on the golden sands had become a generic magazine – and there was no sign of any thanks or acknowledgement either. I'm not normally bothered by the acknowledgement aspect. My photo-library may not be up to Ken Coton's extraordinary standards but you might be surprised at how many of my pics have been used in the various FFC publications over the years, so I'm used to helping out in this way. But, bearing in mind the specific approach this time around, this was all very petty – and, apparently, all down to the intervention of a small-minded individual.

When you hear of the stand-off between the Club and Ken Coton's Ashwater Books you realise some aspects of "friendly old Fulham" may have disappeared forever. Of course, should Mr Mackintosh get wind of these sentiments he'll no doubt imagine that the author is a senile, ranting, rebellious anti-Club man (okay, I'll grant you "senile" perhaps!). Had he met me any time during the last couple of years, he'd have realised that I'm anything but. ⚽

Way Below Par

Here's the third, and final, editorial for this season – a poor return from TOOFIF Towers. Much has happened since Issue 123: we've slipped out of the Europa League in disastrous fashion; dipped out of the FA Cup; lost our English International centre-forward to our near-neighbours; and have bumbled along in the League. On the upside, we've got a new no.9 who's keen to play for the club, seen Clint Dempsey move ever-closer to FFC legendary status with two wonderful hat-tricks, watched as Mousa Dembélé continues to add a brilliant work ethic to his supreme ability to beat people at will, and seen the Club come up with spectacular plans for a new Riverside Stand that looks set to modernise the place and increase the capacity without overwhelming the ground's traditional feel.

So how's the 2011-12 season gone? Well, here's an understatement: it's been a frustrating campaign thus far. Oh, it'll all come good, suggest the more satisfied followers amongst us. Well that's precisely what we all want of course, but when? It's all very well shrugging your shoulders and writing off point after point because we're getting there in the grand scheme of things, but shouldn't someone admit that we've performed way below par this season?

Of course when a performance like Arsenal comes along – in which we were forced on to the front foot for 90 minutes having gone behind to Koscielny's first-half goal only to recover brilliantly thanks to that rousing finale – you feel we've turned the corner. Certainly had this twaddle been written after that encounter then it would have been a whole lot more upbeat. It's not as if we haven't seen decent periods of

play this season, but unfortunately they've not been maintained. Our next League game after that excellent show against the Gunners was away at Blackburn. 'Nuff said!

The TOOFIF stance since the Club made it back into the top flight has always been to be mindful of the dark days but to look forward with relish. [In the really dark days, the TOOFIF stance towards our on-field affairs was generally along the lines of "you cannot polish a turd", but that was then…] We know we're unlikely to win the Premier League any time soon; even so, that doesn't mean we can't have realistic hopes and ambitions. And there's no doubt that we've been able to raise our expectation levels since Roy Hodgson raised our profile.

This season we should have pushed on again, in the light of Mark "Ambition" Hughes taking us to eighth place last term. But we've stuttered alarmingly. Going out of the Europa League in the manner that we did was unacceptable. Dipping out of the FA Cup without seeming to care is a nonsense. Losing to Chelsea on penalties in the League Cup was disappointing too come to that. The sum total is we're heading into February with little or nothing to play for, save the vital matter of our Premier League status.

It's the manner of all of this that grates. The general level of performance has been so humdrum; so matter-of-fact. Who cares? Well we do actually. And before anyone says, "Hey what about the Arsenal game?", let's get to the issue that really frustrates: we have a decent squad of players who have massively underperformed. Some of the football played this season has been technically superb. And the Arsenal game was a brilliant example of how much better we are playing on the front foot. Trouble is, for whatever reason, we've often tended to drop deeper and deeper (as opposed to being forced deeper) with the end result that we've come a cropper, as at Norwich for example.

Any decent advancement achieved by playing the ball cleverly through midfield is then generally negated by ponderous play or an inappropriate pass or touch. It's ironic that we're showing great technical ability (even if it's overdone a tad) in moving from defence to midfield only for the supposed "touch" players in the more advanced areas to stumble all too often. Playing to someone's feet when he's got at least one opponent around him takes great skill from the passer (the pass needs to be accurate and well-weighted) as well as the receiver (knowing when to move off or away from his marker and having a good body shape to collect and, if appropriate, move the ball on). Yet we do this time again, often brilliantly, only to see

the move then fall flat. We've had our moments up front, of course, but in general we've lacked a cutting edge in attack.

All these words and no mention yet of Bobby Zamora. Boy did his move stir up a hornets' nest of opinion among supporters! Having slouched around the pitch for much of his game-time this season, it's best that he's gone. It was clear that he wasn't happy, although quite how much of that was down to him carrying a series of injuries and how much was down to a disintegrating relationship with the new regime and tactics is only known to insiders. Or possibly just Bobby himself. But the whole business hasn't helped the team.

Meantime we've just witnessed a more-than-decent debut: a well-struck goal after 16 minutes during an hour or so of honest graft before going off with an injury. But above all else, Pavel Pogrebnyak actually looked bothered. He may or may not prove to be the answer to our striking problem, but what a welcome change to see a player catching the eye by putting in a positive, determined shift. The Pog took his goal superbly – great reactions, excellent touch and crisp left-footed finish. He also stood up well to the battering offered by Ryan Shawcross and his Stoke cronies: welcome to the Premier League, Pav!

So, barring any disastrous involvement with the wrong end of the table, we're heading for what will be labelled season of "transition". A humdrum season that has virtually petered out already. This is in no way being greedy – indeed maintaining our Premier League status for yet another season (assuming we do!) should be championed, especially for a club with our level of resources. No, this is based on the decent quality of our squad, the general standard of the top flight and the levels attained in previous seasons. Make no mistake, there's a good team in there. And when it all comes together we look a class act, with upbeat body language to match. Trouble is, we've only tended to do it in patches or for one half. And, along with the flat feel to our play, at other times the horrid opposition have all-too-frequently punished us. ⚽

Europa League
Fulham 3 NSI Runavik 0
30.06.11   Qual 1 1st leg

NSI Runavik 0 Fulham 0
07.07.11   Qual 1 2nd leg

Crusaders 1 Fulham 3
14.07.11   Qual 2 1st leg

Fulham 4 Crusaders 0
21.07.11   Qual 2 2nd leg

RNK Split 0 Fulham 0
28.07.11   Qual 3 1st leg

Fulham 2 RNK Split 0
04.08.11   Qual 3 2nd leg

Fulham 3 Dnipro Dnipropetrovsk 0
18.08.11   Play-off Round 1st leg

Dnipro Dnipropetrovsk 1 Fulham 0
25.08.11   Play-off Round 2nd leg

Fulham 1 Twente 1
15.09.11   Gp Stage (Group K)

Odense 0 Fulham 2
29.09.11   Gp Stage (Group K)

Wisla Krakow 1 Fulham 0
20.10.11   Gp Stage (Group K)

Fulham 4 Wisla Krakow 1
03.11.11   Gp Stage (Group K)

Twente 1 Fulham 0
01.12.11   Gp Stage (Group K)

Fulham 2 Odense 2
14.12.11   Gp Stage (Group K)

League Cup
Chelsea 0 Fulham 0
21.09.11   Round 3;
Chelsea win 4-3 pens

FA Cup
Fulham 4 Charlton Athletic 0
07.01.12   Round 3

Everton 2 Fulham 1
27.01.12   Round 4

Full of Hope Before Kick-off

> "It'll be hard for us fans to adjust to life after Danny Murphy. It may well have been the right time for him to move on given his seniority, but he was as influential as ever last season, on and off the park."

Season 2012-13 beckons for the mighty Whites, these days deemed an established Premier League outfit. That in itself is well worth celebrating. For a club of our size to be more than holding its own in the top flight is a mighty achievement. News that approval had been gained for a new Riverside Stand, and thereby increasing the ground capacity to 30,000, can only help matters further.

As for on-field matters, it's hard to gauge what's in store with Martin Jol having shuffled the pack considerably during the close season. And who knows how much further activity is likely – in and out – before the transfer window closes on August 31? We finished last season on a high, with the team showing genuine glimpses of Jol's dream of sexy football, the like of which hasn't been seen round these parts since Jean Tigana masterminded our promotion into the top flight. At the heart of these displays last term were Mousa Dembélé, Clint Dempsey and skipper Danny Murphy. The latter has of course been snapped up by Blackburn this summer, while the two "Dems" have for months been the subject of much transfer speculation.

As I write, Clint Dempsey is still on Fulham's books – although reportedly flogged to Liverpool weeks ago according to some sources! Here's hoping he stays at the Cottage where his ability, determination and versatility have been allowed to shine, but, if not, "Deuce" has put in a huge shift for us since arriving from New England Revolution in 2007 and would leave with our good wishes. However, that saga rumbles on...

While his contribution to FFC has been immense (who will ever forget that majestic time-stopping chip against Juventus?), Dempsey is an easier cog to replace than Dembélé, who has the potential to become a true superstar. Yep, he needs to deliver the final ball or shot more regularly, but the way he ghosts past opponents opens all sorts of possibilities for the team. Since being deployed deeper, Dembélé hasn't shirked his defensive duties either and it's hardly a surprise that he's linked with other clubs.

However, if he remains at Fulham he's likely to be a first-team fixture, and possibly the springboard of our attacks, whereas he might only be a squad player elsewhere (the same principle applies to Dempsey in my opinion) and his ever-improving relationship with Jol might well be enough to persuade him stay for at least another season – substantial bids from "big" clubs notwithstanding. Who knows, a successful season at Fulham might even temper that reported wanderlust!

It'll be hard for us fans to adjust to life after Danny Murphy. It may well have been the right time for him to move on given his seniority, but he was as influential as ever last season, on and off the park. Murphy's enormous input to the Club's steady improvement has been invaluable – an unlikely scenario had the captain himself not

Lewy for England

It's a well known fact that England only win major football tournaments with a Fulham player in the side. The England squad heading for the Euros this summer was lacking in that department (er, lacking in quite a few departments as it turned out) so they went for the next best thing: call for the Fulham management. Okay so Roy Hodgson's been away from the Cottage a while, but wasn't it great to see him and Ray Lewington reunited at England level? It'll be odd not to have Lewy at the Cottage now that he's joined the England set-up on a full-time basis. Little did he know when he swapped Wimbledon for FFC in 1980 that his footballing career would be intrinsically linked to his new club.

Give or take the odd spell away (for good behaviour?) Ray Lewington has been at Fulham ever since, becoming player-manager at just 29 and subsequently being the man the Club turned to whenever things turned sour. Which was often. The classic tale of players getting into their cars and driving a short distance away from the Club's Banstead training ground until the (supposed) manager had departed and then driving back to have a proper training session under Lewington pretty much sums up how bad things became at FFC.

In 2005, following managerial stints at Crystal Palace, Brentford and Watford, Lewy returned to Premier League Fulham as reserve team manager. He held the first-team reins once again after Sanchez was sacked then became Assistant Manager to the new man, Roy Hodgson. The picture of Lewy consoling a tearful Zoltan Gera after the final whistle in Hamburg in May 2010 is an enduring image. Stunning that Lewington could be involved in such an occasion with the Club that he helped to prop up when times were distinctly more dismal. Joining the England ranks with Roy

FULHAM'S PLANS TO TAKE OVER INTERNATIONAL MANAGEMENT POSITIONS GATHERS PACE...

We gotta make a change – what do you reckon, Ray?

I'm a little teapot, short and stout....

Chris Coleman
Wales

Kit Symons
Wales

Billy McKinlay
Northern Ireland

Hodgson is a deserved promotion for a "proper" football man. Here's hoping the pair do well at International level – good grief, they've already lifted England to third in the world rankings!

popped up to score that vital header at Portsmouth in May 2008 that kept us in the top flight. His spell at the Cottage did wonders for his own career, too, after indifferent spells at Charlton and Spurs.

As things stand, others who have left are Dickson Etuhu (linking up again with Murphy at Ewood Park), Pavel Pogrebnyak (Reading), Orlando Sá (Limassol), Bjorn Helge Riise (Lillestrom), Marcel Gecov (Gent) and Andy Johnson (some Mickey Mouse outfit). Farewell fellas. New boy Mladen Petric (from Hamburg) has already been among the goals in the pre-season games; others new to the squad are Sascha Riether, on loan from Cologne, and former Wigan wideman Hugo Rodallega. Welcome, guys!

Now the pre-season games are over, it will be interesting to see what Martin Jol considers is his best starting eleven. And to see if the new set-up, with Diarra presumably taking charge in midfield, can not only hit the ground running but also deliver the attacking stuff craved by the manager while retaining our defensive stability. Hope so.

News that the Club had, at long last, been given the thumbs-up from Hammersmith & Fulham Council to redevelop the Riverside Stand came too late in the year to allow work to start during the close season. But it's great news nevertheless. Tenders for the project are currently being sought with work due to start as soon as it's practical to do so. Much of the to-ing and fro-ing of materials will be done by river barges so as not to clog up the busy streets surrounding the Cottage.

The project will give the ground a wonderfully modern feel, while retaining its unique homely setting, and t will also raise the ground capacity to 30,000. With so little scope for expansion on the site this is a triumph for the Club and underlines its determination to operate a competitive football club at Craven Cottage. Locals will benefit by having an uninterrupted river walkway on non-matchdays. Well done Alistair Mackintosh et al.

A Chat With Diddy

Had TOOFIF existed in the early 1950s, a young David Hamilton might have been writing for it – or even running the show! As it was, his jottings were published in *Soccer Star* magazine, at least until the editor discovered how young his correspondent was at the time. After a long and varied broadcasting career, our genial matchday MC at Craven Cottage has put pen to paper once again, teaming up with Ken Coton at Ashwater Books to produce his *A Fulhamish Tale*. There's no doubting Diddy's allegiance – his many anecdotes detail how the life and times of Fulham FC have intertwined with his 73 years on the planet.

What was the inspiration for the book David, and why now?
It focuses on my time as a Fulham supporter.

I've been a fan since I was nine, so the book's been a long time coming! I became a Director of the club in the '70s and have been the matchday MC for the last 16 seasons – Fulham's most successful period – and so there were quite a lot of stories to tell, my own experiences together with tales of what's gone on behind the scenes. Also I wanted to put the record straight about one or two things.

That would include the time you got sacked. The whole affair seemed rather shabby...
Let's just say it was done by someone with a personal agenda.

Hmm, sounds like your very own "Who shot JR?" moment...?
Yeah, you could say that! In the event it was all very short lived. I only missed one game – although it was a massive one in my eyes. It was our first game back at Craven Cottage after our spell at QPR and it was a lovely day with a carnival atmosphere, and we won as well, so I was very sad to have missed being out in the middle. But *The Sun* launched a campaign that triggered my return.

Were you surprised that there was a reaction?
Yes I was. Dave Kidd, who these days of course contributes a column to your fanzine, was at *The Sun* in those days. He's a big Fulham supporter and he ran an article under the banner "Diddygate" and a huge majority voted that I should have my job back; ultimately, though, it was the Chairman who stepped in. Unfortunately (or perhaps fortunately) during the game that I missed quite a lot of things went wrong and the Chairman called me up to his office at Harrods and during what turned out to be an amusing encounter he gave me my job back. And a pay-rise too, actually!

It's a few years down the line since then, but I hear you're now planning to hang up the mic?
There's a big clue in the last chapter. I put the finishing touches to the book at the end of last season and there's a line that says: "As my own final whistle draws near I'm glad that I chose Fulham as my club all those years ago and I'm glad to have been part of the roller-coaster journey that has brought the Club to where it is today." In that reflective mood it would have been easy to have made 2011-12 my last season but I'm doing one more before stepping down. Let's be fair, by the end of next season I'll be 74. If Fulham were to advertise for someone to do my job they wouldn't bc looking for a 74-year-old. And from my perspective, freezing my nuts off for three-and-a-half hours during the winter months is probably not the best thing to do at my age!

You're not selling it, David...!
It has been – and still is – a terrific gig. And I

"What an astonishing win that was over Juventus. I confess that I stood pitchside in amazement, looking at the Hammersmith End with tears in my eyes. People say that the Fulham crowd are a quiet lot. I can confirm that's not the case."

wouldn't like it to finish unpleasantly again, so I've taken the decision – one that will mean we'll all still be friends and I can continue my allegiance as a supporter. And of course I hope that the lads will give me a momentous season to end on.

That "Fulhamish" tag must be directed at the Club's fortunes during your time as a Director and MC. The ups and downs have been many, as have the changes...?
The fans who have swelled the ranks at Fulham have enjoyed their recent seasons of success, but may not be aware of how Fulham nearly went out of business in the 1990s. Before that we had a Chairman (Ernie Clay) intent on running the Club down – and I was a Director during that regime, and I had to resign because I knew he had a particular agenda, and it wasn't one I shared.

The many tales reflect the enjoyment you've had – as well charting the moments of skulduggery – but it must warm the cockles to see the Club recover and go from strength to strength?
There are a load of laughs in the book – many at the expense of Les Strong – but there was one delicious moment when I announced the man of the match (I think it was Chris Coleman who ultimately put paid to the award being announced in this way). Anyway, the matchday sponsors made the decision but often got it wrong, as reflected by the frequent howls of derision from the crowd when I made the announcement. On this occasion, though, it went to a player who'd been kept out of Jean Tigana's squad by injury and who only came on for the final 12 or 13 minutes. He only touched the ball once as I recall, but when I said the name Simon Morgan the place erupted. The crowd loved the humour and the sentiment – and it's something you couldn't easily replicate today.

It's that much more structured and business-like – and necessarily so?
Yes, that's the case. And when we went into Europe things took an even sterner turn. UEFA expect a number of straightforward announcements to be made, reminding people about not tolerating racism, which is very important, and about not smoking, another important safety issue, but the repetitive nature of the announcements made the whole thing so scripted.

What about the changes in the game itself?
When I first came along to watch Fulham, teams played with five forwards in front of three half-backs, two full-backs and a goalkeeper. It was much more attacking in those days, and there were more goals. What you get more with today's 4-4-2

is sideways passing; stroking the ball from player to player until an opening becomes apparent. With the five men up front, the wingers were off and at 'em – players like Les Barrett and Jimmy Conway. Thrilling players and thrilling stuff. At the end of my book I offer my best-ever Fulham XI, a difficult task actually when you consider I've been watching FFC over five decades, but I've gone for the five forwards approach as that's how it was for most of those who made my final eleven. Even so, two of the current squad make it in there. And I've allowed myself the luxury of naming five subs.

You've alluded to the Club's bad times, but what about the high times? Being out in the middle as MC, what have been the moments that've made the hairs stand up on the back of your neck?
Sealing promotion under Micky Adams was a fantastic moment – although that was actually secured away from the Cottage. We enjoyed another terrific promotion under Keegan, so that season too had a number of memorable matches. Shame he had to leave Fulham under something of a cloud – but he couldn't resist the lure of the England job. Under Tigana we played sublime football. We scored goals for fun and plundered a record points haul, but did so playing some truly wonderful stuff. His signings – apart from Marlet perhaps! – were exceptional. Louis Saha was fabulous in a Fulham shirt, and what about Steed Malbranque? He was fantastic.

But you have to make special reference to that astonishing win over Juventus. I confess that I stood pitchside in amazement, looking at the Hammersmith End with tears in my eyes. People say that the Fulham crowd are a quiet lot. I can confirm that's not the case. We needed four goals at one point, but when Dempsey netted our fourth – with an absolute beauty – in the closing stages the place positively erupted. I was so emotional, it was all I could do to scream out Dempsey's name. What a night that was! Going to Hamburg for the final was a bit reminiscent of going to Wembley in 1975, doing so much to get to the showpiece but on the day, for whatever reason, we disappointed.

That little journey put Fulham well and truly on the European map, didn't it?
Oh, it absolutely did. And getting to the final was a supreme achievement – but I didn't relish getting stuck in the "cherry-picker" before the big kick-off. I've never been too good at heights! That season we graduated from being something of a bit player in London football to being the flag bearer in European competition for the whole country. This may be a bit of a generalisation but I don't think anybody dislikes Fulham; I'd even go as far as to say that many football fans would have us as their second club. Apart from Alex Ferguson, everyone loves coming to Craven Cottage (and that's just

because he can't get all of his entourage into our dressing rooms!). We're a lovable set-up, but not so lovable that we're a push-over.

Fergie doesn't like the place because we his lot now and then! We're very solid at the Cottage...
Match of the Day 2 chose a fixture against Man. United at the Cottage to do a mini-feature on me – and we won 2-0! A lucky mascot, perhaps!

Any awkward moments out in the middle?
Not so much awkward as funny. When I introduced Michael Jackson to the crowd they didn't believe it was the real deal. It was only polite applause at best to begin with. You see, we'd not really had a star of that magnitude before at the Cottage. It wasn't until he'd walked halfway around the sun-soaked pitch, under that umbrella, that the penny dropped.

Where does FFC go from here?
We've got a relatively low capacity at the Cottage. Old Trafford by contrast can hold 77,000 spectators, three times the number allowed at the Cottage. So you can see what we're up against just in terms of matchday income. The news that we've had permission to raise our capacity to 30,000 through the Riverside Stand development is fantastic. Apart from anything else it shows that we're staying at Craven Cottage, which is wonderful. Since the stands were revamped at either end the sound of the crowd is that much better. But not only is it the noise factor, the Cottage is such a special place to watch football. As more clubs leave their ancestral homes for new, purpose-built stadiums with drab, unexciting architecture, the Craven Cottage site becomes more and more the jewel in the crown.

It's unique in more ways than one, isn't it?
Certainly! You've got the "cricket pavilion", the listed stand, the superb riverside location and even the Michael Jackson statue; it's unique all right! Actually, regarding that statue and the comments that followed its siting at the club, considering what Mohamed Al Fayed has done for the Club he can have a statue of who he likes where he likes as far as I'm concerned. It's only the people coming up and down the river who can see it regularly after all, and if it becomes a tourist attraction for the pleasure boaters then what's the fuss?

You mentioned earlier that it was Micky Adams who set our recovery in motion, but since then it's the Chairman who's overseen the club's remarkable rise...
It could quite easily have been one promotion and then a case of treading water. We've seen some very good examples recently of football clubs getting into the hands of the wrong people – once-big clubs getting fines, relegations

and almost going out of business. We've been extraordinarily lucky that our club is in the hands of the right person. He's bankrolled our rise, spending wisely. Being the size of the Club that we are, you could say we've been remarkable over-achievers. You've only got to look at the Charlton story of years ago, when they were being championed as the "moderate" club to follow: well-run and in the top flight. In the end manager Alan Curbishley left because someone there thought they could do better "under new management" – and look what happened to them! Without a doubt Mohamed Al Fayed is the most successful chairman in the history of FFC. I remember Tommy Trinder as a great publicist for the Club, with all of his stage banter and jokes but then came Ernie Clay who seemed determined to run the club into the ground. We've recovered and moved on wonderfully since then.

Do you interact with the players on a matchday.
Years ago I was told by Ernie Clay not to fraternise with the players. That was during the days of Les Strong holding his own at left-back. He and I were great mates. Les said to me one day: "Since you've become a Director you've become very stuck-up. We don't seem to have a drink with you anymore." So I told him that the Chairman had suggested that I shouldn't fraternise. Les, in his diplomatic way, said: "Well fuck him – we're your mates and you're going to have a drink with us!" And I thought, well, actually they are my mates and actually I *am* going to have drink with them! In later years when things weren't going so well, I'd often end up in Crocs in the Fulham Road with Jim Stannard and Terry Hurlock and we'd have a few bevvies and some laughs. Nowadays the players are much more heavily chaperoned and there isn't the same link. By the same token, in the days that Strongy was playing I was in the same age-range as the players – Les and I even played in some charity games together – but there's a wider gap today! Post-match, we've had a string of players come over to the George Cohen Lounge to do some question-and-answer sessions and the like. Generally it's the older players who are more at home in doing this, so Aaron Hughes was very engaging and Danny Murphy was an excellent talker and ambassador for the Club. He gave us a terrific interview in the Lounge last season. It's a shame he's moved on to Blackburn but Danny will go on to become a good communicator, maybe in broadcasting.

Maybe you could give him some tips?
Only about playing football, not about broadcasting! ⚽

"When I introduced Michael Jackson to the crowd they didn't believe it was the real deal. It was only polite applause at best to begin with. You see, we'd not really had a star of that magnitude before at the Cottage. It wasn't until he'd walked halfway around the sun-soaked pitch, under that umbrella, that the penny dropped."

Below: David Hamilton with his book *A Fulhamish Tale.*

Meeting Ray Lewington

Ray Lewington has pretty much seen it all at Fulham. Having cut his teeth with that lot up the road, Ray has filled most roles at the Club since joining from Wimbledon in 1980. I'm not sure if "tea lady" is on that list, but "kit washer" certainly is. These days he's Roy Hodgson's right-hand man in the England camp, a deserved promotion for someone who fully merits the "Mr Fulham" tag for all that he's done for FFC over the years...

"Ray Lewington: England Assistant Manager" – how long did it take for that to sink in?
[Long chuckle] Sounds good, doesn't it? England were heading for the Euros if you remember and I was still with Fulham. Roy Hodgson had got the top job and was keen to have me alongside him; the initial arrangement was that I'd be loaned to England. In due course that deal became permanent and Fulham received some compensation. Being England Assistant Manager is wonderful, and a tremendous honour.

Long-term Fulham fans have an inkling of what you endured during the Club's toughest times, so what's it like to be at the other end of the scale?
It's brilliant with England. But then it's brilliant nowadays at Fulham, too. What a transformation! When I took over at Craven Cottage we had no training ground. The lads had been training, on the sly, in Bishop's Park. Things were desperate; we had no money and couldn't get even the most basic bits of kit. By contrast, my best mate when we were growing up, Ray Wilkins, had just joined AC Milan. I was on the phone to Ray every day, and he sorted out a deal for football boots with New Balance in return for a page in the programme. We had no keeper. Gerry Peyton was heading to Bournemouth. I called him and had great difficulty making him believe I was Fulham manager. We'd always had a great banter at the Club previously, and when I did – eventually – get Gerry to come for a chat the first thing he did was to get me in a headlock and start banging my head against whatever was near us...

...You commanded respect right away...
Oh yes! Gerry said something like, "I knew you'd get some job of importance, Hitler was a small little runt as well!" – and all this time I'm shouting "Gel, Gel, Gerry, let go!" So not a very dignified way of starting a conversation, even with a good pal. Once we discussed things a bit more seriously there was no way we could come near to matching Bournemouth's offer, and that

was that; we still had no goalkeeper. It was even the bread and butter things that were lacking at the time. I remember me and Terry Bullivant driving round looking for somewhere to train. We used the A3 as our starting point and generally fanned out until we found the Fire Brigade Ground, Banstead. Not what you'd call salubrious, but it was available.

How different is it to coach at national level rather than club level?
The England lads are the best trainers I've ever worked with, both in terms of quality and how they apply themselves. We've never come off after a session and thought: "They've dipped below the line today." In club football, particularly after a bad result over the weekend, you've sometimes had to give the squad a gee-up or lay down the law a bit on the Monday morning. But the England lads have been an absolute dream to work with.

But that means the players must respect the coaches, too…?
Both Roy and I are really coach/managers. Roy is firmly of the opinion that if you're the boss you're passing on the responsibility if you simply tell others to coach. We both like to get involved with the players – and, hey, if you see Roy in action you can only have respect for him. It's a case of [clicking fingers] bang, bang, bang – he's right on the button all the time. So Roy's earned their respect straight away, and I suppose as I'm Roy's choice as his number two then the players respect that too.

How different are the England coaching facilities to, say, the Fire Brigade Ground, Banstead?
[Long chuckle] Actually it's been a funny arrangement with England. Prior to getting the new immaculate facilities at St George's it's been a case of training at, say, Arsenal's training ground, or Manchester City's facilities. Now, at St George's, it's incredible – any footballer going there would fall in love with it. I don't suppose there's any better training facilities in the world. As for the Fire Brigade Ground, with its two dressing rooms, you'd have the two pitches on the side that'd been used that weekend. And I remember the ground there as being rock hard; it was hardly ever waterlogged. Poor Michael Cole broke his neck there in a fall – the ground was like concrete. So yeah, more than just a slight difference!

You teamed up well with Roy Hodgson at Fulham; how long have you known him and what's he like to work with?
He's brilliant and so approachable. Roy is 100 per cent honest; there's no side to him. He knows what

> "When I took over at Craven Cottage we had no training ground. The lads had been training, on the sly, in Bishop's Park. Things were desperate; we had no money and couldn't get even the most basic bits of kit."

Opposite page top: Ray Lewington barks out the orders – and that's even before kick-off!.

Below: Lewy consoles a crestfallen Zoltan Gera moments after the final whistle in Hamburg in 2010.

he wants, but he'll still ask for your opinion on certain matters. If you disagree or have a different slant, he'll come back to you then or later and say that he's thought about it but is sticking to his guns. Or he'll be big enough to admit, "Hey, I'd not thought about that aspect." It's refreshing and I find him so easy to work for. There's no hidden agenda with Roy – but on top of that he's bloody good at what he does and is an excellent coach. When Roy came to Fulham I must admit I expected he'd bring in his own coaching staff, but he said he'd give it a go with me – which was fantastic.

How different is working with Roy Hodgson to, say, Alan Dicks?

[Long schoolboy giggles from interviewer and interviewee…!] Well, for a start, Alan Dicks never coached… The beauty of working with Roy is that he's out there with you. He doesn't simply say, "Do this, do that" and stand on the sidelines and criticise. At Fulham we'd split it up in two; there'd be a routine but we'd mix it up on different days. In general, I'd do the first bit and then he'd come in to do the main session. You might find me drilling the back four while Roy was sorting the front six or whatever, but it was definitely a real coaching environment. And I loved that. I don't like managers who do everything by chat. For me, show them, get out there, which Roy does; so many managers can't or won't do that. It's not a case of long lectures, it's more, "This is what we're doing" and we go out and train. And it works. If you use counters and blackboards you don't get a sense of perspective or distance. Theory is all very well, but it's much more "real" on the training field, so get out there; that's what we're there for. It's a case of working for that result. You can't simply announce

that you're going to play 4-4-2 or 4-5-1 and expect it all to click without working it all out in training.

What you're doing now is a million miles from washing the Fulham kit?

Just a bit! Things were really, really bad. There was a big industrial dryer at Fulham, and it was still there when I came back as player/manager, only it broke down and we had no money to mend it. Our kit amounted to one set of long-sleeved white shirts and one set of short-sleeves, and the same with the red second-choice shirts. If you tore a shirt it had to get mended, there was no replacement. For a three-week period around Easter when the games came thick and fast, as we had no dryer I had to take the kit home to get washed and repaired. It was like looking after a Sunday League club. My wife Ann became a dab hand at repairing the training bibs, too. And, with no replacement shirts, when we stuck these out in the garden to dry we had to make sure they weren't pinched (there's a walkway at the bottom) so that meant moving our settee so that we could sit and be on guard!

It was a terrible time – we had no overnighters for long away trips, couldn't afford it. We'd travel on the day of the game and stop at a service station so the players could have a bowl of cereal. And they were lucky to get that. I can recall at one Board meeting one of the directors was querying why we had to buy our physio a pair of football boots; he thought it was an unnecessary expense. We spent around 15 minutes debating the subject. I chirped up: "So it's matchday, it's teeming down with rain, it's slippery and muddy, and you want our trainer to run on in his plimsolls to treat an injured player, going arse over tit in the process. We'd be a laughing stock." Things were that penny-pinching at the time – and necessarily so I suppose given the state of the Club, but it made it an incredibly difficult operation given we were in the business of trying to win football matches.

Incredibly difficult at the time, but did it help you in the long run?

Oh, without a doubt. For a brief period I got absolutely battered by some of the Fulham crowd. I'd been pretty well liked as a player, I think, and there was also a general agreement on my appointment as manager, but then things turned sour and there were some choice opinions from the Enclosure. But I defy anyone to make a real go of it in such dire circumstances. All I can say is that I really tried, and then tried some more. However, it was a wonderful grounding. We had to do it all ourselves;

Fulham 2 Everton 2 03.11.12 7th	1st 2nd 3rd
Arsenal 3 Fulham 3 10.11.12 8th	4th 5th
Fulham 1 Sunderland 3 18.11.12 9th	6th
Stoke City 1 Fulham 0 24.11.12 9th	**7th** 8th
Chelsea 0 Fulham 0 28.11.12 11th	9th 10th
Fulham 0 Tottenham Hotspur 3 01.12.12 11th	11th 12th
Fulham 2 Newcastle United 1 10.12.12 13th	13th 14th
QPR 2 Fulham 1 15.12.12 13th	15th 16th
Liverpool 4 Fulham 0 22.12.12 13th	17th 18th 19th
Fulham 1 Southampton 1 26.12.12 14th	20th
Fulham 1 Swansea City 2 29.12.12 14th	
West Brom 1 Fulham 2 01.01.13 13th	
Fulham 1 Wigan Athletic 1 12.01.13 13th	
Manchester City 2 Fulham 0 19.01.13 14th	
Fulham 3 West Ham United 1 30.01.13 12th	
Fulham 0 Manchester United 1 02.02.13 13th	
Norwich City 0 Fulham 0 09.02.13 12th	
Fulham 1 Stoke City 0 23.02.13 11th	
Sunderland 2 Fulham 2 02.03.13 10th	
Tottenham Hotspur 0 Fulham 1 17.03.13 10th	
Fulham 3 QPR 2 01.04.13 10th	
Newcastle United 1 Fulham 0 07.04.13 10th	
Aston Villa 1 Fulham 1 13.04.13 10th	
FA Cup Fulham 1 Blackpool 1 05.01.13 Round 3	
Blackpool 1 Fulham 2 15.01.13 Round 3 replay	
Manchester United 4 Fulham 1 26.01.13 Round 4	

there were only three staff on the front line: myself, Jack Burkett and Terry Bullivant. We also had Derry Quigley as scout/youth development overseer and a couple of volunteer scouts – not that we had any money to buy players. Looking back, it was a terrific grounding. If we hadn't had to do it all ourselves I may not have dug so deep and carried on as I did. Now I can appreciate the turn of events that much more.

The fans relate to that too – being in the Premier League these days means that much more to those who toughed it out during those years…
Oh absolutely. It's got to. We've been right to the basement. I wasn't there in the bottom division, but I thought we were dead. No hope; no nothing really. And then came a wonderful turnaround. Listen, I think those fans who stuck around then should get free tickets every week; they not only turned up, they really fought for the Club's future. And you and I know who they are. I meet a lot of people who say they were there regularly back then; they weren't. I've got so much time and respect for those supporters who went home and away. And that even includes those who gave me stick! Bloody hell, if those fans had stopped going there'd be no Fulham today.

You were part of a really good side under Malcolm Macdonald and were an important cog in some brilliant performances, only for it all to come off the rails at Derby's Baseball Ground…
We had a proper footballing side in '82-83 – a small side, and we played it on the deck. Little Paul Parker at the back, Ray Houghton, me, Robert Wilson, Sean (O'Driscoll), he wasn't the tallest, Gordon Davies up front, so yeah a small side. But good. We thought we'd be vulnerable at set pieces, but it didn't turn out that way – we left all that to Roger Brown, after all Galey couldn't head a ball, could he?

Below: Our "pocket-sized midfield dynamo" manages to stay still long enough to be snapped by the TOOFIF camera!

We were in third spot for a long time but things started to go wrong in the closing weeks. We lost three on the trot, including a key game at QPR who went up as champions, and after a 2-0 win over Carlisle in our last home game we needed a win at Derby in our final match. Derby, deep in relegation trouble, had two games to play and needed points.

Unfortunately things didn't go our way. We were superior, without playing too well – but we couldn't get the goal. Had we scored we probably would have got three or four. Perhaps we panicked a bit because of our inexperience; anyway Bobby Davison put them ahead. But you couldn't legislate for the dreadful crowd scenes at the old Baseball Ground.

Obviously Derby were fired up and weren't going to give us anything, but you then had many of the home crowd coming over the fence and standing on the sidelines for the final 20 minutes. It was all very threatening. You wonder what would happen if such scenes occurred nowadays. When what we thought was the final whistle went, we all took a few hits from people who shouldn't have been on the pitch as we tried to get to the dressing room – Jeff Hopkins had his shirt pulled off and was punched in the face. Once everything had calmed we thought we had a fair case for a replay. But it wasn't to be – it made for a sad end to what had, for the most part, been an excellent season.

We blew it before the Derby game, of course, it's just that we still had a last chance on that horrible day. There's no question that we deserved to go up to the top flight based on how we'd performed and it was so very close in the end. So close.

And there's that feeling that we were cheated…
These days you'd get the ground closed down for what the Derby supporters were allowed to do on the day. Many of the home fans surrounded most of the pitch for the last 20 minutes, making a mockery of having fences erected. We had players getting kicked as the fans encroached onto the pitch – while the ball was in play! And still nothing was done. It just wouldn't happen today. It was all incredibly intimidating, but to be fair we'd already lost that head of steam during the run-in.

That side was ripped apart, and you headed to Sheffield United but returned within a year…
It was heartbreaking to see everyone going. Ray Harford was in charge by then. Ray was easily the biggest influence on my career. A great coach, someone who sits alongside Roy in my estimation. After I'd left, he called me and said, "It's all going down the Swannee here and I'm off. But David Bulstrode wants a Player-Manager" (on the basis of having two jobs for one pay packet). Ray said, "I feel I'd be letting you down if I didn't tell you, but I'm advising you not to take it – in fact I'm telling you!" Me, I saw it as a terrific opportunity. Going back to my club as a player-boss! And I told Ian Porterfield, my Sheffield United boss. He didn't want me to go, but there was a real pull for me; it was my club.

You say "my club" – okay that's pretty much established today, but back then…?
I really enjoyed my playing days at Fulham. Chelsea's where I grew up and you obviously have an affection for where you started your career. But once at Fulham I got bitten by the bug and just wanted to do well, and the playing side was fantastic. It was my club and I was keen to go back. Ray said, "There's too many problems and question marks about the place" and he was right!

Do you recall turning out with your assistant Gary Peters in an FA Cup tie at Bath? Wasn't that against medical advice?

I'd stopped playing and my knees were in bits. Gary had collapsed one day and had to have a brain scan. Getting a knock to his head wasn't advised. We were sitting in the office talking about the potential line-up for the game and Gary just said: "Fuck it, let's do it. Let's play." So we did. And we got a 2-2 draw and won the replay at Craven Cottage – with a rare Johnny Watson goal.

John Watson – your best-ever signing?

My worst probably! But what a top bloke. He's the only player I've signed without seeing him play. I confess, I panicked. He was recommended to me as a player scoring lots of goals for Dunfermline – really good in the air and able to hold the ball up and bring others into play. He had no pace, but then again he wouldn't cost much, which was handy! But here's the sort of guy he was: I phoned him up and said quite candidly: "I don't know if I can do the deal, we've got little or no money. Would you be prepared to come to London for a couple of days?" To my amazement he said yes. He was with us for a week and, you know, he did all right. He wasn't athletic, but was willing to give it a right go. We'd just sold Leroy Rosenior for £290,000 and I got something like £25,000 of that back to get a replacement. And the Club didn't lose out as we got that sum back in due course.

There was one evening game at the Cottage and the lads went out to do their warm-up; they needed to, it was freezing cold. A group of six or seven supporters were in the Riverside Stand and they'd made a banner that read "Lewington OUT"; well, as the lads jogged across the pitch John suddenly legged it towards the group, grabbed the banner, tucked it under his shirt and stormed into the dressing room where he threw it into the bin. I'd been up on the Cottage balcony so had seen what had happened. John, who'd been with us for a couple of months by then, opened up and said, "Look Ray, I've been trying my hardest" – which wasn't in any doubt – "why not send me back to Scotland?" So we did. He just couldn't get to grips with the pace of the game in England.

What was the toughest aspect of managing FFC during the tough times?

I always thought we weren't far off as a side and just needed reinforcements, so not getting them was very frustrating. It was all down to the finances.

…We still got to the Play-offs…?

We did. Harry Bassett once said to me "You were the worst side ever to get into a Play-off!" It was meant as a compliment to me! But he was adamant. We played well in the first leg against Bristol Rovers, although going down 1-0 at Bath, and it was all set up for the return leg at the Cottage. But Ian Holloway chipped Jim Stannard for a brilliant goal; 2-0 down and Scotty gets sent off. We needed three, went for it but got picked off, losing 4-0 on the night.

It must've been something of a shock to the system to return to the Cottage as reserve team manager with FFC on an upward curve under Mohamed Al Fayed?

I was amazed when I came back. I'd been sacked from Watford – first time that had ever happened; I'd always left clubs on good terms beforehand. Chris Coleman gave me a call. He said: "I need someone around the place. Billy McKinlay is raw but enthusiastic and learning, and I've got Steve Kean as my number two, so this won't be a first-team role, although I'd be more than happy for you to step in if Keano's away scouting. But I'd like someone to keep an eye on the Academy." It was a strange offer in some ways, but very tempting. Back to Fulham! And he offered a decent salary together with a promise that if something else came up then the Club would be supportive. So back I went, and I really enjoyed it. Cookie's a lovely fella and I appreciated the gesture. And it was the start of something good again.

That upward curve extended to a major European final. That must've been a helluva season?

For three seasons I had to pinch myself. There was that tense game at Portsmouth, when we clung on to top-flight football on the final day, then we finished seventh the following season. A year on and we're in the Europa League Final! As a script it'd be considered far-fetched. It was an astounding achievement for Fulham. I saw Mark Maunders outside the stadium at Hamburg, almost crying with joy and he cuddled me and just said: "All them rotten years, Ray…" It was great, really great.

And getting there wasn't a fluke, either?

We had no right to beat Shakhtar Donetsk. What an unbelievable side. In a one-off game maybe you can fluke a win over a great side, but over two games you have to deserve it. That first 20 minutes at the Cottage by Shakhtar was the best spell of football I've ever seen from any side; it was extraordinary. We were standing on the side uttering such well-known coaching terminology as "Fuck me, they're brilliant!" We just had to dig in and try not to be overwhelmed or mesmerised. Which the lads did. And in a way that was just as brilliant. As the game developed we got better and better. And then Bobby Zamora got a "worldie" and we ended up winning 2-1. Amazing. We thought, "Good result, but we've still got it all to do out there!"

Above: Ray Lewington was a pocket-sized midfield dynamo for Fulham – and a bloody good one, too.

> *"For three seasons I had to pinch myself. There was that tense game at Portsmouth, when we clung on to top-flight football on the final day, then we finished seventh the following season. A year on and we're in the Europa League Final!"*

"Let's be fair, we were beaten by the better side. The 'how' narked a bit, going down to a late deflected goal when we were so close to going to penalties, but there was no shame at all in losing to a tremendous side."

It was backs to the wall to start with over there (was it 12 corners in the first 10 minutes?), but organisation and the players' spirit and determination meant we did brilliantly to earn a 1-1 draw and progress. Getting to the final was a dream and Atlético were another fantastic side, as they're still showing now.

Juventus at home. Explain…
I can't. It was the most emotional night I've ever experienced in football. A mate of mine, Trevor, not a great football fan, was there. Just say Fulham v Juventus in his company and he'll not only start gushing about the whole experience but there'll be tears in his eyes. It was pure theatre. And what a goal to decide it! Demps does that, he'd try all these weird and wonderful things. Roy would often say to him, "Go for the percentage option a bit more," but on that night he pulled that one out! It all seemed a long way from going one-down on the night and then needing to score four. Against Juventus! But I promise you, when we got our second I thought, "We could win this". You could sense something. The atmosphere was unique.

What did you all make of the "Stand up if you still believe" chant?
Excuse the pun, but it was unbelievable. Something spontaneous that got to all of us in the ground. What a noise! The place erupted! And the noise just kept on coming. Will there ever be a night like it at the Cottage ever again? I doubt it. But if there is, I want to be there! Pure emotion and atmosphere – easily the best I've ever experienced. Easily.

What's the dressing room like after such a night?
Yes the lads in there were hugging each other and savouring the achievement. But they were utterly exhausted too. (I've had plenty of instances at Fulham where you couldn't wait to get off the pitch! This wasn't one of them!) Everyone was standing up cheering and clapping, and yet I bet the fans were tired too. Eventually we trooped off and tried to savour the whole experience.

Being at the heart of the action, were you looking onwards and upwards at the time of the final, or were you able to reflect on how far the Club had come?
I did have a moment or two at the final, yes. Mark Maunders encouraged that; we looked around at the setting for the final, reflecting on past times. Looking at the stadium filling for the big game was surreal, I admit. Fulham in a major European final. Watching the Fulham banners and flags being put into place Mark and I agreed on that and reverted to good old football parlance: "This is fucking unbelievable".

There's a touching picture of you trying to raise Zoltan Gera's spirits after the Europa League final defeat in May 2010. How were your spirits after the game? Did anyone have to lift you?
No. I was okay, sort of. I was immensely proud of everyone involved. We'd given it everything. Had I thought we'd gone out there and frozen then I might have been flat. But we didn't. Let's be fair, we were beaten by the better side. The "how" narked a bit, going down to a late deflected goal when we were so close to going to penalties, but there was no shame at all in losing to a tremendous side. Had we gone to penalties we knew we had a man-mountain in goal; Mark Schwarzer may well have given us the edge. As for Zolly, he was the most popular lad in the squad. Everybody loved him. He was funny, and has that lovely accent which resulted in him mispronouncing words but above all he's a lovely bloke. To see him on the ground in a right state at losing was heartbreaking.

With Roy Hodgson tempted by the Liverpool job, what happened when Mark Hughes came in with his entourage?
Yes, Roy took on the Anfield challenge. Fulham told him he couldn't just pinch all the staff; Roy told me this and that was fair enough. Meanwhile Fulham had a good pre-season tour of Sweden under myself and Billy McKinlay. The boys were pro-me, if I'm honest, but the Club wanted more of a "name", which I accepted. When Mark Hughes came in I thought I'd be off, but Alistair (Mackintosh) said there's no way you're going; Mark would like you with him, particularly for the first two months, after which I asked Mark if I could do something more productive. That's when I split my time between the reserves and the kids, something I really enjoyed.

So that was your decision, not Mark's?
Yes, that was down to me.

Is it true the Chairman said you had a job for life at Fulham? That's quite a statement!
I was told he'd said that, but I didn't hear it directly from the Chairman! But that was lovely to hear.

Dimitar Berbatov's the hub of Fulham's attack these days; but he's no George Georgiou, is he?
[Laughs] You're right there! Berbatov is the most subtle of players with a sublime touch. He's not quick but never gets tackled, either.

Which players made the biggest impression on you during your many years at the Club?
Ray Houghton was one of our best players. As was Galey, very unlucky not to play for England. Sean O'Driscoll went under the radar a little, but was a great player. And of course Roger Brown, So sad that he passed away last year; a real character, a proper warrior. Gerry Peyton was the most

Below: Ray, a highly respected coach, loves the day-to-day involvement with players.

Lights out!

Manchester United were determined to do well in the FA Cup in 2013, and they were even more hell-bent on wrenching the Premier League crown from the clutches of their near-neighbours. How did I know this (apart from the fact that it was churned out almost daily in every newspaper)? From Sir Alex Ferguson and his players actually. My day job at this point was Chief Sub-editor on Manchester United publications (well, if Fulham wouldn't have me...) and the vibes were clear: Rooney, van Persie and co were out to win every game. Not a good time, then, for Fulham to face them twice in a week.

Our lot were going through a mind-bogglingly inconsistent spell. Having offered glimpses of utter class earlier in the season, with shades of the supreme Tigana championship-winning side, the level reached as we headed into 2013 was more akin to something served up by Dicks or Mackay. A gritty if unspectacular third round replay victory on Blackpool's heavy pitch earned us an away tie at Old Trafford. And it seemed that either Dicks or Mackay had taken the reins one more time as we barely bothered to compete at the Theatre of Dreams, even gifting the hosts a second-minute lead. No coming back from that, and we stumbled out of the Cup, losing 4-1. In hindsight, the only highlight was doing an interview with the ever-jovial Les Strong for the United programme!

A midweek win over West Ham, our bogey team for many years, split the two fixtures with the Reds. We were lucky that our opening goal against the Hammers was allowed to stand given that Berbatov was offside when he neatly headed home. But it could be argued that our vastly different approach meant we possibly deserved that bit of good fortune, especially as a stack of Hammers' indiscretions went unpunished.

Berba's reward was picking up a hamstring injury that would keep him out the clash with his former employers. The 3-1 victory over the Hammers was vital in that a run of just two wins in 15 League games had seen us plummet down the table. So, which Fulham, sans Berbatov, would turn up at the weekend? The very least a football team should offer, wrote some pillock in a certain fanzine editorial, is a "set of committed players, a concerted team approach and intelligent (and ideally inspirational) leadership." We'd been out-fought and out-thought at Old Trafford – not in itself a travesty, although the lack of passion shown was an insult to all those Fulham fans who'd travelled – but then shown a far better attitude to beat the Hammers.

As it happened, the contest with Sir Alex's lot at our place was an absolute cracker that had a bit of everything. Okay, we lost. But, unlike the Cup game and several others during the season, that hardly seemed to matter. The encounter swung more ways than a naughty suburban party. The pulsating contest served up a host of near misses, goal-line clearances galore and several strikes against the woodwork.

The action was so hot that as half-time approached, the floodlights packed up! Cue learned mutterings on the Hammersmith End "West Ham... League Cup... January 1975... Fulham, 2-1." Another voice piped up: "Doncaster, League Cup, October 1983, kick-off delayed; won 3-1 on the night, 6-2 on aggregate." Okay, enough fellas, no one likes a smart-arse! When the lights came back on in 2013, the game somehow remained goal-less until Rooney steered home a clever winner at the Putney End 11 minutes from time. Somehow the overriding emotion was one of satisfaction, despite the home defeat. We'd played really well and had given it a right go.

dedicated footballer I've ever played with. He was always doing extra training. Strongy would tell him to put the football away and clear off home, but Gerry would simply carry on.

As for the current crop, Mark Schwarzer was the best goalkeeper in the world as far as I'm concerned. Aaron Hughes: very underrated, and a great partner for Brede, another top player. With Roy, the players had to fit a profile. He didn't want any fly-by-nights. The emphasis was on what type of person they were; they had to be able to play, of course. He took a punt on Bobby Zamora; after fighting against Roy for the first year Bobby "got it". That year we got to the Europa League final, Bobby was the best target man in the League. He just clicked. He was unbelievable.

In closing, I'm contractually obliged to ask a question about Les Strong. Would you say he was as good a left-back as he claims?
[Cue 20 seconds of laughter...] I love Les. But

I don't know why! I went to school with Teddy Maybank, sat next to him in class, and was at Chelsea with him. Then followed him to Craven Cottage. When I arrived at Fulham, Bobby Campbell asked Teddy to introduce me to the players. We saw Strongy and Teddy said: "You'll find this out for yourself, Ray, but Les is the worst player in the team by a stretch." Les didn't bat an eyelid. He simply said: "Hello mate; he's bloody right by the way!" He's a great, jovial character. You can't help laughing when you see Les. Which is what I did every time I saw him play. Only joking Les – it was just *most* of your games.

Many congrats on the England job, Ray, and thanks for finding the time for a chat. If you and Roy ever find you're a man short...
Yeah, lovely to have a chat, but we'll know where not to come! Please pass on my good wishes to all the Fulham fans.

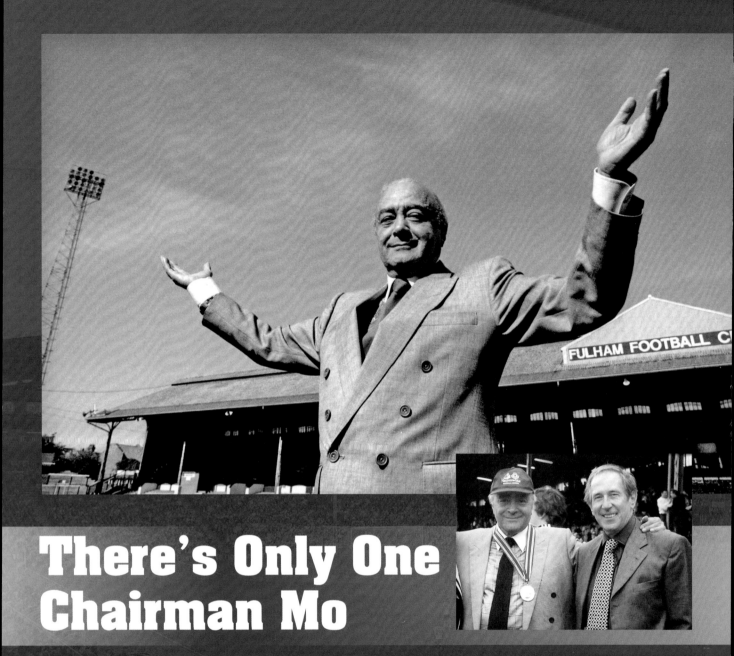

There's Only One Chairman Mo

Above: Never understated, our new Chairman takes stock of his latest purchase: Fulham FC.

Above right: Mohamed Al Fayed, complete with medal, celebrates the Club's promotion to the top flight with Bill Muddyman.

High time we paid fulsome tribute to the magnificent Chairmanship of Mohamed Al Fayed – and wished him happy birthday in so doing. On 27 January [2013], Chairman Mo celebrated his 80th birthday if most Internet sources are to be believed. Check out the Chairman's own website, however, and it says he was born on 27 January 1929, not 1933. But what's four years between friends?! Happy birthday, Chairman, and thanks for overseeing and bankrolling our fantastic Football Club's resurgence. Getting to, and staying in, the Premier League remains a wonderful achievement and we're still enjoying the adventure.

Now this is a fanzine, right? So in the midst of all this revelry and glorification we can't overlook the fact that during our enforced encampment at Loftus Road there were serious designs on taking FFC away from Craven Cottage. Not a crime in itself, of course, but with no alternative sites actually on the table there weren't even grounds

for debate as far as the majority of supporters were concerned. However, the machinations were murky at the time and information to fans was scant. Neither can we ignore one of the Chairman's grand pre-Loftus Road announcements that on returning to the Cottage (to a plush state-of-the-art new stadium that, we were told, ultimately became too costly) the fans would have the best Supporters' Club bar/room possible. Mind you, there's no Supporters' Club these days (to my knowledge), although there *is* a Fulham Supporters' Trust.

And no plush state-of-the-art stadium, either – but what we do have is a gloriously revamped ground generally full to the rafters, and a swish replacement for the dowdy Riverside Stand in the pipeline. We also have a team that's firmly ensconced in the Premier League and which has enjoyed a brilliant dalliance with European football. Such an illustrious status is down to one man – Mohamed Al Fayed, who rode into our corner of SW6 in May 1997.

Having sunk almost without trace to the bottom rungs of the basement division in February 1996, Fulham FC were as far removed from the top flight as the chances of the TOOFIF editor getting a question asked in Parliament. Micky Adams not only righted the ship (with an honourable passing mention for Ian Branfoot), but then steered the Whites to a magnificent promotion on a shoestring budget. By then the Club had resecured ownership of the ground, and despair had been replaced by hope. Even so, at that point, the level of our dreams was pitched at being grateful that we had a future at all and could bumble along in the footballing backwaters at a 15,000 all-seater stadium.

That all changed within weeks once the shy, retiring Chairman Mo arrived on the Craven Cottage pitch in a horse-drawn landau. Premiership football within five years was the cry. By all means go for it, we thought gratefully, if rather incredulously and not a little suspiciously – but don't ruin our wonderful friendly football club in trying.

The rest, as they say, is history. Plenty of bumps along the way, of course, with regard to the ground plus the phenomenal shift in the Club's circumstances and scale of operation, but top-flight football came within four years, not five, during which we won two titles at a canter. And we've since reached the final of a major European competition (two if you include the InterToto Cup), making a host of new friends along the way.

All the while Mohamed Al Fayed has poured his money into Fulham Football Club – primarily into FFC's infrastructure – and done his utmost to ensure we had the best possible manager (and Lawrie Sanchez!). He has made funds available to all who've landed in the managerial hotseat and has generally been hugely supportive to each incumbent.

Never short of an opinion, the Chairman has said his piece when managers have been hired, fired or departed – giving Kevin Keegan "to the nation" for instance and ripping into the over-ambitious Mark Hughes with glorious phraseology – and asking pertinent questions of the authorities as and when, such as his strongly worded letter to the Premier League last April questioning refereeing standards in the wake of us not getting a stonewall penalty at Old Trafford.

Not long after taking ownership of the Club, the Chairman suffered the very public loss of his son, Dodi, who perished along with Diana, Princess of Wales, in that infamous car smash in Paris. Mohamed Al Fayed was moved by the tributes and show of emotion from Fulham supporters – who draped the gates of the Cottage with scarves, shirts and related ephemera – and a bond was sealed. Long may that bond continue.

Thank you Chairman Mo. Hope you're still enjoying it all as much as we are. Keep waving that Fulham scarf. And Happy Birthday! ⚽

"Premiership football within five years was the cry. By all means go for it, we thought gratefully, if rather incredulously and not a little suspiciously – but don't ruin our wonderful friendly football club in trying."

Above left: Mohamed Al Fayed and his famous scarf. The Chairman loved a scarf-waving pre-match sortie around the Craven Cottage pitch before his adoring fans!

Above: Farewell Mo! New owner Shahid Khan takes over the reins at FFC in Summer 2013 and is presented with a Club shirt by the outgoing Chairman, who's sporting a false moustache!

Left: Al Fayed and Jean Tigana in sweeter times, revelling in the Club's promotion to the top flight. The pair's relationship soured in subsequent seasons.

Meeting Cookie (Eventually!)

Ray Lewington gave a cracking interview for TOOFIF 127. Following such a forthright and engaging character such as Lewy would be a tough task. Hmm, I wonder if Cookie might give it a shot…?

Chris Coleman joined third-tier Fulham in late 1997 for £2m from Premier League Blackburn (managed by Roy Hodgson) – this was an enormous transfer fee for a defender dropping down two divisions. And yet it proved to be money well spent, even if his playing days were curtailed by a horrendous car crash in January 2001. By now, though, Coleman was manager of the Wales national team. Plenty to talk about, then, including his time as Fulham manager, but would he be up for it?

Very much so, as it turned out. And yet, having sorted out a time and a place with Cookie by phone ("…11am on the Monday after I get back from my hols…"), that was far from the end of it. I was in Richmond as arranged from about 10.30 on Monday morning, but there was no sign of Chris.

At least not in person. That he'd been on holiday wasn't in doubt as the Daily Mail had splashed pictures of Cookie and his fiancée, Sky presenter Charlotte Jackson, relaxing on a Caribbean beach. But surely he was home by now? I had no idea if he was or wasn't still enjoying the Caribbean sunshine, but, as midday came and went, it was safe to assume he wasn't in Richmond.

It was early evening before Chris Coleman got in touch. He was very apologetic. He'd forgotten that he was moving house that day! He suggested rearranging things for Wednesday lunchtime. I explained that TOOFIF was heading to the printers the following weekend and that I'd rather not send a file that had 6-8 blank pages. Cookie joked that some blank pages might be more interesting than anything he'd have to say, but insisted all was good. So we arranged another meet, again in Richmond, but this time at Les Strong's house.

Strongy is always good value. He was very gracious to offer me his front room for the interview, and did a humorous piece for TOOFIF himself while we were waiting for Chris. He was great company and a genial host – but was there something else going on? As the afternoon wore on, with still no sign of the main man, Strongy was on his mobile phone more and more – and feeding me cake. As teatime approached the sub-plot was revealed – turns out Kit Symons (then Wales' number two), Strongy and Fulham fan Liam Curry had some sort of sweepstake going on, based on what time Cookie would (or wouldn't!) turn up, hence the phone activity and, I'm told, much hilarity. The joke was well and truly on me – and it didn't help that return messages from Strongy were accompanied by pics of me scoffing serious portions of Victoria sponge. As I drove home, sans interview, I wondered who'd won the sweepstake…

A contrite Chris Coleman called later that night. Seems he'd forgotten another trivial event, a divorce hearing. But he could do "tomorrow evening in St Margaret's". Those 6-8 pages were looking blanker than ever so I agreed, but only after telling Chris the sweepstake tale. "Bastards!" he exclaimed with a laugh. "I'll be there tomorrow, don't worry about that!" So it was off to St Margaret's, Richmond, on Thursday evening. Once I'd got there, the ever-organised manager of Wales called me to say he was on his way, albeit in a round-about way. He'd forgotten about some business in Banstead. That's just a couple of miles from my home, and yet I was in Richmond! I very nearly gave up at that point. But I'm very glad I didn't, even though it was almost time for last orders when we finally shook hands and sat down for a chat. "So Lewy was good, right?" he said with

Below. Wales boss Chris Chris Coleman is clearly deep in thought. "Where am I supposed to be today?" perhaps!

gusto. "Dunno if I'll outdo Ray, mind, he's a top, top bloke and Fulham through and through. But I'll give it a crack. Ask me whatever you like…"

When you do media work, you still often refer to Fulham as "us" and "we" – I take it the Club made its mark on you...!

If you spend more than two or three years at a club these days it's considered a long time. I was at Fulham for 10 years, five as a player and then as a coach and manager. I turned professional at 17 and retired from playing at 32 and, with that period as manager, I was at Fulham for a large chunk of my career. On top of that, Fulham is a unique place – with its people behind the scenes, the atmosphere and the brilliant fans. So I still feel as if a part of me is still a part of the Club. When you have a special affiliation with one place, it's very difficult to lose it.

How did the move to Fulham come about in the first place?

I'd gone to Blackburn from Crystal Palace for a lot of money; Kenny Dalglish and Ray Harford signed me. Blackburn had just won the Premiership and for the first 15 games it was great. Then I ruptured my Achilles tendon and it all went downhill. I couldn't get back in the side. Roy Hodgson, a great manager, came in but I didn't fit in with Roy's plans. It was one of those things in football – I respected Roy greatly, but he didn't fancy me and I didn't fancy him. I was from a different era, old school, yet Roy was so forward-thinking and incredibly methodical. There's me (and others!) liking a beer in the week and giving it all at the weekend, but football was moving on. At that stage I would have gone anywhere from Blackburn. I just wanted to play first-team football; I wanted to play for Wales again, something I'd not done for a year and a half. Then came a phone call from Alan Smith. Alan's looked after me for 20 years. He signed me for Crystal Palace, but by now he was Academy Director at Fulham. He said Ray Wilkins and Kevin Keegan wanted to bring me to Fulham. Ray was player-coach at Palace for a while and I had great respect for him – he's an amazing fella. I didn't really know Kevin beforehand; I joined because of my regard for Ray.

What did you expect when you got there?

Do you know what, I didn't really care! I'd had four or five seasons in the lower divisions with Swansea, so that aspect didn't worry me, and I certainly wasn't afraid of a physical battle. Football's different today. Nowadays it's much more technical and tactical. In my time it was much more physical, and I could handle that.

A gamble, nevertheless...?

Of course it was. But I wanted to be a part of that. There was Mohamed Al Fayed backing the Club;

Ray Wilkins was the boss and I was eager to play for him; and Kevin Keegan was, well, Kevin Keegan. The signs were good. Bottom line was I just wanted to play and get my career back on track. It was a bit of a gamble for Fulham, too. My Achilles injury had scared off some clubs. Four or five Premier League clubs wanted me, but they wouldn't meet the £2m+ fee. Second Division Fulham went for it! I phoned my dad to tell him. He said: "Finnegan (he's Irish and calls everyone that!), you worked so hard to get out of the lower divisions, why are you going back?" I said I had a gut feeling it was the right move. Four years later we were in the Premier League, so it worked out well.

What about those early days at Fulham, with better-quality, better-paid players coming into a camp that had won promotion the season before. Surely that affected the spirit of the camp?

Ah, my first meeting with Simon Morgan, who I love to bits! Some of the lads at Fulham – this is 16 years ago remember – were only on about £200-300 a week. I'd been on very good money at Blackburn and had only taken a slight drop in coming to Fulham. On my first day in the dressing-room, over came Morgs who introduced himself with the line, "So Cookie, apart from the £10,000 a week, what attracted you to Fulham?" Typical Morgs! It broke the ice right away. But as I've said, I'd done a decent shift at Swansea and was fully prepared to get back into that environment.

I was no special case. Seriously, the best thing we had at Fulham was a great team spirit. And Simon Morgan was at the very heart of it. Look, he was captain under Micky Adams and had proudly led the team to promotion. With the advent of Mohamed Al Fayed, Micky lost his job and, with Ray the new man in charge, Simon lost the captaincy to Paul Bracewell. Simon always put Fulham first, the team first. And that rubbed off on me, even though I think that's the way I am too. Fulham then signed the right players with the right character at the right time, including Kit Symons from Manchester City. Morgs carried on as normal, doing his stuff on the field but also having digs at me for earning so much money or suggesting I'd spent too much time on sunbeds (never did, it's the colour of my skin!) or accusing Kit of living off my reputation.

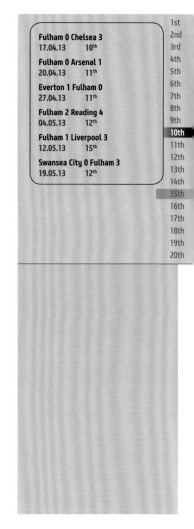

Fulham 0 Chelsea 3	
17.04.13	10th
Fulham 0 Arsenal 1	
20.04.13	11th
Everton 1 Fulham 0	
27.04.13	11th
Fulham 2 Reading 4	
04.05.13	12th
Fulham 1 Liverpool 3	
12.05.13	15th
Swansea City 0 Fulham 3	
19.05.13	12th

1st
2nd
3rd
4th
5th
6th
7th
8th
9th
10th
11th
12th
13th
14th
15th
16th
17th
18th
19th
20th

> *"Morgs was much more than a journeyman pro: he understood the dressing-room; he understood the art of defending; and he understood the value of being a team player. He was invaluable to us. But don't tell him that – we won't hear the last of it!"*

Morgs was quick to take the piss out of Paul Peschisolido for marrying Karren Brady – "Must be difficult for you Paul, having to go home and wash the dishes and do the beds because Karren wears the trousers!" Kit, Morgs and I stuck together and understood what the dressing-room needed. There were no big-time Charlies. I eventually took the Fulham captaincy, and I really enjoyed it, but I always said I had plenty of captains around me.

You three were the heart of the Fulham defence...
Simon was much more than a journeyman pro: he understood the dressing-room; he understood the art of defending; and he understood the value of being a team player. He was invaluable to us. But don't tell him that – we won't hear the last of it! In fact when Jean Tigana came along, Jean didn't know much, if anything, about Fulham, didn't know me, and didn't know Simon. But he kept him on; he was a smart man, Jean, and he valued Simon Morgan's presence and influence at the Club and his positive attitude...

And he could write a book, too...?
He could write a book, that's true, but he could never buy a pint!

The Ray Wilkins and Kevin Keegan partnership didn't work out...
We got into the Play-offs that year, just, having lost our last three games, but it was still a huge shock to hear that Ray had been sacked before the Play-off game with Grimsby. I was gutted. But the Club had made its decision and, as players, you just had to get on with it.

The next season was a little more successful...
We hammered the League. On top of that we beat Villa, top of the Premier League, at Villa Park in the Cup, only lost 1-0 to United at Old Trafford, beat Southampton and Spurs in the League Cup. Kevin did really well before taking the England job.

A good man-manager?
Yes, and a very good motivator. But then so was Ray, and not many realised that. You see Ray on the telly now, smart, dapper, articulate and a very intelligent man. But he can also look you straight in the eye and tell you exactly what he's thinking – to great effect! Even though I'd known him for a while, he was now my boss. If things went well he'd build you up by saying you'd been different class. However, he'd also tell me very pointedly if I'd been below par. Stuff like, "I didn't pay £2m of this club's money for you to play like that!" With his integrity, when he looked you in the eye you knew he meant it. Kevin had a bit of mystique about him, in that you didn't always know what he was thinking. A good motivator though, no question. He would call you into his office and tear you off a strip. But with Kevin you could also say what you thought, which I did on numerous occasions. Often these would turn into blazing rows. Yet once it all cleared over he'd be telling me I was the best defender outside the top flight, so I'd go from wondering why the hell I'd signed for Fulham to be managed by a guy I hated to suddenly thinking he was the best manager I'd ever had.

We won silverware under KK, something us Fulham fans hadn't been used to, and your career was on the up again. So was the gloss taken off when he took the England job?
In a way. We won that last game 3-0, Paul Moody hit a hat-trick against Preston, but it was against the backdrop of Kevin leaving. It was a tough ask of Paul Bracewell to step into the role – the Club's expectations were so high, and it was Paul's first job in management. We finished ninth which, looking back, wasn't bad. But as we didn't make the Play-offs, Paul lost his job.

After the flamboyance of KK, Paul Bracewell was much more cautious...
That's exactly right. Paul had won the League with Everton, don't forget, but had done so playing a certain type of football. Let's be fair though, he was trying to do things his own way – which is the only way to approach these things – and he may well have fine-tuned things had he had a bit more time. But that's football. We all liked Paul, and had great respect for him, but we didn't get the results for him.

So another crossroads; before we talk about the next chapter, what are your best memories as a

Cookie Confesses...

In your time at Fulham, were you aware of the fanzine?
Oh yes. No one likes criticism, but if it's done tongue in cheek – and don't forget that banter was always flying around our dressing room – then it's easier to accept, or at least tolerate. Thankfully, things were on the up during my time at Fulham. Players who say they don't look at a fanzine are liars! And the manager will generally be at the head of the queue, end of story.

Now then, Chris, did you ever call Luis Boa Morte a "rucking flanker"?
[Laughs] Probably! He'd have called me something similar loads of times, too! Luis, what a great guy. We had many a falling out, but so what? He's a top fella – I took him out to Larissa in Greece and I made him my captain. Boa was brilliant for me. They loved him out there for the way he played, with passion, style and talent.

Fulham player. Who were the real characters?
My debut was against Brentford at home. I had a shocker. Really dreadful...

...Bobby Moore had a poor Fulham debut...!
Ha-ha – at least I'm in good company then! One or two of the Brentford strikers had a right go at me verbally, telling me I was rubbish (they weren't wrong, even if they phrased it a lot stronger than that!) and not worth the money. We managed a 1-1 draw. So I looked forward to the return game at Griffin Park. By the time we went there I'd grown into the Fulham way of things and was enjoying my football. I was all ready for Brentford away, no problem. And we pulverised them. Paul Moody got our goals in a 2-0 win. I enjoyed that – and may have mentioned it once or twice to the home forwards! Beating Gillingham at home 3-0 to clinch the title was another good day. I got on the scoresheet that day with a truly magnificent strike (oh, okay, it was from a yard or two out with my right foot, but I enjoyed it). But on the grander scale, I thought "We're on our way now."

We enjoyed that season, too!
I don't know what it is about Craven Cottage; it's like no other ground. Selhurst Park is a football ground, not an arena. In the same way the Cottage is a traditional ground but there's an extra element. I really hope Fulham retain that traditional feel, whatever happens in the future, as it's unique. And it's wonderful to see the place hosting Premier League football. Let me tell you, when I ran out onto the pitch as captain – and especially prior to that game with Gillingham – I had the same "tingly" feeling as I had captaining Wales. We battered Gillingham, it was a full house, our fans were amazing and as for the spirit in the dressing-room, I've never seen the like, I really haven't.

And the characters?
Neil Smith was a top fella. You saw the best of him when your backs were to the wall. When you're winning every week it's harder to judge character, but Smudger had courage in abundance. He was a tough kid, not very big, but prepared to get hurt if it made the difference to his team. A top guy and a great team-mate.

It's all very well being good players, but having that "edge" helps...
Kevin was very clever. He'd quickly sussed out which players held the sway in the dressing-room – in terms of who played, who never missed training and who was ready to give his all. Kevin would join us after training and there'd be a group of us: me, Simon Morgan, Kit Symons, Neil Smith, Stevie Haywood, Paul Peschisolido, Geoff Horsfield, Maik Taylor, Alan Nielson, Rufus Brevett – I'm bound to have left one or two out – but all very good

pros. We thought he was just enjoying a cuppa with us, but he was letting the influential players get on with it. He'd get the vibes from the dressing-room, while letting us lot boss or lead the dressing-room. Don't get me wrong, he was the boss, and he let us know it in no uncertain terms at times, and yet he helped foster a strong, winning camp with a wonderful atmosphere, probably the best I've been involved with.

Along the way, the Taffia came to the fore: you, Kit, Alan Nielson, Andy Melville, Paul Trollope...?
[Laughs] Good job they didn't ask us to sing! The only downside was Andy Melville's dress code – it was so dreadful he put everyone in a bad mood! Morgs picked up on that right away! But, as I've said, the camaraderie was fantastic.

After the Taffia came the French revolution. Jean Tigana's training regime surprised the squad, but it paid immediate dividends...
By the time Jean was announced as Fulham's new manager I knew there was interest in me from other clubs – that's the way things work. I spoke to KarlHeinz Riedle, who we'd signed from Liverpool; he was not only one of the very best players I've ever played with, he was also one of the best people I've met in the game. He told me what to expect from the new French regime. The training was going to be the toughest I'd experienced for a start. And we'd be doing so two or three times a day! I was old school, and this wasn't me. I admit I was unsettled by it. Others were too – players such as Morgs, Kit, Andy Melville, Rufus, Lee Clark all thought we were in big trouble. Training two or three times a day? With us it was more like two or three times a week! So I went to see Jean when he arrived and he told me through his interpreter that he still wanted me to be captain. I said I wasn't sure I could do it, that my ways were different to his and that I had the chance to move to other clubs. I said that I loved Fulham, but I wasn't sure that he could get the best out of me as a player. Jean remained very calm. He just said, "Give me two weeks, see what you think, if you don't like it you can leave, no problem." Let me tell you, I'd bought into his methods within two days! Jean was very

Above: Chris Coleman, the "best young manager in the League" according to Sir Alex Ferguson. But only when United won!

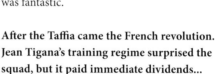

"Kevin Keegan was very clever. He'd quickly sussed out which players held the sway in the dressing-room – in terms of who played, who never missed training and who was ready to give his all."

methodical, very scientific, but he had a lot of feeling also – for the players, for the people and for the Club. It was all way, way ahead of anything we'd ever witnessed.

Okay, so it wasn't the top flight, but I don't think we've had the full credit for the quality of football we played that season...
It must have been brilliant to watch; it was fantastic to play. We had great players, and a great way of playing. Watford clung on to our shirt-tails as we streaked away with the league. Then we thumped them 5-0. Jean took me off with about half an hour to play. Turned out it was my last game as a player at the Cottage. In those six months with Jean Tigana I was in a side that played the most scintillating brand of football, winning game after game in real style – and I was in the best physical and mental condition of my life.

You weren't the only "old-school" player to benefit, though?
No, Rufus, Lee Clark, Andy and others, we were of a certain type, with a certain mentality, yet Jean Tigana and his staff changed us for the better. He also brought in John Collins; what a top-quality player. As was Luis Boa Morte. Pick of the bunch, mind, was Louis Saha. In that season we all did well; how could we fail? But there were three above all the rest: Steve Finnan, Lee Clark, Louis Saha. A class above – with Louis the pick of those three.

Your season came to an abrupt halt. Looking back now at that horrific car smash, do you consider you were unlucky as it cost you your playing career, or lucky that you survived?
When we lost at Stockport a few days earlier I'd taken a bang to my leg. We were top of the League and should never have lost; we were better than that but had an off day and, as captain, I felt responsible for the defeat. So I was a bit flat. In the last five minutes of that game I'd gone in hard on one of the Stockport guys, looking to hurt him if I'm honest in winning the ball. But I was the one who got hurt. When I saw our physio the next day, he said: "Cookie, you're not going to be fit for two weeks." I said: "But we've got Man United in the Cup at the weekend! Fucking hell... I'm not missing that one."

That night I crashed my car, badly. When I woke up the next morning in hospital, the doctor began to outline the extent of the damage. It sounds stupid now, but I barely took in a word of what he said. The only thing concerning me was "Have I got a chance of making Saturday?" Meanwhile I was being told that I had a 50:50 chance of playing again. Broken tibia, and smashed fibia in two dozen places, ruptured ankle ligaments, ruptured cruciate ligaments... Their lips were moving but

nothing was going in. United on Saturday did seem a little unlikely though. Shit!

You're making light of it, but things were serious...
In those first two weeks I was having operation after operation, plus blood transfusions – I was in a different world, and in a lot of pain. As I came round a bit more the reality sank in. My mum and dad showed me all the letters and emails that had come in from Fulham fans – something like 3,000 get well wishes! It was very humbling. When mum and dad left, I was lying there fretting. I was tearful; it concerned me that I'd never be able to reply to all those who'd taken the trouble to write to me. The one thing I could do was to use all the good wishes as a prop for my recovery – and to get back playing. That crash was disastrous – it was horrible and extremely painful. But, if it had to happen, I couldn't have been at a better club. Everyone was so helpful and supportive: Mohamed Al Fayed, Jean Tigana and his staff, the people behind the scenes at Fulham, the players and the wonderful fans. Realistically I was never going to get back playing given the damage I'd done, yet I was stubborn and had a big ego and so was absolutely determined to go for it. I did play reserve football later, but that was it. The people in and around Fulham Football Club were fantastic to me. Fitness coach Roger Propos is the best I've ever worked with. Jean Tigana is the best manager and Christian Damiano the best coach. What a dream team to have at Fulham! Roger pushed me and pushed me, and thanks to him I'm able to lead a normal life today. My playing career ultimately had to stop but I was in good hands.

How did the players help you?
You know who I'm going to start with – Morgs! On the training field before the smash he'd have some choice phrases to describe me: "Big Welsh tart", or "Pretty boy". I was in my hospital bed, looking a bit rough when he came to see me. He looked me up and down and announced, "Not so good-looking now, are you big fella?!" I pulled back the blankets to show him my leg, which wasn't in a good way. Morgs just curled his lip a bit and said drily, "I've seen worse." (When Steve Finnan had a peek, he nearly passed out when he saw the damage!) I have to repeat, I was at the right place, the players were so supportive and even people at the Club who I only knew to say hello to came along to wish me well.

Mark Hughes isn't flavour of the month with our fans just now, but as manager of Wales he gave you one more cap. That was one helluva gesture!
I'm the manager myself now of course. I have to

"That night I crashed my car, badly. When I woke up the next morning in hospital, the doctor began to outline the extent of the damage. It sounds stupid now, but I barely took in a word of what he said. The only thing concerning me was 'Have I got a chance of making Saturday?'"

say that if my side had a 1-0 lead over Germany I really don't know if I could do the same thing. I can never thank Mark enough for what he did. Never! I was named in the squad despite being crocked. Making the bench was a massive surprise and I thought it was Mark's generous way of giving me a last blast of the atmosphere. I was in tears when he said I'd be on the bench – proud Welshman you see. I was soaking up the atmosphere as the game drew to a close when Mark said, "Get stripped, you're going on." This was unreal. Two minutes to go, Wales 1-0 up. In my head I was telling Mark, "You must be bloody mad. Don't put me on. Don't put me in defence – I've only got one leg. I'll lose the game for us." But that never came out. In a daze, what came out was, "Yes gaffer, I'm ready," as I was so desperate to get on the pitch. So on I went – on the right wing. I must go down as the largest right-winger in world football. With no right foot.

You stepped into management at Fulham and it must have seemed easy – ninth in the Premier League and a 3-1 win at Old Trafford?

If you remember I got the job for five games as caretaker the previous season and we managed to stay up. We had a very good squad and I was determined to do things my way; then, if it all went tits-up, it'd be down to me. So I changed the formation and the personnel a little. Meantime, as the division's youngest manager I was the favourite for the sack and Fulham were probably regarded as easy pickings. In Saha, Steed Malbranque, Boa Morte, we had quick players in attack, Lee Clark with great ingenuity in midfield along with Junichi Inamoto, plus great holding players like Martin Djetou, Sylvain Legwinski and Sean Davis. I knew what formation I wanted: 4-5-1; counter attack.

I reasoned that everyone reckoned we'd go down so, in effect, every point would be a bonus. And when we saw the fixtures we took them in blocks of five games and didn't look any further ahead. We targeted those games we ought to win while, if visits to places like Old Trafford, Anfield and Stamford Bridge were looming, then it was a case of being fairly relaxed and doing as well as we could. With the reverse fixtures against those types of club the object was not to lose at home. Hardly rocket science when you think about it, but the plan was very much in place. It seemed to work.

What did Fergie say after we won up there?

Not a lot! I went to his room afterwards and he was gracious enough to ask, "Do you want a drink?" When I said, "Yes please", he said, "The fridge is over there". Which meant get it yourself! The next season when they beat us he was very chatty, telling me I was the best young manager in the League!

"I pulled back the blankets to show him my leg, which wasn't in a good way. Morgs just curled his lip a bit and said drily, 'I've seen worse.' (When Steve Finnan had a peek, he nearly passed out when he saw the damage!)"

Saha top of shops for Fergie

LOUIS IS PRICELESS

SA-HAVE IT . . . Louis celebrates his first goal

Hands off Saha says Coleman

By **Richard Tanner** and **Mark Fleming**

ANGRY Chris Coleman finally snapped over Manchester United's continued interest in Louis Saha by delivering a "hands off" message to Sir Alex Ferguson last night.

Saha has admitted he wants to move to Old Trafford and United have already had one bid rejected but they are bound to be back in again after the French striker hit two more goals in the 2-0 win over Southampton that moved Fulham back up to fourth.

SAHA: Double

United stayed top with a 3-2 win over Everton, but Coleman is determined they won't be adding to their squad from his players.

He said: "Louis is not for sale, and that is that. He is flattered that Manchester United are interested, but he has two and a half years to run on his contract

Left and above: Louis Saha's goalscoring exploits weren't going unnoticed at Old Trafford, and the whole issue, as reported here in *The Sun* (*left*) and the *Express*, became a thorny issue for Chris Coleman.

"We'd had a good year at Loftus Road to be fair, but going back to the Cottage was an important step. I always remember coming out onto the pitch as a player and it was an uplifting experience, especially as captain. Fulham's identity is Craven Cottage."

Looking back, would you have done anything differently as Fulham manager?

Lots. Especially in that last year. I made loads of mistakes. The key is to learn from those mistakes. I hope I'm a much better manager now having clocked up the experience and learned how to deal with certain things.

That infamous line of yours, "Over my dead body", when United came in for Saha – was that a mistake?

No. I knew when I said it that United would have to up their bid. I also knew it would put a bit of pressure on Mohamed with regard to how best to deal with it. As for the fans, I reckoned that they'd like hearing me say it, knowing that the manager of their Club meant business. And I did mean business. Louis Saha was our best player. I remember saying to Mohamed, "Don't sell him, he's got 15 goals already, he's heading for 25. If he gets 25 we'll finish in Europe. Sell him at the end of the season." United came back with an overall bid of £12.85m, so it was only going to end one way. The Chairman explained that the bulk of that would be spent on the new stadium, and I understood. My 'cut' was £500,000, which I used to buy Brian McBride, and he was fantastic for Fulham.

Heading back to Craven Cottage was emotional for long-term Fulham fans – did you get caught up in all of that?

Yes, I did. We'd had a good year at Loftus Road to be fair, but going back to the Cottage was an important step. I always remember coming out onto the pitch as a player and it was an uplifting experience, especially as captain. Fulham's identity is Craven Cottage. Once the chance came to go back to an improved Craven Cottage it had to be taken. And then to improve it further as and when. I know it was never always that simple, but to me it was a no-brainer. The place is unique, and unique in a very good way. I still say the atmosphere for an evening game at a packed Craven Cottage is superb. I covered the Juventus game for Sky, and I remember looking at Roy Hodgson and wishing that I was still the manager – and that was just soaking up the early atmosphere. As the game developed, what a result! What a night! And what fantastic support! As I drove away a little while after the game I saw pockets of Fulham fans looking so elated. When I joined the Club my first game was against Brentford. Now Fulham were heading towards a major European final. Fantastic!

Now you're managing Wales, with Kit Symons by your side. A proud moment tinged with sadness taking over from Gary Speed...

Managing Barcelona – and my chances of getting

that one aren't great – might be a bigger job, but there's no greater honour than managing your country. It's a tough job, very tough, but it's a massive thrill. I knew Gary Speed from the age of 10. I was captain of Swansea boys and he was captain of a North Wales team, Deeside, and they beat us 3-0. My dad said "Finnegan, if that no.10 doesn't make it as a professional player then no one will!" Gary was that good even then. We became great pals soon after that and played together for Wales U18s. So we went back a long way.

I was in Greece when I got a text message from Lee Clark; I couldn't take it in. It was an hour before my team kicked-off but this was awful – I rang Clarkie and got the terrible details. When I got back to Wales I realised the enormity of the tragedy and how deeply it had affected so many people. In taking the Welsh job subsequently, I felt my hands were tied to an extent, because of the love and respect I had for Gary; I couldn't shift too far from Gary's methods partly because they'd been so well received and he'd also got some good results but also because of the great esteem in which he'd been held. I felt stuck. I also felt guilty at wanting to change one or two things. I've known Gary's parents for 30 years so the whole thing was very, very personal for me and a desperate time for Gary's family and friends. Being asked to take over from Gary was as bittersweet as things come. I'm determined to carry on in his honour, but to do things my way now. ⚽

Could do Better

It's been a frustrating campaign, hasn't it? We hurtled out of the blocks with that 5-0 win over Norwich and put up a good show at Old Trafford. Supporters who went to Sheffield Wednesday witnessed a meek effort in the Capital One Cup, a tournament that's produced some great games this season and which, for a club like Fulham, represents a realistic chance of silverware and with it a place in Europe. Bet Swansea are glad they bothered to give it a go.

Losing Dempsey, Dembélé – brilliant at Old Trafford, and on that showing surprising that he went to Spurs rather than United – plus the ageing yet still-influential Murphy was bad enough. Failing to replace them proved a major error of judgement. Bringing in the sublime skills of Dimitar Berbatov (ostensibly) up front is all well and good, but he needs some sort of reliable supply line otherwise cue that disinterested look and flailing of arms. Losing Mahamadou Diarra was a big blow, while the acquisition of Karagounis did at least bring some guile and enthusiasm into the midfield. Even at 35!

At the back it's been worrying how the form of the previously steadfast Hangeland and Hughes dipped alarmingly. Senderos, for all his obvious

TOOFIF turns 25

As TOOFIF made its softly, softly bow at Aldershot in late March 1988, Wimbledon, Sheffield Wednesday and Luton Town sat in the top 10 of Division One. Some of you may not have heard of Division One because, according to today's football guv'nors BSkyB, not a lot happened before the creation of the Premier League in 1992. Not that we were overly concerned with such matters. Back then, the chances of Division Three Fulham ever competing again in the top-flight was about as likely as Kevin Keegan becoming manager at Craven Cottage and doing such a good job that he'd be lured away to manage England. As if...

Any thoughts that we'd bottomed out (this was just after the collapse of the hideous Fulham Park Rangers proposals, remember) were soon booted into touch as we plummeted not only into the basement division but down it too. Ray Lewington recalled recently just how bad things became behind the scenes and how skint the Club was. Lewy and Terry Bullivant would go round local parks to nick footballs off young kids just so the Fulham players could train (all right, they didn't, but the Club was that skint they may well have thought about it!). Meanwhile the depressing ground saga just went on and on. Times were really tough and it gradually dawned that there was a distinct chance that the Club and ground might disappear altogether.

In the intervening years the Club has enjoyed a miraculous transformation. It didn't happen overnight, and there were a number of aggravations along the way. But TOOFIF somehow managed to stick around to cover and reflect on the amazing ups and downs, and to merrily chart that the former gradually outscored the latter. Mohamed Al Fayed has clearly been the main man in all of this, but we shouldn't forget that the upswing really got going on a shoestring under Micky Adams and the GMB.

Quite why there's still a call for TOOFIF today, given the wall-to-wall sports coverage available and the immediacy of news and reaction on the Internet and social media, is a mystery. Fulham Football Club is a fixture in the Premier League these days, playing at a transformed yet still traditional Craven Cottage before sell-out crowds – with a flashy new riverside stand and increased ground capacity on the way. Our gallant European run helped to put Fulham FC well and truly on the international stage and we made many new friends along the way. Seeing the sold-out, revamped ground rocking on all sides as we progressed to the Europa League final was a sight to behold. And if TOOFIF helped, even in the smallest of ways, to ensure that the Club lived to breathe again during the bleak times then its been a worthwhile exercise.

And guess what? In spring 1988, *Man in the Mirror* by Michael Jackson from his *Bad* album topped the Billboard Hot 100. It was the first time that a solo artist had celebrated four No.1 singles from the same album (a fifth followed). Such an intrinsic link between fanzine and King of Pop had to be marked somehow, especially with a 25th anniversary coming up; so now you know why we have that flipping statue. Funny thing is, while the Jacko likeness is clutching a microphone in his left hand, there's no sign of Issue 1 in his right hand. Er, must put that right...

passion, is a ricket waiting to happen. Point is, the unity at the back went walkabout – whether that's down to being chopped and changed, the attitude/form of the individuals or being afforded less cover from the midfield is open to debate. Mark Schwarzer, supreme of late, had a serious dip, too. Hangeland hasn't looked happy as captain. Thankfully his form's improved this year and hopefully he'll sign a new contract (at the time of writing that's very much up in the air). Hope, too, that Sascha Reither's here next season. He's been superb.

Turning point of the season was Sunderland (home). We so nearly turned that one around despite having only nine men for a while. With Hangeland red-carded, Berbatov played like a man possessed. On that showing – bordering on the Karagounis-scale of effervescence – he should be captain. No languid sulks, just masses of effort and eye-boggling skills (that last quality is a given) and leadership by example. Trouble is, it's generally been Mr Languid for the rest of the time; 11 league goals or not. And poor body language. Imagine Berba's goals return (and smiley face) with a dynamic, astute midfield feeding him the bullets...

No apologies for mentioning the away game at Loftus Road once again, and the similar lack of guts a week later at Anfield. You can accept defeats – grudgingly! – when we've given everything (such as Man United at home) and days when nothing seems to go right (Sunderland, also at home), but not a fundamental lack of effort and apparent disdain for the job in hand (and for the travelling fans who'd made huge efforts to support the team). The QPR-Fulham derby had all the passion of a soggy corn flake. Compare that to the determination shown at White Hart Lane; captain Hangeland described it as a "near-perfect away performance". Hard to disagree, and it's a sweet feeling when everyone's obviously pulling the same way.

Welcome, Mr Khan

The Ed went to meet and greet Fulham's new owner when he was unveiled to the media at Craven Cottage. Shahid Khan was on good form – very measured, media savvy (as you'd expect) and lapping up Craven Cottage in the sunshine.

What do you see as your aims for Fulham FC, pushing them towards the top four, perhaps?
Mr Al Fayed took the Club from the third tier of English football to where it is today. And my aims are to stablilse, sustain the Club and have it move forward, be a great part of the community, be a civic asset and win on the pitch.

Are you willing to back those aims by putting a lot of money into the project?
There is a great team here overseeing the whole football operation, they have a plan… I've only been here a day and I'd like to understand that, and I'd like to give them all the resources they need and then hold them accountable.

Why have you bought Fulham – running a football club is expensive and time-consuming?
Because I love sports. And I think the Premier League is at a certain level right now, it's shifting gears; it's the perfect club at the perfect time.

Will you be bringing in your own people at executive level or leave things as they are for the moment?
First of all, you have to remember that Jacksonville and London are two distinct operations that stand alone. Obviously there are some synergies, some best practices and we would want to understand those; some things we'll be able to scale up but Fulham will remain Fulham. We want to have the best people here, so we'll see…

What are your impressions of Fulham and Craven Cottage?
It's a historic place and very impressive in this bright sunshine – by the way, Mr Al Fayed tells me it's like this all the time!

Martin Jol's had to part with some of his favourite players in past seasons – will that be the case now that you're here?
That will be up to Martin and Alistair [Mackintosh]. I'm not a micro-manager and some of the lessons that I've learned in my time in America, going from one guy in a garage to where we are today with more than 17,000 employees, well, how do you get to that level? It's by finding the best people, empowering them, giving them the resources, holding them accountable and not micro-managing. As yet I've not spoken to Martin.

Have you looked at how the other owners of Premier League clubs have fared since taking over, such as Randy Lerner at Aston Villa then there's Sunderland and QPR where they've made mistakes. One or two have spent a lot of money and got carried away; some lessons to be learned, maybe, now you're at Fulham?
Certainly you can learn from history. And of course I've looked at that situation – and yes, you certainly don't want to repeat the same mistakes. I have met Randy a couple of times in the past when he was in the NFL, but I haven't spoken to him this week. I have spoken to Stan Kroenke this week, and the Glazers at length.

Will there be a lot of activity on and off the pitch now that you're here? Fulham have signed a few players already this summer, but are you the sort of person who sits back and takes stock for a while or will you be involved right away?
Well, I don't have first-hand knowledge of what the plan is – hopefully I'll be learning that over the next couple of days. And then it'll be a case of putting that plan in motion.

Craven Cottage is a historic ground, but it's a prime site. Lots of people have tried to knock it down in the past and build houses or whatever on the site – do you see that as a long-term prospect for your plan?
Craven Cottage is something precious, and I see it as something that needs to be sustained and developed. The plan for the Riverside Stand is very, very important. You need a commercial intake so you can spend on players, etc. So it's a virtuous site and, as I say, developing it is very important. ⚽

Here's Hoping…

Another season, another set of hopes and aspirations. That valuable win at the Stadium of Light changed the script for these ramblings. One scrappy if stoic victory doesn't prove anything, but it's a great start. Up to that point, for all the decent transfer business done early in the close season, we'd been quiet on that score as the game at Sunderland approached, and the squad had a distinctly unbalanced feel to it. We'd been linked with a host of players for weeks, as football writers almost everywhere went into scattergun mode, predominantly in an attempt to fill their columns rather than inform. As per normal, very few bullets found their supposed target.

> "Craven Cottage is something precious, and I see it as something that needs to be sustained and developed. The plan for the Riverside Stand is very, very important."

Opposite page right: Pre-season predictions from *The Observer*.

Below: New Fulham owner Shahid Khan, who's not into micro-managing.

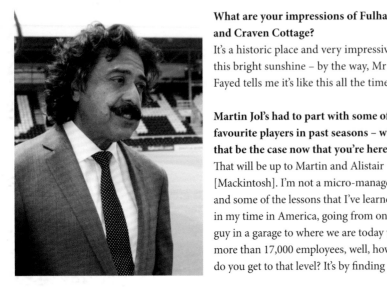

FULHAM
DAVID LLOYD
toofif.co.uk

We were quick out of the blocks this summer to sign Fernando Amorebieta, Maarten Stekelenburg and Derek Boateng, and the purchase of Sascha Riether following his excellent displays while on loan last season is great business. And yet it's all gone quiet since. The calm before the storm perhaps? What we really need is creativity/dynamism in the middle of the park and a foil for Berbatov (below). Taarabt has joined on loan, but is he the answer? A couple of potent signings will make all the difference.

Key player If we can maintain a smile on Berba's face, via a decent supply of the ball and support up front, then things will be going well. Watch out for Noe Baba and a lad called Moussa Dembélé (yes, really) from the U-18s and, wait for it, Buomesca Tue Na Bangna from the U-21s, who is hoping to oust some of the OAPs.

Weak links The squad's attitude was very poor at times last season. QPR away, say, was unforgivable, and the apparent lack of interest once we'd hit 40 points was unprofessional and almost cost us dear.

Headline generator Jol will deserve praise if he can forge a united, never-say-die (and winning) team. The jury's still out on that one – as will Jol be if new owner Shahid Khan isn't impressed.

If you could sign one player from the club's past... Tosh Chamberlain – he'd be guaranteed to bring along best mate and our maestro, Johnny Haynes.

Prediction An optimistic **10th**

As far as TOOFIF Towers was concerned, those hopes and aspirations were not particularly high as we headed towards the big kick-off. And it's now up to Martin Jol and the boys to change that perspective with further unified showings and, hopefully, a little more pace and panache when going forwards.

We're all well aware, as we're quick to pick up on such things, that we lost the influential Dembélé and Murphy at the start of last season, and that the stand-off with Dempsey culminated in him being shipped off to Spurs and not, as anticipated, Liverpool. Understandably we struggled to recover from those losses. In case all of this had somehow escaped us, though, that became the manager's mantra for a good while – more than likely making a point to his employees given that we'd had to "make do" with a clutch of loanees last term. We were all too aware of the dearth of midfield creativity and spark last season, and that Berbatov demonstrated his frustration at a lack of nous around him and general support on many an occasion. We'll have to see if those failings have been addressed with the latest flurry of additions.

Last season was desperately frustrating. In a poor Premier League, it just needed a little consistency to earn a top-half finish, and accordingly that much more prize money. Yeah, we hadn't replaced those important players, but even so we had enough quality to finish so much higher up the table. What hurt is that on too many occasions the team didn't seem unduly bothered. The desperately poor showing at QPR was a disgrace. And we were all over the place at Anfield just days later; 0-4 was bad enough, but we were lucky to escape a proper drubbing. In the closing weeks of the campaign, having reached apparent safety on 40 points we seemed to switch off. By

that yardstick, it wouldn't matter which players were selected; if the squad's attitude, confidence and tactics are poor on matchday, chances are we'll come off second best, superstars or not.

Why did we try to defend slender leads so often, for example? Especially as we'd become a lot less secure at the back. No one expects an over-the-top gung-ho approach, but why so negative? And why so slow and laboured on the ball?

There were also times when we played well; very well, actually. And on the face of it, finishing 12th isn't a poor return. But the fact remains we were off the pace far too often. So yes, this is a "could-have-done-so-much-better" review of 2012-13, and a quick glance at last season's final table reveals that two more decent wins would have propelled us into eighth spot. Attainable, had we been bothered.

Dimitar Berbatov's previous club is famed for plugging away for the full 90 minutes (plus generous add-ons!) even when they're not on-song. While they operate on a level that's substantially higher than ours, with expectations to match, that attitude and belief has served them well. If it's good enough for them…

Pre-season friendlies are rarely a guide to the real campaign to follow, especially given the glut of substitutions. If the Parma game showed us anything, it's that our first XI is actually pretty good. And that's with new-boy Amorebieta waiting in the wings. It's no good having the ability, though, if that leads to an unrealistic sense of arrogance; we can cruise through this, no problem. No we can't.

Resilience and Adel Taarabt don't usually go hand in hand, but there he was making his first League start for us in that gutsy if unspectacular effort at Sunderland (seriously couldn't believe that he got booed by some of our lot when he came on against Parma; each to their own, but how does that help exactly?). "Old timer" Brede Hangeland was dominant and the defence, with Aaron Hughes also starring, looked pretty solid. The hosts weren't the strongest side we'll face this campaign, but getting an away win, despite losing your left-back after just 19 minutes (Richardson limping off early again!), as well as your goalkeeper in the second half, suggests a modicum of mettle. If new loanee Darren Bent fits in and proves anything like the predatory goalscorer of not so long ago then we might have a tasty squad capable of a successful season after all!

Can't sign off without wishing Mohamed Al Fayed all the best in his retirement; massive thanks, Mo, for all your input over the last 16 years. So it's welcome to FFC's new owner, Shahid Khan, who from day one has talked of being a custodian of the Club and of admiring the history of the Craven Cottage site. He's keen to see through the plans for the new Riverside Stand while retaining the site's unique appeal. His has been a softly-softly approach thus far and yet, given his background, I'm sure he'll step in should the need arise. ⚽

Sunderland 0 Fulham 1	1st
17.08.13 4th	2nd
	3rd
Fulham 1 Arsenal 3	**4**
24.08.13 11th	5th
Newcastle United 1 Fulham 0	6th
31.08.13 16th	7th
Fulham 1 West Bromwich Albion 1	8th
14.09.13 13th	9th
Chelsea 2 Fulham 0	10th
21.09.13 18th	11th
Fulham 1 Cardiff City 2	12th
28.09.13 18th	13th
Fulham 1 Stoke City 0	14th
05.10.13 17th	15th
Crystal Palace 1 Fulham 4	16th
21.10.13 13th	17th
Southampton 2 Fulham 0	**18th**
26.10.13 13th	19th
	20th
League Cup	
Burton Albion 2 Fulham 2	
27.08.13 Round 2;	
Fulham win 5-4 on pens	
Fulham 2 Everton 1	
24.09.13 Round 3	
Leicester City 4 Fulham 3	
29.10.13 Round 4	

Papering Over the Cracks

Over the last quarter-century TOOFIF has often been accused of being negative, with some justification, even though the mag was merely reflecting the views from the terraces. It's also fair to say that had the in-house accusers directed their attentions at the root causes of the fans' moans then we may not have sunk down the divisions so feebly.

This column has often said it would far prefer to be trumpeting about how well the Club is doing, front and back of stage. "Doing well", of course, can be subjective, but scaling the divisions in style and reaping the plaudits and the silverware along the way is success in anyone's book. Retaining its friendly image, returning to a revamped Craven Cottage, enjoying a pulsating run in Europe (two, if you include the InterToto!) are among the bonuses we've all enjoyed along the way. And the mag has been pleased and proud to champion such achievements in its pages.

Having reached the giddy heights of the Premier League, the priority has to be to stay

there, something we've done by and large with aplomb since 2001. However, can't say I'm feeling too secure about that record being extended right now, even though, as I write, two clubs are already somewhat adrift at the foot of the table. Worse still, I can't see too many people on the field who are overly bothered about our plight.

And there's the rub, the vast majority of us may not have coaching badges nor are we being paid tens of thousands of pounds to supposedly orchestrate matters. But we've a lifetime's experience of watching our club week in, week out, and can detect when things are going pear-shaped. Like now, for instance.

Kasami's extraordinary strike at Selhurst Park (and yours too, Ginge) was a belter and rightly celebrated. But there's no escaping the fact that the troops in the stands are restless. Our diehard fans cheered on Micky Adams and his men all those years ago for galvanising the whole set-up on peanuts and giving us back some long-lost pride in the Club. And we looked on, often in disbelief, at how Jean Tigana and his staff masterminded a glorious return to the top flight. We also studiously admired how Roy Hodgson and his trusty sidekick Ray Lewington honed the squad, improving every player and forging a genuine team ethic. Right now, though, we can see all-too-clearly how the current set-up is awful by comparison. Little wonder we're upset. However, it's not a case of moaning, but caring.

In the above examples, the men at the helm reaped the reward of considerable hard work behind the scenes, and, "hey presto", earned the success that came their way. There was also a clear plan in operation in each instance. Any idea what the plan is today, folks? Go out there and do your thing (whatever that is), perhaps? Stroll about; something will come our way...? Flicks and tricks will please the crowd, it's sexy football they want...?

Sexy football is the icing on the cake. When it does come off – and we had months of the sexiest football possible under Tigana – it's a joy to behold. But even that apparently off-the-cuff stuff was underpinned by a basic structure that was bolstered by having other basic qualities in abundance: pace, strength, leadership, professionalism, team spirit – and no little skill!

Watching one of our games recently I remarked that we were all over the place: the marking was non-existent; the tracking back was poor; the body language was dreadful; we were second to the ball just about every time; we gave our opponents a big confidence boost by largely sitting back; and it was no surprise at all when

Opposite page right: Steve Sidwell, whose wonderstrike at Crystal Palace in October 2013 was overshadowed by Pajtim Kasami's worldie, was a terrific and often undervalued player for the Club.

Below: As Vikki Orvice's report in *The Sun* confirms, we ended up hammering Palace at Selhurst Park. Such a terrific result should have boosted the confidence levels and led to more of the same. Instead, it just papered over the cracks.

JOLLY GOOD
Fulham give Ollie's strugglers what four

SPECIAL K ... Kasami controls the ball (inset) before firing wonder goal

PAJTIM KASAMI unleashed a wonder goal to put Fulham on a Swiss roll — and pile the pressure on struggling Palace.

Eagles boss Ian Holloway has raised eyebrows this season by taking his wife on the team bus.

Short of parking that very bus in front of their goal last night, he could not have stopped Kasami, never mind the rest of Martin Jol's marvellous Fulham team.

The Swiss winger, 21, signed from Palermo two years ago for £5million, controlled a long pass from Sascha Riether with his chest then, with the next touch, unleashed a superb volley which screamed into the top of the net on the 19th minute.

It prompted Arsenal star Jack Wilshere, who netted a sublime goal in their 4-1 win over Norwich on Saturday and who was watching at home on TV, to tweet: "Well, there's my goal of the month prize gone."

This was a match which had been dubbed 'El Sackico' before kick-off, with both Holloway and Jol under pressure to get a result. Palace, second from bottom with just one win this season against fellow strugglers Sunderland, are now seven points from safety – and

VIKKI ORVICE

co-chairman Steve Parish's patience must surely be running out.

Victory at least ensured that Fulham, fourth from bottom before kick-off, climbed to 14th.

Jol said: "It was unbelievably important to get a result and for them it was a game of importance too. We needed the three points and are in a better position now.

Support

"I played Berbatov, Bent, Ruiz and Kasami at the same time and people knew before the season if it would be difficult to do that.

"But good players should play together and I was happy it came off. It's one of the best results in recent years. The owner is a happy man, too.

Midfielder Steve Sidwell, who bagged a brilliant second, added: "First of all it was a lot of hard work. Going one down so early was a blow, but we got the chances and took them."

After a 3-1 defeat at Anfield in

VERDICT **PALACE** were stopped in their tracks by not one, but two Fulham wonder goals after first taking an early lead.

Palace's last match before the international break, Holloway dropped Marouane Chamakh and Cameron Jerome and handed winger Yannick Bolasie his first Prem start to support Dwight Gayle.

It was the Eagles who started the brightest, Gayle shooting straight at Fulham No 1 Maarten Stekelenburg – back after injuring a shoulder on the opening day of the season.

And just six minutes later the home side took the lead.

Jose Campana picked up a half-cleared corner and fed Jason Puncheon, whose cross from the left found Adrian Mariappa.

The former Reading defender rose above Brede Hangeland and headed the ball into the net.

Palace were soon surging forward again, Stuart O'Keefe shooting wide. But then came Kasami's Marco van Basten-like spectacular to floor Holloway and the home fans.

The midfielder, who spent last season on loan back home at Luzern, almost got a second five

minutes later but his left-foot effort was blocked by Mile Jedinak.

Seconds before the break Sidwell scored another stunner.

Bolasie gave away a needless free-kick 20 yards out. Bryan Ruiz's set-piece hit the wall, but Sidwell fired the rebound into the top corner with the outside of his right foot.

Even a fire alarm, which forced stewards to clear the Selhurst Park executive boxes, could not prevent Fulham owner Shahid Khan from beaming as he watched on from the top of a stairwell.

Misery

Worse was to come for Palace five minutes after the restart.

Keeper Julian Speroni parried away an effort from Darren Bent only for Dimitar Berbatov to head in the resulting corner from Ruiz.

The Palace defence failed to learn and five minutes later conceded from another Ruiz corner, this time Philippe Senderos driving in a volley which crept over the line through the legs of Speroni.

To add to the home side's misery, Gayle had an effort disallowed for offside. And if you think Holloway's week cannot get any worse ... next up are table-topping Arsenal.

Tweet @vikkiorvice

they took the lead. Not that anyone appeared particularly bothered.

These comments were made as Crystal Palace took control of the opening 20 minutes at Selhurst Park. Pajtim Kasami (yes, yes, and you Steve Sidwell!) changed the mood in an instant, demoralising the home side and, as we took charge, highlighting how poor a side they were. Winning 4-1 away from home is a decent achievement, but just as we hoped that result would turn out to be our "hey presto" moment and a reality check that it takes hard work and a game plan to chisel out victories if wonderstrikes aren't forthcoming, so we headed off to play Southampton; with "play" being a gross misnomer, of course.

There was stuff going on that afternoon that wouldn't be tolerated by a badly hungover pub second XI on windswept Hackney Marshes. It's a serious slight to the supporters – particularly those hardy souls who regularly travel to away games. Just as our heroes are being handsomely rewarded for their so-called efforts, the fans (so desperate to back them to the hilt) are having to fork out ever-more exorbitant sums to watch what is currently the square root of not a lot. It all smacks of the Club's desperate days in the lower divisions when the most enjoyable part of a matchday was the pre-game gathering in the pub – so much so that on more than one occasion some guys cut out the "match" bit altogether on an awayday, tucked their tickets into an inside pocket and remained in the friendly confines of the pub, before getting news of the latest slap-dash showing and customary defeat as they boarded their transport home.

While making reference to those dismal days it's worth recounting the editorial words

of TOOFIF back then that defined a footballing crisis as being a time when the Club is seemingly on its last legs, languishing in the depths of the league with no money, no direction and virtually no hope. A genuine crisis is not simply losing a top-flight game here and there. It was a reaction to, if I recall, Spurs fans whingeing at their darlings having an uncomfortable time. It was toys out of pram stuff.

That's not the case in the here and now. This isn't a blip, it's been a steady disintegration of the codes and values laid down by previous managers. At the moment, if we don't get a wondergoal we ain't gonna win. And it's the manner of the defeats that is so hard to take. There seems to be an arrogant approach – get out there and strut your stuff; we're gifted footballers, we can walk the ball into the net at any time. Don't think so! One or two individuals are busting a gut for the cause (if you want names, I'd lob in Riether, Kasami, Sidwell and Parker), but it's a concerted team approach that is required, with an informed game plan together with a back-up Plan B. Stating the bleedin' obvious really, and yet the shambles in evidence on the field is every bit as obvious.

This is no knee-jerk reaction. At a recent game a guy near me in the Hammersmith End suggested a school report card on FFC would say: "Must try harder". His mate was a lot more damning; he snapped back that it was much more a case of "Must try".

Can't imagine Shahid Khan being too impressed with the negative vibes (even if he's somewhat used to it with the Jaguars!). The Club's new owner will surely get involved soon unless things improve sharpish. ⚽

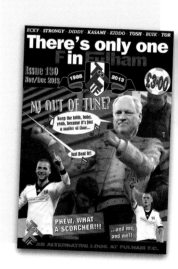

"We've Got Three Managers"

First that incongruous statue was shipped out; then the manager. While most of us probably wished the former had never been there in the first place, as 2013 drew to a close, it seemed remarkable that it was the statue that went first. Quite why Martin Jol and Fulham FC never worked out remains something of a mystery. The Dutchman's CV suggested he would do a decent job at Craven Cottage. And it wasn't as if he wasn't wanted (at least, to begin with!) – Jol had long been courted by Fulham, having been first-choice before the oh-so-ambitious Mark Hughes attempted to move the Club onwards and upwards following the departure of Roy Hodgson. Maybe Jol's plans for expansive football (and presumably expensive signings) was a step too far for a modest club such as ours?

We had our moments under Jol, of course we did; when it clicked there was a magical quality about our interplay. All that stardust disappeared a while back, though. I would track the first serious blip back to our feeble exit from the Europa League in December 2011. As with so many poor performances in the past 12 months, it wasn't the disappointment itself but the manner of it. After going two-up against Odense in the final group-stage game, we allowed a team that was already heading out of the competition to make it 2-2 with the last kick of the game. We'd somehow contrived to exit the tournament from a near-invincible position. Out with a whimper; and with barely a shrug of the shoulders.

And yet… At the start of 2012-13 Fulham FC were, in my humble opinion, just a couple of significant signings from being a top-eight side. Okay, so a key factor in making such a bold remark was that the Premier League comprised a fair few "iffy" teams. Even so, had we secured a Saha, Finnan or Malbranque (potent stars each, for relatively little outlay) then we may well have had the potential to go on to greater things. Instead, we lost Dempsey (at loggerheads with Jol) to Spurs, then Dembélé (on the verge of legendary status at FFC) also to Tottenham, and then our midfield linchpin and team leader Danny Murphy (arguably the greatest loss of the three, old legs and all, given his input and inspiration). Unfortunately, comparable replacements didn't materialise and the downward path was set in motion.

Far from lowering the average age of the squad as promised, Jol, given precious little money to spend – the sale of Dembélé alone brought in £15m – made us the oldest side in the Premier League. And, as discontent spread

across the squad, far from being golden oldies the vast majority displayed as much movement and verve as a geriatrics hospital ward XI. And with as much interest in team affairs as a startled group of pigeons, scattering to all points. Now this column concedes the Dutchman was given precious little money to spend – the 2011 purchase of Bryan Ruiz for £10.6m notwithstanding – but a manager's job is to make the most of what he has, not effectively throw in the towel.

Man-management didn't seem to be Jol's thing – rumours abounded about his fallings-out with players – and in the latter months of his tenure he didn't seem overly bothered about anything, an attitude matched by most of his players. Little wonder, then, that we slumped lower than Berba's shoulders and into the bottom three. Only the powers-that-be know why it took so long to take action. Maybe René Meulensteen's ultimately brief flirtation with Russian club Anzhi Makhachkala prevented an earlier appointment. However, the new man's eventual appointment, as assistant to Jol, seemed bizarre – all the more so given that Jol was sacked within days.

"It was a privilege to manage Fulham, one of the great clubs in the Premier League or anywhere in the world," said Jol after his dismissal. "I am disappointed in this season, but know there are better days ahead for Fulham and its supporters. I will always treasure my experience here and want to thank Mr Khan and everyone at Fulham for the opportunity." Gracious words indeed. Or some PR spin?

So it's welcome to René Meulensteen – and indeed to the other additions to the FFC

> *"We had our moments under Jol, of course we did; when it clicked there was a magical quality about our interplay. All that stardust disappeared a while back, though. I would track the first serious blip back to our feeble exit from the Europa League in December 2011."*

Right: FFC's three amigos – although they weren't around for long!

hierarchy: Alan Curbishley (technical director) and Ray Wilkins (assistant head coach). Welcome, too, to a brand new chant from the fans: "We've got three managers!" Mind you, after the Sunderland debacle it seemed a case of "too many cooks"!

And yet what an immediate turnaround when Meulensteen took over! Jol's final game in charge was a lamentable defeat at West Ham. But the difference was best gauged by two successive home defeats, both by two goals to one. No change in the number of points gained (zero, again), it's true, but at least the unlucky home loss to Tottenham paraded a regalvanised Fulham team that offered some hopeful pointers for the months ahead. Ten days previously we'd put on a leaden show as we slumped to a fifth successive defeat.

The above paragraph is in stating-the-bleedin'-obvious territory to anyone who was at the Cottage for both games. But the change in attitude only underlines how slack the previous regime had allowed things to become. And this malaise can be traced back to when we reached 40 points last season and then all but switched off – an outlook that saw us dragged back into the relegation battle. So much for putting on a show for the paying customers ("top-level footballers deserve their high wages because they're top-rate entertainers" goes the mantra; well, on what we've had to witness in 2013, you can file that one under "Bollocks"). So much for scrapping for every point in a professional manner. And so much for striving to get as high up the table as possible to earn maximum payback from the Premier League. But how dare we criticise; we're just the hapless souls who fork out to watch such rubbish week after week. Why should we expect a concerted effort in return? Why should we want players giving their all or looking as if they give a damn? Frankly, what we've been offered in return for our hard-earned cash for much of 2013 has been disgraceful.

Now here we are in 2014 perilously poised just one slot above the relegation places. Okay, grab a couple of victories and we'll move up a fair few places, but we've found it tough to win matches up to now, even under the new regime; so that's not a given. As this drivel heads off to the printers, we've not exactly been rolling out the black and white carpet to welcome new additions via the transfer window, have we? Maybe it'll all happen in the final 48 hours, but there's no doubt the squad could do with an injection of fresh blood and us supporters could do with a lift from that as well as an indication of how seriously the new owner is taking the threat of relegation.

One bonus has been the blooding of the youngsters. We may not have got the result we wanted at Bramall Lane in the FA Cup, but it was terrific to see the young lads performing so well. Muamer Tankovic was very cool in possession while Josh Passley and Ange-Freddy Plumain showed up well too. Ironic, though, that old boys Karagounis and emergency left-back Duff were our best players on the day.

Dan Burn has also come to the fore, not only looking assured but confident too. The return of Brede Hangeland, already looking a different player to the flaky version we witnessed last autumn, is both welcome and timely.

Main focus will have to be on performing well enough to not only stay in the top flight but to move up the table. That said, we now also have a wonderful opportunity to progress further in the FA Cup. Handled properly, we could use the whole experience to inject and impart that winning mentality, and the confidence that goes with it. We have three experienced men at the helm who should be able to use their collective nous to guide us to safety at the very least.

And a trip to Wembley would cheer us up no end, too. So no pressure, guys! ⚽

Dennis Turner 1946–2014

As Issue 131 was heading to the printers, so came the terrible news that Dennis Turner had passed away. Cue screech of breaks. If anyone merited an 11th-hour amendment in TOOFIF it was Fulham superfan Dennis: FFC Director, Author, Historian, Programme Editor, Supporter and, as far as I'm concerned, mentor and friend. Dennis would no doubt have managed such a "stop press" situation with much more aplomb than yours truly. So, if you're looking down from above, Dennis, apologies for the hurried approach! **DL**

Fulham has lost one of its finest sons just at the time we needed his peerless knowledge of our Club.

David Roodyn

I've got all his books! Real top quality, naturally. But the pinnacle for Dennis was being made a Director of Fulham; he absolutely loved it. It's a new owner's prerogative to change things around, and Dennis was disappointed to have to stand down, but he accepted the situation.

Dennis has written many a piece about me, and they were always funny. He loved Malcolm Macdonald's comment – "I made Strongy captain because he's so incredibly consistent: equally bad with either foot!" It cracked him up for some reason. Dennis and I would always talk in depth about what we thought was going wrong (or right!) at our favourite football club; and he never held back with his views.

Dennis was a wonderfully gifted speaker. Reasonably quiet and reserved away from the lectern, he really came into his own when called to deliver a speech. And on Fulham

Match	Date	Position
Fulham 1 Sunderland 4	11.01.14	16th
Arsenal 2 Fulham 0	18.01.14	17th
Swansea City 2 Fulham 0	28.01.14	17th
Fulham 0 Southampton 3	01.02.14	20th
Manchester United 2 Fulham 2	09.02.14	20th
Fulham 2 Liverpool 3	12.02.14	20th
West Bromwich Albion 1 Fulham 1	22.02.14	20th
Fulham 1 Chelsea 3	01.03.14	20th
Cardiff City 2 Fulham 1	08.03.14	20th

FA Cup		
Norwich City 1 Fulham 1	04.01.14	Round 3
Fulham 3 Norwich City 0	14.01.14	Round 3 replay
Sheffield United 1 Fulham 1	26.01.14	Round 4
Fulham 0 Sheffield United 1	04.02.14	Round 4 replay; aet

1st 2nd 3rd 4th 5th 6th 7th 8th 9th 10th 11th 12th 13th 14th 15th 16th 17th 18th 19th 20th

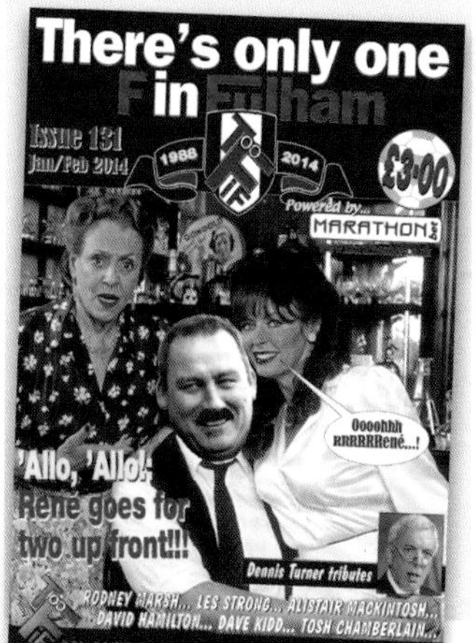

matters he could call on his vast historical knowledge. If anyone was synonymous with Fulham over the decades, I'd say that man was Dennis – a true Fulham man through and through, and a sad loss.

Les Strong

Dennis was a mentor to me after I joined the Fulham programme team in season 1983-84. Subsequently we worked together on several projects including the *Fulham Facts & Figures* book and *The Footballer* magazine, of which he was (naturally) editor. He was knowledgeable and opinionated in the areas of sport, music and politics. I was able to pay Dennis back for starting my sports-writing career by setting up an interview with one of his musical idols, singer-songwriter John Stewart. John, a former Kingston Trio member, was a member of Bobby Kennedy's entourage in 1968. Their one-hour slot developed into an afternoon, and he later said it was a memorable experience. Oh to have been a fly on the wall…

As a Board member, Dennis offered an impartial and Fulham-centred view. His knowledge and decorum will be much missed by the Club, as well as by his friends. A kind, honourable man.

Michael Heatley

Many years ago I wrote to the editor of the Fulham programme to complain about the standard of English in one of its articles. Two days later I was telephoned by a young man who worked in a bank. He told me he was the volunteer editor of the programme, and invited me to join the team. I happily agreed, and met Dennis Turner for the first time outside the Cottage the following Saturday. Those meetings, just outside or just inside the hallowed gates, were to be a regular part of my life on alternate Saturday afternoons during the season for a very long time.

I had never met anyone quite like Dennis. He was totally committed to the Fulham cause and even though he was to become a high-flying economist and had a variety of other interests, his enthusiasm for the Club, the programme, and the many Fulham books he went on to write, co-write and edit, never waned.

This high-flying economist and lecturer on matters financial, was rumoured to have a four-foot-high photograph of Johnny Haynes on his bedroom wall.

Dennis was determined that the Fulham programme would be the best in the country, and I believe he achieved his aim. Led by Dennis, the clutch of us who formed the writing team, certainly did our best. His enthusiasm was infectious.

Dennis Turner will be sadly missed. He was Fulham. Old Fulham. Real Fulham.

Chris Mason

Very sad news, and a real shock. I had the privilege of interviewing Dennis at his home last year for TOOFIF; his passion for our club was extraordinary, as was his knowledge of all things FFC. A true loss to the Club and generations of fans alike.

Mark Hillier

Like so many others, I was shocked to hear of the death of Dennis Turner. Only a few weeks ago we were chatting happily in the Riverside Stand, Dennis confirming to me that our game at Norwich on Boxing Day was Fulham's 4,000th league match, and he was the same Dennis Turner I'd known for many, many years. You'd have to go back a long way to find a Fulham programme without one of his articles in it. He was, of course, a former programme editor and also a director during the last years of Mohamed Al Fayed's ownership. As the Club's historian, he's written the definitive books about Fulham. *Fulham – A Complete Record*, and *Fulham Facts & Figures* are here on my bookshelf, a constant source of reference and useful information. Quite simply, he is irreplaceable.

David Hamilton

So sad to learn of the sudden passing of Club Historian and ex-Director Dennis Turner. I knew him for 35 years and worked with him on numerous FFC books: a perfectionist who wanted everything just right and who worked hard to achieve this; a real Fulham man whose knowledge of matches played over the years couldn't be surpassed. In his "spare" time he was HSBC chief economist and head of business development. RIP Dennis.

Dave Gardner

Dennis was a good friend and a true Fulhamite in every way. I'll always have a part of Dennis with me because there is a photograph that Fulham fans may remember from years ago of a special goal against Chesterfield at the Cottage. It's a Ken Coton special; I have it at home and it's a treasured possession. The picture shows the ball just over the line, but the top left-hand corner is obliterated by a black "smudge". You've guessed – just as the ball went in, a certain Mr Turner

Thank You

A big thank you to everyone who chipped in with advice and assistance after I was stopped from trading by the police before the Swansea City home game. What a nonsensical saga! A WPC, backed up by her male colleague, insisted that I needed a Street Traders' Licence; I insisted that I did not – that is unless there had been a change in the law in the previous few weeks.

However, it became a one-way conversation; I was told very pointedly that I was to be reported to Trading Standards. I'd had very little sleep for three days because of family health issues, and I admitted to being somewhat "crabby". I said that I'd nearly not turned up at all, but that having been made redundant I was relying on the sales of TOOFIF, however limited, to bring in some much-needed revenue before Christmas. All this fell on deaf ears.

Despite everything, I did not lose it; neither did I swear. Exasperated, I tried to point out that I'd been selling TOOFIF for more than 25 years and that, just supposing she was right, then that would mean someone hadn't been doing their job properly for around 700 home games! Unlikely, right? Didn't even seem to register.

Only about six or seven fellow fans saw and heard the whole episode play out, although many noticed as they passed. During the following week, though, I had countless messages of support, plus loads of surefire advice from Fulham-supporting policemen, legal-eagles and publishing folk. You see, nothing had changed: the vending of newspapers and periodicals remains one of the few exemptions, and you're free to go about your business unless you are causing an obstruction.

I wrote to the Borough Commander saying that, for the first time in years, I hadn't carried paperwork with me that substantiated the exemption because of the circumstances on the day. There was no legal requirement for me to do so; it was purely a safeguard. But there I was being told, bluntly, that I was guilty even though I'd not infringed anything. So much for basic rights.

I used the line that I'd been prevented from earning a legal pittance while the touts were seemingly given carte blanche to make their illegal fortunes.

The actions of that WPC had unpleasant consequences in the days that followed, so this wasn't something I was going to take lightly. Anyway, the excellent news is that the matters alluded to are much-improved by now, and that following a cordial meeting at Hammersmith Police Station the whole issue has now been sorted and an apology issued – and accepted.

Thanks again for the backing that came so swiftly plus the professional advice that arrived just as readily. It was very much my responsibility, and my "battle", but, once again, the Fulham "family" rallied around superbly.

---

decided to jump up, arms outstretched, and celebrate the goal wildly, and was caught by Ken on camera! So you see whenever I look at that photo I smile and think of a true Fulham legend who never even wore the shirt. Dennis you will be truly missed by all.

Gordon Davies

I'd known Dennis since I was a player at Fulham – yes, that long! He was "just" a fan in those days, but it was evident from our post-match conversations in the Riverside that he was deeply interested in the Club, its heritage and history. In time he'd be on the phone often, eager to prise some information or opinions for the matchday programme or one of his superb books, and he was kind enough to send me numerous photos taken during my time at the Cottage. It was such a shock to hear that he'd passed away – he was such a nice guy, a very understated person and was incredibly knowledgeable about all things Fulham.

It was Dennis who had the idea of putting on a special night at the Cottage for dear Roger Brown, shortly before Browny passed away. He let Strongy and I run the show on the night and we had a wonderful evening, raising a decent sum of money for Roger and his family as well as having a whole load of fun along the way – yes, Les and I played it for laughs, but I stress that the instigator was Dennis who, typically, kept in the background.

He was always bothered about the former players and was keen to keep them in the fold, inviting them back to the Cottage for games and organising numerous reunions. I'd say Dennis is right up there when you talk about the people that Fulham Football Club is all about; in fact, through his series of books, he probably earns the title of Mr Fulham. I didn't know he was a such a high-flier in the City until fairly recently – Dennis wasn't one to talk himself up – but having learned he was a Chief Analyst in the City you'd have to say that "Chief Analyst of Fulham Football Club's history" sits very nicely alongside his name too.

Tony Gale

Below: Gordon Davies steers home an amazing match-winner against Chesterfield from near the corner flag and ace lensman Ken Coton is there to capture it – complete with the flailing right arm of Dennis Turner!

Omnishambles!

It's fair to say that this season's not exactly gone to plan. And that's being generous in assuming that there was a plan in the first place. What a total shambles as FFC lurched from one indifferent performance to another, changing managerial personnel willy-nilly (no, that's not the name of the latest incumbent!) and, frankly, being perceived as something of a joke for acting out of desperation and in a most unFulham-like manner. In short, what a total PR disaster! Okay, so the ruthless discarding of René and co may yet – hopefully – save the day and, more importantly, our hard-earned top-flight status. But as things stand, I wouldn't bet on it. In fact, with another three points going down the drain after a limp showing against second-bottom Cardiff (our latest "must-win" encounter), all bets are now surely off.

Such ruthlessness should have been employed many months ago with the hapless Martin Jol having long outstayed his welcome. It seemed that with a Club takeover imminent no one wanted to be seen to rock the boat. And with the new owner in place, er, no one wanted to rock the boat. Still, no harm done with such a head-in-the-sand approach, eh? That is unless our Premier League berth counts for nothing. And what about us lot, the supporters, who have forked out enormous sums to follow our heroes, only to be rewarded with excruciatingly bad performances – many of them lacking the very basics in terms of heart, teamwork and tactics. We've suffered no end of slaps in the face and latterly have been on the receiving end of a deluge of mockery as the FFC Christmas panto nosedived into pure farce. Hmm, don't remember that being in the pre-season marketing guff imploring us to buy our season tickets.

Supporters are so very important when it suits the Club (or when the fans have taken it upon themselves to ensure there's still a club left to support), but when there's a moral duty to pass on information (the basics, not the stuff that's best kept at Boardroom level) then we're at the bottom of the pile it would seem. For example, there have been no updates this season – to my knowledge at least – regarding the proposed Riverside Stand, let alone some explanation about the extraordinary managerial merry-go-round – but, hey, you can get first-team replica shirts for a knockdown £20. If our downward trend continues the promised new stand won't be required anyway!

What hurts is that the current situation falls into the "utterly avoidable" category. Much has been made of the effort put in by the players in recent games. At West Brom, for example, several players made brave challenges as we tried in vain to hold on to our one-goal lead – Heitinger hurling himself at a goalbound shot is one determined block that springs to mind. But hang on: effort. Surely that is the very minimum they should be putting in? Every time they take to the pitch. Isn't that the ethos of a professional sportsman? Especially those earning absolute fortunes for performing in front of others who have shelled out relative fortunes to watch and support them. Dips in form and injury problems are one thing (two things, actually), but not being particularly bothered once you've put on the shirt is another matter entirely.

Had we shown such effort earlier in the season that would surely have been converted into more points – even if it would ultimately have turned out to be just papering over the underlying cracks. And that's without considering other fundamental aspects such as team selection and tactics – *whoever is in charge of the team.*

A club of Fulham's stature has no divine right to stay in the top flight. However, by putting in the hard work and making (on the whole) decent appointments we'd become an established Premier League outfit. That's no mean feat. Having done so, though, that's all been allowed to melt away with no one being apparently bothered. The thinking, it would seem, has been: "Okay, we might not be firing on all cylinders, but we'll be okay, there's always three clubs in a worse state than us." Wrong. And it's by no means been an overnight thing, either.

Funny how the media only latched on to our plight once we'd hit the bottom of the division and had played so appallingly against Sheffield United in the FA Cup, whereas the malaise has been in the camp for months. And it's been face-slappingly evident to all the regular supporters. A TOOFIF reader commented that most of today's sporting media are interested more in scandals and shocks than the sporting aspect itself. And it's hard to disagree.

Our standards have dropped alarmingly over a spell of months – think of that inexcusable, insipid display at The Loft last season, and the ensuing pathetic effort at Anfield, or consider how we got the beach towels out last spring once we'd reached 40 points, with almost dire consequences.

And remind me, how many managers ago was that? But, because Fulham FC don't sell papers, we, like so many other middling top-flight clubs, are broadly overlooked. Until there's major trouble afoot, that is, at which point the vultures

> *"A club of Fulham's stature has no divine right to stay in the top flight. However, by putting in the hard work and making (on the whole) decent appointments we'd become an established Premier League outfit. That's no mean feat."*

Below: The Club's outlay of £11.5m on the lesser-spotted Konstantinos Mitroglou was hardly money well spent. And it did nothing to halt our sorry slide into the Championship.

come a-hovering. But we're not "middling" any more, of course, and it now looks likely that we'll be ditching the "top flight" bit too. Unless Felix "We won't go down" Magath pulls off mission improbable.

Personally, I feel our supporters have been remarkably tolerant. Radio phone-ins go into meltdown when certain clubs lose two or three games; I'm pleased to say that we're a lot more dignified than that. We remain as fiercely ambitious as the next set of fans, but we retain our roots and rarely throw our toys out of the pram. Even then, it's generally no knee-jerk reaction but a reasoned plea for someone to listen to our plight. In this case, perhaps we should have shown our displeasure more vocally and much sooner; but then we also know that's not really the Fulham way and we've put our trust in the Board to iron out any awkward creases. After all, the Club had steered a comfortable course in recent seasons and, let's face it, Martin Jol seemed a great choice as Mark Hughes' replacement. But Jol's regime went pear-shaped a long while ago. Still we suffered in relative silence.

Our dignified patience counted for nothing, though. If slagging off the Club and its manager(s) at the merest upset is not the Fulham way of doing things, then neither is the farcical way we ditched Meulensteen, Wilkins and Curbishley. Magath's CV is as impressive as the tales of his fearsome reputation and he could yet save us. Up to now, though, he's struggled to get to grips with the requirements of the Premier League and the players at his disposal. Not really his fault, I suppose, having been dropped in to salvage a badly listing vessel, and yet if he doesn't pull it off you can't help but think that René had at least got to know his squad. Meulensteen patently should not have been appointed to the hotseat, and the fact that we were still letting in goals galore points to the fact that he probably wouldn't have kept us up either. But, by the same token, he might have. Instead, the new appointment has led to more turmoil, a further shuffling of the pack and, following that loss at Cardiff, Fulham FC losing ground at the foot of the division.

I guess with Meulensteen and co struggling to make any real impact, the FFC decision-makers were at that point of being damned if they do and damned if they don't. Most supporters are just damned angry that any damned decision wasn't taken a lot sooner.

Magath has been left with Meulensteen's squad – or at least one that René had tried, via the transfer window, to bolster and rejuvenate from the debris left by Jol. Don't know why, but the phrase "You can't polish a turd" comes to mind... You simply cannot expect Magath – or anyone – to hit the ground running in such circumstances.

Alas, we've not even seen the customary "new-manager" impact. Maybe that's because the players are still shell-shocked after just getting to know the previous new one (or three new ones!).

Clint Dempsey's loan spell was, unfortunately, a disaster. Having left the Club under a cloud to escape Jol, he's now left FFC for a second time having hardly been noticed. The downturn in the Club's fortunes is best epitomised by Dempsey who struggled to make any sort of impression against lowly League 1 opposition, whereas his greatest moment for Fulham was that wonderful goal in that remarkable team effort against Juventus. Oh yes, times have changed all right. Meantime, that League 1 side, Sheffield United, have just reached the FA Cup semi-finals. Hey-ho!

So, who's the new Clint Dempsey? Well, one of the new arrivals is Greek. An acknowledged goal machine with Champions League pedigree. Our potential saviour. Glory be; we're gonna be okay after all. So what if he cost us a record sum? Around 12 million quid? Pah: that'll be deemed peanuts when he keeps us up in the big-business enterprise that is the English Premier League. Eh, what's that? He's injured? Or not match fit – or not up to the rigours and intensity of the Premier League? Especially a hurly-burly relegation scrap. Un-bloody-believable! Who countenanced that one, then?

It's not the fault of Kostas Mitroglou; it's down to whoever got him to sign on the dotted line. Whatever happened to the famous Fulham FC medical? As somebody, somewhere, once said: "You couldn't make it up."

Now that we're properly in the brown stuff, the Club's PR machine has suddenly gone into overdrive. Subsidised travel, uplifting messages from the players, free t-shirts (given away at Cardiff), an acceptance that our vociferous support can serve as the team's "12th man", oh yes, and we all still BELIEVE... Brilliant, of course. And full marks for whoever's coming up with such initiatives, any initiatives. But where the hell was this PR machinery and the acknowledgement that the fans matter earlier in the season? We've been here for the duration you know. Having met several marathonbet folk recently, I can vouch that they truly want to engage with the Fulham fans. It can't be an easy job when the showcase, on-field affairs are going so poorly. We're not down as yet, and a win over Newcastle may raise our hopes once more, but I'm sure I can hear Beth Ditto gargling.

TOOFIF regulars (both of you!) will recognise the tone of this editorial is unusually stern, but in the words of Roy "Catchphrase" Walker: "Just say what you see." It's not been fun watching Fulham fall apart this season. Especially when it could all have been checked a while back. ⚽

Fulham 1 Newcastle United 0 15.03.14 20th	1st 2nd 3rd
Manchester City 5 Fulham 0 22.03.14 20th	4th 5th
Fulham 1 Everton 3 30.03.14 20th	6th 7th
Aston Villa 1 Fulham 2 05.04.14 18th	8th 9th
Fulham 1 Norwich City 0 12.04.14 18th	10th 11th
Tottenham Hotspur 1 Fulham 0 19.04.14 19th	12th 13th
Fulham 2 Hull City 2 26.04.14 18th	14th 15th
Stoke City 4 Fulham 1 03.05.14 19th	16th 17th
Fulham 2 Crystal Palace 2 11.05.14 19th	**18th** 19th 20th

There's only one F in Fulham

Issue 132
Mar/Apr 2014
£3.00

What a F*#!%$ OMNISHAMBLES!!!
FFC RIGHT IN THE THICK OF IT!
AN ALTERNATIVE LOOK AT FULHAM FC

Dear Chairman...

An open letter to Shahid Khan:

Can't imagine you'll ever get to see this, Mr Khan, or if you do that it'll make a smidgen of difference, but here goes. What the hell happened last season? And is there any chance of getting OUR Fulham back?

This is no wild-eyed rant from an occasional fan, it's more of a heartfelt plea from a regular supporter who rarely gets over-emotive or angry when watching a game of football. Someone who, like thousands of others, handed over a sizeable wedge of hard-earned cash to witness last season's pitiful efforts on (and off) the pitch. In some cases "efforts" was very much a misnomer. But yes, I'd say "angry" sums it up rather well.

With the new season now upon us – and yes, I've renewed my season ticket – it could well be that all is now in order; that Felix Magath has brought together a squad of players who are worthy of wearing our shirt and are prepared to give maximum effort; and that the apparent disharmony within the camp is a thing of the past. Hope so.

Looking into the past is often a futile exercise, since nothing can be changed, even if lessons can be learned. Yet all through last season (at which point it was "the present" not "the past"!) there was barely any evidence that anyone at FFC cared a jot. That there was a steady hand on the tiller. That someone was in control. That OUR Fulham was in safe hands. For a club of our scale, relegation from the top flight can never be summarily dismissed, but this one was wholly avoidable. We went down with barely a whimper and with tensions all too apparent. So this is one perennially supportive punter who still needs convincing, given that it's the same set of decision-makers at the helm.

Magath had comparatively precious little time to reverse the downward trend initiated by previous managerial regimes, along with the general malaise that seemed to have escaped the attention of everyone at the Club. Bar us lot watching week in, week out. But with a clutch of other clubs also seemingly hell-bent on self-destruction (and with Norwich having the nightmare of Premier League run-ins) we had enough chances – undeservedly so, many might say – to stay up.

With the margins so very tight it all came down to a goal or two in the end. Even so, it was at that point still a whole lot easier to make a real fist of trying to stay up than hope to return via a successful campaign with a revamped squad in the Championship, a notoriously difficult division to contest and from which to gain promotion.

As things turned out, we still had a glimmer of a chance of staying up as late as the Stoke game. Has there ever been a more embarrassing capitulation in what was an absolutely final "must-win" fixture? And what on earth was the game Dan Burn, a left-footed, gangly centre-half, doing at right-back? That ploy didn't work as the Stoke winger had a field day. What about switching Burn with Heitinger? What about bringing on Reither, a right-back for heaven's sake? Oh well, what do we know...?

This magazine's editorial has invariably been optimistic, and particularly so on the eve of a new campaign. It's that time of year when supporters of clubs up and down the country, in whatever division, are hoping that maybe, just maybe, this could be their year. When, just perhaps, a modicum of success can come their way.

Success can be measured in so many ways. At Fulham we've never expected a cabinet full of silverware – hoped for, yes, but never expected. No, success for us supporters has been measured over the past couple of decades in varying degrees. For a while it was having a club to support at all, as all the signs in the early '90s seemed to be pointing towards "oblivion". With that as a worst-case scenario, it was sheer bliss to watch Micky Adams' side pull together, scrap for their lives and gain promotion from the bottom tier. That's success. In the ensuing years, by now backed by Mohamed Al Fayed, we enjoyed a magnificent surge back to the top flight of the English game via the exciting football under Kevin Keegan and the brilliance of Jean Tigana's promotion side – breaking numerous records in so doing. That's success.

Along the way we regained ownership of the Craven Cottage site and the ground received a much-needed revamp. That's success.

Staying in the Premier League for 13 seasons is, in itself, a huge achievement for a club of our scale and recent history. Getting to the final of a major European competition – and thereby spreading the name of Fulham FC and making more and more friends around the globe – was something quite extraordinary and something we'd all love to repeat some day. That's success. Naturally, we yearn for more of the same, but we don't expect it as a right.

What we do expect, though, is a group of players worthy of wearing the shirt. A manager who not only shows that he is passionate about the job in hand, but who also has the man-management skills and footballing expertise to forge a meaningful team spirit and who has the respect of the players (they don't have to like him!!) – and who also knows that the Chairman and other powers-that-be are helping rather than hindering him.

Reaching that Europa League final with Roy Hodgson at the helm was extraordinary. Things were far from perfect at Fulham under the current

> *"With the margins so very tight it all came down to a goal or two in the end. Even so, it was at that point still a whole lot easier to make a real fist of trying to stay up than hope to return via a successful campaign with a revamped squad in the Championship, a notoriously difficult division to contest and from which to gain promotion."*

England boss; it's sometimes easy to forget the many poor away showings in the League, for example, given the obvious highlights, but the general trend of onwards and upwards wasn't an overnight thing. The squad evolved under Hodgson through hard graft, organisation and a brilliant team ethic. On an individual basis you could see players improve and grow in stature and confidence by the week. All of which is the complete antithesis of last season's omnishambles.

At the start of last season, Mr Chairman, you promised that: "We are about to write a new chapter in the story of Fulham"; well meant, no doubt, but words that now smack of a previous Chairman's comment when we were last relegated from the top flight. In 1968, Tommy Trinder promised we'd only be in the second tier for a single season. He was right – we fell straight through the trapdoor into the third!

You also mentioned last summer that the fans and the Club should have "goals that are meaningful and attainable, on and off the pitch." Far be it for me to be churlish here, but dare I suggest that relegation, while very much "attainable", shouldn't be one of those "meaningful goals".

You added: "A wonderful journey is ahead for all of us." Okay, I'm rubbing it in now, but last season was anything but wonderful. As it transpired, the awful end result was wholly avoidable – and the "journey" was so depressing. There's us screaming for a left or right turn, but the Club refused to change course and over the edge we went.

Over the course of our 13-year tenure in the top division we had, with a couple of scares admittedly, managed to create a successful template for how a progressive, medium-sized club could not only survive but thrive in the Premier League. Far from being smug, we even thought of ourselves as established in the top flight. And yet all of that was undone at a stroke. And, regrettably, in a most unFulham-like way. Those ideals were merely tossed aside as cock-up followed cock-up; no one to blame, apparently, hey-ho, slight shrug of the shoulders, these things happen.

A clean slate, then, for 2014-15, albeit with the same senior management figures at the Club. I shall be supporting FFC with the same vigour and enthusiasm as in previous seasons. Despite the overriding gloom of these notes, there's much to look forward to – not least not having to put up with the massive hype, big business and basic bollocks of the Premier League (even if that's the place to be if you want to mix it with the best). There'll be plenty of other grounds to visit, some for the first time. We have a group of exciting youngsters coming through, each eager to make their mark. Pre-season games have suggested we'll be playing at a much higher tempo and with more smart interplay and passion than last term (not too difficult!!). And, of course, we'll be incredibly fit!

The signing of Ross McCormack from Leeds for a reported £11m looks to be far better business that our previous £11m buy who only seems to be fit when Greece have World Cup fixtures to play. What the hell was that all about? Oops, another "cock-up" reference; sorry! Anyway, if we now have a squad of players who are willing to run through brick walls for this manager (they probably do so every day in training if reports are true!), then it might well be fun to watch Fulham once again. That's the hope. That's a measure of success.

I'm desperately hoping the current regime is determined to make the best of what we have. And then to improve it. No more self-implosions. No more rancour. No more half-arsed performances. Oh, and a few wins would be nice. In short, I want our Fulham back. Surely that's not too much to ask?

David Lloyd, Editor, TOOFIF

A bit of a rant above, but hey-ho. Welcome to a new season, in the Championship! It could well be that Felix Magath is the man to get our great Club back on its feet; it could be that the introduction of youth (thanks to our excellent Academy) is indeed the way forward; it could be that everything in the Cottage garden is actually rosy.

A 2-1 defeat at Portman Road wasn't the ideal way to kick things off. There were flashes of promise as well as warning signs. We had lots of possession – some of the interplay was slick, confident and showed no little skill – but we barely troubled their keeper. Ipswich, by contrast, got stuck in, closed us down well and, while looking fairly ordinary, made the most of their experience in this division. It was men against boys at times.

Pat Roberts gave us a terrific late cameo that almost earned a draw, while Emerson Hyndman had a fine debut in the middle of the park. Fielding eight debutants didn't bode well for a fluid start and, despite all good intentions, the goals we conceded were poor and highlighted our naïvety.

By now I'm all sweetness and light, though. I'm a changed man, having been instructed by that most learned of journos, Darren Lewis of *The Mirror*, during a chat on LBC, not to display negative emotions. FFC life is good, I was told – nothing to be angry about. Course not! The pompous Lewis only wanted to discuss one set of opinions: his own! He continued to slag me off on air after I'd put the phone down. And all because I dared to have an opinion that didn't match his. There was no debate, no discussion. He was the expert; he knew Fulham; and everything was okay. Okay, let's see shall wc, Mr Lewis?

Here's to a few more smiles returning to our faces this season. Here's to a whole lot of positive emotions around Craven Cottage. And here's to all at Fulham Football Club realising their mistakes and getting it right. Okay, take it from the top, Mr Chairman! ⚽

Ipswich Town 2 Fulham 1	
09.08.14	17th
Fulham 0 Millwall 1	
16.08.14	21st
Fulham 0 Wolverhampton Wanderers 1	
20.08.14	23rd
Derby County 5 Fulham 1	
23.08.14	24th
Fulham 1 Cardiff City 1	
30.08.14	23rd
Reading 3 Fulham 0	
13.09.14	24th
Nottingham Forest 5 Fulham 3	
17.09.14	24th
Fulham 0 Blackburn Rovers 1	
20.09.14	24th
Birmingham City 1 Fulham 2	
27.09.14	23rd
Fulham 4 Bolton Wanderers 0	
01.10.14	22nd
Middlesbrough 2 Fulham 0	
04.10.14	22nd
League Cup	
Brentford 0 Fulham 1	
26.08.14	Round 2
Fulham 2 Doncaster Rovers 1	
23.09.14	Round 3

1st
2nd
3rd
4th
5th
6th
7th
8th
9th
10th
11th
12th
13th
14th
15th
16th
17th
18th
19th
20th
21th
22th
23th
24th

Jimmy Conway

Forty years ago Fulham FC were about to embark on a meandering path to their only FA Cup final appearance; two goals from West Ham's Alan Taylor ultimately quashed the Whites' dreams at Wembley in May 1975. That was also the year that Portland Timbers made their bow in the North American Soccer League. With neat symmetry, the Oregon franchise reached Soccer Bowl '75 only to go down by the same 2-0 scoreline to the Tampa Bay Rowdies.

What links those seemingly disparate statements is Jimmy Conway, a distinguished performer for Fulham from 1966 to 1976 and who later played out his footballing career in Portland. Seasoned Fulham supporters will remember Jimmy as a scheming top-flight inside-forward who was transformed into a flying winger when the Club dropped a couple of divisions. And the Whites' icon went on to become every bit as popular in the States where he settled with his wife Noeleen.

So it's tough to acknowledge that the once super-fit Jimmy has entered the latter stages of dementia and no longer recognizes family or friends. Jimmy's former Timbers team-mate Mick Hoban became more of a soul-mate as the devastating condition took a grip. Jimmy and Mick

are two of the more notable figures in Timbers' history – team-mates who became pals after their footballing careers, casual and cordial to begin with, but now tied by something much deeper. "Noeleen asked if I'd speak with his then employer – Oregon Youth Soccer Association [OYSA] – about his condition, 'Trauma Induced Dementia' which had been diagnosed in late 2009," explains Mick. "I met the OYSA and promised Noeleen I'd make sure Jimmy was treated appropriately for someone who, by then, had been State Coach for more than 28 years. From there I pulled together a 12-strong volunteer committee and we planned Jimmy's 'Testimonial', which took place in 2010.

"From the off, Noeleen insisted that all the money raised should go towards research into dementia. We raised $21,000 from the testimonial activities, which was presented to the Alzheimer's Association. Since then we've participated in the annual 'Walk to End Alzheimer's' and have raised more than $50,000 over the past five years."

Mick, who hails from Staffordshire, was a decent midfielder himself. He was on Aston Villa's books although the nearest he got to a first-team spot for Villa was being an unused substitute against, of all clubs, Fulham at the Cottage in November 1970.

Above: One for the family album – Jimmy Conway (*left*) is joined by brother John.

Below: Mick Hoban, a former team-mate of Jimmy's at Portland Timbers, has been instrumental in drumming up support for Jimmy and his family once our former winger's health began to deteriorate.

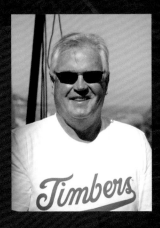

He moved to Atlanta Chiefs and in 1973 was called up to the US national team.

"When a good friend, Noeleen Conway, asked us for help we did what any good friends would do," says Mick. "Personally, I did it because Jimmy has done so much for soccer in Oregon. He did so without any fuss. He didn't ask for any recognition. And he broke new ground in many ways, such as establishing coaching licenses and managing college programs.

"Jimmy was, and still is, the epitome of a Football Man. He loved his game. He excelled at it. Plus he had the knack of infusing others with the same level of passion and commitment. On top of this he was a good mate with a wicked sense of humour and was a truly great family man."

Mick recalls that while Jimmy was an "intense player" and deeply professional. "Jimmy arrived in Portland as an outstanding, accomplished International. As such, along with Clyde Best (ex-West Ham), he was the equivalent to what is called a 'Designated Player' in Major League Soccer today. There was no such designation back then.

"Jimmy was a quick player who was economical in his use of the ball (he didn't like to give it away!). He had a low centre of gravity, quick feet and good acceleration, which could take him past a defender, usually on the right wing, to deliver crosses. Jimmy loved the heat of battle and was no shrinking violet.

"He was, all too briefly, a team-mate of mine in 1978 and right from the start he took his role as a 'senior player' very seriously and would spend lots of time with his younger team-mates, including me, encouraging and advising us on our play."

Jimmy took that professional approach into coaching – in that unassuming way of his. "There's no doubt that Jimmy was an 'old school' coach, says Mick. "He believed in discipline, organisation and team-work. He didn't take too warmly to those who weren't willing to 'put in a shift'. Jimmy also believed in a certain distance between a coach and his players. He wasn't looking to be their friend; he was only interested in being their coach.

"Having said all of that, each year at the Walk to End Alzheimer's we have many of Jimmy's former players who talk warmly about how he helped them both on and off the field. They speak passionately of his integrity, fervour, humour and that tough love."

As a player, Jimmy Conway was never one to boast about his footballing achievements nor his pile of international caps for the Republic of Ireland, but, if pressed, was happy to reflect on his wonderful decade at Craven Cottage. "He often spoke about what he and Noeleen described as his most happy and productive period in his career in the UK," says Mick Hoban. "The friendly fans. That historic and 'quaint' stadium by the banks of the Thames. The great players as team-mates. I'd often ask him about playing alongside Bobby Moore,

Alan Mullery and other 'greats' and his face would light up when he recalled stories of their tours, training and matches.

"I was about 26 when Jimmy, five years older and much more experienced, arrived in Portland," acknowledges Mick. "We called him 'Peter Perfect'! People couldn't believe the degree to which he was just a regular guy – he didn't drink; he didn't smoke; he didn't chase women. The rest of us, we all had our foibles. Even so it wasn't like Jimmy was priestly, or in any way aloof. He was the epitome of a damned good pro!"

Big Brother

It's something of a rarity to have a pair of brothers playing for the same football club. However, five Conway brothers turned out for Bohemian FC in Dublin, although not all at once – and two, Jimmy and John Conway went on to play for Fulham.

Jimmy, originally an inside-forward, became a well-established figure at Craven Cottage, playing in the old First Division alongside former England captain Johnny Haynes, future England manager Bobby Robson and 1966 World Cup-winner George Cohen in the sixties. He was subsequently a key member of the Second Division team that reached the FA Cup final in 1975.

Four years before Fulham's trip to Wembley, Jimmy had been joined at the Cottage by younger brother John, a talented winger who'd won the FAI Cup with "the Bohs" in 1970 before going on to make a couple of appearances in the UEFA Cup Winners Cup against Czech side FASTAV Zlín.

Former Fulham team-mate Les Strong remembers the duo well. "Jimmy's a legend at the Cottage and was the quiet type who did his talking on the pitch. He provided no end of memorable moments in his ten years at Fulham. It's such a shame he's not in the best of shape at the moment.

"John was in the same mould as Jimmy, an excellent wide midfielder, but more slight in build and unfortunate with injuries in his time with us. John respected his elder brother for his impact in the game and for playing for his country; the pair came from a very good family background.

"I became good friends with John. I holidayed with him, a friend of his and our team-mate John Richardson. All four of us squashed into a VW Beetle with four lots of luggage; it was cosy! And boy, John could talk – oh yes, pretty much non-stop all the way from England to Southern Italy!"

Above: Jimmy was proud to play International football for the Republic of Ireland. He's pictured here at the Cottage in the team's kit for a photo that graced the cover of the *Jimmy Conway Football Annual*, no less!

> *"As a player, Jimmy Conway was never one to boast about his footballing achievements nor his pile of international caps for the Republic of Ireland, but, if pressed, was happy to reflect on his wonderful decade at Craven Cottage."*

"Jimmy scored a spectacular goal on his Fulham debut as the Whites secured a 5-1 victory over Wolves in the League Cup in October 1966, and retained his place to make his first League outing in a 2-2 draw with Liverpool at Anfield."

The Conways hail from Cabra, a suburb to the north-west of Dublin. Little did parents James and Mary Conway realise that they'd be responsible for not only raising a grand Irish family but also for establishing a footballing dynasty that would make its mark at home and abroad. "My mother was, and is, an angel, says John Conway, these days a Master Goldsmith based in Lörrach, southwest Germany. "Unfortunately she suffers from the same type of sickness that has latterly affected Jimmy, and is in a home. Back then she was not only our queen but was also the king of the family in many ways."

James Senior ensured his boys were brought up to play football the right way. "My father was a huge influence," confirms John. "He was very strict about how we should play the game, and drummed it into us that we should be disciplined and do things properly." That approach paid dividends and Bohemian FC reaped the benefit. "Tom, a left-back, played for Athlone Town and Bohemians, Paddy was another left-back, and Roddy was a winger, while Jimmy, an inside-forward later converted to a winger, was the pick of the bunch," adds John who joined the Bohs in 1969.

"It was always Jimmy's aim to make it in England. Football was in our blood, and to succeed the next step up was England. Jimmy was a schoolboy International and had a several trials with English clubs, including one with Manchester United. Jimmy started it all for us; seeing him playing for his country from the age of 14 gave us an immense source of pride. He had three years with the Bohs before moving to London. By the time Jimmy joined First Division Fulham in 1966 and made the first team, he was a big, big star in Ireland."

Jimmy scored a spectacular goal on his Fulham debut as the Whites secured a 5-1 victory over Wolves in the League Cup in October 1966, and retained his place to make his first League outing in a 2-2 draw with Liverpool at Anfield.

John, five years Jimmy's junior, was following in his footsteps. "People said at the time that I was just as talented as Jimmy, but I guess I'm made a little differently. Jimmy was totally focused and committed to football and his career, whereas I didn't quite have that level of commitment; even then, I was keen to do other things in life.

"Let me explain it this way. When I was at Fulham I shared digs with a seasoned centre-back called Reg Matthewson. Or to put it another way, Reg thought I was popping down to the pub rather too often and, after having a word in my ear, he suggested I move in with him! Reg was a lovely and genuine chap and they were great times. Jimmy, meantime, was famously teetotal."

It wasn't long before Jimmy gained his first cap for the Republic of Ireland, against Spain in the European Nations Cup. "It was quite a moment for the family, let alone for Jimmy himself," says John. "There were a number of top Irish players

in the English top division – and at Fulham there was Turlough O'Connor, who'd travelled over with Jimmy, John Dempsey, who also made his senior debut in that match against Spain, plus Jimmy Dunne, a hugely under-rated centre-back.

"Jimmy became a firm part of the Irish scene, one of the first names on the team-sheet, at least until Johnny Giles took over as manager. It was difficult to ruffle Jimmy – he was so professional that he'd go along with any team instructions. But he found things difficult under Giles."

Even so, in a 12-year International career during which the Republic played far fewer matches than nowadays, Jimmy made 23 senior appearances (that total includes a couple of amateur/unofficial fixtures). Along with Dempsey and O'Connor, he was in the Irish side that scored a shock 2-1 away win in Czechoslovakia in November 1967. Jimmy scored a belter in West Berlin against West Germany in May 1970 and was on target against Italy at Lansdowne Road a year later, although the Irish lost both games 2-1. By the time he finally stepped down from International football in 1977, Jimmy was his country's 18th most-capped player.

Fulham, meantime, slipped out of the top flight – Jimmy scored their last First Division goal in a 5-1 defeat at Everton. And a season later they were in Division Three! Fulham manager Bill Dodgin converted Jimmy into an out-and-out right-winger at the start of the 1969-70 campaign and unleashed him and left-winger Les Barrett down the flanks. Striker Steve Earle was a major beneficiary – the trio were known as the "Three Musketeers" – and both Earle and Conway scored 23 times that season. For the second time in three campaigns Jimmy Conway was ever-present for the Cottagers.

During an eight-game run early in that season Jimmy netted 11 times – the run included an 8-0 away win at Halifax in which Earle scored five and Conway twice. As a consequence the talented musketeers were targeted by rugged Third Division defenders and Conway suffered as much as anyone. A knee injury resulted in three months on the sidelines and a cartilage operation. In due course, Fulham won promotion in 1971, gained another Conway (John) that summer and appointed a new manager, Alec Stock, within 12 months.

"Fulham was a happy-go-lucky club," admits John Conway. "A couple of good wins here and there to keep us in the middle of the Second Division pack and some entertaining performances seemed to be the main goals. No one talked about promotion; that sort of ambition wasn't there, not even when Bobby Moore came to the Club. It was a homely club and a lovely place to be playing your football, but without any real direction."

Jimmy Conway racked up 360 appearances for Fulham – during which he was never cautioned or sent off. He weighed in with 76 goals and was a huge favourite of the Fulham fans. Even nowadays

Trauma Induced Dementia

Noeleen Conway, Jimmy's wife, says: "Jimmy's diagnosis is Trauma Induced Dementia. It became apparent in his 50s and was caused by injuries he received while playing football. I don't think there is enough research being done to look into this. Traumatic brain injury is very, very real – the main causes are concussions and repeated blows to the head. In those days the leather footballs were laced and not waterproof; they became very heavy in the rain or when caked in mud.

"Hopefully, some time soon, the football community will address this issue more seriously and publicly. The American NFL have had to acknowledge this and there is certainly a case to be made for football (soccer) to do so too."

In the UK, the issue has gained more prominence thanks to the campaigning work done by the family of West Brom legend Jeff Astle, who died in 2002 aged 59 as a result of degenerative brain disease (DBD).

Under the banner "Justice for Jeff", the family are urging for more research into the matter. As Jeff Astle's daughter, Dawn, says: "The Football Association and Professional Footballers' Association promised to conduct a ten-year joint study into DBD and the medical links associated with head trauma through heading footballs. Twelve years on, this research has never been concluded or published." Baggies fans have responded by holding a minute's applause in the ninth minute (Astle was a typically brave no.9) of each of their Premier League games.

"Jimmy loved every minute of his career – minus the injuries," says Noeleen Conway. "I don't think that even given a crystal ball he'd have changed anything. I'll always be grateful that football gave us opportunities we might otherwise never have had; however, the toll it has taken on us has been devastating. Dementia, Alzheimer's, call it what you will, has generally been associated with older folk; clearly with Traumatic Brain Injury this isn't the case."We still do the "Walk to End Alzheimer's" event here in Portland each year to raise money and awareness. Mick Hoban, a friend and former team-mate of Jimmy's, spearheads this effort wonderfully. He keeps the Facebook page – Fans of Jimmy Conway – current with details.

"Sometimes I look at Jimmy's eyes and it's like someone's pulled the shades down," Noeleen admits. "And that's the hardest part. We've been married for 45 years. We worked together. We were in each other's pockets 24/7. And he just went away... but he is still here – and he'll always be my funny, handsome guy."

you'll still hear the occasional rendition of "We've got Jimmy, Jimmy, Jimmy, Jimmy Conway on the wing, on the wing…" from the Fulham faithful at Craven Cottage. He had a 13-game stint at Manchester City before heading with wife Noeleen to Portland in Oregon in 1978, first as a player but ultimately as a coach. The couple have three children, Paul, Laura and Mark – Paul played over a hundred games for Carlisle United in the 1990s before finishing his career at Portland in 2005, Jimmy's final season as assistant coach at the club.

John never made the same impact at Fulham as his big brother – mainly due to injuries and the fact that he was often competing for the same shirt. "I made 37 starts for Fulham [plus eight outings as a sub]," he recalls, "and remember scoring twice at Portsmouth to secure a 2-1 win in 1975, but I think my best game was one of my last – in the FA Cup third round replay at Hull. I was buzzing at that time and full of confidence having had a decent run of games. It was great to know that I was likely to be in the team each week, and it was also great to be playing in the same side as my big brother. I set up our first goal for Viv Busby at Hull and could have had a hat-trick. The match finished 2-2; another replay on the road to Wembley. But that was my last game in the FA Cup.

"I had another good game in December 1973 away at Sheffield Wednesday. I scored the first goal as we ran out 3-0 winners. But things didn't always go to plan – I broke my arm at Bristol City and as soon as I came back got a bad knee injury at Cardiff. I suppose I should be flattered that the

Cardiff player went out to get me – and he got me all right! "I did well enough at Fulham to be invited along by Johnny Giles to the Republic of Ireland training sessions but he never picked me for any squads, more's the pity. We clashed to be honest. I could see why Jimmy, who's so much calmer than me, had been upset by him previously. As my later business life has proved I'm more of an individual than an integrated team player – that's my character, that's how it is. I was more than happy to do my bit and more for any team, but I was never keen on being dictated to."

"Nowadays Jimmy is struggling with Trauma Induced Dementia, and it's such a shame. Take the brotherly thing out of the equation: if there's one guy who deserved to get older gracefully and enjoy his later years then it's Jimmy. He's always been 'the good guy', the genial, likeable fella who's lived his life by the rules, the ultimate footballing professional who kept himself in fantastic shape – he's always been ready and willing to help out anyone, any time, and despite being brilliant at what he did, he's always shunned the spotlight.

"Jimmy suffered some horrific injuries, and had lost some of his lightning speed in his last few seasons at Fulham. But he readjusted, went back to his original position of inside-forward, and just got on with it. The shame was that we didn't play too many times in the same Fulham side. But when we did we enjoyed it. Now and again we'd link up almost magically – one of us would do something 'blind' and it would come off because of an innate understanding." ⚽

Above: Noeleen Conway looks lovingly at husband Jimmy – "my funny, handsome guy" – at a charity gathering.

Below: A snapshot of Jimmy playing indoor football for Portland.

Hopping Mad

It'll never be proven, but it's hard to imagine that René Meulensteen and his management team would have served Fulham as disastrously as Felix Magath and Co have done had they been given the chance. If only the German megalomaniac was afforded the same short shrift as René we may not have tumbled so far as we undoubtedly have. Still, we don't make the decisions, do we?

A further painful glance back at last season and you'll recall that, despite our short-comings and a campaign chock-full of cock-ups, we were somehow still in with a chance of staying up as the other teams around us continued to flounder. Surely Meulensteen, with or without his cohorts, would have conjured a better points-return than Magath managed. If so, and with margins so tight (except where our goal difference was concerned!), the former Man. United man could well have kept us up. It "only" needed a point or two here and there.

Conjecture? Of course it is. But there's no doubt the spirit in the camp would have been much higher under Meulensteen, dismissed after just 75 days, than Magath. What better way to foster unity, team spirit and a never-say-die attitude in a struggling football team than to alienate most (all?) of those around you. And that's before we go anywhere near the basics of team selection and tactics!

Also not up for debate, is that "Mad Mag" was allowed more rope, more time and more control than his predecessor – which he utilised to make an already bad situation very much worse. And yet, despite everything, no one intervened until we'd not only dropped a division but had slumped to the bottom of the Championship – and after the close of another transfer window thereby shackling any new boss. Nothing should surprise us given the past couple of years I suppose, but this was straying into "You couldn't make it up" territory!

This is no cute, wise-after-the-event summation. Things have stunk of a whole lot more than a slab of overripe cheese for months and months. And even discounting the ever-more bizarre tales leaking from Motspur Park, the evidence was there for all of us regular fans to see week after week. And all rubberstamped by our pitiful league position.

And there's the rub. Apart from the tiny minority of supporters with inside knowledge by whatever means, the vast majority had no idea of what was really happening, of who is actually pulling the strings and who is responsible for the spectacular downturn of fortunes. But the evidence was there for all to see – on the field of play, in our goals against column and in our ever-lower League position.

Very much in the know were the players, and a number of those who departed the sinking ship – some having been forced to walk the plank – vented their feelings. It made for desperately sorry reading and yet only reinforced what we'd suspected for some time. Fulham FC, Europa League finalists in 2010 and, for a brief time at least, the darlings of Europe, had been allowed to implode. Now, though, rather than being darlings of Europe, nobody seems to give a jot.

Except the fans. It was hardly surprising the troops were getting restless. But who could they get restless with? General debate on social media quickly turned into arguments, some of which became trashy slanging matches. But with so many of the highly charged opinions based on supposition and, frankly, guesswork, how could any decent conclusion be approached anyway?

It was all Mackintosh's fault. Possibly. But then had he been squeezed out of the loop? *It's all down to Khan.* Again, a good shout, but surely the CEO must have countenanced the managerial appointments? *How could Mackintosh get the signing of Mitroglou so wrong?* How indeed – or was it Khan (or his son?) who did the deal? *Surely those at Motspur Park must have been aware of the damage being done by Magath?* But if Magath was reporting directly to Khan, based across the pond in Jacksonville, the German would surely have been giving his own rose-tinted version of events, wouldn't he? *Is there anyone at the Club even remotely bothered?* Obviously yes – especially those who subsequently lost their jobs when the axe fell following our demotion to the Championship – but it was hard to tell. In fact, the silence was deafening. Fans were simply left to fight it out amongst ourselves. Civil war was in full swing.

In amongst it all, though, our supporters may have played a key role in Magath's eventual departure. It could even be that the pen was mightier than the sword on this occasion. Contact details for Khan's PR man, Jim Woodcock, were circulated on the Internet. Given the vitriol flying about on social media, that could easily have pre-empted a volley of abuse in Khan's direction. Instead, as illustrated by the examples subsequently posted on the fans' messageboards, the missives were full of feeling, forthright and frank, but without crossing a line.

> *"Despite our short-comings and a campaign chock-full of cock-ups, we were somehow still in with a chance of staying up as the other teams around us continued to flounder."*

Opposite page right: Madcap goings-on at FFC under Felix Magath, as revealed by Andrew Dillon in *The Sun*.

Below: The stuff of nightmares, not dreams! All heady stuff, according to Paul Johnson.

MAD MAG
Axed Felix used to 'stare out' players

Magath... SHUSH!

FULHAM are now picking up the pieces in the wake of Felix Magath's 'blinking mad' regime.

SunSport can reveal some of the bizarre methods employed by the hardline German oddball following his sacking on Thursday.

Magath *(right)*, 61, alienated many of his players with his weird approach to coaching and man-management.

A club insider said: "Felix was odd to say the least – many others would have said awful to deal with.

"He used to test the players' mental strength by calling you into his office.

"Then he would just sit and stare at you in complete

EXCLUSIVE by ANDREW DILLON

silence for three minutes to see if you'd blink. It happened to a lot of the lads and no one quite knew what it was supposed to do.

"But if you blinked it was considered a sign of weakness."

Magath, who was likened to Dangermouse character Penfold *(left)*, ruled with an iron fist and tried to control every aspect of the club – demanding to know everything his players did.

Striker Hugo Rodallega found that out to his cost during last season's run-in.

The insider claimed: "It was the penultimate game of last season away at Stoke.

"Hugo had been scoring goals but the club was in trouble at the bottom of the Premier League.

"Hugo had an upset stomach and took a pill for it – but hadn't told the manager. When

Felix found out, he dropped Hugo from the squad completely."

Fulham Under-21 coach and former Cottagers defender Kit Symons is in charge of the team for today's home match against Blackburn and faces a huge task.

The West London club have just one point from seven Championship games this season and sit at the foot of the table.

But that has not put off former Tottenham boss Tim Sherwood and ex-Celtic manager Neil Lennon, who both want the job.

Danny Murphy would also welcome the chance to get his old club out of the mire.

The former midfielder, 37, said: "I care about the club deeply.

"If they did want to speak to me, of course I'd be open-minded to that."

To his immense credit, Jim Woodcock dealt with this sudden avalanche of appeals with aplomb. No "stock" replies, but personal ones, individually tailored. And Magath was shown the door soon after! There's no way of knowing if these appeals tipped the balance. However, the bad press after our dire FA Cup "performance" against Sheffield United is said to have "done it" for Meulensteen – the subsequent battling efforts against Man. United and Liverpool effectively counted for nothing.

So it's feasible – if, I admit, just supposition (that word again!) – that, by fuelling the fire with the correct gas, the actions of these Fulham supporters nudged our owner into taking action.

The dealings of last season made us a big joke in football circles. Not simply the losing of football matches – that's bad enough, but we've been there before – but the manner of how we were allowed to freefall from those gloriously high standards previously set. What a way to run a business! It goes back to Al Fayed's tenure, of course. A better Chairman for Fulham FC would be hard to find, but the lack of investment in the latter part of his stewardship hardly helped. And it was a case of "as you were" when Shahid Khan took over.

Fast forward to this season: a Sunday League manager would be hard pushed to field as many players in so few games as Magath managed. And that assumes that today's professional footballers haven't made the squad because of atypical Sunday league reasons: getting off with the barmaid at the King's Head; taking an impromptu trip with the lads to Southend, and being awol ever since; or suffering broken bones after losing a drunken bet based on jumping over garden walls.

Most of us would prefer never to have heard of Felix Bingo – the never-popular game of second-guessing the squad numbers to be called out for that day's line-up. In the same way as Brede

Hangeland would prefer never to have heard of Magath's cheese therapy. We knew something stunk. The only good thing, I guess, is that the German has gone and we move on.

"We've got our Fulham back" sang the crowd as we thumped lowly Bolton 4-0 at the Cottage. It was only Bolton said some. By the same token it was "only" Fulham, one place below the visitors before kick-off. Even so, it was great to sense that everyone was pulling together once again. And only Bolton or not, there was plenty to suggest that we can climb the table. Who's to say if caretaker boss Kit Symons will get the permanent gig? Well, the five-man panel actually. But there's no doubting that Kit has got us back on track. By "doing the bleedin' obvious" according to *The Mirror*'s (and TOOFIF's!) Dave Kidd. Maybe so. Just highlights how bleedin' obvious it was to us that the previous incumbent had got it all wrong!

And now we have that panel – with no sign of Alistair Mackintosh. Did he help set up the panel then take a back seat? Or has he been shunted to one side? Yet more conjecture. The famous five – two ex-Whites in Danny Murphy and Brian McBride, FFC Academy Director Huw Jennings, Nike Director and Fulham fan David Daly plus all-round good egg Niall Quinn – have a key decision to make. And soon, hopefully. Whoever gets the nod, it's vital the new set-up makes FFC a going concern once again and demonstrates that we're not in the League just to make up the numbers. We have seen how far we can progress with a respected managerial team, just as we've seen how quickly we can fall when it's omnishambolic.

As yet, we've had no thumping of big red buzzers (*X Factor*), no turning of chairs (*The Voice*), or even a magnificent "Seven!" from Len (*Strictly*). Mind you, if there's a Louis Walsh in there any sort of decision may be a long while in coming. ⚽

Fulham 1 Norwich City 0	1st
18.10.14 22nd	2nd
	3rd
Rotherham United 3 Fulham 3	4th
21.10.14 22nd	5th
	6th
Fulham 3 Charlton Athletic 0	7th
24.10.14 19th	8th
	9th
Wigan Athletic 3 Fulham 3	10th
01.11.14 20th	11th
	12th
Fulham 2 Blackpool 2	**13th**
05.11.14 21st	14th
	15th
Fulham 3 Huddersfield Town 1	16th
08.11 14 17th	17th
	18th
Brentford 2 Fulham 1	19th
21.11.14 17th	20th
	21th
Brighton & HA 1 Fulham 2	22th
29.11.14 16th	23rd
	24th
Fulham 0 Watford 5	
05.12.14 16th	
Leeds United 0 Fulham 1	
13.12.14 14th	
Fulham 4 Sheffield Wednesday 0	
20.12.14 13th	
Bournemouth 2 Fulham 0	
26.12.14 15th	
Fulham 0 Brighton & HA 2	
29.12.14 17th	
Cardiff City 1 Fulham 0	
10.01.15 18th	
League Cup	
Fulham 2 Derby County 5	
25.10.14 Round 4	

The Fulham Way

In a recent matchday programme, FFC Chairman Shahid Khan concluded his piece by quoting from an email received by his offices as Felix Magath was being shown the door at Craven Cottage. It was written by Fulham fan Mark Norman and is well worth reproducing here.

"We don't expect to win trophies at Fulham Football Club, we don't expect to win every game, we don't expect to be playing in the Premier League or in European competitions (although, of course, we would love to see all of the aforementioned, but we don't demand it). What we do expect is to enjoy seeing our team perform, see our players perform with pride and see that the staff that are employed by the Club stay true to our principles and lead us with pride and passion."

As previously mentioned, such sentiments were typical of the many missives sent to Khan's PR man Jim Woodcock as we sunk ever lower under the alleged direction of the mad German. Despite our profound exasperation at the whole avoidable mess (someone referred to the mess as an "omnishambles" I believe!) the missives sent to Woodcock were, to quote TOOFIF 134, "full of feeling, forthright and frank, but without crossing a line". It was, quite possibly, no coincidence that Magath was sent on his way soon after.

So, full kudos to Mark (and others) for expressing their angst so passionately and yet without abuse. Not generally our way, of course, but then in these last 2-3 years you can't say that the Club has been run "our way" or even close to the way we'd come to expect our club to be run. And there's the rub. Full marks to the Chairman and his people for recognising the Fulham fans' way of doing things; but with regards to the team and what we've had to put up with at games, he and the Club have short-changed us for a while, and – certainly as far as the latter section of Mark Norman's perspective is concerned – they're still short-changing us. Big time.

Yes, things took a well overdue and most welcome upwards swing when Kit Symons was appointed. Yes, there was a real feeling that thanks to Kit's affection for the Club and his huge success with the junior ranks that we now had a "decent" guy in charge and, to slightly misquote an oft-sung chant, "We had our Fulham back".

However, can anyone say right now that, to use Mark Norman's words, they're "enjoying seeing our team perform"? It's four games without a goal now, hardly surprising given the dearth of shots on target in those encounters. It all looked so promising after that 4-0 win over Sheffield Wednesday. The score may have flattered us that day, but it was a solid victory gained by good teamwork and no little flair. Here's a teaser: have we ever lost 5-0 at home (v Watford) and then bounced back by winning the following game at the Cottage 4-0? There's one for Anne O'Raque and Statto to work on. Not that the "bouncebackability" has been maintained.

We've missed Lasse Vigen Christensen, our star performer so far this season, as he recovered from a hamstring injury. And the positive input by the much-criticised Bryan Ruiz has been noticeable by his absence. Sure, there's a lot about his approach to the game that doesn't fit comfortably with the rigours of the Championship (translation: he can be a right pansy!), but he's unquestionably talented and has suffered in the past by being made to play out wide. Given the right blend of players, he'd always be in my team. Another who's shone is Marcus Bettinelli; not the finished article but looking a decent goalkeeper. The shame is he's had so much shot-stopping practice! Big-money signing Ross McCormack is as industrious as Berbatov was idle and has provided several moments of real class. But why is he being played so deep? If he drops back any further he'll be behind Bettinelli.

However, while it's all very well acknowledging and praising those players who have done well, and conceding that, unlike many performances under Magath, most of the players are putting in a shift, there's no doubt that the end result is disappointing. We've just lost at Cardiff and, not for the first time, it was "Fulham nil". And lucky to get nil. We're hovering above the relegation places and are already a massive 20 points behind pacesetters Bournemouth and Derby. So it's hardly surprising that the (remaining) troops are getting fidgety. These next few weeks could well make or break our season – our activity in the transfer window should indicate how serious the Club are at trying to rectify the calamitous cock-ups of recent seasons.

The soundbites so far this campaign have been about getting promotion; the reality is that we're going nowhere fast. Certainly not upwards. And it hurts. There have been flashes of excellence: Christensen's terrific goal after running the length of the field to finish off a superb breakaway against Sheffield Wednesday shows what we're capable of. Some of the interplay through midfield has been a joy to watch, but it's hardly been a consistent feature. In fact, in recent games, even when we've put together a promising move we've then all too often tried to walk the ball into the net. Is it a lack of confidence or team instructions? If it's the former getting in the way of having a shot at goal then it's evidently knocking those confidence levels even further. If you don't buy a ticket you can't win the raffle. Take a bloody shot when there's an

"The soundbites so far this campaign have been about getting promotion; the reality is that we're going nowhere fast. Certainly not upwards. And it hurts."

opening, guys! Oh, and get it on target!

Certainly we're playing very narrow, which might well be a reaction to leaking so many stupid goals earlier in the season. The goals we're conceding may still be stupid but there are fewer of them thank goodness. Trouble is, our shot-shy team aren't troubling the scorers at the other end of the field. Dull and dour is (possibly) all very well if we're picking up points. But we're not, and as things stand a double demotion isn't out of the question – we need to buck up sharply. Any talk of promotion or making the Play-offs has to be a joke right now.

I find it staggering that Kit Symons is taking so much flak. And that statement has nothing to do with blind support for our latest manager, nice guy that he is. Kit may yet prove to be a fine manager; by the same token he may not. He may not have got things running to his satisfaction up to now and he may indeed prove not to be good enough to do so. But such talk is surely missing the point completely – he is striving to get to grips with the dismal set-up he's been left. We're not doing very well, that's a no-brainer, but the level of vitriol directed (mainly anonymously) at him is totally unfair. Poor as we are at the moment, that sense of frustration should be directed elsewhere.

Kit Symons is by no means responsible for the mess we're in. In fact, he's been responsible for keeping some semblance of sanity in the Club while the mad German was not only ripping the squad apart but also, and most crucially, crushing the last crumbs of squad spirit. Little wonder we went down. Symons, meantime was fostering an excellent crop of youngsters – many of whom are now first-teamers – and doing his level best to retain his dignity by carrying on even though Magath was keen to bring in his own man.

The blunt message to the Chairman is, if Kit's your man (and how can a five-man panel possibly be wrong?!), then back him. After all, I think we're all agreed that we want the "staff employed by the Club [to] stay true to our principles and lead us with pride and passion". That pride and passion must go all the way to the top. Splashing the cash would be a good way of showing this – we're not demanding extravagant purchases or even buying for buying's sake, but a statement or two of intent would be most welcome. Our playing set-up is in dire need of bolstering. No, not another game of musical chairs that results in the players' names on their shirts being indentifiers for playing colleagues rather than spectators. What we need is the addition of a clutch of key players who are then integrated into the squad/team. And yes, in order to get the right calibre of players, that will involve some financial outlay. If we really have designs on doing more than just consolidating our position in the Championship (let alone the dreadful thought of another relegation) then whoever's in the manager's chair has to be backed. He deserves that.

And, for heaven's sake, WE deserve that.

Up to now it seems that the Club are taking the line of not mentioning the recent past in an attempt to pretend that the nightmare never happened. It did. And the ever-growing number of empty seats in the stands at Craven Cottage is a reflection of how badly orchestrated the governance of the Club has been. It's time to get those heads out of the sand and give us what we deserve. Back the manager!

What is a manager anyway? Okay, so the team boss is being described more and more as the "first-team coach" or "head coach". But let's not try to be clever for the minute. He's the manager. He (or she) manages. They manage.

Or not if you're a mad German. Loads of stories have since emerged confirming what we suspected to be true: that for whatever presumably well-meaning reasons, Magath and his methods tore the dressing room apart. Rather than foster a decent squad spirit, albeit a brittle one if necessary, until the key objective of staying in the Premier League had been achieved, his ways caused such a poor atmosphere that even though other clubs in the relegation dogfight were pushing hard at their own self-destruct buttons, we still hurtled through the trapdoor. That's no way to manage.

Brede Hangeland was a supreme player for us; his centre-back partnership with Aaron Hughes was the stuff of dreams. At their peak the duo could easily have walked into a top-four side. However, Hangeland was past his peak last term and ultimately departed with his status tarnished. Being bothered by a niggly back injury hardly helped. And yet he was named in the side pretty consistently, despite not playing well. Why wasn't this situation "managed"? With the big fella's performances so evidently below par, why wasn't he told to get his fitness (and confidence) to an acceptable level before he could be considered for first-team action? No doubt the player wanted to play, but the way it was managed (or rather, not managed) resulted in the worst-case scenario: him losing form even more and with it that cool assurance (as well as seemingly not being able to jump, surely a pre-requisite for a centre-back!); us leaking goals and ultimately being relegated; and his place as a club legend and stalwart tainted.

In the world of football, the current way of being able to shuffle your pack is mainly limited to a couple of transfer windows. Until then, football managers have to manage with what they've got. Make the best of it. Take appropriate measures. Select the best available team. Employ the most suitable tactics. Ensure that, broadly, everyone is pulling the same way. Use powers of persuasion (or fear!) to get the very best out of the staff at your disposal. Underscore one's own importance to the Club by making a success of things. Ensure that whoever made the managerial appointment is

Fulham 2 Reading 1	
17.01.15	15th
Fulham 3 Nottingham Forest 2	
21.01.15	14th
Blackburn Rovers 2 Fulham 1	
31.01.15	15th
Fulham 1 Birmingham City 1	
07.02.15	15th
Bolton Wanderers 3 Fulham 1	
10.01.15	18th
Fulham 1 Ipswich Town 2	
14.02.15	19th
Millwall 0 Fulham 0	
21.02.15	19th
Wolverhampton Wanderers 3 Fulham 0	
24.02.15	20th
Fulham 2 Derby County 0	
28.02.15	19th
Watford 1 Fulham 0	
03.03.15	20th
Fulham 1 Bournemouth 5	
06.03.15	20th
Sheffield Wednesday 1 Fulham 1	
14.03.15	20th
Fulham 0 Leeds United 3	
18.03.15	21st
Huddersfield Town 0 Fulham 2	
21.03.15	20th
Fulham 1 Brentford 4	
03.04.15	20th
Charlton Athletic 1 Fulham 1	
07.04.15	20th
FA Cup	
Fulham 0 Wolverhampton Wanderers 0	
03.01.15	Round 3
Wolverhampton Wanderers 3 Fulham 0	
13.01.15	Round 3 replay; aet, Fulham win 5-3 pens
Sunderland 0 Fulham 0	
24.01.15	Round 4
Fulham 1 Sunderland 3	
03.02.15	Round 4 replay

1st
2nd
3rd
4th
5th
6th
7th
8th
9th
10th
11th
12th
13th
14th
15th
16th
17th
18th
19th
20th
21th
22th
23th
24th

"I went to the Cottage with Viv and we had a chat with Alec before Mullers came along; he took us on to the terraces and told us all about the Club – its history and its characters. He sold us the Club completely. I couldn't wait to get started. That was the start of a truly wonderful period in my career."

shown to be correct for making the decision. Earn brownie points all round. MANAGE!

Given that our previous incumbent failed miserably on these counts it's a wonder that he was allowed to stay so long. By that particular yardstick, René Meulensteen must have committed something dark and dreadful to have been given the boot after a mere matter of days! ⚽

A Chat With Alan Slough

Want a record-breaker? Step forward Alan Slough – first man to kick-off a League game on a Sunday and the only guy to net a hat-trick of penalties at an away ground – plus he was ever-present as Fulham took a record 11 games to reach Wembley in 1975. Just recently, though, renowned fitness fanatic "Sloughie" (rhymes with Fluffy!) has been diagnosed with a form of Parkinson's. The Ed got the full lowdown from the man himself.

You left the professional game in 1982, Alan, but found it pretty hard to hang up your boots...
The simple fact is that football has been my life; I loved playing the game so carried on in non-League circles for quite a while.

...From Torquay to Weymouth, Yeovil and Minehead – roles that included coaching – as well as running soccer schools...?
Yes, the soccer schools went well. I tried my hand at coaching, I went to Torquay as first-team coach – and, as it turned out, physio, plus so many other jobs. I had two years there with my best mate Bruce Rioch. It was tough but we had good times. At Christmas we were flying high in the League – extraordinary given that the previous summer we had just eight professionals on the books. We eventually finished in about fifth or sixth, so all in all a good job done in difficult circumstances. But it was utterly exhausting and so I left to set up the soccer schools and to run a little business. I'm a Luton boy, but I got to love Torquay – it's a really beautiful place to live – so I settled down here.

Was it just your best mate that lured you to Torquay in the first place?
I was at Peterborough and was going to go to Barnet as first-team coach with Barry Fry. Meanwhile Peterborough needed a manager and I was on the six-man shortlist. Then I got that call from Bruce, who I've known since schooldays, and it was a case of "Let's give it a go!"

Mention Torquay to Fulham fans of a certain age and they'll think of Robbie Herrera, who had five years at the Cottage.
Oh, I know Robbie! He's a smashing lad! A left-footed player who played over a hundred games for Torquay; he's back there looking after

the youth set-up. Robbie often checks in on my grandchildren to see how they're doing, so yes I know Robbie very well.

You were a left-back too, originally..?
Yes, a right-footed left-back for many years under Alec Stock at Luton.

All these years later and you have been diagnosed with Parkinson's – how have you been able to deal with such unwanted news?
I hadn't been quite right for a while. I was shuffling my feet in getting around to such an extent that any friends who met me would say to my family, "Alan's struggling, isn't he?" After a bit of to-ing and fro-ing with the hospital I met a wonderful specialist who said I had a form of Parkinson's and got me on the appropriate tablets right away. He made no promises but, after dabbling a little with the dosage, it's worked. They have really picked me up, and I'm very grateful for that. For someone who's been so fit – my game was as much about having such a strong engine as anything else – what I miss is being able to run. Unfortunately, that's out of the window for sure; the old brain doesn't like it! It's a question of getting on with it; okay, one day it's all going to catch up on me, but my way of thinking is that it might not be until I'm 90-plus! So all in all I'm counting my blessings.

What was it that led to you joining Fulham back in 1973? Your Luton team-mate Viv Busby joined at the same time...
We had a lovely team at Luton and I was great mates with most, including Viv. Harry Haslam was Luton manager by then and I wasn't Harry's sort of player. I had the sense that he wanted me out, but I had no inkling of anything until my mum phoned me. She said, "What's this? You're going to Fulham – it's in the *Daily Express*!" I couldn't believe it. I got the paper and there was the headline "Slough and Busby go to Fulham" with Alec Stock saying in the article "It's great to have the boys back with me." My initial thoughts were that it must be true if my former boss at Luton now wanted me to join him at Fulham – and that if I said I didn't want to go he might offer me a much better contract [laughs]!

...Ever the professional!
I went to the Cottage with Viv and we had a chat with Alec before Mullers came along; he took us on to the terraces and told us all about the Club – its history and its characters. He sold us the Club completely. I couldn't wait to get started. That was the start of a truly wonderful period in my career.

Did the fact that you were linking up with your former boss make it any easier?
With Alec, he was generally either for you or

against you. I seemed to tick a fair few boxes for him, whereas Harry Haslam didn't rate me. If you weren't "in" with Alec, or crossed him, then you'd find yourself not being involved. I liked Alec and we got on well. He had his whimsical ways, though. He'd come to me in training or whatever and say quite sharply, "Pull your socks up!" I'd be thinking this is just like being back at school. Then he'd give you a hint of a smile. With or without that smile you got on with it and did as you were told. Years later after I'd given up full-time playing I met Alec again, when I was involved in a charity game. Do you know he said the same thing, "Pull your socks up!" – before adding "You haven't got any shinpads on" and giving me a disapproving look. He was a lovely man and a great manager and it was a privilege to play for him at two clubs.

How were those early days at Fulham?

Freddie Callaghan was the left-back and one of the heroes at Craven Cottage. Yet Alec put me straight in the team in Fred's position. I did quite well and, luckily, the crowd took to me. Fred was fantastic; he told me to just get on with it. Things worked out well for me at Fulham – we got to the FA Cup final. And you can't take that away from me! I kissed the medal (the only Fulham player who did, I think) and, despite losing on the day, that medal meant so much to me then and still does today.

Can you remember your first Fulham goal – here's a clue: it was in September 1973?

I can. "The two mates" were facing each other at Villa Park – Bruce Rioch and yours truly. I'm playing at the back and Bruce has gone past me so I've grabbed his shirt. He didn't like it and lashed out, giving me a proper bloody nose. As I was getting treatment Bruce winked at me – I thought, "Thanks very much Bruce, I'm coming to your house for dinner afterwards!" Anyway, Bruce went and scored for Villa and I did the same at the other end. Honours even.

What about 20 January 1974 – and an indelible place in football history?

Ah yes, kicking off the first League match played on a Sunday, at Millwall. I played the captain's card that day. I'd never kicked-off a game before and don't recall doing so ever again, but as captain I pulled rank! I got there first! My other "first" was as a Peterborough player – scoring three penalties in the same match away from home – at Chester.

Another record, a collective one this time, came when Fulham took 11 games to reach Wembley. I don't suppose you were thinking about the stadium's twin towers when you scored the Third Round decider against Hull City at a neutral venue, Filbert Street?

After a 1-1 home draw we outplayed Hull in the

replay, even so we were two minutes from going out of the competition – Viv equalised right at the end of extra-time to make it 2-2. In that third game I made a break into the box and hammered home a cross from Viv just before half-time; it finished 1-0 and next on the list were Nottingham Forest. As the FA Cup games clocked up we developed a belief that we couldn't get beaten.

You needed that grit to get past Forest – four games then that titanic tussle at Everton, with Fulham supposedly there just to make up the numbers...

We got stronger and stronger as an outfit. Then to go to Everton, best team in the country at the time, and beat them a little more convincingly than the scoreline suggests, was a wonderful achievement. We played really well on the day.

How good was Bobby Moore at Goodison Park? From a spectator's perspective he seemed supercool whenever Bob Latchford, Mick Lyons and co put him under pressure.

Bobby was brilliant; his presence was so influential. His coolness rubbed off – at least on the training ground – he was so calm and cool that we tried to copy him. He gave us an extra layer of confidence. Bobby was also great at giving us pearls of wisdom; and there were few wiser on a football field than Bobby. A superb footballer and a marvellous man.

So when was it – after that result at Everton perhaps – that you realised a trip to Wembley was a distinct possibility?

I don't think any of us had considered it before that game at Goodison – apart from the habitual dreams at the start of any campaign – but, yes, that was such a good performance that we could at least revisit those dreams!

Did it help that the Everton game came so soon after finally knocking Forest out of the Cup?

Yes it probably did. We only had a few days to prepare for the game and we dealt with it magnificently. Not long after that we travelled to Carlisle, nicked a 1-0 win thanks to Les Barrett at one end and Peter Mellor's outstanding goalkeeping display at the other; suddenly Fulham were in the semi-finals of the FA Cup!

...Where Birmingham City lay in wait...?

Above: We won the Cup! Not in 1975, alas, but we came out tops in the "replay" staged 20 years later in aid of Fulham 2000. Alan Slough, Captain on the night, was more than happy to strike a pose with the famous trophy.

It was the draw we wanted. We were in the car outside Craven Cottage on the Monday morning – Viv, John Mitchell and myself – listening to the draw on the car radio, really hoping that we'd get Birmingham. Anyone passing by when we heard we'd got what we wanted must have had a shock – three grown men shouting and cheering loudly... but that's how confident we were. We fancied ourselves to beat Birmingham, and to reach the final.

Nothing's guaranteed in football, though, is it?
You're right; and we did it the hard way. If you check out the recording of that first semi-final there's no question that we deserved to win it – especially with Mitch's super strike. Conversely, the replay at Maine Road was all Birmingham but they couldn't score, even as extra time ticked away. Then we won a throw-in and, as we prepared to take it, I asked the ref how long there was to go and he said: "It's time, we're there, it's time." I received the ball and, given what the ref had just told me, my intention was to head to the corner and ensure we had the 0-0. But one of their defenders dived in at me so I took him on the inside and whacked the ball into the box instead, in went Mitch and next thing the ball is rolling into the net. First we screamed with delight then we screamed at the referee: "You said it was time – blow up now, ref; come on, it's time!" Birmingham were allowed to kick off and Gordon Taylor received the ball and came straight at me. Luckily, despite playing 120 minutes of tense football, my brain was still in gear. I always liked a tackle but on this occasion I just got out of the way; I didn't want to give Birmingham even the remotest chance of winning a free-kick thereby giving them one last chance of knocking the ball into our box. Forty years on, that still gives me the shivers – an FA Cup semi-final and there's me letting a dangerous player run past unchallenged. But that was that, as soon as Gordon ran by the ref blew his whistle and we'd made it! Somehow we still had enough energy to jump up and down to celebrate.

Not a great match perhaps, but a night of huge drama and a dream result?
Absolutely. And Gordon Taylor was the first to come over to me to say well done – what a magnificent gesture by the fella. We'd just eclipsed his Wembley dream in the most dramatic of ways but there he was retaining his composure and wishing us well. You don't forget such moments.

Next stop: Wembley. Did the whole lead-up to the Cup Final and the big day itself flash by in a haze?
I remember it all very well actually. And it brings back lots of little memories, not just the facts of the match. I remember being interviewed by Barry Davies beforehand on the pitch alongside Alan Mullery. I was asked about the pitch. I came out with the classic lines: "It's terrific; it's really wonderful," and as I did so I looked down at the surface and noticed that the mud had been painted green. Other events staged at the famous old stadium had left the pitch a lot worse than it looked. I wasn't used to talking on the telly and blindly came out with what I was expected to say – not the cleverest moment of my life!

You didn't reach such heights the following season and manager Alec Stock was shown the door...
That was sad. But these things happen in football.

In stepped Bobby Campbell; how did you get on with him?
We had our ups and downs, that's for sure. There was one particular one-to-one at the end of which he said, "I've a good mind to take the captaincy off you." My response was, "Well you can do that if you want, you're the manager." To be fair, despite our differences, he never did and I thought he was a big man for not doing so. It was Bob who had offered me the captaincy in the first place. I was honoured and said that I'd be more than happy to be skipper, at least until Bobby Moore returned from America. When he came back I told him the captaincy's all yours but he was having none of it. "It's yours for the keeping," he said. "You're the captain of Fulham but if you need any advice I'm here alongside you on the pitch." What a man!

As Fulham captain you had to contend with a couple of big-name arrivals – did George Best and Rodney Marsh give you any problems?
Not at all! In fact I looked after George who, believe it or not, was a really shy fella. On the field George was full of tricks, but off it he'd ask me to stand by him at functions and gatherings, at least until he'd familiarised himself with those in attendance. It was the same when we played abroad. Now George was world famous, of course, and yet he remained most comfortable among those that he knew. Mind you, there was one occasion when I happened to remark that we were low on ready cash. "Hang on," he said, "I'll nip over there to do an interview for the papers," and returned with our bills settled. George could be exceptionally generous. So no, I didn't fall out with them and they didn't fall out with anyone either. Rodney was an amazing character too, he'd be doing all sorts of tricks in the dressing room just 15 minutes before kick off – flipping coins up and catching them on the back of his neck; throwing a ball up, catching it, then standing on it while another ball was thrown at him which he'd chest away, all sorts of unbelievable juggling just before we were due on the pitch. It epitomised Fulham's

image as entertainers back then – clubs would have their biggest gates when Fulham came to town.

For me, probably the most vivid memory of George Best in a Fulham shirt was his stunning goal at Peterborough...

When he flipped the ball up and belted it into the top corner from the edge of the box? I knew the goalkeeper well and he must have thought, "Hey it's George Best and he's having a shot, but he's hemmed in and anyway I've got it covered," … just as the ball flew over his shoulder! Few people will remember this but I scored the other goal for Fulham that night – we won 2-1 – but mine wasn't world-class. My goal had shades of John Mitchell's bundled effort that took us to Wembley. I ran into the box made a decent connection with the ball only for the keeper to make a save; the ball pinged back at me and went in off my arm – it was probably the luckiest goal of my career.

Bestie, of course, scored in the first minute of his Fulham debut against Bristol Rovers at the Cottage…

That's right. I know because I gave him the ball! George was alongside me saying, "Pass me the ball, pass me the ball!" So that's what I did. I'm sure the goalie was frightened to death at facing George Best because it wasn't the sweetest strike of his career, but in it went and George was up and running again.

Having Best and Marsh in the ranks didn't reap the expected number of League points, but when it all clicked there were plenty of magic moments...

And not just on the pitch. Here's a story that says a lot about George Best in his time at Fulham. We'd finished training and Bestie asked me if I wanted to have some shooting practice with him. So, with everyone else back in the showers, the pair of us and Gerry Peyton headed off to one of the goals. "What's the drill?" I asked. "We'll hit them from the 18-yard line," replied George. No one else was around, so this was a private session and all very low key except for the normal competetive element between fellow professionals. I started things off and curled the ball into the top corner with Gerry flat-footed. Up stepped George, and he did likewise. It got to about six-all and it dawned on me that I was taking on the great George Best. It's hard enough to beat Gerry Peyton at the best of times! We got to nine-all and Gerry, top goalie or not, hadn't come close to making a save. With that, I took my tenth dead-ball kick from the edge of the box and this time Gerry flew across to make a fine flying save. George took his tenth shot and his aim was as true as ever: George Best 10 Alan Slough 9. For George, this was a valuable practice session and not a case of getting one

over a playing colleague. For me, it was a magic moment – seeing a genius at work was brilliant as well as a privilege. But that was George, a normal, shy individual until he put on his football boots, at which point his genius took over.

Fast forward to an away game at Blackburn Rovers. You and Bobby Moore played your last games for Fulham that day; it was widely known that Bobby was retiring – did you realise it would be your final game for the Club?

No, not really. There were changes afoot – Bobby was retiring and George and Rodney had already left – but then things moved very quickly. Peterborough came in for me and I was on my way. In fact, Les Barrett was in the car with me but they decided not to take Les for whatever reason. My wonderful time at Fulham was over but Peterborough was another enjoyable chapter.

In closing, can I remind you that you DID lift the FA Cup for Fulham!

[Laughs] I did, in a friendly game played against West Ham years later at Craven Cottage. I was in my mid-forties and still playing in a local league but once I and the others got back to the Cottage I think we all thought we were years younger! Everyone was running around as if our lives depended on it. There were a fair few substitutions made during the game in an attempt to preserve our legs and lungs, and at one point I was playing at the back. I looked quite good doing that, even at 45 – but once I was back in midfield and expected to run back and forth it became a bit more of a struggle! It was a lot tougher for Jimmy Dunne – Jimmy was making a long-awaited return to Fulham but had to go off injured within a minute of going on! It was another great night with the lads. And we won, and I was able to lift the Cup. ⚽

Above: Having pulled rank, Alan Slough kicks off the very first League match on a Sunday – at The Den in January 1994.

Below: Rodney Marsh and George Best are pictured in the US. In the middle is football agent Ken Adam, a Fulham fan. The maverick footballers played for FFC in the 1970s alongside Alan Slough.

Tracking Down John Cutbush

Fulham's right-back at Wembley in 1975 was John Cutbush. He made 160 appearances for the Club between 1972 and 1977 before moving to Sheffield United and then to Wichita Wings in the States. Once he'd hung up his boots, John settled in Doncaster and remained away from the Fulham fold – apart from resurfacing briefly for the fundraising cup final "replay" at the Cottage in 1995. Even former pal and fellow full-back Les Strong had lost contact.

"I had three years in the States playing indoor football before crowds of 25-30,000. It was different, but brilliant. After that it was back to Doncaster. People would ask, 'What will you do when you've finished playing football?' My reply was: 'Struggle!' And it *has* been a struggle at times. I spent 15 years working for BMW; I finished off in the bodyshop – in a semi-skilled position, actually. But I've done all sorts, including working on building sites.

"Football's such a transitory career. Once I'd moved north to Sheffield I became detached from my mates at Fulham, where I'd spent five happy years, and even more so when I went to the USA. I've never been an extrovert so settling for a quiet family life back in Doncaster just seemed natural."

How did the move to Fulham come about, John?

I joined in August 1972, and absolutely loved it. Alec Stock was the first manager to gave me a real chance in the game. Before that I was at Tottenham, but never made the breakthrough. I was at Spurs for about five years too long, just hoping to be given my chance either at right wing or at full-back. When the time came to move I had the choice of ten clubs, but Fulham was my first option. I was genuinely thrilled to join the Club, and I found that its reputation as a friendly set-up was fully justified.

Who was there at the time?

If I remember rightly, I joined just as Les Strong and John Mitchell were breaking into the Fulham team. We lost the first game of the season (away at Sheffield Wednesday) 3-0, then drew 1-1 at home to Burnley – I played on the right-wing in that one – before we won 2-1 at Middlesbrough. I enjoyed that game, picking up not only maximum points but also my first win bonus! In those days we got £10 appearance money and £20 a point. It's all very different today! Great times, a great club and a great manager. I was loving every moment. I respected Alec Stock a lot. He gave me a few rollickings that I wasn't too happy about. But that was his job.

It must have been great to play alongside Alan Mullery and Bobby Moore?

If it was an honour to play for Alec, it was certainly that to be in the same side as Bobby Moore and Alan Mullery. I knew Alan from my time at Spurs. I recall him turning up to the training ground at Cheshunt in his [Ford Cortina] 1600E England car – England's 1970 World Cup squad players each received one as part of the sponsorship deal – to watch us young 'uns. He was a brilliant player and a brilliant captain too; he certainly proved that at Fulham. Bobby Moore was different class in everything he did. When you're that good you don't simply toss that to one side when you join another club in the latter stages of your career. He was never the quickest of players anyway, and coming to Fulham seemed to give him a new lease of life rather than offer an easy time in a lower division.

And you got to Wembley!

Bobby still had his pride and, who knows, maybe it was his way of showing the West Ham hierarchy that he still had so much to offer. Fortunately

"Alec Stock was the first manager to gave me a real chance in the game. Before that I was at Tottenham, but never made the breakthrough. I was at Spurs for about five years too long, just hoping to be given my chance either at right wing or at full-back."

Below: John Cutbush cuts infield against Crystal Palace.

Below right: A wave to the crowd – against the Manager's orders! – at Wembley in 1975.

Fulham benefited from that. It was incredible that he should not only get to the FA Cup final with Fulham but that we'd meet West Ham at Wembley. Bobby was so calm and assured. He was a great mentor but that calmness was something I couldn't master – I think you have to be born with it. Me? I was always a nervous wreck! The funny thing about Mooro was that he barely said anything on the pitch – unlike Mullers, who was always barking orders or giving encouragement – he simply got on with the job in that unflustered way of his.

It was a decent team all said and done?

You're right, it wasn't all about those two. In goal was Peter Mellor who, on his day, could save absolutely anything – he could be world class. Peter was also incredibly brave. Alan Slough was another. "Sloughie" was such a lovely guy and a very good pro; he wasn't necessarily pretty in what he did, but could run all day and boy did he always put in a shift. If a chance fell his way, Alan could hit a ball superbly. In short, he was every manager's dream.

As that Cup run progressed we all showed that we were good players, and we made our mark as a team. We surprised quite a few neutrals with our performance at Everton. In no way was it easy, but we played superbly against a side that was top of the tree and expected to swat us aside. We stood up to the task magnificently. From a personal perspective I proved I could do it – playing to such a high level away from home and in front of 50,000 spectators was a real highpoint of my career. It wasn't the same story at Wembley, unfortunately.

I got the old newspaper reports out the other day; we received so many plaudits, and rightly so. And that's the frustrating point all these years later. We had it in us to beat anyone, and to do so with tenacity and style. But our showing at Wembley, sound though it was, was sterile by comparison.

It didn't quite go to plan though as the possibility of a trip to Wembley loomed...?

No! Not long after the highs of that Everton game I had a real low point – injuring my knee at Sunderland. I felt the "bang" and it hurt, but within five minutes I was back on the pitch having more or less run it off. It was still a bit sore, but when I tried to get up the following morning I couldn't walk. I suppose a surge of adrenaline had seen me through the game; this, though, was horrible.

I'm not a good spectator of games that I should be playing some part in. It hurts. You want to be out there. My leg hurt, but it was more a case of hurting inside. There's absolutely no doubt that you want the players to do well, it's just that you have that empty feeling of missing out, of not being able to do your bit. And, for heaven's sake, we're talking about the quarter-final and semi-final of the FA Cup. I was devastated not to be playing an active part. Once again, the lads were great, digging deep

at Carlisle and coming out on top after two tough games against Birmingham.

As the final neared I was named sub against Portsmouth, where poor Strongy got injured and on I came. In my absence John Fraser had taken my slot, now he stood in for Strongy. I was back in the team – for the last couple of League games but also for the Cup final too.

What about the whole Wembley experience?

Alec told us not to wave to our family and friends as we walked out, yet I was one of a few that did – not to disobey Alec, it was just such a natural thing to do. The game was so surreal. It was genuinely like being in a dream. We'd had an odd preamble with the fuss with the boots, meaning we all had to blacken out all the white markings, then suddenly we were walking onto the pitch, and with that we'd kicked off. I'd been playing for about 20 minutes and the whole occasion seemed to hit me: where I was; what I was doing.

A sudden realisation…?

Yeah, we'd settled first – I didn't do anything special but was doing all right. Then suddenly, bang, the realisation dawned on me. John Mitchell went close with a shot and the famous Wembley roar went up – and with it, it was like someone had slapped me around the face. I woke up; it was no dream. This was real. The nerves kicked in, I suppose.

The irony in all of this is that throughout my career I tended to get better as a game wore on. I was always naturally fit so that was never a real issue – my confidence grew as I relaxed into the games. For whatever reason that wasn't the case at Wembley, and it's something I'll have to live with.

That's a bit harsh?

I'm still tough on myself all these years later for making that ricket. It's largely my fault that I've got a runners-up medal and that Mullers didn't lift the trophy. I've lived with it for 40 years and, to be blunt, I've got it for life. Peter [Mellor] took a lot of stick for the way the goals went in, but I know only too well that I was at fault for the first of Alan Taylor's goals. That's the reality.

Did you drown your sorrows afterwards?

Not really, although we did enjoy the "do" that had been arranged for us afterwards at the Dorchester, even if the atmosphere would have been so much livelier had we won. We were each presented with a pair of cufflinks. My reaction was, "These are nice but, you know, thirty bob's-worth…" It was our other halves at our table who pointed out that they were real gold and "absolutely fantastic". I soon changed my view to, "These are nice and, you know, worth a fair bit too"! My son's got 'em now, as well as my medal. ⚽

Above: Peter Mellor, a top-class goalkeeper in his day. He's now based in the States, cpmplete with a "forehead full of wrinkles"!

A one-on-one with Peter Mellor

Where's all the time gone, Peter?

You tell me! It was 1981 when I finished playing [with Portsmouth]. After a season with the Edmonton Drillers in the NASL, I moved to Tampa, where I've lived ever since. I'm the National Technical Director for the United Soccer Leagues (USL). I'm also a staff instructor for US Soccer and the NSCAA in their National coaching education programmes. I live in a beautiful part of the world, and I can go fishing a whole lot more than I used to when I was at Fulham!

Do you still cast your mind back to Wembley '75?

Oh yes! My forehead is full of wrinkles and those memories are firmly etched in there somewhere! It was a special time. We were a Second Division outfit and yet we operated as a First Division club, certainly that was the feeling in the dressing room. Having the experience and abilities of Alan Mullery and Bobby Moore was a huge bonus, and both were great leaders. Alan was the more verbal of the two whereas Bobby led by example. That sort of leadership gave the more bread-and-butter players wonderful guidance and confidence.

It must have been a great experience to play behind those sort of players?

It was brilliant. Except, perhaps, at Carlisle! There wasn't much cover around that day, experienced or otherwise! Goalkeepers tend to be in the spotlight when things don't go to plan – as I know only too well – but on that day I had to step up to the plate. Luckily things went well for me at Brunton Park.

Fulham were fortunate in having some top characters behind the scenes as well...?

Alec Stock was a tremendous leader – not technically or tactically perhaps, that was down to Bill Taylor and John Collins – but he was such a gifted man-manager. I learned so much from Alec. The respect Alec had from the players, each and every one of us, was tremendous. His skill was in being able to keep the whole group together while still being able to focus on each of us individually. I must mention Ron Woolnough, too – the best physio I ever worked with.

Sounds like you were pretty impressed!

Fulham was a very special place, and the characters in the dressing room were incredible. It was a great all-round team – on the field, off the field and even including the support staff in the offices. I never played anywhere else that came close to having such an atmosphere. Underpinning it all was having the right mix of characters in the dressing room.

Les Strong… now there's a character!

I was settled here in Florida and hadn't heard from him in years until the phone rang and a voice said: "Hey, it's Strongy! I'm a national team coach now." I figured on him doing a number of things, but this wasn't one of them! "I'm in Anguilla," he continued. My response was, "Where the hell is Anguilla?" Strongy explained he was based in the Caribbean and was coaching their national team – he wasn't getting paid, though. "I've got a house, a fabulous lifestyle, plenty to drink and all the ladies I want." Can't imagine that's in Roy Hodgson's England contract! Les said that his side had played in the Shell Cup and "didn't do very well" – in fact they'd let in something like 30 goals in three games and 25 were down to the goalkeeper! Would I pop over and give him a hand with the coaching?

First Florida then Anguilla... another tough gig!

Yeah, life can be really tough!! But we had a brilliant time, so much so that I took my wife, Valerie, out there too. In amongst the coaching Les and I swapped so many stories about our time at Craven Cottage. In fact, I was never fired so I assume that I'm still the Anguillan goalkeeping coach. I'd better check that one out with Strongy!

You returned for the Fulham 2000 "replay"

I did, and despite being out of the country for 20 years the banter kicked off immediately. "Hey, here comes Baldy," shouted Strongy as I walked in. Charming! But in that split second it was as if I'd been training with the guys the previous day and this was simply the regular gathering. As the saying goes, it was as if I'd never been away.

And such tomfoolery helped get Second Division Fulham to Wembley?

At the time, getting to the FA Cup final was the biggest single honour a club player could achieve. If you were an International player then there were higher goals. But playing at Wembley was something really special.

Did that add to the nerves?

No. Although it might have worked in reverse. I was pretty calm about the whole occasion and felt I'd taken in all the team instructions and was geared up for the game. With hindsight maybe I was too relaxed. I'd come off a good run of performances so my confidence was good, and yet maybe I should have felt a bit more nervous. Maybe I was over-confident.

Either way, you were in the spotlight!

That's how it is for 'keepers. Few people talk about Johnny Cutbush losing the ball on the halfway line...

...John Cutbush does...

...And I'm looking forward to reminding him about that when I see him! I'll give him a hug first, mind! But that's what the game's about, isn't it – a goalkeeper makes an error and it's all too apparent to everyone in the stadium. But I thoroughly loved my time as a goalkeeper, and those five years at Fulham in particular.

The object of this chat isn't to dissect the events of 3 May 1975, Peter!

[Laughs!] Fair enough. But there's one lighter aspect to it all. I have used that particular mistake for years as part of my coaching education programme in talking about the psychological role of the goalkeeper. I'll show that clip to a class of 30 or 40 candidates who are taking their national license and then explain how I had to deal with the error in the days and months that followed. You have to come to terms with it, learn from it, and move on.

Okay, let's go back to that game at Carlisle. What's it like when everything goes right?

Keeping a clean sheet is the first objective. Do you remember Timmy Howard's spectacular performance in the World Cup for the USA against Belgium? I was watching that, as he pulled off save after save, and thinking how similar the circumstances were to that day at Brunton Park 40 years ago, even though Timmy was performing on a grander stage. I must say I was especially proud of Timmy because I'd identified him as a goalkeeper of significant promise when he was 14 and with my coaching status I've had close dealings with him since then. With all the emotions filling my head as Timmy made that record number of saves it was hard not to reflect on the Carlisle game.

Do you ever show those clips as part of your coaching programme?

I've have tried so many times to get footage of that game but without success – so I have to rely on my memory! There was an appeal made to the Fulham fans a few years ago; nothing emerged unfortunately. For obvious reasons, I'd love to hear from anyone who has access to that footage.

Maybe Les Barrett has stockpiled all the footage so that he can take all the glory for knocking home the winning goal?

I'll ask him! We were convinced we'd do well at Carlisle though. We prepared extremely well and the team spirit was excellent. We were sure we'd do all right, even if that meant earning yet another replay. However, we were largely second best. We got through, but not in the way we'd envisaged. Watching Timmy Howard do his stuff struck a chord – I could truthfully reflect and say, "I had a game like that once."

It must have been a great trip home?

Oh, it was! We had a bit of a sing-song – and dear old Alec even let us have some extra cans of lager on the way back! ⚽

Staying Up – Probably!

It's a risky thing to say given the club we support and what happened last season, but we may have enough in the tank to stay up. That "lucky" win at Huddersfield not only put three much-needed points on the board but also provided an injection of confidence – for the players, management and beleaguered supporters. Relegation from the Premier League was hard to stomach and yet, far from making a concerted bid to get back to the top flight we've suffered a further demoralising campaign that's given us few positive vibes. However, if we show the attacking intent that was on display against Leeds and the sheer doggedness shown at Huddersfield in our remaining games we should be safe. Probably.

That home defeat to Leeds just days before our trip to Huddersfield was a hammer-blow given that we should have gone into half-time several goals to the good. The fact we didn't was down to wasteful finishing and – not for the first time – calamitous defending seconds before the break. Or, in fact, no defending at all. What a gift of a goal that was. The guilty party, Kostas "The Match" Stafylidis then compounded that error early in the second half with one of the most senseless sendings off ever.

Yes, it should have been our throw-in, but to show such dissent meant just one thing, a yellow card. If that was daft, what followed was brainless. To foul that guy seconds later under the noses of both the referee and his assistant was as stupid as it was unprofessional. Second yellow = red card. Cue a group of our players surrounding the ref and earning the Club a fine. Failing to control the players. Guilty as charged. If only we'd had that level of fire in the bellies from the start of the season!

If all that goes down as bog-standard refereeing and bog-standard consequences, I suppose that's to be expected. After all, the standard of refereeing has been bog-standard all season. The performance of Mark Brown, allegedly in charge of our home game with Reading, is a case in point. He was incredibly inept; and that's being incredibly polite.

Failing to control the players, eh? Hmm, I'd say Brown was guilty as charged too – except he wasn't charged. Double standards, I'd say.

The officiating in that Leeds game was supreme by comparison. But can someone explain why that tackle by Stafylidis merited a yellow card when the guy who scythed down Scott Parker in the first half didn't even get a finger-wagging?

Grasping for positives this season is difficult, but it's great to see Cauley Woodrow and Marcus Bettinelli earning call-ups to the England Under-21 set-up. Marcus has certainly had plenty of practice this season! Overriding good news, though, is that vital win at Huddersfield and with it the likelihood of staying up. Here's hoping there's a healthier vibe around our club between now and August. ⚽

"Despite being out of the country for 20 years the banter kicked off immediately. "Hey, here comes Baldy," shouted Strongy as I walked in. Charming! But in that split second it was as if I'd been training with the guys the previous day."

A Chat With Roy Hodgson

Roy Hodgson has enjoyed a long and varied managerial career during the course of which he stopped off at Craven Cottage for a memorable 30 months as Fulham boss – preserving our top-flight status via a magical "Great Escape" in May 2008, taking us to a seventh-place finish the following season before, incredibly, steering us to the Europa League final in May 2010. Evidently keen to keep a bit of Fulham by his side, Roy took Ray Lewington with him when the England job came a-calling. So, lots to talk about when the England manager graciously found time in his busy schedule for a Fulhamish chat with TOOFIF...

Let's go back to late 2007, Roy; how did the move to Fulham come about?

I wasn't aware that Fulham were on the lookout for a new manager. I'd been managing Finland since the previous June and we'd just finished the Euro 2008 qualifiers; our draw with Portugal meant we just missed out on qualification and I was set to go to Inter in an advisory role. Then I received a couple of phone calls that made me question whether I really wanted to retire from the field and take on a directorial position. I was in Helsinki preparing to come home for Christmas when I took a call from David McNally at Fulham and we agreed to meet as I'd be in London anyway. There

was another job in the offing, and I had a meeting about that one as I was heading back to Finland. So lots to think about, and an important decision needed to be made about the way my career was heading. Given what's happened since I'm pleased to say that I wasn't given too much thinking time; Fulham got back to me and officially offered me the job. Given Fulham's position in the table, time was of the essence.

Okay, two different roles, but it's intriguing that you chose Fulham over Inter...

I'd just turned 60 and the job at Inter would have meant semi-retirement. Despite the lure of working with Massimo Moratti at Inter, I suppose I wasn't really ready for that and, as it worked out, I made the right choice; in fact, I couldn't have made a better one!

Were you still thinking that two or three months down the line when Fulham were still 19th and relegation seemed a given?

We thought we were progressing, but without getting enough points on the board. Certainly not in the first few games, a tough run that included defeats to Chelsea, Arsenal and Manchester United – top teams, and a tough start!

What did you see as your main challenges once you took the reins?

The teamwork had to be better and we needed to be more tactically astute. We had to inculcate the right mentality for what was obviously going to be a battle to stay up. That meant working hard on the training field – working hard on specific things that might give us a chance, while developing the mental strength to deal with any knockbacks that might come along the way. Above all of that was to have a belief and trust that if we did all of the above and attacked better as a team while defending better as a unit too, then success would come; we had to believe and hope that such success would arrive quickly enough to preserve our status.

You couldn't have left it any later. Two-down at Manchester City at half-time; we were effectively relegated! The 3-2 victory was the first of many stand-out results in your time at Fulham. What on earth did you say?

There wasn't that much to say, to be honest. I remember saying there was no point in giving a Churchillian speech or simply saying "Don't worry, it'll all be fine; it'll be all right on the night." No, we had to focus on playing better than we had in the first period and to stick to the principles that we believed in. It was all pretty level-headed and realistic; no promises of miracles, just a question of taking the field with the right mentality and, with a bit of fortune, we could get some sort of reward. We had to set a simple goal, an achievable one: we're gonna win the second half. We can't take their two goals away (more's the pity!), but what we can do is to put that real bummer of a first-half score to one side, one that put us even further in the shit, and take to the field for the second 45 minutes with great resolve. That's within our control and, who knows, it could give us a chance.

The spectacular comeback at City was a major achievement but was just one aspect of the "Great Escape" – after all, there was still Birmingham to come at home and Portsmouth away. Still no sign of Churchill...?
Frankly, I don't think that approach works. The focus has to be on the work you've been doing as a group and the various conversations you've had with the players at the training ground collectively and individually. Suddenly expecting to find the right two or three words that might inflame people while glossing over a multitude of sins that might be affecting the team or the Club is naïve in my book.

I had the privilege of being in the Portsmouth press box for that final game of the 2007-08 campaign after which you were quick to commiserate with the managers who'd been relegated. The press lapped up that classy gesture!
It wasn't that difficult as I'd had plenty of time – months, in fact – to contemplate our possible relegation! I always believed our team was good enough to find a way through, but with every passing week things looked that much worse. We missed a massive opportunity at home against Sunderland when we conceded some sloppy goals; it was a blow going 3-1 down near the end after getting ourselves back into the match. A win that day would have seen us move in the right direction; instead it was a plunge the opposite way. Thankfully we had plenty of strong characters at the Club, underestimated characters – Hughes and Hangeland were a great pairing at centre-back, Danny Murphy was a big influence in midfield as was McBride up front. Plus Simon Davies, Paul Konchesky... thank heavens we had players with such strong personalities.

Having stayed up, albeit only on goal difference, that dramatic upswing must have served as a platform for what was to follow?
It was proof that what we'd been working on, and what we believed in, was the way forward. What's more, we would start the following season on a higher footing; instead of starting the campaign halfway through the season and already struggling, now we would have a full pre-season then a full Premier League programme plus Cup games to

look forward to, and to prepare for. Then, once you've secured your safety you can look upwards. And that, to be honest, is the outlook of most of the clubs in the Premier League. It's only a select few who can envisage competing for the major prizes. The dream is for top ten finishes; in reality it's safety first for the vast majority.

You took "safety first" to a new dimension, taking us to seventh the following season! And you did so by maintaining and enhancing that squad belief in the "boring" basics of organisation, discipline, collective hard work, no little skill...
That probably underestimates the quality of the players in terms of their technical ability, but, yes, those are some of the key buzzwords that apply to any sort of successful teamwork, whatever the sport. I suppose you could say it's boring to those who believe football is somehow magical and that everything falls into place with a click of the fingers – and that the difference between success and failure is whether the manager you've appointed has a magic wand or not. But of course that's so different to being a professional in this footballing world when you realise early on that magic wands simply don't exist! And furthermore, there are no managers out there who possess qualities that other top managers don't have; okay, they might encourage the press to believe that they do have special qualities, and they may even manage to get the press to write along those lines.

However, in the world of football we don't subscribe to that theory; no, any successful outfit will be based on a foundation of hard work. And, even then, that doesn't guarantee success, at least in the short term, because football matches all have a story of their own as they unfold and people's judgement comes from the result at the end of the match. And the result at the end of the match doesn't always coincide with the quality of the work that's gone into the match preparations and then during the game itself.

A case in point is a game I watched at the weekend: Manchester City versus West Ham. The judgement after West Ham's victory was that Bilic's work was fantastic and that his side was brilliantly well organised and it was a defensive

Cardiff City 1 Fulham 1	
08.08.15	10th
Fulham 1 Brighton & HA 2	
15.08.15	17th
Hull City 2 Fulham 1	
18.08.15	21st
Fulham 1 Huddersfield Town 1	
22.08.15	21st
Rotherham United 1 Fulham 3	
29.08.15	14th
Fulham 2 Blackburn Rovers 1	
13.09.15	11th
Sheffield Wednesday 3 Fulham 2	
19.09.15	16th
Fulham 4 Queens Park Rangers 0	
25.09.15	11th
Fulham 0 Wolverhampton Wanderers 3	
29.09.15	14th
Charlton Athletic 2 Fulham 2	
04.10.15	13th
Middlesbrough 0 Fulham 0	
17.10.15	13th
Fulham 1 Leeds United 1	
21.10.15	13th
Fulham 4 Reading 2	
24.10.15	11th
Bristol City 1 Fulham 4	
31.10.15	10th
Burnley 3 Fulham 1	
03.11.15	11th
Fulham 2 Birmingham City 5	
07.11.15	12th
MK Dons 1 Fulham 1	
21.11.15	12th
Fulham 1 Preston North End 1	
28.11.15	13th
Nottingham Forest 3 Fulham 0	
05.12.15	16th
Fulham 2 Brentford 2	
12.12.15	17th
Fulham 1 Ipswich Town 2	
15.12.15	17th
Bolton Wanderers 2 Fulham 2	
19.12.15	18th
Derby County 2 Fulham 0	
26.12.15	18th
Fulham 4 Rotherham United 1	
29.12.15	18th
Fulham 0 Sheffield Wednesday 1	
02.01.16	19th
Wolverhampton Wanderers 3 Fulham 2	
12.01.16	19th
Huddersfield Town 1 Fulham 1	
16.01.16	19th
League Cup	
Wycombe Wanderers 0 Fulham 1	
11.08.15	Round 1
Fulham 3 Sheffield United 0	
25.08.15	Round 2
Fulham 0 Stoke City 1	
22.09.15	Round 3
FA Cup	
Sheffield Wednesday 2 Fulham 1	
09.01.16	Round 3

1st
2nd
3rd
4th
5th
6th
7th
8th
9th
10th
11th
12th
13th
14th
15th
16th
17th
18th
19th
20th
21st
22nd
23rd
24th

masterclass. My judgement was that it was a result and performance that comes along maybe every 100 matches. City were so much better in every respect. Sure, West Ham toughed it out if you like, but City had so many goal chances; there were several occasions when, having thrown bodies at shots, the ball went just centimetres the wrong side of the Hammers' post...

...That aspect was conveniently overlooked...?

...Exactly! My idea of brilliant defensive organisation is when the opposition don't get the chance to shoot. It's not brilliant organisation if the opposition are allowed 25 shots at goal from in and around your penalty area – that bothers me! Sometimes the game unfolds that way, but if it happened every week you'd be in trouble more often than not. When we played Shakhtar in 2010 they had something like 80 per cent possession. Their ability to pass and keep the ball was extraordinary – we simply couldn't get near them for long periods. That's when the qualities you've instilled into your squad can see you through, if you're lucky.

The hard work DID pay off for Fulham in your second full season. It was evident that players were improving week by week – gaining confidence both in their own abilities and contribution plus the team structure. Paul Konchesky was a prime example. "Little" Fulham were being properly managed, and the results – literally and figuratively – were just reward...

"Structure" is the right word there. And results are crucial. You can't push a team forward without getting good results. When a player feels that the structure around him and his game is solid, and he is "at one" with that structure, then it becomes that much easier to improvise, to test yourself more, to take a few more risks and to do things that you may not have been doing for a while – because you know that, if the worst happens, the structure is there and you can go back to that solid base should something not quite come off. When there's no structure then it's very, very difficult. In such circumstances, if a player tries to do something that he thinks his manager, his fans or the club want him to do and is unsuccessful then there's no cover and nothing for him to fall back on. I must say I was fortunate in the quality of players I found at Fulham; they were of the right type to accept that the qualities we've already spoken about were the right way to go. Similarly, with anyone we brought in, it was made very clear to them that they had to buy in to that philosophy. We'd simply say: "If that isn't for you then don't bother joining us!".

Whatever it was, it worked. We were beating the Liverpools and Manchester Uniteds of this world...

Yes, we had a good team. And those boys deserve a lot of credit. They may not all have been household names but in some ways they became so through their efforts. Players such as Danny Murphy and Simon Davies had found themselves in the footballing backwaters after previously playing in successful teams, but at Fulham they had the qualities we required, and they benefited. Zoltan Gera, Damien Duff, Mark Schwarzer are other great examples. We believed in them, that's for sure, and fortunately they produced for the Club.

Those you named, plus other "characters" such as Zamora, Dempsey, Baird and Pantsil, still needed managing, though...?

We had plenty of good characters. In fact, I think Lawrie Sanchez was unlucky, at least in terms of his player recruitment. He was vilified in some quarters, but players such as Hughes, Baird, Stephen Davis and even David Healy, who didn't have the greatest success here, were good players and good lads. Steve we let go only because we had a few players like him so he was finding it hard to nail down a definite place in the team. We'd have been more than happy to keep him, but once we got that big offer from Glasgow Rangers it was hard to do so.

Which of these caused you the most bother – the 2010 Icelandic ash cloud or Jimmy Bullard?

[Laughs...] Make no mistake, Jimmy was a very talented footballer. But not a player for whom team structure and tactical restraints came naturally. He wanted the ball, and wanted to see what he could do with the ball – top qualities. He could certainly pass the ball well, and when he returned from injury he was a key figure in our staying up. To answer your question seriously, I wouldn't say Jimmy caused us problems, it was more the way we were going. He then got that opportunity to move to Hull where he thought he could pull the strings a little bit more than he was able to do here. That ash cloud was a massive blow; the whole wretched business affected our Europa preparations and gave us another unwanted obstacle to overcome.

Dealing with the effervescent Jimmy Bullard was one thing but you also had an eccentric Chairman to contend with at Fulham...

Mohamed? He was very good, actually. In fact, if he was ever problematic it was more with the Chief Executive than the Manager! The football team is the shop window of the Club but Mohamed oversaw all the club dealings, the running of the Club, focusing on the finances and proposed expenditure – and that's the CEO's domain. After David McInally left, the Club appointed Alistair [Mackintosh] and I'd have to say that the backing both Alistair and I got from the Chairman was good. Mind you, he'd ask lots of questions – it was never simply a case of getting out the chequebook. He always wanted an explanation as to why we wanted to bring in a particular player, for example.

He wanted to know what the reasoning was, what that player would bring to the Club and how the proposed purchase would make his club a better club. I'd say I got along very well with the Chairman and to this day I wouldn't hear a bad word said about Mohamed Al Fayed; for Fulham, he was fantastic. He moved Fulham Football Club away from the threat of extinction and then put in enough money – plus considerable time and effort – into overseeing a climb up the divisions. Make no mistake, he wanted to run the football club properly and to see it run properly. In short, he wanted to run it like Harrods – successfully. It was hard for me to leave Fulham and the Chairman – and he certainly made it very clear that he didn't want me to leave – but at my age when a club like Liverpool comes calling you don't know how many more of those opportunities will come along. I think most of the people at the Club understood the situation; I don't think Mohamed did – for him, Fulham was a Bayern Munich or a Barcelona!

Another decent partnership was the one you built up with Ray Lewington, so much so that he's now your assistant in the England set-up. What are his qualities?

He's a very good coach and a very good person! He shares my thoughts and philosophy about football, which is important, but he's very much his own man. Ray is a perfect assistant in the sense that he assists fully. He's really good on the training field and his enthusiasm for the game is always evident. We make such a good team because he's assists me enormously – I can share an idea or suggestion with him and be sure of getting not just an educated answer but an honest one. So much so that it might even change my original opinion.

Putting the amazing highs you achieved at Craven Cottage to one side for a moment, us fans got to thinking that Roy Hodgson and Fulham Football Club was a perfect fit for as long as it lasted. I know you're something of a footballing pragmatist, but did you ever come close to feeling that?

Yes... Yeah, I think I probably did. It's close to where I was born and close to where I live. I loved the atmosphere around Motspur Park and everything around the Club. I loved the way I was treated – I could easily have seen myself attempting to be a long-term servant...

...That's not your record by and large though, is it? You've generally had shortish spells in charge here and there...?

More recently, perhaps. In the beginning, though, it was more four years here and five years there. I had 12 years in Sweden at three clubs and then five years in Switzerland with the national team. The game's moved on somewhat though, hasn't it?

Above: Roy Hodgson joins a group of Fulham supporters for a snapshot in Basle.

I mean, four or five years anywhere these days is seen as a long-term stay and is equivalent to maybe a 10- or 15-year stay in days gone by.

High time we focused on some of the many highs you engineered at Fulham. One came around after Dickson Etuhu netted the scruffiest of goals in Italy against Juventus, paving the way for a truly remarkable return leg at the Cottage...

A great night! And all the more so after a going a goal down – we had it all to do once Trezeguet scored in the opening minutes. At that stage we required three goals – against Juventus! – to take the game into extra-time. We did play well that night; the noise was tremendous! Euphoria's a funny thing, sometimes it comes along from nowhere and people just get carried away with it...

Ray has said that, once we scored, he thought we might be on for something special – and said as much to you at the time – even if overall victory might have been a little too fanciful....

Yeah, I think he did. But then I'm always a bit more circumspect! It developed into a great night and we pulled off a major result. The great thing is that it became one of those footballing occasions that you can always look back on fondly and treasure. The ensuing win against Wolfsburg was fantastic too and the mood had been high, of course, after we'd beaten Portsmouth in 2008...

You've rather summed up the scale of that result against Juventus there – we went on to defeat German champions Wolfsburg but, by comparison, did so in such a matter-of-fact way...

In fact, we were much better than Wolfsburg in both of those games...

...that must have given you great satisfaction...?

Yes, I suppose it did! And do you know the funny thing is that Mohamed and others at the Club

> *"We tried to always remain humble; tried to do our job properly vis-a-vis the community and the younger teams in the Club and also our statements in the press – we always tried to behave correctly. If you can ally all of that with achieving some good results then I'd say it's a job well done."*

weren't all that keen on us taking part in the competition in the first place! They were worried – and rightly so – that doing everything that was required in taking the Europa League seriously would impinge on the bread and butter of our domestic competitions. As I recall, we also did quite well in the FA Cup that season, so to compete so effectively on so many fronts with the budget and player pool that we had was considered a difficult proposition. In fact, we finished 12th in the Premier League that season, a drop from our seventh place the previous season, so I suppose there's your proof that the further we went in Europe our League programme became a bit of a grind by comparison. By the same token, when you've got the possibility of making a final in Europe, whether you finish 10th or 12th tends to be a little less important.

That possibility famously became a reality and, even with an injury-hit squad, we more than matched Atlético Madrid in that Hamburg final – only being pipped by a late, late goal, and a flippin' deflected strike at that...
Yes, and against a team of such big names, too: everyone's aware of Aguero and De Gea today, of course, while Forlán, who proved such a thorn in our side, played at the very top level. A terrific team, and a line-up that formed the basis of the Club's subsequent forays in the Champions League. So that really unfortunate deflection – the ball squirmed through Brede's legs and clipped his back leg to go beyond Mark's dive was cruel, especially as it was only four minutes from the end of extra-time. Atlético had some very good players but I think had it gone to penalties we would have stood a very good chance, simply because Mark Schwarzer was so good (although, to be fair, I suppose De Gea was a good keeper even then!). Having lost a UEFA Cup final on penalties as manager of Inter Milan and then to see Fulham go down to a late, deflected goal in extra-time

I'd have to say that I've not been lucky in that respect. But the whole experience at Fulham led, of course, to other things for me – it's thanks to Fulham and the fact that I returned to England to take on their offer that I've subsequently got to the pinnacle of my career: managing England. I'm sure it wouldn't have happened had I taken either of the other jobs on the table; it certainly wouldn't have happened had I gone to Inter.

Your achievements with Fulham lifted the Club's profile around the world. The warmth of feeling towards FFC in the spring of 2010 was extraordinary. And we did it (or almost did it!) the

Below: Roy Hodgson chose Fulham over Inter milan – and it proved to be a wise career move.

Fulham way, if there is such a thing. We picked up Fair Play awards, fan behaviour awards, a Barclays Spirit Award and even Manager of the Year. Brilliant stuff, and brilliant times – and all from inculcating a little structure...
It's back to the people at the Club – we believed in fair play. Everything we did was football orientated in that we never tried to gain advantages by doing anything outside of the world of football. We tried to always remain humble; tried to do our job properly vis-a-vis the community and the younger teams in the Club and also our statements in the press – we always tried to behave correctly. If you can ally all of that with achieving some good results then I'd say it's a job well done.

In the sometimes controversial world of sport it's always a great treat to see "the nice guy" come first. We may have had to settle for second in Hamburg but we remained champions in many people's eyes...
I think that's a fair assessment. We were certainly a lot of people's second favourite team for a while – which is some achievement.

I must thank you for that achievement. I don't represent anyone, I'm simply a nutty long-time Fulham supporter who happens to edit a fans' magazine. But, on this occasion it's only fair to pass on the thanks of all Fulham fans for what you did at the Club. Special thanks also for finding the time to speak so openly to TOOFIF.
It's thanks from me too; I've enjoyed the chat. And I must say the Fulham fans all played their part in helping us do so well.

One final comparison, Roy. Just five years on from our fantastic European exploits, here you are at the peak of your profession – manager of England, and ably assisted by "our" Ray Lewington. Meanwhile Fulham are struggling to make headway in the rough and tumble of the Championship...
I suppose that highlights the volatile nature of football. Fulham are just one of a great number of clubs who have reached very, very high only to fall very quickly subsequently. It all goes to show how important "structure" and "doing the right thing" and getting the right people at a football club are. The choice of manager is always going to be a pivotal decision because he will affect so much of the mentality and philosophy at the Club. If you don't get that right – if, for whatever reason, the "fit" isn't right – things can very, very quickly go wrong...

Fair to say that "fit" wasn't right for you at Liverpool...?
...Possibly, although I think the change of ownership had a lot to do with it. The people

who brought me in left after a couple of months. But then that's just one of the risks involved in taking on such a job.

When did the approach come from Liverpool?
It was pretty soon after the final actually – I certainly didn't have it "lined up" beforehand.

In the interim, were you contemplating another season with Fulham? And if so, what do you think you could have achieved?
Oh, very much so. In the world we live in today, the only way a club such as Fulham could have advanced in perhaps the way the supporters would have wanted would have been via massive financial investment. I didn't really expect Mohamed to do much more than he'd already done, so I don't think there'd have been

£100-200m made available to me! But we were an ageing team and we'd have had to make some changes. That said, I'm confident we could have continued along the same path; maybe we might not have topped that special run in Europe, but there's no reason to think that we couldn't have done well in the domestic cup competitions while holding our own in the League. I like to believe we could have kept ploughing a very steady furrow while gaining the rewards for doing so.

Here's hoping you and Ray continue to do well with England. However, I'm sure I'm not the only selfish Fulham supporter who – especially given what's happened in the meantime – wishes you were still ploughing that furrow at Fulham! ⚽

The Great Escape of 2008: Roy Hodgson's views at the time...

Fulham 1 Sunderland 3
"I'm pretty low at the moment. The only thing in our favour is that we are still six points behind. But it's a bitter blow. In the first half, just before their goal, I had every hope that our performance was going to give us a result.

"It was always uphill after their second goal. We got in good crossing positions but our final ball wasn't good enough.

"The only lifeline is that football is not played on paper – on paper it looks very, very bad for us."

Reading 0 Fulham 2
"It was a good victory because we played well enough to deserve it and we hit the woodwork three times. We defended more solidly than last week and we kept them at bay.

"We would have a far better chance of staying up if there were eight or so games left. We have 12 points to fight for and this performance has given me hope that we might get some miraculous escape."

Fulham 0 Liverpool 2
"We matched them quite well but once they got their first goal we were chasing the game and when they got the second goal it put us out of contention. We can retain hope of staying up. The task gets harder because we have not recovered any points on the teams above us and we have lost another game and another opportunity.

"We have given a good account of ourselves, but we do not have anything to show for it."

Manchester City 2 Fulham 3
"It was a splendid victory for us, one we so badly needed. It looked bleak at half-time, and we had a mountain to climb – we didn't deserve to be losing. But we did it.

"At 0-2 I honestly thought we weren't out of it. I never lost hope, but to win it was extraordinary. We've given ourselves a chance now."

Fulham 2 Birmingham City 0
"A game we had to win – and we did so in some style in front of our home crowd. When you've been at the bottom of the division for so long, virtually all season, you don't really expect your fans to turn out in such great numbers and to give you that sort of magnificent support.

"And credit to the players too – they kept their shape, they kept to the pattern from the first minute to the last. But let's not get ahead of ourselves, there's one more crucial victory still required."

Portsmouth 0 Fulham 1
"I knew it would be tough, and we were aware throughout the game of how the results were going elsewhere. But then up popped Danny Murphy with a bullet header that kept us up. "For much of the game I was contemplating this post-match interview and dreading the fact that we could well be facing life in the Championship, so my thoughts are with the managers and players who have not been so fortunate this afternoon.

"Everybody at Fulham deserves great praise and we'll enjoy the moment for a couple of days. Then it'll be a case of getting our feet back on the ground and preparing for next season to ensure we have a better platform so that we don't face the same predicament."

Left: Diomansy Kamara, a 64th-minute substitute, netted twice as Fulham staged a remarkable recovery to win 3-2 at Manchester City having been 2-0 down – and effectively relegated – with 20 minutes left to play.

George Cohen

If there's one stat Fulham fans love to spout every four years, it's this: England only win the World Cup when there's a Fulham player in the side. England's right-back in 1966, and ever-present during the march to the final and the fantastic 4-2 victory over West Germany at Wembley, was George Cohen. A one-club man, "Gentleman George" made 459 appearances for FFC (scoring six goals) and would have added more but for a freakish injury picked up in 1967 when still at his prime. He's still a one-club man – hosting the George Cohen Lounge on Fulham matchdays with customary genial charm. High time for a TOOFIF chat. After all, next year marks the 50th anniversary of 1966. Worth celebrating, don't you think?

What was it like to be on Fulham's books as a youngster?
I was scouted by former Fulham winger Ernie Shepherd. Ernie said I'd be well looked after at Fulham, my local club. I was 15 – and I was indeed looked after. I got on with everyone famously.

A full Fulham debut wasn't too long in coming?
I was 16 and we faced Liverpool at Craven Cottage. Before that, though, manager Dug Livingstone needed a full-back for the Reserves. I was a wing-

half but, with our full-back injured, he switched me to right-back where I had to mark a nippy winger. I did quite well, matching him for pace and reading his moves. After that Dug insisted that I was a full-back. He warned, "I want you back every afternoon, after your work; you'll be training with me or Joe Bacuzzi. You're going to be a full-back – and a bloody good one!" So I was comprehensibly trained in how to defend in the old W-M formation.

Were you nervous before your full debut?
The only time I was nervous – really nervous – was before a certain match at Wembley Stadium in 1966. On that day the magnitude of the occasion got to me. But otherwise no, not even as a 16-year-old. The confidence of youth kicked in. I had to wait until the following season for my next run-out [against Huddersfield], but before that Liverpool game I was given the standard safety-first mantra from several players: "If in doubt, kick it out!" Well, it's fair to say I was in doubt a lot of times that day! I think I even found the Thames a couple of times. But when I came off the pitch at the end they all seemed pleased enough with me. The manager told me I'd be offered full professional terms before long. I was a right-back. I was also pretty confident in my abilities, or at least in my pace. Being quick, I reckoned that if I was ever beaten by an opponent

I'd be quick enough to recover and get back at him. Speed was always my main asset, although as I filled out I became stronger too.

Which key people at Fulham helped you to learn?
There were many! Roy Bentley was terrific; Arthur Stevens was great; Joe Bacuzzi was marvellous – and there was always advice from Johnny Haynes. John was five years older than me. He was not only a sensational player but he was always prepared to help out during matches or in training. Sometimes forcibly! But that's only right – you don't become a player by people patting you on the back and saying "Never mind". You do so by taking criticism and learning from it. There was a huge amount of experience at the Club – Eddie Lowe, a terrific player, was one who'd come over during a lull in the game and suggest, "If you do this..." or "If you do that..." – simple words of wisdom that you'd be daft to ignore. Make no mistake, though, once you got into the first team it was a man's world.

You've mentioned a few names there. Great characters – and they could play a bit too...?
Could I have been anywhere better? I doubt it! As a lad it was tough at times, but what a group of players! Roy Bentley was phenomenal; he organised my overlapping full-back role, which wasn't the done thing at the time. Mind you, the onus was on me to get back and defend; that was the priority.

Back then, people would receive around £10 for working a 48-hour week. Once I'd signed professional in October 1956 I received a £20 signing-on fee and was earning £8-10 a week. I went home with that month's wages – about £50 after tax! – and was pretty excited. I marched in at home and in my exuberance blurted out what I'd received. Right away I could have bitten my tongue off. Good news though it was, to announce it like that in front of my father wasn't a subtle move.

...What would he have made of the enormous sums involved today...?
Indeed! In 1956 players were only getting about £10 a week; that was the case until 1961, when it went up to £20. In my early days at the Club some guys would have to do a morning's work to supplement their income – and up and down the country that could mean a shift down the mines. Not me, thank goodness, I was well paid by comparison, especially once Johnny Haynes got his £100 a week.

Enter Jimmy Hill...?
Jimmy did a magnificent job. As Chairman of the Professional Footballers Association, Jimmy, along with Cliff Lloyd, the PFA Secretary (and former Fulham full-back), did a great job; the Football League and the FA did not. I believe they offered a £5-a-year increment. But in the end they capitulated and Johnny was the first to benefit,

famously being the first player to receive £100 a week – and I don't blame him, he was worth it!

Today's bowling-green pitches are a world away from the mud-heaps you and Johnny faced...
When you're running at speed, the level of skill you need is higher – that was certainly the case in my day when the churned-up playing surface meant you couldn't rely on the ball running consistently. If you're trying to cross a ball at speed on a bumpy pitch it could be very difficult indeed. Let's just say that I must have encountered a number of bumps! But seriously, it *was* difficult. Johnny would have revelled on surfaces that allowed him to play first-time passes with ease. He was brilliant anyway, but had he been able to play the ball first time with confidence, rather than sometimes having to take a touch, he'd have created even more openings.

Did you simply accept Johnny's abilities and skills after a while, or were there occasions when he still managed to surprise you?
He was skilful; he was strong; he was two-footed; he knew where he wanted to put the ball, and invariably it hit the spot; he had the marvellous ability of creating time for himself; I could go on. John was a truly gifted player with magical qualities. He did have bad games, though. He was human in that respect! But John was his own worst critic. He could be vitriolic on the pitch when mistakes were made – he was famously voluble when things weren't going well – but he always included himself in that equation. Perhaps the best way to sum John up is to look at his relationship with his schoolboy pal Tosh [Chamberlain]. They'd have blazing rows, they were like two brothers in that respect, but once the game was over any differences of opinion were forgotten. John had such high standards; and he expected others to strive for those same standards. As for his skill level, well I've been quoted as saying

> *"Johnny was skilful; he was strong; he was two-footed; he knew where he wanted to put the ball, and invariably it hit the spot; he had the marvellous ability of creating time for himself; I could go on. John was a truly gifted player with magical qualities."*

Below: An iconic shot of George Cohen and Craven Cottage in 1962, courtesy of Ken Coton. Fulham's opponents on the day were Nottingham Forest.

> *"We've had so many changes on and off the field – owner, managers, players, that it's been tough to get that required stability. So many youngsters have been introduced, don't forget. No matter how good they are potentially, it's always a big ask of a youngster to make a seamless transition into the first team."*

that Johnny could give you goosebumps on a wet night in a match that didn't matter. That opinion hasn't dimmed with the passage of time.

At today's Fulham, standards have been allowed to drop over the past few seasons. You are still passionately involved at the Cottage, so it must have hurt to see us slide out of the top flight?
It's been a disastrous time. Here isn't the place to apportion blame, but it's been an unfortunate period. Make no mistake, Fulham is a fantastic club. All those who come to my lounge feel that the Club is giving them something. The match is the main focus of the day, naturally, but all the guests are made to feel extremely welcome and wanted.

We've had so many changes on and off the field – owner, managers, players, that it's been tough to get that required stability. So many youngsters have been introduced, don't forget. No matter how good they are potentially, it's always a big ask of a youngster to make a seamless transition into the first team. And we've blooded so many in such a relatively short period. I was a regular in the team at 17, Alan Mullery also made the breakthrough at about the same age, alongside several senior pros. You may well get a word of advice here and there, but in essence there's no quarter given. You're a professional footballer in a team of professionals who are relying on each other for their bonuses and such-like. You're there to do a job. Your age has very little to do with anything. That's what I mean about it being a tough profession. You need fitness and skill, naturally, but you also need character.

You need the strength of character to show that you belong...?
Precisely. If one of your team-mates is having a poor game or carrying an injury then it's up to those around him to recognise that and chivvy him along (no substitutes back in my day of course) and maybe offer more cover than usual. There's a great story of a dressing-room "discussion" from my day that was threatening to get quite raucous. Bobby Keetch was getting it in the neck, right, left and centre. It all got a bit comical; not that Bob found it funny. Every time he opened his mouth to defend himself someone else chipped in with, "Well, you didn't do that; you didn't do this..." Then, all of a sudden from the back of the room came this crusty "cor blimey" voice of Jimmy Langley. "Now I'm going to be honest with you, Bob," said Jim earnestly, before continuing, "Two years ago, when I had a bad game..." End of discussion! He wasn't allowed to finish as we were all rolling around with laughter. Our manager, Beddy

Below: George Cohen is flanked by John Fraser (left) and Les Strong after receiving the Freedom of the Borough of Hammersmith and Fulham in October 2016.

Jezzard, simply put his head in his hands. But it only underlined the team's fantastic camaraderie.

And it wasn't a bad set-up. You got to two FA Cup semi-finals (four if you include replays!)...?
I don't dwell on it, but it still rankles that we didn't get to Wembley in 1962. Against Burnley at Villa Park, Maurice Cook was clean through. He steamed into the area and the goalkeeper upended him. We've got the next best thing to a goal – a penalty. Only the ref didn't give it! We couldn't believe it – it was such a blatant foul, and such a straightforward decision to make. Fair to say that Johnny Haynes went potty; actually we all went potty! The referee was adamant that Maurice had tripped. It might seem a bit righteous to say so, but back then we didn't have any of the faking that's crept into the game today. Maurice had neither dived nor tripped. He'd been cleaned out.

The semi-final against Manchester United four years earlier was rather surreal, coming so soon after the tragedy at Munich. It was also a sensational match. We went to Villa Park as underdogs. Even though United had lost so many players in the disaster they'd brought in several excellent replacements. The match was contested in front of about 65,000, but the surprising factor on the day is how many were evidently rooting for us. And, once again, we were desperately unlucky not to go through. Johnny [Haynes] put the ball into the net but he was adjudged to have handled it. The thing is, you generally only get one chance against the great teams. We'd had ours and didn't take it – we lost the Highbury replay 5-3. Tony Macedo had a poor game that day, but then he'd been outstanding in the earlier rounds and was as instrumental as anyone in getting us there...

...Shades of Peter Mellor in 1975...?
Yes indeed. Tony was an agile, brilliant goalkeeper, and capable of pulling off the most unlikely of saves. Just not in the Highbury replay!

Ah, it was only the FA Cup. You were obviously saving yourself for the big one: Wembley in '66!
I wish I knew that at the time!

Who was your most difficult opponent?
Cliff Jones. I still see him from time to time today and we always exchange a man-hug. And he'll always say, "This is the closest you ever got to me!" That camaraderie is so very important.

You clocked up 459 games for Fulham – and scored six goals. Do you remember them?
I remember scoring against Brighton, my first goal for the Club. Both Jimmy Langley and I scored, so both full-backs were on target. [Mike Johnson scored the other in a 3-1 win.] I also stuck one away from about 25 yards against Wolves [in October

1964]. Johnny Haynes put me through from the half-way line and I had a clear path on goal. As their players chased back I panicked and just hit it! The ball hit the bar and went it, so it looked good! As I headed back for the restart, their captain, Ron Flowers, who I knew pretty well by then, said, "You'll never score another goal as good as that one as long as you've got a hole in your, er, proverbial." He wasn't far wrong as I only scored one after that [in a 4-1 home win over Manchester City in 1966].

We'll come to your World Cup stories in a mo, George. Let's skip to the grisly bit a year or so after your Wembley exploits: that knee injury against Liverpool.
That freak injury halted me in my tracks. Their goalkeeper volleyed the ball clear and I went to make a fairly routine connection. I simply didn't get there in time and put undue pressure on my left knee. And that was it. No collision; no opponent involved. Nearest guy to me was Peter Thompson, the Liverpool winger. When I eventually got up it just gave way again. Diagnosing and treating such injuries are much more straightforward these days, but back then even the specialist didn't realise it was a cartilege problem. I had blood in the joint. As the cartilege doesn't have a blood supply it was thought that a vein had snapped or whatever. Anyway this all went on for months, and it was only when I went to Harley Street that I was told quite bluntly, "You're finished, my boy." I went to see Club Director Eric Miller and he said the Club would look after me. In due course I went to work as a land buyer for a friend introduced to me by Jimmy Greaves. That involved studying for two years at an architect's in London before moving to Tunbridge Wells where I've been ever since.

While preparing for life in the property business you had a spell as Fulham Youth team manager...?
I'm proud to say that one or two of my players made a real mark at the Club. Former England cricketer Mickey Stewart [Alec's father], a talented footballer, was coaching the London Universities side at, ironically, Motspur Park. He asked if I'd like to take over from him as he had to get back to cricketing duties. The honorary role offered a great chance to get some coaching experience. While I was there, two boys stood out. One was John Lacy; the other was Mickey Nairn. Mickey was a hot prospect but he picked up a nasty injury so Fulham's loss was industry's gain. John had a fine footballing career; he played for us in the 1975 FA Cup final and subsequently left for Tottenham for about £200,000. We had various training sessions at Fulham at which at triallists came along. I was with my old pal Ken Craggs (Ken's wife introduced me to Daphne, my lovely wife, so we go back a long way!) when John Fraser turned up. They say there's not too much sentiment in football, but

Above: A young George Cohen sports a full head of hair – he hadn't met Les Strong at that point!

John was a man you desperately hoped would make it. He made himself a footballer – he listened to everything and never questioned anything. He wanted to give himself the best possible chance. I was delighted he had such a good career.

You also discovered Les Strong...?
[Laughs] Don't blame me! Les...what can I say? What a character! And what a stalwart he became to Fulham! When Les turned up for training we asked, "Where do you play, son?" He replied, "I'm a scheming inside-left." So we gave him a run-out. After about half an hour it was all too obvious that he was neither an inside-forward nor a schemer. We called him over and asked if he'd played anywhere else. "Oh yes," he insisted, "I can also be a bit of a destroyer at left-half." So we reshuffled the side and said, "Okay, away you go." In one sense he didn't do too badly, but on the other, his fouls were so damned obvious no referee would let him stay on the park. Between us, though, Ken and I thought he had the makings of a player. So we persevered and Les went on to be a decent left-back.

Here you are still serving FFC so well!
I had a great career. It finished abruptly, but I had a terrific time. As for being a one-club man, I know there were several offers – or at least a number of back-door approaches – I gather Tommy Trinder turned down an offer of £82,000. I know Everton were after me. They wanted to pair me up with my England left-back Ray Wilson. Arsenal wanted to do a swap with Don Howe plus cash. But why would I want to leave? I was enormously happy at Fulham. It wasn't as if the other clubs could tempt me with more money – I was lucky enough to be one of the highest-paid players in the League at that time. So I was more than happy to stay put.

Hearing you having such a good laugh puts so much of what you've been through health-wise into perspective. Your grim battles with cancer have been well documented and it's fantastic to

> "That freak injury halted me in my tracks. Their goalkeeper volleyed the ball clear and I went to make a fairly routine connection. I simply didn't get there in time and put undue pressure on my left knee. And that was it. No collision; no opponent involved."

Above: George Cohen in World Cup-winning action for England against West Germany in 1966.

see you looking so well with that particular issue a thing of the past. Today it's the effects of the extreme doses of chemotherapy that plague me – but having a laugh is so important. In my days at Fulham we had so many laughs.

Wembley, 1966. England 2 West Germany 2. The World Cup Final is set for 30 minutes extra-time and England manager Alf Ramsey rallies his troops: "Look at the Germans – their shirts are out, their socks are down. They're finished. You've won it once, now go and win it again." So George Cohen and co did just that.

It's 50 years since that World Cup Final, George. You must get a warm glow from being one of the select few to have got your hands on the trophy.
Fifty years, goodness me. I don't know about "warm glow" but I had butterflies on the day of the final. It wasn't simply the magnitude of the Wembley final that got to me, though, it was more that our regular pre-match preparations went right out of the window. While there was none of the "hype" that has become something of an industry these days with the wall-to-wall television coverage, you could still sense the nation's growing expectation levels thanks to the media coverage.

When did those nerves kick in?
From when I got up for breakfast! The magnitude of the game hit me. When, at last, we were on the coach to the ground the tension eased a little. The streets were packed and there were flags everywhere – quite a sight! But it underlined the importance of the game. As kick-off approached there was no way of easing the nerves by doing our regular warm-ups and sprint exercises – no, we had all the ceremonial stuff, anthems and presentations, which heightened the anxiety. I managed some warm-ups in the dressing room, but it was all so cramped. We were all in the same boat, but it wasn't an ideal way to prepare for your biggest-ever game. Then we walked down the tunnel and onto the pitch – well, the noise was unbelievable. As we lined up I could sense that I wasn't the only one who was anxious. I remember saying to myself, "Don't bugger things up now, George." With that, I prepared myself to meet the Queen!

Was the confidence instilled by Alf Ramsey still there?
Oh yes. Ours was a supremely professional outfit. Alf had made damned sure of that. And we had every confidence that we'd beat the Germans if all went to plan; it's just that we'd have to do so despite the whole ballyhoo of the fragmented build-up.

As the World Cup progressed Argentina gave England some problems...?
They were a good team; stacked with good players with great technical ability. They didn't need to resort to the stupid tactics they famously employed. Their captain, Rattin, was at the heart of it all. If I'd wanted to see one of their players being sent off, it was him – he was that good a player, and so influential. But he instigated his own downfall, and that of his team's, by his unsavoury actions. There was a great story that concerned Nobby as he came out for the second half. One of their players said he was going to kick him in the teeth. Nobby replied: "You'll have a job – they're in a glass of Steradent in the dressing room!" [Laughs!]

Then came Portugal, and Eusebio, in the semis...?
What a player! That game was one of the best of the whole competition. They'd kicked Brazil, and Pelé, out of the competition – literally! They were such talented footballers, and in Eusebio they had one of the world greats – an extremely powerful player, and so quick. Nobby, much smaller and way slower, played him out of the game, so much so that Eusebio's input became limited to taking dead-ball kicks, including the penalty from which he scored. Poor Eusebio left the pitch crying because he realised he hadn't been allowed to contribute in the way he'd wanted to because of Nobby's presence. In a later World Cup Alan Mullery did a similar brilliant man-marking job on Pelé.

You had no reason to cry at the final whistle – you were in the World Cup Final...?
I have to correct you there! You're right, I wasn't crying. We were all exhilarated by the performance and the 2-1 victory. But you never assumed you were in the team! A decent performance increased your chances, naturally. But you couldn't take anything for granted under Alf. I was only told I was in the team the night before the Final. It was only 11 players back then, don't forget, no subs.

So only 11 England World Cup winners, then – to date – and you're one of them!
Yes, and I'm immensely proud of that, especially as I played in all six games. I had a scare in the weeks before the tournament when I cut my knee to the bone. When I eventually joined the squad we were trained incredibly hard, nothing was left to chance, and I was kept behind by Les Cocker for extra training. Little Les was a real tyrant and I was absolutely shattered. But it paid dividends.

It must have been a different type of "shattered" after playing 120 minutes against West Germany. Winning 4-2, Geoff Hurst's hat-trick, "people on the pitch"... you'd won the World Cup!
I don't think any of us could enjoy it right away; we were all too knackered after running our legs and

lungs to the limit on that heavy Wembley playing surface! But it soon sunk in. Nobby found an extra ounce of energy from somewhere – he jumped on me and gave me a big open-mouthed kiss...

...a nightmare moment amid the exuberance...?
...it was like being kissed by Mick Jagger! And before long we were jogging around Wembley holding the trophy aloft. I say "we", but Bob didn't want to let go of it! It was a wonder any of us could run at all after grafting so hard on that spongy, energy-sapping surface. Alf famously told us to "Go out and win it again" after we'd been pegged back to 2-2 in the 90 minutes – he then instructed us to go for them, harry them, not to let them settle right from the start of extra-time. That was a lot easier said than done; but we did so and it was a defining moment. Alan Ball tore into the Germans, just as he'd done all game. He was nothing short of magnificent. Bally was just a little kid, but stuck to his task brilliantly. It was easy to spot his non-stop running up and down the pitch – it wasn't just his red hair, it was because he was so damned effective – but he also did more than he share of covering. If I made a move that took me away from right-back defensive duties he'd be covering me in a flash....

...Giving you extra confidence...?
...You have no idea how much. To have Nobby and Alan performing so selflessly in and around my position was the stuff of dreams. In that Final I was up against two sprinters: Sigi Held and Lothar Emmerich. It was fantastic to have Nobby and Alan on hand to help nullify them.

You were privileged to play under two supreme England captains: Johnny Haynes and Bobby Moore. How did they compare as skippers?
As far as Bobby was concerned, he was leading a side stacked with other captains. For example, I was captain of Fulham. Bobby was quieter on the pitch than Johnny. But Bobby had some strong characters around him. Let's be honest, if anyone criticised Jackie Charlton they'd be risking a whack around the head! Bobby wasn't one to bark orders on the pitch, although he'd offer plenty of advice. Johnny, as has been well documented, was louder and much more critical. He was as hard on himself as he was with others around him. John was a quiet fella off the pitch. And what he said on it stayed out there, too. Back in the bar after the game there'd be no repercussions. He was such a big name at the time, which we all respected. He was captain of England. And he was some player!

That England team of 1966 was stacked with good players, but with a strength of character and team ethic to match...?
Not half! In goal we had Gordon Banks, the best keeper in the world. Ray Wilson: what a left-back!

Bobby [Moore] was a supreme player and reader of the game and forged a great partnership with Jack [Charlton]. Mooro was the glacial presence whereas Jack, one of the most under-rated of our players, offered rough authority. Neither could be described as "nippy", though – which is where Ray and I came in. It was a strong defensive unit. Oh, and there was Nobby! He was our policeman who'd patrol in front of our back four. Nobby could read a game superbly, and yet, unlike Mooro, he'd rarely get the praise for that. Alf was fully aware of this. On the field I'd always know where Nobby was and had the reassurance of knowing that if I'd have to move away from my patch then Nobby would instantly provide the cover. He did have the knack of getting in the midst of any aggro mind. In fact, as we progressed through the competition there was quite a thing going on about Nobby backstage. He'd put in a tackle against Jacques Simon that put the French playmaker out of the game and some people didn't want to see him involved in the quarter-final against Argentina. But Alf saw to that.

Sounds like that defensive unit was good enough to win the World Cup!?
It was, and we did! Just as Alf had told us we would. ("Gentlemen," he'd told us, "there is no question about it – we can win the World Cup.")

Alf Ramsey was clearly the driving force...?
He was. But he knew only too well that he had a set of players who could not only play but who'd also stand up and be counted on the field of play. As I said, we were all leaders really. Although he was only 21, Alan Ball came from a footballing family and was already a forceful character. Bally was a pocket dynamo and was simply superb in the Final against West Germany. Mooro certainly didn't bawl us out; it wasn't his style, but it wasn't generally required. We all knew our responsibilities. Mind you, if things needed to be said then they were. Things were dealt with there and then in the dressing room after which it was matter closed.

As a result of staying at Fulham you only picked up one major honour through your whole career. Not a bad one, though!
Indeed, the top of the pile! But I'd have liked a few intermediate ones too, mind! At Fulham, we were unlucky not to make two FA Cup Finals – having got so far twice we certainly didn't have the rub of the green in either of those semi-finals, which was a great shame. ⚽

Below: George Cohen and his "magnificent" wife, Daphne.

> *"Alf famously told us to 'Go out and win it again' after we'd been pegged back to 2-2 in the 90 minutes – he then instructed us to go for them, harry them, not to let them settle right from the start of extra-time. That was a lot easier said than done; but we did so and it was a defining moment."*

Welcome, Slaviša

A former work colleague used to say of Lord Lichfield: "He takes that many photos it's little wonder that now and again one or two turn out to be okay." That may or may not be harsh. But that comment sprang to mind when Slaviša Jokanović was (eventually) appointed. A decent decision at last! At least it looks that way. Slav's been universally welcomed in and around SW6, and the general consensus is he's the best we could have hoped for given our lowly status in the Championship. Certainly, the mood around Craven Cottage was undeniably much improved prior to the evening game with Rotherham, even though Slav didn't officially take charge of the squad until after that fixture. The 4-1 win helped, too!

Our first few performances under the new boss have served to highlight what a difficult job he has ahead of him. Those games also demonstrated that rookie manager Kit Symons was doing a reasonable job, having inherited an appalling mess from Felix Magath. That's not to say things were going well under Kit; the Club's supposed top-six aspirations were looking fanciful to say the least, and were undermined further by that thumping handed out by Birmingham at the Cottage. At that juncture the decision to change managers seemed not only sensible but also merciful.

The ensuing farce, though, blew a massive hole in the supposition that there was any sensible decision-making involved. Kit Symons was sacked because he and his charges hadn't gleaned sufficient points from the games played up to then to satisfy the senior management. Indeed, without that remarkable second-half comeback against Reading, the Kitman would have been booted out two weeks beforehand. Symons was well aware of the points requirements and had reputedly cleared

his desk well before what turned out to be his final day at the Club – which hardly smacks of a happy state of affairs behind the scenes. Nor does it suggest an environment in which the manager had the full backing of those above him.

Kit paid the ultimate price for his side being consistently inconsistent. We were treated to some fleeting flashes of brilliance from his players during his tenure but those tantalizing moments were easily outweighed by periods at the "drab" end of the scale. Silly errors were commonplace and we conceded shedloads of stupid goals. Even when playing well we rarely looked capable of closing out games; a "routine" away win at Charlton became two points lost as we somehow allowed the hosts to score two late goals. Good bloke or not, Kit wasn't delivering and was increasingly looking out of his depth.

Still, at least a decision had been made; no harm done, right? Wrong. It took 49 days to appoint the new man; 49 days during which just about every out-of-work manager was linked with the post, as were a number of in-work managers, including the soon-to-be-sacked Steve Clarke at Reading, Exeter's Paul Tisdale plus some guy at Maccabi Tel Aviv. Worst of all, though, those 49 days embraced seven fixtures from which we took just four points (four draws; three defeats). A measly four points from 21; that's well below Kit Symons' points ratio – he gleaned 20 from 16 games and we were in 12th spot, eight points off a Play-off space following that shocker against Brum. Weeks later, and prior to the Rotherham game, we'd plummeted to 19th and were 13 points adrift of a Play-off berth. Good work, everyone!

What a fall from grace. Fulham FC, the multi-million-pound business astutely steered to the giddy heights of a firmly established club in the multi-billion-pound Premier League, has since been allowed to slump not just from the top flight but to a position where a further drop into the third tier isn't out of the question. Astonishingly, this has been achieved by totally mismanaging the core of its business: football. It's rather like Rolex losing track of time, Gillette taking suicidal short cuts, Lego bricking it or Google suffering engine failure. Talk about taking your eyes off the ball.

And who suffers? Well it's not those who continue to be handsomely paid to make the important decisions, that's for sure. The impression is that it's been a lot more about protecting their jobs rather than protecting the Club's status. And, given our downward spiral, you're left with the impression that the largely absent Shahid Khan isn't overly bothered either – even if the well-advanced plans for the Riverside Stand suggest that our

> *"Kit paid the ultimate price for his side being consistently inconsistent. We were treated to some fleeting flashes of brilliance from his players during his tenure but those tantalizing moments were easily outweighed by periods at the 'drab' end of the scale."*

Below: With Fulham continuing to stumble, TOOFIF came up with a couple of alternative covers for Issue 139.

owner is here for the long term. No, it's us fans who have suffered; big time. We've forked out our hard-earned cash to get in return a host of hollow promises and the destructive transformation of a well-run Premier League club into a glorified Sunday League set-up in just a few seasons. Not that a Sunday League club could ever manage to accommodate the number of players we've somehow managed to use in that time.

Don't suppose the powers-that-be will enjoy this assessment. Truth hurts, right? Well it hurts to write such an assessment; especially as our slump hasn't been down to outside forces.

This is no petulant toys-out-of-the-pram rant. This column has often acknowledged that our support doesn't crave world domination (unlike other parts of the Borough!). But that shouldn't be misconstrued as a lack of ambition. We may have a billionaire owner and we certainly enjoyed the advancements made thanks to our previous owner's largesse but, given our fairly recent history, we're also only too aware of our roots and accept that for a club of our scale to prosper it needs to be firing on all cylinders, on and off the pitch.

Our pathetic slump cannot be attributed to bad luck. Unless, of course, you consider that it's our bad luck to have the current lot in charge! Us fans may not have the coaching badges (some do, mind!), but we're there every week to witness the latest end-product of this regime. The evidence is there for us all to see for ourselves; the League table merely backs that up. Just as it was magnificent to watch and recognise the steady improvement made by the squad under Roy Hodgson – individually and collectively – so it's been a depressing exercise traipsing to games to witness another episode in what's been a steady decline.

Over the past few months especially, standing at TOOFIF corner has been something of a chore. Even the most level-headed of supporters and those who generally keep their opinions to themselves have congregated in and around the area to vent their spleen. Fair to say they've not been happy! Point is, we can see and chart the decline only too clearly. The big question is: why has it been allowed to happen? And is it down to incompetence or ignorance? Either way, there are no gold stars in the offing.

As with all the other new appointments, here we are welcoming Slaviša Jokanović to Craven Cottage and wishing him all the luck in the world. As he's already discovered, he'll probably need it! Not much in the way of a points haul thus far under the new Head Coach, but there's a gritty determination about him that bodes well. Slav took a while to get going at Watford, too, before guiding them to promotion. More of that, please, Slav!

I commented earlier that truth hurts. Well, so do lies. And it seems that certain Club officials are quite prepared to operate in that manner. The extraordinary thing is that in each example I've been made aware of, there's been no apparent reason to lie in the first place! One example involved me directly. Another involved a top-notch group of respected supporters involved in a no-brainer project to benefit all parties involved, including FFC. The third concerned the Fulham Supporters' Trust and the FFP cock-up that's led to a transfer embargo.

On top of hearing that a fervent Fulham supporter with a slight speech impediment was mocked by a club official in the Club Shop, and seeing at first hand how a 12-year-old lad was refused a glass of water at a charity game at the Cottage, then it's no wonder that people are complaining that the whole Fulham FC ethos and its famed friendly image have taken a severe downward turn. The Americans are supposed to be top of the tree PR-wise. But while they're over there, what I've related is happening over here.

You may recall reference to an "imminent press release" from FFC in the last issue, regarding a project that "ticks all the Fulham boxes". Last I heard on the previously extremely urgent matter was that it had been held up "slightly" but that it remained ongoing and would be dealt with very soon, hopefully by Christmas. Well, we're still waiting. Maybe they meant the festivities of 2016?

Point is, these are the sort of cock-ups and glitches that happen at other clubs, not ours. The nature of the footballing network is that it's always been the done thing to poke fun at other clubs in a mess – not those in a financial crisis or in danger of going under; that's when the good nature of football fans generally comes to the fore. Ridiculous transfers; managerial merry-go-rounds; crazy team policies; poor communications with the Club's supporters; issuing rallying cries relating to Play-off aspirations without doing anything to back them up. That's been us, not "other clubs". And, alas, the jokes are well and truly on us.

This wonderful football club of ours could really do with a massive positive shot in the arm. Here's hoping that Slav can do his bit by making the most of what's at his disposal. Although we've shown remarkable patience over the last few seasons, that'll be the key word once again as we show our support for the new Head Coach. (Slav had an inauspicious first visit to Craven Cottage, getting sent off in the 1-1 draw with Chelsea in 2001. Let's just say it was good old Graham Poll at his finest!) It's early days as yet, but he seems to have the qualities to become a heroic managerial figure here – if he doesn't become overwhelmed with the internal politics, that is! At this stage, any sort of improvement will be greatly welcomed given our current lowly League position.

A run of decent performances plus a stack of points in the bag would be a good way of lifting the mood. Go for it, Slav – and good luck! :·:

	1st
Fulham 0 Hull City 1	2nd
23.01.16 19th	3rd
	4th
Fulham 1 Derby County 1	5th
06.02.16 19th	6th
Queens Park Rangers 1 Fulham 3	7th
13.02.16 19th	8th
	9th
Blackburn Rovers 3 Fulham 0	10th
16.02.16 19th	11th
Fulham 3 Charlton Athletic 0	12th
20.02.16 18th	13th
	14th
Leeds United 1 Fulham 1	15th
23.02.16 18th	16th
Fulham 0 Middlesbrough 2	17th
27.02.16 20th	**18th**
	19th
Reading 2 Fulham 2	20th
05.03.16 19th	21st
Fulham 2 Burnley 3	22nd
08.03.16 19th	23rd
	24th

Fall From Grace

In March 2010 Fulham FC overcame Juventus in the Europa League, following an epic contest at Craven Cottage full of guts, teamwork and no little skill. Roy Hodgson's team fought back magnificently against all odds and were rewarded with a famous, and thoroughly deserved, victory – and with it the most marvellous cacophony of sound from our jubilant supporters. That remarkable performance paved the way for an astounding run that went all the way to the final, putting Fulham FC well and truly on the world footballing stage. Back in 2010 Fulham were the Leicester City of the day, winning the hearts of most neutral fans for their honest approach to the game and for squeezing every ounce from the squad's resources.

In March 2016, several managers and umpteen players later, Fulham FC hosted fellow Championship strugglers Bristol City at the Cottage and, even after getting off to the most wonderful of starts, the team utterly lost its bottle and were ultimately outfought by City who grabbed a vital away win that took them above us in the table. Fulham's unremarkable performance put them firmly in the relegation dogfight.

A few boos rang out from the stands, but it was the relative silence that was deafening – a stunned bemusement at how far we'd fallen in both standards and stature. These days, given the drop in attendances, even a lot of the Fulham "faithful" aren't bothered about their Club, a reflection of the apparent apathy from the powers-that-be and the squandering of a hard-earned lofty footballing status. As for neutral football fans, and the general football community at large, well they couldn't give a flying fig about FFC nowadays.

The last Boredroom piece was something of a rant. And it seems that this old fart's witterings about our Club's feeble fall from grace struck home, as the feedback was not only substantial but also in total agreement. (Normally any such feedback falls into the "insignificant" or "non-existent" category!) The general consensus was that it's hard to argue against the claim that, one after another, the Club's wounds have been self-inflicted.

We were in a position of strength in 2010 and, for all the stuff about "punching above our weight", we improved as a team beyond the Europa League highs. We finished the following season in a solid eighth position in the top flight, and backed that up by finishing ninth 12 months later.

I've always felt that a couple of astute buys at that time – think of how we got Louis Saha for a relative snip, or Van der Sar, Legwinski, Volz or Malbranque – would have cemented us as a top-eight side. Okay, that's quite a claim, but that assumption is based on

the decent set-up we'd established back then and, just as relevant, the poorish state of the top flight's "middling" clubs at the time. Instead, we sold the exciting Mousa Dembélé (mk.1!) and the influential Danny Murphy, both prodigious workers, and replaced them, in effect, with the enigmatic Dimitar Berbatov, whose ability and ball-skills were phenomenal, but who was to workrate and commitment what the Michael Jackson statue was to beauty and movement. Alas, the rest is history.

And so, here we are being told that we're facing a run of cup finals in order to save our Championship status. "Every game is important now", said Scott Parker before the away game at Birmingham. "We have nine left and every single one of those is a cup final for us."

Leaving aside the fact that our record in cup finals is lousy, what a curious statement to be punted out by the Club by email under the "news" banner. I think all of us regulars had already realised we were in a bit of a pickle weeks ago. Important games? We're in danger of being relegated to League One? You don't say! And it begs the question, if the remaining matches are to be regarded as cup finals, what have all the previous games been regarded as, pre-season friendlies?

This isn't a dig at Scott Parker. It's been all-too-evident that he's been trying his best ever since he returned from injury. Some of his crunching tackles and last-ditch blocks have epitomised his mind-set and really ought to have inspired all those around him to apply themselves in similar fashion. Unfortunately, a Scott Parker "shift", worthy though it is, doesn't last for 90 minutes these days. Even so, his determined efforts have still put many of those around him to shame.

Cup finals or not, if our starting 11 display Parker's appetite for the fight, we'll be okay. Given our lofty ambitions for this season – "challenging for promotion" according to the Chairman, don't forget – it's almost unfathomable that we're now in grave danger of being relegated. ⚽

Gentleman George on a Pedestal

So, the secret's out of the bag at long last – George Cohen MBE, our World Cup-winning full-back, is to have a statue at Craven Cottage to honour his footballing achievements and allegiance to FFC.

Esteemed sculptor Douglas Jennings – who did the brilliant Johnny Haynes statue – has been commissioned to come up with something every bit as good, depicting George in a "typical" pose. The finished article will be unveiled at Craven Cottage in October 2016, commemorating the 50th anniversary of England's famous (and, up to now, only) World Cup success in 1966.

Opposite page right: Four members of England's World Cup-winning team of 1996 – George Cohen, Gordon Banks, Martin Peters and Sir Geoff Hurst – are reunited with the famous Jules Rimet Trophy.

Below: Here's the *Sunday Mirror's* take on Fulham's home defeat to fellow strugglers Bristol City in March 2016.

FULHAM 1
McCormack 2

BRISTOL CITY 2
Pack 69, Tomlin 90

Slav: We've Cott to fight

🔶 SKY BET CHAMPIONSHIP

at Craven Cottage

SLAVISA JOKANOVIC believes his Fulham strugglers can survive, despite being dragged into big trouble by one of their relegation rivals.

Just one point separates the Cottagers and the drop zone after this latest setback following Lee Tomlin's last-gasp winner for Bristol City.

And the Fulham manager conceded his side are now up against it.

He said: "We started the game very well and scored a good goal. But we didn't control the last 30 minutes in the second half. We got confused and started making mistakes.

"Then we had problems. They put us in big trouble. It's disappointing for us and our fans. We were talking about the last 10 games when we must go to war.

"Our supporters are unhappy. They don't deserve this at this moment at the level we are now. We are in a relegation battle and our situation is really clear.

"I can say sorry to the fans as they push us and try to help us. I don't want to think about relegation. It's in our hands, so we must be brave to resolve this situation."

It looked so good for Fulham after Ross McCormack's second-minute chipped opener.

But City were a different side after the break when Lee Johnson's double change reaping rewards.

Their pressure told in the 69th minute when Marlon Pack drove home from distance. And on-loan striker Tomlin curled home a 90th-minute free-kick to pile on the misery for Fulham.

Robins boss Johnson said: "For Lee to get it up and over like he did, it always had a chance. It was a very big feeling when that nestled in the bottom corner.

"Lee can bend it like Beckham. But he can't run, so he has to!"

MATCH STATS opta

	FUL	BRI
Possession	50%	50%
Shots On Target	6	5
Shots Off Target	8	4
Blocked Shots	2	1
Corners	3	5
Fouls Conceded	12	12
Offsides	8	4
Yellow Cards	2	1
Red Cards	0	0

The statue was the brainchild of Fulham fan Ed Vanson who, in late 2014, recognised that almost 50 years had passed since England's momentous achievement at Wembley and was well aware of the adage: "England only win the World Cup with a Fulham player in the side." Ed canvassed several influential supporters and by the start of 2015 there was a working group in place. "We didn't use the word 'committee' as that sounded too pompous," said Ed. "In essence we were just a group of fans who were determined to see George honoured in some way. And, to be frank, for it to be done during George's lifetime so he could see how much his efforts on behalf of club and country have been appreciated. Before long we had a fantastic group of supporters involved and, with George's long-time pal Bob Howes acting as our chairman, things really began to move in the right direction."

Given the downturn in the Club's fortunes and the associated fans' disenchantment, the group was determined that this would be a supporter-led initiative to bring some much-needed cheer and unity to the Club's supporter base.

"Honouring George was a complete no-brainer," added Ed. "But it was only once the group got together that the enormity of the task struck home – there was a huge sum of money to raise and an incredible amount of work involved in doing so.

"We soon agreed that a Douglas Jennings statue was the best option, but we also wanted to ensure that there was some sort of legacy that revolved around George's work in the community.

"The World Cup commemorations present an ideal timeframe as the spotlight will be on George (and, therefore, Fulham FC) plus just one or two other players, as, sadly, the majority of that World Cup-winning team have either passed away or are suffering ill-health. But for all of that, the statue will be of George in his Fulham kit – it's a Fulham celebration, and he's our hero!"

As Ed hints above, George has been a great ambassador for FFC's community work. So, the fundraising process embraces two initiatives planned in his name with the aim of improving men's health through local dementia care and health preventative programmes. FFC Chairman Shahid Khan has pledged to match whatever is

raised, pound for pound, to not only ensure that the statue is erected but also so that the Foundation can deliver the health initiatives supported by George.

The recent two-part TOOFIF interview with George Cohen – along with the glowing endorsement of George's footballing pedigree from England manager Roy Hodgson – was intended to run alongside the statue announcement. However, rather like the direction of our favourite football team, the whole business seemed to run into a cul-de-sac once the Football Club seized the reins.

Intriguingly, the long-awaited press release in March announcing the statue stated that the "supporter-led group proposed the statue to Fulham earlier this year", when this had, in fact, been done in early March last year! It was shortly after this that former FFC Vice-Chairman Bill Muddyman and Bob Howes asked me to join the group – thereby bringing down the tone instantly! Others involved included Ed Vanson (naturally!), Heather Wilson (widow of former FFC full-back Tom Wilson), Sir Paul Kenny and David Hamilton along with another former FFC director David Shrimpton in the wings and Ken Coton happy to let us raid his photo archives. Extra drive was provided by Sue Prebble, Ollie Hicks, Emily Samonas, Roger Russell, Ray Roberts and Ed Holford.

It became the epitome of a serene swan: all grace and dignity on the surface (calling for diplomatic tact and patience) and yet belying the furious activity going on out of sight. This included pulling in all sorts of favours to ensure the peripherals (e.g. website, logo, headed paper, various contact lists, etc.) were not only put together speedily but that they were accurate and professionally presented. It was a fantastic effort by all concerned and the ideas presented were outstanding.

With Douglas Jennings eager to get started, and also to ensure he had sufficient lead-time to produce something as resplendent as his likeness of Johnny Haynes (and eager to receive an initial payment for what is hardly a "two-bob job"), there was another pressing issue: keeping any mention of the project from George himself before it was officially sanctioned by the Football Club. Thankfully George was none the wiser until the appropriate juncture, at which point he was "gobsmacked".

In the event, the Football Club not only sanctioned the statue – once the Chairman was informed, rather belatedly apparently – but also took control of the project. And with it our urgency was seemingly replaced by, shall we say, a far steadier approach.

Thankfully, there was fresh impetus once FFC Foundation CEO, Steve Day, became involved and, by whatever means, the bottom line is that Ed Vanson's initial idea and the ensuing hard work and determination of a clutch of dedicated Fulham supporters has ensured that the Club not only did get on board but have embraced the project. ⚽

Fulham 1 Bristol City 2 12.03.16 20th	1st 2nd 3rd
Birmingham City 1 Fulham 1 19.03.16 21st	4th 5th 6th
Fulham 2 MK Dons 1 02.04.16 21st	7th 8th
Preston North End 1 Fulham 2 05.04.16 19th	9th 10th 11th
Fulham 2 Cardiff City 1 09.04.16 17th	12th 13th
Brighton & HA 5 Fulham 0 15.04.16 17th	14th 15th 16th
Ipswich Town 1 Fulham 1 19.04.16 19th	**17th** 18th
Fulham 1 Nottingham Forest 3 23.04.16 21st	19th 20th
Brentford 3 Fulham 0 30.04.16 21st	21th 22th
Fulham 1 Bolton Wanderers 0 07.05.16 20th	23th 24th

The Whole Kit and Kaboodle

No sooner had the Ed popped over to have a cosy chin-wag with Kit Symons than the news came out that our former manager had rejoined the Wales ranks as number two to another former Whites boss, Chris Coleman. One moment Kit was living in hope then, by the next morning, he was officially back in work. Ah, the power of TOOFIF!

> *"Giving the place a lift was the easy bit, and the training sessions and the matchday performances perked up right away. Sustaining that was almost impossible with the squad of players we had."*

It's almost a year now since you left Fulham, Kit – how are things?
I'm in the process of going back to the Wales set-up. When I left Fulham it was all very amicable, the finances were all sorted out, and there was nothing to stop me getting another job should an opportunity come along. The Welsh job is a great position – it was difficult to give it up in the first place because it was clear things were going so well in the camp. As things transpired, I left Wales in the June after we'd beaten Belgium and then I got sacked by Fulham at the start of November. So from running around trying to do two jobs, I was left high and dry not long afterwards – that's the way it goes in football.

You got the FFC job in similar fashion to Cookie – rookie manager, first job, struggling club...?
It was a fantastic opportunity. I'm just disappointed with how it panned out, and that my time was up after a relatively short spell. I've absolutely no regrets about taking the position, none at all. Funny thing is, I was out having a meal with Cookie when he got the call offering him the Fulham job for the last five games of the [2002-03] season.

Would you say you were the right man, but perhaps at the wrong time?
You rarely get to choose the circumstances. As it was, someone had to try to keep the Club in the Championship. Let's be fair, the Club was in a real mess. Having been relegated, we'd got a measly one point from seven Championship games, and yet even that dreadful return didn't tell half the story. The squad of players simply wasn't suitable for the Championship. The atmosphere around the place was dreadful and the

players and staff were desperately unhappy; the place was on its knees. So yes, I'd say I was the right person to lift the place.

You'd been in the background at FFC for quite a while before being appointed...?
When I returned to the Club I was doing the scouting (during Roy Hodgson's time in charge) for the Europa League games, then joined the Academy staff, assisting Gary Brazil with the Under-18s, taking over from Gary when he left for the Premier League. So, having then taken charge of the 21s you could say it was a natural progression [to get the first-team job] – and it was something I'd always wanted to do. But, as I say, it was all a proper mess. Then again, the relatively easy bit was to lift the morale. Any new face could have made a fist of that – people were so disconsolate, the only way was up! It wasn't long before people started to enjoy coming in to work again. In a business where you want, and need, the players to express themselves and to go the extra mile for themselves and those around them, the last thing you want on your hands is a group of disillusioned, inhibited people.

How can things have been allowed to sink so low?
There were players who'd been ostracised – Bryan Ruiz, Hugo Rodallega and Fernando Amorebieta, for example, had been pushed aside and made to train on their own. The first thing I did was to get everyone together – hardly rocket science is it? But I knew it would be tough, and it was!

Your spell as Caretaker-Manager went pretty well...?
Giving the place a lift was the easy bit, and the training sessions and the matchday performances perked up right away. Sustaining that was almost impossible with the squad of players we had. Let's be clear, they weren't bad players, far from it, but that group weren't set-up for the rigours of the Championship. Thank goodness we got the points on the board when we did because, although the League table suggests we stayed up fairly comfortably in 17th spot, those last few games were horrible. It was a case of sacrificing my footballing principles in order to keep the Club in the division. That home game against Wigan near the end of the season was truly awful as a spectacle, but we got a point. It was a case of "needs must".

Had you thought relegation to League One was a possibility?
Definitely! Our position in the table answers that question. However, I still thought we had

enough to get to safety a lot sooner than we did. The legacy of that awful start, the appalling confidence levels and the drastic culling of the squad proved a lot more difficult to rectify.

In essence you'd been left with a clutch of junior players – albeit ones that you knew well – to do a man's job…?
Had things been handled differently it would have been a very different story. People such as Brede [Hangeland], Sidders [Steve Sidwell], Stocko [David Stockdale], Aaron Hughes and Damien Duff were not only top players but fantastic characters too. They were leaders in their different ways. Okay, they wouldn't have been happy at being relegated, but they were the sort to knuckle down and get the Club to a decent footing in the table. They were great professionals and they cared for the Club with a passion, even in these more mercenary days, but over time they'd been worn down. These were exactly the sort of individuals you'd want at a football club – leaders, the sort that would fight and scrap for the cause; instead, they were pushed out.

But they were high wage-earners too…?
I think players should be on contracts that include a clause that should they be relegated then their wages have to be reviewed accordingly. It was great that Fulham were in the Premier League for so long, but I think some people thought we had a divine right to stay there and not get relegated. Yet it all went downhill fast and down we went. That's what happens if things aren't done properly.

I'd say that's the fans' viewpoint. FFC took their eye off the ball in the wake of the change of owner and then three seasons of overall mismanagement led to a drastic change of fortunes: a superbly well-run club was allowed to implode. You don't need to be on the Board to know that, it's been all-too-visible in what's been on view, week in, week out, on the pitch…
It's no coincidence that when things are done properly on and off the pitch then you have a real chance. Getting to the Europa League Final in 2010 is a case in point. Okay, we may have exceeded all expectations in getting to Hamburg, but we did so because there was a genuine structure in place and everyone was pulling in the same direction. It was a fantastic achievement by everyone.

So, the million-dollar question: "What happened?"
My big thing with Fulham is that we had a massive warning shot that went unheeded. In Martin Jol's last full season, our last home game was against Liverpool, and when the players came out afterwards for the customary lap of appreciation so many supporters had already drifted away. That's not like the Fulham fans at all. But it had been such a poor, disappointing season and it was evident how disillusioned they were. We went to Swansea a week later; they'd already won the League Cup and were safe in the league so they were already "on the beach". But because we won there we finished 12th, our budgeted position; had we lost we'd have finished 17th. That's when we should have taken action. Instead it was all deemed okay when, in actual fact, the Club was clearly in decline.

Stats aren't everything then?!
That's right! The warning shot was ignored. With the takeover still fresh, I can understand that there may have been political reasons for not rocking the boat. However, as a football club we needed to take notice and make sure we rectified the situation.

You were with the Academy players at the time and must have been pleased with the team's progress and also the progression of individuals into the first team?
The whole Academy set-up at Fulham is excellent. I really enjoyed my time there.

Did you have to work to the philosophy of the first-team boss?
No, not really. There's not been a "Fulham way" under recent managers – we've gone from Roy Hodgson to Mark Hughes, to Martin Jol to Felix Magath; all very different in their styles and outlook. In that time there's not been a specific style of play that's filtered down to the junior sides. And I think I was naïve in thinking there was a "Fulham way" when I took over the first team. I'd been at the Club on the coaching side for a while and before that had enjoyed a fantastic spell as a player so I felt I knew what the fans wanted. Looking back, I possibly didn't gauge things right. With Ross and Moussa around I knew we'd score goals, but I also knew we weren't strong enough at the back and we didn't have a designated holding midfielder (something I'd been promised on a few occasions!) so it was a question of trying to do the best with what we had. I knew the fans liked free-flowing football so we tried to think in those terms, knowing that we were almost guaranteed to

score; the real test was to shore up the defence as best as we could.

We got goals, that's for sure...
Yeah, at both ends! Believe me, we worked really hard on the defensive stuff during training. Perhaps because we all knew we could score (a situation all clubs crave) we paid too much attention to that rather than adopt a more dour, defensive approach. One of the issues was that we had Ross McCormack who, for me, can only really play in "a two" upfront – and he'll guarantee you goals in that system – but that meant we were not strong enough behind; we had no holding midfielder and our centre-backs weren't robust enough and the result was there for all to see…

Can you say why there was such an impasse when the weaknesses were so evident? Was it the purse-strings being tightened or did it go deeper than that?
We knew there was a likely transfer embargo on the horizon so I only had one summer to improve things. We got Tom Cairney – a top player who's got the ability to play in the top flight – but other than that it was free transfers pretty much...

...Were they your choices...?
...I had a say. It's important to state that a successful set-up is down to the players at your disposal. The manager, while he has an influence in getting the right players, sets and creates the environment and the tone of the whole Football Club and, of course, selects the side. But ultimately it's about the players you've got. Looking back to the start of the 2015-16 season, we were doing okay but giving away such silly goals. We battered Brighton in the second half, yet it was still 1-1 going into added time only for "Hutch" to give away a penalty. Then we went to Hull and Bodurov gives away a goal late on when it was 1-1. Neither player meant to do what they did, naturally, but they were stupid mistakes by players who, perhaps, weren't at the right level. But it was just the way it was – I mean, we had to play Kay Voser at left-back on the opening day against Cardiff as we had nobody else.

As a former defender, was it frustrating that you couldn't sort out the defence – a charge that was also levelled at your fellow centre-back Cookie when he was Fulham boss? It was Roy Hodgson who organised things and stopped the conceding of daft goals…
That all comes down to the players at your disposal too – massively so. Roy had a "box" of four in front of his keeper – usually Brede Hangeland and Aaron Hughes, and ahead of them Danny Murphy and Dickson Etuhu. Brede and Aaron were two top quality centre-halves – and forged a

great partnership – while Danny and Dickson just sat in there. With all the other players schooled in what was expected of them it was going to take something special to break down that unit: good players and a good team structure.

Like everyone else, I'd hoped to have got a few more points in the bank by the time we hosted Birmingham; even so we were top scorers in the division and were in 12th place. I was called in after that Birmingham defeat and told that they wanted the Club to go in a different direction. They finished 20th – so it went in a different direction all right! It was the same group of players involved after my departure and, on paper at least, they had an easier run of games.

But I can understand the criticism of our defensive play. We did a helluva lot of work in an attempt to improve things but, again, it's down to who you've got. For all the honest effort put in by the lads in my squad, we were never a team defensively. Even so, we were generally on the up having gone from 24th, to 17th, to 12th; had we plateaued or taken a real dip then I'd have understood the Club looking at things the way they did.

So, did you have doors closed on you with regard to shuffling the defensive pack, or was it down to the embargo, etc?
The transfer embargo presented us with problems, obviously – but that was coming in the January so it was a case of doing our business the summer before. I'd been promised defenders and a holding midfielder – Kevin McDonald was in the frame – and there were three central defenders in the mix, too, and I'd been promised two of the three. As you know, none of these materialised. We had to make the best of what we had.

Okay, let's flip back to 1998. You joined Fulham and the Club's quest for the big time… starting at Macclesfield away…
[Laughs] …Yeah, 1-0. John Salako. In fact, my first game in a Fulham shirt came two days after I'd signed – we went over to Hamburg for a friendly. Naturally, Kevin Keegan was mobbed over there and, to coin a phrase, "He loved it"! We played well and won the game so I realised right away that we had a decent squad: good players, and great lads. You've no idea the lift you get on joining a new club to find that there's a good team spirit and a great atmosphere about the place. Stats, all joking apart, are very important and they have a key part to play in the modern game (I'm no dinosaur; you'd be stupid not to use them) but you can't get away from the things that are always right, in whatever era. If the dressing room's right you can get that indefinable extra something that no stats can register. I'm one to embrace any new science info or methods if they can benefit you or

the Club but there are some elements that are just as valid today as they were forty of fifty years ago.

Keegan put together a great squad of players – and Simon Morgan…!

Ah, Morgs was brilliant. He was the only player, I think, who managed to go the whole journey with Fulham as we headed up the divisions. Simon was a very good player. We had a huge squad that season as "New Fulham" progressed very quickly. Somehow it remained a harmonious camp – and massive credit must go to those players who were pushed to one side so soon after earning promotion from the bottom division. Keegan had a plan and a vision of what he wanted – and he was going to get there.

Looking from the outside in, that crossover period was handled pretty well. Cookie and Pesch, for example came in for decent money and were immediately rubbing shoulders with Micky Adams' freebies…?

It helped that Keegan was straight with all the players. It was no surprise to find that the players who'd got Fulham promoted were all good guys – that good squad spirit again – and so, even though they were bound to be miffed at being sidelined, it was handled well and they took it on the chin. Then again, the big-money buys – and Cookie was a massive signing – integrated right away too. Chris is a rough-arse Swansea boy and as down-to-earth as you can get, so there were no big-time Charlies to potentially upset things. Cookie was there to do a job, as we all were.

You, Cookie and Morgs made a dominant trio at the heart of the defence, but were among the goals, too…?

In joining Fulham I was playing at the lowest level in my career, but it was the best time ever. It was just brilliant. We worked our socks off at training and on the pitch, but with it came so many laughs. We became a real tight group. The three of us did well. Frank Sibley did loads of work with us, defensively and also in an attacking sense with set pieces. Stevie Hayward would take the corners or wide free-kicks and hang the ball up for me to head for goal or back across the box to, usually, Morgs or Cookie. We scored shedloads that first season. Stevie's delivery was fantastic and he was something of an unsung hero that year.

Morgs has a Welsh name but played for England Under-21s; you and Cookie, though, go way back with Wales…?

Cookie's a year older, but yes we go back to the Under-17s, the U-21s, then the full Welsh squad, so we were quite pally before coming to Fulham. It was Cookie who rang me, actually, before passing the phone to Kevin. I was leaving Man

City and had received a good offer from Sheffield Utd, in a higher division to Fulham, so there was more money on the table. All the common sense in the world suggested I should go to Sheffield – I wouldn't have to move house, we'd just had a baby, plus there was the money factor; and yet Fulham sounded right. Cookie sold it to me, as did Kevin. CEO Neil Rodford, too, was excellent. I bought into the Chairman's five-year plan straight away. It was definitely the right move.

He was a bit of a boy, the Chairman…?

He was about all the time and was great fun. I did well with the "gold" chocolate bars – for my nieces of course!

Kevin left for the England job at the end of the season, and Paul Bracewell took over...

Very different in character, and yeah, it was a big change when Kevin went; he was a hard act to follow. Actually, that end-of-season game against Preston made for quite a day. It was Kevin's last game and we were champions. I was chasing Roger Brown's goalscoring record and I'd been assigned penalty duties. Then along came Paul Moody: 0-0 at half-time, Moods scores two then we get a spot-kick. He was on a hat-trick so he took the kick and scored; I was okay with that. At the training ground, years later, outside my office hung that iconic Ken Coton picture of Big Roger, bloodied head all bandaged up, cigar in one hand and mug of something in the other. It's a brilliant photo of a top, top character… I'd always look at it and think, "D'you know, some records are meant NOT to be broken!" Anyway, one of my goals – against Millwall – was an own goal but they gave it to me. So I wouldn't have deserved it anyway.

It's pretty evident that you caught the "Fulham Bug", whatever that is?

I did, no question. I'd had a brilliant eight years or so at Portsmouth, then moved to Man City for another 100+ games. I'm the sort to give 100 per cent wherever I go, even if I don't have the frills. That first season at Fulham, especially, was wonderful.

I guess getting 101 points twice in three seasons helped…?

We had good players and gained lots of wins.

Below: "Dirty Kit – oh, very funny!"

Kit's Stuff

So, your best moments, Kit?
There are so many. Millwall away was a good one. Tony Roberts (who's just joined the Welsh camp as goalkeeping coach) was in goal for Millwall. Anyway, Stevie Haywood sends in a decent free-kick towards me and I can see Tony coming off his line. I thought "I could get a battering here" and sure enough he pretty much punched my head off. But I'd got there first and the ball trickled over the line for the winner. The Fulham fans seemed to rise as one... "Yeeeeaaahhhh..." then, just as quickly they deflated. You could see it in their faces: "What have you done? What chance have we got now of getting back to the station in one piece, you idiot?!" A fair few have spoken to me about it subsequently and said "What were you thinking?" I found myself apologising for scoring the winner (and for getting a right thumping from Tony!). Ah, the joys of Millwall away!

Oddest moment?
Oh, Wigan at home. Another goal that day, and who's in the dressing room afterwards but Michael Jackson. (There's me scoring

for fun and they put up a statue of Jacko – scandalous!) I was getting treatment after the match when Mohamed Al Fayed walks in with Michael Jackson, and Jacko says "Hey, great game." I should've said, "Yeah, not BAD, but hardly a THRILLER" but no, I was dumbfounded. A short while later the lads came back into the dressing room and I blurted out: "You'll never guess who's just been in here..." "Michael Jackson!" they shouted back "And we've all just had a team photo taken with him." We all got a copy of the photo and when my little girl, a big Jacko fan, saw it later she said "Where are you, daddy?" "I was in the changing room." "So you didn't meet him then..." So there you have it, no photographic evidence, no proof.

Funniest characters?
Cookie was always hilarious; he just couldn't help it. Morgs was fantastic to have around, a proper character. Every morning I'd walk in and say, "All right Morgs, how are you?" Without fail he'd reply "Rubbish!" So that's what I call him, even today: "Rubbish". Pesch was the moaniest person ever – but that was simply a front and an example of his dry humour. It was his idea of banter.

Best players?
A special mention for two fantastic goalkeepers, Maik Taylor and Edwin van der Sar. But as for the very best, I've already highlighted him: Louis Saha. So strong, so quick, so good in the air and with two great feet. He was astonishing.

Best game as FFC manager?
Beating QPR 4-0 was special, it's always good to win a local derby and we played some good stuff that day, too. But it was also satisfying to score four in successive weeks, at home to Reading then away at Bristol City. We then lost 3-1 at Burnley, a difficult fixture for Fulham at the best of times, then came Birmingham! So while we all knew that things were far from perfect we were at least mid-table and looking upwards rather than down.

But it was more about the way we won and the brilliant spirit about the place. That first season there was still the customary drink or two with the fans in the Riverside bars after the game – which helped you feel a part of the Club. Shame it doesn't happen today but, like it or not, the game has changed. I must say that I liked that side of things.

Even Keegan began purring about the Club – he'd seen much grander times and stadiums – but he loved the floodlit games down by the river…

It's a special place, without a doubt. Fulham's a great club that has seen plenty of ups and downs; I'm big pals with Strongy and Galey and it's clear that the Cottage has always been strong on characters and home to a string of great players too. Although I don't mean those two, naturally!! Keegan, twice European football of the year, bought into the whole Fulham thing. There's a perception that it's little Fulham by the river – and it isn't the largest ground in the land – but when it all clicks the place can be rocking.

I had an interesting exchange with Kevin during a training session at the Bank of England ground. I was on a decent goalscoring run and, as he went to walk past, he said: "Playing well just now, and scoring goals too!" So I replied, "Cheers, gaffer." He continued, "Bit of a purple patch, eh?" I said something like "Thanks, boss" then, as he walked away he shot back, "I had a purple patch once – it lasted for 15 years!" And he kept on walking. Basically, what he was saying was "Keep your feet on the ground pal – you ain't done anything yet." I thought: "Point taken. Nice one gaffer." If he took to you then you'd get on famously. I liked Kevin and he was brilliant for me.

After Bracewell, enter Jean Tigana…

And what a phenomenal entrance. Big changes in outlook and attitude, and it was simply superb. That first season under Keegan we were quite relaxed but it became more serious, more professional I suppose, in that the training was different and there was much more focus on things like our diet. It was fantastic – even the extra-early-morning training! If anyone doubted his methods those doubts soon went out of the window as we started like a runaway train – we were unstoppable. Some of the football we played was spectacular, and we reeled off one win after another.

As you say, some of the football was "pure" – at least until Christmas or just beyond?

We played Brentford at Griffin Park in pre-season. Tigana just said: "Play, play, play…" So there's me and Rufus Brevett, not exactly in the twinkletoes category, expected to play it out from the back. Later in that game, with Brentford having pushed four up to shadow our back four, Maik Taylor had to kick the ball long. Tigana went mad! When we queried what it was he expected us and Maik to do, he snapped back: "Find a solution! Find the next free man; they can't mark everyone." So he'd encourage us to take chances, and he'd often go mad if we didn't. He believed in us, and, let's be fair, we had a bloody decent crop of players. John Collins and Lee Clark, fantastic in midfield. And Louis Saha up front – wow, he was special. In that first season for Fulham in the Championship, his was the best performance I've ever seen from an individual – he was consistently brilliant – and he was backed up by being part of an exciting squad. In some ways Louis was a freak. He was so athletic, so quick and able to control the ball outrageously at times. The way he'd take the ball on his chest at whatever angle and pace was unbelievable. Ironically he'd had injury issues before coming to Fulham and he was subsequently plagued with injuries later in his career. For Louis, though, everything came together at Fulham, and the training regime clearly suited him. We were all exceptionally fit, though – probably as fit as any of us had ever been.

By that season, Andy Melville was first-choice centre-back with Cookie, and you only regained your place after Cookie's awful accident…

Losing Chris in those dreadful circumstances was a terrible blow, but as far as the football was concerned it was business as usual really. Yes, we'd lost our captain and a top lad, but he was that much of a presence that his misfortune galvanised us; we were all determined to finish the job for Cookie. It was a horrific accident and a terrible time for him and his family, and yet we stuck together. On the night we got that famous victory at Blackburn and effectively won the league, I was lucky enough to be judged man of the match, and in the televised interview afterwards I said that we'd done it for Cookie – and that's how it was. ⚽

"Fulham's a great club that has seen plenty of ups and downs; I'm big pals with Strongy and Galey and it's clear that the Cottage has always been strong on characters and home to a string of great players too. Although I don't mean those two, naturally."

Opposite page far left: Wigan at home – and who should pop along for the game but pop superstar Michael Jackson. Photographer Javier Garcia was on hand to confirm Jacko was the real deal, and not a look-alike!

Opposite page right: Maik Taylor – a "fantastic goalkeeper".

Opposite page bottom: Kit Symons looks to his right with a degree of apprehension, just in case there's a Millwall fan or three in the vicinity.

Below: Kit is flanked by two stalwart Fulham fans, Cath and James Goldthorpe.

Brede Hangeland

Ten years ago Brede Hangeland signed for Fulham. He didn't know it back then, but it was the start of a glorious spell for player and football club. As Brede explains, it was, for the most part, the perfect place to play football and he had the perfect mentors in Roy Hodgson and Ray Lewington. If you ever take a photo of the genial giant, however, don't ask him to say "cheese"!

How did you land at Fulham, Brede – was it because you already knew Roy Hodgson? Did you know anything about the Club at that point?
It was very much down to Roy. I didn't know much about Fulham, but I had been to Craven Cottage before. At the end of the football season in Norway, I'd come over with a group of friends to see some games. We came to Fulham before the Putney End had a stand, and watched the game from there. When Roy got in touch, I was playing for Copenhagen and the Premier League was a huge attraction. I must be honest, I'd have joined any Premier League club but the huge draw at Fulham was the chance to link up again with Roy, who'd been my boss earlier in my career at Viking. This was my big chance.

You left a winning team for one that was, well, not doing quite so well…
Oh yes, it was something of a shock! Copenhagen was the best team in Scandinavia so our defensive unit invariably lined up on the halfway line, and I was something of a playmaker centre-back. At Fulham, we were back on the six-yard box and defending for our lives. It was a baptism of fire, I suppose, but for all the early trials and tribulations I soon felt at home at Fulham. In fact, for me at least, it became the ultimate place to play football – the perfect fit, if you like.

….Even though, given the chance, you'd have been more likely to win medals elsewhere…?
That's possible. I want to win as much as anyone – that's the point of playing any sport – but the whole package is so important. The matches are the main focus, naturally, but it's also about the long spells in-between; it's about where you live; the type of people you work with. It's about the staff, the players, the fans, the sponsors. Without a doubt, moving to Fulham was the perfect move for me.

That "baptism of fire" developed into a relegation scrap. Dubbed "The Great Escape",

where did that extraordinary run of results come from? Was it because the pressure was perceived to be off?

I joined the Club in the January and slowly but surely things began to improve under Roy. I soon realised we weren't a great team by Premier League standards but we could all sense the improvement. Really, it became a question of whether we could turn things around quickly enough. Before we knew it, the end of the season crept up on us and time was running out. The harsh reality was that, with four or five games to go, relegation was staring us in the face. I remember Roy telling me at the start of the year that joining Fulham was a gamble – that we could be a Championship club within months. But he said that if we could sort things out it had the makings of a great, great story. That really appealed to me. With a few games to go, though, the gamble looked to have failed.

Ah, so you're a gambler…?

No, not by nature! But Roy was insistent. He said everything was in place – it was a great location with terrific staff and fantastic fans. The potential was there for the Club to progress, and we had an owner who was hugely supportive. However, we had to get points on the board, and quick.

That win at Manchester City offered a glimmer of hope. I've watched that game since and we adopted a risky strategy – we were so open! – they were "nothing-to-lose" tactics. That victory gave us some belief. The pressure at the time was enormous, really intense. We were all bothered about keeping the Club in the top flight, and that pressure racked up considerably as the Portsmouth game approached. I may not have won anything at Fulham, but beating the drop was a huge achievement and almost like winning a trophy.

That's quite an admission!

None of us wanted to be relegated. But it went way beyond that. Had the Club gone down so many backroom staff would have been affected; some would have lost their jobs. Even that early in my Fulham career I felt at home there and I didn't want all the decent folk caught up in the knock-on effects of us being relegated. So the pressure built up for sure – our predicament was the first thing on my mind on waking up and it was still there going to bed!

So, when you're 1-0 up at Portsmouth and there's still 14 minutes to go and they're launching balls into our box, there's so much riding on you not making a mistake. When that final whistle went it was the greatest feeling – pure delight at getting the vital win, plus massive relief all round.

When did that become a sense of determination to build on that escape, and not to get dragged into such a position again the following season?

There were a few changes in personnel in pre-season, but by the start of the new campaign I was already convinced we wouldn't get relegated. That gradual improvement I spoke about earlier was even more evident; you could sense we were on the right track. We made key signings – Mark Schwarzer, notably – but we were stronger as players and as a team.

And the fabled repetitive training sessions were in full swing?

[Laughs!] Oh yes! Roy is the person who's taught the most about defending, by a mile. So much so that I felt that after working with him nobody could teach me anything new. He was so incredibly detailed. The defensive drills that Aaron Hughes and I did with him were intense but ever so constructive. Aaron and I forged a phenomenal understanding, one that became almost telepathic. In fact, Aaron and I barely spoke on the pitch; we didn't have to as we got to know each other's game and strengths incredibly well. We had no "unknowns". Sure, we conceded goals because we were up against top quality players every week, but we shored things up considerably. Roy's coaching and our understanding of our respective roles meant that we were rarely caught out, and that was borne out of increased confidence and the knowledge that we'd cover each other automatically.

We noticed that from the stands – and the by-product of having an organised defence was that we cut out conceding those scrappy, unlucky, "iffy" goals at a stroke…

Football can be a complicated game, but the key is to get rid of as much of the "x-factor" as you can

"Roy is the person who's taught the most about defending, by a mile. So much so that I felt that after working with him nobody could teach me anything new. He was so incredibly detailed. The defensive drills that Aaron Hughes and I did with him were intense but ever so constructive."

Below: For big Brede, pictured here in pre-season action at Wycombe, it was a case of "practice makes perfect" at FFC.

Above: Brede Hangeland is pictured after a man-of-the-match showing at Portsmouth. Our 1-0 win at Fratton Park in May 2008 completed a wonderful Great Escape and secured our top-flight status.

by organising yourself, which is what Roy is all about. He will organise the team and get the players fully tuned in so that we're prepared and have a strategy for just about any eventuality. And the way Roy goes about doing that is more comprehensive than anyone else I've seen in the game.

It doesn't fall into the "sexy football" bracket, perhaps, and yet it can prove the bedrock from which sexy football can emerge, particularly in a club of our stature. Your partnership with Aaron Hughes was one of the fantastic by-products of Roy's structured approach…
Having the system is one thing, but you've then got to have the vital ingredients – players who have the ability and the right mental approach to make the plan work. You've only got to look back at that squad; they're all good guys, there was no "star" mentality, we were all team players, and we were all prepared to do the necessary groundwork and listen to the instructions. The key to it all was that we could see the improvement for ourselves; in fact, it was fantastic to sense that we were getting stronger by the week. So "sexy" it wasn't! Repetitive? Oh yes! Doing the same sort of stuff day after day in training was certainly that. But "boring"? No, because we could see that it was working – both in training and, especially, in matches – and that we were being schooled brilliantly.

Paul Konchesky was one player who benefited enormously…
Without a doubt. Paul, like everyone else in the team, knew he'd have two or three options when he was in possession. In Paul's case, he could expect Clint Dempsey to move off the line or for one of the central midfielders, very often Danny Murphy, to make himself available so he'd feel confident in possession knowing that he'd have team-mates ready to help out. Paul could then play that pass and then move to offer support himself. It all came from the training field; most options were covered.

You mention Danny Murphy. Now there was a guy with a decent CV but prior to joining Fulham he'd been treading water, so to speak, at Charlton and Spurs; he was signed by Lawrie Sanchez, but once Roy came along he became the team's linchpin…
Danny's an intelligent man. He probably spotted as early as anyone that if we all bought into Roy's methods then we could be successful. You're right about Danny's CV: at the time he was probably the only one of us who'd been successful at a

big club. And yet he was level-headed and a key player – and a key person – in our camp. If he made a mistake, for example, he was especially keen to win the ball back or to take possession as soon as possible afterwards in order to go again with another telling pass. He never shirked his responsibilities and never hid; and that rubbed off on all of us. The bigger the game, the more Danny liked it. He had an important role to play, both as a central midfielder and captain, and he did so wonderfully.

Your first Fulham goal, against Arsenal, was a match-winner – a good way to open your account?
It was a big day for me. It was still quite early in my Fulham career and simply being in the line-up to play a big team like Arsenal was a thrill in itself. We were beginning to feel that if we did our jobs well then we could not only stand up to the bigger clubs but maybe beat them (despite losing at Hull the previous week!). I remember the goal – I got on the end of a cross from Jimmy Bullard midway through the first half – and we held on for a fantastic victory.

We also clocked up wins against Spurs and Manchester United on the way to finishing seventh – no "Great Escape" that season!
The difference was amazing. We'd been transformed, within 12 months, from being okay players in a poorish team to confident and capable players in a strong team. It's a wonderful feeling to be a part of something so special. Now we'd even qualified for the Europa League, too.

Ah, the unforgettable European Tour! One game that often gets overlooked because of the fantastic events that followed is the home game with Shakhtar Donetsk. They were a bit tasty, weren't they? How the hell did you beat them?
Shakhtar were superb – the best team I've ever faced. Technically brilliant and fantastically quick. They had us on the rack at the Cottage early on. Rather than defend on the 18-yard line, we were defending on the six-yard line and our midfielders were patrolling the edge of the box. Bobby Zamora and Andy Johnson also did their bit, but generally from fairly deep in our half! Mentally, though, we were fully switched on and were confident of our team structure, but this was something else! They were really, really good.

Back to the value of those training drills, then?
Exactly! We somehow managed to fend off wave after wave of attacks after Zoltan Gera had given us the lead, before gradually working our way into the game. I'm absolutely convinced that had Shakhtar managed to break our resolve and put us out then they'd have gone on to win the competition. To beat them was some performance.

Bobby Zamora's glorious second-half strike (and a fantastic late save from Mark Schwarzer) earned us a 2-1 victory that night and a 1-1 draw in Donetsk meant we were through. That away goal was useful, Brede?

It was another tough game; one in which everyone played their part. I got my head to Damien Duff's corner and that goal [after 33 minutes] knocked them out of their stride – for a while, at least!

How do you explain a night like the one we experienced against Juventus at the Cottage?

The previous weekend we played Manchester United at Old Trafford, and lost 3-0. I dislocated a rib and was in all sorts of trouble. The pain was unbearable and that was it; I wouldn't be playing against Juve. On the Tuesday I couldn't walk, and there was absolutely no chance of doing any training. What happened next was amazing, and it sums up Fulham for me. The medical team did absolutely everything in a bid to get me sorted, and that included seeing experts at Harley Street, and I got plenty of advice and followed their recommended treatments. On the Wednesday I was able to train, albeit in considerable discomfort, and by Thursday I had much more movement and was prepared to give it a go. When Trezeguet scored for them so early in the game I remember standing there in pain and thinking "We're 4-1 down, this looks like being a long night!" So how *DO* you explain what happened next? Well, it was like we went into this zone, one in which everything you tried works. It WAS surreal; it was like being in a movie and the whole thing was scripted in your favour. I recall thinking at one point, "We're battering them here; we're battering Juventus!" It was an incredible feeling. From a footballer's perspective it was perfect. We could see that they couldn't contain us. We had the momentum and were playing the perfect game; "Hey, we could win this!". And then the moment when time seemed to stand still – when Clint Dempsey's chip sailed into the net…

And then the noise…!

Wow! There was a moment of silence then a tumultuous roar – and that was just Clint! What a noise, and what a fantastic feeling. In amongst all that, though, was an air of professionalism. There were still ten minutes or so to go and – rather like that game at Portsmouth – now wasn't the time to make any mistakes. Then again, we'd been well drilled to deal with such moments. We had a very strong feeling of togetherness, on and off the pitch. We were in it for everyone, from the management to the fans. Everybody who was there that night was lucky to share in the experience.

During that season, Bobby Zamora reinvented himself from a more-than-decent target man

struggling for goals to an absolute world-beater. He must have been a right handful in training?

When he was on his game, which was most weeks, Bobby was unplayable. And even during that glorious purple patch I'd say he was terribly underrated outside the Club. He was one who'd whinge about the repetitive training drills now and again, but it was a front, he just had to have his say. He loved the fact that we were doing well. I got to know Bobby very well on the training pitch! They could be tough sessions. Don't forget that our attacking players were also drilled by Roy, so, with all of us fully aware of our responsibilities, they could be tough but rewarding sessions.

We've mentioned Roy Hodgson a fair few times, but what of Ray Lewington, who knows Fulham inside out – what were his strengths?

Both are gentlemen, so you respect them as people first and foremost. But they're excellent coaches too. They complement each other fantastically well and, as well as getting their coaching points across well, both could tell you off, too! However, that was all part of being at work. Ray was a perfect foil for Roy and we all learned so much from them.

Roy used to say that a player might only be in possession of the ball for a total of two or three minutes in a game. That means there's another 88 or so minutes in which he's moving and thinking. You can't switch off. You've always got to consider as the play develops, "Am I in the right spot now?" or "What's likely to happen here" and position yourself accordingly. The beauty of working with Roy and Ray was they never gave you mixed messages; there was no confusion.

"Shakhtar were superb – the best team I've ever faced. Technically brilliant and fantastically quick. They had us on the rack at the Cottage early on."

Below: Thou shalt not pass! Brede's on the spot to thwart this Norwich attack.

By this time Fulham were a match for anyone, in the League or in Europe. We enjoyed further epic nights at the Cottage against Wolfsburg and Hamburg – and we've not mentioned Zoltan Gera or Simon Davies as yet…?

Just as I described Bobby Zamora above, Zoltan, Simon and others may have been regarded as average players by some; those at the Club knew that wasn't the case. They were top, top players playing key roles in a magnificent adventure. They could play all right, and proved that time and again. Within the game, Fulham were highly regarded. I'd often speak with players from other Premier League clubs and none fancied playing us – they acknowledged our standing at the time and knew they'd be in for a tough test, no matter who they were. We were a compact set-up, with hard-working players who knew what they were doing. I promise you, our would-be opponents hated the prospect of playing us. And within our team ethic we had players who could really play and who could offer moments of sheer brilliance.

Unfortunately we had to field a patched-up team for the big day and had to settle for the "plucky losers" tag – but what was it like to play in a major European final and nearly pull off a shock?

It's one of the very few regrets I have in my career. I can slo-mo that cross in my mind; had I reacted a split-second earlier I'd have snuffed out the danger. It was a routine part of my game and I can't explain it. Perhaps it was fatigue or the occasion, but I hesitated for a fraction of a second and Forlán's effort glanced off me and beyond Mark [Schwarzer] into the net. I know others don't regard it as a mistake; however, I really should have prevented that goal. The really painful aspect is that we'd nearly seen out extra-time and I'm absolutely convinced that we'd have won the penalty shoot-out. I know they had [David] De Gea in goal, but then we had Mark, a fantastic keeper, and five really strong penalty takers.

Having put Fulham on the world map, Roy Hodgson went off to manage Liverpool. Was that a surprise?

Realistically, Roy was very unlikely to turn that job down. We're all ambitious, and this was a fantastic opportunity for him.

And along came Mark Hughes. We finished that following season well, but only after a hint of player-power – is that correct?

I enjoyed working with Mark. As the season went on we seemed to click and things augured well for the future. The first half of the campaign was challenging. Mark inherited a squad of players that was drilled to perfection – anyone could have managed that squad, even my grandmother! Instead Mark wanted to change a few things. For example, whereas previously we were encouraged to show the attacking players the inside option where we'd have others ready to pick them off, Mark wanted us to show them outside. A minor detail, you might think, but it was quite a big switch for us defenders. My view was that Mark had a great chance of simply picking up where Roy left off; there was no need to change anything, any new manager could simply walk in and be successful. Some of the key players got together and basically said, "We know what to do here". This wasn't really a case of being rebellious, more of knowing where our true strengths lay. With that, we went from skirting with the relegation places to a solid eighth-place finish. I have a lot of respect for Mark Hughes, he's an intelligent man, and he could see that things were working that much better. We had a great run of results in from January, and we were training well. Mark should take great credit for that.

So were you surprised when he left?

Yes! I was both surprised and disappointed. I've since heard via one of his colleagues, Mark Bowen, that he considers that decision a mistake in retrospect. Had he stayed I've no doubt that Fulham would have remained a solid mid-table Premier League at the very least, and his CV would have been enhanced. He'd have been a much better bet than those who followed.

We had a spell under Martin Jol that promised much – with Mousa Dembélé looking a real find – but, with Mohamed Al Fayed selling to Shahid Khan, the Club seemed to drift. Was that a frustrating time?

My career at Fulham was like a game of two halves – the first half was on the up, the other half was going down. Martin Jol was keen to oversee a more expansive style. He said we were strong defensively but his mistake was to assume that would remain so. We knew we couldn't simply turn up on a matchday and maintain our standards without putting in the hard work on the training field. And this was made that much more difficult when he changed the personnel – Philippe Senderos came in for Aaron Hughes, for example. Make no mistake, Senderos was a good player, but why would you break up a proven, successful partnership for no good reason? On top of that, as players came and went – and we had a number of very good players – so you could sense that the high values set by Roy Hodgson and Ray Lewington were gradually being eroded. It meant that we were now just as good as the sum of the individual players, there wasn't that fantastic team mentality that had given us such an edge.

With Martin Jol having outstayed his welcome, in came René Meulensteen, yet in the blink of an eye he, too, was replaced. Enter Felix Magath…!
I liked Meulensteen. However, I think the Club made a big mistake. Rather than reset the bar and consolidate Fulham's position as an established Premier League club, they looked to become a top team. That's a laudable ambition, but it's one that a club of Fulham's size and stature has to manage very carefully. If you take away the foundations of a solid team and bring in too many "flair" players then you run the risk of knocking the house down. The upshot is that when you find yourself in a relegation battle you haven't got enough grit, you haven't got enough players who really care when it really matters. Meulensteen was a nice man, a top coach, but wanted us to play like a top team, almost overnight. When you're down there you have to keep it simple, be well organised, work hard and galvanise the whole set up to stand a chance of avoiding the drop. You can't really hope to outplay teams; that doesn't work.

Hmm, point taken. But might he have been the better option to the one that followed?
Oh! Please! *ANYONE* would have been a better option!

If Hodgson was the perfect fit for FFC, surely Magath was the polar opposite?
They were desperate times. But yes, he was the worst fit imaginable! And that's in terms of personality, in terms of values, in terms of ethics, everything. BUT, I'm prepared to accept anything if it means staying in the League. We had two players from German football in Sascha Riether and Ashkan Dejagah and they were almost crying when they heard that Magath was coming in. I listened to their stories, but the fact remained we needed a strong personality to take charge and so long as his methods worked, even if he was this perceived madman I was hearing about, then so be it; I'd give it my best shot. Within a week I knew he was the wrong appointment; if we were to save Fulham from relegation we'd have to do it despite him.

His CV was sound, though…?
As a German-mentality coach perhaps, and one who was used to working with German players. But he was now in charge of an English Premier League team. Things work differently here; there has to be mutual respect between the players and the coaches, even if the final word still lies with the man in charge. You cannot operate some Army-style regime and bark out nonsensical orders. I'm sorry to say it was a disastrous appointment and it developed into a nightmare scenario that made staying up that much more difficult, if not impossible. Given that we were such a solid team just a few years before I'd say it was scandalous that we were relegated. I know this a selfish outlook, but I'd have liked nothing more than to have been able to play out my career at Craven Cottage as part of a stable set-up in the Premier League. Unfortunately, after all the hard work put in by so many people to make Fulham such a wonderful top-flight club, some form of malaise set in. That relegation could and should have been avoided.

And so to the crackers cheese episode. Has this been, er, overcooked?
No, it's all true. And it's not really my style to speak out in such a way, but there you go. When I left Fulham I was aggrieved at how badly "my" club had been mismanaged and I was keen to help out in some way. In order to get rid of Magath I had to tell my story to as many people as possible. That cheese story – I was advised by Magath to put a lump of cheese soaked in alcohol on my leg to cure an injury – is simply one of many madcap episodes during those infuriating months. The Club Doctor, Steve Lewis, an experienced frontline doctor in football medicine, was completely overruled (as well as totally bemused!). They were sad, sad times.

Okay, let's close on a brighter note. What are your abiding memories of your time at Fulham?
During the Magath era I'd say to myself, "This isn't Fulham, it's something freakish." I had a fantastic time at the Club. I returned quite recently and watched a game from the Hammersmith End, and it rekindled all the wonderful memories. Fulham is the perfect place to play football. You get a feeling of being part of something special, of being part of the Club and of having a bond with all those who love it. There's a lovely charm about the place and yet, when things are going well it can be a rousing fortress on matchdays. That "Stand Up If You Still Believe" chant in 2010 was astonishing! And I've yet to meet a rude Fulham fan! I'm so very grateful for having had such a great time at the Club.

I made so many great friends and played with so many players who, like me, felt a genuine affinity with Fulham and its supporters. It's a very special place. I may have arrived somewhat randomly, but now I feel there's a connection there for life. ⚽

"Perhaps it was fatigue or the occasion, but I hesitated for a fraction of a second and Forlán's effort glanced off me and beyond Mark [Schwarzer] into the net. I know others don't regard it as a mistake; however, I really should have prevented that goal. The really painful aspect is that we'd nearly seen out extra-time and I'm absolutely convinced that we'd have won the penalty shoot-out."

Small Talk

The whole point of supporter forums – whether online or in printed fanzine form – is that they offer an outlet for opinions. And if someone else has their own point to make, whether in support of said comment or in total disagreement, then that's how a discussion unfolds.

From time to time mischief-makers add their two-penn'orth and fuel the flames, or quash the argument with a well-timed or well-observed comic retort.

Then there are those who totally miss the point (in my humble opinion, naturally!) and whose vehemence comes across as sheer ignorance. One such case came recently on The Fulham Independent forum when a poster innocently remarked, with a degree or two of pride, that it was 20 years since Micky Adams led FFC to promotion from the bottom division. The response was as swift as it was wide of the mark. Why hark back to celebrate something so puny as a minor promotion, one that didn't even come with the basement division's championship trophy? It was all so "little Fulham" blah-blah-blah, all you small-minded Fulham fans living in the past blah-blah-blah and happy to dwell on traipsing around the lowlier footballing outposts chalking

By George, it's Another Statue!

When England won the World Cup in 1966 George Cohen was ever-present at right-back. To mark the 50th anniversary of that significant achievement plus, of course, his long and distinguished association with FFC, George has been honoured by the Club and the Borough.

In October a statue of George was unveiled at the Hammersmith End and just days later he was made an honorary freeman – the highest civic distinction a borough can grant – at a special meeting of Hammersmith and Fulham Council. Here are some pictures of how it all went...

Below left: Some day my plinth will come...! Ace sculptor Douglas Jennings, also responsible for the brilliant Johnny Haynes statue, gets a random passer-by to inspect his work...

GEORGE COHEN MBE
FULHAM PLAYER
WORLD CUP WINNER
GENTLEMAN

Right: "Looks a bit like Bobby Moore," said a fair few at the unveiling. The statue's current elevated position doesn't perhaps show it off in all its glory but the plan is to move it to an improved vantage point as and when the Riverside Stand is redeveloped. The words on the plinth are particularly classy.

Right: After receiving the Freedom of the Borough, George is congratulated by Nick Cusack (left), former FFC player and these days Assistant Chief Executive of the PFA, and long-time pal Bob Howes.

up the points. How noble; how bloody heroic! Blah-de-blah – you get the drift!

How bloody sad is he? Or let's just say "misguided"! Our hard-fought victories 20 seasons ago might not have been against the much more glamorous and mightier Arsenal, Chelsea, Manchester United or Liverpool – or, come to that Shakhtar Donetsk, Juventus or Hamburg – but they paved the way for the glorious wins over those aforementioned leading lights.

Also, given the appalling plight of the Club in the preceding years, that promotion season gave us a massive injection of hope (of not merely surviving, but doing so with a degree or two of dignity) as well as an explosion of enjoyment and genuine camaraderie. Here was a group of players giving their best under a rookie manager doing his utmost to forge a winning package. It wasn't always pretty and there were a fair few blips along the way, but we loved it. And, as was all too evident, they loved it, especially once we'd got over the finishing line.

I can't imagine there's a single Fulham supporter who'd relish going back to those days – but there's plenty to be said for the methods that underpinned our success, which was at the same time modest (promotion from the bottom tier, but no championship) yet bloody extraordinary. And there was a real connection with the players – often literally so given the close confines of the basement division grounds – which added to the joyous celebrations as we hit the home straight. Carlisle away (while on a different scale to, say, beating Man Utd at Old Trafford!) was a blast; Mansfield away was as miserable a 0-0 as you'll ever have to endure, but the point gained with tired legs ensured we'd be waving bye-bye to Division Three; Cambridge away, at which we swamped the Abbey Stadium in all manner of fancy dress, was a hoot, tempered only by the news that Wigan had done enough to pip us on goal difference (by a single goal!). The measure of our achievement was underlined by the fact that Micky Adams was named the division's Manager of the Season despite us finishing as runners-up. All in all, the boys done good!

"Little Fulham" mentality? I don't think so! That '96-97 campaign was very much the springboard for what was to follow. Without those wins at unglamorous outposts such as Rochdale, Exeter, Darlington and Scunthorpe there'd have been no Keegan, no Tigana and no Hodgson. (There'd have been no Sanchez or Magath either, but let's gloss over those!) Living in the past is one thing, but remembering and celebrating significant historical events is another thing entirely.

In this instance it also helps to keep our feet on the ground somewhat. Our focus as supporters should always be on the here and now, with a modicum of consideration as to the future. But what's wrong with treasuring our past achievements and admiring those who were instrumental in achieving them? With no slur intended on our newer supporters, I'm damned sure that our amazing exploits in getting to the Premier League and on to the European trail were appreciated that much more by those who'd stuck by the club when things looked very bleak indeed.

Funnily enough, Micky Adams himself was eager to preach in the mid-'90s that games were won on the pitch and not courtesy of a club's past glories and legendary figures. And here we are feting him and his troops. Can't imagine, though, that he'd be keen to hear any of us describing his input to FFC's history as "little" or that in applauding that campaign we're revelling in being "Little Fulham". Come to think of it, best not to use the word "little" in any context when he's around...!

Talk of '96-97 puts how far we've come since that season sharply into focus. Unfortunately it also serves to highlight how all the hard graft put in on and off the pitch in not only getting us to the Premier League but staying there relatively comfortably (and all the joyous moments along the way) has been snuffed out almost in an instant.

It's rare for a badly run club to deliver the goods on the field. By the same token, there's no guarantee that a club will reel in silverware simply because it's well run; but it certainly helps!

Money talks these days, most notably in the top flight where the rich just keep on getting richer – although you wouldn't say that the fans' enjoyment levels are going up in the same proportions. FFC's achievement in mixing it for so long with the big boys was fantastic. There were some "iffy" periods but, by and large, the Club was well run and FFC reaped the rewards for that.

The statisticians amongst us claim that we're "at our level" now; that, historically at least, we're a second-tier team. Well that's all right then. For me, that's "Little Fulham" thinking. I disliked many aspects of our Premier League adventure, especially as the top flight became ever-more corporate and the considerations of loyal supporters became less and less important to the fat cats running the show. However, in any sporting context, the top flight is the place to be, or at least the place to aspire to be. Pootling along in "Division Two" is a very poor second best. Being allowed to slip so far and so quickly as to almost drop into the third tier is, frankly, a disgrace and an insult to all those who worked so hard to get us into the top flight in the first place – and to all those loyal supporters who've shelled out their hard-earned cash believing (and being told ad nauseam!) that the Club officials were pulling out all the stops to get back among the big boys. Sadly, the evidence of what we've had to endure these past few seasons tells another story entirely. ⚽

Fulham 5 Huddersfield Town 0	
29.10.16 11th	
Brentford 0 Fulham 2	
04.11.16 7th	
Fulham 1 Sheffield Wednesday 1	
19.11.16 8th	
Brighton & HA 2 Fulham 1	
26.11.16 10th	
Fulham 5 Reading 0	
03.12.16 10th	
Wolverhampton Wanderers 4 Fulham 4	
10.12.16 9th	
Fulham 2 Rotherham United 1	
13.12.16 9th	
Fulham 2 Derby County 2	
17.12.16 9th	
Ipswich Town 0 Fulham 2	
26.12.16 7th	
Fulham 1 Brighton & HA 2	
02.01.17 10th	

1st
2nd
3rd
4th
5th
6th
7th
8th
9th
10th
11th
12th
13th
14th
15th
16th
17th
18th
19th
20th
21st
22th
23th
24th

Uplifting Experience

First things first: many thanks and congrats to Slaviša Jokanović for raising the footballing bar at FFC. In the past few weeks, so many supporters have commented (sharing my view) that, at long last, coming to watch Fulham play has become a pleasurable experience once again. Some of the sparkling attacking moves have reminded many of the brilliance of Jean Tigana's promotion-winning team; praise indeed!

True, over the course of the season we've often failed to turn the high percentage levels of possession and ever-improving attacking prowess into victories, but at least it's been rewarding to witness the positive upswing. When all's said and done, we've been making chances. Loads of them! The fact that it's no longer a drag to drag oneself along to the Cottage has surely been down to a sense that, despite the all-too-frequent blips, there's a successful team evolving.

In fact, some of the sparkling interplay through midfield has bordered on the extraordinary, requiring supreme levels of skill and understanding. Pivotal to this has been Tom Cairney, who has blossomed in the playmaker role. However, while his clever close control and passing skills make him the most eye-catching and headline-grabbing midfielder, he wouldn't shine anything like as much but for the prodigious shifts put in by Stefan Johansen and Kevin McDonald. When all goes to plan, it's an entertaining blend and an increasingly solid one, amply backed up by the wing-backs as well as the lively trickery of Sone Aluko.

So, with all this glowing praise flying about, why is it that many of us are still feeling short-changed? It might be because there's a real sense that Slaviša Jokanović has orchestrated the fantastic upswing despite the Club's input rather than because of it. His outburst earlier this season about the lack of support from those supposedly charged with bringing in new signings was clear evidence that all was not right.

The Chris Martin saga has developed into a major issue because of the Club's indifferent transfer activity. Over the past few seasons the turnover of players reached ridiculous proportions and it was anyone's guess how the influx of players would gel – if at all! Back in August, though, the key acquisitions were surely a couple of strikers. You didn't have to be Sherlock Holmes to detect that both Dembélé and McCormack were off. So, if the Head Coach reckoned that neither Cauley Woodrow nor Matt Smith were up to the task, then the cupboard was pretty bare.

> *"Tom Cairney has blossomed in the playmaker role. However, while his clever close control and passing skills make him the most eye-catching and headline-grabbing midfielder, he wouldn't shine anything like as much but for the prodigious shifts put in by Stefan Johansen and Kevin McDonald."*

Top right: Kevin McDonald's "prodigious shifts" has helped Fulham's midfield, and Tom Cairney in particular, to shine.

Opposite page top: Paul Johnson presents: The Theatre of (We Can) Dream!

Below: The team's dramatic shift in style and substance thanks to Slaviša Jokanović's methods gets an airing in the *Standard*.

Jokanovic: I've found best way to succeed

SLAVISA JOKANOVIC says Fulham have found a winning formula ahead of tomorrow's west London derby against QPR, *writes Giuseppe Muro*.

Fulham are eighth in the Championship having lost just one of their past seven matches and can move to within three points of the play-off places with a win in the lunchtime kick-off at Loftus Road.

Jokanovic (*right*) said: "I have to be happy because we created a style and an identity. I believe our supporters start to recognise it is a great way to try and win the game.

"We are more solid, we are dominating games, we control many things and create many chances. But the most important thing is always to win the game.

"I believe, and my players believe, this is the best way to fight for the victory, and at QPR we are going to try and do something similar."

QPR, meanwhile, have picked up under Ian Holloway by winning their past three games to pull away from the drop zone.

Holloway said: "The results early on were not anywhere near what I expected.

"But it is a really good place to be right now.

"How Fulham are doing is tremendous. Their manager deserves a massive pat on the back. It is a big test for us but I believe we can make it four wins in a row."

Our ridiculously wealthy Chairman has been reluctant to splash the cash on the squad, so I doubt if anyone expected him to rubberstamp huge outlays but there does seem to be a chasm between what he says and what he does – or at least what his charges do.

Losing two prolific strikers such as Dembélé and McCormack could be construed as careless, even if their departures were maybe down to circumstances, but to come nowhere near to replacing them for so long smacks of cackhandedness; something we've become accustomed to in recent seasons, unfortunately. It certainly smacks of a lack of ambition from the top.

Once he'd got himself fitter, Chris Martin has done well for us. He's more than capable. Then he went on strike. (How ironic: there's us desperate for a striker and he goes and does precisely that!) Matt Smith, shortly to depart for QPR, was hurriedly reinstated as central striker but, for all his genuine effort and endeavour, was just as off the pace as Martin when he was trying to get to grips with Slav's ways. To have no cover is plain daft! Thing is, had Martin got crocked in that time it would have been the same situation: no acceptable cover.

Once the transfer window rolled along it was, even more incredibly, a case of more going out than coming in. Signing Gohi Cyriac may prove to be a masterstroke, we'll see, but at this juncture you'd have to say that our transfer activity fell into the "uninspiring" category. Again. ⚽

Crazy, then, that it wasn't until the very final knockings of the Autumn transfer window (very late on Aug 31) that we brought in Martin on a year-long loan from Derby. So much for being on the case! We'd played nine games by the time the loanee made his debut at home to Birmingham. What's more, Martin was patently carrying a few extra pounds, not match fit, and also had to tune in to Slav's way of playing. This wasn't a case of hitting the ground running, more like doing so at a gentle stroll!

Above, right and below: When Chris Martin, on loan to FFC from Derby, was unsettled by Steve McLaren, new Manager at Martin's parent club, Slaviša Jokanović came out with several pearls of wisdom, as shown here...

Spot of Bother

> *"Try as we might, we couldn't get back in the game. Alas, we looked jaded; beaten by the occasion. Even Cairney's radar was off, misplacing a couple of passes as we struggled to break down the stoic home defence."*

How ironic that it took a penalty, and a debatable one at that, to halt our march to the Championship Play-off Final. It's fair to say that most of us expected to get to Wembley – which is a tribute to Slaviša Jokanović's methods and the way his players had responded as the season progressed. Sealing sixth spot only to then lose out over two legs to Reading was tough to take. There were loads of talking points; bottom line, though, was that, when push came to shove, we couldn't deliver.

There was plenty of pushing and shoving in the first leg at the Cottage; the visitors not only blatantly slowed down proceedings at every opportunity, but also weren't averse to dishing out niggly fouls. Unfortunately, referee Stuart Attwell decided to issue reprimands rather than yellow cards. "How many 'final warnings' are you going to give them, Attwell?" was a typical Hammersmith End cry. That said, Japp Stam's lot were doing a fine job in stifling our attacking instincts. Their legitimate tactics were spot-on; shame the borderline stuff was deemed acceptable too.

When Obita opened the scoring for Reading early in the second half it was evident the Fulham players reckoned they were hard done-by. Johansen may well have been fouled by McShane on halfway, and there was certainly a handball by Williams as the ball broke loose. Attwell, though, allowed play to continue and, while we momentarily froze, Obita took possession in front of the Cottage and put his team ahead.

A lovely move, less than ten minutes later, put Malone clear and his low cross-shot was parried by Al-Habsi. As the ball looped up in slow motion, Tom Cairney had time to comb his precious barnet before nodding home the equaliser. All to play for. And when Reading skipper McShane was given a straight red with ten minutes to go, there was every chance that our superior fitness and numerical advantage would pay dividends. Us Fulham fans did our bit, maintaining a fantastic atmosphere, but despite several openings (and a decent appeal for a penalty when Fredericks was felled) we couldn't fashion a winner.

With no chance of getting tickets for the return game at the Madjeski, it'd have to be Sky TV instead, with my two sons joining me on the sofa. Before kick-off I posted this on Facebook: "Here's hoping it's us bullying the opposition tonight – legitimately, of course. If we aren't intimidated, play to our strengths and take the game to Reading then we'll be heading to Wembley. We're good enough, but we've got to 'turn up', and show that we're good enough. A stronger ref than Saturday would be a bonus (and getting the rub of the green would be doubly so!). COYW!"

Unlike Saturday, the three of us were pretty nervous. Surely we could do this. Just like Saturday, several of our players looked edgy. Great save by Betts, ditto Al-Habsi to deny Fredericks; 0-0 at the break. Then the turning point: a flipping penalty. Kalas, under pressure from Kermogant, nudged the ball with his arm. It's a stonewall pen; had it been at the other end, we'd have been screaming for a spot-kick. Referee Martin Atkinson had little

TASTY COTTAGE TIE

FULHAM 1
Cairney 65

READING 1
Obita 53

By Kieran Gill

Reading skipper McShane sees red as Fulham are frustrated

THE race for Premier League promotion is finely poised after free-scoring Fulham were kept quiet by the 10 men of Reading in their Championship play-off semi-final first leg yesterday.

No one scored more than Fulham in English football's second tier this season and they thumped Reading 5-0 at Craven Cottage before Christmas.

Yet Slavisa Jokanovic's side were unable to inflict any further misery on Jaap Stam's Reading, who lost Paul McShane to a straight red.

They will have to do without their club captain for the second leg at the Madejski Stadium on Tuesday after McShane stuck his studs into the knee of Kevin McDonald.

'We trust all our players,' Stam said. 'McShane is an important piece of the puzzle but other players can do that job as well and we are still confident. I'm not talking about advantage Reading. We know what we can do.'

Reading, who finished third in the Championship, took a surprise lead through Jordan Obita but Tom Cairney cancelled that out.

Fulham, though, left feeling frustrated. 'We cannot be completely satisfied,' Jokanovic said. 'I believe we deserved to score more and win the game but everything is now open for Tuesday.'

Craven Cottage is one of English football's gems, with its old-fashioned charm and positioning by the River Thames. Yet for this visit of Reading, with almost 24,000 fans in attendance, it was rocking.

Reading came with a plan to counter-attack and try to take a clean sheet back to the Madejski.

They wasted time throughout — much to Fulham's frustration — and could not manage a single shot on or off target in the first half.

That changed in the 53rd minute when Obita received the ball to the left of the box and unleashed a shot that went in off the far post.

Fulham's players surrounded referee Stuart Attwell, feeling a free-kick should have been awarded in the build-up when Stefan Johansen was brought down by McShane.

Fulham levelled in the 65th minute when Reading goalkeeper Ali Al-Habsi made a hash of a Scott Malone cross and gifted it to Cairney, who headed home.

McShane was sent off for his foul on McDonald on 80 minutes, with replays showing that his studs did connect with his opponent.

So Reading had to play out the final 10 minutes one man down. They survived and so there is everything to play in Tuesday's second leg.

HANDLE WITH CAIR: An error by Reading goalkeeper Ali Al Habsi leads to Tom Cairney's equaliser for Fulham

FULHAM (4-2-3-1): Bettinelli 6; Fredericks 6, Ream 6.5, Kalas 6, Malone 6.5; McDonald 6, Cairney 7; Aluko 5.5 (Cyriac 87min), Johansen 6, Ayite 6; Martin 5.5 (Kebano 6, 61). Subs (not used): Button, Odoi, Parker, Piazon, Sessegnon. **Booked:** McDonald, Malone.
READING (3-4-2-1): Al Habsi 6; Moore 6, McShane 5, Blackett 6, Gunter 6, Williams 6, Evans 6.5, Obita 6.5 (Grabban 5.5 (Mendes 68, Ilori 82), Swift 6 (van den Berg 6, 74); Kermogant 6. Subs (not used): Jaakola, Beerens, McCleary, Popa. **Booked:** Swift, Kermogant. **Sent off:** McShane (80min).
Referee: S Attwell (Warwickshire) 6.

choice but to give it. Thing is, replays showed it was far from nailed-on – as the players locked horns, Kermogant punched the ball first and there were even suggestions that the Reading man had used his arm to nudge Kalas on to the ball. Hmm, not sure about that one. But it was certainly nowhere near as clear-cut as the handball before Reading's first goal at the Cottage. Had this one been entrusted to a video ref the decision would surely have been a free-kick to Fulham for the blindside handball. Rats.

Try as we might, we couldn't get back in the game. Alas, we looked jaded; beaten by the occasion. Even Cairney's radar was off, misplacing a couple of passes as we struggled to break down the stoic home defence. Even so, Al-Habsi took the plaudits for keeping the home side in it, tipping over a rising effort from McDonald (when the Fulham man – one of the few who refused to buckle – should have shot low and hard). Aluko inexplicably shot high and not so handsome from a great position and in added on time sub Martin headed well wide when his nearest challenger was the yellow-clad Bettinelli.

On the final whistle I posted this: "Hoping for Wembley, but instead we get Middlesbrough! Too many players not good enough when it mattered. Or simply knackered. Too many misplaced passes; even Cairney was at it. We know we had the ability to be the better team, but we weren't the stronger team over the two games. Stam's tactics won out. We weren't sharp enough at the death. A lacklustre end to a great season. Big shame."

Don't forget that our season started much later than other teams. We only got things together in the autumn, having gone six games without a win between the two International breaks (against Birmingham, Burton, Wigan, Bristol City, Nottm. Forest and QPR – hardly heavyweights in the division). After this we were treated to some sparkling football, and supporters were heard to say that they were enjoying coming to Fulham again. Full credit to Slav and his gang for our wonderful renaissance. The big question is will he be given the backing to not only keep the core of this squad together but to bolster it in key areas. A recognised penalty taker would be handy, too! ⚽

A Bit of Banter With Leroy

For our former centre-forward Leroy Rosenior, two phrases kept cropping up during his career: "It's Only Banter", the title of his excellent, recently published autobiography, and "Keep your powder dry", the wise words of his father Willie about how it's best not to react impulsively when faced with a difficult situation. One such situation came very early in Leroy's career at Fulham and is outlined in the book's prologue. Two unnamed opponents dished out an appalling tirade of racial abuse at him – the supposed "Banter" mentioned above – in an attempt to unsettle the teenage striker. It worked to the extent that after the final whistle Leroy was not only close to tears, he was close to quitting the game. He could easily have "decked" the obnoxious pair, either on the pitch in front of the 30,000 crowd or at the final whistle when they offered their hands for a handshake, muttering that it had just been banter. Instead, Leroy kept his powder dry; in doing so his mental strength went up a few notches.

Leroy not only went on to have a successful career that led to management and media punditry but was also chuffed that one of his sons, Liam, followed in his footsteps in donning the white shirt of Fulham. The Ed spent an engaging half-hour with Leroy – who's warm, relaxed and witty – directly before our former No.9 headed into Wogan House for an interview with Simon Mayo on Radio 2. Good to see that you put TOOFIF first, Leroy…!

So Leroy, apart from enjoying a coffee opposite the Radio 2 HQ, what are you up to these days?
I'm working on a freelance basis with IMG, the global sports company, on the Premier League Productions. I also write for some newspapers and I'm an ambassador for "Show Racism the Red Card" so I'm keeping busy. Previously I was with the BBC for six years; that was great while it lasted, but it meant some very late nights!

Have you seen much of Fulham this season?
Not too much, no. I've seen a fair few bits and pieces, and I've caught a couple of live games.

Fulham 1 Wolverhampton Wanderers 3	
18.03.17	7th
Rotherham United 0 Fulham 1	
01.04.14	6th
Derby County 4 Fulham 2	
04.04.17	7th
Fulham 3 Ipswich 1	
08.04.17	7th
Norwich City 1 Fulham 3	
14.04.17	7th
Fulham 3 Aston Villa 1	
17.04.17	6th
Huddersfield Town 1 Fulham 4	
22.04.17	6th
Fulham 1 Brentford 1	
29.04.17	6th
Sheffield Wednesday 1 Fulham 2	
07.05.17	6th
Championship Play-offs	
Fulham 1 Reading 1	
13.05.17	Semi-final 1st leg
Reading 1 Fulham 0	
16.05.17	Semi-final 2nd leg

1st
2nd
3rd
4th
5th
6th
7th
8th
9th
10th
11th
12th
13th
14th
15th
16th
17th
18th
19th
20th
21st
22nd
23rd
24th

I saw the game at Newcastle where they played exceptionally well. I've also seen a few features on Ryan Sessegnon, and he looks a real talent. From my perspective, the manager has done a great job. He's brought in a lot of players and they seem to have gelled; they're playing a good style of football and, importantly, they're now competing at the right end of the division.

The football's been great on the eye and we're still in the mix despite a couple of poor results. Our fear is that we might yet fall short because we didn't bring in another couple of players in January. We could certainly have done with having a goalscoring centre-forward – a Leroy Rosenior, perhaps – from day one…

If only…! Sometimes you can't get players when you want them, and traditionally the January window is not a good time to get a centre-forward – unless he's an out-of-contract 52-year-old! From where Fulham were at the start of the season, I'm really pleased to see them doing so well. There's some solidity in the set-up now whereas previously I'd been concerned they might drop out of the division. It's fingers crossed now for a strong finish to the season.

How did the book project come about? Was it something you'd been thinking about for a while?

I've been travelling the country as an ambassador for Show Racism the Red Card and giving talks. At one of these events someone approached me and said that, as I had so many tales to tell, that I should consider putting them in a book. idea struck a chord. My father, who died a few years ago, was a really good story-teller. He was something of an extrovert who dealt with the 1950s racism – both everyday and life-threatening – with wit and charm. So really the book is about me, my father and Liam – I wanted to give a snapshot of our experiences, going from the fifties

when my parents came over from Sierra Leone to where we are now and everything we've been through. I wanted to show people how I dealt with the abuse, bringing people together rather than alienating them. I suffered a lot of racial abuse during my playing career and I wanted to note everything down on paper. That was the notion, anyway. As I'm not a household name like Rooney or Beckham it took about four years for the book to become a reality.

Your dad comes across well…

I hope so, as he was a huge influence on me. My story begins with my father, and I hope I've done him proud. I also hope that the book comes across as something different, and as a social commentary that provokes some healthy debate. We'll see…

The racism aspect forms only part of your "commentary" anyway, but unsurprisingly that's the aspect flagged by many reviewers…

I'm glad you've said that. It's about a whole lot more than that. Neither is it about "digging out" people for being racists, it's more about how we dealt with the issue in a positive way. I'm very much hoping that the anecdotes will make people smile as well.

It's an extension of your ambassadorial role…

Yes, offering help and finding solutions rather than getting on any soapbox.

It might sound a bit creepy to say so, but your warm and relaxed manner is bound to help get the message across…

I hope so. It's a potentially difficult area, but the best thing to do is to talk about it and not be confrontational. It's a question of adopting the right tone. I've been delighted with the feedback to the book – and especially to its tone. I didn't

Leroy on… Fulham Football Club

"Fulham FC. Perhaps not the most acclaimed of our capital's football clubs but to me and so many like-minded followers, the magic that shines from the place is as blinding as any floodlight over one of Spurs' many glory, glory nights, and as perfect as the feel of Arsenal's old marble halls.

"Trophies and glory have never been regular or willing visitors to that famous Cottage in SW6, but there has been no shortage of wonderful footballing individuals who have opened their kitbags and brought both romance and memories to its famously Grade II-listed façade.

"Johnny Haynes, that dapper playmaker of the late 1950s and early '60s, his

Brylcreemed hair as perfect as his distribution. Jimmy Hill as a player, administrator, chairman and ultimately saviour who so summed up the place with his friendly enthusiasm and fervour. And it's no surprise that legends of the game came here to see out their glory days. Bobby Moore, Rodney Marsh and George Best rightly chose Fulham as the Club for which to show off their talents without the pressures of the clubs they had previously represented.

"There's something about the place. The walk through the park from Putney Bridge. The red-bricked terraced houses and the ground itself. Unwilling

to modernise, unapologetic for its friendliness. For this football-lover, it was the perfect club to stroll into as a starting point for my career. I was a Tooting boy, but so was Citizen Smith – Robert Lindsey's character in the sitcom of the same name, and he proudly wore his black and white scarf while declaring "power to the people" on our television sets at the time.

"I remember Derry Quigley picking me up in his white van and driving me to the Cottage {for my trial]. Sure, I'd played for England Schoolboys in stadiums before but this was different. This could – if things went well – become my home."

want to come across as bitter – because I'm not. I didn't want to come across as unhappy – which I'm certainly not. I really wanted people who've read it to judge it as a heart-warming, thought-provoking, non-confrontational tale. It's fantastic to get feedback that [ghost-writer] Leo Moynihan and I have hit the right mark.

On a much lighter note, we know you as Leroy but the book also reveals that your first name is actually Willie, same as your dad…
Can you imagine me walking into a football dressing room and announcing "Hello, I'm Willie!"? So I stuck with Leroy!

Footballing dressing rooms are potentially awkward places if you haven't the character to deal with the regular banter, right down to Sunday League level…
I suppose at grass-roots level you can choose to walk away if it's not for you – not that I'd necessarily advocate doing so. If you did that in the professional game you'd be losing your career. You have to have a strong character to deal with any issues and rise above it – and the same applies when you walk out onto the pitch. Football has become more and more glamorous, but it can be extremely tough. I can vouch that it was certainly tough in the 1980s!

So how many times did you swing your elbows?
A lot! I had to learn quickly. There were fewer cameras, if any, back then and a lot went on off the ball. Do you remember those defenders wearing headbands? Well they'd wear those so they could nut you in the back of the head! If those were the rules I'd give them a chance to nut my elbow instead. That was part of the game at the time – and do you know what, we relished it. It was physical, brutal even, but it wasn't sly. It was a battle; an up-front, honest, man-to-man battle. Unlike the racist stuff, this was honest combat, rather like a boxing match in which the fighters respect each other, set about their rugged business and then share a pint or two afterwards. The downside, of course, is that we picked up a whole host of injuries along the way. I'm glad today's players don't have to suffer in that way – but that's just the way it was.

Something that comes through in the book is the warmth you felt, and still feel, for Fulham FC – you had three separate spells at the Club for goodness sake!
And that all kicked off with Club Scout Derry Quigley. I'd played a representative game at the Richardson Evans ground in Roehampton Vale and a Chelsea scout had left his business card for me. It's always nice to be wanted! That was when Derry approached me. He told me how impressed

he was and that with the right coaching I could make it – he asked if I'd like to go to Fulham for a three-month trial. Here was a guy willing to stay and talk to me. No business card, but real conversation. I soon discovered that Derry had a wonderful way about him – he was Fulham to the core – and had unbelievable footballing knowledge. My life would never be the same again.

Derry certainly fell into the "unsung hero" category, didn't he…?
Without a doubt! You can't think of Derry without having a picture of him driving around in that minibus picking up and dropping off players – a tangible way of giving them a helping hand as they started their careers. I was at Derry's funeral and it was gratifying to see so many players he'd helped as youngsters paying their respects to a wonderful man. As we swapped stories afterwards it was evident how much he'd affected our lives, not just as players but after we'd hung up our boots, in fact right up to the day he died. Derry could be stubborn. When I went to see him in hospital, by which time he was suffering from dementia, he refused to let me make a cup of tea. That was his job. He was shaking, but so determined. Even though it seemed like half-an-hour in the making, that was a great cup of tea. That was Derry.

Derry was always a behind-the-scenes man, getting on with some great things, but unseen. And yet his genial manner (together with a superb track record) sums up the Fulham FC way of doing things…?
Definitely. He would influence people, make no mistake, but he'd do it quietly and without looking for any sort of limelight.

Things might not have been settled during your time at Fulham – particularly off the field with the future of Craven Cottage increasingly in doubt – but you had some great players around you…
The funny thing about football is that you don't fully appreciate such things until later in your career. There I was playing with Paul Parker, Dean Coney, Gordon Davies, Tony Gale, Ray Houghton, Ray Lewington – and those are just the first names that spring to mind – and it's the norm. You're focusing on doing your best to break into the side, and to stay there, and these top players are simply your team-mates and it's your norm. You only realise later how good they really were. That was reinforced by the time I was playing for West Ham – I'd be up against Ray Houghton at Liverpool, Paul Parker at Manchester United, but they learned their trade with me at Fulham. We had Jim Stannard and Gerry Peyton, two very good goalkeepers, as well as a host of others, such as Cliffie Carr, who were terrific players and good guys to be around.

"I soon discovered that Derry had a wonderful way about him – he was Fulham to the core – and had unbelievable footballing knowledge. My life would never be the same again."

Was your management duo of Malcolm Macdonald and Ray Harford a dream team? Two different personalities who blended well perhaps?

Yes, a perfect combo in many ways. Different, but they brought out the best in each other. Malcolm was an unbelievable motivator – he could make you feel ten-foot tall – and ultra-confident in himself, which came across positively to the players, whereas Ray was a quieter operator (you would be, compared with "Supermac"!) but also a very confident guy – which didn't always come across in public – and very innovative in training. In fact, Ray was anything but quiet. He was a joker. He also didn't mince his words in getting his message across – in that distinctive deep voice of his!

When you played alongside Ray Lewington (and were subsequently managed by him), did you think, "Hey, here's a future England No.2 in the making"?

Nice things happen to nice people! It's a bit trite to simply say "what goes around comes around" but it's a fact that the way you treat people has a great bearing on what's around the corner. Ray was fantastic. So while none of us were thinking in England terms way back then, it was no surprise to see Ray in the England dug-out. The game needs more people like Ray – he's got the character to get the best out of others. His family were always around at Fulham, so I got to know them well. So when he got the England job I was really pleased for him, his wife Ann and the family.

He's certainly done his bit at Fulham!

Clubs need a constant thread. It's a transient business but you need that common denominator. Ray has worn many hats at Fulham but has done so with a passion. Fulham have been very lucky to have Ray, to have that constant thread. Just look at how Eddie Howe is doing much the same in keeping things going at Bournemouth.

Back in December 1982, you must have been hoping for a dream goalscoring debut. Instead you broke your collarbone!

Yeah, I broke it in the first half, but played on. Amazing what a rush of adrenaline can do! It was only on the coach afterwards that the pain really set in. I was in a figure of eight bandage for six weeks after – and it was about a year before I got another chance in the first team. That was frustrating, but in that year I'd grown up physically. I managed to get on the scoresheet against Derby – getting both our goals in a 2-2 draw.

Cue the chant...

The Fulham crowd were magnificent. Not only did I get the "LEE-ROY" chant regularly but when I was playing for West Ham later in my career, I'm told that when news of my goalscoring debut came over the radio there was a big cheer from the Fulham faithful. Now that's a classy thing to do, and at great variance to the stuff that I and others had to put up with at other grounds! That relationship with the Fulham supporters was special, and was a big factor in me returning to the Club, twice!

All football fans think their club is special. We're biased at Fulham, naturally, but there does seem to be something different, something special about Fulham FC...?

It's a place where I feel comfortable. And I think it's a place where all returning players feel comfortable. It's a unique environment – in a nutshell, there's no other football club like it. The fans are passionate, but passionate in a different way to those of other clubs. Even though they've been in the Premier League recently – and, with a bit of luck, are heading back there – the Club seems grounded, and are closer to their fans than other clubs are. The fans, too are special. You have to be a special sort of person to be a Fulham supporter. I was back at the Club just the other day and I went up the steps into the Cottage for the first time since I was 17 and about to sign my three-month trial papers. (I'd been to the players' lounge in the Cottage to meet Liam after a game, and had also met Andy Cole there, but not up the main steps.) It brought back so many good memories.

I suppose you could say it's all changed but remained the same somehow...?

Exactly! When you move it can have a detrimental effect. There was a distinct, unique feel about Highbury, for example. And it's no surprise that Liverpool are staying put at Anfield. West Ham found this out. You lose that attachment, the history. Fulham is all about being by the river. There's a smell that comes off the Thames; the air, when you walk round the back of the ground, seems different; it can certainly be colder! And the walk to the ground along the river from Putney Bridge can be magical. And when you arrive at the ground and see the "Fulham" lettering on the Cottage in black and white, it almost brings a tear to your eye. It's an amazing place – here's hoping it never loses those unique qualities!

Do you still see any of your former team-mates these days?

Galey! You always hear Galey if he's in the vicinity. I see Tony quite often because of our media work. Paul Parker, too. I was really close to Paul before he went off to Singapore – we did a show on Setanta together. These days I do a show called Kick Off on a Saturday morning and Ray Houghton came on it about two weeks ago. I hadn't spoken to Ray for years before that so it was great to catch up. He still talks as fast as ever – it comes at you fast and furious. Ray was never one for full stops!

So here we are all these years later – what are your abiding memories of your times at Fulham?
I probably shouldn't admit to this, but I can't remember much about scoring my hat-trick for Fulham at Grimsby. I was asked about it the other day, but couldn't recall any specifics. I do recall those two goals on my home debut against Derby, though. I had Tony Sealy as a strike partner that day – he was shorter than me but he acted as my minder, looking after the "young lad". I was really proud to score 20+ goals one season, and got the Player-of-the-Year award, even though I left the Club again in March.

In due course another Rosenior came along to FFC, your son Liam.
I'd not been back to the Club until Liam started playing under Chris Coleman. I went with Liam when he got to sign the contract with CEO David McInally. Liam had a tough baptism, he was up against Cristiano Ronaldo and Manchester United, but he did really well. When Lawrie Sanchez came in things didn't work out on a lot of levels and it didn't finish well. Liam's involvement though means I have my own fond memories of Fulham as well as top memories of Liam doing well for the Club. It's a good place to learn your trade, a good place to play football. Liam loved his time at the Cottage – he definitely didn't want to leave. ⚽

Playing the Numbers Game

Did you know that FFC used more than 100 players from the start of 2013-14 (our relegation season from the Premier League) to the end of 2016-17? Here's the full list, with those somehow managing to last more than one season listed in italics on subsequent mentions. How many had you forgotten? And how many do you wish you'd not been reminded of? What chance consistency? What chance stability? Little wonder it's been something of a struggle...

PLAYERS 2013-14
1. Maarten Stekelenburg
2. John Arne Riise
3. John Heitinga
4. Brede Hangeland
5. William Kvist (loan from VfB Stuttgart)
6. Steve Sidwell
7. Pajtim Kasami
8. Mahamadou Diarra
9. Lewis Holtby (loan from Spurs)
10. Alexander Kačaniklić
11. David Stockdale
12. Giorgos Karagounis
13. Kieran Richardson
14. Damien Duff
15. Matthew Briggs
16. Konstantinos Mitroglou
17. Ryan Tunnicliffe
18. Hugo Rodallega
19. Larnell Cole
20. Elsad Zverotić
21. Derek Boateng
22. Ashkan Dejagah
23. Cauley Woodrow
24. Patrick Roberts
25. Sascha Riether
26. Scott Parker
27. Chris David
28. Clint Dempsey (loan from Seattle Sounders)
29. Dan Burn
30. Ange-Freddy Plumain
31. Fernando Amorebieta
32. Mesca
33. Lasse Vigen Christensen
34. Darren Bent (loan from A. Villa)
35. Muamer Tanković
36. Moussa Demhélé
37. Josh Passley
40. Dimitar Berbatov
41. Bryan Ruiz
42. Philippe Senderos
43. Aaron Hughes
44. Adel Taarabt (loan from QPR)

PLAYERS 2014-15
45. Gabor Kiraly
46. Tim Hoogland
47. Kostas Stafylidis (loan from Bayer Leverkusen)
48. Shaun Hutchinson
49. Nikolay Bodurov
    Scott Parker
50. Matt Smith
    Bryan Ruiz
    Alexander Kačaniklić
51. Seko Fofana (loan from Manchester City)
52. Danny Guthrie (loan from Reading)
    Patrick Roberts
    Kay Voser
    Cauley Woodrow
53. Michael Turner (loan from Norwich City)
    Ryan Tunnicliffe
    Hugo Rodallega
    Lasse Vigen Christensen
54. James Husband (loan from Middlesbrough)
    Moussa Dembélé
55. George Williams
56. Jazz Richards (loan from Swansea City)
57. Emerson Hyndman
58. Sean Kavanagh
    Dan Burn
59. Adil Chihi
60. Jack Grimmer
61. Ryan Williams
62. Marcus Bettinelli
63. Jesse Joronen
64. Ross McCormack
    Elsud Zverotić
65. Mark Fotheringham
    Fernando Amorebieta
66. Thomas Eisfeld
    Chris David
67. Stephen Arthurworrey
68. Cameron Burgess

PLAYERS 2015-16
   Marcus Bettinelli
   Jazz Richards
69. Luke Garbutt (loan from Everton)
    Shaun Hutchinson
70. Richard Stearman
71. Ryan Fredericks
    Scott Parker
    Matt Smith
72. Tom Cairney
    Alexander Kačaniklić
73. Joe Lewis (loan from Cardiff City)
74. Tim Ream
75. Sakari Mattila
76. Michael Madl (loan from Sturm Graz)
    Cauley Woodrow
    Ryan Tunnicliffe
77. Zakaria Labyad (loan from Sporting Clube de Portugal)
    Lasse Vigen Christensen
78. Chris Baird (loan from Derby County)
79. Jamie O'Hara
80. Andy Lonergan
    Moussa Dembélé
    Emerson Hyndman
81. Rohan Ince (loan from Brighton & Hove Albion)
    Dan Burn
    Ross McCormack
    Fernando Amorebieta
    Nikolay Bodurov
    George Williams
82. Ben Pringle
    Jack Grimmer
    Sean Kavanagh
    Larnell Cole
    Kay Voser
    James Husband (loan from Middlesbrough)

PLAYERS 2016-17
83. Scott Malone
84. Denis Odoi
    Richard Stearman
85. Kevin McDonald
    Scott Parker
    Matt Smith
    Tom Cairney
86. Floyd Ayité
    Tim Ream
    Michael Madl
    Cauley Woodrow
    Ryan Tunnicliffe
    Lasse Vigen Christensen
87. Jozabed
88. Sone Aluko
89. Tomas Kalas (loan from Chelsea)
90. David Button
91. Ryan Sessegnon
    Sean Kavanagh
92. Dennis Adeniran
93. Luca de la Torre
94. Tayo Edun
    Jesse Joronen
95. Neeskens Kebano
96. Stefan Johansen
97. Chris Martin (loan from Derby County)
98. Ragnar Sigurðsson
99. Lucas Piazon (loan from Chelsea)
100. Ryan Fredericks
101. Stephen Humphrys
102. Cyriac (loan from Oostende)
     Marcus Bettinelli
103. Thanos Petsos (loan from Werder Bremen)

Close, but no Cigar

Just as it looked as if we might well regain our Premier League status, thanks to that fantastic effort orchestrated by Slav over the latter months of the season, we came up a fraction short. It's true we weren't at our best in the Play-off matches against Reading, who "did a job" on us, but neither did we get the rub of the green. The upshot of those disappointing couple of games was that we didn't even get that longed-for day out at Wembley. So it's back to the grind of the Championship instead. And, hopefully, to get it right this time around!

Despite our lamentable record in previous Play-offs, I was convinced we'd make it in May. That wasn't down to typical optimism or the relative hype stirred up by the media who'd not only suddenly noticed our presence in the top six but were championing us (all of a sudden) because we were playing the best football in the division. We'd looked good for quite a while, of course, and were a decent shot because we had the momentum, had a strong squad spirit and were making plenty of openings. We were playing well and with belief. We were realistic contenders. Slav and co had restored our belief in the set-up too – for which he deserves a medal – and it was fun to support FFC for the first time in a while.

Unfortunately – and there's no delight or smugness in saying this – the editorial of Issue 144 got it about right. *"With the immense improvement shown this season under Slaviša Jokanović's stewardship and the (at times) super-slick football played by the team, it would be heartbreaking if we fell just short ... For all the improvement, though, our squad doesn't have sufficient strength in depth. Neither is the spine of the team sufficiently settled nor resilient. Surely the centre-back and centre-forward positions, in particular, were crying out for back-up in the January window. None came."*

We were a smidgen short at the death. There's no denying that the last two-thirds of the season were exciting and highly profitable points-wise. However, the season started in August, not November. The points squandered in the opening months cost us automatic promotion. The poor activity in the transfer windows cost us dear. Jokanović almost pulled off a miracle; he got us damned close and oversaw an attractive brand of football *despite* the FFC hierarchy, not because of it.

In fact, you could sum up Fulham's season in one microcosmic moment. It came in the closing seconds of the Play-off second leg at Reading. On-loan centre-forward Chris Martin had a chance to go from zero to hero as that cross came in – it was a more-than-reasonable chance for a

more-than-reasonable player – but he nodded the ball wide. It HAD to be on target. It was what he was there to do, head the ball at goal. But he couldn't deliver. A goal then would have levelled the scores and given us fresh momentum. That missed opportunity served to demonstrate all-too-clearly how poorly we'd done in replacing goal machines McCormack and Dembélé, despite the fact that their departures had been flagged for months. Martin was signed as a loanee in the closing minutes of the autumn transfer window, then had the temerity to go on strike when his parent club indicated they wanted him back. No wonder Jokanović bemoaned the lack of transfer activity. He was badly let down. And we were badly let down.

The quality of the football we played last season brought understandable comparisons with the Jean Tigana squad of 2000-01. The huge difference though was that Tigana's squad was all set to go from the off. We kicked off that season with 11 straight victories, achieved with a stunning playing style that was as entertaining as it was effective. Compare that with our set of results between the two International breaks last autumn when we faced a clutch of poor sides and failed to beat any of them. While we were struggling to find the right formula, Newcastle and Brighton were making a habit of winning football matches. Consequently we had to play catch-up, doing so convincingly but ultimately unsuccessfully. It grates a little that Huddersfield, who we battered 5-0 and 4-1, took the third promotion slot via the Play-offs. Still, better them than Reading!

Those two Play-off encounters weren't easy on the eye, were they? And it took a controversial penalty award to separate the sides. Mind you, it was only contentious because of what the match officials didn't see – Kermogant handling the ball in the first place as he pressed Kalas who then nudged it with his left arm. Kermogant's sly interference was on the blind side of referee Martin Atkinson; from his perspective, once he'd deemed that Kalas had handled the ball deliberately, he had to give it. It wasn't utterly clear-cut, but had the roles been reversed we'd all have been clamouring for a spot-kick, right? So, was it a penalty? Most definitely, as the referee gave it! But was it the correct decision? Given Atkinson's sightline, most probably.

But by the same yardstick, the referee of the first leg – Stuart Attwell – got it hopelessly wrong at Craven Cottage. Did Williams handle the ball in the lead up to Reading's goal? "Most probably"! And yet he allowed the goal to stand. Even more frustratingly, though, he failed to clamp down on Reading's timewasting tactics, which were blatant from the off ("They were bloody at it from the moment they got off the team bus" said a guy near me). Were they breaking the rules? Most definitely!

With all the visitors' niggly fouls and brazen game-slowing tactics the ball seemed to be barely in play. Yet the officials turned a blind eye until Swift was booked for getting out his string vest and deckchair when he should have been taking a 40th-minute corner. We'd had about 25 minutes of actual football by that point; astonishing!

Let's not lose sight of the fact that we ultimately failed to get to Wembley because we didn't take our chances, and there were several good ones (and Al-Habsi denied us on several occasions in the second leg). Also we looked increasingly "leggy" in that second match. And how ironic, having squandered so many spot-kicks last season, that it took a penalty kick to split the teams.

Even so, what's the point of being good guys if the bad guys aren't punished? Reading only got away with blatant cheating because they were allowed to do so. ⚽

Stats Not the Way to do it

One has to assume that, despite being an 11th-hour loan signing, Chris Martin had ticked all the relevant boxes and satisfied FFC's stringent stats-led recruitment policy before signing on the dotted line. If so, then his case showcases flaws in the system so admired by our US owners.

Overall, his performances were decent. Even though he was more mobile than Matt Smith (although not as good in the air), Martin didn't fully fit into the system employed last season. He made no end of runs off the ball as we counter-attacked, only to be frequently ignored – and he often let his exasperation show. To his credit, though, he continued to "show" and his input – including those aforementioned sprints that were sometimes used as effective dummy runs – was above average. Chris Martin is a good player, but in Slav's system he wasn't a fabulous fit.

I know next to nothing about the specifics of FFC's stats-gathering and how they're used. The likelihood, though, is that Martin probably delivered on what was expected (penalty-taking excepted!). But no end of stats research can reveal the inner workings of a player's character. Martin went on strike when Steve McClaren made noises about recalling him to Derby, despite being contracted to Fulham for a season. It follows, then, that stats cannot possibly tell the whole story.

I imagine any stats rolled out for one Dimitar Berbatov would be mighty impressive. We were privileged to see several examples of Berba's extraordinary ball control, his quickness of thought and eye for goal. He no doubt developed his famous languid arrogance because, technically at least, he is a footballing natural and it all came so easily to him. When things were going his

way, that is. The Bulgarian is another who downed tools, refusing to play for Spurs as he angled for a move to Old Trafford. And, once things weren't to his liking at FFC he may as well have gone on strike again, such was his negative input. Worse than that, though, his bad influence seemed to pervade through the squad. His footballing ability – and his presumably sky-high stats – was never in question, but his attitude most certainly was.

For us long-in-the-tooth supporters none of the above is much of a bombshell. In fact, it could be filed under "flippin' 'eck, he's stating the bleedin' obvious once again!" And yet it doesn't seem to fit with the stats approach currently in vogue at FFC. On the face of it, it seems crazy that an experienced head coach can effectively be barred from bringing in a player he considers would bolster the squad (Manchester United's midfielder Andres Pereira was the case in point, having been offered to us on loan by Jose Mourinho) because the stats don't add up. And even when they do, as with the cases mentioned above, a player's character can potentially make a mockery of all the ticked boxes.

This "outburst" is borne from the frustration of having to suffer our club being allowed to fall apart in bizarre fashion over the past few campaigns. Slaviša Jokanović put his mark on the Club last season and came desperately close to overseeing a promotion campaign despite such a stuttering start. For much of this close season it has looked to be more of the same – other clubs making moves in the transfer market while we drag our heels.

This is the time of year when supporters of ALL clubs up and down the country are hopeful that this might be THEIR season. That's the way football works. Having got so close last season, surely the Club would want to make the most of that upswing in fortunes and build on it. The fact that Tom Cairney, Ryan Sessegnon and others are keen to stay demonstrates the faith they have in the Head Coach, and ensuring we hang on to our jewels is undoubtedly great business by the Club. Frustratingly, though, we've been slow off the mark once again this season in plugging the gaps. Pre-season training isn't simply about getting fit, it's about making full preparations for the campaign ahead, a key part of which is integrating new players into the squad.

This isn't an all-out attack on the stats-led approach, believe it or not. No, the use of statistics in sport is more important than ever – with so much information available nowadays it would be plain daft not to use it and all the cutting-edge technology that comes along with it. Thing is, while you can be 100 per cent in favour of the use of stats, they surely cannot tell 100 per cent of the story; neither can they be deemed 100 per cent foolproof. ⚽

Fulham 1 Norwich City 1		1st
05.08.17	10th	2nd
		3rd
Reading 1 Fulham 1		4th
12.08.17	14th	5th
		6th
Leeds United 0 Fulham 0		7th
15.08.17	16th	8th
		9th
Fulham 0 Sheffield Wednesday 1		10th
19.08.17	19th	11th
		12th
Ipswich Town 0 Fulham 2		13th
26.08.17	14th	14th
		15th
Fulham 1 Cardiff City 1		16th
09.09.17	13th	17th
		18th
Fulham 2 Hull City 1		19th
13.09.17	13th	20th
		21st
Burton Albion 2 Fulham 1		22nd
20.09.17	14th	23rd
		24th
Fulham 1 Middlesbrough 1		
23.09.17	14th	
Nottm Forest 1 Fulham 3		
26.09.17	11th	
QPR 1 Fulham 2		
29.09.17	8th	
Fulham 2 Preston NE 2		
14.10.17	9th	
Aston Villa 2 Fulham 1		
21.10.17	11th	
Fulham 1 Bolton Wanderers 1		
28.10.17	13th	
Fulham 0 Bristol City 2		
31.10.17	15th	
Wolverhampton Wanderers 2 Fulham 0		
03.11.17	16th	
Fulham 1 Derby County 1		
18.11.17	17th	
Sheffield United 4 Fulham 5		
21.11.17	14th	
Fulham 1 Millwall 1		
25.11.17	12th	
Brentford 3 Fulham 1		
02.12.17	15th	
Fulham 1 Birmingham City 0		
09.12.17	12th	
Sunderland 1 Fulham 0		
16.12.17	12th	
Fulham 2 Barnsley 1		
23.12.17	11th	
Cardiff City 2 Fulham 2		
26.12.17	11th	
Hull City 2 Fulham 2		
30.12.17	12th	
Fulham 4 Ipswich Town 1		
02.12.18	10th	
League Cup		
Wycombe Wanderers 0 Fulham 2		
08.08.17	Round 1	
Fulham 0 Bristol Rovers 1		
22.08.17	Round 2	

Play-off Charge in Limbo

I don't suppose Hannibal Smith was ever a Fulham supporter. Had he been, the oft-disguised leader of the A-Team (played on TV by George Peppard) would be as peed off as the rest of us. His famous catchphrase – "I love it when a plan comes together" – can hardly be applied to Fulham this season. In fact, there's barely any semblance of a plan at all from the owner and senior management – which is utterly astonishing given last season's exciting charge for the Play-offs that had us dreaming of regaining our top-flight status. What on Earth is going on at the Club? Who is responsible for our indifferent, unbalanced squad and scratchy performances thus far?

Only those in the know would have any chance of answering the first of those questions. However, everyone it seems has an opinion (or three!) as far as the second one is concerned. One thing's for sure, most of us are extremely perplexed.

What's indisputable is that the head of steam built up so magnificently last season has been allowed to dissipate into the ether – and it's us, the supporters, who've suffered, naïvely supposing that the Club would make a concerted effort to push on from that excellent vantage point. But far from building on our exhilarating form of last season we've been allowed to drift. Far from enhancing that squad with key players in key positions, we have been left with an unbalanced group (one that's been hit by a succession of injuries). Far from "doing whatever it takes" to ensure we have a fighting chance of winning promotion, the silence from our owner Shahid Khan and his son has been deafening. Tony Khan, so voluble and so keen to take so much of the credit when we were doing well last spring, has scuttled back to the US and is nowhere to be seen (or heard) now that we're in the mire, comparatively at least.

Fulham FC hit the headlines for all the wrong reasons when data specialist (sic) Craig Kline was dismissed a few weeks ago. Kline, at loggerheads with Slaviša Jokanović for ages, didn't go quietly, making a series of serious allegations on Twitter and calling the police who, according to reports, interviewed him on a "picnic bench" at Motspur Park. Kline's job title by then was Assistant Director of Football Operations, having been promoted from his role as Director of Statistical Research in February – at which point Brian Talbot became the other Assistant Director of Football Operations, reporting to FFC Vice-Chairman and Director of Football Operations Tony Khan. FFC's Chief Operating Officer is of course Alistair Mackintosh, who joined from Manchester City in 2008.

All of the above (bar Hannibal Smith!) have been roundly denounced by Fulham fans, particularly in recent weeks. And that includes our Head Coach. We've had our share of crises over the years at this Club, and no one's suggesting this mess falls under that banner. Neither are we in "omnishambles" territory; then again, perhaps we're not far off. Who's running the show? Maybe no one is. That's the impression given, anyway. We're "merely" supporters, with varying degrees of footballing nous. But we all care. At the moment it doesn't appear that the FFC powers-that-be, some of whom are on hefty salaries to get things right, care a jot. The evidence is there for all of us to see: out on the pitch.

Last season Scott Malone and Sone Aluko were key players, making a host of positive contributions (whatever their other failings!); neither has been adequately replaced. Malone chipped in with regular sorties down the left flank and a clutch of goals (while allowing teenage sensation Ryan Sessegnon to play further forward); Aluko's pace and trickery carved open opposition defences on a regular basis. Neither are world-beaters, but both were excellent fits in Slav's chosen system of play, and both are sorely missed. Also as things stand, we have no obvious goal-scorer, whether an out-and-out old-fashioned centre-forward, nippy striker or false number nine. Neither are we scoring anything like as freely as last season. Oh, and our defence is all-too-easily breached. Hardly a recipe for success, is it? Us simple supporters can identify these deficiencies all too clearly and yet we're not the ones paid thousands of pounds for our supposed expertise to solve such issues; we do, though, pay thousands to watch our heroes, having been "reassured" that everything's hunky-dory.

So who's responsible? Cue shoulder shrugs.

Our loss at Brentford was described as "spineless". A good description, especially after that poor second half against mediocre, but better organised, rivals. But that's a literal definition of our team: no spine – surely the pre-requisite for any team hoping to do well in the rugged Championship. Credit Jokanović for introducing the slick football of last season that not only masked some of our squad's shortcomings but, thanks to those numerous wins, also raised confidence levels in the camp. And there's nothing wrong with the "slick football" approach, even in the Championship; we didn't do badly under Tigana, did we? Then again, our side that cantered to 101 points in 2000-01 with an even better and more consistent brand of exhilarating football was underpinned by a spine of Maik Taylor, Chris Coleman (Kit Symons), Andy Melville, Lee Clark, Sean Davis, Barry Hayles and Louis Saha.

"At Brentford, Denis Odoi was a sending-off waiting to happen. Gentleman Jim said so (so it must be true!). Jokanović acknowledged afterwards that he was contemplating replacing Odoi before the second booking (with the Belgian having already had a 'final' warning from the ref)."

At Brentford, Denis Odoi was a sending-off waiting to happen. Gentleman Jim said so (so it must be true!). Jokanović acknowledged afterwards that he was contemplating replacing Odoi before the second booking (with the Belgian having already had a "final" warning from the ref): "In one moment, we are thinking about avoiding this kind of situation and making some movement from the bench," he said. "But I cannot change all the players with one yellow card." Maybe so, but it's one of a number of head-scratching decisions of late.

Veteran journo Brian Glanville, a regular at the Cottage, wasn't convinced with our set-up at Griffin Park. He wrote that Joka had opted for a "dubious line-up" and that he was "technically awry". Glanville pointed out that Fonte was "ineffectual" and left-back Sessegnon, when going forward, "left space behind [for Brentford] to attack".

On top of that, the ordinary fan has no idea precisely why some squad members never get a sniff of first-team action – presumably a snub at those signed by Kline. Is such stubbornness a strength, or is such bullishness affecting our chances?

This isn't an out-and-out attack on Jokanović, far from it, merely an attempt to show that he's not blameless either. As for "his" squad, he may well have decided that several of the Club's purchases (instigated by whom?) aren't good enough, in which case isn't it about time he was given the tools to do the job? Our player recruitment under the Khans has been, er, interesting with the revolving-door policy doing nothing for stability. The number of player ins and outs has been staggering – a policy that's been proven to be as unproductive as it's been nonsensical, and that's before any mention of stats, tick-boxes and age restrictions. Meanwhile, the much-vaunted re-signing of Club "jewels" Ryan Sessegnon and Tom Cairney last summer was reckoned a couple of masterstrokes and led us to surmise that all was well in Joka's camp, which, given Cairney's recent upbeat comments about being happy at the Club, may indeed be true. Thing is, if we carry on as we are, not only will they be prised away but Joka will be off as well, without getting the chance to prove if he's capable of doing the job or not. At which point it'll be a further merry-go-round, more destabilisation and yet more time lost. Cue further frustration from us lot, and, presumably, yet more shoulder shrugs from Khan and co.

What exactly is Alistair Mackintosh's role in all of this? A decent fella by all accounts (until recently I've been barred from meeting him) but given our less-than-stellar record on the pitch under his stewardship, he surely falls into the "could do better" category. And what of Brian Talbot, another who didn't care for Kline? Taking a step back, that shouldn't necessarily matter. Sometimes a clash of characters can produce better results than having a couple of "yes men" – differing views can lead to a healthy debate particularly if there's someone

with a casting vote; in this case, Tony Khan. (Then again, you're not likely to get a healthy debate if the respective parties detest each other and one is a close long-time friend of the arbiter!) But once again, the evidence is there for us all to see – we're not exactly moving onwards and upwards, are we?

Some of the reporting surrounding Kline's departure was whimsical, not least the "picnic bench" reference. (Wonder how many picnics it's hosted?) The suggestion that the disgraced stats man had planned to hijack a press conference in a Sumo wrestler's suit and challenge Jokanović to a mock fight (supposedly to show that they got on famously despite a difference of views) was as incredulous as it was hilarious. And perfect fodder for a fanzine cover! Then again, we don't like being perceived as a joke, Mr Khan.

To discover that our squad could have been augmented by Aaron Mooy, Glenn Murray and Tammy Abraham but for Kline's intervention beggars belief. Instead, in came a clutch of so-so players who've failed to set our first team alight either because our Head Coach doesn't rate them or because he's stubbornly refusing to select (presumably) Kline's choices. Or maybe it's a combination of the two. Either way, the pool of players available for first-team action according to Jokanović is markedly different to what's on the Club's books. What a strange, sorry state of affairs.

Former captain Danny Murphy waded into the argument recently, suggesting that the owners have been repeatedly let down by "a couple of people at the Club". He said: "They have now got themselves into a real pickle because parachute payments are dwindling, they are struggling to make an impact because a couple of their best players have gone."

Murphy is also upset at FFC's decline: "The Club has gone from being [in] a really healthy place to a really difficult place. I feel for the owners as they bought the Club in good faith as a Premier League club. It was in good condition.

"A couple of the people at the Club at the time decided they walked on water, went against all the advice they were getting and messed it up. It's a shame because it was a fantastic club to be around."

I've a lot of time for Murphy, a superb FFC player and captain, and these days an articulate pundit. Quite how much he knows about the inner workings of the Club these days is another matter, but he's entitled to his views. In any case, he might still be a bit miffed that FFC (and, who knows, those same "couple of people") didn't retain him as his playing days at the Cottage petered out. He's also stretching things to suggest that – presumably – Malone and Aluko were two of our "best players".

Match	Score	Date	Position
Middlesbrough 0 Fulham 1		13.01.18	8th
Fulham 6 Burton Albion 0		20.01.18	7th
Barnsley 1 Fulham 3		27.01.18	6th
Fulham 2 Nottingham Forest 0		03.02.18	5th
Bolton Wanderers 1 Fulham 1		10.02.18	5th
Fulham 2 Aston Villa 0		17.02.18	5th
Bristol City 1 Fulham 1		21.02.18	5th
Fulham 2 Wolverhampton Wanderers 0		24.02.18	5th
Derby County 1 Fulham 2		03.03.18	4th
Fulham 3 Sheffield United 0		06.03.18	4th
Preston North End 1 Fulham 2		10.03.18	4th
Fulham 2 Queens Park Rangers 2		17.03.18	3rd
Norwich City 0 Fulham 2		30.03.18	3rd
Fulham 2 Leeds United 0		03.04.18	3rd
Sheffield Wednesday 0 Fulham 1		07.04.18	3rd
Fulham 1 Reading 0		10.04.18	2nd
Fulham 1 Brentford 1		14.04.18	3rd
Millwall 0 Fulham 3		20.04.18	2nd
Fulham 2 Sunderland 1		27.04.18	2nd
Birmingham City 3 Fulham 1		06.05.18	3rd

Championship Play-offs
Derby County 1 Fulham 0
11.05.18   Semi-final 1st leg
Fulham 2 Derby County 0
14.05.18   Semi-final 2nd leg
Fulham 1 Aston Villa 0
26.05.18   Final; Wembley

FA Cup
Fulham 0 Southampton 1
06.01.18   Round 3

1st
2nd
3rd
4th
5th
6th
7th
8th
9th
10th
11th
12th
13th
14th
15th
16th
17th
18th
19th
20th
21th
22th
23th
24th

Effective, definitely, but hardly irreplaceable once it was known that they were keen to move on. For our "best players" look no further than our Captain and talisman Tom Cairney and, as a fantastic prospect who's excelling while learning the ropes, Ryan Sessegnon. Keeping them at the Club, while the media were intent on selling them on, was great business. With little else to go on bar perception and body language, the fact that they're still at FFC suggests that all remains good behind the scenes. As hinted above, Cairney has reassured us that he remains very happy at the Club.

"You can't put a price on happiness," Cairney told *Standard Sport*. "Last season I was extremely happy on and off the pitch and that's when you play your best football. I wanted to show my happiness to the fans, let them know that I want to be here and try to take Fulham forward. I love playing football here. That's what I want to do. I feel a responsibility to Fulham. It's been great ever since I arrived. I enjoy playing football, I really enjoy playing it at the Cottage and long may it continue."

As I write, another transfer window approaches. Hopefully, there's much more scope to get things right this time now that Kline has departed. Not for the first time, Jokanović has conveyed his concerns via the media. Is it me, or does he seem to be more positive this time around? For all the negativity in this little rant, we're only a smattering of key purchases away from being capable of launching another Play-off charge. For "key" read "astute" rather than "expensive". Surely our scouting network can come up with something special and prove this particular cynic wrong.

Then again, with all the money swimming about in the top flight, even an expensive signing would cost effective *if* promotion was somehow achieved. Jokanović said: "I have the targets and it's clear what we need. The Club has agreed what positions we need to improve in the future and now it's a question of how we are going to [achieve it].

"I prefer [to do our business] at the beginning of January, not at the end of this month. The intention is to try to find an element that we are missing in these few months and try to be stronger, more solid and more competitive."

Should we make the signings hinted at above there's still no guarantee of a dramatic upswing; football doesn't work like that. But there's a chance. And if Jokanović retains the trust of the players then there's every chance with a squad bolstered in the right places. With the present set-up we're simply languishing; going through the

motions even. It's all so unacceptably humdrum following the yardstick set last season. We dream of success rather than demand it. In terms of results, we hope for the best rather than expect it as some sort of right. What we do expect from a professional organisation, though, is a concerted effort from the management and a group of first-team players prepared to play for the shirt and for their manager/head coach. You can't fault the players for their efforts, by and large, this season but confidence levels have dipped whereas this time last season they were all set to rocket. The end product of having a disjointed squad is, surprise, surprise, a series of disjointed performances and results (and it doesn't help that our engine room's been hit by injuries, either).

This column is being put together in the wake of another disappointing defeat, this time at Sunderland. At least most of us were prepared for that one – we knew only too well that Sunderland hadn't won at home since the beginning of time and had just installed Chris Coleman and Kit Symons as their new management team. Long-in-the-tooth Fulham fans had that one down as a home banker well before kick-off! ❖

Willo Talk

With the current Fulham set-up going up through the gears and setting their sights on promotion to the Premier League, who better to ask about how they're doing than Robert Wilson. Not only was Willo a midfield linchpin in the Fulham side that so nearly went up to the top flight in 1982-83, but he's also been a regular at our games up and down the country over the past few seasons. The Ed enjoyed a cozy chat with Robert on the eve of our away game at Derby County – our opponents for that infamous contest at the Baseball Ground in 1983. Willo was kicked in the leg by a Derby fan that afternoon as, incredibly, hundreds of home fans were allowed entry to the pitch surrounds and even onto the pitch while the game was in progress. With Willo eager to cheer the current side to promotion, he admitted this was to be his first return to Derby since that highly charged encounter of '83.

So, you're London-born, and Fulham were your local team, but here you are with a Yorkshire accent. What's that all about?
You're right, I was born in 1961, and moved north in 1989 when I left Fulham for the second time to sign for Huddersfield; I've been up here ever since. And yes, I've picked up the accent a bit – "Galey" always gives me a lot of stick about it!

You joined FFC as an apprentice – as a right-back?
I signed as an apprentice in July 1977, as a defender. In my second season as an apprentice I was switched to a holding midfielder and things

Above: Robert Wilson models the 1984-85 Fulham kit, complete with the Club's very first shirt sponsor – Scottish brewers William Younger.

Below: Unsavoury antics at Derby's Baseball Ground in May 1983 as "Willo" gets a boot from a home fan. Incredibly the end-of-season encounter – vital for both sides – was allowed to continue despite the encroachment of home fans.

went from there. Bobby Campbell was Fulham manager and he watched me play a few times. I signed professional terms in June 1979 and Bobby selected me for the first team when we were drawn against Blackburn in the FA Cup in January 1980. I was asked to mark their Player-Manager Howard Kendall, a very experienced pro and, at the time, still an influential midfielder.

Do you still recall that first game?
Yeah, I remember the build-up and the nerves. I was being asked to stifle their playmaker – a big challenge. But we didn't do badly, drawing the game and so it was a replay at the Cottage the following week. Howard was a terrific player and he went on to have an excellent second career in management.

Malcolm Macdonald soon took the reins at Fulham and the Club enjoyed something of an upswing in fortunes…
That's right. Bobby had given me a couple of League outings but by the time the 1980-81 season kicked off, Malcolm was in charge. It was the start of a two-and-a-half year adventure under Malcolm, one that was enjoyed by the Club, the players and the supporters. He forged a young side (with a few old heads like Strongy and Peter O'Sullivan!) that did really well. Malcolm was what he was – the figurehead. He had two fantastic coaches alongside him in Terry Mancini and Ray Harford; and later on George Armstrong. Malcolm was great at taking the limelight and dealing with the press but generally we didn't see him from Monday to Thursday – he'd turn up on a Friday for the five-a-sides! – but we understood that and it worked fine. The overall set-up was great.

By then you'd become a fixture in the side. With things going well so early in your career, you must've thought, "hey, this is okay…"?
A number of young players were coming through at the same time, which helped. Then there were those such as Galey and Roger Brown, not much older than us but with a fair few games already under their belts, who were great guys to have around. Ray Lewington was another top guy and Malcolm brought in Sean O'Driscoll from Alvechurch, so things began to take shape. Ray Harford got us playing some fantastic football, even on the muddy pitches we had to put up with in the '80s. (Even our own pitch was bad as they played Rugby League there most weeks!) If that side in their prime could play on today's fantastic pitches, I reckon it would be like watching our current first team when they're playing in full flow, I really do. I'm really enjoying watching us at the moment, just as the older supporters enjoyed watching our side play the one- and two-touch football we were renowned for; I know because so many have told me so!

As Malcolm and his coaches got things going, confidence levels grew and you improved…?
I was basically playing in the No.10 role and the goals started to flow, so what's not to like about that? In the season that culminated in that brilliant game with Lincoln, I had a licence to break forward so was able to join in with Ivor and Dixie who were forging a terrific partnership. I'd be the "third man" safe in the knowledge that Lewy would be "sitting in" behind the ball. With Ray Houghton and Noisy supplying the ammo, it was a joy to be in the thick of the action. We created so many chances – so much so that I was top scorer one season [1984-85 with 11 goals]. If I look at a YouTube clip now that shows me scoring, it's all too evident how much I enjoyed putting the ball into the back of the net!

Enthusiastic…? Over-exuberant…?
Oh yes. But then it was the same when any of our side scored. I celebrated them all.

And why not, that's the whole objective, isn't it?
Of course it is! With one or two players today it's become a bit muted, all rather "expected". And it's why I love the way Ryan Sessegnon celebrates, tapping the badge (although we didn't do that in our day as it wasn't relevant) and savouring the moment with the fans. There's a real passion there, and it reminds me so much of what it was like to enjoy the moment. Ryan's got so much going for him. He's so much better already than I ever was, but it's fantastic to see a youngster go through the same system that I did and it's nice to see a home-grown player not only establish himself but enjoy doing so. He'll be a £50–70m player within five years.

…And so level-headed too…?
Ryan comes from a great family background and it's a joy to see him develop. Despite all the media speculation, it's great to see him keeping his feet on the ground and continuing to do the business for Fulham. Only last night he picked up two awards – Young Player of the Year and EFL Player of the Year at the London Football Awards – which is fantastic for him, his family and the Club.

Back in 1982-83 you very nearly managed successive promotions; we probably only fell short because of a lack of cover…?
It's no secret we had something of a skeleton squad with other youngsters coming in as and when, such as Cliffie Carr and John Reeves. Even so, we were flying high. People will pinpoint that Leicester game at the Cottage, which we lost 1-0 – a guy called Wilson scored for them, believe it or not, Ian Wilson's shot deflected in off Galey's arse – and that contentious offside call that struck off Ivor's "goal". Even a point would've been invaluable. We'd been 12 points clear at one stage, but fell away. I have nightmares about the games against Sheffield

"Ryan's got so much going for him. He's so much better already than I ever was, but it's fantastic to see a youngster go through the same system that I did and it's nice to see a home-grown player not only establish himself but enjoy doing so. He'll be a £50–70m player within five years."

Wednesday (lost 2-1) and QPR (lost 3-1) in the final run-in; two massive defeats. We beat Carlisle 2-0 [Wilson 2!], then came Derby away.

Memorable for all the wrong reasons…
I can recall that one all too vividly. I remember travelling up on the coach, the build-up to the game, let alone the bizarre events in the match itself. Do you know it hurts me to watch the YouTube footage (which I was sent this week with our match with Derby coming up tomorrow).

How surreal was it, with so much resting on the game, to be out there with so many home fans surrounding much of the pitch? Many were on actually on it during that second half!
It was horrific. Derby fans didn't have the greatest of reputations and here they were swamping the touchline. We were a goal down, not playing great, but trying to work our way back into the game. Now we had an extra, nasty element to contend with. At half-time Malcolm had told us to remain patient – it was 0-0 at the break – and that the chances would come. Even in that first 45 minutes there was an intimidating atmosphere. They scored through Bobby Davison with 15 minutes to go which meant we were chasing the game. By that time someone had opened the perimeter gates and the home fans were surrounding large chunks of the pitch.

I attended all the subsequent hearings and heard that it was the done thing at Derby to open the gates at the end of the last home game of the season to allow supporters to celebrate the campaign with their "heroes". But they did so too early; there must've been at least 20 minutes still to play. It was a fiasco, and the encroachment only made the intimidation that much worse.

We didn't play particularly well on the day, but so much rested on that game – at both ends of the table. How did you manage to stay reasonably calm with so much going on?
I think we did fairly well given the provocation. It was almost impossible to concentrate on playing football – which is all we should have been concerned with. Instead, it was hard not to be distracted by hordes, many of whom were actually on the pitch. How do you keep your composure in such circumstances? On the one hand we knew that if we could nick a goal then we'd be right back in it. Then again, we realised that the odds were stacking up against us through no fault of our own. As the minutes ticked away, I was attacked in the corner of the pitch by a Derby fan. I had the ball at my feet and was trying to fend off a Derby player when a guy in the crowd swung a kick at my knee. If you watch the footage you'll see that I wasn't best pleased and thought of going into the crowd; but I checked myself, and Lewy was quickly on the scene to make sure I didn't do anything silly. Even that wasn't the end of it. When Gerry [Peyton] took a goal kick and the ref blew for an infringement, the crowd thought it was the final whistle and streamed onto the pitch. Our next problem was to leg it back to the dressing room in one piece; not all of us got back unscathed. It was an absolute nightmare.

By this point Malcolm was going mental and we were all badly shaken – Jeff Hopkins was in a terrible state; his shirt was ripped and he'd been punched a few times. Once the dust had settled, we fully expected some sort of action to be taken. Our case was strong: we expected a replay. In saying that, we knew full well that another game would give us the advantage of knowing precisely what we had to do. It would affect Derby (who went on to win their outstanding game to stay up) and Leicester who'd clinched that third spot at our expense. But we were innocent. While there was no easy solution, we were very hard done by – nobody

Below: Going up? Willo thinks so! Fulham's latest victory – this one a less-than-convincing 2-1 comeback win against Sunderland – gets a write-up in the *Daily Mail*.

The joy boys: Mitrovic (left) with Ryan Sessegnon and Rui Fonte (right) REUTERS

Mitrovic puts Fulham back in promotion slot

FULHAM owner Shahid Khan may be buying Wembley but he wants his club to avoid having to visit the stadium in their pursuit of the Premier League.

Fulham came from behind to beat Chris Coleman's Sunderland last night and pile the pressure on Cardiff, their competitors for the final automatic promotion place.

It was Aleksandar Mitrovic, the striker on loan from Newcastle, who completed the turnaround as Fulham try to steer clear of the play-offs.

Mitrovic has now scored 12 goals in 13 games and he left Fulham's supporters singing: 'Cardiff City, we're coming for you.' Neil Warnock's Cardiff side now trail by two points and travel to Hull today.

Fulham appeared nervous under the Friday night

CHAMPIONSHIP

FULHAM	2
SUNDERLAND	1

KIERAN GILL
at Craven Cottage

floodlights. Sunderland did not look too bothered about going forward but nevertheless scored in the 28th minute and an upset was on the cards.

Joel Asoro, on his 19th birthday, turned Matt Targett and shot from distance. The ball slid beyond Marcus Bettinell on the slick surface.

It was a goal that would have been celebrated in Cardiff as a Fulham loss would have left Warnock's team one win away from confirming

TOP OF THE TABLE

	P	W	D	L	F	A	GD	Pts
Wolves	44	30	8	6	82	36	46	98
Fulham	45	25	13	7	78	43	35	88
Cardiff	44	26	8	10	67	39	28	86
Aston Villa	44	24	10	10	71	40	31	82

automatic promotion. But the home side levelled just before the break with a move that exemplified their pleasing passing style before the ball was buried by Lucas Piazon.

Sunderland were furious. They felt Ovie Ejaria had been brought down in the box before Fulham's break-away but referee Peter Bankes showed no sympathy.

It was all Fulham in the second half and Mitrovic sealed the win with a header.

Over to you, Cardiff.

got punished as far as I'm aware. As for getting that vital third spot, those two defeats in the final run-in probably put the mockers on that. Even so…

It was probably the worst-ever case of what could go wrong at the last-chance saloon. We'd been 12 points clear as you've said. Were you aware of the Club's penny-pinching stance as we got to the "business" end of the season?
Oh yes! We all know the Andy Thomas story! He'd come on loan from Oxford and given our forwards, notably Dixie (Coney) a bit of a breather. But Ernie Clay wouldn't give Malcolm the money to buy him, even though Andy had done well. Dixie was terrific, but he was still very young and he was desperately in need of a break. Signing Andy could have been the answer, although we'll never know for sure!

On a brighter note, there was still enough quality at the Club to take Liverpool to three games in the Milk Cup in 1984-85. Good games…?
I was talking to a pal of mine about this recently. He'd found a picture from one of those games that showed me with the ball but surrounded by Hansen, Lawrenson and Souness! We played very well in all three games, even the 1-0 defeat at the Cottage. It was fantastic to pit ourselves against a team full of superstars and a stark reminder that we could well have held our own had we gone up to the top division – the type of football we played was certainly suited to the top tier. Don't forget that not long after, with the Club struggling, we lost 10-0 at Anfield in the same competition!

You were sold (to Millwall) in 1985, but came back in 1987 – was that wise?
They say it's never the same second time around, but I loved playing for Fulham – even if the Club was very different by 1987. I came back because Ray (Lewington) was manager; he's one of my best mates and was doing his best in trying circumstances. Despite everything we got to the Play-offs in my second season back. We did okay at Bristol Rovers in the first game only to get battered at home 4-0, and had Peter Scott sent off. That was my final game for the Club. I've always felt privileged and honoured to wear the shirt of my home team.

What were your stand-out moments for FFC, Rob?
I'll always remember the Lincoln game. We were under a fair bit of pressure to get over the line, but there was a fantastic atmosphere – night games at the Cottage are generally special – and the image of big Brownie powering in endures today. We got the draw we needed; then came the celebrations on the Cottage balcony in front of so many fans. A great, great night. As for favourite goals, there was the one I got at Shrewsbury where I beat four or five players (bear with me, as it goes up every time!) before putting the ball in the net. A

clipping in one of my scrapbooks likened it to the Ricky Villa goal at Wembley! To be fair, there were lots of highlights playing for that wonderful side under Malcolm – beating Newcastle away 4-1 was another special occasion, with Ray Houghton scoring the goal of the season. One of Ivor's two that day got shortlisted as well. It was another good effort; I know, as it was me who played him in!

What do you make of the way Fulham have fought back from nearly going out of business?
Yeah, a lot's happened, hasn't it? Things looked dodgy in the late '80s and early '90s. More recently, I was at Stoke when the Club was relegated from the Premier League – a dire afternoon. Then again, I was at Huddersfield when we were promoted under Jean Tigana – so I've seen lots of ups and downs over the years. And here we are challenging for promotion once again. I've watched the team a lot over the last couple of seasons. My son is a mad Fulham fan and wants to go as often as possible and I'm only too happy to be there with him.

Given that you're an ex-player, do you get "involved" as a fan?
Oh yes. You get involved with that fan intensity – you know, willing them to do well every week. I've seen some poor performances – up at Sunderland, for example; and at Middlesbrough we got out of jail. By the same token, it's a sign of a good side to play poorly, as we did at Boro, yet sneak the win. There have been many fantastic performances, like the game at Sheffield United, when you can't help but get excited.

The fulcrum of those good showings is the midfield three…
Yeah, and it reminds me a lot of our "three" – me, Ray Houghton and Ray Lew…

Which trio is better, Rob?
[Laughs…] I'd give it to Cairney, McDonald and Johansen. Cairney's a class apart. His ball control and ball retention is phenomenal; and he can brush opponents off, too. He's got so much composure. It's been a shame for him – and us! – that he's had to dip in and out this season because of his injury. But Kevin's stepped up to the plate, playing more of a captain's role when Tom's been out. I was one of many who were slagging Stefan off for a while, up to about 12 to 14 games ago. For whatever reason, he's was having "second season-it is", as he did at Celtic. But that's disappeared. You watch him in the latter stages of games now and he's still running to close people down. I'm sure Slav must have given him a bollocking, because his whole body language has changed in the last three months.

You're talking us up – so can we go up?
I think so, yes. I don't think it's out of our reach

Above: One of the above went on to appear in a longstanding advertising campaign for crisps and front *Match of the Day*. The other, Robert Wilson, continues to support The Whites from his base in Huddersfield.

"By this point Malcolm was going mental and we were all badly shaken – Jeff Hopkins was in a terrible state; his shirt was ripped and he'd been punched a few times. Once the dust had settled, we fully expected some sort of action to be taken."

Above: Robert Wilson – these days Assistant Manager at Shaw Lane AFC in the Northern Premier League.

to finish second. We're on a fantastic run in terms of points and team showings, so why not? The signing of Mitrovic set a nice benchmark and he's made a helluva difference, and looking fitter and more involved in every game. The way we play we need a striker who can play a "wall-pass" and who can hold the ball up when necessary; Mitro looks the part. But for all out attacking prowess, the key factor in our fantastic run has been the improvement at the back. We'd been prone to giving away cheap goals, but that's no longer happening and we're looking a lot more solid. Tim Ream has been truly outstanding in recent games, while we look more confident and assured with Bettinelli in goal, even though there's not a lot between him and Button as goalkeepers – again, probably a confidence thing.

Rumour has it you're back in football?
I've been out of it recently because I wanted to watch Fulham play as much as anything. My last post was coach at Brighouse Town, where my son was playing. Now I've just been made Assistant Manager at Shaw Lane AFC, based in Barnsley and who are in second place behind Altrincham in the Northern Premier League. We were due to play Altrincham tomorrow, but the snow's put paid to that, so I'll be at Derby! And I fancy us to win it!

In closing, Rob, what triggered that fearsome tackle on a poor, beleaguered fanzine editor at Fulham's less-than-salubrious training gound in Banstead all those years ago?
(Laughs…) Hey, I had a hard-man reputation to maintain! I was letting you know I was there – that's the phrase, isn't it? If you ever played five-a-sides with Vinnie Jones or Razor Ruddock, you'd know that those sort of challenges were par for the course, team-mate or not! That was just regulation five-a-side stuff! ⚽

Forward Thinking

It's often said that a week is a long time in politics. By that yardstick, the general four-to-six-week lifetime of a TOOFIF is a bloody eternity. Several readers of the last issue, when subsequently passing the fanzine sales pitch, commented that things were looking up on the pitch and that the "current" editorial (penned in late December!) was looking more outdated by the day. Each such remark was made with a knowing twinkle, thankfully! And it's certainly true that today's wall-to-wall social media outlets win the immediacy crown hands down.

Fulham's resurgence has been brilliant to watch. It's a different set-up to the one that dazzled their way up the division and into the Play-offs in the latter months of last season. The sparkle's still there, thank goodness, but this season's improvement and accompanying surge up the table is built on more robust foundations. We look

a decent outfit, and one that's full of self-belief. At last we've got a centre-forward to spearhead our attacks. True, we'd also done pretty well up to now by fielding false number nines and the like, but having the option of an out-and-out striker has improved things immeasurably. It's about having a balance to the squad – as mentioned last time out – and the manager having options.

Aleksandar Mitrovic has slotted in fantastically well, in terms of performance and application. If, as suggested by the front cover, he turns out to be the key acquisition as we strive for promotion then the wait for a genuine No.9 will have been worth it. Fact is, though, that despite tracking him for a while, we only actually rubberstamped the loan move in the very final minutes of January's transfer window. It was a damned close call!

The Serb's late, late switch to SW6 was described by Adam Hurrey, writing for *The Sportsman*, thus: "Mitrovic's stalling Premier League career was about to make a sideways move. A deal with Bordeaux was agreed. Then his former club Anderlecht stepped in, and Mitrovic flew to Brussels, only for the collapse of an outgoing transfer to scupper that deal too. The chaos theory of the transfer window worked in Fulham's favour." And how!

Another to have slotted in seamlessly is Matt Targett, whose defensive capabilities have allowed teenage goal-machine and all-round-good-egg Ryan Sessegnon to move forward and do what he does best. Cyrus Christie looks to be a useful acquisition, too, and has made a telling impact in his comparatively few outings.

So, our bolstered squad is now looking a match for any in the division. We not only have an excellent starting line-up available on any given day, but also several players who can make a real difference to proceedings when called upon from the bench. Also evident is the fantastic squad spirit, for which Slaviša Jokanović (and the players themselves!) must take huge credit. Having banked yet another win, at Preston, we're looking a real force – a confident set-up that can win matches with immense style or, as at Preston, with sheer willpower. As the old adage goes, a good team knows how to win ugly, too.

A poster on one of the FFC messageboards has been banging on for months and months about how Jokanović has been short-changed by the Khans (unwittingly or otherwise). The bottom line was that we were having to watch sub-standard fare because Jokanović was hampered by the Club's poor management structure and transfer dealings (hmm, now where have I read that before…?). The incessant posts jarred – and caused many a verbal ruction – even if the basic message was valid: we simply didn't have a balanced squad, and it showed – ah yes, the basis of the last editorial!

With Craig Kline and his infernal algorithms and stats a thing of the past, we've enjoyed our most successful transfer window in ages. Coincidence? Hardly! And with it, hey presto, we've gone on an astonishing unbeaten run. The look of the squad now compares to what we should have had at the start of the campaign, not two-thirds of the way through it. The real bonus is that we've been able to attract Mitrovic to the Cottage, albeit on loan, a player who in all likelihood wasn't available to us last Autumn even had we made the call.

I found one messageboard reply (after the 3-0 win over Sheffield United) to the aforementioned poster rather strange. "Sometimes the right formula takes a while to create… Struggle can be creative… Why do we need to go through this 'blame game' all the time? Can't we just enjoy this resurgence?" First things first, all these comments are perfectly valid too, and perfectly reasoned. Personally I think they're skewed in this instance because it's been all-too-obvious to us regulars that the whole recruitment process has been warped and that the squad has been neither strong enough nor balanced enough to put up a reasonable challenge over much of the past two campaigns. You can't simply get rid of two goalscoring machines in Dembélé and McCormack – who gave ample notice of their intentions to leave – and not provide some sort of replacement(s). Not if you've any hope of "pushing on" at any rate. And you can't simply allow two key players in last season's sparkling side to depart (Malone and Aluko) without redressing that balance. Now that we have, we're flying!

I can't stand moaning for moaning's sake. And, to be fair, some Fulham fans have made that an art form! We've had some desperate times at FFC over the past two or three decades, when it was only natural to be concerned at the Club's plight and when some of the on-field performances were that bad they defied description. Thankfully that dreadful period has been consigned to history and we've subsequently enjoyed a fabulous surge up the divisions and a decent period back in the top flight – plus that fantastic European tour. Didn't stop one or two of the moaners, mind. That's when many of the points raised by the responder above were more than valid. Taking a negative stance when so much else is going well is an odd way of looking at things – but each to their own, naturally!

I've had reason to read old copies of TOOFIF recently (NOT something I do on a regular basis!) and the tone of the editorials during the better years do reflect the enjoyment. It was a joy to be able to react to our Club's success and to chart our amazing rise and change in circumstance – as well as the manner in which it was achieved. TOOFIF stalwart Roger Scoon reminded me recently that between October 2009 (Kagisho Dikgacoi, three-match ban) and November 2012 (Chris Baird, one-match ban) we didn't have a single player suspended. That's an astonishing stat! (Okay, if you're going to be pedantic, there was one – Matt Saunders who,

in Nov 2009, received a three-match ban while on loan at Lincoln – but that's still a whole three years without a suspension!)

Personally, I didn't like much of the Premier League "experience", but if, as with any sport, you're striving to achieve, then you've got to challenge the very best, and that means doing so in the top flight, warts and all. As things stand, we're hardly likely to set the Premier League alight – at least not in the way we've managed to charge up the Championship table these past couple of seasons. Should we get there, we'll probably find an even more marked gulf between the "haves" and the "have-nots" than last time. Or, just maybe, that'll be where our billionnaire owner might come into his own! Hey, he might even get his own song if that happens!

I'm not generally one to get ahead of myself, but it's also worth considering that should we fail at the last hurdle this season then our best players – and even perhaps our Head Coach– may be off to pastures new. Given the way football operates these days, it would be naïve not to think otherwise. Promotion might well check such thoughts in the minds of the players (and their agents!) and persuade them that there's a good thing going on at FFC – so why not hang around for a while longer. Ryan Sessegnon, for example, would surely benefit from having a season as a guaranteed starter with us in the Premier League rather than being a relative bit-part player elsewhere. Yeah, yeah, we've got to get there first! Even so...!

Tom Cairney, too, would surely continue to thrive with the freedom afforded to him by our Head Coach and the system he operates. Would he get that enjoyment factor elsewhere? Probably not. For all his talent, there's certainly no guarantee that he'd slot into another side's system so comfortably and be so effective. The fact that TC's remained loyal to FFC and Jokanović (and has announced in terms that transcend the usual PR-speak that he's enjoying himself here) suggests that he'd hang around if the Club continues to move in the right direction. Then again, this is purely conjecture!

If we do go up, might it not also suggest to a certain Mr Mitrovic that he could do a job for us in the top flight? If he keeps on scoring for us so freely then he could well be the guy to get us there – and become an almost-instant Fulham legend. (Must chuck in another stat here: Mitro has scored more goals for us in his loan spell so far than the whole Newcastle side has managed in the same period; thanks, Rafa!).

Anyway, here's where I DO agree with that fella on the FFC messageboard. Now that we've got a TEAM to admire, let's enjoy the resurgence, support them loud and proud and see what happens. At this juncture we have nine regular Championship games left, so there's heaps to play for. We're on a roll and the top teams still have to play each other. Come on you Whites! ⚽

"If we do go up, might it not also suggest to a certain Mr Mitrovic that he could do a job for us in the top flight? If he keeps on scoring for us so freely then he could well be the guy to get us there – and become an almost-instant Fulham legend. "

Jean Tigana

An almost throwaway question – "Are you still in contact with Jean Tigana?" – prompted an exchange of phone calls that culminated in a mind-blowing meeting with our media-shy ex-manager at his base in the south of France. That question was posed, somewhat sheepishly, to Bill Muddyman in Stevenage Road before one of our home games in Spring 2018, with the explanation that it would be fantastic to get Jean's assessment of his time at the Club. The Frenchman's tenure at FFC had kicked off in amazing fashion in 2000, but ultimately ended on a more downbeat note three years later after his relationship with Mohamed Al Fayed had soured.

"Leave it with me," said Bill. Within a couple of weeks Bill had kindly arranged to host a Skype call; then, almost at once, he decided that a face-to-face chat in the south of France would be a much better option, and would I be up for it. Hell, does Tom Cairney favour his left foot?

It's said that you should never meet your heroes. If there's any semblance of truth in that remark, then it certainly didn't apply on this occasion. Jean Tigana, in relaxed mode thanks to Bill's presence – and his kind assurance that I could be trusted – was on great form. Meeting him at his newly refurbished vineyard HQ just outside the seaside resort of Cassis was both a privilege and a pleasure.

Astonishingly, all these years later – and especially after having been taken to court by our former owner – Tigana's affection for Fulham FC and its supporters remains almost boundless. As to those allegations (Tigana was cleared in the high court of any wrongdoing in 2004), in my humble opinion there's more chance of yours truly being selected to play for France than there is of JT behaving unscrupulously; he's a class act. Over and above all of that, though, Jean remains a key figure in Fulham's history and was responsible for overseeing a squad that gave a footballing lesson to all the other Championship sides as we stormed into the Premier League in 2001. Eleven wins on the bounce wasn't a bad way to announce the arrival of a new regime; little wonder it was tagged the "French Revolution"!

Jean Tigana was appointed in early April 1999, although he didn't take the reins until after the 1999-2000 campaign had finished. With Paul Bracewell having been sacked in March – a victim of his measured approach – we'd seen out the season under the joint stewardship of KarlHeinz Riedle and Roy Evans. As we tabled a ninth-place finish in the old First Division, Tigana was preparing to say au revoir to the south of France and was drawing up plans on how to make an impact in London SW6.

"At Fulham there was the feeling that everyone was pulling the same way and that there was a genuine family spirit to the Club. Do you know, I made so many friends in my time at Fulham; I still get cards from some of the backroom staff even today. We were made incredibly welcome and I'll always remember that."

Above right: Jean Tigana, who oversaw a magnificent record-breaking campaign in 2000-01 that took Fulham back into the top flight of English football.

Fulham FC on the banks of the Thames is a long way from your long-time base in Cassis [about 20 miles from Marseille] – what was the appeal of managing in England, and how did the move come about?

I met Bill and Tim Delaney in Marseille and we discussed the possibility of me coming to Fulham as manager. I confess I knew little about Fulham FC. I went to see two games at Craven Cottage, a picturesque, homely stadium rather than a large one. During that trip I had a meeting with Mr Al Fayed; after that I made the decision to join the Club. This was going to be a whole new experience for me, and a real challenge if I'm honest. I'd managed before, of course – at Lyon and Monaco – and at Monaco we'd won the French League title and reached the Champions League semi-final; but working in a new country and in very different circumstances was an exciting challenge.

What were your thoughts about your new club?
Some aspects were a mess. For example, on taking a look around the Club I noticed that some players were training alone; Rufus [Brevett] was one. The Club had wanted me to start right away but I'd said: "No way. Next season." There was so much to organise. And so I assembled my staff and we started to prepare for what lay ahead.

Were Christian Damiano and Roger Propos on board from the start?
Yes. Both are fantastically good [at what they do] and both men are committed in their approach and are really hard workers. It worked very well. We were hugely encouraged by the reaction of the Club – whenever I asked for something, the answer was always yes. Don't forget, we were trying to change so much, from the training methods to the on-field

approach. But there were no problems; from the Chairman down, the Club was always supportive. This was hugely encouraging for Christian, Roger and myself; it meant that we were even more determined to succeed and repay this faith.

Are things done differently in France, then?

It's much more of a battle! At Fulham we were asking for a new doctor, a new methodology or for the pitch to be prepared differently and much more. These were big considerations, but the answer was always yes. In France you might get a yes but with the caveat that it might be done tomorrow, or next year! At Fulham there was the feeling that everyone was pulling the same way and that there was a genuine family spirit to the Club. Do you know, I made so many friends in my time at Fulham; I still get cards from some of the backroom staff even today. We were made incredibly welcome and I'll always remember that.

Your methods may have been, by British standards, revolutionary, but did you and your French colleagues have any difficulties in getting to grips with the British way of life?

No, no – for me it was very easy! It was incredible really. I've subsequently worked in Turkey and in China as well as France. But in England, and at Fulham, they opened the door immediately. We were made so very welcome. It was genuinely refreshing. But we had a vital job to do – our part of the bargain was to win football matches.

The Club had finished ninth in the second tier in 1999-2000, so what was needed to spark a promotion push?

I'd seen those two games, and I'd watched the tapes, and to my mind the players weren't ready. Several were too heavy and a number had been struggling with niggly injuries. We also needed a striker. So it was clear that as part of the pre-season preparations we needed the players to undertake a comprehensive series of tests – medical checks, blood tests, radiographies – to ensure we'd be in peak condition. That also meant reminding the players about the importance of looking after their bodies, which included a change in diets and, to the displeasure of quite a few, no alcohol! I mentioned Rufus earlier; well, he was one who'd had to train alone because of injuries. In the time I was at Fulham he had three fantastic seasons.

Your training regime was very different to the norm, at least here in Britain…?

Yes the methods were different, but Arsène Wenger (who I succeeded at Monaco) was already adopting a similar approach at Arsenal. The outlook on matchdays had to change, too. Some people thought I was crazy to insist on such a footballing philosophy in the second tier in England. That division has always been renowned for its toughness – it's a long season of players kicking and fighting each other! But we changed all of that at Fulham thanks to many, many training sessions. Everyone, players and management, worked incredibly hard on changing that philosophy.

Famously, one or two baulked at some of your proposals – to begin with! – such as having to do report at the crack of dawn, then facing three training sessions a day…

[Laughs] Yes! But that didn't last long. From our perspective, though, we had a group of fantastically committed players. In France, when you start a training session things tend to start slowly. In England, when we expected a slow start for a warm-up game, the players tore into each other! It was like a furious rugby match! But we harnessed that commitment and channel all that energy. Once we'd got every one fit, that is. [More laughs!] It was great to take the squad to Clairefontaine [France's national football centre] as part of the change in their culture – it was there that we explained about the importance of an athlete's body, how an injury problem in the leg could be down to an inflammation elsewhere in the body. So we introduced regular dental checks. I was able to demonstrate what I'd learned throughout my French football upbringing.

You turned to your French connections for your two main signings – Louis Saha from Metz as your main striker and midfielder John Collins from Everton. You knew John from your time at Monaco…

Yes, both were very important signings. We also took Luis Boa Morte and Fabrice Fernandes on loan. I didn't want to spend too much money, but by the same token we had to make quality signings. I'd worked with John at Monaco and we'd won the League. His experience was invaluable, but he also knew how I operated, and was able to express that to the players at Fulham. He was my first choice on a number of levels.

You kicked off with 11 wins from 11 games; that's quite a statement of intent!

Yes, it was fantastic – but you see I was disappointed at not winning the 12th match. I wanted to win them all, however unlikely that may have been in reality.

Fulham fans couldn't believe our eyes – the new style of football was stunning…

There were good performances, yes, but it wasn't only fast, attractive football, that squad of players had real heart and desire, too. They could fight and dig deep when necessary. That great victory at Blackburn was proof of that!

Don't worry, we'll discuss that in great detail in a moment…!

[Much mischievous laughter!] Good, good!

Leading the line was the extraordinary Louis Saha: he was dynamic, athletic, brave and lightning fast.

Yes, I agree! He also had a great mentality; that was very important. Louis integrated with the existing players very well.

Actually, that squad was full of players with sound mentalities – although maybe not Fabrice Fernandes…?

[Laughs] Fabrice was crazy! A crazy man who could play good football.

You could hardly have two different physiques than those of Saha and Hayles – do you know Barry Hayles is still playing today, albeit at non-League level?

Still playing? Wow – that's incredible! Barry started to understand my methods right away. I told him, bluntly, that he was too fat! Well, too stocky, anyway! I explained that your body is your temple and if you fuel it the wrong way then you'll suffer. Who likes to drink bad wine? I know I don't. I told Barry that I'd carried on playing until I was 36. We'd won the League title and got to the Cup final and I was still pretty fit. That was no boast to Barry, I was simply demonstrating that I'd looked after my body and that if Barry did the same he'd not only be sharper but could extend his career. Still playing today? That's incredible.

Were you surprised at how good Saha was?

No, not at all. Louis was a fantastic player for us. His only problems were to do with his physique and these had to be managed very carefully at the training complex. His body was rather fragile – that wasn't his fault – and he was prone to suffering muscle strains. Once we'd developed a programme that suited him, which included a stretching regime as well as a dietary plan, everything was fine. Louis was perfectly suited to our quick counter-attacking game.

One day, after I'd stopped managing Fulham, I went to see Alex Ferguson. He asked me about Saha. I told him he was a top player with a fantastic mentality. I said that I didn't have to tell him, a great manager, about a player's qualities but I was happy to endorse Saha's character. "Why are you asking?" I enquired. Quick as a flash he said: "Because I want to buy him!" Apparently he'd asked his defenders who'd given them the most problems, and they'd all said "Saha".

He made his mark early on, scoring twice for us at Old Trafford in our first Premier League match…
Two good goals, yes, but we lost 3-2. And they had that goal by Beckham from a free-kick. That was never a free-kick; if anything Finnan was fouled. [Cue a look of derision that confirms that the ref's decision still rankles all these years later!] Steve Finnan was another very important player. When we had our first training camp at Clairfontaine, Finnan always seemed to be injured. At the time he wasn't an automatic choice for the right-back position, or so he thought. But he was as far as I was concerned. Steve was a classy player, so much so that I told Arsène Wenger: "You should take a look at him – he's your sort of player."

So many players blossomed under your stewardship: Finnan, Haynes, Sean Davis to name but three – was this mainly down to increased confidence levels?
I love to manage young players, and to help them improve. I like to iron out any problems and instil confidence. I like to help them with their positional play. Sean Davis got to know that. [Huge chuckle!] We'd be training and I'd call out sharply: "Sean!" and he'd look round and move to where I thought he should be. Within seconds it would be "Sean!" again, and he'd respond once more. That scenario continued and, to his credit, Sean was a good listener and a really good learner. [With apologies to Sean Davis, that particular tale bore a striking resemblance to another story told by Jean later, that of training a Rhodesian Ridgeback. The dog's name – I kid you not! – was Fulham, and it got plenty of the "Sean!" treatment. Jean trained Fulham to prize-winning levels in record-breaking time.]

In later years Roy Hodgson's repetitive training drills paid dividends at Fulham. Barry Hayles has said that there was a lot of repetitive work with you in charge, and that you always made it fun. That organised approach became the bedrock of our scintillating performances…
You must be organised; always! And fit! We'd get to the last 20 minutes and we'd still be looking hungry for more goals. I thing we were better prepared than the other teams, so we were in better shape to see the match out – by that time, though, we'd generally run the opposition ragged with our style of play: quick one-twos and lightning counter-attacks. It was no surprise that we'd score one or two extra goals in the latter stages.

Football isn't complicated, you know, if your organisation is sound: good control, good positioning, good pass. That's it! When all your players are on the same wavelength it can look easy – and it can be easy – as long as we have organised things properly beforehand in training. But management involves a bit of cunning, too. Rufus used to love getting stuck in; he loved a tackle. If I thought he was getting a bit carried away I would get the reserve left-back to warm up and make sure Rufus was aware of this. Rufus got the message: keep battling but don't overstep the mark, and stay focused. I loved Rufus, he had such heart. He was another great listener.

As your first season in charge progressed, losing Chris Coleman must have been a big shock?
It was a big blow for the team. For Chris, it was devastating – his injuries were dreadful. Right away I said: "We keep him!" His playing career looked well and truly over (although he made a typically brave attempt to return), but I was determined that he should stay and be considered one of the squad. He was a big character, a passionate Welshman and so full of spirit. Some people thought I was crazy [to keep him]. Okay, it was unlikely that he'd ever return to the first team but, once he'd recovered from the worst of his injuries, his presence was important. On top of that I wanted to teach him the management ropes. I recognised that he was a natural leader. One day I would have to leave Fulham, and I wanted Chris to take my place in due course. At Lyon I had Guy Stéphan all set to take over from me, and it was the same at Monaco, where Claude Puel stepped up, so I have a history of schooling my assistants to replace

me. Such continuity is important and it's one of my footballing philosophies.

Another philosophy is making the most of your young players. If they have the talent it's vital that you nurture the youngsters. Why spend millions on players when you have a crop of decent youngsters at your disposal? You need to make key signings from time to time, but my philosophy is to school the young players so that, when it's time for me to move on, I'm leaving behind something of a legacy. As they mature, those players either continue to thrive with the Club or can be sold for good money. Fulham did very well from the sales of players from my time at the Club: Sean Davis, Louis Saha, Luis Boa Morte, Steve Finnan. I love to see players improve.

Okay, let's talk about that game at Ewood Park – as we approached the business end of the season we headed north to play Blackburn. Would you say Graeme Souness prepared your team wonderfully?
Souness was a bit crazy [suggesting that Blackburn were a better team than Fulham]! So many emotions were involved that night, especially after Rufus was sent off in the first half. When Sean got that late winner I lost it – for the first and only time in my career I raced down the touchline to celebrate. Maybe I was a bit crazy too [huge giggles]! It was a fantastic performance by the team; lots of fight, lots of real character. When we got back to the hotel I even let the players have a beer. But only one [more giggles]!

You sent on Alan Nielsen for Barry Hayles after Rufus was sent off, and we got something of a lifeline when Brad Friedel gave Saha a sniff of a chance just before half-time: 1-1, game on! The ten men battled hard in that second period and then, in the closing stages… Sean Davis. What was HE doing in such an advanced position?
[Excited giggles.] That was Sean!

Lee Clark was heavily involved in that late break, showing great determination and resolve to carry the ball so far upfield…
Clark was a fine player; great intelligence and good positioning. But with that team you could go anywhere and adapt accordingly. We could brush teams aside or stand up to be counted.

At Blackburn it was the latter, and the ball fell to Sean who slotted home the winner…
A good moment, right? He enjoyed it.

I enjoyed. We all enjoyed that moment as it proved a point and all but assured promotion.

We went up as Champions having racked up 101 points. At that stage the Chairman must have been enjoying things too…?
Yes, he was happy. We were in the Premier League. I know the fans were happy because of the quality of the football we'd played. It was incredible to see (and hear!) so many supporters on the streets of Fulham when we paraded the trophy on the open-top bus. I'll always remember and treasure those scenes – the smiles and waves from so many fans. Yes, incredible! I never thought so many would be there; it was wonderful.

I worked really hard for Fulham, but the supporters gave it back to me by 200 per cent! Not just to me, but Roger and Christian too. We truly felt part of the Fulham family and were really enjoying being part of the Fulham adventure.

The Chairman may have hoped for a second successive title, but what were your hopes for Fulham in the top flight?
Tenth place was a realistic target. We'd come a long way, only now we'd be taking on the really big clubs. For all of our joy at getting promoted, we could only celebrate for a few days. We had to start planning right away for what was a much bigger test.

And they don't much bigger than Manchester United (away). We put on a great show at Old Trafford in our first Premiership game, twice taking the lead before United won 3-2. Your Gallic shrug to the media who were talking up Fulham's performance and your words "But we lost", summed up your mood…
We had played well. However, so much hinged on that free-kick from which Beckham scored. It was Finnan who'd been fouled. In my experience, key decisions tend to go the way of the big teams; I'd had the benefit of that as a player. So it was really a question of getting on with and to start preparing for the next match.

In the event, we qualified for the InterToto Cup and also got to within one game of reaching the FA Cup final…

I thought we were unlucky against Chelsea [in the FA Cup semi-final]. Had we reached the Final things could have been very different, but that's football. We had plenty of possession but couldn't make the breakthrough – I remember Legwinski and Marlet going close and we also had chances

to equalise after they'd scored just before half-time. That defeat was tough to take.

It's a while ago now, but that still seems to grate…?
The mood had changed. Directly after we lost that semi-final the Chairman came into the dressing room and made his feelings very clear! He said, "Today you lost me £10m!" There were no congratulations to the players for reaching the semi-final or anything like that, no he was seething. I hate losing. And I hate losing semi-finals. But the Chairman's remarks smacked of hatred. I could easily have walked out there and then; I was angry and I was upset. You see the players were bitterly disappointed at losing the match and at that point the right thing to say was, "Okay, let's regroup and get it right next year." But no, he was only interested in the money. I distanced myself from the Chairman after that outburst; from then on I concentrated wholly on team affairs rather than being concerned with what he might think.

What had changed, Jean? Why was Al Fayed so embittered towards you?
The crazy thing is, he was jealous. I had a fantastic relationship with the supporters at Fulham. And when the crowd chanted my name, the Chairman didn't like it. He felt they should have been chanting his name. All the time. His face would scowl when the crowd chanted TI-GA-NA, TI-GA-NA! Things got quite awkward. But despite all of that nonsense, if you offered me the chance to do it all again I would drop everything to do so. It was a magnificent experience and one that I'll always treasure. And that's all down to the people involved at the Club – and that includes the wonderful supporters. I had incredible support, even when things got difficult in 2003 and also during the court case that followed [2004].

You won that court case, but let's not dwell too much on that here. How were you able to focus on the job of managing FFC in 2002-03 and how is it that the whole High Court business hasn't soured your affection for Fulham?
For me, the priority was always Fulham Football Club. Not Tigana; and not Al Fayed. I was only going to be there for a limited time – three, four or five years, perhaps – but the Club would always be there. That's always been my philosophy wherever I've worked. But at Fulham that outlook was strengthened by the support

I'd received. So I had to remain focused on my job; that was the priority. My views on Al Fayed haven't changed. He's a bad man in my opinion. He thinks because he has the money that he's the king. For me, he's the king of nothing! So for me it's been easy to separate Al Fayed from Fulham. My affection for Fulham remains unaffected. No problem.

The signing of Steve Marlet became a major talking point (and it's fair to say that Chairman had a view!), but what were his strengths as a player?
I felt the team needed someone quick, a player who could cross the ball accurately, and Marlet fitted the bill perfectly. He was already a French International and we had high hopes that he'd improve our team. Unfortunately, almost as soon as he'd signed for Fulham, Steve got injured on International duty. He recovered, but had lost that vital acceleration. He was still a very good player, and he continued to play for France, but he didn't shine for Fulham in the way I had hoped he would.

Is it true that you considered returning to Fulham in 2013?
Yes, I was contacted. And it would have been the three of us – Christian, Roger and myself. I was keen to help Fulham get out of trouble, and I would have done it for free. At that point I told Bill [Muddyman], don't worry about the contract, we can sort that out in due course. There was a good chance that Thierry Henry could have been involved in that package, as a player short-term, but one who'd be learning the management ropes. But it didn't happen. ⚽

Resounding Victory

As the final whistle blew at Wembley, that explosion of noise from the white wall of Fulham supporters was extraordinary – particularly as our volume levels were already between "raucous" and "positively thunderous". The guys on the pitch had done us proud, and yet in that special moment, amid all the pandemonium and general mayhem, I think every one of us felt we'd also done our bit to help them get over the line. That glorious feeling of total unity and solidarity doesn't occur too often and was well worth savouring – after belting out another rousing rendition of "Mitro's On Fire", naturally!

Our Wembley success was the culmination of an amazing record-breaking season. Despite all the records, and unlike the last time we gatecrashed the top flight under Jean Tigana's stewardship, we achieved our target having played a remarkable game of catch-up. Right to the last there was the distinct possibility that, team of the moment or not, we might slip up at the final hurdle. Could we hold our nerve? Did we have the legs? Could we do it when it really mattered? Fair play (and congrats) to all concerned: not only were such questions answered in the most positive way possible, but the climax to the season will live long in the memory and will be forever etched in Fulham folklore.

Being Fulham, though, we didn't do it the easy way. After losing to Chris Coleman's Sunderland in mid-December we sat in 12th spot, eight points shy of Sheffield United in 6th place, and 18 adrift of second-placed Cardiff. Hell, we'd need a 23-match unbeaten run to stand any chance of gate-crashing any promotion party. Astonishingly, that's precisely what this Fulham squad managed to put together: 18 wins and five draws. Our Play-off berth was now secure. But, tantalisingly, with one regular game left to play, second place was still within reach.

Maybe there wasn't enough belief that Reading could go down the M4 to stem Cardiff's promotion charge; maybe our 24th game since that loss at the Stadium of Light was one fixture too far. Either way, we looked leggy and lethargic for much of our 3-1 loss at Birmingham. Third place with 88 points was a superb return given the way we'd started the season. The nagging fear was it could yet all count for naught.

We were much improved, if far from firing on all cylinders, in the first Play-off match at Derby. Had Kevin McDonald's second-half shot hit the net rather than the bar then maybe we'd have considered it a decent result; instead the hosts held a one-goal advantage going into the second game at the Cottage. Could we do it? Of course we could! But *would* we do it? Ah, more nagging doubts. Come on Fulham!

What a night that was at Craven Cottage. What a noise. What an atmosphere. What a performance. Even so, at 0-0 at the break, there was still the small matter of having to score a couple of goals against resilient opposition. But we were giving it a real go and playing well; the crowd, on their feet from the off, were going through their full repertoire; surely Derby had to crack. Two minutes after the break, no sooner had some idiotic fanzine editor uttered the words "Sessegnon's having a quiet game", young Ryan popped up to belt the ball home and bring the scores level. Our unlikely hero on the night was Denis Odoi, whose near-post header from Sess's corner flashed into the far corner of the net. With that, noise levels at the often sedate Craven Cottage cranked up another few notches. We were going flippin' barmy. We were going to Wembley! All in all, not a bad time to record your first-ever Play-off victory. One more and we'd be in the top flight.

For all the joyous scenes at the Cottage, we'd only got one step closer; we'd achieved nothing. There was still one more huge obstacle to overcome – unbeaten runs counted for little now, neither did the fact that we'd finished above our Wembley opponents, Aston Villa. Even so, that win over Derby provided a terrific injection of confidence and belief. If the team could get to grips with Wembley and the occasion then surely we'd stand a good chance.

The media hyped up what we already suspected. This was shit or bust time for FFC; at least for the current set-up. Parachute payments from our last period in the top flight were about to dry up, while this Wembley fixture was said to be worth a colossal £170m to the winners; on top of that, several of our players, and even our Head Coach, were, according to the media, being linked with other clubs should we fail to go up. No pressure then!

Wear white, came the cry. And most got the memo. As the teams took to the Wembley pitch our white wall was already in good voice. In fact, our fantastic supporters were creating a stupendous racket and a phenomenal atmosphere. Go for it fellas, and we'll be supporting you all the way.

Our superiority was evident from the off; we were on top and looking confident and classy. Things got even better when Johansen found Sessegnon and he slotted a clever, well-weighted pass through the Villa defence, allowing Cairney to steer the ball past Johnstone with that trusty left foot. A goal up, 23 minutes gone; we're on our way.

Villa upped their game after the break, but didn't look good enough – only Grealish offered any real threat. Then came a potential game-changer: Odoi,

---

"After losing to Chris Coleman's Sunderland in mid-December we sat in 12th spot, eight points shy of Sheffield United in 6th place, and 18 adrift of second-placed Cardiff. Hell, we'd need a 23-match unbeaten run to stand any chance of gate-crashing any promotion party. Astonishingly, that's precisely what this Fulham squad managed to put together. "

Opposite page top: Mission accomplished – well, the first bit anyway! The Fulham crowd invade the Craven Cottage pitch after cheering their heroes to a Play-off semi-final victory over Derby.

Below: Wembley, May 2018. Wear white, someone suggested. And the players were backed all the way by a raucous white wall of noise. Tom Cairney's well-taken goal was enough to defeat Aston Villa; Premier League, here we come!

already booked, rashly swung a boot at the ball but caught Grealish instead. Ref Anthony Taylor had no option but to red card our semi-final hero. Twenty minutes left on the clock for Fulham to protect their lead. Those 20 minutes added a heroic element to the proceedings. Yes, we were well worth the lead, but now we had to show the footballing nous and resolve to keep Villa at bay – and us lot in the stands had to double our resolve and cheer our boys home. It was a supreme effort all round, and we got there. Little wonder, then, that when a shrill blast of the ref's whistle signalled the end of the game we went into maniacal overdive. This was an unbelievable achievement by Slaviša and his players, and didn't we all know it!

Frankly, winning the game was all that mattered on the day, on so many levels. But what made our Wembley visit so special was that it snowballed into such a brilliant occasion. The result underpinned everything, of course. But the whole Fulham contingent – management, players and supporters – looked properly at home on such a big stage; we all "turned up", did our bit and had an absolute ball. Post-match interviews were conducted in a jubilant yet dignified manner, and were a great advert for Fulham FC. The players' remarks suggested that, far from heading off elsewhere, there was much more to come from this particular squad. And, given the unity shown on and off the pitch as the well-chosen post-match playlist was enjoyed to the full, why wouldn't anyone not want more of the same?

Barry Hayles, 2018

What were your first impressions on joining Fulham in November 1998, Barry?
I was joining a big club for a big fee. It was a shock to the system, and it took a while to settle into my new environment. It was all very exciting.

Kevin Keegan was in charge – a big name in football – did he help you?
It was a privilege to join Fulham and even more so to have been brought to the Club by someone who was a legend in the game. Kevin was fantastic with me. He'd make a point of explaining why he wanted you in the team – he'd tell me to go out and express myself. Kevin was great with the players, not only in building up our confidence but in detailing what he expected from us.

You took a while to settle…
Some fans thought I'd been brought in to replace Pesch [Paul Peschisolido], the fans' favourite…

…You're so similar in stature…
[Laughs] Hardly! I was a little taken aback by the few boos I received when my name was announced so I just had to get my head down and work hard to prove any doubters wrong. I spoke to Kevin about the situation. Deliberately or otherwise I ended up being paired with Pesch for a while and we did quite well, and I gradually won the fans over.

At what point did you feel settled and confident?
It's well known that Kevin liked us to attack. In the FA Cup game against Southampton [13 January 1999], we had a fair few strikers on the pitch. When Kevin made some substitutions he left me and Dirk Lehmann on the field, having subbed Geoff Horsfield and Pesch. That was a real confidence booster and when Matty Brazier's shot was parried five minutes from time I was on the spot to smash

Fulham 0 Crystal Palace 2	1st
11.08.18 19th	2nd
Tottenham Hotspur 3 Fulham 1	3rd
18.08.18 19th	4th
Fulham 4 Burnley 2	5th
25.08.18 12th	6th
Brighton & Hove Albion 2 Fulham 2	7th
01.09.18 11th	8th
Manchester City 3 Fulham 0	9th
15.09.18 15th	10th
Fulham 1 Watford 1	**11th**
22.09.18 15th	12th
Everton 3 Fulham 0	13th
29.09.18 16th	14th
Fulham 1 Arsenal 5	15th
07.10.18 17th	16th
	17th
League Cup	18th
Fulham 2 Exeter City 0	19th
28.08.18 Round 2	20th
Millwall 1 Fulham 3	
25.09.17 Round 3	

Torturous Ticketing

For all of the euphoria at the business end of the season, FFC's ticketing system was a disgrace – note, that's a pop at the system, not the staff at the Club. Having to deal with Ticketmaster for the Play-off final was a nightmare. After it took me an age to get through, the guy at the other end was as irritatingly useless as he was gratingly polite. "No, sir, I can't book five seats together in any part of the stadium." This was on the first morning of sales, so that made no sense whatsoever.

"Can you do three together and two in front (or behind)?" No, sir, we can't deal with that configuration." "What do you suggest I should do, then?" "I'm sorry, sir, I don't know – oh hang on, I've found five in a row." "Great, I'll take them." "Sorry, sir, they've gone." Good grief. He may have been new to the job, who knows, but he then asked me to hold, and after getting yet more canned music blasted into my lugholes for what seemed like an eternity, he eventually got back to me

and started the whole booking process all over again.

It could have been a different fella, I suppose, but if so he sounded exactly the same. Either way he now seemed to know his way around the system and before too long, hey presto, he'd discovered five seats together and we were in business. "Thank you, sir." "No, thank you, sir." What an appalling system, but job done at least; phew! Let's hope Tom Cairney and co have better luck in finding the net come the big day!

home the winner. There was a great atmosphere, and it was great to knock out a Premier League team.

What's this about Keegan lending you his car?
That was on my third or fourth day at the Club. My car was getting repaired and I asked for a lift to the station. Quick as a flash, the gaffer said I could use his for a few days. This was amazing – I'm the new boy and my manager, Kevin Keegan for heaven's sake, is lending me his car. And no beat-up banger, but a top-of-the-range BMW. I used it for two or three days (very carefully!); it was a helluva gesture.

Did the Keegan-for-England thing rock the camp?
Yes. I didn't think he'd go, even though it was the England job. I thought, "We're going places, we've got the right Chairman, the right Manager, the right squad to go on and do things…" But I suppose you can't turn down England.

Any managerial switch can lead to doubts and, I gather, Paul Bracewell didn't rate you too highly?
Once Kevin left, Bracewell told me I didn't figure in his plans. That's his prerogative! He wanted to ship me out to Bristol City – all very interesting as I'd previously done pretty well for Bristol Rovers – with Ade Akinbiyi coming to Fulham. I had to speak to City boss Tony Pulis. His first words were: "This is a magnificent deal – I'm getting you and £2m." His next words were, "But there's a stumbling block…" I'd have to take a pay-cut. I wasn't keen on the move and I certainly wasn't keen on any cut in pay. So I went back to Fulham determined to prove my worth.

Bracewell only lasted the best part of a season and in came Jean Tigana. Was that a shock?
My first thoughts were, "I'm out of the door now!" I was sure he'd bring in a load of new faces. But that never happened. I was nervous before our first one-on-one meeting, but Jean said "I like what I've seen on the videos. You're an aggressive player; maybe you should tone it down a bit." My response was that I wasn't intentionally feisty but that the aggression was part of my game. He understood that, and it was the start of a fantastic relationship. Jean was brilliant, and he helped so many of us to improve. He got the best out of me without a doubt.

Didn't he say at the start that you were too stocky?
He told me bluntly that when I finished playing I'd be a fat man unless I sorted things out there and then. He mentioned it a few times in the days that followed, often with that little laugh of his. There were so many changes going on at Fulham at the time, with dietary arrangement high on the agenda, so these weren't throwaway lines or insults. He was on my case for all the right reasons.

And the benefits were there for all of us to see…
It was a joy to be a part of it all. Jean would chop

and change, so Luis Boa Morte might come in and I'd have to watch – but it was a genuine delight to be part of that set-up.

We played sublime football in those first months under Tigana, but the stand-out game in the closing weeks was Blackburn away…
Yeah, and I've still got the scar [under the left eye] to prove it, thanks to David Dunn! When Rufus got sent off, Jean took me off and put Alan Nielson on at left-back. I could barely see out of my left eye.

Bad eye or not, could you have sprinted down the touchline like Jean Tigana did, or danced like Sean Davis when he stabbed home the winner?
Jean's sprint was so funny – and so out of character! Although I'd been subbed by then, that Blackburn performance was a stand-out game. It's the sort of game that you want to be involved in, and why you play football. We showed such character. We had a fantastic squad that could play supreme football, but we showed we had plenty of heart too.

What was it like to partner Saha?
Louis is the best player I ever played with – the perfect striker. He a great touch, great pace, good in the air, two good feet and was really skilful in one-on-one situations. He was a nightmare to play against in training, but a dream to partner on the pitch. I was the battering ram, whereas Louis had all the finesse. We practised hard in training and it paid off. We'd have a midfield diamond that would spring into action whenever a counter-attack was possible and it was all done at such a speed that we'd frequently have an overload of players. With Lee Clark and John Collins orchestrating things we were majestic and so fluid going forwards.

Despite what you may have read or heard about extra training sessions in pre-season, they weren't the toughest pre-season sessions either. We were put through it, of course we were, but it was so considered and so focused. With Jean and his guys it was the whole package of measures that was so impressive and which made such a difference. And we flew out of the blocks. It was a magical time.

It may not have been so sparkling in the top flight, but we still had our moments…
We had that exciting game at Old Trafford to kick off our first Premier League season. Louis was on fire and we only lost 3-2 when we probably deserved something. I almost had to pinch myself that I was involved. I was proud to score in our first home game in the top flight, a 2-0 win over Sunderland. Scoring against Chelsea was sweet, too, and I also got both goals in our 2-0 win over Everton.

You scored twice against your boyhood idols?
Spurs are still my team! That match was memorable for so many reasons. I wasn't in the side at the time

[August 2003], but Chris Coleman got to hear that I tended to score against Spurs (back in my Stevenage days we'd often play friendlies against Spurs and I'd often get on the scoresheet). Anyway on the Thursday after training, Coleman called me in and said I'd be in the side on the Saturday. Normally the team wouldn't be named until Friday, so this was unusual. Also, we'd won the previous game so it was odd to change a winning line-up. But I was in – and managed to get those two goals.

How was your relationship with Chris Coleman?
Initially it was excellent. Things took a turn when I was selected to play for Jamaica. Chris wasn't too pleased. "It only a friendly," he said. "I don't want you getting injured." But I was keen to play so off I went, only to get crocked – I was out for two months. That didn't go down too well.

I was offered another years at FFC, but on the same money. This was around the time Louis was heading to Man Utd. I was keen to stay, obviously, but did the standard thing of asking for a slight pay rise or a two-year deal. Thing is, they never got back to me at all, at least not until Lee Hoos told me later that season, "You must have guessed that we'd withdrawn that contract offer." It was quite a shock. I felt let down by Chris Coleman at that point. He should have told me sooner that the Club were prepared to let me go and that I should start to look around. I felt I'd been hung out to dry. Anyway, there I was at the end-of-season do with the fans but with a face like thunder. The guys on my table soon twigged and I had to tell them, "Sorry fellas, but believe it or not I won't be here next season." I didn't want to be at the do, but it was expected of me. The last thing I wanted was to be moody in the company of supporters who'd been great to me, but that's how it was.

You might have been mightily peed off at that point but, Spurs fan or not, you remain a firm follower of Fulham. Why?
Simple, really: I had such a great time with Fulham. The fans were so genuine with me and there were so many fantastic moments.

And it was during your time at Fulham that you tugged Emmanuel Petit's ponytail…
My mum showed me the picture the next day and asked "What were you doing?" I just said, "Well it was there, waiting to be pulled – and, anyway, he's got Arsenal links. Us Spurs fans aren't impressed by that sort of thing!

More recently you went to Wembley to see our Play-off victory. According to YouTube you were everywhere – and your name was sung almost as many times as Tom Cairney's…
It was a great day. The fans were unbelievable – in the way they supported the team so well, and the

way they welcomed me. I was just there minding my own business really, but somehow I became part of it all. I got bombarded by all and sundry; it was so surreal to be mobbed all these years later. All day the atmosphere was fantastic – and the result was brilliant.

Today's team has shades of Tigana's title-winners?
Similarities, yeah! The players are comfortable on the ball and the ball-retention is fantastic. The signing of Mitrovic was so important as his presence gives the team another dimension. With Mitro in the team there's always another option; if they're unable to break a team down with the passing game then they can choose to by-pass the midfield and bring the big striker into play. Mitro's hold-up play was terrific, as were most of his lay-offs. His goals were so valuable too. Every team needs a big man! ⚽

Meeting Tom Cairney

With the 2018-19 season approaching, how better to spend an hour than in the company of Fulham captain Tom Cairney? While memories of that wondrous day at Wembley remained fresh, it was evident that there was now a steely resolve to make the most of our return to the top flight. Indeed, Fulham announced the signings of Nice duo Jean Michaël Seri and Maxime Le Marchand just a couple of hours after the chat with TC at Motspur Park. So, "on the up" in more ways that one…

You were pretty hacked off 12 months ago, Tom, after we'd lost to Reading, but the whole Play-off experience went a lot better this time around…?
That Play-off defeat to Reading was tough – it was the worst I've ever felt on a football pitch. We'd put together that winning run in the second half of the season, had made it into the Play-off slots and, despite finishing sixth, were favourites to go up thanks to the momentum we'd built up. It was such a shame the season ended that way. It was also Scott Parker's last game for us, and his last game before hanging up his boots, so it was sad for him, too. Now, 12 months on, it's all turned around; not only did we gain promotion but Scott's returned as coach.

Automatic promotion would have caused fewer butterflies, but you went for the glory route…!
Other players who've gained promotion via the Play-offs have said it's the best way to do it – but you can't plan it that way! For peace of mind, and to avoid the heartache we suffered last year, finishing in the top two had to be the objective. But it wasn't to be. We celebrated like crazy after the Play-off semi-final win over Derby, not because we were ahead of ourselves, it was more a sense of relief that we'd overcome a major hurdle and had got to Wembley. At the very least we'd get the day out that everyone connected to the Club deserved. If all went to plan we could top that day out with a famous win.

Above: The Ed meets Tom Cairney, whose affection for the Club and its traditions is as genuine as it is uplifting. "It felt like home to me as soon as I arrived, and you can't put a price on happiness."

Above: Tom Cairney races towards the Fulham end as soon as he hears the final whistle – cue scenes of delirium on and off the Wembley pitch.

Going back to that semi-final, did you ever think Fulham fans could make such an incessant racket?
We've had our moments at the Cottage, but I've never heard the crowd make such a noise. As far as making a difference, of course it did; one hundred per cent. It was almost as if the crowd sucked the ball towards the goal, especially during the second half when we were attacking the Hammersmith End. We'd done everything apart from score in the first half but, in that atmosphere and the way we were playing, I couldn't see Derby holding out.

That word "momentum" again…
Oh yeah, we were piling on the pressure and found a way through, thank goodness. I wasn't around for the famous Juventus game, but this was easily my most special night at the Cottage. It was a brilliant outcome and the celebrations were just as fantastic. But we'd only done one part of the job at that point.

Astonishingly, those noise levels were more than matched at Wembley – 38,000 Fulham fans and the whole White Wall giving raucous support even before you stepped onto the pitch…
The build-up to the Final was awesome. There was plenty of talk of Villa being more experienced than us, but we had a lot of belief and confidence. We set out to dominate, and I think we did that in the first half. It was a bit backs-to-the-wall once we went down to ten men, but even then our crowd were sensational, even cheering when we cleared the ball down the pitch. The noise was so great you'd have thought we'd scored not just cleared our lines.

Our goal – your goal! – came midway through the first half. Ryan Sessegnon spotted your run and sent a peach of a pass behind the Villa centre-back and your left peg did the rest…
It was a surreal moment. Scoring at Wembley; that doesn't happen every day. I can barely remember anything about the goal itself. Sounds silly, I know, but I can remember everyone piling on me. And there was a fantastic roar coming from the other end of the ground – I wish I could have scored in front of the Fulham fans; we could all have milked the moment together that much more!

I take it that special effort has pushed your goal against Leeds [March 2017] into second spot?
Oh yeah! That late goal against Leeds at the

Cottage and the mayhem that followed was amazing, but nothing can top scoring a winner at Wembley! The Wembley win was so important. So much was riding on the game – getting promotion, naturally, but also the money that comes with it. It was vital to get this Club back to where it belongs.

And going down to ten men gave the winning performance a heroic aspect…?
It did. But it was strange; we may have had a brief "oh heck" moment when Dennis [Odoi] was shown the red card. And yet we regrouped right away. In fact we were incredibly calm. Sometimes in a match you get a feeling that the opposition aren't going to score. It's not something you can explain – but I certainly felt like that. I honestly thought we'd hold out, even with ten men.

It seemed an age to us, but eventually that final whistle went: cue pandemonium…!
If I could relive any two minutes I'd choose those moments after the final whistle. For some reason it was even a better feeling than scoring. I'd cleared the ball and, with Ollie [Norwood], was right by the ref when he blew for full time, so I reckon I was the first to hear the whistle – so I was off! Ollie tried to catch me as I raced towards the Fulham end but I swear it's the fastest I'd run all season. I've never had a feeling like it – relief, joy, pride, delight; a mixture of everything. We went mad, the crowd was going loopy. It's so hard to describe the high. Then came the pile-on – the players, some of the under-23s, the physios. It was amazing.

Even those who didn't play enjoyed the moment to the full – that's a sign of a decent spirit, right?
You don't get promoted if you don't have that. The bench, the other staff – everyone involved with FFC it seemed – were celebrating wildly. That's exactly how it should be. We were so together in all respects.

Let's talk about your specific role in the team – you were switched from a wide berth to being a midfield pivot. You've taken to the central position superbly and seem to be having a ball?
For years I've said that the central role should be my position – but it's Slaviša who's given me the chance to prove it. I've got certain qualities that British coaches or managers might regard as a luxury. I'm quite languid – you could say lethargic! – at times

Below: Members of the Lloyd clan enjoy their day out at Wembley – along with the rest of the Fulham family.

in the way I play. So I owe a lot to the manager for seeing qualities in me that maybe others didn't.

That all needs to be coordinated within a unit?
Stefan [Johansen] and Kevin [McDonald] have been amazing too. We've enjoyed two fantastic seasons and the three of us have complemented each other. The boss trusts me to get on the ball and make us tick, make us play. He tells us to be brave. There's different sorts of footballing bravery; some players put their heads in where it hurts and others try to help the team play by being prepared to take possession in potentially challenging areas.

Is that a big part of the Head Coach's philosophy?
One hundred per cent. He takes the pressure off us – if we give the ball away or make mistakes he insists that he's the one to pay the bill. It's his philosophy and it's the way he wants us to play.

Us fans hadn't seen that sort of approach since Jean Tigana took us up in 2001…!
I've had a few fans suggest to me that, if it were possible, a clash between Jean Tigana's side and our current one would make for a great game!

As good as Tigana's players were – and we blitzed the division that season – we weren't able to show anything like that form in the top flight. There was a tendency to try to walk the ball into the net, leading to a string of sterile, unfulfilled performances.
That's a good point – and it's a big set up we're facing. But we'll be playing the same way, I'm sure – but hopefully with a cutting edge.

It's not a bad time to be captain of Fulham…?
Not at all! And it's a massive privilege. It all fell into place for me at Wembley, didn't it? There I was leading the team out, scoring the winning goal, getting man of the match, lifting the trophy plus all those mad celebrations – it doesn't get any better than that. Those fantastic memories will stay with me forever.

Can Fulham cause a few surprises in the top flight?
There's every chance we can surprise people with the way we play: we could well go to one or two potentially difficult grounds and surprise them by dominating possession. The important thing, though, is to ensure that such performances are translated into victories. It remains to be seen if we can do that, but I'm sure we'll surprise a few people with our approach. We won't be timid, and we won't be there as a newly promoted side just to make up the numbers.

Ever thought of using your right foot?
[Laughs!] I think about it sometimes, but then use my left foot anyway!

You've said many a time that you're happy at Fulham (and have just signed a new contract); but why, specifically?
Since I arrived here it's felt like home to me. I know that sounds like a cliché, but that's the truth. I'm very happy off the pitch, which is an important, settling factor when you're looking to do good things on the pitch. Seriously, you can't put a price on happiness. So, while I'm aware that there's been interest, I've signed two contract extensions in the last couple of years, so this is what I want to do and this is where I want to stay. The way we performed in getting to Wembley and then getting promotion has only strengthened my feelings; I want to stay, a hundred per cent.

It took the winter galvanising of the squad to really set us on our way, though…
If we'd had even an average start then we'd have been up there with Wolves, I'm sure of that. Once we got into our stride we were comfortably the best team in the division. Mitrovic and Targett were key acquisitions, but had we started better we'd have been right up there.

That had been our worry: being the "best team" and yet, for whatever reason, missing out at the death having started so slowly…
It's a scary thought! I couldn't have taken another Reading! Thank heavens it worked out well. We all knew the score before the Villa game: we had to go out and play, really play. Losing wasn't an option.

There's a fine line between confidence and arrogance, but the latter can be self-destructive?
Absolutely! We were never arrogant. But putting together such an amazing unbeaten run – half a season unbeaten! – boosted our confidence massively. Even so, we just went about our business as usual. It was never a question of simply turning up and assuming we'd win. We were never arrogant, even when we faced teams near the bottom of the division. If we could, we'd put them to the sword but it took a team performance to do that. It was vital that we played with confidence but that was borne of hard work and commitment.

The new season's almost upon us…
I'm really looking forward to it. However, we realise that it'll be tough. Our first job will be to make sure we stay in the top flight. I'm not that naïve to expect that we'll do anything special. The objective is to stay in the Premier League and to build on that year by year. It's not that long ago that this great club was a force to be reckoned with in the top flight. I want that to be the case again.

One thing's for sure: no Play-offs this season…
[Laughs!] No Play-offs means we'll get an extended holiday! ⚽

"Since I arrived here it's felt like home to me. I know that sounds like a cliché, but that's the truth. I'm very happy off the pitch, which is an important, settling factor when you're looking to do good things on the pitch. Seriously, you can't put a price on happiness."

The Here and Now

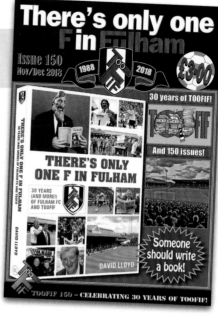

Having swept into the Premier League on the back of that supreme 23-game unbeaten run and those emotional scenes on and off the pitch during the Play-offs, we've come back down to Earth with a bump once the 2018-19 season kicked off. And this despite an astonishing £100m sepnding spree. Full marks to the Khans for backing the Head Coach – although it does leave him with the slight headache of formulating his best line-up and forging a squad spirit that was so evident last season. A cruel run of injuries has, up to now, hampered things too. Our defensive unit is anything but united – it's had more changes than the Thameslink timetables, and is currently operating a less than satisfactory service. We need to get back on track, and soon. As any football pundit worth his salt will tell you, make a mistake in the Premier League and you'll be punished.

We gained promotion thank to a decent group of players able to deliver the possession-based attacking football demanded by the Head Coach. There wasn't too much strength in depth, though, and once the loanees headed back to their parent clubs the need for extra acquisitions to bolster our Premier League ambitions was all too apparent. The upshot is that we've hardly hit the ground running and, as this little lot heads off to the printer, we've just suffered a hardly uplifting 1-5 thumping by Arsenal. Two things: a) we've recovered from poor starts for the last two seasons, and there's more than enough quality in the squad to suggest we'll do so again; b) while it's all so unsettling after last year's heroics, it's much more preferable to be taking on such challenges in the Premier League with a supportive Chairman rather than scratching around in the basement division wondering if there'll even be a footballing tomorrow. Times, and circumstances, certainly have changed!

Who knows what tomorrow will bring? However, if the last 30 years of watching FFC has taught us anything, it's that if everyone's pulling in the right direction and we've got a decent Manager in the hotseat then we're in all likelihood going in the right direction. Slaviša Jokovic has a decent track record here, and the players (as far as I know!) love playing for him. The beaming faces on the Wembley pitch last May bear testament to that; and not just those who did their bit during the macth but, significantly, those players who didn't. It was a genuine squad effort on the day and during the whole campaign. It's

not naïvety or blind optimism to suggest that if that spirit's still there then we'll be okay this season. Time for a stating-the-bleedin'-obvious remark: bottom line for this campaign is not to get relegated. Anything better than that will be a bonus. And good to note the following from Shahid Khan's missive to the FA Council members on 5 October. "Work on the new Riverside Stand at Craven Cottage will begin in May, as pledged, ensuring stability and sustainability for our Club and a future on the banks of the Thames longed for and deserved by our supporters."

So there it is, a personal appraisal of the last 30 years of being a Fulham supporter. As it's *my* book, I've been able to address one or two issues that had been left hanging along the way. The end product is far from comprehensive – there were many others I'd have liked to speak to, for example – but it's pretty fulsome all the same. You won't all share my opinions, naturally, but that's at the heart of being a football fan. We care; we support; we're bothered; we have opinions! I've tried to present an honest account of the goings-on and I hope that no one gets the hump about anything contained in these pages. Here's to the next 30 years – COYW! ⚽

Below: A quick appraisal of the season so far in *The Observer*.

Below right; Overheard in Stevenage Road: "First time I've seen that plonker without a stack of mags in his hand. P'raps he's trying to flog scarves now!"

Fulham
David Lloyd
Toofif.co.uk

1) Best performance? Believe it or not, the first half against Arsenal is a contender. But the best was against Burnley. Seri's opener was a peach and, with Mitro netting two, it seemed we'd turned the corner. Apparently not.

2) And the worst? That second half against Arsenal.

3) Happy with the manager? He's done reasonably well given the injury list and the big influx of players. But does he know his best XI? And has he had the chance to field it as yet?

4) Why I love ... Aleksandar Mitrovic With all the chopping and changing, he's been one of the few constants. Given how many are flying in at the other end, we need the big Serb to remain upbeat.

5) What is "the Fulham way?" Solid and successful under Hodgson; attack-minded and successful under Jokanovic. A fusion of the two styles would serve us well just now.

6) Which figure from the past would you most want to bring back now? Brede Hangeland and Aaron Hughes. A phenomenal centre-back pairing.

7) Funniest moment so far ... We're 3–1 down against Arsenal and the guy behind me, who's been loudly bemoaning all and sundry from the very first whistle, offers this nugget: "Just look at the body language out there. It's all so negative."